GUIDE
gs

The Westfjords
p158

North Iceland
p187

East Iceland
p238

West Iceland
p134

The Highlands
p285

Reykjavík
p44 ✪ **Southwest Iceland & the Golden Circle**
p85

Southeast Iceland
p263

Iceland: Nature's Wonderland >p179

Language

Icelandic belongs to the Germanic language family, which includes German, English, Dutch and all the Scandinavian languages except Finnish. It's related to Old Norse, and retains the letters 'eth' (ð) and 'thorn' (þ), which also existed in Old English. Be extra especially when you're trying to read bus timetables or road signs, that place names are often spelled in several different ways due to specific grammar rules. ... Icelanders speak English, so you'll ... problems if you don't know any Ice-... many attempts to speak the ... greatly appreciated.

How are you?	
Hvað segir þú gott?	kvadh se
Fine. And you?	
Allt fínt. En þú?	al feent.
What's your name?	
Hvað heitir þú?	kvadh h
My name is ...	
Ég heiti ...	Yg hay-t
Do you speak English?	
Talar þú ensku?	ta-lar th
I don't understand.	
Ég skil ekki.	Yg skil e

THIS EDITION WRITTEN AND RESEARCHED BY

Brandon Presser,

Carolyn Bain, Fran Parnell

welcome to Iceland

A Symphony of Elements

Iceland is, literally, a country in the making – the natural elements work in harmony to power its veritable volcanic laboratory: geysers gush, mudpots gloop, Arctic gales swish along silent fjords, stone towers rise from the depths of an indigo sea, and glaciers grind their way through cracked lava fields and the merciless tundra. The sublime power of Icelandic nature turns the prosaic into the extraordinary. A dip in the pool becomes a soothing soak in a geothermal lagoon, a casual stroll can transform into a trek across a glittering ice cap, and a quiet night of camping means front-row seats to either the aurora borealis' curtains of fire, or the soft, pinkish hue of the midnight sun.

A Deeply Personal Experience

Beyond the torturous clash of ecological anomalies, it's hard not to be deeply touched by the island's awesome beauty – few leave the country without a pang and a fervent vow to return. Iceland has that effect on people – it turns brutes into poets, and sceptics into believers. Perhaps it's the landscape's austere bleakness, or maybe it has something to do with the island's tiny

A mythical kingdom ruled by elves and Arctic energy, Iceland is where the past meets the future in an elemental symphony of wind, stone, fire and ice.

(left) Glacial lake, Landmannalaugar (p121)
(below) Reykjavik rooftops, with Hallgrimskirkja (p46) in the background

population, but a soul-stirring visit is as much about the people you meet as it is about the ethereal landscape. The warmth of the Icelanders starkly contrasts the frigid climate – expect complimentary cakes and cookies, friendly intellectual banter, invites to pub crawls, eager hiking buddies and 50 new Facebook friends when you return home.

Scandinavian Sensibilities & Sagas

Iceland's climate and environment is as charged as the scrolls of its ancient sagas; electrifying legends of heroes and thieves during a time when the rest of the European continent was mired in disease and ignorance. The era's mystic ruins, crumbling turf houses and haunting cairns act as the cultural and tactile counterpoints to the islanders' modern set of visual pursuits. Influenced by its Scandinavian brethren, Iceland's current spectrum of style embodies the airiness of a crisp Arctic evening. The relative ease of life allows for an aesthetic that draws on the desolation of the surrounding land and mixes it with the whimsy of the collective imagination.

❭ Iceland

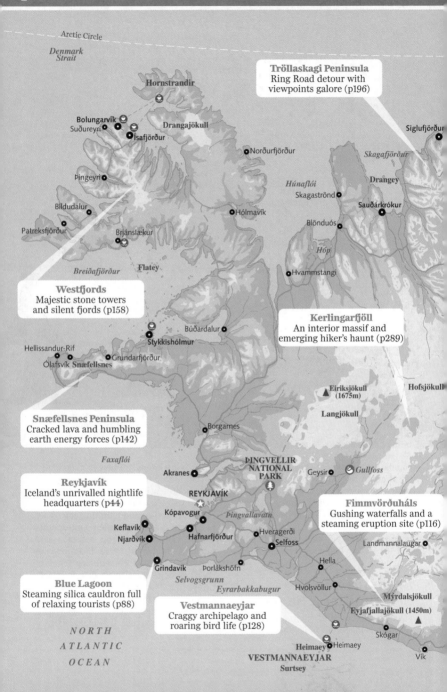

Arctic Circle

*Denmark
Strait*

Hornstrandir

Bolungarvík
Suðureyri
Ísafjörður
Drangajökull

Þingeyri

Norðurfjörður

Tröllaskagi Peninsula
Ring Road detour with
viewpoints galore (p196)

Siglufjörður

Skagafjörður

Húnaflói
Skagaströnd
Drangey
Sauðárkrókur

Bíldudalur

Patreksfjörður

Brjánslækur

Hólmavík

Blönduós

Hóp

Hvammstangi

Breiðafjörður   Flatey

Westfjords
Majestic stone towers
and silent fjords (p158)

Búðardalur
Stykkishólmur

Kerlingarfjöll
An interior massif and
emerging hiker's haunt (p289)

Hellissandur-Rif
Ólafsvík Snæfellsnes   Grundarfjörður

▲ Eiríksjökull
(1675m)

Hofsjökull

Langjökull

Snæfellsnes Peninsula
Cracked lava and humbling
earth energy forces (p142)

Borgarnes

Faxaflói

ÞINGVELLIR
NATIONAL
PARK

Akranes

Geysir ☼ Gullfoss

Reykjavík
Iceland's unrivalled nightlife
headquarters (p44)

REYKJAVÍK

Kópavogur *Þingvallavatn*

Fimmvörðuháls
Gushing waterfalls and a
steaming eruption site (p116)

Keflavík
Njarðvík Hafnarfjörður
Hveragerði
Selfoss

Landmannalaugar

Grindavík Þorlákshöfn

Hella

Blue Lagoon
Steaming silica cauldron full
of relaxing tourists (p88)

Selvogsgrunn

Eyrarbakkabugur

Hvolsvöllur

Mýrdalsjökull

Vestmannaeyjar
Craggy archipelago and
roaring bird life (p128)

Eyjafjallajökull (1450m) ▲

NORTH

ATLANTIC

OCEAN

Heimaey Heimaey

Skógar

Vík

VESTMANNAEYJAR
Surtsey

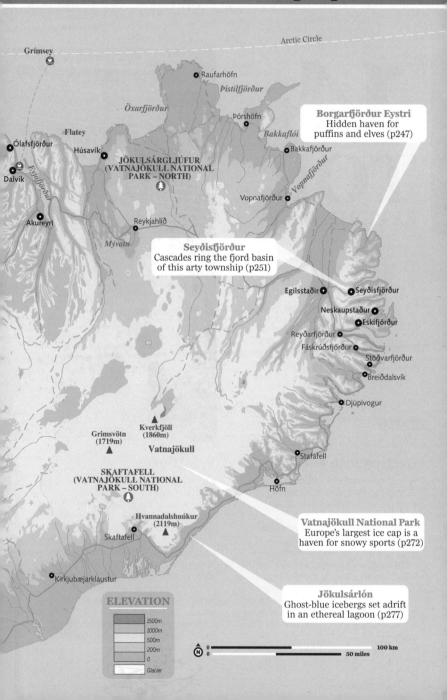

Arctic Circle

Grímsey

Raufarhöfn

Þistilfjörður

Öxarfjörður

Þórshöfn

Bakkaflói

Flatey

Ólafsfjörður

Húsavík

Bakkafjörður

JÖKULSÁRGLJÚFUR
(VATNAJÖKULL NATIONAL
PARK – NORTH)

Dalvík

Eyjafjörður

Vopnafjörður

Vopnafjörður

Akureyri

Reykjahlíð

Borgarfjörður Eystri
Hidden haven for
puffins and elves (p247)

Mývatn

Seyðisfjörður
Cascades ring the fjord basin
of this arty township (p251)

Egilsstaðir

Seyðisfjörður

Neskaupstaður

Eskifjörður

Reyðarfjörður

Fáskrúðsfjörður

Stöðvarfjörður

Breiðdalsvík

Djúpivogur

Grimsvötn
(1719m)

Kverkfjöll
(1860m)

Vatnajökull

Stafafell

SKAFTAFELL
(VATNAJÖKULL NATIONAL
PARK – SOUTH)

Höfn

Hvannadalshnúkur
(2119m)

Skaftafell

Vatnajökull National Park
Europe's largest ice cap is a
haven for snowy sports (p272)

Kirkjubæjarklaustur

Jökulsárlón
Ghost-blue icebergs set adrift
in an ethereal lagoon (p277)

ELEVATION

1500m
1000m
500m
200m
0
Glacier

N

0   100 km
0   50 miles

14 TOP EXPERIENCES

Getting into Hot Water

1 Iceland's unofficial pastime is splashing around its surplus of geothermal water. There are 'hot-pots' everywhere – from downtown Reykjavík to the isolated peninsular tips of the Westfjords – and not only are they incredibly relaxing, they're a great way to meet the locals (and cure a mean hangover!). Everyone knows that Blue Lagoon (p88) is the big cheese; its steaming lagoon full of silica deposits sits conveniently close to Keflavík International Airport, making it the perfect send-off before flying home. For more information, see p19. Blue Lagoon

Westfjords

2 Iceland's sweeping spectrum of superlative nature comes to a dramatic climax in the Westfjords (p158) – the island's off-the-beaten-path adventure par excellence. Sweeping beaches flank the southern coast, roaring bird colonies abound, fjordheads tower above and then plunge into the deep, and a network of ruddy roads twists throughout, adding an extra sense of adventure. The region's uppermost peninsula, Hornstrandir, is the final frontier; the sea cliffs are perilous, the foxes are foxier, and hiking trails amble through pristine patches of wilderness that practically kiss the Arctic Circle.

NIGEL PAVITT / GETTY IMAGES ©

JOHNATHAN AMPERSAND ESPER / GETTY IMAGES ©

Jökulsárlón

3 A ghostly procession of luminous-blue icebergs drifts serenely through the 18-sq-km Jökulsárlón lagoon (p277) before floating out to sea. This surreal scene (handily, right next to the Ring Road) is a natural film set: in fact, you might have seen it in *Batman Begins* and the James Bond film *Die Another Day*. The ice breaks off from Breiðamerkur-jökull glacier, an offshoot of the mighty Vatna-jökull ice cap. Boat trips among the 'bergs are popular, or you can simply wander the lakeshore, scout for seals, and exhaust your camera's memory card.

Northern Lights

4 Everyone longs to glimpse the Northern Lights, the celestial kaleidoscope known for transforming long winter nights into natural lava lamps. The lights, also known as aurora borealis, form when solar flares are drawn by the earth's magnetic field towards the North Pole. What results are ethereal veils of green, white, violet or red light, shimmering and dancing in a display not unlike silent fireworks. Peak aurora sightings occur in the depths of winter, but look for the lights in clear, dark skies anytime between October and April.

SUBTIK / GETTY IMAGES ©

ARCTIC-IMAGES / CORBIS ©

Driving the Ring Road

5 There's no better way to explore Iceland than to hire your own set of wheels and loop around Rte 1 – affectionately known as the Ring Road. The ovular strip of cement loops around the island in a clock-like fashion, passing through verdant dales decked with tumbling chutes, haunting glacial lagoons with popcorn-like icebergs, desolate strands of sea coast and arid plains of parched lava fields. Don't forget to take some of the detours – use the Ring Road as your main artery and then follow the veins as they splinter off into the wilderness. For more information, see p30.

Vatnajökull National Park

6 Europe's largest national park covers 13% of Iceland and safeguards mighty Vatnajökull, the largest ice cap outside the poles (three times the size of Luxembourg). Scores of outlet glaciers flow down from its frosty bulk, while underneath it are active volcanoes and mountain peaks. Yes, this is ground zero for those 'fire and ice' clichés. You'll be spellbound by the diversity of landscapes, walking trails and activities inside this supersized park. Given its dimensions, access points are numerous – start at Skaftafell in the south (p272) or Ásbyrgi (p232) in the north. Dettifoss waterfall

Borgarfjörður Eystri & Seyðisfjörður

7 A tale of two east-side fjords. Stunning Seyðisfjörður (p251) garners most of the attention – it's only 27 (sealed) kilometres from the Ring Road, and it welcomes the weekly ferry from Europe into its mountain-lined, waterfall-studded embrace. Beautiful Borgarfjörður Eystri (p247), on the other hand, is 70km from the Ring Road, many of them bumpy and unsealed. Its selling points are understated: puffins, hidden elves, rugged rhyolite peaks. They both have natural splendour in spades. We can't help but love 'em both. Seyðisfjörður

Fimmvörðuháls

8 If you haven't the time to complete one of Iceland's multiday treks, the day-long Fimmvörðuháls walk (p116) will quench any wanderers' thirst. Start at the shimmering cascades of Skógafoss, hike up into the hinterland to discover a veritable parade of waterfalls, then gingerly tiptoe over the steaming remnants of the Eyjafjallajökull eruption before hiking along the stone terraces of a flower-filled kingdom that ends in silent Þórsmörk, a haven for campers, hemmed by a crown of glacial ridges.

Tröllaskagi Peninsula

9 Touring Tröllaskagi (p196) is a joy, especially now that road tunnels link the spectacularly sited townships of Siglufjörður and Ólafsfjörður, once end-of-the-road settlements. The peninsula's dramatic scenery is more reminiscent of the Westfjords than the gentle hills that roll through most of northern Iceland. As well as top-notch scenery and hiking, pit stops with pulling power include Hofsós' perfect fjordside swimming pool, Lónkot's fine local produce and Siglufjörður's outstanding herring museum, plus ski fields, whale-watching tours, and ferries to offshore islands.

HOLGER LEUE / GETTY IMAGES ©

AEVARG / GETTY IMAGES ©

Reykjavík's Cafe Culture & Beer Bars

10 Iceland's capital is rather wee by international standards, but the city's ratio of coffee houses to citizens is nothing short of staggering. In fact, the local social culture is built around these low-key hang-outs that crank up the intensity after hours, when tea is swapped for tipples and dance moves break out on the sticky floors. Handcrafted lattes and designer microbrews are prepared with the utmost seriousness for accidental hipsters sporting well-worn *lopapeysur* (Icelandic woollen sweaters), uneven hair and clunky boots. For details, see p72.

Snæfellsnes Peninsula

11 With its cache of wild sand-strewn beaches and crackling sulphur lava fields, the Snæfellsnes Peninsula (p142) is one of Iceland's best escapes – either as a day trip from the capital, or as a relaxing long weekend. Jules Verne was definitely onto something when he used the area as his magical doorway to the centre of the earth. New Age types have flocked to the region to harness its natural power and energy, and even if you don't believe in 'earth chakras', you'll undoubtedly find greater forces at play along the stunning shores. Kirkjufell, Grundarfjörður

Heimaey & Vestmannaeyjar

12 An offshore archipelago of craggy peaks, Vestmannaeyjar (p128) is a mere 30-minute ferry ride from the mainland, but feels miles and miles away in sentiment. A boat tour of the scattered islets unveils squawking seabirds, towering cliffs and postcard-worthy vistas of lonely hunting cabins perched atop patches of floating rocks. The islands' 4000-plus population is focused on Heimaey, a small town of windswept bungalows with a scarring curl of frozen lava that flows straight through its centre – a poignant reminder of Iceland's volatile landscape.

Kerlingarfjöll

13 Accessible for only a handful of months each year (and we use the word 'accessible' loosely), this pristine mountain range lies deep in Iceland's highlands, off the Kjölur route. Historically, myths of trolls and fearsome outlaws spurred travellers speedily along the highland routes, and Kerlingarfjöll (p289) remained unexplored until last century. Today, increasing numbers make use of long, bumpy bus routes or 4WDs to reach this remote 150-sq-km range. What awaits is a hiker's paradise: geysers and hot springs, glaciers and dazzling, autumnal-hued rhyolite mountains.

13

ARCTIC-IMAGES / GETTY IMAGES ©

14

HARRY PRESSER ©

Puffins & Whales

14 Iceland's two biggest wildlife drawcards are its most charismatic creatures: the twee puffin, which flits around like an anxious bumblebee, and the mighty whale, which heaves its awesome power as it glides through the frigid blue. Opportunities to see both abound on land and sea. For details, see p35.

need to know

Currency
» Icelandic króna (Ikr)

Language
» Icelandic (Íslenska)

When to Go?

Warm to hot summers, mild winters
Mild summers, cold winters
Cold Climate

Ísafjöður
GO Jun–Aug

Akureyri
GO Jun–Aug

Egilsstaðir
GO Jun–Aug

Reykjavík
GO Jun–Oct

Þórsmörk
GO Jul–Sep

High Season
(Jun–Aug)
» Visitors descend en masse to all corners of the country – especially Reykjavík.

» Endless daylight and midnight merriment abounds.

» The arid interior welcomes eager hikers.

Shoulder
(May & Sep)
» Breezier weather and occasional snows in the interior.

» Optimal visiting conditions for those who prefer crowdless vistas to cloudless days.

Low Season
(Oct–Apr)
» Most minor roads shut down due to severe weather conditions.

» Northern Lights shimmer across the sky.

» Brief spurts of daylight betwixt endless stretches of night.

Your Daily Budget

Budget less than Ikr15,000 (€100)
» Camping: Ikr900–1500

» Dorm beds: Ikr2900–6000

» Grill bar grub or soup lunch: Ikr1500

» Hitching, ride-sharing or bus tickets (one way Reykjavík–Akureyri): Ikr11,800

Midrange Ikr15,000–30,000 (€100–200)
» Farmhouse accommodation: Ikr10,000–15,000

» Cafe fare or meaty mains: Ikr2000–3000

» Small private vehicle: Ikr16,000

Top end over Ikr30,000 (€200)
» Boutique sleeps: Ikr28,000–40,000

» Multi-course meals: Ikr6000–10,000

» 4WD rental: Ikr40,000

Money

» Credit cards reign supreme, even in the most rural reaches of the country. ATMs available in all towns.

Visas

» Citizens from the EU, Australia, Canada, Japan, New Zealand and the US do not require visas for entry into Iceland.

Mobile Phones

» Visitors with GSM phones can make roaming calls; purchase a local SIM card if you're staying awhile.

Driving

» All traffic circulates on the right side of the road; the steering wheel is on the left-hand side of the car.

Websites

» **Visit Iceland** (www.visiticeland. com) Iceland's official tourism portal.

» **Icelandic Met Office** (http://en.vedur. is) Best resource for weather forecasts.

» **Icelandic Road Administration** (www. vegagerdin.is) Details road openings and current conditions.

» **Icelandic Farm Holidays** (www. farmholidays.is) Countryside accommodation network throughout Iceland.

» **Lonely Planet** (www. lonelyplanet.com/ iceland)

Exchange Rates

Australia	A$1	Ikr132
Canada	C$1	Ikr127
Europe	€1	Ikr162
Japan	¥100	Ikr156
UK	UK£1	Ikr202
US	US$1	Ikr127

For current exchange rates see www.xe.com.

Important Numbers

Emergency services, and search and rescue	☏112
Directory enquiries	☏118

Arriving in Iceland

» **Keflavík International Airport (KEF)**
Iceland's only fully dedicated international airport is 50km from Reykjavík. The flybus (www.flybus.is/flybus; Ikr1950) has regular service to the BSÍ – the capital's central bus terminal – in conjunction with flights. Connecting service to your accommodation can be easily arranged. Cars can be rented from the airport upon arrival – prebooking highly recommended. There's no taxi culture linking KEF to Reykjavík.

Changing Prices

The so-called currency 'crash' of 2008 seems to have opened Iceland's doors to all types of visitors. In fact, the island nation has seen roughly a 20% increase in tourism during each summer since the króna's decline. As a result, local prices have been on a sharp upward incline ever since, especially as the government tacks on exorbitant hospitality taxes. As inflation rates continue to hover well above the international average, one can only assume that prices will continue to grow at a rather rapid rate. Thus, the listings reflected in this book should be primarily used as a base guideline and a point of comparison between the various options offered – not as the exact price point of the item in question. For more details, see the boxed text, p333.

if you like...

Wildlife

Iceland's noticeably small citizenry has allowed for large populations of other animals to flourish – photo ops abound as whales breach, foxes bark, and colourful birds soar overhead.

Vestmannaeyjar's puffins
The largest puffin colony in the world lives in this eye-catching archipelago. During summer thousands of these clowny creatures flit overhead as the ferry pulls into the harbour at Heimaey (p128)

Húsavík's whales View underwater marvels and bird life on a boat expedition from Iceland's whale-watching heartland (p225)

Hornstrandir's Arctic fox Iceland's only native mammal thrives in the faraway kingdom of towering cliffs and mossy stones (p173)

Lake Mývatn's birds Twitchers adore the marshy surrounds of the lake, a magnet for migrating geese and all kinds of waterfowl (p215)

Vatnsnes Peninsula's seals Take a seal-spotting cruise from Hvammstangi or drive the peninsula scouting for sunbaking pinnipeds (p190)

Stunning Scenery

Of all the enticing elements that draw visitors to Iceland, nothing beats the island's surreal landscapes. To choose between incomparable vistas is like picking a favourite child; we've given it our best shot below.

Þingeyri to Bíldudalur The drive between these two townships may be jaw-clenchingly rutty, but the zipper-like fjordheads resemble fleets of earthen ships engaged in a celestial battle (p164)

Breiðafjörður Thousands of anthropomorphised islets dot the sweeping bay as rainbows soar overhead during the occasional summertime sun shower (p143)

Höfn to Skaftafell Glittering glaciers, brooding mountains and an iceberg-filled lagoon line the 130km stretch along the Ring Road's southeast coast (p277)

Eastfjords Supermodel Seyðisfjörður steals the limelight, but her fine fjord neighbours are just as photogenic (p251)

Þórsmörk Magnificent forested kingdom nestled under harsh volcanic peaks, wild stretches of desert and looming glaciers (p126)

Hiking

There's something particularly magical about exploring Iceland by foot – each mountain pass and fjordhead reveals itself slowly, almost purposefully, leaving an indelible mark in one's mind.

Landmannalaugar & Þórsmörk Accessible only by 4WD, Iceland's favourite hiking centres are striking realms offering endless foot fodder, and the hike between them – known as Laugavegurinn – is the original flavour of wilderness walking (p121)

Hornstrandir Pristine nature as far as the eye can see in this hiking paradise orbiting the Arctic Circle (p173)

Skaftafell Follow trails through twisting birch woods or don crampons to tackle offshoots of the mammoth Vatnajökull ice cap (p272)

Jökulsárgljúfur A veritable smorgasbord of geological wonders, including thundering waterfalls and Iceland's 'Grand Canyon' (p230)

Kerlingarfjöll A remote highland massif with a growing reputation (p289)

EDUCATION IMAGES / UIG / GETTY IMAGES ©

» Turf houses and church, Laufás (p215)

Hot-Pots & Swimming Pools

Put on those swimsuits – the 'land of fire and ice' flows with endless amounts of geothermal water. And a soothing soak is definitely what the doctor ordered after a long day of active exploration.

Blue Lagoon As touristy as it may be, it's hard not to adore a soak in the steaming silica soup surrounded by dramatic flourishes of frozen lava (p88)

Mývatn Nature Baths Ease aching muscles at the north's answer to the Blue Lagoon (p216)

Krossneslaug A geothermal Valhalla at the edge of the world where the lapping Arctic waters mingle with a toasty geothermal source (p178)

Lýsuholslaug Swim in this pool, filled with mineral-rich waters, and you'll emerge with smooth, baby-soft skin – it's like soaking in a warm gin fizz with a twist of algae (p154)

Hofsós swimming pool The most perfectly sited fjordside swimming pool puts this sleepy northern town on the map (p197)

History

Carefully documented in tomes of elaborate sagas, Iceland's history is as captivating and complex as its varied landscapes.

Reykjavík 871 +/-2 Brilliantly curated exhibit constructed around an excavation site of an ancient Viking hall (p48)

Settlement Centre Offers excellent insight into Iceland's settlement and one of the more famous sagas (Egil's Saga) through beautiful wooden sculptures (p139)

Siglufjörður Herring fishing once brought frenzied activity and untold riches to town; today an outstanding museum re-creates the fish-flavoured heyday (p198)

Víkingaheimar A fresh-faced museum whose centrepiece is a perfect reconstruction of the oldest known Viking-age ship, which sailed to America to commemorate a thousand years of Viking settlement (p90)

Keldur The only truly remaining turf structure from Iceland's Saga Age is usually closed, but glimpsing the exterior is still a must for history buffs (p111)

Lakagígar Attempt to comprehend one of the most catastrophic volcanic events in human history (p269)

Architecture & Design

Iceland mixes Scandismooth design roots with its weather woes and dreams of fairies, creating a unique design dialogue that seamlessly mingles with its citizens and surrounds.

Churches Some of Iceland's most bizarre architectural flourishes are – strangely – its churches; check out churches in Stykkishólmur (p143), Blönduós (p191) and, of course, Reykjavík (p46)

Harpa Reykjavík's newest architectural iteration is a sweeping cultural centre that glows like the switchboard of an alien ship after dark (p48)

Skyr-konfekt The product of a prize-winning partnership between a farmer and a design firm, this carefully crafted confection might be the most delicious thing you try during your stay (see boxed text, p156)

Turf houses A paradigm of pre-modern Iceland, these hobbit houses are wonderfully whimsical and offer an interesting insight into Iceland's past (p247)

If you like... elves and trolls, you'll quickly uncover a secret world of stone churches and sacred sea stacks. A 'hidden people' map can be purchased in Hafnarfjörður for earnest enthusiasts (p81)

Local Food

The best way to get to the heart of Iceland is through its stomach – the fresh-from-the-farm ingredients and a host of bizarre traditional edibles will make it a memorable journey for your tastebuds.

Fish soup Any restaurant worth its salt has a savoury fish soup on the menu – head to the Snæfellsnes Peninsula and try Narfeyrarstofa (p146) or Gamla Rif (p151)

Lamb Iceland's headliner meat is a locavore's dream, and it falls off the bone at myriad restaurants around the country – our favourite is Heydalur (p172)

Hákarl A pungent tribute to Iceland's unpalatable past – try a piece of this spongy-soggy oddity at Bjarnarhöfn, then check out the shed of fetid meat out the back (p147)

Langoustine The Höfn fishing fleet pulls countless crustaceans from the icy local waters; Höfn's restaurants simply grill and add butter (p281)

Skyr A delicious yoghurt-y snack available at any supermarket in Iceland

Hverabrauð Around Mývatn, sample this cake-like rye bread, baked underground using geothermal heat (p220)

Waterfalls

With hundreds of spots to shoot your very own shampoo commercial, Iceland has no shortage of falling water – picking a favourite will undoubtedly start a debate among fellow travellers.

Dettifoss Stand back! With the greatest volume of any waterfall in Europe, thundering Dettifoss demonstrates nature at its most awesome (p234)

Goðafoss The 'Waterfall of the Gods' is loaded with spiritual symbolism and looks like it's been ripped straight from a poster on your travel agent's wall (p215)

Skógafoss Camp within spitting distance of this gorgeous gusher – easily spotted from Rte 1 – then hike up into the highlands to discover 20 more waterfalls just beyond (p115)

Dynjandi A veritable welcome sign to the Westfjords' central peninsulas, Dynjandi's veins of arctic water cascade outward over terraces of stone that look like the side of a Bundt cake – turn around and you'll be afforded some of the most gorgeous fjord views in all the land (p164)

Unique Sleeps

Lay your head down and dream of tomorrow's magical pursuits at one of the following memorable options.

Hótel Egilsen A rundown merchant's house has been brilliantly transformed into a gorgeous harbour inn with boutique-chic fixtures (p145)

Hótel Djúpavík Set on the site of an abandoned herring factory, this legendary bolthole will fulfil all of your fjord fantasies; Sigur Rós shot part of their documentary here (p177)

Dalvík HI Hostel Dalvík's charming, vintage-inspired hostel is like no other we've encountered. Budget prices happily belie the boutique decor (p201)

Sólbrekka Two cottages proffer tranquil isolation with knockout views in ultra-remote Mjóifjörður (p255)

Álftavatn The halfway point on the Laugavegurinn hike, this lakeside base is a sight for sore eyes after a long day of trekking – the remoteness is palpable and there's a great backpacker vibe (p123)

month by month

January

After December's cheer, the festive hangover hits. The first few weeks of the year can feel a bit of an anticlimax – not helped by the extra-long dark nights and inclement weather.

Þorrablót

This Viking midwinter feast (late January to mid/late February) is marked nationwide with stomach-churning treats such as *hákarl* (putrid shark meat), *svið* (singed sheep's head) and *hrútspungar* (rams' testicles). All accompanied by generous amounts of *brennivín* (a potent schnapps nicknamed 'black death'). Hungry?

February

The coldest month in many parts of Iceland, though everyday life in the capital can seem untouched. The countryside may be scenic under snow, but mostly dark – there's only seven to eight hours of daylight per day.

Winter Lights Festival

Mid-month, Reykjavík glows with a celebration of light and darkness. This wide-ranging festa encompasses Museum Night and Swimming Pool Night (late-opening museums and pools), illuminated landmarks, cultural events and concerts, and celebrations to mark International Children's Day. See www.vetrarhatid.is.

Food & Fun

International chefs team up with local chefs and vie for awards at this capital feast. Teams are given the finest Icelandic ingredients (lamb and seafood, natch) to create their masterpieces. See www.foodandfun.is for a list of participating restaurants.

March

Winter is officially over, but it's not quite time to start celebrating. The country awakes from its slumber and winter activities such as skiing become hugely popular as daylight hours increase.

Beer Day

Hard to imagine, but beer was illegal in Iceland for 75 years. On 1 March, Icelanders celebrate the day in 1989 when the prohibition was overturned. They need little prompting, but pubs, restaurants and clubs all around Reykjavík are especially beer lovin' on this night.

April

Easter is celebrated in a traditional fashion (Easter-egg hunts, roast lamb), and spring is in the air. Days lengthen and the mercury climbs, meaning lots of greenery after the snow melts, plus the arrival of thousands of migrating birds.

Sumardagurinn Fyrsti

Rather ambitiously, Icelanders celebrate the first day of summer (the first Thursday after 18 April) with carnival-type celebrations and street parades, particularly in Reykjavík. Before you accuse them of winter-induced madness, note that Icelanders previously used the Old Norse calendar, which divided the year into only two seasons: winter and summer.

Puffins on Parade

To the delight of twitchers and photographers, in April the divinely comedic puffin arrives in huge numbers (an estimated 10 million birds) for the breeding season, departing for warmer climes in mid-August. There are puffin colonies all around the country; read up at www.puffins.is.

May

May is shoulder season, and it's not a bad month to visit, just before the tourist season cranks up in earnest. Enjoy prices before they escalate, plus lengthening days, spring wildflowers and first-rate birdwatching.

Listahátíð í Reykjavík

Culture vultures flock to Reykjavík Arts Festival, Iceland's premier cultural festival. It showcases two weeks of local and international theatre performances, film, dance, music and visual art. See www.listahatid.is/en for the program.

Whale Watching

Some 23 types of whale reside in the waters around Iceland; the best time to see them is from May to September. Whale-spotting boat tours leave from the Reykjavík area, and from a few towns north of Akureyri, but Húsavík is the country's whale-watching heartland.

June

Hello summer! The short, sharp, three-month-long tourist season begins. Pros: the best weather, near-endless daylight, the pick of tours and excursions, the best choice of accommodation. Cons: big crowds, peak prices, the need to book all lodging.

Sjómannadagurinn

Fishing is integral to Icelandic life, and Seafarers' Day is party time in fishing villages. On the first weekend in June, every ship in Iceland is in harbour and all sailors have a day off. Saltydog celebrations on the Sunday include drinking, rowing and swimming contests, tugs-of-war and mock sea rescues.

Hafnarfjörður Viking Festival

The peace is shattered as Viking hordes invade this tiny seaside town near Reykjavík for a five-day festival in mid-June. Expect little by way of raping and pillaging – more like staged fights, storytelling, archery and music.

National Day

The country's biggest holiday commemorates the founding of the Republic of Iceland on 17 June 1944 with parades and general patriotic merriness. Tradition has it that the sun isn't supposed to shine. And it usually doesn't!

Opening of Mountain Roads

The highland regions of Iceland are generally blanketed in snow well into the warmer months. The opening of 4WD-only mountain roads is highly weather dependent, but generally occurs around mid-June (some roads may not open until early July); they're often closed again by mid-September. The website www.vegagerdin.is keeps you updated.

Midnight Sun

Except for the island of Grímsey, Iceland lies just south of the Arctic Circle. Still, around the summer solstice (21 June) it's possible to view the midnight sun (when the setting sun doesn't fully dip below the horizon), especially in the country's north.

Midsummer

The longest day of the year is celebrated with solstice parties and bonfires (staged anytime between 21 and 24 June), although the Icelandic midsummer isn't as major an event as in the rest of Scandinavia. Some superstitious souls roll naked in the midsummer dew for its magical healing powers.

Humarhátíð

There's lots to love about the tasty *humar* (often translated as lobster, but technically it's langoustine), pulled fresh from Icelandic waters and served a delectable number of ways in the fishing town of Höfn. The town honours the *humar* each year in late June/early July, with crustacean-centric festivities.

(above) Hallgrímskirkja (p46) lit up during the Winter Lights Festival
(below) Crowd enjoying a concert during Menningarnott

July

Iceland's festival pace quickens alongside a (hopefully) rising temperature gauge and a distinct swelling of tourist numbers. Expect busy roads, busy campgrounds, busy guesthouses etc, and book ahead.

Listasumar á Akureyri

The northern capital of Akureyri hosts a summer arts festival spreading over 10 weeks from late June to late August. It draws artists and musicians from around Iceland, with exhibitions, concerts, theatre perform-ances, street parties and a parade.

Þjóðlagahátíð á Siglufirði

The tiny but perfect five-day folk-music festival in Siglufjörður welcomes Icelandic and foreign musi-cians. As well as the tradi-tional tunes, enjoy courses on Icelandic music, dance and handicrafts. It's held in early July.

Sumartónleikar í Skálholtskirkju

The cathedral at the his-toric religious centre of Skálholt hosts around 40 public concerts, lectures and workshops over a six-week period from July to mid-August. The focus is on contemporary religious music and early music. See www.sumartonleikar.is.

Eistnaflug

The eastern-fjord town of Neskaupstaður goes off in the second week of July, when the popula-tion nearly doubles to celebrate the heavy-metal festival Eistnaflug. Metal, hardcore, punk, rock and indie bands share the stage. See www.eistnaflug.is.

Bræðslan

The beloved Bræðslan pop/rock festival has earned itself a reputation for great music and an intimate atmosphere. Some big local names (and a few international ones) come to play in tiny, out-of-the-way Borgarfjörður Eystri on the third weekend in July. Check out www.braedslan.is.

August

The tourist season continues apace, with Southern Europeans flying north for vacation. By mid-month the puffins have departed (and some whales, too); by late August the local kids are back at school, and the nights are lengthening.

Verslunarmannahelgi

A bank-holiday long weekend (the first weekend in August) when Icelanders flock to rural festivals, family barbecues, rock concerts and wild campsite parties.

Þjóðhátíð

This earth-shaking event occurs in Heimaey, Vestmannaeyjar, on the August bank holiday, commemorating the day in 1874 when foul weather prevented the islanders from partying when Iceland's constitution was established. More than 11,000 people descend to watch bands and fireworks, and drink gallons of alcohol. See www.dalurinn.is.

Herring Festival

Also on the August bank holiday, Siglufjörður celebrates its heady herring-induced heyday with dancing, feasting, drinking and fishy-flavoured activities.

Kántrý Dagar

Yep, 'Country Days' is an unexpected one. This country music festival (p193) is held on the third weekend in August in Skagaströnd, and is organised by Hallbjörn Hjartarson, the eccentric, self-styled Icelandic Cowboy.

Menningarnótt

On Culture Night, held mid-month, Reykjavíkurs turn out in force for a day and night of art, music, dance and fireworks. Many galleries, ateliers, shops, cafes and churches stay open until late. See www.menningarnott.is for a full program of events and guided tours.

Reykjavík Marathon

Your chance to get sporty and sophisticated on the same day: this event is held on the same date as Menningarnótt. There are full- and half-marathon opportunities, as well as fun runs. More than 13,000 people got sweaty in the 2012 event. See www.marathon.is.

Reykjavík Jazz Festival

From mid-August, Reykjavík toe-taps its way through two weeks dedicated to jazz, man. Local and international musicians blow their own trumpets in venues across town, with lots of events staged at Harpa. Check out www.reykjavikjazz.is.

Gay Pride

Out and proud since 1999, this festival brings Carnival-like colour to the capital on the second weekend of August. Its highlight is Saturday's gay-pride march, followed by a concert. Needless to say, there's lots of dancing and flirting. See www.gaypride.is.

Tango on ICEland

Tango has really gripped the Icelandic soul. In Reykjavík, this three-day annual event at the end of August is composed of dance workshops and performances. See www.tango.is.

September

Tourist arrivals have plummeted and prices drop, making this a good time to visit. The weather can still be agreeable, but summer-only hotels, attractions and services are closed. Highland roads are generally closed by mid-month.

Réttir

An autumn highlight, the *réttir* is the farmers' round-up of sheep and horses that have grazed wild over summer. The round-up is often done on horseback and the animals are herded into a corral where the sorting takes place (participants and spectators welcome). Naturally, it's all accompanied by much rural merrymaking.

Reykjavík International Film Festival

This intimate 11-day event from late September features quirky programming

that highlights independent film-making, both home-grown and international. There are also seminars, workshops and a 'talent lab' for young film-makers. Check the program at www.riff.is.

October

October marks the official onset of winter, with cooler temperatures, longer nights and the appearance of the Northern Lights. Reykjavík parties hard, with big crowds gathering for its music festival.

⊙ Northern Lights
Also called aurora borealis, these colourful, dancing lights are caused by charged particles from solar flares colliding with the earth's atmosphere. They're only viewed in the darkness of night with no cloud cover. The best months for viewing are October to April (maybe Sep-

tember if you're very lucky), with peak visibility from December to February.

☆ Iceland Airwaves
You'd be forgiven for thinking Iceland is just one giant music-producing machine. Since the first edition of Iceland Airwaves was held in 1999, this fab festival has become one of the world's premier annual showcases for new music (Icelandic and otherwise). Check out www.icelandairwaves.is.

November

Summer is a distant memory. November is a bleak-ish month, with nights lengthening (sunsets around 4pm) and weather cooling. Warm up in a hot-pot and hope for Northern Lights sightings.

⭐ Dagar Myrkurs
East Iceland (Egilsstaðir and the fjords) perversely celebrates the

onset of winter over 10 days in early November, with dark dances, ghost stories, magic shows and torch-lit processions during its un-usual Days of Darkness festival. See 'Events' on www.east.is.

December

A festive atmosphere brings cheer to the darkest time of the year. Christmas markets, concerts and parties keep things bright and cosy, followed by New Year's Eve celebrations. Note that many hotels are closed between Christmas and New Year.

⭐ New Year's Eve
Festivities aplenty on 31 December, with din-ners, bonfires, fireworks, parties and clubbing till the early hours of New Year's Day to celebrate the arrival of a brand-new year.

itineraries

Whether you've got three days or 30, these itineraries provide a starting point for the trip of a lifetime. Want more inspiration? Head online to lonelyplanet.com/thorntree to chat with other travellers.

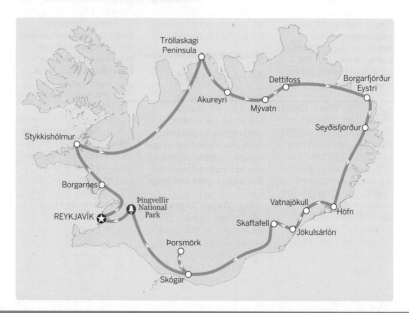

10 Days
Intro to Iceland: Classic Ring Road

Depart **Reykjavík** in a clockwise fashion, stopping in **Borgarnes** on the way to **Stykkishólmur**, an adorable village overlooking an isle-ridden bay. Rejoin the Ring Road, breaking away once more to uncover the quaint townships and coastal vistas of the **Tröllaskagi Peninsula** before gliding through **Akureyri**, Iceland's unofficial northern capital. Onto mysterious **Mývatn** next, with a stop at **Dettifoss** to experience the awesome power of nature. Push eastward to **Borgarfjörður Eystri** for summer puffins galore. Slow down in **Seyðisfjörður**, then tackle the long journey through the rest of the east as the road curls along dozens of magical fjords. Pause in **Höfn** for langoustine, jump on a snowmobile to discover **Vatnajökull**, then putter along the glacial lagoon at **Jökulsárlón**. Warm up your hiking legs in **Skaftafell**, then tackle the awesome trek from **Skógar** to **Þórsmörk**, a verdant interior valley. Find your way back to the Ring Road and as you continue west, veer away one last time to check out the yawning continental divide and the island's ancient government seat at **Þingvellir National Park** before rolling into **Reykjavík** to spend the remainder of your holiday enjoying the capital's treasures.

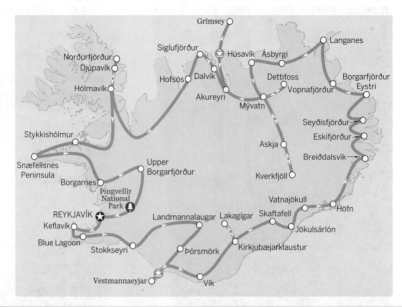

Three to Four Weeks
The Grand Tour

Pick up your own wheels after arriving in **Keflavík**, and head to **Blue Lagoon** to slough off the hours of tiring travel. Follow the coastal road through maritime **Stokkseyri**, then it's on to **Landmannalaugar** for the legendary multiday hike down into the secreted valley of **Þórsmörk**. Back near the Ring Road – as the anti-clockwise journey continues – you'll find the boat out to **Vestmannaeyjar**, where puffins flit like buzzing bees above fresh lava flows. Hang out in verdant **Vík**, then push onward to **Kirkjubæjarklaustur**, where you can venture up to **Lakagígar** to learn about the devastating effects of the Laki eruptions. Further on, **Skaftafell** offers a slew of hiking and biking possibilities. Don't miss a boat ride among oversized ice cubes at **Jökulsárlón** and a snowmobile safari on **Vatnajökull**, Europe's biggest glacier. Pause in **Höfn** for some legendary langoustine, then relax in hushed **Breiðdalsvík** before negotiating the hairpin fjord roads leading up to peaceful **Eskifjörður** and inspiring **Seyðisfjörður**. Follow the rhyolite cliffs down to **Borgarfjörður Eystri** to snap photos of puffins and turf houses, then climb through **Vopnafjörður** to the grassy plains of **Langanes**, Iceland's 'tail'. The quiet northeastern circuit rolls through **Ásbyrgi** before dropping off in the charming town of **Húsavík** for some serious whale watching. Wander around scenic **Mývatn**, which makes a great base for exploring the pounding waterfall, **Dettifoss**, and Iceland's inland treasures like the glittering caldera at **Askja** and silent ice caves at **Kverkfjöll**. Stop for a slice of civilisation in **Akureyri** before touching the Arctic Circle in **Grímsey**. Wander up through **Dalvík**, check out **Siglufjörður**, then treat yourself to a relaxing swim in **Hofsós**. Learn about ancient witchcraft in **Hólmavík**, sleep fjordside in **Djúpavík** and bathe in **Norðurfjörður**'s geothermal spring. Base yourself in the charming village of **Stykkishólmur** to explore the myriad treasures of the **Snæfellsnes Peninsula**, from golden beaches and craggy lava fields to glistening ice caps and hidden hot-pots. It's on to **Borgarnes** next, followed by **Upper Borgarfjörður**'s blend of saga sites and hidden caves. Continue the history lesson at **Þingvellir National Park**, where you can also glimpse the shifting continental plates. Then end the epic journey in **Reykjavík**, Iceland's charming cultural stronghold.

» (above) Svartifoss waterfall (p272), Skaftafell
» (left) Town houses along Grettisgata, Reykjavík

MARTIN MOOS / GETTY IMAGES ©

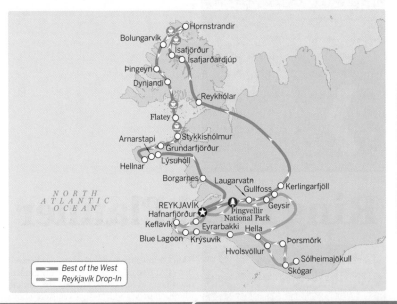

Legend:
- Best of the West
- Reykjavík Drop-In

Two Weeks
Best of the West

Start in **Reykjavík**, enjoying the city's cafes, bars and museums. Head to **Þingvellir National Park** to witness the tearing apart of continental plates, then take in the rosy sunsets in **Laugarvatn** before completing the so-called Golden Circle with stops at spurting **Geysir** and glittering **Gullfoss**. Rev up the 4WD for a ride along the deserted Kjölur Route, stopping in **Kerlingarfjöll** to admire the striking landscapes. Slide west for a soothing seaweed bath in **Reykhólar** before negotiating the sawtooth fjords of **Ísafjarðardjúp**. Use spunky **Ísafjörður** or scruffy **Bolungarvík** as a launch pad to explore the ethereal wilderness of **Hornstrandir**, Iceland's most majestic hiking reserve. Crawl through the heart of the Westfjords, using **Þingeyri** as a base to check out the region's photogenic features, like the gushing waters of **Dynjandi**. Hop aboard the Baldur ferry and pause in **Flatey** to disconnect from the world, then alight in charming **Stykkishólmur**. Swing through **Grundarfjörður**, meditate atop one of the earth's chakras at **Hellnar**, link up with a glacier safari in **Arnarstapi**, soak your weary bones at **Lýsuhóll**, then learn about the sagas in **Borgarnes** before returning to the capital.

Three to Four Days
Reykjavík Drop-In

If you're on a lengthy layover or enjoying a long weekend away, try the following route, which takes in some of the top attractions located within a stone's throw of the capital. After landing in **Keflavík** make a beeline for **Blue Lagoon** to soak away the jetlag. Wander through the steaming earths at **Krýsuvík** before barrelling down the coastal highway for fresh seafood in **Eyrarbakki**. Choose a base near **Hella** or **Hvolsvöllur** to enjoy a spot of horse riding and Northern Lights viewing (in the colder months). Active bodies will enjoy the stunning hike from **Skógar** up through the ridge between two brooding ice caps (and the site of the Eyjafjallajökull eruption in 2010) then down into **Þórsmörk**, a silent kingdom filled with wild Arctic flowers. Those who are tighter on time can trek along the glacial tongue of **Sólheimajökull** instead. Swing through gushing **Gullfoss**, spurting **Geysir** and the rift-ridden **Þingvellir National Park** on your way to **Reykjavík**. Iceland's capital bustles with an all-star assortment of trendy boutiques, galleries and clubs. Don't forget to stop in **Hafnarfjörður** to cavort with 'hidden people' before returning to the airport.

Ring Road Planner

Best Ring Road Detours

Snæfellsnes Peninsula A veritable ring road unto itself that passes through haunting lava fields, wild coastline and an ominous ice cap; 200km detour (p142).

Tröllaskagi Peninsula Follow Rte 76/ Rte 82 along the jagged coast as it climbs up towards the Arctic – scenic vistas, reminiscent of the Westfjords, await; 100km detour (p196).

Borgarfjörður Eystri Take Rte 94 through rhyolite cliffs and down into this quiet hamlet of visiting puffins and chocolate-box houses; 150km detour (p247).

Vestmannaeyjar Hop on the ferry at Landeyjahöfn to discover a rugged archipelago of lonely islets; 30km detour plus a 30-minute boat ride each way (p128).

Þórsmörk Park at Seljalandsfoss and take the bus into the forested kingdom rife with scenic walks; 50km detour along a rutty road accessible only by certified vehicles; hiking also an option (p126).

Don't beat yourself up – dear intrepid traveller – if you've never heard of any town in Iceland beyond Reykjavík. Outside the capital, there's barely a village that registers above 10,000 inhabitants. As such, it can be a tad tricky to plan a loop around the island when 99% of the country is vast and unknown.

Fortunately, there's a clear path that ploughs along the circumference of the island, taking in most of its highlights. The Ring Road, so to speak, wraps around in a circular fashion, its 1300km of mostly paved highway (which should not be confused with the Golden Circle) is the main thoroughfare from which secondary roads sprout away leading to further-flung adventures. See p26 for more inspiration.

When to Go

The Ring Road is accessible year-round, but the country's secondary roads are closed during the colder months. Expect the island to be *fully* accessible during July and August, though most roads thaw out in late May and June.

If you're planning to drive, check out www.vegagerdin.is for details of road closures, and www.vegur.is for information on forecasts and weather trends.

Clockwise or Anticlockwise?

It doesn't matter which way you tackle the Ring Road – the landscape reveals itself in an equally dramatic fashion from both directions. If you're travelling during the latter part of summer (July through September), we recommend completing the loop in a clockwise manner – check off your northern must-sees first as warmer weather sticks around a tad longer in the south.

How Much Time Do I Need?

If you were to drive the Ring Road without stopping, it would take approximately 16 hours during the warmer months. Thus, a week-long trip in the countryside would mean an average of about 2½ hours of driving per day. While this might seem a bit full on for some, it's important to remember that the drive is extraordinarily scenic and rarely feels like a haul. For travellers planning an Iceland itinerary that's less than seven or eight days, we recommend committing to one or two regions in the countryside rather than trying to hoof it around the island.

By Car

Discovering Iceland by private vehicle is by far the most convenient means of transport. It is, as expected, the most expensive way to get around the island as well.

Renting a Car

According to Bergþor Karlsson, the general manager of Reykjavík's Bílaleiga Akureyrar (Europcar; www.holdur.is), it's best to start as early as possible when searching for low fares. The internet is your best resource, but one should always take care to ensure that the name of your rental service appears on your booking, and to double-check that all fees are included in the quoted price. In general, it's less of a hassle to arrange a vehicle with a service of international repute.

Breaking Up the Journey

The most important thing to remember about travelling along the Ring Road is that one should use it as a conduit to explore many memorable detours. We recommend choosing five mini-bases along the journey to break up the drive – to make things simple, try selecting one stop in each of our chapters in which the Ring Road passes through: the west, north, east, southeast and southwest. (Those who are tight on time should skip an overnight stop in the southeast.) Depending on the length of your trip, you can spend several nights at each base, engaging in the

area's best activities and detours (see p30) before moving to the next one.

F Roads

Iceland's 'F Roads' (mountain roads) take your adventure to another level. These roads lead to some of the most scenic and far-flung spots on the island, but these paths are horribly bumpy and unsuitable for most cars. If you plan on taking an F road, you *must* rent a proper 4WD. If you opt for a 4WD, you can consider trimming down your Ring Road tour by taking one of the interior routes (see p288).

By Bus

Far less convenient than car rentals, Iceland's limited bus service is the most cost-effective option for solo travellers, but one should budget double the time of a private vehicle to loop around, lest you spend the majority of the trip staring at the countryside through a scuffed up window.

For comparison, a bus pass that rings two travellers around the island in one direction equals the price (without petrol) of a rental car for four or five days. For more information about bus passes and trends, see p346.

By Bicycle

We don't want to dash your dreams of an active holiday, but cyclists will have a tougher time than expected travelling on the Ring Road. Although the path is mostly paved, there is hardly any room on the road's shoulder to provide a comfortable distance from vehicular traffic. And lonely patches of highway mean that drivers tend to speed, kicking up dust and debris. Cycling can be a great way to explore more rural regions (see p345).

By Hitching & Ridesharing

The most cost-effective way to venture around the Ring Road is to stick out your thumb. Many hostels have rideshare poster boards in their lobbies, on which travellers can request rides or offer room in their car in exchange for petrol money. Check out www.samferda.is, an online rideshare message board. In summer it's quite easy to hitch all the way around the Ring Road; see p350 for details and potential risks involved.

Outdoor Adventures

When to Go...

For Multiday Hiking Wait for spring thaw; trekking is at its best from July to mid-September.

For Horse Riding Ride during the shoulder seasons (April to May and September to October) when the weather is cooler but mild, and tourist numbers are down.

For Northern Lights You'll need dark, cloudless nights; winter is best, but aurora borealis can occur anytime between September and April.

Best Activity Bases

South Coast Choose your rural digs somewhere between Hella and Höfn, and you'll be a stone's throw from glacier hikes, mountain biking and volcano treks.

Ísafjörður Stay in or around the Westfjords' largest town to access Hornstrandir, the kayak-friendly fjords of Ísafjarðardjúp, and the rugged central peninsulas.

Akureyri Iceland's northern capital is the gateway to Mývatn, up-and-coming Tröllaskagi, and whale watching on the northern seas.

Iceland's breathtaking natural beauty and rarefied air put colour in your cheeks, a spring in your step and passion in your soul. This unspoilt island contains Europe's largest national park and the mightiest ice cap to be found outside the poles, a sea full of whales and the world's biggest puffin colonies, lonely mountains, hidden valleys, sinister canyons, pristine lakes, twisting rivers and sawtooth fjords. Break away from Reykjavík's orbit and launch yourself into this spectacular landscape with a range of adventures and activities.

Activities

Boating & Kayaking

Boating (commonly known as RIB boating in Iceland; rigid inflatable boating) offers a completely new perspective on Iceland's natural treasures. At sea you belong to an entirely different kingdom ruled by rolling waves and mammoth whales lurking beneath.

Best Boating Hot Spots

» **Heimaey** (p128) Zip across the Vestmannaeyjar archipelago taking in the craggy cliffs and swooping birds.

» **Stykkishólmur** (p143) Wind through the myriad islands of silent Breiðafjörður.

» **Húsavík** (p225) Traditional wooden ships bob in the cool Arctic waters at the harbour – lovely trips to the neighbouring islets are popular in summer.

Best Places to Paddle a Kayak

» **Hornstrandir, Ísafjörður & Ísafjarðardjúp** (p167) Sea kayaking at its finest; try multiday tours through Arctic covers or a one-day adventure to Vigur, an offshore islet.

» **Seyðisfjörður** (p252) The charismatic (and legendary) tour guide will leave you wondering what's more charming – the fjord or him.

Cycling

Short cycling excursions can be a fun and fit way to explore the island's varied natural treasures. In Reykjavík you'll find a couple of biking outlets (p52) – some offering day trips to nearby attractions such as the Golden Circle. Bike hire is possible in many other towns around the country as well – consult the On the Road chapters for specifics.

Travelling around Iceland by bicycle can be more of a challenge than it might seem – shifting weather patterns and a lack of a solid biking infrastructure mean that you'll often be struck by heavy winds and you'll be forced to ride alongside intimidating vehicular traffic on the Ring Road. If you wish to explore large swaths of the country, we recommend the south, where new biking trails were being developed away from the Ring Road at the time of research. You'll also find a variety of bike operators, from Hveragerði (p102) all the way to Skaftafell (p272).

For more information about the logistics of cycling in and around Iceland, see p345.

Glacier Walks & Snowmobiling

Trekking across a piercing white expanse can be one of the most memorable and ethereal experiences during your time in Iceland. Lucky for you, the island has several snowy options that offer a taste of winter even on the warmest of days.

Best Glaciers & Ice Caps to Explore

» **Eyjafjallajökull** (p114) The site of the volcanic eruption in 2010; take a super-Jeep to discover the icy surface then wander over to Magni, nearby, to see the still-steaming earth.

» **Vatnajökull** (see the boxed text, p282) Europe's biggest ice cap is an endless expanse of white; perfect for snowmobile rides.

» **Snæfellsjökull** (p151) Jules Verne's *Journey to the Center of the Earth* starts here; try the snowcat tour from Arnarstapi.

» **Langjökull** (p141) Close to Reykjavík; perfect for dog sledding.

» **Sólheimajökull** (p117) Ideal for an afternoon trek – strap on the crampons!

Hiking

The opportunities for hiking in Iceland are virtually endless, from leisurely hour-long strolls to multiday wilderness treks – leaving your wheels behind opens up vast reaches of untouched nature that will undoubtedly leave an indelible mark in your mind and memory. However, the unpredictable weather is always a consideration, and rain, fog and mist can turn an uplifting hike into a miserable trudge – for proper packing tips, see p34.

For a definitive list of Iceland's best multi-day treks, see p179.

Useful Hiking Resources

» **Ferðafélag Íslands** (Icelandic Touring Association; www.fi.is) Runs huts, camping grounds and hiking trips throughout the country. Offers solid advice on hikes – especially Laugavegurinn.

Top Short Walks

» **Skaftafell** (p272) Everyone's favourite part of Vatnajökull National Park offers a slew of short walks around glinting glaciers, sparkling waterfalls and verdant hillocks.

» **Þórsmörk** (p126) An emerald kingdom tucked between the unforgiving hills of the interior; moderate to difficult walks abound.

» **Skógar** (p115) Hike up into the interior for a parade of 20-plus waterfalls; continue on to Fimmvörðuháls and down into Þórsmörk for one of Iceland's most rewarding day-long hikes.

» **Snæfellsnes Peninsula** (p36) Half-day hikes galore through crooked lava fields; don't miss the coastal walk from Hellnar to Arnarstapi.

» **Mývatn** (p216) Flat and easy, the marshy lakeshore at Mývatn plays host to a variety of curious geological anomalies as well as migrating birds.

» **Borgarfjörður Eystri** (p247) Low-key wandering among the rhyolite cliffs, or hiking up to the fjordhead for views.

HIKING CHECKLIST

The following list represents some of the most important ingredients for a successful outdoor adventure in Iceland. For more packing ideas, visit https://www.mountainguides.is/PracticalInformation/EquipmentLists/AlpineMountaineering DayTours.

Clothing

When planning for your hiking excursion, remember that you can purchase all of your weather-appropriate clothes upon arrival in Iceland. Infuse the economy with a little extra cash and check out **66° North** (www.66north.com), by far Iceland's best outerwear brand, which produces high-quality apparel for sub-Arctic conditions. Other options to check out include **Cintamani** (www.cintamani.is) and **zo-on** (www.zo-on.is).

Basics and undergarments abide by the 'cotton-killer' rule; look for merino-based materials that are ecologically sensitive and amazingly comfortable.

☐ down- or fibre-filled jacket

☐ breathable rain shell

☐ light wool sweater

☐ merino T-shirts

☐ exercise underwear

☐ wool socks

☐ lightweight, loose trousers (never jeans)

☐ breathable snow trousers or wind trousers

☐ wool hat or tuque

☐ long johns

Footwear

Hybrid footwear is the key to packing light in Iceland. The best shoes are ones that are weather resistant, well suited to walking, but can also withstand the glares from fashion-savvy Reykjavík residents.

☐ weatherproof shoes

☐ hiking shoes

☐ lightweight sandals/thongs

Camping Equipment

☐ polar sleeping bag for negative Celsius temperatures

☐ tent

☐ foldable duffle for camping supplies

Miscellaneous

Proper navigation tools (topographical maps and GPS) are essential, as many routes are only loosely marked. Keep toiletries to a minimum, but make sure you have all of the essentials, including a small first-aid kit and sunscreen. High-contrast polarisation sunglasses are useful for glacier treks; extra plastic bags are handy for separating wet and dry items. Umbrellas are useless as Arctic winds tend to destroy them within minutes.

Note that you will be required to carry your food and waste in and out of all treks (including toilet paper). Energy bars are light and create little rubbish, while stainless-steel water bottles are a good solution for liquids. **SteriPen** (www.steripen.com) is a handy portable water purifier; it doubles as a torch.

Horse Riding

Horses are an integral part of Icelandic life and you'll see them all over the country. Riding is popular and the naturally gentle breed is ideal even for inexperienced riders.

Horse fanatics might be interested in the **Landsmót** (National Horse Festival; www.landsmot.is/en), which takes place every two years (next being held in 2014) in Skagafjörður in the north of Iceland.

Iceland's Best Horse-Riding Regions

» **Southern Snæfellsnes** (p36) The wild black- and blonde-sand beaches under the shadow of a glinting glacier are perfect places for a ride. Several award-winning stables are located here.

» **Hella** (p109) The flatlands around Hella that roll under brooding Hekla host a small constellation of horse ranches offering multiday rides and short sessions for newbies.

» **Skagafjörður** (p192) The only county in Iceland where horses outnumber people has a proud tradition of breeding and training.

Long Trips

For those who have a serious case of the trots, a multiday journey through Iceland's wilderness will be just what the doctor ordered. Generally, multiday trips on horseback must be booked well in advance, as trip schedules are usually set by each stable in advance. These trips tend to be full-package affairs, with transport, guiding, accommodation and meals included. The horse-riding regions listed above each have several reputable horse farms – check the relevant On the Road chapters for contact info.

Short Rides

The Icelandic breed of horse is truly unique, and having a friendly encounter with these gentle beasts is an experience that should feature on everyone's holiday itinerary. Many farms around the country offer short rides for neophytes – there are a handful of stables within a stone's throw of Reykjavík (p55) – figure around Ikr4000 for an hour's ride. See the On the Road chapters for specifics.

Scuba Diving & Snorkelling

Little known but incredibly rewarding, diving in Iceland is becoming increasingly popular. The clear water (100m visibility!), great wildlife, spectacular lava ravines, wrecks and thermal chimneys make it a dive destination like no other. The best dive sites are Silfra at Þingvellir (p97) and the thermal cones in Eyjafjörður (p207).

Scuba virgins can enrol in a PADI course with **Dive.is** (www.dive.is); everyone else should have 10 or more dives under their belt and understand the basics of diving with a drysuit.

Swimming & Spas

Thanks to Iceland's abundance of geothermal heat, swimming is a national institution, and nearly every town has at least one *sundlaug* (heated swimming pool). Most pools also offer hot-pots (small outdoor heated pools), saunas and jacuzzis. Admission is usually around Ikr400 to Ikr500 (half-price for children) for an unlimited swim session.

Icelandic swimming pools and natural hot springs have a strict hygiene regimen, which involves a thorough shower without swimsuit *before* you enter the swimming area.

Best Resources for Getting into Hot Water

» **Friends of Water** (www.vatnavinir.is/home)

» **Swimming in Iceland** (www.swimmingin iceland.com)

» **Thermal Pools in Iceland** (by Jón G Snæland) Comprehensive guide to Iceland's naturally occurring springs (with images); sold in most Icelandic bookstores.

» **Blue Lagoon** (www.bluelagoon.com) Iceland's favourite hot spring and undisputed top attraction.

» **Visit Reykjavík** (www.visitreykjavik.is) Click through to find the clutch of pools in the capital region.

Wildlife Watching

Iceland's range of wildlife is small but bewitchingly beautiful. There are few better places for whale watching, and the towering bird cliffs that frill the land's edge are a twitcher's dream. Placid Icelandic horses are perfect for beginners, and the wild eyes of the Arctic fox will haunt you forever.

Arctic Foxes

Loveable like a dog but skittish like a rodent, the Arctic fox is Iceland's only native

» (above) Horse riding on the beach, Snæfellsnes (p142)
» (left) Arctic foxes (p311)

THOMAS SCHMITT / GETTY IMAGES ©

mammal. A sighting is rare, but these are the best spots to try your luck:

» **Hornstrandir** (p173) The Arctic fox's main domain – join the team of researchers who set up camp here each summer.

» **Suðavík** (p171) Home of the Arctic Fox Center – there are often orphaned foxes living in a small habitat on-site.

» **Breiðamerkursandur** (p276) One of the main breeding grounds for skuas, the area has drawn a rising number of Arctic foxes hungry for a snack.

Puffins & Seabirds

On coastal cliffs right around the country you can see huge numbers of seabirds, often in massive colonies. The best time for bird-watching is between June and mid-August, when gannets, guillemots, razorbills, kitti-wakes and fulmars can be seen. Puffins are spotted from the end of April until mid-August, when they suddenly take to the sea en masse.

The best bird cliffs and colonies:

» **Vestmannaeyjar** (p128) Puffins swarm like frantic bees as you crawl into the harbour at Heimaey. Chirpers nest on virtually every turret of stone emerging from the southern sea.

» **Hornstrandir** (p173) Delightfully removed from civilisation, this preserve offers an endless wall of stone that shoots down from the verdant bluffs straight into the lapping waves – countless birds have built their temporary homes within.

» **Borgarfjörður Eystri** (p247) This delightful township offers one of the best places in Iceland to spot surly puffins, who build their intricate homes a mere metre from the viewing platform.

» **Látrabjarg** (p162) Famous in the Westfjords for the eponymous bird cliffs – an assortment of species awaits.

» **Mývatn** (p215) A different ecosystem than the towering bird cliffs cloaking the jagged fjords, Mývatn's swampy landscape is a haven for migratory avians.

» **Skálanes** (p255) Ziggurats of stone offer endless terraces for visiting birds, including playful puffins. You'll have to ford a river to get here, so you're likely to be the only onlookers around.

Seals

Seals aren't as ubiquitous as Iceland's birds, but seeing these blubbery beasts bark at each other on sun-drenched rocks and swim around in the icy seas provides endless mirth to onlookers.

» **Hvammstangi & Vatnsnes Peninsula** (p190) A seal museum, viewing tours and a craggy peninsula studded with the lazy, sun-loving characters.

» **Ísafjarðardjúp** (p170) Curling fjordlings and rock-strewn beaches are the spot for these jovial creatures to bask in the Arctic sun.

PLAN YOUR TRIP OUTDOOR ADVENTURES

SEEING THE NORTHERN LIGHTS

The Inuit thought they were the souls of the dead; Scandinavian folklore described them as the spirits of unmarried women; and the Japanese believed that a child conceived under the dancing rays would be fortunate in life. Modern science, how-ever, has a much different take on the aurora borealis.

The magical curtains of colour that streak across the northern night sky are the result of solar wind – a stream of particles from the sun that collides with oxygen, nitrogen and hydrogen in the upper atmosphere. These collisions produce the haunt-ing greens and magentas as the earth's magnetic field draws the wind towards the polar regions.

Catching your own glimpse of the Northern Lights requires nothing more than a dark, cloudless night and a pinch of luck. It's as simple as that. In recent years many Icelandic tour companies have been offering pricey 'Northern Lights safaris' – we do not recommend these, as they are essentially taking you to an area with little or no light pollution to increase your viewing odds. Instead, try booking a few nights at a rural inn where you can enjoy the surrounds during the (short) day and wait calmly for the light show in the evening – many hotels offer viewing wake-up calls should the lights appear in the middle of the night while you're asleep.

The best time to see the Northern Lights is between October and April, though it is possible to see them in September.

Whales

Iceland is one of the best places in the world to see whales and dolphins, and tours on quiet oak-hulled boats minimise disruption so you can get astonishingly close. The most common sightings are of minke whales, but you can also spot humpback, fin, sei and blue whales, among others.

Prices hover around €50 for a two- or three-hour tour. Sailings do in fact run all year, with the best chances of success from mid-June to August.

Iceland's best spots for whale watching:

» **Húsavík** (p225) Iceland's classic whale-watching destination, complete with interesting whale museum; 99% success rate during summer.

» **Tröllaskagi** (p196) Plying the same seas as the boats from Húsavík, this is the new kid on the block.

» **Reykjavík** (p53) Easy viewing for visitors to the capital; boats depart from the old harbour right downtown.

Tours

Although joining a bunch of other travellers on an organised tour may not be your idea of an independent holiday, Iceland's rugged terrain and high costs can make it an appealing option. Tours can save you time and money and can get you into some stunning but isolated locations where your hire car will never go. Many tours are by bus, others by 4WD or super-Jeep, and some by snowmobile, quad bikes or light aircraft. Most tours give you the option of tacking on adventure activities such as white-water rafting, snowmobiling, horse riding and ice trekking.

If you're planning to base yourself in Reykjavík and hoping to use day-long tours to explore the countryside, it's vital to note that you will spend (dare we say waste) a significant amount of time being transported from the capital out to the island's natural treasures. If a series of short tours is what you're after, you are better off choosing a base in the countryside closer to the attractions that pique your interest.

The following list represents some of the largest tour operators around Iceland; check out their websites to get a sense of what is on offer. You'll find almost all other tour operators and tour offerings in the destination chapters (trips from Reykjavík are on p52).

» **Air Iceland** (www.airiceland.is) Iceland's largest domestic airline runs a range of combination air, bus, hiking, rafting, horse-riding, whale-watching and glacier day tours around Iceland from Reykjavík and Akureyri. Also runs tours to Greenland from Reykjavík.

» **Eskimos** (www.eskimos.is) Caters to higher-end clientele with personalised touring services.

» **Ferðafélag Íslands** (Icelandic Touring Association; www.fi.is) Leads summer hikes from Landmannalaugar to Þórsmörk, and also runs some bus tours and cross-country skiing trips.

» **Iceland Excursions** (Gray Line Iceland; www.grayline.is) A bus-tour operator with comprehensive day trips plus horse-riding, whale-watching, diving and self-drive tours.

» **Icelandic Mountain Guides** (www.mountainguides.is) Offers a wide range of hiking and mountain- or ice-climbing tours. It also provides equipment rental and private guiding for more serious climbers.

» **Reykjavík Excursions** (www.re.is) Reykjavík's most popular day-tour agency, with a comprehensive range of year-round tours.

» **Útivist** (www.utivist.is) Runs friendly, informal hiking trips and covers just about every corner of Iceland.

regions at a glance

Reykjavík

Culture ✓✓
Nightlife ✓✓
Activities ✓✓

The Culture Capital
With miles and miles of nothing but nature all around, Reykjavík is Iceland's confirmed repository of all things cultural, from winning museums and super-sleek gallery spaces to a roaring music scene and a colourful guild of craftsfolk and designers. Festivals roll on through the year, brightening even the bleakest of winter nights with heart-warming celebrations of every shape, size and colour of the rainbow.

p44

White Nights
Reykjavík, if anything, is notorious for its small but fierce nightlife. And while legions of foreign bachelor parties are common, the best nights out in the capital start with coffee at one of the dozens of quaint cafes, 'pre-gaming' drinks at a friend's apartment, an unholy pilgrimage between several beer bars, and a 4am sticky-floored romp to Top 40 beats when a makeshift dance floor suddenly materialises.

Long Weekend Extravaganza
Perfectly positioned halfway between Europe and North America, Reykjavík has done an impressive job of establishing itself as the perfect layover between continents. Urban walking and biking tours take in the top sights of the capital, but the magic of Iceland unfolds just beyond – and the city's well-oiled travel machine can instantly launch you into the wilderness via car, bus, jeep, boat or foot.

Southwest Iceland & the Golden Circle

Landscapes ✓✓✓
Activities ✓✓✓
Wildlife ✓✓

In the Path of Destruction
If the southwest printed bumper stickers, they would say 'the further you go, the better it gets' – wander into the interior and you'll find vistas of mythic proportions sitting under the watchful glare of several grumbling volcanoes.

Hiking, Biking & Vikings
High in the hills a hiker's paradise awaits, while down along the shores of the south coast and the Reykjanes Peninsula bikers will find plenty of trails in suitable weather. Toss in a smattering of interesting Saga-era relics and you have endless itinerary fodder for every type of tourist.

For the Birds
The stunning Vestmannaeyjar archipelago has the largest colony of puffins in the entire world, and they offer a spirited welcome as they shoot over the arriving ferries like wobbly firecrackers.

p85

West Iceland

Landscapes ✓✓
Activities ✓✓
Wildlife ✓

Infinite Islets
The Snæfellsnes Peninsula is a technicolour realm marked by exotic splashes of frozen lava, Caribbean-clear water, and a haunting ice cap casting ghostly shade. The most impressive vista, however, is Breiðafjörður – a wide bay specked with thousands of isles that refract the cloud-filled skies above.

Sand, Stone & Sagas
The Snæfellsnes' long peninsular arm offers endless options for active souls – long coastal walks, hikes through lava fields and rides on its infamous ice cap. History buffs can take a trip back in time; the west is often dubbed Sagaland for its rich Viking history.

Off Course by Horse
The southern shores of the Snæfellsnes Peninsula are one of the best places in the country to ride the famous Icelandic horse – follow the crests of beige sand or trot into the wild hills to find hidden geothermal sources.

p134

The Westfjords

Landscapes ✓✓✓
Activities ✓✓✓
Wildlife ✓✓✓

Welcome to Mordor
A dramatic enclave of sea and stone, the Westfjords' landscape inspires fables of magical, faraway lands. Not to be missed is the undulating coastline; each fjord finger is like an earthen ship lining up to do battle on a sea of reflected twilight.

Explore the Arctic
Sitting at the edge of the Arctic – its jagged peninsulas eagerly gripping north – Iceland's final frontier is the perfect setting for rugged mountain biking, sea kayaking, sailing, springtime skiing, and jaw-dropping hiking through the desolate Hornstrandir reserve.

Foxy Friends
Roving horses clip-clop throughout, but the main draws are the scattered bird cliffs that scallop the Arctic edges and the lonely foxes that scurry between grassy hillocks. One can even volunteer to help monitor and protect Iceland's only native mammal.

p158

North Iceland

Landscapes ✓✓
Activities ✓✓✓
Wildlife ✓✓✓

The Works
What landscapes *doesn't* north Iceland offer? There are offshore islands, lonely peninsulas, icy peaks, pastoral horse farms, belching mudpots, sleepy fishing villages, epic waterfalls, shattered lava fields, breaching whales...

The Active North
Horse riding is best in the northwest. Birdwatching around Lake Mývatn is world-class, but remote Langanes and Arctic Grímsey hold their own. Hike the northern reaches of Vatnajökull National Park, or ski the Tröllaskagi Peninsula.

Whale Wonderland
Seals inhabit Vatnsnes Peninsula; puffins and seabirds nest all over. Waterbirds take to Mývatn like ducks to water. The biggest draw lurks beneath: Húsavík is the whale-watching master; towns along western Eyjafjörður, including Akureyri, are its apprentice.

p187

East Iceland

Landscapes ✓✓✓
Activities ✓
Wildlife ✓✓

Fan-fjord-tastic

The Eastfjords' scenery is particularly dramatic around the northern fjord villages, backed by sheer-sided mountains etched with waterfalls. Inland, the scenic lake Lagarfljót (and the forest on its eastern shore) is ripe for exploration, as is the 1833m mountain Snæfell, part of Vatnajökull National Park.

On Land & Water

Kayaking in Seyðisfjörður is a highlight, while mountain biking in this fjord is a good landlubber's option. Birdwatching and horse riding at Húsey are first-rate. Hikes in and around the fjords are highly praised.

Roaming Reindeer

Wild reindeer roam the mountains, and Iceland's version of the Loch Ness monster calls Lagarfljót home. Bird life is prolific, at the remote farms of Húsey and Skálanes, or the perfectly placed puffin-viewing platform at Borgarfjörður Eystri.

p238

Southeast Iceland

Landscapes ✓✓✓
Activities ✓✓
Wildlife ✓✓

Glacial Glory

Containing glittering glaciers, toppling waterfalls, the iceberg-filled Jökulsár-lón lagoon and Iceland's favourite walking area (Skaftafell), it's little wonder the southeast is among Iceland's most-visited regions. Contrasting this beauty is the stark grey sands of the eerie sandar.

Ice-Cap Endeavours

Various places offer ice climbing, glacier walks, snowmobiling, quad biking and hiking. Boat trips among the 'bergs of Jökul-sárlón are popular, you can mountain bike in Skaftafell, or there's the underrated activity of cracking langoustine claws in Höfn.

A Bevy of Birds

Seals are a photogenic addition to the camera-friendly waters of Jökulsár-lón, while great skuas make their homes in the sandar and harass visiting humans and birds. Ingólfshöfði is overrun with nesting puffins and other seabirds.

p263

The Highlands

Landscapes ✓
Activities ✓
Wildlife ✓

Barren Beauty

Touring the highlands will give you a new understanding of the word 'desolation'. The solitude is exhilarating, the views are vast. Some travellers are disappointed by the interior's ultrableakness and endless grey-sand desert, others are humbled by the sight of nature in its rawest, barest form.

Hard-Core Hiking

It's immensely tough but equally rewarding to hike or bike interior routes. Kerlingarfjöll and the Askja region have first-class hiking; Hveravellir has hot springs. Many visitors may be happiest touring the sights from the comfort of a 4WD tour!

Lifeless Land?

This region is practically uninhabited – there are no towns or villages, only summertime huts and accommodation. You may see the odd sheep, but that's likely to be all.

p285

> **Every listing is recommended by our authors, and their favourite places are listed first**

> **Look out for these icons:**

 Our author's top recommendation

 A green or sustainable option

 No payment required

See the Index for a full list of destinations covered in this book.

On the Road

Reykjavík

POP 202,300

Best Places to Eat

» Bergsson Mathús (p69)
» Snaps (p69)
» Kaffismiðjan (p68)
» Sægreifinn (p69)

Best Places to Stay

» Icelandair Hotel Reykjavík Marina (p66)
» Hótel Borg (p66)
» KEX Hostel (p64)
» Reykjavík Downtown Hostel (p64)
» AirBnB (p64)

Why Go?

The world's most northerly capital combines colourful buildings, quirky people, eye-popping design, wild nightlife and a capricious soul to devastating effect. Most visitors fall helplessly in love, returning home already saving to come back.

In many ways Reykjavík is strikingly cosmopolitan for its size. It is, after all, merely a town by international standards. But on the flip side of the coin, the island's capital is also very much a global city in disguise – peek under the shiny holiday veneer to find a place that is utterly quaint and embraces its know-your-neighbours smallness.

It's that striking contrast that gives the city its charm; the two sides, like tectonic plates clashing against one another, create an earthquake of energy. Add a backdrop of snow-topped mountains, churning seas, air as cold and clean as frozen diamonds, and fiery nights under the midnight sun, and you'll agree that there's no better city in the world.

Road Distances (km)

	Reykjavík	Borgarnes	Ísafjörður	Akureyri	Egilsstaðir	Höfn
Borgarnes	74					
Ísafjörður	457	384				
Akureyri	389	315	567			
Egilsstaðir	698	580	832	265		
Höfn	459	519	902	512	247	
Vík	187	246	630	561	511	273

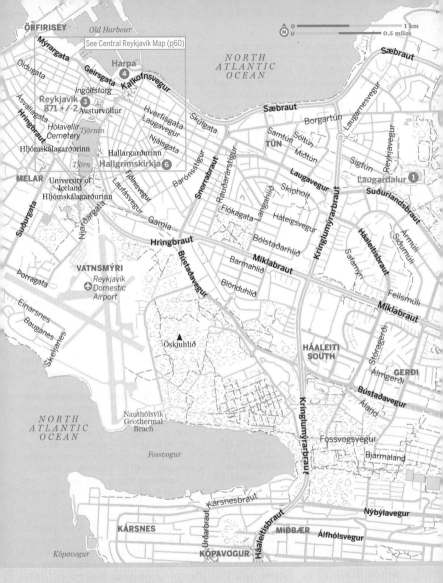

Reykjavík Highlights

1 Do as the locals and enjoy an afternoon soak at one of the city's public geothermal pools, such as **Laugardalur** (p53)

2 Don your *lopapeysa*, grab your MacBook and join the legions of accidental hipsters sipping quarts of coffee at one of the city's awesomely quirky **cafes** (p68)

3 Immerse yourself in Icelandic history at the brilliantly curated **Reykjavík 871 +/-2** (p48) set atop the excavated ruins of a Viking hall

4 Enjoy a performance or simply relax in the comfy lounge chairs at **Harpa** (p48), the capital's sparkling new cultural centre

5 Join the **djammið** (p47), a wild pub crawl through Reykjavík's tiny but oh-so-cool bars and clubs

6 Survey the city from the heights of **Hallgrímskirkja's** (p46) modernist steeple

History

Ingólfur Arnarson, a Norwegian fugitive, became the first official Icelander in AD 871. Myth has it that he tossed his *öndvegissúlur* (high-seat pillars) overboard, and settled where the gods washed them ashore. This was at Reykjavík (Smoky Bay), which he named after steam rising from geothermal vents. According to 12th-century sources, Ingólfur built his farm on Aðalstræti, and excavations have unearthed a Viking longhouse there (see p48).

Reykjavík remained just a simple collection of farm buildings for the centuries that followed. In 1225 an important Augustinian monastery was founded on the offshore island of Viðey (p80), although this was destroyed during the 16th-century Reformation.

In the early 17th century the Danish king imposed a crippling trade monopoly on Iceland, leaving the country starving and destitute. In a bid to bypass the embargo, local sheriff Skúli Magnússon, the 'Father of Reykjavík', created weaving, tanning and wool-dyeing factories – the foundations of the city – in the 1750s.

Reykjavík really boomed during WWII, when it serviced British and US troops stationed at Keflavík. The city grew at a fast and frenetic pace, until recently when it took a slamming after the global credit crisis of 2008 (see p307). Angry protests outside Parliament eventually led to the resignation of Prime Minister Geir Haarde in February 2009. Today, with the continuous rise in visitor numbers, central Reykjavík can feel like a bit of tourist town – especially in summer.

◎ Sights

The city is spread out along a small peninsula, with Reykjavík Domestic Airport and the long-distance bus terminal BSÍ in the southern half, and the picturesque city centre and harbour occupying the northern half. The international airport is 48km away at Keflavík (a special airport bus provides connections to the centre of Reykjavík).

The city centre is very compact, and contains most of Reykjavík's attractions. The commercial main street is Laugavegur. At its eastern end is Hlemmur bus terminal, one of the two main city bus stations. Moving westwards, this narrow, one-way lane blossoms with Reykjavík's flashiest clothes shops, bars and eateries. It changes its name

to Bankastræti, then to Austurstræti as it runs across the centre. Running uphill off Bankastræti at a jaunty diagonal, the artists' street Skólavörðustígur ends at the spectacular modernist church called Hallgrímskirkja.

The highway-like Lækjargata cuts straight across Bankastræti/Austurstræti. To its west is the so-called Old Reykjavík. To the northwest lies Reykjavík's working harbour. Tjörnin lake and the domestic airport are to the southwest.

For information on the popular 'volcano shows', see p73. And for details on Iceland's design scene, see the boxed text, p319.

📦 Hallgrímskirkja CHURCH

(Map p60; ☑510 1000; www.hallgrimskirkja.is; Skólavörðuholt; ⏱9am-9pm Jul & Aug, 9am-5pm Sep-Jun) Reykjavík's most attention-seeking building is the immense concrete church Hallgrímskirkja, star of a thousand postcards and visible from 20km away. You can get an unmissable view of the city by taking an elevator trip up the 75m-high **tower** (admission Ikr600).

In contrast to the high drama outside, the church's interior is puritanically plain. The most startling feature is the vast 5275-pipe **organ**, which has a strangely weapon-like appearance.

The church's radical design caused huge controversy, and its architect, Guðjón Samúelsson, never lived to see its completion – it took a painstaking 34 years (1940–74) to build. Those columns on either side of the tower represent volcanic basalt – a favourite motif of Icelandic nationalists. Hallgrímskirkja was named after the poet Reverend Hallgrímur Pétursson, who wrote Iceland's most popular hymn book.

If you come after 5pm during summer, the money from your tower ticket supports an array of local charities. There are many opportunities to hear church music as well – from mid-June to mid-August there are noontime concerts on Wednesdays, Thursdays and Saturdays, and on Sundays at 5pm. Sunday services are held at 11am sharp; the last service of the month is in English. There is also a small service held on Wednesday mornings at 8am.

Gazing proudly into the distance out front is a **statue** of the Viking Leifur Eiríksson, the first European to stumble across America. It was a present from the USA on the 1000th anniversary of the Alþing (National Assembly).

REYKJAVÍK IN...

One Day

Start your visit with a walk around Tjörnin and the Old Reykjavík quarter to get yourself oriented (doesn't hurt to swing by the main tourist information centre nearby to pick up some supplemental material about the city). Then follow Bankastræti and meander up arty Skólavörðustígur, poking your nose into its crafty little galleries. At the top of the hill is the immense concrete church Hallgrímskirkja, Reykjavík's most dramatic building. For a perfect view of the city, take an elevator trip up the tower.

Take in a couple of the city's best museums, like the impressive Reykjavík 871 +/-2, or the National Museum, then head down to the Old Harbour for a wander and a whale-watching tour if the mood strikes.

The afternoon is all about people watching – a favourite pastime among Icelanders. Sit yourself down at one of the top cafes, like Kaffismiðjan or Tiú Droppar, and watch the world go by. Or, better yet, head to Laugardalslaug and soak in the rich mineral waters while listening to local gossip.

Keep dinner plans loose for the evening, as many of the more laidback restaurants – like Vegamót – turn into wild party beasts in the evening. Once the bill's been settled, you might want to head back to your hotel for a kip and a freshen-up: you're going to need some energy if you're going to djammið; joining Reykjavík's notorious Bacchanalian pub crawl. Rather than cosying down in one venue, it's the done thing to cruise from bar to bar. To get you started, visit perennial favourite Kaffibarinn first, then tag along with locals in the know as they drag you to the latest and greatest drink-holes.

Two Days

After a late night out, sleep in and enjoy a relaxing brunch at Bergson Mathús, Grái Kotturinn or Laundromat Cafe.

Next, catch bus 18 from Lækjartorg bus station to Perlan. There are two excitements here: first is the superb Saga Museum, which brings Iceland's early history to life. Second is the hexagonal viewing deck, where you'll get tremendous views.

Head back to the city centre to shop for some designer wares, but make sure you've booked a table at one of the capital's finer restaurants. Then, splash out on an authentically Icelandic feast with added riffs by the city's foremost chefs. Dill, Friðrik V or Fiskfélagið make good choices.

After dinner treat yourself to a show at Harpa; if nothing's on check out one of the volcano shows (but have a late dinner after the show, as these popular screenings tend to end around 8pm).

Three Days

If you're only in Iceland for three days, make sure to spend some time in the countryside before you leave. A whole day in the desolate landscape that surrounds Reykjavík is a must – try combining a bus or super-Jeep trip to the Golden Circle with a variety of exhilarating activities. Most tour operators offer a bevy of combined packages that weave the countryside wonders together. It's also a cinch to tackle it on your own – see the DIY box on p95.

If you're planning to devote some time to exploring the countryside after your third day in town, then use your time to really feel like a local. Head out to Mosfellsbær for discounted lopapeysur (Icelandic woollen sweaters), and check out the local geothermal pool at Árbæjarlaug. It's also very much worth heading down to Hafnarfjörður, home to one of Iceland's greatest concentrations of hidden people; there are some excellent museum and dining options to be had here as well.

'What about the Blue Lagoon?' we hear you ask. Well, here's the clever part – you can visit Iceland's number-one attraction on your way back to the airport tomorrow. Wallowing in its warm, sapphire-blue waters is certainly a fantastic last memory to take home.

map p60; http://en.harpa.is; Austurbakki 2) An architectural beacon of prosperity in a post-crash economy, Harpa is Reykjavík's sparkling new concert hall and cultural centre. Giving the Sydney Opera House a run for its money both in scope and allegory, Harpa dazzles the eye with an intricate lattice of convex and concave glass panels that sparkle like the switchboard of an alien spaceship at night. To some it's an acquired taste, but to most – especially locals – it's a symbol of progress and a harbinger of wonderful events and artist endeavours still to come.

In addition to a season of brilliants shows, it's worth stopping by to check out the design boutiques on the lobby level, lounge on the plush chairs along the auspicious staircase, dine at a gourmet restaurant on the upper level, or take a tour of the grounds (Ikr1500; 3.30pm daily).

Old Harbour NEIGHBOURHOOD
(Map p60; Geirsgata) Largely a service harbour until recent years, the so-called Old Harbour has blossomed into a hot spot for tourists that borders on a mini adult Disneyland. Photo ops abound as boat bells ding while bobbing up and down; views of snowcapped mountains scallop the horizon. Whale-watching and puffin-viewing trips depart from the pier, as do many of the city's walking tours. Swing through to check out a cluster of excellent restaurants and cafes, shop for souvenirs, and watch a documentary about Iceland's temperamental tectonics.

Reykjavík 871 +/-2 MUSEUM
(Settlement Exhibition; Map p60; ☏411 6370; www.reykjavik871.is; Aðalstræti 16; adult/child Ikr1100/free; ☺10am-5pm) The city's best-curated museum is based around a single 10th-century Viking house but shows what miracles can be achieved when technology, archaeology and imagination meet. Through 21st-century wizardry, a fire leaps from the hearth, while around the walls ghostly settlers materialise to tend crops, hunt, launch a boat and bury their dead. The information on the display panels is refreshingly objective, providing a balanced and uninflated account of Iceland's settlement. It's interesting to note that scientists have found no evidence of religion among the earliest settlers.

Across the street you'll find an active excavation site where archaeologists are in the process of uncovering new artefacts from the Viking era. Ask at the ticket booth about daily tours of the new dig – they usually run in English at 11am on weekdays.

Tjörnin & Old Reykjavík NEIGHBOURHOOD
With a series of sights strung together like a precious necklace, the area dubbed Old Reykjavík is in the heart of the capital, and is largely the focal point of the many historic and introductory walking tours about town. The area is anchored around **Tjörnin** (Map p60), a placid lake at the centre of the city. It echoes with the honks, squawks and screeches of over 40 species of visiting birds, including swans, geese and Arctic terns; feeding the ducks is a popular pastime for the under-fives. Pretty sculpture-dotted parks line the southern shores, and their lacing paths are much used by cyclists and joggers. In winter, hardy souls strap on ice skates and turn the lake into an outdoor rink.

HOW TO BE A REYKJAVÍKUR

Six simple ways to blend in:
» When talking about partying in the capital, don't call it the 'runtur' – that's reserved for youngsters in the countryside who drive around to socialise in lieu of drinking. Call it 'djammið (p47).
» Refer to the different areas of Reykjavík by their postal code. The city centre is '101'.
» Never carry an umbrella. Locals never do; the wind will inevitably tear it apart.
» Be a fan of cats; there's a serious stray cat problem in the city – you'll see them poking their heads out of every nook and cranny.
» Refer to blatant demonstrations of frivolous wealth as being 'so 2007' (as in, before the country's currency crash).
» Learn how to pronounce 'Eyjafjallajökull'. It's kinda like saying 'hey I forgot my yoghurt' very fast, or – more precisely – *ay-ya-fiat*-la-yo-gootl.

Nearby, grassy **Austurvöllur** (Map p60) was once part of first-settler Ingólfur Arnarson's hay fields. Today it's a favourite spot for lunchtime picnics and summer sunbathing, and is sometimes used for open-air concerts and political demonstrations. The statue in the centre is of Jón Sigurðsson, who led the campaign for Icelandic independence.

Sitting between the park and the pond are several buildings of interest, including Reykjavík's waterside **Ráðhús** (City Hall; Map p60; Vonarstræti; admission free; ⊙8am-7pm Mon-Fri, noon-6pm Sat & Sun), a postmodern construction that divides all who see it into 'hate-its' or 'love-its'. Concrete stilts, tinted windows and mossy walls make it look like a half-bird, half-building rising from Tjörnin. Inside there's a fabulous **3D map of Iceland** – all mountains and volcanoes, with flecks of nothing-towns disappearing between the peaks.

Also of note is the **Alþingi** (Map p60; www.althingi.is; Túngata), which was originally sited at Þingvellir some thousand years ago. The modern Alþingi (Icelandic parliament) moved here in 1881; a stylish glass-and-stone annexe was completed in 2002. You're welcome to attend **sessions** (⊙4 times weekly Oct-May) when parliament is sitting.

When compared to the sky-scraping hulk of Hallgrímskirkja, Iceland's main cathedral, **Dómkirkja** (Map p60; www.domkirkjan.is; Lækjargata 14a; admission free; ⊙10am-5pm Mon-Fri) is a modest affair, but it played a vital role in the country's conversion to Lutheranism.

Perlan & the Saga Museum   MUSEUM

(Map p54; www.perlan.is; ⊙10am-10pm) Looking like half of Barbarella's bra, Perlan is a complex based around the huge hot-water tanks on Öskjuhlíð hill. It's about 2km from the city centre (take bus 18 from Hlemmur).

The main attraction is the endearingly bloodthirsty **Saga Museum** (www.sagamuseum.is; adult/child Ikr1800/800; ⊙10am-6pm Apr-Sep, noon-5pm Oct-Mar), where Icelandic history is brought to life by eerie silicon models and a soundtrack of thudding axes and hair-raising screams. Don't be surprised if you see some of the characters wandering around town, as moulds were taken from Reykjavík residents (the museum's owner is Ingólfur Arnarson, and his daughters are the Irish princess and the little slave gnawing a fish!).

The hexagonal **viewing deck** offers a tremendous 360-degree panorama of Reykjavík and the mountains; multilingual recordings explain the scenery. There's a busy **cafe** (⊙10am-9pm) on the same level, so if it's brass-monkey weather, you can admire the same beautiful views over coffee and crêpes. The mirrored dome on top of the tanks contains the like-named Perlan, a fine dining venue in the evenings.

Two **artificial geysers** will keep small children absolutely enthralled; the one inside blasts off every few minutes, while the outside geyser comes on in the afternoon. There are numerous walking and cycling trails on the hillside, including a path to Nauthólsvík hot beach.

National Museum   MUSEUM

(Þjóðminjasafn; Map p60; www.nationalmuseum.is; Suðurgata 41; adult/child Ikr1200/free; ⊙10am-5pm May–mid-Sep, 11am-5pm Tue-Sun mid-Sep–Apr) Displays at the National Museum are well thought out and give an excellent overview of Iceland's history and culture. The strongest section delves into the Settlement Era, with swords, silver hoards and a great little bronze model of Thor on display. However, the most treasured artefact in the museum is a beautiful 13th-century church door, carved with the touching story of a knight and his faithful lion. Upstairs, you really get a sense of the country's poverty over the following 600 years. Simple, homey artefacts utilise every scrap; check out the gaming pieces made from cod ear bones, and the wooden doll that doubled as a kitchen utensil.

Þjóðmenningarhúsið   MUSEUM

(Culture House; Map p60; www.thjodmenning.is; Hverfisgata 15; adult/child Ikr1000/free, free Wed; ⊙11am-5pm) Creeping into the darkened rooms of the Culture House is a true thrill for saga lovers. A permanent exhibition covers saga history, from a who's who of Norse gods to a tragic account of Árni Magnússon, who devoted his life to saving Icelandic manuscripts, and died of a broken heart when his Copenhagen library went up in flames.

Sun-Craft   MONUMENT

(Map p54; Sæbraut) Reykjavík is littered with fascinating statues and abstract monuments, but it's Jón Gunnar Árnason's ship-like Sun-Craft sculpture that seems to catch visitors' imaginations. Its seaside positioning may have something to do with it; there's also an oddly skeletal shape about it, as though it were some strange combustion between human ribs and the hull of a boat. Stop by late at night during summer for a

REYKJAVÍK SIGHTS

colourful photo shoot with the snow-topped mountains in the distance.

FREE **Reykjavík Museum of Photography** MUSEUM
(Ljósmyndasafn Reykjavíkur; Map p60; www.photo museum.is; 6th fl, Grófarhús, Tryggvagata 15; admission free; ☺noon-7pm Mon-Fri, 1-5pm Sat & Sun) Despite its grand name, the Reykjavík Museum of Photography is really just an exhibition room above Reykjavík City Library. It's definitely worth dropping in, though – its quintessentially Scandinavian exhibitions are free and usually thought-provoking. If you take the lift up, walk down the stairs, which are lined with funny old black-and-white photos.

Víkin Maritime Museum MUSEUM
(Víkin Sjóminjasafnið; Map p54; www.sjomin jasafn.is; Grandagarður 8; adult/child Ikr1200/ free; ☺10am-5pm Jun–mid-Sep, 11am-5pm Tue-Sun mid-Sep–May) Based appropriately in a former freezing plant for fish, the small Víkin Maritime Museum celebrates the country's seafaring heritage, focusing on the trawlers that transformed Iceland's economy. Much of the information is in Icelandic only, but silent film footage of trawler crews in action is worth a look. Your ticket also allows you aboard the coastguard ship *Óðín*, a veteran of the Cod Wars (of the 1970s when British and Icelandic fishermen quite literally came to blows over fishing rights in the North Atlantic), as part of guided tours that take place at 1pm, 2pm and 3pm (2pm and 3pm only at weekends during winter, closed in January and February). There's also an adorable on-site cafe called **Bryggjan** (mains Ikr800-1790) that is open during museum hours and offers quaint views of the boat-filled harbour.

Iceland Phallological Museum MUSEUM
(Hid Íslanska Reðasafn; Map p54; www.phallus.is; Héðinsbraut 3a; adult/child Ikr800/free; ☺noon-6pm) Oh, the jokes are endless here. This unique museum houses a bizarre collection of penises. From pickled pickles to petrified wood, there are over 300 different types of family jewels on display. Featured items include contributions from a walrus, the silver castings of each member of the Icelandic handball team and a singular human sample from the museum's previous owner who recently passed away. But don't rush to

volunteer – three other donors-in-waiting have already promised to bequeath their manhood (signed contracts are mounted on the wall). Quirky sidenote: all displays are translated into Esperanto.

Einar Jónsson Museum MUSEUM
(Map p60; www.skulptur.is; Njarðargata; adult/child Ikr600/free; ☺2-5pm Tue-Sun Jun–mid-Sep, 2-5pm Sat & Sun mid-Sep–Nov & Feb-May) Einar Jónsson (1874–1954) is Iceland's foremost sculptor, famous for his intense symbolist works. Chiselled allegories of Hope, Earth, Spring and Death burst from basalt cliffs, weep over naked women, sprout wings and slay dragons. For a taster, the **sculpture garden** (admission free) behind the museum is dedicated to the artist and contains 26 bronze casts; they're particularly effective at dusk. If these appeal to your inner Goth, you'll find gleaming white-marble sculptures on similar themes inside the museum itself. The building was designed by the artist and contains his austere penthouse flat, with unusual views over the city.

FREE **Reykjavík Art Museum** MUSEUM
(Listasafn Reykjavíkur; www.listasafnreykjavikur. is) The excellent Reykjavík Art Museum is split over three sites: Ásmundarsafn, Hafnarhúsið and Kjarvalsstaðir.

There's something immensely tactile about Ásmundur Sveinsson's monumental concrete creations – see for yourself in the **garden** outside the rounded, white **Ásmundarsafn** (Ásmundur Sveinsson Museum; Map p54; Sigtún; ☺10am-5pm May-Sep, 1-5pm Oct-Apr). Duck inside the museum for smaller, spikier works in wood, clay and metals, exploring themes as diverse as folklore and physics. Ásmundur (1893–1982) designed the building himself; getting into the spirit of things, the council later added an igloo-shaped bus stop in front. Buses 14, 15, 17, 19 and S2 pass close by.

Hafnarhús (Map p60; Tryggvagata 17; ☺10am-5pm Fri-Wed, to 8pm Thu) is a former warehouse now converted into a severe steel-and-concrete exhibition space. Pride of place is usually given to the distinctive, disturbing comic-book paintings of Erró (Guðmundur Guðmundsson; 1932–), a political artist who has donated several thousand works to the gallery. The rest of the industrial interior holds temporary modern-art installations: for example, fluorescent paintings of moss, a kaleidoscopic coffin and works by Japanese Pop artist Yoshitomo Nara have appeared over the last few years. The cafe has great harbour views.

Jóhannes Kjarval (1885–1972) was a fisherman until his crew paid for him to study at the Academy of Fine Arts in Copenhagen. He's one of Iceland's most popular artists, and his unearthly landscapes can be seen inside the angular glass-and-wood **Kjarvalsstaðir** (Map p54; Flókagata; ⊘10am-5pm), alongside changing installations.

National Gallery of Iceland   MUSEUM
(Listasafn Íslands; Map p60; www.listasafn.is; Fríkirkjuvegur 7; admission Ikr1000; ⊘11am-5pm Tue-Sun) Surreal mud-purple landscapes are intermingled with visions of trolls, giants and dead men walking at the National Gallery of Iceland's main art gallery. Overlooking Tjörnin, it certainly gives an interesting glimpse into the nation's psyche. As well as a huge collection of 19th- and 20th-century paintings by Iceland's favourite sons and daughters (including Ásgrímur Jónsson, Jóhannes Kjarval and Nína Sæmundsson), there are works by Picasso and Munch.

Sigurjón Ólafsson Museum   MUSEUM
(Map p60; www.lso.is; Laugarnestangi 70; adult/child Ikr500/free; ⊘2-5pm Tue-Sun Jun–mid-Sep, 2-5pm Sat & Sun mid-Sep–Nov & Feb-May) The Sigurjón Ólafsson Museum is a peaceful little place showcasing the varied works – portrait busts, driftwood totem poles and abstract football players – of sculptor Sigurjón Ólafsson (1908–82). A salty ocean breeze blows through the wooden rooms, which also contain Reykjavík's only shoreside cafe. On Tuesday from early July to August there are classical concerts at 8.30pm. Buses 12 and S5 pass close by.

Árbæjarsafn   MUSEUM
(www.reykjavikmuseum.is; Kistuhylur 4; adult/child Ikr 1100/free; ⊘10am-5pm Jun-Aug, by tour only 1pm Mon-Fri Sep-May) Quaint old buildings have been uprooted from their original sites and rebuilt at the open-air Árbæjarsafn, a kind of zoo for houses, 4km east of the city centre beyond Laugardalur. Alongside the 19th-century homes are a turf-roofed church and various stables, smithies, barns and boathouses – all very picturesque. There are summer arts-and-crafts demonstrations, and it's a great place for kids to let off steam. Take bus 12.

REYKJAVÍK'S ART GALLERIES

Reykjavík has many small contemporary art galleries. The following are of note:

ASÍ Art Museum (www.listasafnasi.is/english/; Klapparstígur 33)

Gallerí Fold (www.myndlist.is; Raudarar stigur 14-16)

i8 (www.i8.is; Tryggvagata 16)

Kling & Bang (http://this.is/klingog bang; Hverfisgata 42)

NÝLO (Nýlistasafnið; www.nylo.is; Skúla gata 28)

Studio Umbra (studio.umbra@isl.is; Lindargata 14)

FREE **Reykjavík Botanic Gardens**   GARDENS
(Map p54; www.grasagardur.is; Skúlatún 2; ⊘green-house 10am-10pm Apr-Sep, to 3pm Oct-Mar) Reykjavík Botanic Gardens contains over 5000 varieties of subarctic plant species, colourful seasonal flowers, a summer cafe serving coffee and waffles, and lots of bird life (particularly grey geese and their fluffy little goslings).

Laugardalur   NEIGHBOURHOOD
(Map p54) Laugardalur was once the main source of Reykjavík's hot-water supply – the name translates as 'Hot-Springs Valley'. It encompasses a large stretch of land in the very eastern part of the city. Most tourists venture out to the area to take advantage of the large public pool fed by a steamy geothermal source. There are a few other items of interest in the area including a **farmers market** and some relics from a bygone era, like an old wash house. Buses 14, 15, 17, 19 and S2 pass within a few hundred metres of Laugardalur.

Seltjarnarnes   NEIGHBOURHOOD
(off Map p54) Visiting the coast at Seltjarnarnes is a strange feeling. Head 1.5km west from the bustle of Lækjartorg, and you reach a red-and-white **lighthouse**, a strip of lava-strewn beach and a windswept golf course. Waves rush in, the air has that salt-sea tang, fish-drying racks sit by the shore and Arctic terns scream overhead – it all feels a million miles away from Reykjavík.

Seltjarnarnes is a haven for birdwatching – 106 visiting species have been recorded here. The offshore island **Grótta**, where the lighthouse stands, is accessible at low tide but closed from May to July to protect nesting birds. Across the water of the fjord there are super views of Esja (909m).

One of the nicest ways to get here is along the good coastal path, popular with walkers, joggers and cyclists. You can also take bus 11 from Hlemmur or Lækjartorg bus stations.

 ## Activities & Tours

As lovely as the capital's sights are, Reykjavík's real wonders are its activities; consider it a cosmopolitan base camp to the natural wonders that lie beyond. Activity-focused tours have taken the city by storm; there are heaps of other touring possibilities as well, which focus on the region's best attractions and destinations (see the boxed text, p58). Super-Jeeps and buses usher tourists to a variety of destinations – some are worth the buzz, others can feel a bit like a tourist trap during the warmest months of the year. These trips cater brilliantly to individuals spending only a few days in Iceland, but should not be undertaken by those planning on spending more than a long weekend, who can explore by themselves.

Walking Tours

Little Reykjavík is perfect for exploring under your own steam, but if you'd like a little guidance, the main tourist information centre has brochures that can bring the city's popular attractions to life.

Companies and private walking guides are always evolving and changing their tours to suit the tourists' needs (especially during summer). At the time of research the **Free Walking Tours** (www.freewalkingtour.is) was running strong, offering tours at noon and 2pm during the warmest months. **Go Ecco** (www.goecco.com) also leads walks of the capital, as does **Haunted Iceland** (www.hauntedwalk.is), which offers themed excursions.

Stop by the tourist information kiosk along the Old Harbour – amid the whale-watching ticket booths – for the latest on walking tour options. You can also sign up for hikes in the region here – a 'white night hike' (Ikr22,500 per person) takes in the steaming Reykjadalur area (departing at 5pm, returning at midnight; wine and soup included).

Bicycle Tours

Reykjavík Bike Tours
BICYCLE TOUR

(Map p60; ☏694 8956; www.reykjavikbiketours. is) A fantastic Icelandic-German outfitter offering active tours of the capital and the surrounding attractions, Reykjavík Bike Tours specialises in the following options: the Classic Reykjavík Bike Tour (2½ hours, 7km), which takes in the city's top attractions; the Coast of Reykjavík Bike Tour (2½ hours, 18km), which follows the coastal areas around the city revealing beautiful vistas; the Golden Circle & Bike (eight hours, 25km of cycling), which explores Gullfoss, Geysir and Þingvellir on wheels; and Vestmannaeyjar & Bike (12 hours, 11km of cycling), which is a wonderfully unique way of exploring the beautiful offshore archipelago further down in the south coast. Prices start at Ikr4800. You can also rent a bike and go at it on your own (Ikr3000/5000 for a half-/whole day).

Kría
BICYCLE TOUR

(Map p54; ☏5349164; www.kriacycles.com) Reykjavík's hipster answer to the bike trade, Kría is a sleek boutique, coffee kiosk, and cycle hot spot offering rentals and rural daytrips. Excursions start at €95.

Season Tours
BICYCLE TOUR

(www.seasontours.is) With electric bike tours and scooter excursions, this small company offers trips that explore the history of Iceland, its Viking settlement and various curiosities about town. A variety of walking and driving tours are also available.

Quad Biking Tours

While bike tours focus on the sights and attractions of Reykjavík and nearby destinations, quad biking is all about the thrills of offroading on ATM vehicles. Most tours take place on the acrid lava fields of the Reykjanes peninsula. Figure around Ikr9000 for an hour's tour, and Ikr42,000 for a six-hour safari.

Quad Safari
QUAD-BIKING

(☏414 1533; www.quad.is) Run in partnership with one of the bespoke tour operators, Eskimos, Quad Safari is based in Mosfellsbær and offers a variety of bouncy ATV outings in the hills nearby. During summer it's a lot of fun to go in the evening after dinner to check out the midnight sun and the twinkling lights of the capital from far above.

Whale-Watching Tours

Although the northern waters near Akureyri and Húsavík are known for their whale-watching tours, Reykjavík holds its own, making it a great option for tourists on shorter visits to Iceland.

Prices start around Ikr7500 for a two- to three-hour trip. Note that if you do not see whales, you will be given a voucher for a second trip at no cost. Tours generally run all year, though service greatly increases with demand during the warmest months. This also coincides with the prime season for viewing.

At the time of research, Zodiacs (or RIB boats) were taking the country by storm; check the section of the docks with the whale-watching operators for the season's iteration of speed boat service.

The following companies also offer sea angling opportunities for fishing enthusiasts, and special puffin viewing trips (though you'll often see puffins on a small islet while sailing out in search of whales).

Elding Whale Watching   WHALE WATCHING

(Map p60; ☎555 3565; www.elding.is) Elding is the original flavour of whale watching off the coast of the capital. It is also considered the most professional and the most ecofriendly, limiting its power expenditure on its wooden boats. Refreshments are sold onboard, and every trip is staffed by a scientist. Guests walk through a small museum as they board the boat, which gives a bit of background to the life of the local whales. Elding also runs the ferry to Viðey (see p80); the noon departure leaves from the Old Harbour.

Life of Whales   WHALE WATCHING

(Map p60; ☎562 2300; www.hvalalif.is) The cheapest whale-watching option, and sporting the largest boat in the area, Life of

---

REYKJAVÍK'S GEOTHERMAL SOURCES

Reykjavík's naturally hot water is the heart of the city's social life; children play, teenagers flirt, business deals are made and everyone catches up on the latest gossip at the baths. Volcanic influence keeps the temperature at a mellow 29°C, and most of the baths have *heitir pottar* (hot-pots), Jacuzzi-like pools kept at a toasting 37°C to 42°C. Admission usually costs around Ikr500 for adults (about half-price for children); bring your own towels and bathing suits – they cost extra. For further information, see www.spacity.is.

Reykjavíkurs get very upset by dirty tourists in their nice, clean pools (for good reason – the city's pools are free of chemicals). To avoid causing huge offence, visitors *must* wash thoroughly without a swimsuit before hopping in.

Laugardalslaug (Map p54; Sundlaugavegur 30a; ⊙6.30am-10.30pm Mon-Fri year-round, plus 8am-10pm Sat & Sun Apr-Oct, 8am-8pm Sat & Sun Nov-Mar) is the largest pool in Iceland, with the best facilities: an Olympic-size indoor pool, an outdoor pool, four hot-pots and a whirlpool, a steam bath, and a curling 86m waterslide. The state-of-the-art gym and Laugar Spa (Map p60; www.laugarspa.is; ⊙6.30am-10.30pm Mon-Fri year-round, plus 8am-10pm Sat & Sun Apr-Oct, 8am-8pm Sat & Sun Nov-Mar) is next door. Take bus 14.

Our favourite geothermal pool is the slickly designed Árbæjarlaug (Fylkisvegur, Elliðaárdalur; ⊙6.30am-10.30pm Mon-Fri year-round, plus 8am-10pm Sat & Sun Apr-Sep, 8am-8.30pm Sat & Sun Oct-Mar), well known as the best family pool. It's half inside and half outside, and there are lots of watery amusements (slides, waterfalls and massage jets) to keep the kids entertained. Take bus 19; it's a ways out of town towards Mosfellsbær.

In the centre of town you'll find Sundhöllin (Map p54; Barónsstígur 16; ⊙6.30am-9.30pm Mon-Fri, 8am-7pm Sat & Sun) Reykjavík's oldest swimming pool with a definite 'municipal baths' feel; it's the only indoor pool within the city. There's also Vesturbæjarlaug (Map p54; Hofsvallagata; ⊙6.30am-9.30pm Mon-Fri, 8am-7pm Sat & Sun) within walking distance of the centre (or take bus 11 or 15) that has a very local feel, with a large 25m pool, a kid's swimming area and a clutch of hot-pots.

In addition to the pooled geothermal sources, Reykjavík also has the dinky Blue-Flag Nauthólsvík Geothermal Beach (Map p54; ☎511 6630; ⊙10am-8pm mid-May–mid-Aug), on the edge of the Atlantic. It's packed with happy bathers in summer, thanks to golden sand imported all the way from Morocco, and an artificial hot spring that keeps the water at a pleasant 18°C to 20°C. There are sociable hot-pots, a snack bar and changing rooms (Ikr200). Get there on bus 19.

REYKJAVÍK ACTIVITIES & TOURS

Reykjavík

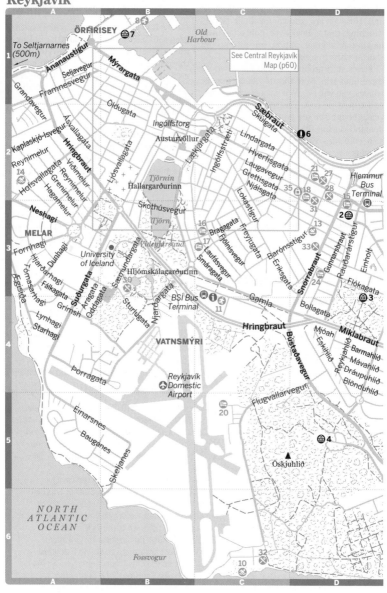

Whales takes about 30 to 40 minutes to reach the sweet spot in the sea to see whales.

Special Tours
WHALE WATCHING

(Map p60; ☏892 0099; www.specialtours.is/whale-watching) The smallest and fastest boat in the fleet of operators, Special Tours takes 20 minutes to reach the prime viewing spot in the bay. The 60-passenger vessel gets up close and personal with the mammoth beasts; they use an even smaller vessel for their puffin tours. In the height of summer

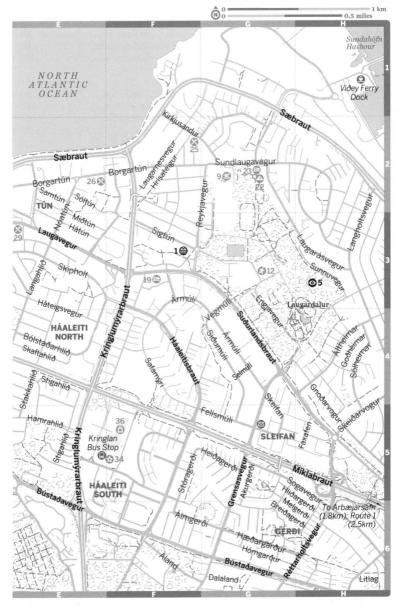

they run puffin trips five times a day and whale-watching trips three times a day.

Horse-Riding Tours

Trotting through lava fields under the midnight sun is an unforgettable experience. Horse farms around Reykjavík offer tours for all ages and experiences, and can collect you from your hotel. Most offer some form of activity or tour year-round.

The stables are very flexible, offering a variety of services from 90-minute outings to

Reykjavík

full-day adventures and multiday tours. You can also combine riding with a variety of activities, like touring the Golden Circle or visiting the Blue Lagoon. If you plan on touring around by bus anyway, it is cost effective to combine riding with other pursuits. Figure around €50 for a 90-minute ride.

Eldhestar HORSE RIDING
(☑480 4800; www.eldhestar.is; Vellir) Located near Hveragerði, Eldhestar is one of the most established riding outfits in Iceland. Trots take place on the flat, surrounding grasslands.

Íshestar HORSE RIDING
(☑555 7000; www.ishestar.is; Sörlaskeið 26, Hafnarfjörður) One of the oldest stables in the country, Íshestar is also one of the largest, with well-organised trots through crumbling lava fields. It's a favourite among German visitors.

Laxnes HORSE RIDING
(☑566 6179; www.laxnes.is; Mosfellsbær) Small and family-owned, Laxnes is run by an older couple whose nephews take mostly newbies out for very relaxed trots.

Íslenski Hesturinn HORSE RIDING
(☑434 7979; http://islenskihesturinn.is; Fjárborg) A newer addition to the horse-riding offerings in the capital area, this company takes special care to match you with a horse that suits your capabilities.

Viking Horses HORSE RIDING
(☑660 9590; http://vikinghorses.is; Kópavogur) Run by a small family, this stable is very popular in summer when they offer their acclaimed 'white night' rides during the midnight sun.

Scuba Diving & Snorkelling Tours
You wouldn't think it, but Iceland has some of the best and most unique snorkelling and scuba diving in the world. Imagine a crystalline fissure so clear that while diving you actually feel like you're flying – the following operators can make your scuba dreams come true at Silfra, a fissure near Þingvellir on the Golden Circle.

Prices are kept competitive across all operators at Ikr11,900 for a snorkel session, and Ikr29,900 for scuba. In June and July it's possible to do a midnight dive when the sun is still shining bright.

Dive.is (☎663 2858; dive.is) is the oldest operator in Iceland, Scuba Iceland (☎892 1923; www.scuba.is) has garnered a good reputation for its small groups, and Arctic Adventures (☎562 7000; www.adventures.is) caters to younger travellers, while also offering a spate of other water sports including river rafting.

Advance booking is essential; the aforementioned outfitters can pick you up in town, or you can meet them on site.

Rafting & Speedboating Tours

The Hvitá river, located along the Golden Circle, is the top spot for white-water rafting and speedboating near Reykjavík. Fun for the family, these trips run from Reykholt (p100; see for details) but pickups can be easily arranged from the city centre. A morning tour runs for around Ikr9900; afternoon trips go for Ikr15,900 and include a barbecue.

Snowmobiling Tours

There are many opportunities to jump on a snowmobile around the country; the best lie far beyond the capital. If you're basing yourself Reykjavík there are several operators that can take you to Langjökull nearby; the following options operate their own skidoos. Note that there are no day trips to Mýrdalsjökull, and day trips to Vatnajökull are done by air. The best operators in Reykjavík for snowmobiling are Mountaineers of Iceland (☎580 9900; www.mountaineers.is) and Arctic Adventures (☎562 7000; www.adventures.is).

Glacier Walks & Ice-Climbing Tours

Crunching across an empty ice cap can be an exhilarating experience that starkly contrasts with the quaintness of the capital. Tours take visitors out to Sólheimajökull, one of the glacial tongues of the massive Mýrdalsjökull. Walks run year-round; ice climbing is only from September to April. For ice climbing you have to be in reasonable shape (able to pull your own weight up). Figure Ikr19,900 for a short glacier walk, and Ikr26,900 for ice climbing. Prices are significantly lower if you tackle the ice locally and base yourself somewhere on the southern coast.

The Reykjavík-based operators are Arctic Adventures (☎562 7000; www.adventures.is) and Icelandic Mountain Guides (☎587 9999; www.mountainguides.is).

Caving & Lava Tunnel Tours

Exploring the wild underground world of Iceland's tortured terrain is a wonderful way to learn about the geological history of the island. It's impossible to explore many of these fissures and caverns by oneself, so attaching yourself to a tour is your best bet.

REYKJAVÍK IN WINTER

It's bitterly cold and the sun barely rises, but there are *some* advantages to wintery Iceland. The major joy, of course, is watching the unearthly glory of the Northern Lights (see p59).

The Reykjavík Skating Hall (Map p54; ☎588 9705; www.skautaholl.is; Múlavegur 1, Laugardalur; adult/child Ikr850/500, skate hire Ikr400; ☉noon-3pm Mon-Wed, to 3pm & 5-7.30pm Thu, 1-8pm Fri, 1-6pm Sat & Sun Sep-Apr) throws open its doors in winter. Some people also skate on Tjörnin (p48) when it freezes.

The ski season runs from November to April, depending on snowfall. The three ski areas close to Reykjavík (Bláfjöll, Hengill and Skálafell) are managed by the organisation Skíðasvæði (☎530 3000; www.skidasvaedi.is; Pósthússtræti 3-5). Iceland's premier ski slopes are at 84-sq-km Bláfjöll (☎561 8400; ☉2-9pm Mon-Fri, 10am-5pm Sat & Sun), which has 14 lifts and downhill, cross-country and snowboarding facilities. It gets swamped by eager city dwellers when the snow begins to fall. The resort is located about 25km southeast of Reykjavík on Rte 417, just off Rte 1. A shuttle bus leaves from the Mjódd bus stand southeast of town once per day in season – check with Skíðasvæði for departure times.

More bus tours (p59) operate in winter than you might imagine, offering a startling vision of familiar places: a white and frozen Gullfoss, caves full of icicles and snow-covered mountains.

DESTINATION DAY TRIPS

For travellers with the luxury of time, it's best to visit many of the following attractions under your own steam – you'll spend far less time moving back and forth from the capital to the island's other wonders sprinkled further afield.

These are the most popular destinations to visit during a guided day trip from the capital:

» **Golden Circle** (p95) Comprising three beloved attractions – Þingvellir, Geysir and Gullfoss – the Golden Circle is the ultimate clutch of attractions beyond the city limits that gives short-stay visitors a taste of the Icelandic countryside. It's simple, and cost effective, to combine a tour of this region with virtually any activity, including ATVs, snowmobiling, snorkelling, rafting and caving. Full-day trips generally depart around 9am returning at around 6pm; trips also leave around noon and return at 7pm. In summer you can do an evening trip (7pm to midnight) if you're tight on time.

» **Blue Lagoon** (p88) A must for most travellers; not visiting the Blue Lagoon is like going to the Louvre and not seeing the Mona Lisa. Many day trips from the capital can tie in a visit to the lagoon; however, it's perfectly seamless to tack it on to your journey to/from Keflavík International Airport instead.

» **South Coast** (p102) It may not look like much from the Ring Road, but once you step off the paved track, you'll uncover a wild assortment of geological wonders from active volcanos, glorious hikes, and shivery ice caps ready for exploration. Tours run throughout the year.

» **Jökulsárlón** (p277) This glacial lagoon is truly a sight for sore eyes; it is, however, quite far from the capital, making this one of the longest day trips available. Be prepared to spend the majority of the day in the bus, and you'll be visiting the lagoon at its most crowded. Often a visit to Jökulsárlón is combined with other activities, but it is better to base yourself on the south coast if you're going to tackle something this far out.

» **Snæfellsnes Peninsula** (p142) The Snæfellsnes Peninsula provides a less-travelled circuit to the popular Golden Circle, although it's slightly further away. Expect short hikes along crunchy lava fields, snowmobiling on the glacier, adorable seaside villages and a boat tour of offshore islets. Tours run year-round.

» **Landmannalaugar** (p121) For day trippers, a visit to Landmannalaugar can only be done on a super-Jeep tour, and you'll spend the majority of the day bouncing around the car. You reach this geothermal region after much anticipation and several stops at other geological attractions along the way, often including Hekla. It's the starting point for the famous Laugavegurinn hike to Þórsmörk and is thus very crowded. Visiting on a day trip is a bit of a tease – you'll only have about two hours to enjoy the surroundings. Tours only run during summer.

» **Þórsmörk** (p126) It's almost a tragedy to visit beautiful Þórsmörk on a day trip from the capital, as there are so many hiking routes to explore. Easily tackled on a super-Jeep tour, it's also possible to visit under your own steam in summer by taking the perfectly synced bus which arrives around midday and gives you until the early evening to walk through the verdant valley.

Many of these caves and lava tubes lie along the desolate Reykjanes peninsula, though it's also possible to do a trip out to Upper Borgarfjörður (p142). **Arctic Adventures** (☑562 7000; www.adventures.is), **Iceland Excursions** (☑540 1313; www.grayline.is) and **Icelandic Mountain Guides** (☑587 9999; www.mountainguides.is) are the best places to scout out your caving expedition. Figure around Ikr9500 for a three-hour excursion.

Inside the Volcano　ADVENTURE TOUR
(☑863 6640; www.insidethevolcano.com; admission Ikr37,000) Iceland's media darling when it opened its veritable doors in 2012, this one-of-a-kind experience takes a limited number of adventure-seekers down into one

of the only perfectly intact magma chambers in the entire world. From a geological perspective this is truly a mind-blowing experience; a mining cart lowers visitors in groups of four deep down into the bottom of a vase-shaped chasm that once gurgled with hot lava. The lights are dim and time is very limited, but those who can use their imagination will be dazzled. The trip also includes a hearty bowl of home-made lamb stew after returning from the bowels of the earth. Whispers about altering the experience to make it more tourist-friendly (allowing greater amounts of visitors) were circulating during the research of this guide; check the website for regularly updated details.

Northern Lights Tours

Wholly hokey in every way possible, Northern Lights trips are the latest tour trend to hit Reykjavík. Operators (usually the super-Jeep tours) take onlookers out into the countryside during the colder months to escape the urban light pollution in order to find these magnificent curtains of light. Trips last around four hours – usually from 10pm to 2am – and there's no light show guarantee.

There's no special recipe to seeing the aurora borealis, and no special place in the country that has better lights than others, so rather than linking up with a Northern Lights trip from the capital, we recommend spending a night or two in the quiet countryside to maximise your viewing possibilities. (For the record, the aurora borealis can indeed be glimpsed from the capital.) Many rural hotels offer Northern Lights wake-up calls, so that you don't miss out.

Bus & Activity Tours

A day-long bus tour from Reykjavík is one of the best and most cost-effective ways to see some of the country's spectacular natural wonders, especially if you're on a short holiday. They're also good if you want to combine sightseeing with activities, be it snowmobiling, horse riding, rafting or scuba diving.

Tours need to be booked in advance (either at the tourist office, at your hotel or hostel, or directly with the company) and they may be cancelled if there are insufficient numbers or if the weather turns rancid. Young children generally can travel free or at discounted rates.

Every year more and more tour operators pop up, but following are some of the better-established ones.

Iceland Excursions   BUS TOUR
(Gray Line Iceland; Map p60; ☑540 1313; www.grayline.is; Hafnarstræti 20) A bus-tour operator with comprehensive day trips that often combine destinations and activities such as white-water rafting and horseback riding. Book online for the best prices; expect large groups.

Reykjavík Excursions   BUS TOUR
(Kynnisferðir; Map p54; ☑580 5400; www.re.is; BSÍ bus terminal, Vatnsmýrarvegur 10) The most popular bus-tour operator has summer and winter programs. Extras include horse riding, snowmobiling and themed tours tying in with festivals.

Iceland Horizons   BUS TOUR
(☑866 7237; www.icelandhorizon.is) A smaller tour bus operator with only 14 seats, this company gets rave reviews, especially when humorous David helms the wheel.

Gateway to Iceland   BUS TOUR
(☑534 4446; www.gatewaytoiceland.is) Gateway to Iceland gets great reviews by backpackers because their minibus tours are smaller than the mass market ones, but larger than the exclusive super-Jeep options, making it a strong choice for penny pinchers looking for an extra bit of service.

Bustravel   BUS TOUR
(☑511 2600; www.bustravel.is) Very popular among the hostelling crowd about town, Bustravel has a good selection of informative driver-guides. Groups are large and prices are kept very low.

Arctic Adventures   BUS TOUR
(Map p60; ☑562 7000; www.adventures.is; Laugavegur 11) With young and enthusiastic staff, this company specialises in action-filled tours – rafting, horse riding, quad bike tours, glacier walks and so on.

Guðmundur Jónasson Travel   BUS TOUR
(☑511 1515; www.gjtravel.is; Borgartún 34) Offers tried-and-true day excursions along the Ring Road and into the highlands, and can arrange super-Jeep trips, self-drive holidays and group travel.

Super-Jeep & Supertruck Tours

If your holiday budget allows it, a super-Jeep tour (rather than a bus tour) can be a more

Central Reykjavík

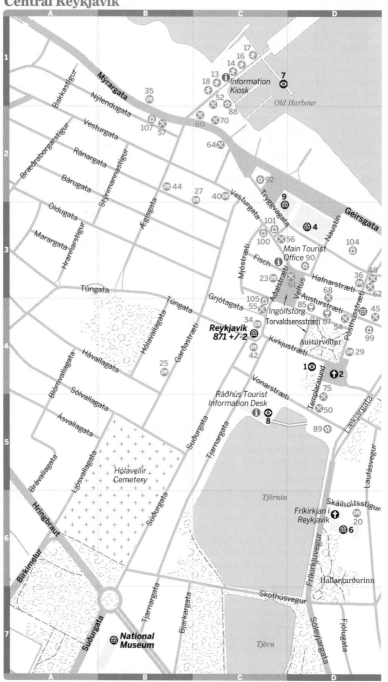

REYKJAVÍK

Bakkastígur

Mýrargata

Nýlendugata

Vesturgata

Bræðraborgarstígur

Ránargata

Styrimannastígur

Bárugata

Öldugata

Ægisgata

Marargata

Hávallagata

Hávallagata

Túngata

Túngata

Hólavallagata

Garðastræti

Vesturgata

Grjótagata

Mjóstræti

Fischer

Aðalstræti

Tryggvagata

Geirsgata

Nauslin

Hafnarstræti

Austurstræti

Veltus

Pósthússtræti

Hafnarstræti

Information Kiosk

Old Harbour

Main Tourist Office

Ingólfstorg

Torvaldsensstræti

Reykjavík 871 +/-2

Kirkjustræti

Austurvöllur

Vonarstræti

Templarasund

Lækjargata

Ráðhús Tourist Information Desk

Blómvallagata

Sólvallagata

Ásvallagata

Bráavallagata

Ljósvallagata

Suðurgata

Tjarnargata

Hólavellir Cemetery

Suðurgata

Hringbraut

Birkimelur

Suðurgata

Tjarnargata

Bjarkargata

Tjörnin

Skothúsvegur

Fríkirkjan í Reykjavík

Skálholtsstígur

Fríkirkjuvegur

Hallargarðurinn

Laufásvegur

Sóleyjargata

Fjólugata

National Museum

Tjörn

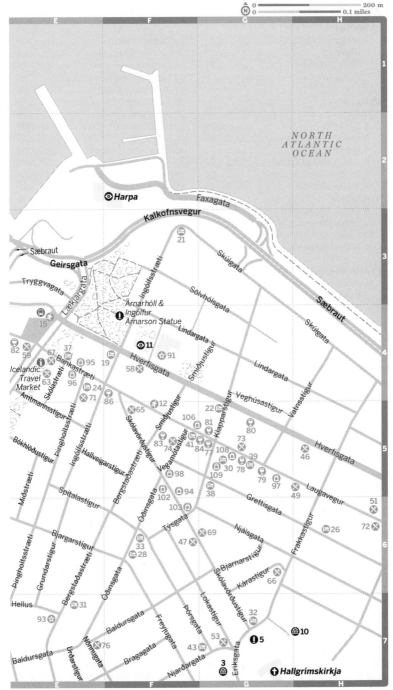

0   200 m
0   0.1 miles

NORTH
ATLANTIC
OCEAN

Harpa
Faxagata
Kalkofnsvegur
21
Skúlgata

Sæbraut
Geirsgata
Tryggvagata
Sölvhólsgata
Sæbraut
Lækjargata
Ingólfsstræti
Skúlgata

Árnarhóll &
Ingólfur
Arnarson Statue
Lindargata

15
11
Lindargata

82 59
67   37
Bankastræti 95 19
Hverfisgata
91
Smiðjustígur

Icelandic
Travel
Market
63 Skólastræti
58
Veghúsastígur
Vatnsstígur

96   24
Amtmannsstígur 71
86
65
12
22
80
Hverfisgata

Bókhlöðustígur
Þingholtsstræti
Ingólfsstræti
Hallveigarstígur
Skólavörðustígur
Smiðjustígur
106   81
83 74   41 84 77
108
73
39
46

Miðstræti
Spítalastígur
Bergstaðastræti
Vegamótastígur
98
30 78
79   97
Laugavegur
49
51
72

102   94
109
38
Grettisgata

Bjargarstígur
Grundarstígur
Bergstaðastræti
Óðinsgata
103
Týsgata
47   69
Njálsgata
Frakkastígur
26

33
28

Hellus
31
Skólavörðustígur
Skthjarnarstígur
Kárastígur
66

93
32
10

Nönnugata
76
Baldursgata
Freyjugata
Þórsgata
Lokastígur
53
5

Baldursgata
Urðarstígur
Bragagata
Njarðargata
43
Eiríksgata
3
Hallgrímskirkja

Central Reykjavík

intimate and customised experience. Generally you'll reach your points of interest a lot faster, and you can get out further into the wild terrain to uncover less visited attractions as well. These tours tend to have very small groups (around four to six people) and are a cost-effective way to see the countryside if you were planning on exploring with a 4WD.

Eskimos   ADVENTURE TOUR
(☑414 1500; www.eskimos.is) A high-end operator offering a variety of tailor-made super-Jeep services based on guests' requests. It also acts as a travel agency, providing transport for Reykjavík-based travellers who want to experience activities, such as ice caving and dog sledding, in the countryside. It can even create multiday super-Jeep excursions.

Mountaineers of Iceland   ADVENTURE TOUR
(☑580 9900; www.mountaineers.is) Excellent, knowledgeable guides, many of whom have experience working on the national rescue team. These are real nature enthusiasts and outdoor fanatics that will inspire Icelandic devotion as well.

Other companies of note: **Gateway to Iceland** (☑534 4446; www.gatewaytoiceland. is), **Ice Limo** (☑554 4000; www.luxurytravel.is), **Superjeep.is** (☑660 1499; www.superjeep.is).

Air Tours
Iceland is surprisingly large, and driving distances to beautiful spots outside Reykjavík can be daunting if you're only here for a short time. Larger budgets will delight in the possibility of day trips and shorter tours by air to such destinations as Akureyri, the

steaming earths of the south coast and highlands, Vestmannaeyjar, and even a day trip to Greenland (p77).

Two companies offer sightseeing flights: **Eagle Air Iceland** (☎562 4200; www.eagleair.is), which is more activities focused, and **Air Iceland** (☎570 3000; www.airiceland.is), which has seamless connections to most major destinations in the country. Both are based at Reykjavík Domestic Airport.

🎓 Courses

The **Icelandic Culture and Craft Workshops** (☎566 8822; www.cultureandcraft.com) offer half-day knitting workshops using pure Icelandic wool. They meet in the mornings at 9am in changing locations around the city. See the website for details.

🎊 Festivals & Events

For the city's list of festivals, many of which are celebrated with gleeful enthusiasm in Reykjavík, see Month by Month (p21). For forthcoming live music, see www.musik.is.

🛏 Sleeping

Reykjavík has loads of accommodation choices, with midrange guesthouses and business-class hotels predominating. From June through the end of August accommodation fills up very quickly; reservations are a must. Most places open year-round (though we've noted where accommodation is summer only) and offer significant discounts from October to April; summer prices are listed here.

SLEEPING WITH THE LOCALS

As Reykjavík continues to transform into a full-fledged tourist town during summer, the price of accommodation is ever on the rise. Enterprising locals have begun to capitalise on the capital's prize neighbourhoods by offering up space in their centrally located homes or apartments. These apartment and room rentals are undercutting the rack rates for the area's hotels, providing better value for money, but without any of the hotel perks (no cleaning, concierge service etc).

Compare the address of your home-to-be with the maps in this chapter; you don't want to end up too far from the city centre, especially if you're visiting for a short stint. Check out **Airbnb** (www.airbnb.com) and **Couchsurfing** (www.couchsurfing.org).

Budget

Budget digs in the capital are priced much like a major European capital – expect hostels and camping if you're looking to pinch pennies.

KEX Hostel HOSTEL€
(Map p54; ☎561 6060; www.kexhostel.is; Skúlagata 28; 4-/16-person dm Ikr5100/3200, d without bathroom Ikr14,400; ☜) Like some kind of unofficial headquarters of backpackerdom, KEX is a mega-hostel with heaps of style (think retro Vaudeville meets rodeo) and sociability. Overall it's not as prim as the other options in this category – and the bathrooms are shared by many – but if you're searching for a friendly vibe with a fun lobby bar, look no further.

Reykjavík Downtown Hostel HOSTEL€
(Map p60; ☎553 8120; www.hostel.is; Vesturgata 17; dm from Ikr9400; @☜) Squeaky clean and well run, this effortlessly charming hostel gets such excellent reviews by the backpacker crowd that it regularly lures large groups and an older legion of penny-pinchers.

Reykjavík Loft Hostel HOSTEL€
(Map p60; ☎553 8140; www.hostel.is/Hostels/Reykjavikloft; Bankastræti 7; dm/d Ikr5300/18,400; @☜) Reykjavik's newest addition to the hostel scene opened in the spring of 2013, and is perched high above the action on busy Bankastræti. Attracting a decidedly younger crowd, this sociable spot comes with prim dorms, plenty of chill-out space and a special Japanese coffee maker that apparently makes the best cup on the planet. Discounts are available for HI members.

Reykjavík Backpackers HOSTEL€
(Map p60; ☎578 3700; www.reykjavikbackpackers.com; Laugavegur 28; dm/d from Ikr4990/17,490; @☜) A major player in the capital's hostel scene, this place has spic-and-span rooms (try to score one on the upper floors), quirky bus seats in the lobby, a fantastic roof deck, and a climbing wall tucked in the back.

Reykjavík City Hostel HOSTEL€
(Map p54; ☎553 8110; www.hostel.is; Sundlaugavegur 34; dm from Ikr6400; P@☜) Reykjavík's original hostel is a large, ecofriendly complex that retains a fun backpacker vibe despite being 2km out of the city centre.

Reykjavík Campsite CAMPGROUND€
(Map p54; ☎568 6944; www.reykjavikcampsite.is; Sundlaugavegur 32; sites per person Ikr1400; ☺mid-May–mid-Sep; ☜) The only camping option in the city (right next door to the city hostel, 2km east of the centre in the Laugardalur valley) gets very busy in summer, but with space for 650 people in its three fields, you're likely to find a place. Facilities include free showers, bike hire, a kitchen and barbecue area.

Salvation Army Guesthouse HOSTEL€
(Map p60; ☎561 3203; www.guesthouse.is; Kirkjustræti 2; dm/d Ikr3500/11,500; ☺Jun-Aug; ☜) This is the nearest thing Reykjavík has to a Japanese capsule hotel! The tiny rooms at this Christian 'guest house' are highly functional and frill-free, if a bit rundown. Step outside and the whole of Reykjavík is at your feet.

Midrange

Reykjavík is packed with *gistiheimili* (guesthouses), and there are new places opening every year. Most are in converted houses, so rooms often have shared bathrooms, kitchens and TV lounges. Some offer sleeping-bag accommodation. Short-term apartments rentals in Reykjavík are often very good value.

Most of the hotels rooms in this category are places built for and favoured by business travellers or large groups, and are thus pretty bland.

Grettisborg Apartments APARTMENTS €€
(Map p54; ☑694 7020; www.grettisborg.is; Grettisgata 53b; apt from €145; ☎) Like sleeping in a magazine for Scandinavian home design, these thoroughly modern apartments come in 50 shades of grey (no, not like that), sporting fine furnishing and sleek built-ins.

Baldursbrá Guesthouse GUESTHOUSE €€
(Map p54; ☑552 6646; baldursbra@centrum.is; Laufásvegur 41; d incl breakfast from Ikr16,000; @☎) This exceptional little guest house, on a quiet street close to Tjörnin and the BSÍ bus terminal, stands out thanks to the care and kindness of its owners. The decent-sized, comfy rooms all have washbasins, and the additional facilities are admirable – a sociable sitting room-TV lounge, and a private garden with a fab hot-pot, sauna and barbecue.

Castle House & Embassy Apartments GUESTHOUSE €€
(Map p54; ☑511 2166; http://hotelsiceland.net; Skálholtsstígur 2a & Garðastræti 40; apt from Ikr20,500; ☎) Turn to these pleasant self-contained apartments for satisfyingly central and commendably quiet accommodation. The two sets of apartments (located on opposite sides of Tjörnin) are much more personal than a hotel, but come with room service: fresh towels appear daily and washing-up seems to magically clean itself.

Guesthouse Butterfly GUESTHOUSE €€
(Map p60; ☑894 1864; www.kvasir.is/butterfly; Ránargata 8a; d with/without bath €130/105; ☺mid-May–Aug; ☎) On a quiet residential street within fluttering distance of the centre, Butterfly has neat, simply furnished rooms. There's a guest kitchen, and the friendly Icelandic-Norwegian owners make you feel right at home. The top floor has two self-contained apartments with kitchen and balcony.

Sunna Guesthouse GUESTHOUSE €€
(Map p60; ☑511 5570; www.sunna.is; Þórsgata 26; d/apt from Ikr18,500/31,500; ☎) Rooms at this guesthouse are simple and sunny with honey-coloured parquet floors. Nine have private bathrooms, and several at the front have good views of Hallgrímskirkja. Families are made to feel welcome; choose between neat studio apartments holding up to four people, or more spacious apartments with accommodation for up to eight.

Galtafell Guesthouse GUESTHOUSE €€
(Map p54; ☑551 4344; www.galtafell.com; Laufásvegur 46; d/apt Ikr16,600/20,200; ☎) In the quiet, well-to-do 'Embassy District', and within easy walking distance of town. The four spruce apartments here each contain a fully equipped kitchen, a cosy seating area and a separate bedroom, and there are three doubles with access to a guest kitchen. The only drawback is that they're basement rooms, so there are no views of anything but the pavement!

Guesthouse Óðinn GUESTHOUSE €€
(Map p60; ☑561 3400; www.odinnreykjavik.com; Óðinsgata 9; s/d incl breakfast Ikr13,500/16,900; ☎) This family-run guest house has simple white rooms with splashes of colourful artwork. An excellent buffet breakfast is served in a handsome room with sea views. Some en-suite rooms are available.

Forsæla Guesthouse GUESTHOUSE €€
(Map p60; ☑551 6046, 863 4643; www.apartmenthouse.is; Grettisgata 33b; d/apt from Ikr17,200/26,800; ☎) This is a really lovely option in Reykjavík's conservation area. Star of the show is the 100-year-old wood-and-tin house for four to eight people, which comes with all the old beams and tasteful modcons you could want. Three apartments have small but cosy bedrooms and sitting rooms, fully equipped kitchens and washing machines. There's a minimum three-night stay.

Three Sisters GUESTHOUSE €€
(Þrjár Systur; Map p60; ☑565 2181; www.threesisters.is; Ránargata 16; apt from €133; ☺mid-May–Aug; @☎) A twinkly-eyed former fisherman runs the Three Sisters, a lovely town house in old Reykjavík, now divided into eight studio apartments. Comfy beds are flanked by old-fashioned easy chairs and state-of-the-art flatscreen TVs. Each room comes with a cute fully equipped kitchen (including fridge, microwave and two-ringed hob).

Room With A View APARTMENTS €€
(Map p60; ☑552 7262; www.roomwithaview.is; Laugavegur 18; apt from Ikr28,000; ☎) This ridiculously central apartment hotel offers one- to four-bedroom apartments, decorated in Scandinavian style and with private bathrooms, kitchenettes, CD players, TVs and washing machines. Half have those eponymous sea and city views, and most have access to a Jacuzzi. Rooms vary – check the

website for a wealth of details. It has a bang-on-centre location; the downside is Friday- and Saturday-night street noise.

Hótel Frón
HOTEL €€

(Map p60; ☎511 4666; www.hotelfron.is; Laugavegur 22a; d incl breakfast from Ikr22,900; @🛜) This bright blue hotel has lots in its favour – particularly its excellent location overlooking Laugavegur (although rooms at the front can be noisy at weekends), and the stylish apartments in a newer wing. Older rooms are less inspiring.

Hótel Leifur Eiríksson
HOTEL €€

(Map p60; ☎562 0800; www.hotelleifur.is; Skólavörðustígur 45; d incl breakfast from Ikr25,500) This hotel glories in one of the best locations in Reykjavík: it's slap on the end of arty Skólavörðustígur, and more than half its 47 rooms have inspiring views of Hallgrímskirkja. They're fairly small and basic, but you're paying for the hotel's coordinates rather than its interior design.

4th Floor Hotel
GUESTHOUSE €€

(Map p54; ☎511 3030; www.4thfloorhotel.is; Laugavegur 101; d incl breakfast from Ikr20,900; @🛜) Close to Hlemmur bus station, the 24 rooms at this 'hotel' (really a guesthouse) are a mixed bag. Economy rooms fit these accoutrements into a tiny space and have shared bathrooms, while more expensive en-suite rooms are larger: four have sea views and two have balconies. The smart studio apartments here are worth every króna.

CenterHótel Plaza
HOTEL €€

(Map p60; ☎595 8550; www.plaza.is; Aðalstræti 4; d incl breakfast from €215; @🛜) A full service hotel guarding an enviable spot in the Old Reykjavík quarter, this fresh-faced member of the CenterHótel chain has business-oriented rooms with polished wooden floors, and great views from the higher levels.

CenterHotel Klöpp
HOTEL €€

(Map p60; ☎595 8520; www.centerhotels.is; Klapparstígur 26; d incl breakfast from €180; 🛜) Scandi-sleek detailing borders on spartan at this central sleeping option. The facade's rather dreary and dated, but the rooms are fresh-faced; many sport bay views.

Snorri Guesthouse
GUESTHOUSE €€

(Map p54; ☎552 0598; www.guesthouserey kjavik.com; Snorrabraut 61; d with/without bath Ikr21,200/15,400; 🛜) On the corner of a big road intersection, this pebble-dashed building doesn't look too promising. However, its

clean rooms in muted shades – particularly the more expensive 'family' variety – make for a decent base. It's about a 20-minute walk into the city centre.

Top End

Expect good service and lovely digs, but nothing here truly compares to the high-end hotels of major metropolitan cities.

TOP CHOICE Icelandair Hotel Reykjavík Marina
BOUTIQUE HOTEL €€€

(Map p60; ☎560 8000; www.icelandairhotels.is/ hotels/reykjavikmarina; Mýrargata 2; d Ikr30,000; @🛜) A gorgeous addition to the capital's accommodation scene sits next to the Old Harbour, with excellent sea views from the even-numbered rooms on the 4th floor. Captivating murals, blonde-wood trimming, up-to-the-second mod cons, and clever ways to conserve space make the small rooms a winner overall. The lobby also benefits from the eye-catching design scheme with a menagerie of strange furniture and a live satellite feed to Blue Lagoon.

101 Hotel
BOUTIQUE HOTEL €€€

(Map p60; ☎580 0101; www.101hotel.is; Hverfisgata 10; d from Ik53,000; @🛜) The 101 aims to tickle the senses – with yielding downy beds, iPod sound docks and Bose speakers, rich wooden floors and glass-walled showers – it may mean you skip the bars and opt for a night in instead. A spa with masseurs, a small gym and a glitterati restaurant-bar add to the opulence. Some people have been underwhelmed by the service, but all in all this is one of the city's boutique-iest places to stay.

Hótel Holt
LUXURY HOTEL €€€

(Map p60; ☎552 5700; www.holt.is; Bergstaðastræti 37; d from €255; @🛜) Cross the threshold and enter a world of luxury. Original paintings, drawings and sculptures adorn the rooms (Holt houses the largest private art collection in Iceland), set off by warm-toned decor and rose-coloured carpets. Downstairs is a handsome amber-hued library, a bar with flickering fire and a huge selection of single-malt whiskys, and one of the country's best restaurants.

Hótel Borg
LUXURY HOTEL €€€

(Map p60; ☎551 1440; www.hotelborg.is; Pósthússtræti 9-11; d from €325; @) The city's most historic hotel was completely overhauled in 2007. Super-smart beige, black, and cream decor, parquet floors, leather headboards and flatscreen Bang & Olufsen TVs are now standard throughout, lending the hotel an elegant (if rather masculine) feel. It may have lost some of its art deco charm, but thankfully it's retained the enormous showerheads in its bathrooms. Quadruple-glazed windows cut down on drunken weekend street noise.

REY Apartments
APARTMENTS €€€

(Map p60; ☑771 4600; www.rey.is; Grettisgata 2a; apt €145-330; ⑨) For those leaning towards private digs rather than hotel stays, REY is a very handy choice with a huge cache of apartments scattered across several Escher-like stairwells. It's a full service affair, and easily trumps the growing Airbnb market.

Icelandair Hotel Natura
HOTEL €€€

(Map p54; ☑444 4503; www.icelandairhotels.com/hotels/reykjaviknatura; Nauthólsvegur 52; d Ikr27,600; @⑨) The name might be slightly misleading at first, since it's next to the domestic airport and not in the countryside, but Natura impresses with its unique design developed by local artists who drew their inspiration from the Icelandic countryside. Perks include free city bus tickets, an indoor geothermal pool and a 'bedtime story' (you'll see).

Hilton Reykjavík Nordica
HOTEL €€€

(Map p54; ☑444 5000; www.hilton.com; Suðurlandsbraut 2; d from Ikr28,000; @⑨) Bring your autograph book to the Nordica – visiting celebs often stay here. Cool Scandinavian chic oozes from every part, with amenities such as 24-hour room service, gym, spa and the gourmet restaurant Vox (p71). Light-filled rooms with enormous beds are decorated in subtle shades of cream and mocha; those on the upper floors have super sea views. The hotel's about 2km from the city centre, but it runs a free city-centre shuttle service.

Radisson SAS 1919 Hotel
HOTEL €€€

(Map p60; ☑599 1000; www.radissonblu.com; Pósthússtræti 2; d from €199; @⑨) Although this is part of a large chain, the catchily named Radisson SAS 1919 Hotel is a boutique place with plenty of style. Attractive rooms sport wooden floors, large beds, flatscreen TVs and wireless access. Keep walking up the carved iron stairwells to the 4th floor and you'll reach the large, comfy suites. Other bonuses include a fantastic location, a gym and the cool Gullfoss bar-restaurant.

CenterHótel Arnarhvoll
HOTEL €€€

(Map p60; ☑595 8540; www.centerhotels.com; Ingólfsstræti 1; d from €500; @⑨) A sleek hotel on the waterfront, Arnarhvoll offers unimpeded views of the bay and Mt Esja in the distance. Cool, Scandinavian-designed rooms with clean lines and large windows let in all that lovely Nordic light; it's definitely worth paying extra and getting one with a sea view. Rooms are on the small side, but the extremely comfortable beds more than compensate for this common Icelandic shortcoming. A small sauna and steam room in the basement add novelty.

CenterHótel Þingholt
HOTEL €€€

(Map p60; ☑595 8530; www.centerhotels.com; Þingholtsstræti 3-5; d from €220; @⑨) Compact, quirky and full of character, Þingholt opened in 2006 and still retains a fresh, new feel. It was designed by architect Gulla Jónsdóttir, who used natural materials and some very Icelandic ideas to create one of Reykjavík's most distinctive boutique hotels. Rooms are compact, but feel cosy rather than cramped. This snuggly effect is heightened by moody lighting, stylish dark-grey flooring and black-leather headboards and furniture.

Hótel Óðinsvé
HOTEL €€€

(Map p60; ☑511 6200; www.hotelodinsve.is; Þórsgata 1; d from Ikr28,900; @) A boutique hotel with bags of personality, Óðinsvé contains 43 sun-drenched rooms with wooden floors, original artwork and classic furnishings. They're all very different – some are split-level, some have balconies and many have bathtubs – but only room 117 has a resident ghost! The hotel also owns some stunning apartments, which overlook the prison a short walk away on Skólavörðustígur.

Hótel Reykjavík Centrum
HOTEL €€€

(Map p60; ☑514 6000; www.hotelcentrum.is; Aðalstræti 16; d from €300; ⑨) This central hotel has striking architecture – mezzanines and a glass roof unite two buildings, giving the whole place a spry, light feel. Its 89 neatly proportioned rooms come in two styles: 'traditional', with patterned wallpaper and white-painted furniture; and 'deluxe', with leather seats and a more contemporary feel. Both have safes, minibars, pay TVs (with films to order), tea-making facilities and wi-fi internet access.

✕ Eating

From take-it-to-go hotdogs to gourmet platters on white-cloth tables, little Reykjavík has an astonishing assortment of eateries. Although you can go around the world in 80 plates, we much prefer the slew of Icelandic and 'new Nordic' restaurants serving up tried-and-true variations of seafood and lamb.

Of all the dining options, it's Reykjavík's cool and cosy cafes that are the city's best features. Lingering is encouraged – many offer magazines and free wi-fi access. They're the best places to go for morning coffee and light lunches. As the evening wears on, most undergo a Jekyll-and-Hyde transformation – coffee becomes beer, DJs materialise in dark corners, and suddenly you're not in a cafe but a kick-ass bar. Magic. Because the dividing line is so blurred at some venues, also see Drinking, p72.

Budget

Reykjavík's budget eateries are few and far between, and usually fall under the cafe category. Although fast food options are relatively abundant, we much prefer cosying up to piping hot coffee and a home-made soup or sandwich for a midday meal. Expect the healthier cafe options to close earlier in the day than fast food venues, so save your pennies for a pricier meal in the evenings after a heady day of sightseeing.

TOP CHOICE **Kaffismiðjan** CAFE €

(Map p60; www.kaffismidja.is; Kárastígur 1; snacks Ikr180-600; ⊙8.30am-5pm Mon-Fri, 10am-5pm Sat) Coffee cupping is now virtually akin to wine tasting in Reykjavík, and leading the trend is the effortlessly hip Kaffismiðjan, easily spotted with its smattering of wooden tables and potato sacks dropped throughout the paved square outside during the warmer months. Swig a perfect latte prepared by award-winning baristas, and snuggle up on velvety sofas when the weather isn't at its finest.

Tiú Droppar CAFE €

(Map p60; Laugavegur 27; soup Ikr1290; ⊙9am-10pm; 🖥) Tucked away in a cosy basement off the main drag, Tiú Droppar feels like granny's den, with floral wallpaper and pictures of seascapes in small gilded frames. Check out the locals' latest footwear fashions through the street-level windows while slurping tasty home-made soup. In the evenings, the quaint space reimagines itself as

the **Château des Dix Gouttes**, offering tipples of the wine variety, instead of coffee brews.

Bakarí Sandholt BAKERY €

(Map p60; www.sandholt.is; Laugavegur 36; mains Ikr250-980; ⊙7.30am-6.15pm Mon-Fri, 7.30am-5.30pm Sat, 8.30am-5pm Sun) Laugavegur's favourite bakery takes bread making to the next level with a generous assortment of fresh baguettes, croissants, pastries and delicious sandwiches that are great to pack in your bag if you're heading off on a day trip or short hike. There's a small sitting area in the back should you want to relax with an espresso.

Grái Kötturinn CAFE €

(Map p60; Hverfisgata 16a; mains Ikr800-1800; ⊙7.15am-3pm Mon-Fri, 8am-3pm Sat-Sun) This tiny six-table cafe (a favourite of Björk's) looks like a cross between an eccentric bookshop and a lopsided art gallery – quite charming! Locals joke that the cafe is never open, as more often then not you'll find the spot closed during the most opportune hours of the day. If you do gain access, you'll be treated to a delicious breakfast of toast, bagels, American pancakes, or bacon and eggs served on thick, buttery slabs of freshly baked bread.

Noodle Station ASIAN €

(Map p60; Skólavörðustígur 21a; mains Ikr1080; ⊙11am-10pm Mon-Fri, noon-10pm Sat & Sun) No-frills noodle soups of ambiguously Asian origin are dished out by the bowlful at this trusty local establishment. There are several other options along Skólavörðustígur (all with 'Noodle' in the name) serving similar items, but everyone seems to gravitate towards this stalwart for their fill of spicy broth.

Hamborgara Búllan FAST FOOD €

(Map p60; www.bullan.is; Geirsgata 1; mains Ikr660-1990; ⊙11.30am-9pm) Although the food is hardly 'fast' by international standards, the Old Harbour's outpost of burger-dom proffers savoury patties that will satisfy your secret desire for McDonald's. Russell Crowe was spotted here a few times packing an artery between takes while shooting on location during the summer of 2012.

Kaffi Mokka CAFE €

(Map p60; www.mokka.is; Skólavörðustígur 3a; ⊙9am-6.30pm) Reykjavík's oldest coffee shop is an acquired taste. Its decor has changed little since the 1950s, and its original mosaic pillars and copper lights either look retro-cool or dead tatty, depending on your mood! It has a mixed clientele – from older folk to tourists to trendy young artists – and a selection of sandwiches, cakes and giant waffles.

Bæjarins Beztu   HOTDOGS €

(Map p60; Tryggvagata; mains Ikr320; ☉10am-1am Sun-Thu, 11am-4am Fri & Sat) Icelanders are utterly addicted to hot dogs, and they swear the best are those from this converted van/portable situated near the harbour that was patronised by Bill Clinton (pre-angioplasty). Use the vital sentence *Eina með öllu* ('One with everything') to get the quintessential favourite with mustard, tomato sauce (ketchup), rémoulade and crunchy onions.

Babalú   CAFE €

(Map p60; Skólavörðustígur 22a; mains Ikr980; ☉8am-9pm) Walk up a flight of stairs to find this quaint cafe, which feels like the den of one of your eccentric friends. Books and board games abound, which seems to lure weary backpackers with nowhere to go. Try the cheap chilli to fill your belly, or overdose on sugar with a slice of home-made cake (the New York–style cheese cake is a local favourite).

Café Haiti   CAFE €

(Map p60; Geirsgata 7b; ☉8.30am-6pm Mon-Thu, 8.30am-7.30pm Fri, 10am-6pm Sat) If you're a coffee fan, this tiny cafe in the Old Harbour is the place for you. Owner Elda buys her beans from her home country of Haiti, and roasts and grinds them on-site, producing what regulars swear are the best cups of coffee in the country.

Midrange

A wonderful crossbreed of cafes and stylish eateries, the capital's midrange choices either make a great lunchtime meal or an abridged dinner repast.

TOP CHOICE Bergsson Mathús   CAFE €€

(Map p60; www.bergsson.is; Templarasund 3; mains Ikr1190-1890; ☉7am-7pm Mon-Fri, to 5pm Sat & Sun) If this prim, Scandi-simple cafe were located in your hometown, we're pretty sure that you'd eat here everyday. Meals are assembled with the utmost care – the owners pride themselves on providing the freshest produce and ingredients available. Stop by on weekends when locals flip through magazines, gossip and devour a scrumptious brunch plate (Ikr1890) with heaped side-portions of bread (the best we've ever tasted; no exaggeration).

TOP CHOICE Snaps   NORDIC €€

(Map p60; www.snapsbistro.is; Óðinstorg 101; mains Ikr1980-3100; ☉11.30am-11pm) Snaps' secret to success is simple: serve scrumptious seafood mains at surprisingly affordable prices. Lunch specials are a reasonable Ikr1690, and you'll score a three-course dinner for wallet-friendly Ikr4800. Seats are squished into a social greenhouse-like space that receives plenty of light; or cosy up to the cute bar with its bold brass rim.

Sægreifinn   SEAFOOD €€

(Sea Baron; Map p60; Geirsgata 8; mains Ikr1190; ☉11am-10pm) This place dishes out the most famous lobster curry soup in the capital. If the eponymous sea baron isn't dishing out bowlfuls to customers then he's probably upstairs taking a nap on one of the bunk beds. Feel free to join him; siestas come free with your meal.

Laundromat Café   INTERNATIONAL €€

(Map p60; www.thelaundromatcafe.com/en; Austurstræti 9; mains Ikr990-3990; ☉8am-1am Mon-Thu, to 3am Fri, 10am-3am Sat, 10am-1am Sun) This Danish import has seen a lot of success after crashlanding on one of Reykjavík's main drags. Locals devour heaps of hearty mains in a cheery environment surrounded by tattered paperbacks. Go for the 'Dirty Brunch' on weekends, to sop up an evening's worth of booze.

Ban Thai   ASIAN €€

(Map p54; www.banthai.name; Laugavegur 130; mains Ikr1690-1890; ☉6-10pm) When it comes to Thai food, Iceland has a surprisingly decent selection of places to get your *pad thai* on. Though it's not the most centrally located, Ban Thai is by far the local favourite – it's located just beyond the Hlemmur bus terminal.

Roadhouse   INTERNATIONAL €€

(Map p54; www.roadhouse.is; Snorrabraut 56; mains Ikr1690-4290; ☉11.30am-9.30pm Mon-Thu, to 11pm Fri-Sat, 1-9.30pm Sun) Like some large homage to Arthur Fonzarelli, Roadhouse delights in its utter American-ness, from the large booth seating and oversized portions to the vintage license plates, old Coca-Cola bottles, and Beach Boys beats playing on the speakers.

Café Loki
ICELANDIC €€

(Map p60; Lokastígur 28; mains Ikr450-2590; ⊙10am-6pm Mon-Fri, noon-6pm Sun) Ignore the garish signage slapped across the exterior of this cafe located close to Hallgrímskirkja, and you'll discover it has a tasteful interior. Café Loki serves up very traditional dishes, from light snacks such as eggs and herring on home-made rye bread to Icelandic platters of sheep's-head jelly and sharkmeat. The food is popular with curious tourists, and with the locals, too.

Svarta Kaffið
FAST FOOD €€

(Map p60; Laugavegur 54; mains Ikr900-1750; ⊙11am-1am Sun-Thu, to 3am Fri & Sat) Order the thick home-made soup (one meat and one veg option daily) at this quirky cave-like cafe – it's served piping hot in fantastic bread bowls.

Vegamót
INTERNATIONAL €€

(Map p60; www.vegamot.is; Vegamótastígur 4; mains Ikr1300-3000; ⊙11am-1am Mon-Thu, 11am-5am Fri & Sat, noon-1am Sun) A long-running cafe-bar-club, but still a voguish place to eat, drink, see and be seen. There's a startling choice on the 'global' menu, including Mexican salad, seafood *quesadilla*, and our favourite, the Louisiana chicken dunked in criminal amounts of barbecue sauce.

Icelandic Fish & Chips
SEAFOOD €€

(Map p60; www.fishandchips.is; Tryggvagata 8; mains Ikr990-1590; ⊙noon-9pm) A reader-recommended restaurant serving hearty portions of...well, have a guess! It's good-value fare (for Iceland, at least), and the owners have put their own singular slant on it with a range of 'Skyronnaises' – *skyr*-based sauces (eg rosemary and green apple) that add an unusual zing to this most traditional of dishes.

Hornið
ITALIAN €€

(Map p60; Hafnarstræti 15; mains Ikr1500-4000; ⊙11.30am-11pm) There's an easy-going air at this bright art deco cafe-restaurant, with its warm terracotta tiles, weeping-fig plants and decently spaced tables. Pizzas are freshly made before your eyes, the prettily presented pasta meals will set you up for the day, and you can sample traditional Icelandic fish dishes.

Café Paris
INTERNATIONAL €€

(Map p60; Austurstræti 14; mains Ikr990-4990; ⊙9am-1am Sun-Thu, to 5am Fri & Sat) An old favourite, Paris is one of the city's prime people-watching spots, particularly in summer when outdoor seating spills out onto Austurvöllur square; and at night, when the leather-upholstered interior fills with tunes and tinkling wine glasses. The mediocre selection of sandwiches, salads and burgers, is very much secondary to the see-and-be-seen scene.

Top End

Reykjavík's upmarket dining experiences pride themselves on being a memorable culinary experience, though an international level of service should not be expected at all establishments. These restaurants fall into one of two distinct categories: either you'll come across local spots that serve carefully curated Icelandic fare, or high-end eateries that transport Icelander's tastebuds to other nations far, far away.

Dill
NORDIC €€€

(Map p54; www.dillrestaurant.is; Sturlugata 5; 3-course meal from Ikr5900; ⊙11.30am-2.30pm & 5-10pm) 'New Nordic' par excellence is the major draw card at this elegant yet simple venue at the local culture house. The focus is very much on the food – locally sourced nibbles served as a parade of courses. The owners are friends with the famous Noma clan, and have drawn much inspiration from the celebrated Copenhagen restaurant.

Friðrik V
ICELANDIC €€€

(Map p54; www.fridrikv.is; lunch mains/3-course dinner Ikr1590/5900; ⊙11.30am-1.30pm Tue-Fri, 5.30-10pm Tue-Sat) One of the top spots to splash out on a gourmet Icelandic meal, Friðrik's eponymous master chef is known throughout the country for championing the 'slow food' movement, and his darling family helps him prepare every meal. Each dish is a carefully prepared medley of locally sourced items presented in a forward-thinking manner. There's *skyr* brûlée, filet mignon carpaccio, rhubarb sorbet, langoustine with roasted vegies, *skyr* mozzarella caprese...the list goes on.

Fiskfélagið
INTERNATIONAL €€€

(Fish Company; Map p60; www.fishcompany.is; Vesturgata 2a; mains Ikr2900-5400; ⊙11.30am-2pm & 6-11.30pm) The 'Fish Company' takes Icelandic seafood recipes and spins them through a variety of far-flung continents. Try the local catch marinated in Asian spices, amid copper lamps and quirky furnishings.

Fiskmarkaðurinn SEAFOOD €€€
(Fish Market; Map p60; ☑578 8877; www.fisk markadurinn.is; Aðalstræti 12; mains Ikr1690-3390; ☺11.30am-2pm & 6-11.30pm Mon-Fri, 6-11.30pm Sat & Sun) Don't let the weird dead-bony-fish logo put you off – this restaurant excels in infusing Icelandic seafood with Far Eastern flavours. Ingredients have a strong focus on local produce. For example, there's the 'Farmers Market' menu, which takes specialities from around Iceland (lobsters from Höfn, salmon from the Þjórsá, halibut from Breiðafjörður) and introduces them to spicy chillis, papaya, mango, coconut, satay glazes and *ponzu* sauce.

Sushisamba FUSION €€€
(Map p60; www.sushisamba.is; Þingholtsstræti 5; mains Ikr1490-8990; ☺5-11pm Sun-Thu, 11.30am-2pm & 5pm-midnight Fri-Sat) The reported location of TomKat's last dinner as a married couple (you can apparently request to sit at their table if you book ahead), Sushisamba throws its hat into the raw fish ring and puts a Latin spin on things. The Icelandic Feast (Ikr5990; six courses) is good value.

Vox ICELANDIC €€€
(Map p54; ☑444 5050; www.vox.is; Suðurlandsbraut 2; mains Ikr4600-5900; ☺6-10pm Tue-Sat) The Hilton's five-star restaurant definitely feels like a hotel venue, and thus a bit passé, but the famous Sunday brunch lures steady streams of locals and tourists alike.

Forréttabarinn TAPAS €€€
(Starter Bar; Map p60; www.forrettabarinn.is; Nýlendugata 14, entrance from Mýrargata; mains Ikr1390; ☺5-11pm Sun-Thu, to midnight Fri-Sat) Tapas restaurants have become wildly popular in the capital, with a handful of hot spots proffering small plates (and high prices). This joint, near the harbour, is our favourite, with its 'appetizers for dinner' theme. The menu is vast and international; you'll want around three plates per person.

Þrír Frakkar ICELANDIC €€€
(Map p60; ☑552 3939; www.3frakkar.com; Baldursgata 14; mains Ikr3000-5300; ☺noon-2.30pm & 6-10pm Mon-Fri, 6-11pm Sat & Sun) Owner-chef Úlfar Eysteinsson has built up an excellent reputation at this snug little restaurant – apparently a favourite of Jamie Oliver's. Specialities include salt cod, anglerfish and *plokkfiskur* (fish stew) with black bread. You can also sample nonfish items, such as seal, puffin, reindeer and whale steaks.

Austur Indía Félagið INDIAN €€€
(Map p60; Hverfisgata 56; mains Ikr2600-4000; ☺from 6pm) The northernmost Indian restaurant in the world is an upmarket experience, with a select choice of sublime dishes (a favourite is the tandoori salmon). One of its finest features, though, is its lack of pretension – the atmosphere is relaxed and the service warm.

Við Tjörnina SEAFOOD €€€
(Map p60; ☑551 8666; www.vidtjornina.is; Templarasund 3; Ikr2200-5900; ☺from 6pm) People return again and again to this famed seafood establishment, tucked away near Tjörnin. It serves up beautifully presented Icelandic feasts such as guillemot with port, garlic langoustine, or the house speciality marinated cod chins (far more delicious than they sound). The restaurant itself is wonderfully distinctive – it feels like a quirky upper-class 1950s drawing room.

Lækjarbrekka ICELANDIC €€€
(Map p60; www.laekjarbrekka.is; Bankastræti 2; mains Ikr3220-5580; ☺11.30am-11pm) This topnotch restaurant has built up its reputation over more than 20 years, cooking traditional Icelandic dishes (game, lobster, juicy pepper steak and mountain lamb) with half an eye on the tourist dollar.

Nauthöll ICELANDIC €€€
(Map p54; www.nautholl.is; Nauthólsvegur 106; mains Ikr2090-6290; ☺11am-10pm Mon-Sat, to 5pm Sun) Out of the city centre beside the geothermal beach, this excellent option for Icelandic faves sits in a delicate glass box with views out to the waterway. The interior is equally as simple, with polished floors and leather high-back chairs.

Argentína STEAKHOUSE €€€
(Map p60; ☑551 9555; www.argentina.is; Barónsstígur 11a; mains Ikr3850-5980; ☺6-10.30pm Sun-Thu, to 11.30pm Fri & Sat) This dark, fiery steakhouse rightly prides itself on its succulent locally raised beef – the best red meat you'll eat in Reykjavík. It also serves tender char-grilled salmon, reindeer, lamb, pork and chicken, with a wine list to complement whatever choice you make.

Humarhúsið SEAFOOD €€€
(Map p60; www.humarhusid.is; tmannsstígur 1; mains Ikr4100-6500) Understated and utterly elegant, the Lobster House is justly celebrated for its succulent shellfish, langoustine and lobster. Although crustaceans feature

in most dishes, you can also sample game, fish, lamb and beef, plus there's a vegetarian option.

Self-Catering

Reykjavík's supermarkets come in handy if you're planning a day trip away from the city and want to stock up on food. There are a slew of international fast-food options if you're looking for something very quick that you can possibly take on the go. Alcohol is pricey in bars and restaurants. The only shops licensed to sell alcohol are the government-owned liquor stores Vín Búð, of which there are 13 branches across the Reykjavík area.

Bónus   SUPERMARKET

Kringlan shopping centre (Map p54; ⊘noon-6.30pm Mon-Thu, 10am-7.30pm Fri, 10am-6pm Sat, noon-6pm Sun); Laugavegur (Map p60; Laugavegur 59; ⊘noon-6.30pm Mon-Thu, 10am-7.30pm Fri, 10am-6pm Sat) This supermarket offers the best value for money.

10-11   SUPERMARKET

(⊘24hr) Austurstræti (Map p60;); Barónsstígur (Map p54); Borgartún (Map p54); Laugalækur (Map p54) The ever-present 10-11 are similar to 7-Elevens in other countries. They're open late, but the prices are inflated.

Vín Búð   LIQUOR STORE

(⊘11am-6pm Mon-Thu & Sat, 11am-7pm Fri) Austurstræti (Map p60; Austurstræti 10a); Borgartún (Map p54; Borgartún 26) The most central branch is on Austurstræti, with another on the way towards Laugardalur at Borgartún.

Hlölla Bátar   FAST FOOD

(Map p60; Ingólfstorg; mains Ikr1290-2190; ⊘11am-2am Sun-Thu, 10am-7am Fri & Sat) Keep it local with a greasy sub sandwich from Hlölla Bátar.

🍷 Drinking

Sometimes it's hard to distinguish between cafes, bars and entertainment venues in Reykjavík, because when night time rolls around (be it light or dark out) many of the city's coffee shops turn the lights down, the volume up, and swap cappuccinos for cocktails. Some even turn into full-blown nightclubs in the wee hours of the night. For the lowdown on how the locals party, check out the boxed text, p47. And don't forget to peruse the Eating section for some of these cafe-to-bar transformers.

TOP CHOICE **Kaffibarinn**   BAR

(Map p60; Bergstaðastræti 1; 🛜) This old house, with the London Underground symbol over the door, contains one of Reykjavík's coolest bars; it even had a starring role in the cult movie *101 Reykjavík* (2000). At weekends you'll feel like you need a famous face or a battering ram to get in. At other times it's a place for artistic types to chill with their Macs.

oKEX Bar   BAR

(Map p54; Skúlagata 28) This might be the only hostel bar in the world where locals actually hang out. And we completely understand why – the vibe is 1920 Vegas, with saloon doors, an old-school barber station, scuffed floors, and the ambient sound of snarky chatter and slot clinks. The food, however, is worth a miss.

Micro Bar   BAR

(Map p60; Austurstræti 6) Boutique brews is the name of the game at this low-key spot near Austurvöllur. Bottles of beer represent a slew of brands and countries, but more importantly you'll discover a handful of local draughts from the island's best microbreweries. Swing by during happy hour (5pm) for Ikr500 tipples.

Slippbarinn   BAR

(Map p60; Mýrargata 2) Jetsetters unite at this Scandi-savvy hotel bar near the Old Harbour. After you grow tired of the city's relentless beer scene, seek refuge here for the best cocktails in town.

Bakkus   BAR

(Map p60; Laugavegur 22) The double-decker dive bar fulfils all of your *djammið* needs with plenty of room to dance and a bar top for swigging swill. Expect all-night romp fests on weekends.

Lebowski Bar   BAR

(Map p60; Laugavegur 20a) Named after the eponymous 'Dude' of moviedom, the Lebowski Bar is smack dab in the middle of the action with tons of Americana smothering the walls, and a long list of white Russians – a favourite from the film.

Boston   BAR

(Map p60; Laugavegur 28b) Boston is cool, arty and easily missable. It's accessed through a doorway on Laugavegur that leads you upstairs to its laid-back lounge, decorated in cool black wallpaper grown over with silver leaves. Expect the occasional bout of live music; you'll also find a DJ spinning beats.

Prikið PUB

(Map p60; Bankastræti 12) The feel at Prikið falls somewhere between a frat house and a saloon – there is a great vibe if you're up for some greasy eats and a round of socialising. Things get dance-y in the wee hours, and if you survive the night, it's a popular place to indulge in a next-day 'hangover sandwich'.

Hemmi & Valdi CAFE

(Nýlenduvöruverslun Hemma og Valda; Map p60; Laugavegur 21) Hemmi and Valdi's Colonial Store is another mismatched, beat-up, heavy-on-the-irony cafe. This relaxed place was originally set up by a couple of young dads to sell coffee, beer and, erm, baby clothes. There are huge windows perfect for street-gaping, comforting pottery mugs, a warm welcome for kids and a short menu of coffees and cakes. At night, this transmutes into a great little bar selling some of the cheapest booze in Reykjavík.

Dillon PUB

(Map p60; Laugavegur 30) Beer, beards and the odd flying bottle...atmospheric Dillon is a RRRRROCK pub, drawing lively crowds. There are frequent concerts on its tiny corner stage, a great beer garden and an unusual DJ, the white-haired white-wine-and-rum-swilling 'rokkmamman' Andrea Jons, a kind of female Icelandic John Peel.

Hressingarskálinn BAR

(Map p60; www.hresso.is; Austurstræti 20; 🛜) Known colloquially as Hressó, this large open-plan cafe-bar serves a diverse menu until 10pm daily (everything from porridge to *plokkfiskur*). At weekends, it loses its civilised veneer and concentrates on beer, bar and dancing; a garden out back provides fresh air. There's usually a DJ or live music on Thursday nights.

Gay 46 GAY

(Map p60; Hverfisgata 46) Reykjavík's gay scene can feel twice as fickle as the rest of the city's nightlife culture; at the time of research this was the venue of choice for boys who want to meet boys. The atmosphere errs on 'warehouse' (but not in the cool way); through a second door there's a men-only room covered in rainbow paint and porn.

☆ Entertainment

Cultural Activities

Reykjavík has several theatre groups, comedy shows, an opera house and a symphony orchestra. Information on current events can be found in *What's On in Reykjavík, Grapevine* or the daily papers. Shows geared towards tourists that explore Icelandic lore, culture and its quirks are run by

---

GAY & LESBIAN REYKJAVÍK

Although Reykjavík has garnered a global reputation as a very gay destination (perhaps due to the fact that the prime minister is openly lesbian), the city itself should be thought of as very gay friendly and not as a destination that actually has a sizeable gay population (how could it with only 200,000 inhabitants!).

Gay establishments come and go with the wind, but you can guarantee that there's always at least one dedicated club or gay in the city centre. At the time of research it was the gloomy Gay 46 (p73). As there's not even a whisper of a stigma towards the gay community, it's very common for people of any sexual orientation to hang out in a sociable spot all together. In fact, the annual pride parade is one of Iceland's most-attended events.

The gay and lesbian organisation **Samtökin '78** (☏552 7878; www.samtokin78.is; 4th fl, Laugavegur 3; ⊕office 1-5pm Mon-Fri) provides information during office hours and doubles as an informal LGBT community centre. Sharing a space with Samtökin is **Pink Iceland** (☏562 1919; www.pinkiceland.is; ⊕9am-5pm Mon-Fri), the nation's only LGBT-focused travel agency. Travellers are welcome to swing by and ask about upcoming events or opportunities to interact with the local gay community. At the time of research, the founders of Pink Iceland were launching a series of walking tours (Ikr3500; 90 minutes) and bimonthly circuit parties – get in touch with them for more details.

Visitors like to get technological to meet others as well – the Apple application Grindr is commonly used, as is **Gay Romeo** (www.gayromeo.com). Visit **GayIce** (www.gayice.is) for general gay news in Iceland.

DJAMMIÐ

Reykjavík is renowned for its weekend party scene that goes strong all night long, and even spills over onto some of the weekdays (especially in summer). Known as *djammið* in the capital, it's the grown-up version of the infamous *runtur*, when Icelandic youth drive around their towns in beat-up cars.

Much of the partying happens in the city's cafes and bistros, which transform into raucous beer-soaked bars at the weekend; there are also dedicated pubs and clubs. But it's not the quantity of drinking dens that makes Reykjavík's nightlife special – it's the upbeat energy that pours from them.

Places usually open until 1am Sunday to Thursday and until 3am or later on Friday and Saturday. 'In' clubs have long queues at weekends, though they tend to move rather quickly due to the constant circulation of revellers.

Thanks to the high price of alcohol, things generally don't get going until late. Icelanders brave the melee at the government alcohol store Vín Búð (see p72), then toddle home for a prepub party. Once they're merry, people hit town around midnight, party until 5am, queue for a hot dog, then topple into bed or the gutter, whichever is more convenient. Considering the quantity of booze swilling around, the scene is pretty good-natured.

Rather than settling into one venue for the evening, Icelanders like to cruise from bar to bar, getting progressively louder and less inhibited as the evening goes on. Most of the action is concentrated on Laugavegur and Austurstræti. You'll pay around Ikr700 to Ikr800 per pint of beer, and some venues have cover charges (about Ikr1000) after midnight. Things change fast – check *Grapevine* for the latest listings. You should dress up in Reykjavík, although there are pub-style places with a more relaxed dress code. The minimum drinking age is 20.

the **Iðnó Theatre** (Map p60; ☏551 9181; www.lightnights.com; Vonarstræti 3) and **Let's Talk Iceland** (Map p60; ☏699 7040; www.letstalk.is; Hafnarstæti 1-3).

National Theatre THEATRE
(Map p60; ☏551 1200; www.leikhusid.is; Hverfisgata 19; ⊘theatre closed Jul & Aug) The National Theatre has three separate stages and puts on around 12 plays, musicals and operas per year, from modern Icelandic works to Shakespeare.

Reykjavík City Theatre THEATRE
(Map p54; ☏568 8000; www.borgarleikhus.is; Kringlan, Listabraut 3; ⊘theatre closed Jul & Aug) Stages at least six plays and musicals per year. The **Icelandic Dance Company** (www.id.is) is in residence there.

Live Music
The Reykjavík live-music scene is chaotic, ever-changing and strangely organic, with new venues mushrooming up over the stumps of the old. To catch up with the current state of Icelandic music, consult the free English-language paper *Grapevine* (widely available), or pop into one of the city's two independent music shops. There

are frequent live performances at the various bars and cafes listed in this chapter.

Volcano Shows
Iceland's eruptive landscape is a source of awe for many, and has been meticulously documented over the last century. There are several spots around town where you can watch brilliantly captured footage of the island's biggest headliners, including Surtsey, Hekla, Katla and the infamous Eyjafjallajökull. Try **Volcano Show** (Red Rock Cinema; Map p60; ☏845 9548; vknudsen2000@yahoo.com; Hellusund 6a; admission Ikr1500), **Cinema No2** (Map p60; ☏899 7953; www.lifsmynd.is/cinemano2; admission Ikr1000-1500) and **Volcano House** (Map p60; ☏555 1900; www.volcanohouse.is; Tryggvagata 11; admission Ikr2000). Shows at all theatres run throughout the day every day in both English and German.

🔒 Shopping
Shopping in Iceland's capital is a great way to access the city's culture of design that act as a wonderful counterpoint to the surrounding nature. From sleek, fish-skin purses and *lopapeysur* to unique beats played from local artists' albums and lip-smacking bottles of the Icelandic schnapps *brennivín*,

it's very easy to take home a piece of Reykjavík's soul, and one needn't settle for a plastic figurine of a troll.

Don't forget – all visitors are eligible for a 15% tax-free shopping refund (see the boxed text, p339).

Eymundsson BOOKS
Austurstræti (Map p60; Austurstræti 18; ⊙9am-10pm Mon-Fri, 10am-10pm Sat & Sun); Skólavörðustígur (Map p60; Skólavörðustígur 11; ⊙9am-10pm Mon-Fri, 10am-10pm Sat & Sun) These are Reykjavík's two biggest central bookshop branches. They have a superb choice of English-language books, as well as newspapers, magazines and maps, and both contain great cafes.

Kraum SOUVENIRS
TOP CHOICE
(Map p60; www.kraum.is; Aðalstræti 10) The brainchild of a band of local artists, Kraum literally means 'simmering' like the island's quaking earth and the inventive minds of its citizens. Expect a carefully curated assortment of unique designer wares, like fish-skin apparel and driftwood furniture, all on display in Reykjavík's oldest house.

66° North CLOTHING
TOP CHOICE
(Map p60; www.66north.is; Bankastræti 5) Iceland's outdoor-clothing company began by making all-weather wear for Arctic fishermen. This metamorphosed into weather-proof but ultra-fashionable streetwear – coats, fleeces, hats and gloves. They even clothe the Icelandic Search and Rescue Organization. Shopping here is a great excuse to leave your arctic apparel at home. The branch at Kringlan shopping centre stays open late on Thursdays.

Leynibuðin CLOTHING
(Map p60; http://leynibudin.is; Laugavegur 21) A consortium of young designers, Leynibuðin is a veritable mini-market of locally crafted apparel. Items border on hipster and grunge – it's a great introduction to the city's made-at-home trend.

Dogma CLOTHING
(Map p60; www.dogma.is; Laugavegur 30) This quirky T-shirt specialist is the go-to spot for scouting out your 'Big in Iceland' shirt or the ever-popular 'Eyjafjallajökull' pronunciation tee.

Netagerðin SOUVENIRS
(Map p60; www.netagerdin.is; Nýlendugata 12) Once a warehouse that stored and produced fishing nets, this unique space near the harbour is now home to three inspired design studios and a local music label. The workshop doubles as a store.

Spark
(Map p60; www.sparkdesignspace.com; Klappastígur 33) This self-proclaimed 'design space' has a rotating selection of exhibitions that focus on unique local partnerships. The gallery sells most of the items on display and has a stockpile of fascinating (and purchasable) items from previous shows.

Geysir SOUVENIRS
(Map p60; www.geysir.net; Skólavörðustígur 16) For more traditional souvenirs, there's no better place to shop than Geysir, which boasts an elegant selection of Icelandic essentials: sweaters, postcards, figurines etc.

Kolaportið Flea Market ANTIQUES
(Map p60; Geirsgata) Held in a huge industrial building by the harbour, this weekend market is a Reykjavík institution; however, the selection of secondhand clothes and old toys leave something to be desired.

Fríða Frænka ANTIQUES
(Map p60; Vesturgata 3) This place is a two-storey treasure trove of everything from antique furniture to '60s plastic kitsch. Items are piled precariously high in tiny side rooms – the art-installation effect adds to the experience.

Gaga CLOTHING
(Map p60; www.gaga.is; Vesturgata 4) Strange knitted goods from designer Gaga Skorrdal.

Handknitting Association of Iceland CLOTHING
(Map p60; www.handknit.is; Skólavörðustígur 19) Traditional handmade hats, socks and sweaters are sold at this knitting collective, or you can buy yarn and knitting patterns and do it yourself. There's a smaller branch (Map p54; Laugavegur 64), which sells made-up items only.

Aurum JEWELLERY
(Map p60; Bankastræti 4) Guðbjörg at Aurum is one of the more interesting designers; her whisper-thin silver jewellery is sophisticated stuff, its shapes often inspired by leaves and flowers.

12 Tónar MUSIC
(Map p60; www.12tonar.is; Skolavörðustígur 15) A very cool place to hang out is 12 Tónar,

responsible for launching some of Iceland's favourite new bands. In the three-floor shop you can listen to CDs, drink coffee and maybe catch a live performance on Friday afternoons.

Skífan Music MUSIC
(Map p60; Laugavegur 26) Reykjavík's biggest music chain store has lots of choice, bargain-bin offers and listening headsets so you can try CDs before you buy. There's a second location at Kringlan shopping centre.

Kringlan SHOPPING CENTRE
(Map p54; www.kringlan.is; Kringlan) Reykjavík's biggest shopping centre, 1km from town, has 150 shops. Take buses S1-4, S6, 13 or 14.

Information

Emergency

For an ambulance, the fire brigade or the police, dial 🖃112.

Landspítali University Hospital (🖃543 2000; Fossvogur) Has a 24-hour casualty department.

Internet Access

Your best bet for internet access is to log on at your hotel, guesthouse or hostel. Most cafes around the capital also have complimentary wi-fi access. Alternatively you can pay Ikr250 per hour for online services at the main tourist information centre and at the libraries.

The following offer internet access:

Aðalbókasafn (🖃411 6100; www.borgarbokas afn.is; Tryggvagata 15; ☺10am-7pm Mon-Thu, 11am-7pm Fri, 1-5pm Sat & Sun) Excellent main library in the heart of Reykjavík.

Kringlusafn (🖃580 6200; www.borgarbokas afn.is; cnr Borgarleikhús & Listabraut; ☺10am-7pm Mon-Thu, 11am-7pm Fri, 1-5pm Sat & Sun) Branch by the Kringlan shopping centre.

REYKJAVÍK WELCOME CARD

The **Reykjavík Welcome Card** (24/48/72hr Ikr2400/3300/4000) is available at various outlets including the tourist office. The card gives you free travel on the city's buses and on the ferry to Viðey, as well as free admission to Reykjavík's municipal swimming pools and to most of the main galleries and museums. It's worth it if you make use of the buses and swimming pools but might not be good value if you're just visiting a few museums and galleries.

Medical Services

Dentist on duty (🖃575 0505)
Health Centre (🖃585 2600; Vesturgata 7)
Læknavaktin (🖃1770) Non-emergency telephone medical advice between 5pm and 11.30pm.
Lyfja (🖃552 4045; Laugavegur 16; ☺9am-6pm Mon-Fri, 11am-4pm Sat) Central pharmacy.
Lyfja Apótek (🖃533 2300; Lágmúli 5; ☺7am-1am) Late-night pharmacy, near the Hilton Reykjavík Nordica hotel. Buses S2, 15, 17 and 19.

Money

Truthfully, you don't need to take money out, as almost every place accepts credit cards (except the municipal buses). The charge for changing currencies at hotels or private bureaus can be obscenely high.

Íslandsbanki (🖃440 4000; www.islandsbanki. is; Lækjargata 12)
Kaupþing (🖃444 7000; www.kaupthing.com; Austurstræti 5)
Landsbanki Íslands (🖃410 4000; www.lands banki.is; Austurstræti 11)

Post

Main post office (🖃580 1200; Pósthússtræti 5; ☺9am-6pm Mon-Fri) With an efficient parcel service, philatelic desk (www.stamps.is) and poste restante service.

Telephone

Public phones are rare in mobile-crazy Reykjavík. Try the tourist office, the post office, by the southwestern corner of Austurvöllur, on Lækjargata, or at Kringlan shopping centre.

Tourist Information

Reykjavík has a very good main tourist information centre, and an increasing number of private centres run by travel agencies that specialise in booking visitors on trips.

With enough brochures and booklets to wallpaper your living room, the capital has no shortage of publications that detail all of the current happenings around town – these are commonly found at the tourist bureaus and in the lobbies of most hotels and hostels.

The excellent English-language newspaper *Grapevine*, widely distributed, has the lowdown on what's new in town.

BSÍ Tourist Information Centre (Map p54; Vatnsmýrarvegur 10) Information leaflets.
Icelandic Travel Market (Map p60; 🖃552 4979; www.icelandictravelmarket.is; Bankastræti 2; ☺8am-9pm May-Aug, to 7pm Sep-Apr) Private office.
Main Tourist Information Centre (Upplýsingamiðstöð Ferðamanna; Map p60; 🖃590 1550; www.visitreykjavik.is; Aðalstræti 2; ☺8.30am-

WORTH A TRIP

A DAY IN GREENLAND

A convenient halfway-point between Europe and North America, Reykjavík has developed quite the reputation as a trendy layover destination. Tourists who are tight on time tend to use the capital as base for scenic day trips. Glacial lagoons, geysers, lava fields, and windswept islands can be tackled before nightfall, but few people realise that a trip to Greenland can easily fit into the itinerary. In summer, Air Iceland offers regular tours to the faraway community of Kulusuk in east Greenland. Hidden in an endless tapestry of icy whites and cool blues, Kulusuk represents the ultimate frontier.

With only 360 inhabitants (and no flushing toilets), the little village slowly reveals itself to day trippers during the stunning walk over from the airport. The distant mirage of brightly coloured wood-box houses suddenly becomes a reality as cameras click furiously. Although the traditional Greenlandic drum dance demo is a tad kitsch, the rest of the experience is like one giant dream sequence. At the end of the tour you have the option of returning to the airport by sea or by land. The boat ride (an extra €25) puts you face-to-face with the popcorn-like ice chunks floating in the bay, while the hike gives visitors one last chance to take in the dramatic scenery of snow-strewn crags.

Prices start at Ikr66,520. OK, so it's pricey, but how many people can say that they have a 'Kalaallit Nunaat' stamp in their passport?

For further information, head to shop.lonelyplanet.com to purchase a downloadable PDF of Lonely Planet's Greenland & the Arctic guide.

7pm daily Jun–mid-Sep, 9am-6pm Mon-Fri, to 4pm Sat & to 2pm Sun mid-Sep-May) Staff are friendly, and there are mountains of free brochures and leaflets, plus some maps for sale. They can book accommodation, tours and activities.

❶ Getting There & Away

Air

Reykjavík Domestic Airport (Innanlandsflug; www.reykjavikairport.is) is based just south of Tjörnin on a wide stretch of fenced-in land. From morning to evening, planes fly between Reykjavík and Akureyri, Egilsstaðir and Ísafjörður; as well as to Greenland and the Faeroes. Internal flight operator **Air Iceland** (Flugfélag Íslands; ✈570 3030; www.airiceland.is) has a desk at the airport, but you can usually save money if you book over the internet (a computer terminal is provided near the check-in desks). **Eagle Air** (✈562 4200; www.eagleair.is) also operates sightseeing services from here.

International flights operate through **Keflavík International Airport** (✈425 0600, 425 6000; www.kefairport.is), 48km west of Reykjavík. The easiest way to get there is on the Flybus. For international airlines, see p344.

Boat

For information on the Viðey ferry service, see p80.

Bus

Almost all long-distance buses use the **BSÍ bus terminal** (✈562 1011; www.bsi.is; Vatnsmýrar-

vegur 10), near the domestic airport – the company name is pronounced *bee ess ee*. The desk here can book you onto bus services around Iceland. You can pick up summer (June to August or mid-September) or winter (mid-September to May) bus timetables, and there's also a rack of tourist information available.

In summer regular direct services include those listed in the table (see p79). There's reduced or no service the rest of the year.

For other destinations on the northern and eastern sides of the island (eg Egilsstaðir, Mývatn and Húsavík), you'll need to change buses in Höfn or Akureyri, which may involve an overnight stop.

For more information about getting to various places around the country, consult the destination of interest.

❶ Getting Around

To/From the Airport

Getting to Reykjavík from Keflavík International Airport is easy: the **Flybus** (✈580 5400; www.re.is) meets all international flights. It is not worth taking a taxi as they are very expensive and take roughly the same amount of time as the bus. One-way tickets cost Ikr1950, or Ikr2500 if you want to be dropped off at your hotel (note that all buses stop at the BSÍ first). Buy tickets before you board from the booth just inside the airport doors (credit cards accepted). The journey to Reykjavík takes around 50 minutes.

On the return journey plan to leave from the BSÍ bus terminal more than 2½ hours before

WORTH A TRIP

FAEROE FORAY

Biweekly flights and ferries (see p77) give Arctic adventurers three or four days to explore the truly magical Faeroe Islands. A half-week is just enough time to check the following highlights off your to-do list:

» **Tórshavn** The first thing you'll notice are the striking turf roofs adorning almost every bright-coloured building in the marina. The quaintness is palpable in the most charming way possible, yet you still know that you're in a capital. Although light on sights, Tórshavn makes a great base if you're planning a series of day trips. While mild summer evenings illicit thoughts of Mediterranean fishing villages or a Caribbean outpost, the faint howl of distant winds confirms that the Faeroes are indeed children of the Arctic.

» **Gjógv** Perhaps the most adorable village in the entire world, Gjógv ('jaykf') may be hard to pronounce, but it's oh-so easy to love. Tiny turf-roofed cottages sit clustered around a naturally formed harbour, which looks as though a lightning bolt has ripped straight through the terrain creating a sheltered cove. There's good hiking here, and an adorable inn should you want to spend the night.

» **Mykines** Marking the western limits of the island chain, Mykines (*mee*-chi-ness) is where the local landscapes come to a dramatic climax – innumerable bird colonies (puffins!), haunting basalt sea-stacks and silent solitary cliffs. Although considered quite remote by Faeroese standards (there are only 11 inhabitants), the island is connected to Vágar by helicopter and ferry services.

» **Hestir** Like a resting horse pausing for a quenching sip of seawater, little Hestir rears just south of Streymoy. The island is best known for its hollow grottos carved into the cliffs by the pounding waves. See www.tutl.com for information about unique, jazz-laced tours of the caves.

international departures. Reykjavík City and Downtown hostels and the main hotels can arrange transfers to the bus station, if you let them know the night before you intend to travel.

The Flybus will also drop off and pick up in Garðabær and Hafnarfjörður, just south of Reykjavík, if you ask before boarding.

From the domestic airport terminal it's a 1km walk into town or there's a taxi rank outside. Bus 15 runs from here to Hlemmur bus station.

Bicycle

Reykjavík has a steadily improving network of well-lit cycle lanes – ask the tourist office for a map. At times, though, you will probably end up on busy roads. Be cautious, as drivers show little consideration for cyclists. Refreshingly, you are actually allowed to cycle on pavements as long as you act sensibly and don't cause pedestrians any problems.

The concierge at any hotel can help arrange bike rentals, or see p52.

Bus

Reykjavík's **Strætó** (☑540 2700; www.straeto.is/english) city bus system offers regular and easy transport around central Reykjavík and out to the suburbs of Seltjarnarnes, Kópavogur, Garðabær, Hafnarfjörður and Mosfellsbær. Recently Strætó has extended its service all along the south coast – see p346 for more.

For the most up-to-date information on bus numbers and routes, pick up a copy of the *Welcome to Reykjavík City Map,* which includes a very clear bus-route map. The map is widely available, including from tourist information centres and bus stations.

Buses run from 7am until 11pm or midnight daily (from 10am on Sunday). Services depart at 20-minute or 30-minute intervals. A limited night-bus service runs until 2am on Friday and Saturday. Buses only stop at designated bus stops, marked with a yellow letter 'S'.

TICKETS & FARES

The fare is Ikr350 (no change is given). One-/three-day passes (Ikr800/2000) can be bought from the two bus stations, Kringlan and Smáralind shopping malls and the bigger swimming pools. If you need to take two buses to reach your destination, *skiptimiði* (transfer tickets) are available from the driver – you have a limited time (usually 45 minutes) in which to use them.

The Reykjavík Welcome Card (see the boxed text, p76) also acts as a free Strætó bus pass.

BUS STATIONS

The two central terminals are **Hlemmur**, at the far end of Laugavegur (the main shopping street), and **Lækjartorg**, right in the centre of town. Check your route carefully, as not all buses stop at both.

Useful routes include the following:

1 Hlemmur bus station, Lækjartorg bus station, National Museum, BSÍ bus terminal, hospital, Hamraborg bus station (Kópavogur), Fjörður bus station (Hafnarfjörður).

14 Lækjartorg bus station, National Museum, BSÍ bus terminal, hospital, Hlemmur bus station, Laugardalur (for swimming pool, City Hostel and campsite).

15 Domestic airport terminal, BSÍ bus terminal, hospital, Hlemmur bus station, Laugardalur, Háholt bus station (Mosfellsbær).

Car & Motorcycle

A car is unnecessary in the city, as it's so easy to travel round on foot and by bus. However, if you want to get into the countryside and don't fancy the bus tours (see p59), it's well worth hiring a car.

The capital's drivers can be inconsiderate: beware of people yattering into mobile phones (illegal, in case you're wondering), drifting across lanes or cutting corners at junctions.

PARKING

Parking is limited and expensive during working hours; it's free between 6pm and 10am from Monday to Saturday and free on Sunday. Most hotels have a couple of parking spaces reserved for their guests, but in general it can be rather difficult to jockey for a spot during the day. And don't bother leaving your vehicle at a public venue like a municipal pool – local law enforcement vigilantly doles out fines.

GETTING IN & OUT OF TOWN

Getting out of town is easy – follow the signs for Rte 1. Getting back into Reykjavík can be more confusing, as there are dozens of exits from the highway and road signs are marked with abbreviations rather than full street names. To help you, the main road into Reykjavík is Vesturlandsvegur, which turns into Miklabraut and then Hringbraut. Exit by the Kringlan shopping centre for the Laugardalur area, at Snorrabraut for the Hallgrímskirkja area, and at Suðurgata for the town centre.

Taxi

Taxi prices are high. Flagfall starts at around Ikr500. Tipping is not required. As an example, taxi service from the BSÍ to the Reykjavík Downtown Hostel costs around Ikr1600.

There are usually taxis outside the bus stations, domestic airport, and pubs and bars on weekend nights (you'll find there are huge queues for the latter). Alternatively, call **BSR** (☑561 0000) or **Hreyfill-Bæjarleiðir** (☑588 5522).

Walking

Reykjavík's compact layout means that it's very easily walkable. Most restaurants, bars, hotels and attractions are clustered within a 1.5-sq-km area.

BUS SERVICES FROM REYKJAVÍK

Note that bus service in winter runs on a reduced schedule.

DESTINATION	PRICE	DURATION	FREQUENCY	YEAR-ROUND
Akureyri	Ikr11,800	6hr	daily	Yes
Blue Lagoon	Ikr1400	45min	several daily	Yes
Borgarnes	Ikr2400	1¼hr	twice daily	Yes
Geysir/Gullfoss	Ikr3800-4400	2½hr	daily	Jun–Aug
Höfn	Ikr13,700	8½hr	daily	Yes
Keflavík	Ikr1400	40min	several daily	Yes
Kirkjubæjarklaustur	Ikr8100	5hr	daily	Yes
Landmannalaugar	Ikr7700	5½hr	daily	mid-Jun–Aug
Ólafsvík	Ikr6200	3hr	several daily	Yes
Selfoss	Ikr1900-2000	1hr	many daily	Yes
Skaftafell	Ikr10,100	6½hr	daily	Yes
Vík í Mýrdal	Ikr5900	4hr	two daily	Yes
Þórsmörk	Ikr6200	3½hr	two daily	Jun–mid-Sep

GREATER REYKJAVÍK

Viðey

If the weather's fine, the tiny uninhabited island of Viðey (www.videy.com/en/) makes a wonderful day trip. It's just 1km north of Reykjavík's Sundahöfn Harbour, but this nugget of nature feels like another world. Strange modern artworks, an abandoned village and shipwreck sites add to its melancholy spell. Here, life slows right down – the only sounds are the wind, the waves and golden bumblebees buzzing among the tufted vetch and hawkweed.

◉ Sights

Just above the harbour, you'll find Viðeyarstofa (which houses a lunchtime cafe inside during summer), an 18th-century wooden church and a small monument to Skúli Magnússon. Excavations of the old monastery foundations turned up some 15th-century wax tablets and a runic love letter, now in the National Museum; less precious finds can be seen in the basement of Viðeyarstofa. Higher above the harbour is Ólafur Eliasson's interesting art installation The Blind Pavilion (2003). Nearby is Yoko Ono's Imagine Peace Tower (2007), a 'wishing well' that blasts a dazzling column of light into the sky every night between 9 October (John Lennon's birthday) and 8 December (the anniversary of his death).

The whole island is crisscrossed with walking paths. Some you can cycle (there are free bikes available at the ferry stop, or bring your own), while others are more precarious. A good map at the harbour shows which paths are which. The whole island is great for birdwatchers (30 species of birds breed here) and budding botanists (over one-third of all Icelandic plants grow on the island). In August, some Reykjavík inhabitants come here to pick wild caraway, which was originally planted here by Skúli Magnússon.

From the harbour, trails to the southeast lead you past the natural sheep fold Réttin, the tiny grotto Paradíshellir (Paradise Cave), and then to the old abandoned fishing village at Sundbakki. Most of the south coast is a protected area for birds and is closed to visitors from May to June.

Trails leading to the northwest take you past low ponds, monuments to several shipwrecks, the low cliffs of Eiðisbjarg and basalt columns at Vesturey at the northern tip of the island. Richard Serra's artwork, made from huge pairs of basalt pillars, rings this part of the island.

❶ Getting There & Away

The summer-only Viðey ferry (☑533 5055) takes a mere five minutes to skip across to the island from Reykjavík. It operates from Sundahöfn from mid-May to the end of September, leaving at 11.15am, 12.15pm, 1.15pm, 2.15pm, 3.15pm, 4.15pm, and 5.15pm, returning 15 minutes later. In winter, there's a reduced weekends-only service (1.15pm, 2.15pm, 3.15pm). A boat also sails from Reykjavík harbour from June to early September, leaving at noon and returning at 3.30pm. The return fare is Ikr1000/500 per adult/child aged 6 to 18 years.

WORTH A TRIP

LITERATURE AND LOPAPEYSA

One of Reykjavík's outer suburbs, Mosfellsbær (www.mosfellsbaer.is) is a great add-on to your Golden Circle or Ring Road adventures.

Nobel Prize–winning author Halldór Laxness lived in Mosfellsbær all his life, and his home is now the Gljúfrasteinn Laxness Museum (☑586 8066; www.gljufrasteinn.is; adult/child Ikr800/free; ⊙9am-5pm daily Jun-Aug, 10am-5pm Tue-Sun Sep-May). Located just outside the suburban centre on the road to Þingvellir, the house is a superb example of an upper-class 1950s home, complete with original furniture and Laxness' fine-art collection. A 25-minute guided audio tour leads you round, highlights include the study where Laxness wrote his defining works; his beloved Jaguar is parked outside.

If you're in need of retail therapy, the township is also home to the factory outlet shop Álafoss (www.alafoss.is; Álafossvegur 23; ⊙9am-6pm Mon-Fri, to 4pm Sat), which is undoubtedly the best place in all of Iceland to purchase handwoven lopapeysur (Icelandic woollen sweaters), made from pure Icelandic wool. Prices are significantly slashed compared to the tourist boutiques in downtown Reykjavík.

Kópavogur

POP 30,000

Kópavogur, the first suburb south of Reykjavík, is just a short bus ride away – but it feels far from the tourist trail. There are a few culture-vulture attractions in the complex next door to the distinctive arched church.

◎ Sights

Menningarmiðstoð Kópavogs   MUSEUM

The cultural complex Menningarmiðstoð Kópavogs contains Kópavogur's **Natural History Museum** (Náttúrufræðistofa Kópavogs; www.natkop.is; Hamraborg 6a; admission free; ⊙10am-7pm Mon-Thu, 11am-5pm Fri, 1-5pm Sat), which takes a look at Iceland's unique geology and wildlife. There's an orca skeleton, a good collection of stuffed animals and geological specimens, and a fish tank housing some of Mývatn lake's weird *Marimo* balls.

You'll also find Iceland's first specially designed concert hall here, built entirely from Icelandic materials (driftwood, spruce and crushed stone). **Salurinn** (⏀570 0400; www.salurinn.is; Hamraborg 6) has fantastic acoustics – see the website for details of its (mostly classical) concert program. Tickets cost Ikr1000 to Ikr4000 depending on the concert.

Gerðarsafn Art Museum   MUSEUM

(www.gerdarsafn.is; Hamraborg 4; ⊙11am-5pm Tue-Sun) Next door to Salurinn, there are changing modern-art exhibitions in the beautifully designed Gerðarsafn Art Museum. Its small cafe has mountain views.

Sundlaug Kópavogs   GEOTHERMAL POOL

(Borgarholtsbraut 17; adult/child Ikr550/150; ⊙6.30am-10pm Mon-Fri, 6.30am-10pm Mon-Fri, 8am-8pm Sat & Sun) If you're testing out the city's geothermal pools, try the Olympic-sized Sundlaug Kópavogs, popular with families, with a children's pool, slide, sauna and hot-pots.

ⓘ Getting There & Away

Buses 1 and 2 leave every few minutes from Hlemmur or Lækjartorg in central Reykjavík, stopping at the Hamraborg stop in Kópavogur (look out for the church). The journey takes about 15 minutes.

HIDDEN WORLDS

Many Icelanders believe that their country is populated by hidden races of little folk – *jarðvergar* (gnomes), *álfar* (elves), *ljósálfar* (fairies), *dvergar* (dwarves), *ljúflingar* (lovelings), *tívar* (mountain spirits), *englar* (angels) and *huldufólk* (hidden people).

Although Icelanders are embarrassed to say they believe, most of them refuse to say hand-on-heart that they *don't* believe. Many Icelandic gardens feature small wooden cut-outs of *álfhól* (elf houses) to house the little people in case the myths are true.

Hafnarfjörður is believed to lie at the confluence of several strong ley lines (mystical lines of energy) and seems to be particularly rife with these twilight creatures. In fact, construction of roads and homes in Hafnarfjörður is only permitted if the site in question is free from little folk.

Hafnarfjörður

POP 26,640

The 'Town in the Lava' rests on a 7000-year-old flow and hides a parallel elfin universe, according to locals. Its old tin-clad houses and lava caves are worth a visit on a sunny summer's day, but in winter, unless the Christmas market is on, tumbleweeds roll.

Hafnarfjörður was once a major trading centre, monopolised by the British in the early 15th century, the Germans in the 16th and the Danes in the 17th. Many of the finest houses in town once belonged to rich merchants. Today the town is spreading like spilt milk, but the endless new-building estates east of the harbour hold little of interest for visitors.

◎ Sights

Reykjavík's baby brother of a town has two excellent museums, but many tourists actually come to Hafnarfjörður to walk through **Hellisgerði** (www.elfgarden.is), a peaceful park filled with lava grottoes and apparently one of the favourite places of the hidden people.

Hafnarfjörður Museum   MUSEUM

(Byggðasafn Hafnarfjarðar; ⏀585 5780; admission free) Hafnarfjörður Museum is divided over

Hafnarfjörður

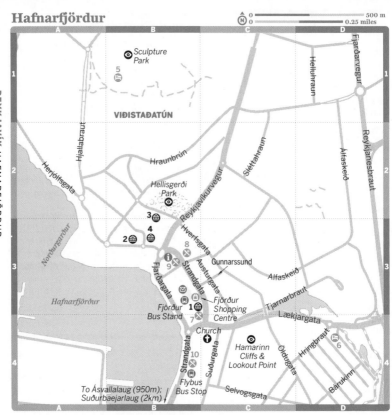

several buildings. **Pakkhúsið** (Vesturgata 8; ⊙11am-5pm daily Jun-Aug, 11am-5pm Sat & Sun Sep-May) is the main section, with three storeys of exhibits. Upstairs, there are displays on the history of Hafnarfjörður, and a small toy museum in the attic.

Next door, but still part of the complex, **Sívertsen's Hús** (Vesturgata 6; ⊙11am-5pm Jun-Aug) is a beautiful 19th-century home belonging to merchant Bjarni Sívertsen, once the most important man in Hafnarfjörður. It's decked out with period pieces – a piano, rich drapes, woven wallpaper, mahogany furniture, delicate crockery and silver spoons.

To take on board the huge contrast between Bjarni's lifestyle and the typical impoverished Icelander's, you can visit another home from the same period – the tiny restored fishing hut **Siggubær** (Sigga's House; Kirkjuvegur 10; ⊙11am-5pm Sat & Sun Jun-Aug), next to the park at Hellisgerði.

Beggubúð (Begga's Shop; Vesturgata 6; ⊙11am-5pm Jun-Aug) presents a shop laid out as it was in 1906; **Bookless Bungalow** (Vesturgata 32; ⊙11am-5pm daily Jun-Aug, 11am-5pm Sat & Sun Sep-May) was once the home of two Scottish brothers heavily involved in Hafnarfjörður's fishing industry, and now contains an exhibition on fishing.

FREE Hafnarborg   MUSEUM
(☑555 0080; www.hafnarborg.is; Strandgata 34; ⊙11am-5pm Wed, Fri-Mon, to 9pm Thu) Well worth a look, this upbeat modern-art gallery has two floors of regularly changing exhibitions, occasional musical concerts and an excellent restaurant inside.

🏃 Activities & Tours

There are three good swimming pools in town, including the mod indoor **Ásvallalaug** (☑512 4050; Ásvellir 2; adult/child Ikr450/110; ⊙6am-10pm Mon-Fri, 8am-8pm Sat &

Hafnarfjörður

⊙ Sights

1	Hafnarborg	B3
	Hafnarfjörður Museum (Beggubúð)	(see 4)
2	Hafnarfjörður Museum (Bookless Bungalow)	B3
	Hafnarfjörður Museum (Pakkhúsið)	(see 4)
3	Hafnarfjörður Museum (Siggubær)	B2
4	Hafnarfjörður Museum (Sívertsen's Hús)	B3

⊟ Sleeping

5	Hafnarfjörður Guesthouse & Campsite	B1
6	Helguhús Guesthouse	D4
	Viking Hotel	(see 10)

⊗ Eating

7	Gló	B4
8	Súfistinn	B3
9	Tilveran	B3
10	Viking Village Fjörukráin	B4
	Vín Búð	(see 1)

Sun) and old-time outdoor favourite **Suður-bæjarlaug** (☑565 3080; Hringbraut 77; adult/child Ikr450/110; ⊙6.30am-9.30pm Mon-Fri, 8am-6.30pm Sat, 8am-5.30pm Sun).

Hidden Worlds CULTURAL TOUR
(☑694 2785; www.alfar.is; per person Ikr3900; ⊙2.30pm Tue & Fri Jun-Aug) Find out if you have second sight on a 90-minute Hidden Worlds tour, a guided storytelling walk around the homes of the hidden people, departing from the tourist office. It's rather pricey, although a copy of the *Hidden Worlds* map is included in the cost, marking the Hafnarfjörður homes of elves, fairies, hermits and dwarves. The information centre sells an elf map for Ikr1500 should you want to search for the hidden people on your own.

⚝ Festivals

In mid-June the peace is shattered as Viking hordes invade town for the six-day **Viking festival**. Its staged fights and traditional craft demonstrations are centred on the Viking hotel.

⊨ Sleeping

Viking Hotel HOTEL €€
(☑565 1213; www.fjorukrain.is; Strandgata 55; s/d from Ikr15,900/18,700; @🛇🛜) This over-the-top Viking village has over 40 rooms and 14 turf-roofed cottages at the back. The 1st-floor rooms are wholly Viking in theme – battle-axe murals and all – while the top floor has traditional bed-and-board rooms.

Helguhús Guesthouse GUESTHOUSE €
(☑555 2842; www.helguhus.is; Lækjarkinn 8; s/d incl breakfast Ikr8500/12,500) Close to a small lake a 10-minute walk out of town, Helguhús is a well-turned-out town house with cosy, cream-coloured rooms (all with shared bathrooms).

Hafnarfjörður Guesthouse & Campsite GUESTHOUSE €€
(☑565 0900, 895 0906; www.hafnarfjordurguest house.is; Hjallabraut 51; sites per person Ikr1100, s/d Ikr7200/9600; ⊙mid-May–mid-Sep; 🛜) Overlooking the strange sculptures of the Víðistaðatún park, this 'guest house', run by the Icelandic Scouts, offers basic hostel-style accommodation in a stylish decking, glass and concrete building. Good facilities include kitchen, washing machine and internet access. The sleeping bag option (Ikr3600) consists of mattresses on the floor of a recreational space.

⊗ Eating

⬛TOP⬛ Gló VEGETARIAN €€
(Strandgata 34; mains Ikr990-1890; ⊙11am-9pm Mon-Fri, to 5pm Sat & Sun) A patch of green in a sea of grey, this health-conscious establishment is a big hit with the locals, and has a couple of branches in the greater Reykjavík area; though this one – set among the sparkling white halls of the local art museum – is our favourite. Hearty mains, like savoury curries, are served à la cafeteria with an eclectic assortment of sides.

Súfistinn CAFE €€
(Strandgata 9; mains Ikr800-1500; ⊙8.15am-11.30pm Mon-Fri, 10am-11.30pm Sat, 11am-11.30pm Sun) This great cafe-bar is the most cheerful place to eat in town – ladies lunch, readers read, kids play chess and half of Hafnarfjörður gathers to gossip about the other half. There's a satisfying selection of salads, sarnies, burritos, crêpes, quiches and coffee on offer, and an all-new outside decking area.

Tilveran   SEAFOOD €€
(Linnetsstígur 1; mains Ikr2100-3700; ⊙11.30am-2pm & 6-9pm Mon-Thu, to 10pm Fri & Sat) On the main pedestrian street, this unassuming little restaurant specialises in seafood, with dishes such as tagliatelle with lobster. The three-course dinner (Ikr4590) is very good value, and features a lobster soup, a fish main and a rich chocolatey dessert.

Viking Village Fjörukráin   RESTAURANT €€€
(www.vikingvillage.is; Strandgata 50a & 55; mains Ikr2500-5600) The tacky but strangely endearing restaurant Fjörukráin is housed in a totally outrageous reconstruction of a Viking longhouse, complete with carved pillars and dragons on the roof. It offers Viking feasts (*hákarl*, dried fish, braised lamb, fish soup and *skyr*; Ikr18,900), served up by singing Vikings.

❶ Information

There are banks with foreign-exchange desks and ATMs at the Fjörður shopping centre, right by the bus station.

Library (Strandgata 1; ⊙10am-7pm Mon-Wed, 9am-7pm Thu, 11am-7pm Fri year-round, plus 11am-3pm Sat Oct-May) Internet access is available at the super library for Ikr200 per hour.

Tourist information centre (☑585 5500; www.visithafnarfjordur.is; Strandgata 6; ⊙8am-4pm Mon-Fri) The tourist office is in the town hall (Ráðhús). At weekends from June to August, there's tourist help at Pakkhúsið from 11am to 5pm.

❶ Getting There & Around

It's an easy 30-minute bus ride from Reykjavík to the Fjörður bus stand at Hafnarfjörður – bus 1 (Ikr280) leaves every 10 minutes from Hlemmur or Lækjartorg – get off at the Fjörður shopping centre.

The **Flybus** (☑562 1011) to Keflavík International Airport will stop in Hafnarfjörður in front of the Viking restaurant.

Hafnarfjörður is small and it's easy to get around on foot. **A-Stöðin/Airport Taxis** (☑520 1212; www.airporttaxi.is) have taxis standing outside the Fjörður shopping centre.

Southwest Iceland & the Golden Circle

Includes »

Why Go?

Geysers spout, waterfalls topple, black beaches stretch into the distance, and brooding volcanoes and glittering ice caps line the horizon. The beautiful southwest contains many of Iceland's most famous natural wonders – and is consequently a relatively crowded corner of the country. But get away from the Golden Circle and you'll find vast stretches of seemingly undiscovered territory.

In fact, as a general rule in the southwest, the further you go the better it gets. Tourist faves like the silica-filled waters of the Blue Lagoon and the earth-rending landscapes of Þingvellir are within spitting distance of the capital. The churning seas of the south coast lie further beyond, leading to the Vestmannaeyjar archipelago offshore. At the far reaches of the region are the remnants of the Eyjafjallajökull eruption, and the hidden valleys of Þórsmörk and Landmannalaugar, accessible only by 4WD or a life-altering hike.

Best Places to Eat

» Gamla Fjósið (p114)
» Lindin (p98)
» Slippurinn (p132)
» LAVA Restaurant (p89)
» Við Fjöruborðið (p106)

Best Places to Stay

» Frost og Funi (p104)
» Efstidalur (p98)
» Laugarvatn HI Hostel (p98)
» Álftavatn (p126)
» Hótel Rangá (p111)

Road Distances (km)

	Keflavík	Selfoss	Gullfoss	Landmannalaugar	Vík
Selfoss	100				
Gullfoss	156	71			
Landmannalaugar	230	130	147		
Vík	226	130	177	218	
Reykjavík	51	57	113	185	186

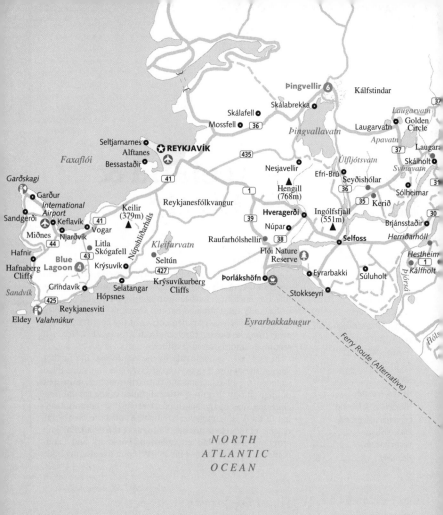

Southwest Iceland & the Golden Circle Highlights

1 Set sail for **Vestmannaeyjar** (p128), with its dazzling stone towers, millions of surly puffins and a small town of citizens nestled between the lava flows

2 Camp in **Þórsmörk** (p126), a green kingdom protected from the harsh northern elements by turrets of brooding glaciers

3 March along the caramel-coloured peaks at **Landmannalaugar** (p121), then set off on Iceland's most famous rite of passage, the Laugavegurinn hike

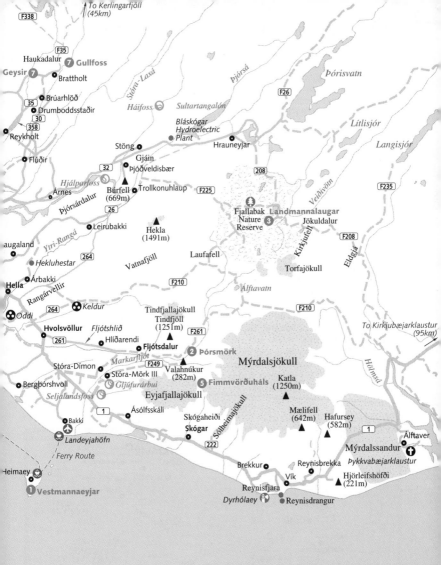

4 Wash away your worries in the turquoise cauldron at **Blue Lagoon** (p88), the Vegas-version of Icelandic hot-pot-ing

5 Hike past a parade of waterfalls, a steaming ash-ridden earth, and a valley bedecked with arctic flowers at **Fimmvörðuháls** (p116)

6 See the continental plates rip away from one another at **Þingvellir** (p96), then dive down one of the fissures for a superlative scuba session

7 Wait for water to shoot skywards at **Geysir** (p98), or watch it tumbling down at **Gullfoss** (p99)

REYKJANES PENINSULA

SOUTHWEST ICELAND & THE GOLDEN CIRCLE BLUE LAGOON

As the first bit of the country that most visitors see, the Reykjanes Peninsula might lead you to wonder why you chose Iceland for your holiday. From the air, or from the bus between Keflavík International Airport and Reykjavík, it can look like the most blighted and disheartening place on earth. But cast off your doubts! Nestling among the grey-black lava fields is Iceland's most famous attraction, the Blue Lagoon; and there are plenty of other marvels hiding in this forbidding landscape. Give it time, and the grey waves, smoking earth and bleak, mournful beauty will mesmerise you.

Most towns are squeezed into Miðnes, a small spur on the northern coast of the peninsula; the rest is wilderness. Near the international airport are the wave-lashed fishing villages of Garður and Sandgerði, lost places where you can watch migrating birds while the wind blows all your thoughts away. A back road runs south from Keflavík along the rugged coast to Reykjanestá, a wonderful spot full of battered cliffs and strange lava formations.

Public transport to Keflavík and the Blue Lagoon is fast and frequent from Reykjavík, but you'll need private transport to reach more remote parts of the peninsula.

Blue Lagoon

As the Eiffel Tower is to Paris, as Disney World is to Florida, so the **Blue Lagoon** (Bláa Lónið; ☎420 8800; www.bluelagoon.com; admission from €33; ☺9am-9pm Jun-Aug, 10am-8pm Sep-May) is to Iceland...with all the positive and negative connotations that implies. Those who say it's too expensive, too clinical, too crowded are kind of right, but you'll be missing something special if you don't go. In fact, you'll almost hate yourself for liking it so much...

Set in a tortured black lava field, just off the road between Keflavík and Grindavík, the milky-blue spa is fed by water (at a perfect 38°C) from the futuristic Svartsengi geothermal plant. The silver towers of the plant provide an off-the-planet scene-setter for your swim; add roiling clouds of steam and people daubed in white silica mud, and you're in another world.

The lagoon has been imaginatively landscaped with hot-pots, wooden decks and a piping-hot waterfall that delivers a powerful hydraulic massage – it's like being pummelled by a troll. There are also two steam rooms, a sauna, a massage pool and a special VIP section with its own interior wading space.

Reykjanes Peninsula

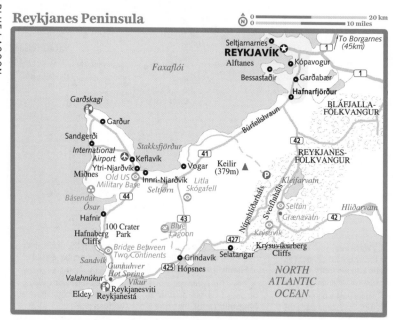

The superheated sea water is rich in blue-green algae, mineral salts and fine silica mud, which condition and exfoliate the skin – sounds like advertising speak, but you really do come out as soft as a baby's bum. The water is always hottest near the vents where it emerges, and the surface is several degrees warmer than the bottom.

For extra relaxation, you can lie on a floating lilo and have a masseuse knead out your knots (per 20/30 minutes €35/50); be aware, though – you need to book spa treatments well in advance.

Three warnings: the Blue Lagoon requires the same thorough naked prepool showering that applies in all Icelandic swimming pools; the water can corrode silver and gold, so leave watches and jewellery in your locker; you'll also need bucketfuls of conditioner afterwards – all that briny water plays havoc with your hair, especially if you get the silica goo in it.

🛏 Sleeping & Eating

In addition to the wonderful water amenities, Blue Lagoon also has an excellent restaurant, a cafe, a hotel, and a gift shop selling all sorts of curative soaps and gels to take home. At the time of research, plans for a large-scale hotel near the lagoon were underway.

Blue Lagoon – Clinic   HOTEL €€€
(☑420 8806; www.bluelagoon.com; s/d incl breakfast €230/280; @🛜) Guests don't have to be undergoing treatment to stay at the Blue Lagoon clinic, a 10-minute walk across the lava field from Iceland's most famous attraction. Rooms are soothing and modern, with heated-floor bathrooms, and each has a small porch from where you can regard the surrounding moonscape. Rates include entry to the lagoon.

Northern Light Inn   HOTEL €€€
(☑426 8650; www.northernlightinn.is; s/d Ikr26,500/34,500; @🛜) Spacious rooms with audacious accent walls sit stacked along a lava field at this bungalow hotel. There's a sunny sitting room, and free transfers are provided to the international airport and the lagoon (although the latter is easily walkable). The on-site restaurant boasts a smattering of Nordic fare; the floor-to-ceiling windows look out over the lava and steam-spewing power plant.

TOP CHOICE **LAVA Restaurant**   ICELANDIC €€
(www.bluelagoon.com; mains Ikr2700-5900; ⊘noon-9pm) Take a break from all of the mediocre table service in the capital, and enjoy a topnotch dining experience at Blue Lagoon's popular restaurant. The dining room feels a bit like a function hall, but the views out to the lagoon are serene, the waitstaff are excellent and the menu features Iceland's favourite dishes prepared with perfected recipes.

❶ Getting There & Away

The lagoon is 50km southwest of Reykjavík, but there are plenty of bus services that run there year-round. You'll need to book in advance. See http://www.bluelagoon.com/Geothermal-spa/How-to-get-there/Bus for detailed information. The best and cheapest option is **Reykjavík Excursions** (☑580 5400; www.re.is), which runs on the hour from 9pm to 6pm for Ikr8000, including lagoon admission.

Keflavík & Njarðvík (Reykjanesbær)

POP 13,000

The twin towns of Keflavík and Njarðvík, on the coast about 50km west of Reykjavík, are a rather ugly expanse of suburban boxes and fast-food outlets – a rather inauspicious welcome to the island. Together they're known simply as 'Reykjanesbær'. Although they aren't somewhere you'd want to spend a massive amount of time, they comprise the largest settlement on the peninsula and make a good base for exploring the area. If you've an early flight, they're handy for the airport.

If you're around at the beginning of September, the well-attended **Night of Lights** (Ljósanótt í Reykjanesbæ; www.ljosanott.is) festival is worth seeing, particularly its grand finale, when waterfalls of fireworks pour over the Bergið cliffs.

⊙ Sights

KEFLAVÍK

The area around the museum Duushús is the prettiest part of Keflavík; just to the east on the seashore is an impressive **Ásmundur Sveinsson sculpture**, used as a climbing frame by the local kids. Just beyond, the larger-than-life **Giantess**, a character from Herdís Egilsdóttir's children's books brought to life by a local art collective, sits in a rocking chair in her black cave.

Keflavík

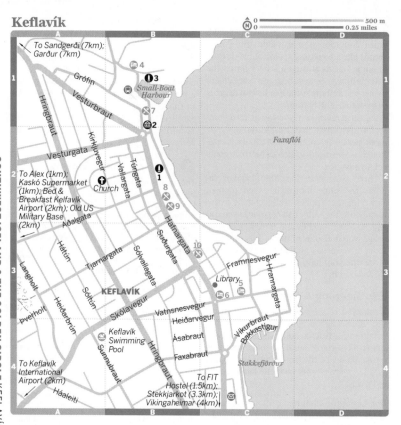

SOUTHWEST ICELAND & THE GOLDEN CIRCLE KEFLAVÍK & NJARÐVÍK (REYKJANESBÆR)

Keflavík

Duushús   MUSEUM

(☎421 3796; Grófin; admission free; ⊗noon-5pm Mon-Fri, 1-5pm Sat & Sun) In a long red warehouse by the harbour, Duushús is Keflavík's historic cultural centre. There's a permanent exhibition of around 60 of Grímur Karlsson's many hundreds of miniature ships, made compulsively over a lifetime; a gallery where seven international art exhibitions are held each year; and a changing local-history display.

NJARÐVÍK

TOP CHOICE **Víkingaheimar**   EXHIBITION

(Viking World; ☎422 2000; www.vikingaheimar. com; Víkingabraut 1; adult/child Ikr1000/free; ⊗11am-6pm May-Sep, 10am-5pm Oct-Mar) At the southern end of Njarðvík, the spectacular Víkingaheimar is a Norse exhibition centre built in one beautiful, sweeping architectural gesture. The centrepiece is the 23m-long *Íslendingur,* an exact reconstruction of the Viking Age *Gokstad* longship. It was built almost singlehandedly by Gunnar Marel Eggertsson, who then sailed it from Iceland to New York in 2000 to commemorate the

1000th anniversary of Leif the Lucky's journey to America. Additional rooms display ancient relics, most likely from the Celtic settlement, and upstairs there's an exhibit about the Norse gods geared towards children. During summer there's a 'settlement zoo' outside showcasing the animals that the original settlers brought to Iceland.

🛏 Sleeping

All the sleeping options listed provide a free airport transfer.

Icelandair Hotel Keflavík   HOTEL €€
(☎421 5222; www.icehotel.is; Hafnargata 57; d incl breakfast Ikr27,600; @🖥) The most comfortable option within the airport's orbit, the Keflavík offering to the Icelandair chain features two multistorey wings and a solid restaurant beside the lobby. Never mind the retro 'Flughotel' sign on the facade, rooms inside are thoughtfully decorated and thoroughly modern.

Hótel Berg   GUESTHOUSE €€
(☎422 7922; http://hotelberg.is; d incl breakfast €130; @🖥) More than a large, homey guesthouse than an airport hotel, Berg's common spaces benefit from charming personal touches and an eclectic selection of old furniture, including stacks of tattered paperbacks on the shelves. It's located at the northern (and most charming) end of Keflavík; it's a wonderfully welcoming place to stay.

Alex   HOTEL €
(☎421 2800; www.alex.is; Aðalgata 60; d with/without bathroom incl breakfast Ikr15,900/13,400; @🖥) The closest sleeping option to the airport has a cornucopia of sleeping styles from sleeping-bag space (Ikr3000 per person) to doubles with private bathrooms, to cottages out the back. An attached car-rental service increases Alex's convenience as a crash pad for travellers arriving in Iceland on a late flight. It's about 1.5km from central Keflavík. Luggage can be stored for Ikr300 per day.

Bed & Breakfast Keflavík Airport   HOTEL €€
(☎426 5000; www.bbkeflavik.com/; s/d incl breakfast €92/119; @🖥) Making excellent use of one of the abandoned buildings on the military base, this large, spruced-up hotel offers an assortment of simple accommodation options for travellers needing a sleepover spot close to the airport. Sleeping-bag accommodation in six-person dorm rooms costs €28.

Hótel Keflavík   HOTEL €€
(☎420 7000; www.hotelkeflavik.is; Vatnsnesvegur 12-14; d incl breakfast €180; @🖥) A sure-fire stunt double for the Icelandair Hotel when it books out, this reliable spot, just half a block away, has a rather gaudy lobby but the rooms are perfectly serviceable. Book online and you'll find discounts of up to 40%. The hotel also runs a small **guesthouse** (r €90) across the street geared more towards budget-conscious travellers.

FIT Hostel   HOSTEL €
(☎421 8889; www.fithostel.is; Fitjabraut 6a; dm from Ikr3800; @🖥) In an industrial estate towards Njarðvík, off busy Rte 41, this hostel feels a bit rough around the edges, but it's the cheapest option near the airport for penny-pinchers . You can catch buses to Reykjavík and Keflavík in front of the hostel, but a car or a love of walking through concrete suburbs would be helpful here. Interestingly, the government uses this hostel for displaced persons and people seeking asylum in Iceland.

🍴 Eating

There are enough drive-through snack bars and greasy grills in Keflavík to give you an instant burger-induced coronary. For more civilised fare, there are several places along the main street; plus the Icelandair Hotel has an excellent restaurant.

Thai Keflavík   ASIAN €€
(www.thaireykjavik.is; Hafnargata 39; mains Ikr1590-3390; ⏱11am-10pm Mon-Sat, 4-10pm Sun; 🖥) Promoting authentic Thai dishes created from Icelandic ingredients, this restaurant is a great choice at the end of your holiday if you're up to your eyeballs in fish and lamb. There's outdoor seating at large wooden tables during the warmer months. It also rents bikes for €5 per hour.

Kaffi Duus   SEAFOOD €€€
(www.duus.is; Duusgata 10; mains Ikr2500-4850; ⏱11am-10pm) This friendly nautical-themed cafe-restaurant-bar, decorated with walrus tusks, overlooks the small-boat harbour and cliffs. It serves generous platefuls of fish, fish, fish, fresh out of the sea, with a few pasta dishes, salads and burgers thrown in. It's a popular evening hang-out.

Ráin   ICELANDIC €€€
(www.rain.is; Hafnargata 19a; mains Ikr1790-6590; ⏱11am-10pm Mon-Fri, 4-10pm Sat & Sun) Decorated like the interior of a wooden cruise

GOODBYE TO THE MILITARY BASE

Keflavík owed a great deal of its former prosperity to the former American military base, which closed down in September 2006.

In 1951 a fear of 'reds under the bed' led the US to establish a military presence in Iceland, which was a handy submarine fuelling stop between the US and Russia. Over the years various passionate protests were made demanding that the troops leave, but all came to nothing. It was only as submarines became more advanced and the Cold War ended that US operations in Iceland were scaled back.

The US eventually made tentative noises about a complete closure. Contrarily, this time many Icelanders demanded that the soldiers stay – the jobs that the base provided and the money it brought into the economy were too valuable to lose; and how could Iceland defend itself without an army of its own?

But the units drifted home and the base powered down, until on 30 September 2006 a simple ceremony took place – the US flag was lowered, and the Icelandic flag was raised in its place, ending 55 years of occupation.

Even today, Keflavík still misses its soldiers; the town now has the highest unemployment rate in Iceland. There are no cohesive plans for the enormous military zone on Reykjanes. The Lego-like barracks are being used as accommodation for Reykjavík University students, but the shooting ranges, warehouses and miles of razor wire all lie abandoned. It's estimated that it will cost the Icelandic government Ikr4 billion to clean up toxic areas and demolish unwanted buildings...but after the economic crisis in 2008, it's unlikely to be a priority for some time.

ship from the '70s, Ráin offers great sea views (when the mist hasn't rolled in!) and serves a selection of Icelandic favourites – go for the 'turf and surf' special.

Olsen Olsen   FAST FOOD €
(Hafnargata 17; snacks Ikr600-1000; ☉11am-10pm) In the 1950s, thanks to American-introduced rock and roll, Keflavík was the coolest place in Iceland. This USA-style diner transports locals back to the glory days, with shiny silver tables, red plastic seats and pictures of Elvis on the walls. Although it's a tribute to all things American, we're pretty sure it's not named after Mary Kate and Ashley.

ⓘ Getting There & Around

To/From the Airport

Most of Reykjanesbær's accommodation options offer free airport transfers for guests. A taxi will cost about Ikr2500 – call **Airport Taxi** (☑420 1212; www.airporttaxi.is) or **Hreyfill-Bæjarleiðir** (☑588 5522; www.hreyfill.is). For information on the Flybus between the airport and Reykjavík, see p77.

Air

Apart from flights to Greenland and the Faeroes, all of Iceland's international flights use Keflavík International Airport. For more information, see p344.

Bus

SBK (☑420 6000; www.sbk.is) runs several daily buses between Reykjanesbær and the BSÍ bus terminal in Reykjavík during the week, with limited service on weekends. You can ask almost any passing bus to drop you off near the town limits on its way to/from the airport when you board.

Northwestern Reykjanes

The western edge of the Reykjanes Peninsula is rugged and exposed – perfect if you love wild rain-lashed cliffs and beaches. There are several fishing villages and some quirky sights to be seen among the lava fields.

GARÐUR

From Keflavík, if you follow Rte 41 for 9km, on through the village of Garður, you'll reach the beautiful wind-battered **Garðsk-agi headland**, one of the best places in Iceland for bird spotting – it's a big breeding ground for sea birds, and it's often the place where migratory species first touch down. It's also possible to see seals, and maybe whales, from here.

Two splendid **lighthouses**, one old and one new, add drama – you can get near-360-degree sea views from the old lighthouse. There's also a small **folk museum** (☑422 7220; www.svgardur.is; admission free; ⊙1-5pm Apr-Oct), filled with a pleasing mishmash of fishing boats, birds' eggs and sewing machines. It contains the balconied **2 Lighthouses Restaurant** (⊙1-5pm Apr-Oct), with superb views over the ocean to Snæfellsjökull.

There's a tranquil, free **camping** area by the lighthouse, with toilets and fresh water.

SANDGERÐI
Five kilometres south of Garður, it's worth stopping at this industrious fishing village to see the interesting **Fræðasetrið nature centre** (☑423 7551; Gerðavegur 1; adult/child Ikr600/300; ⊙9am-5pm Mon-Fri, 1-5pm Sat & Sun Jun-Aug, 9am-5pm Mon-Fri Sep-May), where there are stuffed Icelandic creatures (including a monstrous moth-eaten walrus), jars of pickled things (look out for the freaky Gorgonocephalus), tanks with sea squirts, crabs and anemones, and a fascinating exhibit about Arctic explorer JB Charcot. **Vitinn** (Vitatorg 7; mains Ikr850-8900; ⊙11.30am-9pm), across the street, serves rock crab in shanty-chic surrounds. The lunch buffet (Ikr2100), featuring a veritable aquarium of food, is also quite popular.

There are some pleasant **beaches** on the coast south of Sandgerði, and the surrounding marshes are frequented by more than 190 species of **birds**. About 5km south you'll find a lonely church at **Hvalsnes** featured in a famous Icelandic poem, then 2km beyond, you can walk to the ruins of the saga-age fishing village **Básendar**, which was destroyed by a giant tidal wave in 1799.

100 Crater Park (Keflavík to Valahnúkur)
If you turn off Rte 41 onto Rte 44 just outside Keflavík, you'll first pass the deserted **US military base** before reaching the fading fishing village of **Hafnir**. There's nothing much to see here – just humps and bumps in a field, thought to be a 9th-century longhouse belonging to Ingólfur Arnarson's foster brother, and the anchor of the 'ghost ship' *Jamestown*, which drifted ashore mysteriously in 1870 with a full cargo of timber but no crew.

Pass the bird cliffs at **Hafnaberg**, and you'll reach the so-called **Bridge Between Two Continents**. There's a small sign and a carpet of pavement unfurling through the lava field where you can take a photo on a teeny bridge spanning a sand-filled gulf between the North American and European plates.

In the far southwest of the peninsula the landscape breaks down into wild volcanic crags and craters, hence the name **100 Crater Park**. Several space station–like **power plants** here exploit geothermal heat to produce salt from sea water and to provide electricity for the national grid. **Orkuverið Jörð** (Power Plant Earth; ☑422 5200; www.powerplantearth.is; admission Ikr1000; ⊙12.30-4.30pm Sat & Sun mid-May–mid-Sep) is an interactive exhibition about the world's energy supplies. You also get a glimpse into the vast, spotless turbine hall, and you can meander along a concrete culvert down to the seashore afterwards to watch 67°C waste water steaming into the cold waves. (It's much more exciting than it sounds!)

One of the most wild and wonderful spots is **Valahnúkur**, where a dirt track leads off the main road through 13th-century lava fields down to the most desolate cliffs imaginable. At the time of research, plans were underway to create an understated visitors centre at the foot of the rising cliff. You can clamber up to the ruins of the oldest lighthouse (1878) in Iceland and contemplate the fragility of life. From here you can see the flat-topped rocky crag of **Eldey**, 14km out to sea, which is home to the world's largest gannet colony. Some claim the last great auk was killed and eaten there, though Faeroese dispute this, insisting that the event occurred at Stóra Dímun. Today Eldey is a protected bird reserve.

Back towards the main road is a steaming multicoloured **geothermal area**. This includes the hot spring **Gunnuhver**, named after the witch-ghost Gunna, who was trapped by magic and dragged into the boiling water to her death.

Grindavík
POP 2850
Grindavík, the only settlement on the south coast of Reykjanes, is one of Iceland's most important fishing centres. If this were an English seaside town, its waterfront would be full of B&Bs, pubs and shops selling sticks of rock; here, all flimflam is rejected in favour of working jetties, cranes and warehouses. The busy harbour and tourist-free town are actually quite refreshing.

The town's only tourist attraction is **Kvíkan** (Magma; ☑420 1190; www.visitgrindavik.is;

Hafnargata 12a; adult/child Ikr1200/free; ⊙10am-5pm mid-May–mid-Sep), a museum of limited interest with two exhibits. The 1st floor is dedicated to explaining the fish-salting industry in a well-curated showroom with three videos. Upstairs there's a detailed display about geothermal energy. The museum also has as a small **tourist information centre** (⊙10am-5pm mid-May–mid-Sep).

🛏 Sleeping & Eating

Campsite   CAMPGROUND €
(Austurvegur 26; sites per person Ikr900; ⊙mid-May–mid-Sep) Grindavík's fresh-faced campsite is, by far, one of the best in all of Iceland. Located near the harbour, this patch of green comes with all of the best amenities, including an on-site eating spot and playground.

Heimagisting Borg   GUESTHOUSE €
(☑895 8686; www.guesthouseborg.com; Borgarhraun 2; s/d Ikr8500/13,000; @🛜) Owned by an Icelandic-American couple, Borg is an older home in the centre of town with the cosiness of 'grandma's place'.

🔝 **Bryggjan**   CAFE €
CHOICE
(Harbour; snacks Ikr300-1000; ⊙11am-11pm) Hidden behind a block of warehouses along the harbour, this adorable cafe serves up light meals amid framed photos, portraits, and old fishing buoys dangling from the ceiling.

Salthúsið   SEAFOOD €€
(www.salthusid.is; Stamphólsvegur 2; mains Ikr2300-4500; ⊙5-10pm Mon & Wed-Fri, 12.30pm-midnight Sat, 12.30-10pm Sun) The classy wooden Salthúsið is the first dedicated saltfish restaurant in Iceland. The *baccalao* is prepared in different ways (with ginger, chilli, olives and garlic; au gratin; as nibbly nuggets; or with mushrooms, red onion and capers), so there's plenty of variety. If the idea of saltfish doesn't grab you, fall back on perfectly prepared lobster, chicken or lamb.

❶ Getting There & Away

Three scheduled daily buses travel between Reykjavík and Grindavík.

Reykjanesfólkvangur

For a taste of Iceland's empty countryside, you could visit this 300-sq-km wilderness reserve, a mere 40km from Reykjavík. Its three showpieces are **Kleifarvatn**, a deep grey lake with submerged hot springs and black-sand beaches; the spitting, bubbling geothermal zone at **Seltún**; and the southwest's largest bird cliffs, the epic **Krýsuvíkurberg**.

The reserve was established in 1975 to protect the elaborate lava formations created by the Reykjanes ridge volcanoes. The whole area is crossed by dozens of **walking trails**, which mostly follow old paths between abandoned farms. They're detailed in the good pamphlet map *Walking & Hiking in Krýsuvík* (in English), available from the tourist offices at Keflavík or Hafnarfjörður. There are parking places at the beginnings of most of the popular walks, including the loop around Kleifarvatn, and the tracks along the craggy Sveifluháls and Núpshliðarháls ridges.

KLEIFARVATN

This deep and creepy lake sits in a volcanic fissure, surrounded by wind-warped lava cliffs and black-sand shores. Legend has it that a wormlike monster the size of a whale lurks below the surface – but the poor creature is running out of room, as the lake has been shrinking ever since two major earthquakes shook the area in 2000. For a macabre fictional slant on this event, seek out Arnaldur Indriðason's thriller *The Draining Lake* (2004). A walking trail runs right around the water's edge, offering dramatic views and the crunch of volcanic cinders underfoot.

KRÝSUVÍK & SELTÚN

The volatile **geothermal field Austurengjar**, about 2km south of Kleifarvatn, is often called Krýsuvík after the nearby abandoned farm. Even by Icelandic standards, this area is prone to geological tantrums. The temperature below the surface is 200°C and the water is boiling as it emerges from the ground. A borehole was sunk here to provide energy for Hafnarfjörður during the 1990s, but it exploded without warning in 1999 and the project was abandoned.

At **Seltún**, boardwalks meander round a cluster of **hot springs**. The steaming vents, mud pots and solfataras (volcanic vents) shimmer with rainbow colours from the strange minerals in the earth, and the provocative eggy stench will leave a lasting impression.

Nearby is the lake **Grænavatn**, an old explosion crater filled with weirdly green water – caused by a combination of minerals and warmth-loving algae.

KRÝSUVÍKURBERG

About 3km south of Seltún, a dirt track leads down to the coast at **Krýsuvíkurberg** (marked on the main road as Krýsuvíkur-bjarg). These bleak black cliffs stretch for 4km and are packed with puffins, guillemots and other sea birds in summer. A walking path runs along their length.

THE GOLDEN CIRCLE

An artificial tourist circuit loved by thousands of visitors, the Golden Circle takes in three popular attractions all within 100km of the capital: Þingvellir, Geysir and Gullfoss, offering visitors the opportunity to see the country's most important historical area, a spouting hot spring and a roaring waterfall, all in one condensed, doable-in-a-day tour. Visiting the area under your own steam will allow you to explore some of the exciting attractions further afield.

If you're planning to spend the night in the Golden Circle, you'll be spoilt for choice – the area is relatively small in size, making any of the following options a perfectly suitable

DIY GOLDEN CIRCLE

The so-called Golden Circle is a collection of interesting sights within spitting distance of the capital. Not to be confused with the Ring Road, which wraps around the entire country (and takes about a week or more to properly complete), the circuit's attractions have become exceeding popular in the last decade, especially for long-weekend visitors. During the warmest months of the year, it feels as though hundreds of Reykjavík-based operators offer half-day trips of the circle; however, it's very easy to tackle the sights on your own – you can even tack on additional elements that suit your interests.

The primary points of the Golden Circle are Þingvellir, the site of the continent shift and the ancient Icelandic parliament, Geysir, an erupting geyser, and Gullfoss, a pounding waterfall carving its way through a canyon. Admittedly, they can feel like a rather arbitrary collection of attractions, especially when far more fantastic things lay further beyond.

It's very easy to rent a vehicle and drive between the sights, taking as much time as you'd like visiting each destination. Signs are well marked and the roads are well paved. Figure around four hours to complete the journey. You can also tackle the Golden Circle by bicycle (p52). DIYers should consider adding on the following elements to their tour:

» **Laugarvatn** (p97) Located between Þingvellir and Geysir, this small lakeside town has two must-tries: Lindin, an excellent local restaurant, and Fontana, a brand-new geothermal spa with a sauna steamed by a mini active geyser.

» **Kerlingarfjöll** (p289) You'll need a 4WD to travel beyond Gullfoss – the last stop in the 'circle' – but it's well worth continuing on. This highland reserve, about two hours beyond the falls, is Iceland's upcoming hiker haven. Get here before the masses!

» **Kaldidalur Corridor** (p142) Tiny rentals are prohibited from driving this track, but if you get a sanctioned vehicle, you can explore this lonely road that swerves along a hulking glacier. It starts near Þingvellir and ends near Húsafell, where you can venture into a magnificent lava tube and learn about the nation's rich saga history at Reykholt. Do the traditional Golden Circle in reverse, then head westward.

» **Þjórsárdalur** (p101) Largely unexplored, the quiet valley along the Þjórsá riverbed leads up into the highlands acting as one of the main routes to the steaming earths at Landmannalaugar (the starting point of the famous Laugavegurinn hike; p123) – the road is dotted with ancient Viking ruins and mysterious natural wonders like Gjáin.

» **Eyrarbakki and Stokkseyri** (p105 and p106) After completing the loop, head south of Selfoss to find two seaside townships that are strikingly different than the other towns nearby. Feast on seafood after a long day of driving, and check out some of the local galleries that informally set up shop each year.

» **Flúðir** (p101) If you're curious about Iceland's blooming agrarian movement (no pun intended), check out the farms in and around Flúðir; many offer tours of their greenhouses and horse ranches. Buy all the ingredients (even fresh cuts of beef) to prepare a wonderful feast in your guesthouse's kitchen.

choice. The Laugarvatn area is a good base with several worthy sleeping and eating options; there are a number of solid choices scattered along Rte 35 as well (p99).

Þingvellir

This national park, 23km east of Reykjavík, is Iceland's most important historical site and a place of lonely beauty. The country's first national park, it was finally made a Unesco World Heritage Site in 2004.

The Vikings established the world's first democratic parliament, the Alþing, here in AD 930. As with many saga sites, there aren't many Viking remains to be seen, but the park has a superb natural setting, inside an immense, fissure-ridden rift valley caused by the separating North American and Eurasian tectonic plates.

History

Many of Iceland's first settlers had run-ins with royalty back in mainland Scandinavia. These chancers and outlaws decided that they could live happily without kings in the new country, and instead created district *þings* (assemblies) where justice could be served.

Eventually, a nationwide *þing* became necessary. One man was dispatched to Norway to study law, while his foster brother travelled the country looking for a suitable site. Bláskógur – now Þingvellir (Parliament Fields) – lay at a crossroads by a huge fish-filled lake. It had plenty of firewood and a setting that would make even the most tedious orator dramatic, so it fitted the bill perfectly. Every important decision affecting Iceland was argued out on this plain – new laws were passed, marriage contracts were made, and even the country's religion was decided here. The annual parliament was also a great social occasion, thronging with traders and entertainers.

Over the following centuries, escalating violence between Iceland's most powerful groups led to the breakdown of law and order. Governance was surrendered to the Norwegian crown and the Alþing was stripped of its legislative powers in 1271. It functioned solely as a courtroom until 1798, before being dissolved entirely. When it regained its powers in 1843, members voted to move the meeting place to Reykjavík.

◉ Sights

From the Park Service Centre on Rte 36, follow Rte 361 down to the only standing structures in the great rift. Start at the farmhouse, Þingvallabær, which was built for the 1000th anniversary of the Alþing in 1930 by the state architect Guðjón Samúelsson. It's now used as the park warden's office and prime minister's summerhouse.

Behind the farmhouse, Þingvallakirkja (⊙9am-7.30pm mid-May–Aug) is one of Iceland's first churches. The original was consecrated in the 11th century, but the current wooden building only dates from 1859. Inside are several bells from earlier churches, a 17th-century wooden pulpit and a painted altarpiece from 1834. The Independence-era poets Jónas Hallgrímsson and Einar Benediktsson are interred in the small cemetery beside the church.

Straddling both sides of the Öxará river, you'll find the ruins of various *búðir* (booths), which are clearly marked with interpretive panels. These small stone-and-turf shelters were where parliament-goers camped, and they also acted like stalls at today's music festivals, selling beer, food and vellum to the assembled crowds. Most of the remains date from the 17th and 18th centuries; the largest, and one of the oldest, is Biskupabúð, which belonged to the bishops of Iceland and is located north of the church.

Near the start of the walk up through the dramatic Almannagjá is the Lögberg (Law Rock), where the Alþing used to convene annually. This was where the *lögsögumaður* (law speaker) recited the law to the assembled parliament each year. After Iceland's conversion to Christianity, the site shifted to the foot of Almannagjá cliffs, which acted as a natural amplifier, broadcasting the voices of the speakers across the assembled crowds. The site is marked by a flagpole. Decisions were reached by the Lögrétta (Law Council), made up of 146 men (48 voting members, 96 advisers and two bishops), who are thought to have assembled at Neðrivellir (Low Fields), the flat area in front of the cliffs.

Follow the path through Almannagjá up to the top of the precipice. This slice in the terrain is the area's most dramatic example of the earth-rending forces at play, though it should be noted that you are not technically walking between the two continental plates; they are much further apart and can be seen on the horizon from the lookout at the multimedia centre when you reach the top. Each year North America and Europe tear further away from each other at a rate of 1mm to 18mm.

At the top of the Almannagjá rift is the interesting Interpretive Centre at Þingvellir (admission free; ☺9am-5pm), a multimedia centre exploring the area's nature and history in a 40-minute film. Books and souvenirs can also be purchased here. The small adjacent boardwalk offers great views of the valley.

Filling much of the rift plain, Þingvallavatn is Iceland's largest lake, at 84 sq km. Pure glacial water from Langjökull glacier filters through bedrock for 40km before emerging here. It's joined by the hot spring Vellankatla, which spouts from beneath the lava field on the northeastern shore. Þingvallavatn is an important refuelling stop for migrating birds (including the great northern diver, barrow's golden-eye and harlequin duck). Weirdly, its waters are full of *bleikja* (Arctic char) that have been isolated for so long that they've evolved into four subspecies.

🏃 Activities

One of the most sensational activities in Iceland is strapping on a scuba mask and a dry suit and exploring the crystalline fissures that scar the rift between continental plates. Dive operators explore the Silfra fissure – and while the waters are perfectly clear (it almost feels as though you're flying), the tight space between the submerged cliff walls can feel cramped with other divers during July and August. You can link up with the diving outfits in Þingvellir or join a trip departing from Reykjavík – see p56 for more details.

☞ Tours

If you're travelling to Þingvellir under your own steam you can link up with free one-hour English guided tours (☺10am Jun-Aug), setting off from the church.

🛏 Sleeping & Eating

Unfortunately, the centenarian Hótel Valhöll, the only hotel within Þingvellir National Park, burned to the ground in July 2009 (despite still being on many of the park's maps). In these troubled economic times there are no signs of a rush to rebuild, so for now the five Þingvellir campsites (sites per person Ikr1000; ☺May–mid-Sep), overseen by the Park Service Centre, are the only place to stay at Þingvellir. The best are the two

at Leirar, near the cafe – Syðri-Leirar is the biggest and Nyrðri-Leirar has laundry facilities. Fagrabrekka and Hvannabrekka are for campers only (no cars). The fifth campsite, Vatnskot, is down by the lake side, and has toilets and cold water (no electricity).

Cottages @ Lake Thingvellir   COTTAGES €€
(Skálabrekka; ☎892 7110; www.lakethingvellir.is; cottage Ikr20,000) Offers four pine cottages with views to the lake near the national park entrance along Rte 36.

ℹ Information

Park Service Centre (Þjónustumiðstöð; ☎482 2660; www.thingvellir.is; ☺9am-8pm May-Sep) On Rte 36, the Service Centre has a tourist information desk with helpful details about the national park, as well as a cafe (open from 8.30am to 10pm from February to mid-November). The park's multimedia centre also dispenses information about exploring the area.

ℹ Getting There & Away

The easiest way to get here is on a Golden Circle tour or in a hire car.

From mid-June to August the daily **Reykjavík Excursions** (☎580 5400; www.re.is) bus service 6/6A runs from Reykjavík to Þingvellir, stopping for 45 minutes at the Park Service Centre before continuing to Geysir, Gullfoss and back to Reykjavík.

Laugarvatn

POP 200

Laugarvatn (Hot Springs Lake) wasn't named this way for nothing – this agreeable body of water is fed not only by streams running from the misty fells behind it, but by the hot spring Vígðalaug, famous since medieval times. A village, also called Laugarvatn, sits on the lake's western shore, and it is the best places to base yourself in the Golden Circle area.

◎ Sights & Activities

Fontana   GEOTHERMAL POOL
(☎486 1400; www.fontana.is; admission Ikr2500; ☺11am-10pm Jun-Sep, 1-9pm Mon-Fri, 11am-9pm Sat & Sun Oct-May) Although some locals were rather upset that the crude sauna has been replaced with a skankier soaking spot, Fontana has been steadily luring the masses much like its big brother, Blue Lagoon. There are three wading pools, and a cedar-lined steam room that's fed by a naturally occurring geyser-like vent down below.

SOUTHWEST ICELAND & THE GOLDEN CIRCLE LAUGARVATN

If you want skip all of the hot-pot hoopla, there's a regular geothermal swimming pool next door that costs a fraction of the price but retains none of the glitz.

Tours

Laugarvatn Adventures ADVENTURE TOUR
(☑862 5614; www.caving.is) Laugarvatn runs two- to three-hour caving and rock climbing trips in the hills around town. The company provides boiler suits, but bring a pair of gloves for crawling and scrambling through lava tunnels and up rocky slopes.

▣ Sleeping & Eating

Sunsets in Laugarvatn are particularly spectacular – the sun glows bright red as the dwindling rays bounce off the lake. It's a great place to spend the night, but we recommend skipping the campground, as it has a rather unfortunate reputation for attracting local undesirables.

TOP CHOICE **Efstidalur** GUESTHOUSE €€
(☑486 1186; www.efstadal.is; Efsti-dalur 2; d with/without bathroom Ikr21,400/16,000) Located between Laugarvatn and Geysir on a working dairy farm, Efstidalur seems wholly unassuming at first, but quickly reveals itself to be a wonderfully welcoming option offering cosy digs and tasty meals. Although the farm is on the well-worn Golden Circle tourist circuit, its bucolic surrounds make it feel miles away from the hustle, especially in the evenings. Adorable semi-detached cottages are built from polished strips of wood and have brilliant views of hulking Hekla in the distance. The on-site restaurant (mains Ikr1800 to Ikr5000, open mid-May to mid-September) serves beef right from the farm and trout from the lake nearby.

TOP CHOICE **Laugarvatn HI Hostel** HOSTEL €
(☑486 1215; laugarvatn@hostel.is; dm Ikr3800; @⌘) This large year-round hostel, spread over several buildings along the village's main street, is one of the most professional operations in southern Iceland. The large main building rises up three floors, and has plenty of kitchen space (with great lake views while you're washing up). There's a second large building dedicated to groups with a spate of separate amenities, and, depending on the summer, there are one or two additional buildings that are much smaller and house-like. Breakfast is served at the kindly owners' home.

Hótel Edda HOTEL €
(☑444 4000; www.hoteledda.is; s/d Ikr9500/11,800; ⌖Jun–mid-Aug; @⌘) Laugarvatn's two big schools become Edda hotels in summer. The 98-room **ML Laugarvatn** has the usual serviceable Edda accommodation that will have you reminiscing about your college days (sleeping-bag options available from Ikr2400). **ÍKÍ Laugarvatn** is swankier by far: its 29 rooms (single/double Ikr15,600/18,800) all have private bathrooms, half with beautiful panoramic lake views. Its in-house restaurant (two courses Ikr3900) has great Helka views as well.

TOP CHOICE **Lindin** ICELANDIC €€€
(☑486 1262; www.laugarvatn.is; Lindarbraut 2; 3 courses Ikr5400-8900; ⌖noon-10pm May-Sep, reduced hours Oct-Apr) Owned by Baldur, the Icelandic parliament's official caterer, Lindin is the best restaurant for miles. The front – facing the lake – is purely gourmet, with soft floral patterns and prim tablecloths, while the back of the restaurant has a noticeably different decor and serves international fare at cut prices. We highly recommend the splurge for a true taste of the Icelandic wilderness – try the juicy reindeer burger and finish your meal with what Baldur claims is the best dessert on the planet (you'll see!).

❶ Getting There & Away

There's a year-round bus service to Laugarvatn from Reykjavík, continuing on to Gullfoss and Geysir, and then returning to Reykjavík.

Geysir

One of Iceland's most famous tourist attractions, Geysir (*gay*-zeer) is the original hot-water spout after which all other geysers around the world are named. The Great Geysir once gushed water up to 80m into the air but, sadly, it became clogged in the 1950s when tourists threw rocks into the spring in an attempt to set it off. Large earthquakes in 2000 seem to have shifted some blockage, though the eruptions are very infrequent. Luckily for visitors, the world's most reliable geyser, **Strokkur**, is right next door. You rarely have to wait more than five to 10 minutes for the water to swirl up an impressive 15m to 30m plume before vanishing down what looks like an enormous plughole. Don't stand downwind unless you want a shower.

The volatile earths at Strokkur and Geysir are free, and a large complex **Geysir**

Center (☎480 6800; www.geysircenter.com; ⌚10am-10pm Jun-Aug, to 6pm Sep-May) has been erected to corral the masses across the street. Here you'll find a massive restaurant, a souvenir shop of mall-like proportions, a separate cafeteria space, and **Geysisstofa** (☎480 6800; www.geysircenter.com; adult/concession Ikr1000/800; ⌚10am-5pm May-Aug, noon-4pm Sep-Apr), a mildly interesting audiovisual exhibition about geysers, volcanoes and earthquakes.

🛏 Sleeping & Eating

Hótel Geysir   HOTEL €€
(☎480 6800; www.geysircenter.is; s/d from Ikr17,500/21,900; ⌚Feb-Dec; @🛜) A campus of alpine-style cabins across the street from Strokkur; this busy spot also has a geothermal pool and two hot-pots. During summer, when the port is full of cruise ships, the hotel can be completely overrun with tourists who stop here for the buffet lunch (Ikr2800); in the evening there's a four-course prix fixe (Ikr6900) and a sushi menu. Hótel Geysir also maintains a **campsite** (sites per person Ikr1200; ⌚May-Sep), and can set you up with horse-riding tours upon request.

Guesthouse Geysir   HOTEL €€
(☎893 8733; www.geysirgolf.is; d Ikr15,900; 🛜) This modest block of fresh-faced hotel rooms is geared towards golfers – there are nine well-groomed holes out the back. A kitchen is available for guests.

❶ Getting There & Away

From June to August, scheduled **Trex** (☎551 1166; www.bogf.is) bus 2/2a runs from the BSÍ bus station in Reykjavík to Geysir and Gullfoss (at 8.30am, and also at 11am in July and August) and back, a circuit of around 8½ hours.

Also from mid-June to August, the **Reykjavík Excursions** (☎580 5400; www.re.is) daily bus 6/6a stops at Þingvellir, Geysir and Gullfoss for at least 45 minutes each, before returning to Reykjavík.

Very popular Golden Circle tours run year-round from Reykjavík.

Gullfoss

Iceland's most famous waterfall, Gullfoss (Golden Falls) is a spectacular double cascade. It drops 32m, kicking up a sheer wall of spray before thundering away down a narrow ravine. On sunny days the spray creates shimmering rainbows, and it's also

magical in winter when the falls glitter with ice. On grey, drizzly days, mist can envelop the second drop, making Gullfoss slightly underwhelming.

The falls came within a hair's breadth of destruction during the 1920s, when a team of foreign investors wanted to dam the Hvitá river for a hydroelectric project. The landowner, Tómas Tómasson, refused to sell to them, but the developers went behind his back and obtained permission directly from the government. Tómasson's daughter, Sigríður, walked (barefoot!) to Reykjavík to protest, even threatening to throw herself into the waterfall if the development went ahead. Thankfully, the investors failed to pay the lease, the agreement was nullified and the falls escaped destruction. Gullfoss was donated to the nation in 1975 and has been a nature reserve ever since.

Above Gullfoss is a small **tourist information centre and cafe** (mains Ikr1290-1950; ⌚9am-9.30pm Jun-Aug, 9am-6pm Sep-May), which is famous for its organic lamb soup made from locally sourced ingredients. A tarmac path suitable for wheelchairs leads to a lookout over the falls, and a set of steps continues to the water.

There's accommodation and another eating option a few kilometres before the falls at **Hótel Gullfoss** (☎486 8979; www.hotelgullfoss.is; s/d incl breakfast Ikr22,000/27,500; 🛜), a large, modern bungalow hotel without much personality.

Gullfoss is the final attraction on the traditional Golden Circle tour; you can continue along the road beyond the falls – the Kjölur Route (p288) – which heads deep into the highlands.

Gullfoss to Selfoss (Route 35)

If you're completing the Golden Circle in the traditional fashion, then the route from Gullfoss back to the Ring Road at Selfoss will be the final stage of your trip. Along the way you'll find plenty of interesting items to lure you off the road. This is Iceland's most active agrarian area; there are plenty of spots to try some fresh produce grown in greenhouses or on the local cattle ranches.

Most people follow surfaced Rte 35, which passes through Reykholt, then meets the Ring Road about 2km west of Selfoss. You can detour off Rte 35 to Skálholt, once Iceland's religious powerhouse.

Alternatively, you could follow Rte 30, which is intermittently surfaced and passes through Flúðir, meeting Rte 1 about 15km east of Selfoss.

REYKHOLT
POP 190

The rural township of Reykholt – one of several Reykholts around the country – is centred on the hot spring Reykjahver and has an obligatory geothermal pool. The township is south Iceland's centre for white-water rafting. Both Arctic Rafting (562 7000; www.arcticrafting.is; mid-Apr–Sep) and Iceland Riverjet (863 4506; www.iceland riverjet.com; Apr–mid-Oct) are based in the area, offering a fun day of thrills and spills along the Hvítá river.

The family at Friðheimar (www.fridheimar. is; May-Oct) tend to two interesting projects during the warmer months of the year. They are known in the region for their captivating horse shows, which introduce visitors to the unique Icelandic equine. Fifteen-minute shows (Ikr18000) run daily at 10am from June to September, followed by an informal meet-and-greet. The farmstead also has a massive greenhouse project that is currently producing tomatoes. Groups (Ikr1650 per person, 10-person minimum) are invited on a short tour of the greenhouse, which includes a bowl of spicy tomato soup.

Friendly Guesthouse Húsið (486 8680; www.kaffiklettur.is; Bjarkarbraut 26; d Ikr8500) has sleeping-bag accommodation in a basement on a quiet cul-de-sac; there's a hot tub and a barbecue.

Café Mika (Skólabraut 4; mains Ikr2390-4400; 10am-9pm) has an outdoor pizza oven – a favourite among locals – and sells hand-crafted chocolate at the cash register within.

Kaffi Klettur (mains Ikr1890-4190; noon-9.30pm Jun-Aug, noon-9.30pm Sat & Sun Sep-May) is decorated in a fairy-tale cottage style, with tapestries, old coffee mills and horse bridles. It has a wide selection of pizzas, burgers, crêpes, pasta, and traditional fish and meat mains.

SKÁLHOLT & LAUGARÁS

Skálholt is a hugely important religious centre; it was one of two bishoprics (the other was Hólar in the north) that ruled Iceland's souls from the 11th to the 18th centuries.

Skálholt rose to prominence under Gissur the White, the driving force behind the Christianisation of Iceland. The Catholic bishopric lasted until the Reformation in 1550, when Bishop Jón Arason and his two sons were executed by order of the Danish king. Skalhólt continued as a Lutheran centre until 1797, when the bishopric shifted to Reykjavík.

Unfortunately, the great cathedral that once stood here was destroyed by a major earthquake in the 18th century. Today there's a modern theological centre, a visitor centre (Ikr500; 9am-6pm), a turf-house (9am-6pm) re-creation of Þorlagsbúð, and a prim church (9am-6pm) with a museum (admission Ikr200; 9am-6pm) in the basement containing the stone sarcophagus of Bishop Páll Jónsson (bishop from 1196 to 1211). According to Páls Saga, the earth was wracked by storms and earthquakes when he died. Spookily, a huge storm broke at the exact moment that his coffin was reopened in 1956.

The neighbouring village of Laugarás is essentially a community of farms, many of which sell their fresh produce on-site. Visit Engi (www.engi.is), which regularly sells a selection of top-grade fruits and vegetables grown in greenhouses. Adorable souvenirs – including rocks painted like ladybugs – are also for sale. It's clearly marked at the entrance to the township when arriving from Skálholt.

Sleeping & Eating

Hótel Laugarás   HOTEL €
(486 8600; hotelhvita@simnet.is; sites per person Ikr1000, r €80; May-Sep; @) Located beside the suspension bridge in Laugarás, this basic hotel is shockingly drab from the exterior, but surprisingly pleasant, with parquet-floored rooms inside. The top floor is reserved for local fruit-picking volunteers. There's a grill-style restaurant attached, and horse rentals are possible for €40 per hour.

Skálholtsskóli   HOTEL €€
(486 7088; www.skalholt.is; d Ikr18,000) The Lutheran theological centre at Skálholt is open to guests. It's often booked out by visiting church groups, but if you're seeking clean, plain, twin-bedded rooms with private bathroom in a peaceful hamlet, it's worth calling. A separate building contains sleeping-bag accommodation (Ikr6400), and there's a restaurant.

Getting There & Away

From June to August, scheduled Trex (551 1166; www.bogf.is) bus 2/2a does an 8½-hour circuit from Reykjavík to Geysir and Gullfoss, calling at Reykholt and Skálholt/Laugarás. The bus leaves the city at 8.30am. Outside those months, Skálholt/Laugarás is a request stop only.

To drive to Skálholt, take Rte 35 from Selfoss. After around 30km, turn right onto Rte 31; the settlement is a couple of kilometres further along.

KERIÐ

Around 10km further southwest of Skálholt and Laugarás, Rte 35 passes Kerið, a 6500-year-old explosion crater containing a spooky-looking green lake. Björk once performed a concert from a floating raft in the middle. It's said that some joker has introduced fish to the water.

Up the road on the other side of Rte 35, **Hótel Grimsborgir** (555 7878; www.grimsborgir.com; d incl breakfast €218;) is a Truman Show–like campus of homes that are marketed as fully kitted-out hotel suites.

Flúðir

POP 380

For travellers who don't follow the convenient Rte 35 from Gullfoss back to the Ring Road, the alternate path – Rte 30 – will take you through Flúðir, known throughout Iceland for its geothermal greenhouses that grow the majority of the country's mushrooms. It's also a popular weekend getaway spot for hardworking Reykjavíkurs, who come to throw off their big-city cares at their private cottages.

Sleeping & Eating

Skip the fast food at the petrol station and swing by the **farmers market** (1-6pm Mon-Fri, 11am-6pm Sat & Sun mid-Jun–mid-Aug), located at the village's main cross street, which proffers the best produce of the region: vegies, meat, strawberries and potatoes. There's **Samkaup-Strax supermarket** (9am-10pm Mon-Fri, 10am-10pm Sat & Sun) for self-caterers when the market is closed.

Campers might want to skip the local camping site along the Litla Laxá stream, as it is usually rammed with Icelanders, especially on weekends.

Hótel Flúðir HOTEL €€
(486 6630; www.hotelfludir.is; Vesturbrún 1; s/d Ikr21,200/24,700; @) Icelandair owns this stylish chalet-like row of hotel rooms, which has much more warmth than other hotels in the chain. Comfortable rooms have

parquet floors, duvets covered with embroidered leaves, and soothing prints of fruit and flowers.

Grund GUESTHOUSE €€
(552 6962; www.gistingfludir.is; d incl breakfast Ikr17,000;) Run by kindly Dagný, this adorable guesthouse has a handful of homey rooms filled with antiques. The on-site restaurant (mains Ikr1350 to Ikr4400) prides itself in offering fresh food, like trout from Þingvellir.

Getting There & Away

From June to mid-September, Trex bus service 8/8a runs daily from Reykjavík to Flúðir. Outside those months, the service runs a more limited schedule. Most Flúðir buses run via Árnes.

Western Þjórsárdalur

The Þjórsá is Iceland's longest river, a fast-flowing, churning mass of milky glacial water that runs 230km from Vatnajökull down to the Atlantic. Including its tributaries, it accounts for almost one-third of Iceland's hydroelectric power.

Rte 32 follows the western side of the river, as it moves upstream and into the highlands. This is one of the preferred routes to reach Landmannalaugar by vehicle (via Rte F26) – it's the starting point for the famous Laugavegurinn Hike (p123). As always, you'll need a 4WD to tackle an F road; it's still worth venturing up Rte 32 to discover an oft-overlooked area filled with Viking ruins and hidden waterfalls.

ÁRNES

The tiny settlement of Árnes, near the junction of Rtes 30 and 32, is a convenient base for exploring Þjórsárdalur, or an easy spot to layover on the way to/from Landmannalaugar (located 1¾ hours further on). Be sure to check out the highly informative Þjórsárstofa (admission free; 10am-6pm Jun-Aug) in the large white community centre, which feels more like a makeshift museum about the wonders further on.

Árnes HI Hostel (Nónsteinn; 486 6048; arnes@hostel.is; sites per tent Ikr1000, dm Ikr3800;) isn't the cosiest place on earth, but its two buildings, with twin rooms and dorm space, are perfectly serviceable, plus there's a guest kitchen, and a small octagonal **pool** (Ikr400; Jun-Aug).

Most buses between Reykjavík and Flúðir stop in Árnes – though the buses to

Landmannalaugar tend to follow a route further east and do not stop here.

STÖNG & ÞJÓÐVELDISBÆR

Heading further along Rte 32 from Árnes towards Stöng and Þjóðveldisbær, take a short (2km) detour along a signposted track to the delightful waterfall Hjálparfoss, which tumbles in two chutes over a scarp formed from twisted basalt columns.

Perhaps the most strangely situated swimming pool in Iceland is the open-air Þjórsárdalslaug, which was closed at the time of research but is due to reopen by this book's publication date. It was built from concrete left over from the construction of the Búrfell hydroelectricity plant.

The ancient farm at Stöng was buried by white volcanic ash in 1104 during one of Hekla's eruptions. It once belonged to Gaukur Trandilsson, a 10th-century Viking who lived a tempestuous life. Unfortunately, the centuries have destroyed all traces of his saga; brief mentions in some 12th-century graffiti in Orkney, in *Njál's Saga* and in a scurrilous medieval rhyme hint that he had a fling with the housewife at the nearby farm Steinastöðum and was killed over the affair in an axe duel.

Stöng was excavated in 1939 – Iceland's first proper archaeological dig – and is an important site, used to help date Viking houses elsewhere. The farm ruins are covered over by a large wooden shelter at the end of a bad, bumpy dirt road that branches off Rte 32 about 20km beyond Árnes. You can still see stone-lined fire pits and door lintels made from octagonal basalt columns, and the surrounding lava landscape is impressively desolate. A walking path behind the farm takes you a couple of kilometres to a strange and lovely little valley, Gjáin, full of twisting lava and spectacular waterfalls.

We happen to think it's an atmospheric spot, but Þjóðveldisbærinn (☑488 7713; www.thjodveldisbaer.is; adult/child Ikr500/free; ☉10am-noon & 1-6pm Jun-Aug), a reconstructed Viking-era farm, is more photogenic. The farm exactly reproduces the layout of Stöng and its neighbouring church. The two farms are like a cosmetic surgeon's 'before' and 'after' photos.

South of the reconstructed farm is the high-tech and hands-on Búrfell hydroelectricity plant (☉10am-6pm Jun-Aug), decorated by one of Sigurjón Ólafsson's largest sculptures.

From Stöng you can walk 10km northeast along a 4WD track to Iceland's second-highest waterfall, Háifoss, which plunges 122m off the edge of a plateau. You can also get most of the way there by 4WD.

For remote accommodation in Þjórsárdalur, on the edge of the highlands, base yourself at Hólaskógur (☑661 2503; www.atvtravel.is). It's effectively a mountain hut, big enough for 80 sleeping-baggers, with camping places outside and a great sauna (Ikr500). The company that manages the hut offers quad-bike (ATV) tours.

THE SOUTH COAST

Coming from Reykjavík, this is one of the most exciting bits of the southern coast, simply because of the suspense. Initially Rte 1 trundles through a flat, wide coastal plain, full of horse farms and greenhouses, before the landscape suddenly begins to spasm and grow jagged. Mountains thrust upwards on the inland side of the road and the first of the awesome glaciers appears.

Public transport isn't bad along the Ring Road, which is studded with interesting settlements: Hveragerði, famous for its geothermal fields and hot springs; Skógar, the leaping-off point for Þórsmörk, one of Iceland's most popular hiking destinations; and Vík, surrounded by glaciers, vertiginous cliffs and black beaches.

Treats lying off the Ring Road include the tiny fishing villages of Stokkseyri and Eyrarbakki; brooding volcano Hekla (the gateway to hell!); the great unpronounceable Eyjafjallajökull, site of the 2010 eruption; and farms and valleys rich with saga heritage.

Hveragerði

POP 2320

At first glance, you might write Hveragerði off as a dull grid of boxy buildings. However, spend longer than half an hour here and your ominous muttering should fade away. This friendly town has soul, and lots of small, strange things to see and do.

Hveragerði sits on top of a highly active geothermal field, which provides heat for hundreds of greenhouses. Nationally, the town is famous for its horticultural college and naturopathic clinic. There are also some fantastic hikes in the area, so it makes a good base for walkers.

Pick up the handy *Hveragerði, The Capital of Hot Springs and Flowers* booklet, which details all of the sights, activities and dining options in the area.

🔆 Sights & Activities

Geothermal Fields   PARK
Hveragerði is known throughout Iceland for its accessible geothermal fields – the town has some of the most wildly steaming earths on the entire island. Boreholes and mudpots abound, though the landscape changed a great deal during a sudden earthquake in 2008 (swing by the simulator at the tourist information centre for details).

Today there are two concentrated areas where you can experience the planet's power and heat firsthand.

The geothermal park **Hverasvæðið** (Hveramörk 13; admission free; ⊙10am-6pm Mon-Fri, noon-4pm Sat & Sun Jun–mid-Sep), in the centre of town, has mudpots and steaming pools where visitors can dip their feet. You can also take a guided walk around the spring to learn about the area's unique geology and subsequent greenhouse power.

The second area is situated north of the town's steaming river – make sure you stick to the marked paths (lest you melt your shoes) and wander through seemingly endless fields of stinky sulphur and belching plains. If you keep going past the golf course, you'll reach a car park; from here, it's a 3km walk to unmissable **Reykjadalur**, a delightful geothermal valley where there's a bathable **hot river** – bring your swimsuit.

Listasafn Árnesinga   ART MUSEUM
(☑483 1727; www.listasafnarnesinga.is; Austurmörk 21; admission free; ⊙noon-6pm May-Oct, noon-6pm Thu-Sun Oct-Apr) We highly recommend the large, airy modern art gallery Listasafn Árnesinga, which puts on great temporary exhibitions. It's worthy of a town four times the size of Hveragerði, and has a fine cafe too.

HNLFÍ Health Clinic and Spa   SPA
(HNLFÍ ☑483 0300; www.hnlfi.is; Grænumörk 10) Iceland's most famous clinic, Heilsustofnun Náttúrulækningafélags Íslands, has mainly treated prescription-only patients in the past. However, it has now opened its doors to visitors seeking relaxing massages (Ikr5850 to Ikr9500) and deep-heat mud

Hveragerði

500 m
0.25 miles

To Golf Course (500m);
Reyjadalur (3.5km)

Football
Field

Breiðamörk

Geothermal
Fields

Dynskógar

Laufskógar
Brattahlíð
Hverahlíð
Varmahlíð

Frumskógar
Bláskógar

Varmá

Skólamörk

Geothermal
Swimming
Pool

Hverarmörk

Þelamörk
Hverarmörk
Þórsmörk

Réttarheiði

Breiðamörk
Austurmörk
Reykjamörk
Heiðmörk

Sunnumörk

Grænamörk

To Þorlákshöfn
(20km)
To Selfoss (12km)

Hveragerði

baths (Ikr5200). HNLFÍ has excellent facilities, including indoor and outdoor pools, hot-pots, a sauna, a steam bath and modest accommodation (double Ikr11,000).

Raufarhólshellir CAVE

This 11th-century lava tube is over 1km long, and contains some wonderful (protected) lava columns. You'll need a torch (flashlight) and sturdy boots to explore; the going underfoot can be quite treacherous from earlier cave-ins. In winter, cold air is funnelled down and trapped inside, producing amazing ice formations. You'll find the tube southwest of Hveragerði off the Reykjavík–Þorlákshöfn route (Rte 39), which passes right over the tunnel. It's about 1km north of the junction where Rtes 38, 39 and 427 meet.

Tours

Iceland Activities ADVENTURE TOUR

(☏777 6263; www.icelandactivities.is; ⊙8am-5pm Mon-Fri, 9am-4pm Sat) Specialising in biking, surfing and hiking tours, this family-run adventure company offers wonderful half-day and full-day trips in the southwest at very reasonable prices.

Sleeping

TOP CHOICE Frost og Funi HOTEL €€

(Frost & Fire; ☏483 4959; www.frostandfire.is; Hverhamar; s/d incl breakfast Ikr16,100/22,000; @🐾) Under new ownership, this quirky little hotel sits atop a quaking geothermal field that is constantly belching out boiling water, steam and oozing mud. The rooms stretch along a warm ravine, and are designed with subtle Scandi-sleek details and original artwork. Don't miss the heat-pressured sauna and the simmering hot-pots; both are fed by the hotel's private borehole.

Gistiheimilið Frumskógar GUESTHOUSE €

(☏896 2780; www.frumskogar.is; Frumskógar 3; s/d Ikr7000/11,000; 🐾) Located on a street that once was a veritable colony of Icelandic poets and writers, this cosy guesthouse proffers a hot-pot, steam bath, and apartment-style accommodation in the geometric digs behind the small main house.

Hótel Örk HOTEL €€

(☏483 4700; www.hotel-ork.is; Breiðamörk 1c; d incl breakfast Ikr24,900; @🐾) Dominating the view from the Ring Road, this large hotel looks like some sort of strange architectural relic from Japan in the 1950s. Rooms feel rather dated, but the hotel has a clutch of family-friendly amenities, including a sauna, a nine-hole golf course, billiards, and an excellent swimming pool with a slide and hot tubs. The in-house restaurant is decidedly gourmet and considered one of the town's best.

Eating

In addition to the usual supermarket suspects, there are several busy bakeries – like Hverabakarí (Breiðumörk 10; ⊙8.30am-6pm) and Almar (Sunnumörk 2; ⊙7am-6pm) and fast-food eating options lining the main service street running parallel to the Ring Road. Several spots in town offer meals cooked using the area's geothermal heat – you are even invited to make hardboiled eggs at the town's central spring.

Kjöt og Kúnst INTERNATIONAL €€

(www.kjotogkunst.com; Breiðamörk 21; mains Ikr1490-4390 ⊙noon-9pm Mon-Sat Jun-Aug, reduced hours Sep-May) The big-ticket item here is the bread baked using the natural heat from the earth. Dishes are mostly Icelandic (soup, fish and lamb), though you'll find an assortment of please-all sandwiches and pizzas.

ℹ Information

Tourist information centre (Upplýsingamiðstöð Suðurlands; ☏483 4601; www.southiceland.is; Sunnumörk 2-4; ⊙8.30am-5pm Mon-Fri, 9am-2pm Sat, 9am-1pm Sun Jun-Aug, 8.30am-4pm Mon-Fri Sep-May) Hveragerði contains the regional tourist office for the whole south coast, and shares its premises with the post office and a small exhibit about the earthquake that tore through the area in 2008.

ℹ Getting There & Away

The bus stop is at the N1 petrol station on the main road into town.

Sterna (☏551 1166; www.sterna.is) Runs bus 12b/12c from Reykjavík to Vík stopping in Hveragerði twice daily from mid-May to mid-September.

Strætó (☏540 2700; www.straeto.is) Buses 51 and 52 stop here twice daily on the Reykjavík–Vík/Höfn route and the Reykjavík–Landeyjahöfn route.

Þorlákshöfn

POP 1580

In the past, most people came to this fishing town, 20km south of Hveragerði, to catch the ferry to the Vestmannaeyjar; however, the ferry now departs from Landeyjahöfn on the southwest coast near Hvolsvöllur. When its stormy and the new pier fills with sand, the ferry to Vestmannaeyjar will resume from here. There's very little reason to spend time in town otherwise.

Just outside Þorlákshöfn, Rte 38 runs to Hveragerði, Rte 39 runs to Reykjavík, and Rte 427 runs west along the bottom of the Reykjanes Peninsula to Krýsuvík and beyond.

Eyrarbakki

POP 590

It's hard to believe, but tiny Eyrarbakki was Iceland's main port and a thriving trading town well into the 20th century. Farmers from all over the south once rode here to barter for supplies at the general store – the crowds were so huge it could take three days to get served! Another of Eyrarbakki's claims to fame is that it's the birthplace of Bjarní Herjólfsson, who made a great sea voyage in AD 985 and was probably the first European to see America. Unfortunately, Bjarní turned back and sold his boat to Leifur Eiríksson, who went on to discover Vinland and ended up with all the glory. Today the town is known for its prison – the largest in Iceland.

◉ Sights

Húsið á Eyrarbakka   MUSEUM
(House at Eyrarbakki; ☑483 1504; www.husid.com; Hafnarbrú 3; admission Ikr700, incl Sjöminjasafnið á Eyrarbakka; ☺11am-6pm mid-May–mid-Sep) One of Iceland's oldest houses, built by Danish traders in 1765, Húsið á Eyrarbakka has glass display cabinets explaining the town's history, rooms restored with original furniture (including the oldest piano in Iceland), and a collection of stuffed birds in a separate structure at the back. Keep an eye out for Ólöf Sveinsdóttir's shawl, hat and cuffs, knitted from her own hair.

Sjöminjasafnið á Eyrarbakka   MUSEUM
(☑483 1082; Túngata 59; ☺11am-6pm mid-May–mid-Sep) Just behind Húsið á Eyrarbakka is this small maritime museum with displays on the local fishing community. Its main exhibit is the beautiful, tar-smelling, 12-oared fishing boat, *Farsæll*. Admission to the Húsið á Eyrarbakki also includes this smaller museum.

Flói Nature Reserve   RESERVE
Birdwatchers should head for the estuarine Flói Nature Reserve, an important marshland on the eastern bank of the Ölfusá. It's visited by many wetland birds – common species include red-throated divers and various kinds of ducks and geese – with the biggest numbers appearing during the nesting season (May to July). There's a 2km circular hiking trail through the marshes. For more information, contact the **Icelandic Society for the Protection of Birds** (☑562 0477; www.fuglavernd.is). The reserve is 3km northwest of Eyrarbakki – you'll need your own transport.

🛏 Sleeping & Eating

Rein   GUESTHOUSE €€
(☑693 3543; www.rein-guesthouse.is; Þykkvaflöt 4; d incl breakfast Ikr16,000) Maia the dog welcomes guests to this quiet guesthouse with three wooden-walled attic. Although the creaking timbers and shabby-chic furniture give the house an ancient feel, it was actually only built in 1997.

Eyrarbakki HI Hostel   HOSTEL €
(☑483 1280; www.gonholl.is; Eyrargata 51-53; dm/apt from Ikr3800/20,000; ☎) Although this place falls under the aegis of the Icelandic hostelling association, it's unlike most hostels we've ever seen. It's composed of four lovely apartments, all with warm peach-toned walls, wooden floors, fully equipped kitchen (including dishwasher and washing machine) and cosy sitting rooms. Regular sleeping-bag space is also available for dormitory enthusiasts. The staff also run the dour **Gónhóll**, a strange cafe and superette set inside a warehouse next door.

Rauðahúsið   SEAFOOD €€
(www.raudahusid.is; Búðarstígur 4; mains Ikr1900-3500; ☺11.30am-9pm Sun-Thu, to 10pm Fri & Sat) Arch rival of the lobster restaurant in Stokkseyri, this place operates in an old red house, with cheery staff and great fresh seafood.

Hafið Bláa   SEAFOOD €€
(www.hafidblaa.is; Óseyri; mains Ikr2000-4000; ☺11am-10pm Jun-Aug) Halfway between Eyrarbakki and Þorlákshöfn, this seafood restaurant inhabits a beautifully designed building that looks like an upturned boat, with Arctic terns and gannets diving down from the ceiling. Even if you don't get a table overlooking the ocean, the sweeping estuary views on the opposite side are equally impressive.

❶ Getting There & Away

There are eight buses between Selfoss and Eyrarbakki/Stokkseyri on weekdays only, the first leaving at 6.50am and the last at 10.55pm.

Stokkseyri

POP 490

Eyrarbakki's twin lies east along the shore. It's another small fishing village, with a tourist emphasis less on museums and more on family fun. Winter is not the time to visit, but come in summer and you could easily spend a day enjoying the two villages' attractions.

◉ Sights & Activities

Veiðisafnið MUSEUM
(☑483 1558; www.hunting.is; admission Ikr1250; ⊙11am-6pm Apr-Sep, 11am-6pm Sat & Sun Feb-Mar & Oct-Nov) A small private collection curated by a local hunter, this two-room showcase feels like a museum of natural history, with dozens upon dozens of taxidermic creatures mounted on the walls. A chat with the friendly owner reveals fascinating stories of his expeditions all over the world.

Draugasetrið MUSEUM
(Ghost Centre; ☑895 0020; www.draugasetrid.is; Hafnargata 9; adult/child Ikr1500/1000; ⊙12.30-6pm Jun-Aug) Draugasetrið, on the top floor of a huge warehouse in the village centre, is a veritable haunted house run by a gaggle of blood-thirsty teens. A 50-minute iPod-guide (available in a multitude of languages) recites 24 spooky stories in a series of dry-ice-filled stations. On the side of the building, and run by the same people, is the Icelandic Wonders (adult/child Ikr1500/1000; ⊙12.30-6pm Jun-Aug) centre, which is decorated in a similar vein but walks you into a world of trolls, elves and Northern Lights. Admission to both attractions costs Ikr2500.

Sundlaug Stokkseyrar PUBLIC POOL
(adult/child Ikr500/free; ⊙1-9pm Mon-Fri, 10am-5pm Sat & Sun Jun-mid-Aug, 5.30-8.30pm Mon-Fri, 10am-3pm Sat & Sun mid-Aug-May) The town's popular swimming pool.

☞ Tours

Kajakferðir Stokkseyri KAYAKING TOUR
(☑896 5716; www. kajak.is; Heiðarbrún 24; tour Ikr4350; ⊙Apr-Oct) If you're interested in kayaking, join a small tour with Kajakferðir Stokkseyri, which explores the nearby lagoon (Ikr3750 per hour). It's based at the Sundlaug Stokkseyrar.

🛏 Sleeping & Eating

For cheap meals, there's a grill at the Shell petrol station.

Gaulverjaskóli HI Hostel HOSTEL €
(☑551 0654; www.south-hostel.is; Gaulverjaskóli; sites per person Ikr1000, dm Ikr3800; ⊙Feb–mid-Nov) The friendly owners have poured their hearts and souls into renovating this former school; today it's a clean, quiet hostel with a welcome common space in the attic, and a spacious separate kitchen block. Breakfast and a lamb stew dinner can be ordered in advance (you'll have to self-cater otherwise). It's based in a tiny hamlet marooned in a vast expanse of flat agricultural land, 9km from Stokkseyri along the coastal road leading back towards Selfoss.

Kvöldstjarnan GUESTHOUSE €€
(Evening Star; ☑483 1800; www.kvoldstjarnan. com; Stjörnusteinum 7; d incl breakfast Ikr16,000) The five bright, white rooms here come with washbasins and fluffy feathery duvets with Marimekko-esque prints. There's a small lounge area and sparkling kitchen for guest use. The owner's father has created an impressive garden, in spite of strong ocean breezes and salt-laden air.

TOP CHOICE Við Fjöruborðið SEAFOOD €€€
(☑483 1550; www.fjorubordid.is; Eyrabraut 3a; mains Ikr2050-4850; ⊙noon-9pm Jun–mid-Sep, 5-9pm Mon-Fri, noon-9pm Sat & Sun mid-Sep–May) This upmarket seafood restaurant on the shore has a reputation for serving the best lobster in Iceland. The legendary soup costs Ikr2050 and most people agree that it's worth every penny. Slurp your bisque amid old flagstones, glass fishing buoys and other marine memorabilia. Reservations recommended.

❶ Getting There & Away

For bus info, see p105.

Selfoss

POP 6570

Selfoss is the largest town in southern Iceland, an important trade and industry centre, and witlessly ugly. Iceland's Ring Road is its main shopping street – as a pedestrian, you're in constant danger of ending up as road jam. The only reason to stop in Selfoss is to load up on groceries before heading further on.

Selfoss

🛏 Sleeping

Vatnsholt GUESTHOUSE €€

(☎899 7748; www.stayiniceland.is; Vatnsholt 1-2; d with/without bath Ikr20,000/16,000; @☎) A wonderful place if you have the kids in tow, Vatnsholt is located about 16km southeast of Selfoss, just 8km off the Ring Road. Here you'll find a collection of sun-filled bedrooms scattered throughout a sweeping farmstead with views to Eyjafjallajökull, Hekla, Vestmannaeyjar and the steaming earths at Hveragerði. Bike rentals (Ikr2000), a menagerie of animals (including Elvis the dancing goat) and an elaborate playground could have you staying for days (or weeks). Enjoy fresh food at the on-site restaurant (three courses Ikr4900; open 6pm to 9pm), then check out the 9pm movie about Iceland's dynamic landscape.

Selfoss

Hótel Selfoss HOTEL €€

(☎480 2500; www.hotelselfoss.is; Eyravegur 2; s/d from Ikr25,000/29,500; @☎) This 99-room behemoth near the bridge has business-style hotel rooms and great facilities, including a large spa and an excellent in-house restaurant (mains Ikr1850 to Ikr5900). Make sure you get a room overlooking the broad and lovely river Ölfusá, rather than the drab car park.

Selfoss HI Hostel
HOSTEL €

(B&B Hostel; ✆482 1600; www.bandb.is; Austurvegur 28; dm/d Ikr4500/7100; 🛜) The layout of this hostel promotes maximum sociability, with extra-wide hallways and plenty of common space riddled with large couches and comfortable lounge chairs. We were surprised, however, to find that the staff barely spoke English (or Icelandic for that matter!); the vibe was much more sleep-and-go than stay-and-chill. Members get a Ikr600 discount; linen costs an additional Ikr1100.

✖ Eating

Selfoss is the best place in Iceland to stock up on groceries before setting off for wilder pastures. Virtually all major supermarkets are represented here, including **Bónus** (Austurvegur 42) and **Krónan** (Tryggvatorg). Fast-food chains are abundant as well. Consult the popular *Around Iceland* booklet for additional restaurant options.

Kaffi Krús
INTERNATIONAL €€

(www.kaffikrus.is; Austurvegur 7; mains Ikr890-2390; ⊙11am-10pm) The 'coffee mug' is a popular cafe set in a charming old house along the main road. There's two floors of seating, a ton of outdoor space, and a large selection of Icelandic and international dishes. Prices are a bit steep, all things considered, but budgetarians could split a pizza to keep costs down.

Sunnlenska Bókakaffið
CAFE €

(Austurvegur 22; ⊙noon-6pm Mon-Sat; 🛜) This adorable independent bookshop (selling both new and secondhand books) also offers coffee and cake. It's a great place to escape the maddening crowds of fast-food mongers.

❶ Information

Landsbanki Íslands, Kaupþing and Íslandsbanki all have branches with ATMs on Austurvegur.

Tourist information centre (✆480 1990; http://tourinfo.arborg.is; Austurvegur 2; ⊙10am-6pm Mon-Fri, 11am-2pm Sat mid-May–Aug) The tourist information desk, inside the town library and close to the roundabout on the main road, is staffed in summer; the information office in Hveragerði is better.

❶ Getting There & Away

All buses between Reykjavík and Höfn, Skaftafell, Fjallabak, Þórsmörk, Flúðir, Gullfoss, Laugarvatn and Vík pass through Selfoss. Selfoss is one hour away from Reykjavík.

Reykjavík Excursions (Kynnisferðir; ✆580 5400; www.re.is) Runs bus 20/20a from Reykjavík (departing at 8am) to Skaftafell, stopping here once daily from June to mid-September.

Sterna (✆551 1166; www.sterna.is) Runs bus 12b/12c from Reykjavík to Vík, stopping in Selfoss twice daily from mid-May to mid-September.

Strætó (✆540 2700; www.straeto.is) Buses 51 and 52 stop here twice daily on the Reykjavík–Vík/Höfn route and the Reykjavík–Landeyjahöfn route.

THE EDDAS

The medieval monastery at Oddi, in Rangárvellir about 8km from Hella, was the source of the Norse Eddas, the most important surviving books of Viking poetry. The *Prose Edda* was written by the poet and historian Snorri Sturluson around 1222. It was intended to be a textbook for poets, with detailed descriptions of the language and meters used by the Norse *skalds* (court poets). It also includes the epic poem *Gylfaginning*, which describes the visit of Gylfi, the king of Sweden, to Ásgard, the citadel of the gods. In the process, the poem reveals Norse creation myths, stories about the gods, and the fate in store for men at Ragnarök, when this world ends.

The *Poetic Edda* was written later in the 13th century by Sæmundur Sigfússon. It's a compilation of works by unknown Viking poets, some predating the settlement of Iceland. The first poem, *Voluspá (Sibyl's Prophecy)*, is like a Norse version of Genesis and Revelations: it covers the beginning and end of the world. Later poems deal with the story of how Óðinn discovered the power of runes, and the legend of Siegfried and the Nibelungs, recounted in Wagner's *Ring Cycle*. The most popular poem is probably *Þrymskviða*, about the giant Thrym, who stole Þór's hammer and demanded the goddess Freyja in marriage in exchange for its return. To get his hammer back, Þór disguised himself as the bride-to-be and went to the wedding in her place. Much of the poem is devoted to his appalling table manners at the wedding feast, during which he consumes an entire ox, eight salmon and three skins of mead.

HEKLA

The name of Iceland's most famous and active volcano means Hooded One, as its 1491m-high summit is almost always shrouded in ominous-looking cloud. Hekla has vented its fury numerous times throughout history, and during the Middle Ages it was commonly believed to be the gateway to hell.

Viking-era settlers built farms on the rich volcanic soils around Hekla, only to be wiped out by the eruption of 1104, which buried everything within a radius of 50km. Since then there have been 15 major eruptions – the 1300 eruption covered more than 83,000 sq km in ash.

In recent years, hellish Hekla has been belching out ash in steady 10-year intervals. The main danger comes from the ash, whose high fluorine content has poisoned thousands of sheep. Adding insult to injury, the most recent eruption (in 2000) produced a small pyroclastic flow (a high-speed and highly destructive torrent of rock particles and gas, which typically travels at over 130km per hour and can reach temperatures of 800°C).

Fittingly, locals live in constant fear that the mighty mound will erupt at any moment. Like most of the other volcanos in Iceland, it is long overdue to erupt.

For more information about Hekla, check out the small museum at Leirubakki.

Climbing Hekla

You can climb Hekla, but remember that it's still an active volcano. There's never much warning before eruptions, which are usually indicated by multiple small earthquakes 30 to 80 minutes before it blows! Stick to days when the summit is free from heavy cloud, and carry plenty of water – the volcanic ash makes you thirsty.

There's a small car park where mountain road F225 branches off Rte 26 (about 45km northeast of Hella). Most hire cars aren't insured for F roads and will need to be parked here, but it's a long and dusty walk (16km) to the foot of the volcano (or you could try your luck at hitching).

With a large 4WD you can continue along F225 to the bottom of Hekla. From here, a well-marked walking track starts at Skjólkviar and climbs steadily to the right, up to the ridge on the northeastern flank of the mountain, then onto the summit crater. Although the peak is often covered in snow, the floor of the crater is still hot. From the bottom of the volcano, the return trip takes about five hours. The trip to the summit takes about three hours from the furthest point that one can take their vehicle. Note that small 4WDs will have to park at the Skhólkviar sign – in June all cars will have to park at the sign, as there's simply too much snow to go any further.

Alternatively, you can organise bespoke super-Jeep tours from anywhere in the region, and the taxi service at the Heklusetrið can get you within spitting distance of the summit.

Hella & Around

POP 810

This small agricultural community sits on the banks of the pretty Ytri-Rangá river in an important horse-breeding area. It's also the nearest village to the hulking, shadow-wreathed volcano Hekla, 35km north up Rtes 264 then 268.

◉ Sights & Activities

TOWN CENTRE

There is very little of interest in the town of Hella. Most tourists gravitate towards the horse farms in the plains beyond. The handicrafts cooperative Hekla Handverkshús (☑864 5531; Þrúðvangur 35; ◐9am-6pm May-Sep, 1-5pm Sat & Sun Oct-Apr) doubles as an informal tourist information desk.

RTE 26 (TO HELKA)

Beyond the teeny township of Hella, you'll find sweeping floodplains that extend down to the sea and all the way up to Helka – one of Iceland's most ominous volcanos. The road to Hekla – Rte 26 – winds its way beyond a cluster of horse farms offering a variety of riding trips.

The museum at Heklusetrið (☑487 8700; www.leirubakki.is; Leirubakki; admission Ikr800; ◐9am-9pm Jun-Aug) details the explosive history of brooding Hekla up the track with spooky sounds and dim lighting. You'll learn what to do in case of a sudden eruption, and, unsettlingly, you'll also discover that the mound is long overdue to erupt.

You can organise trips up to Hekla from the museum; a round-trip taxi to Skjólkviar costs Ikr28,000; the driver will wait as you climb up and back. We recommend departing around 9am; you'll be back at the museum by 4.30pm. One-hour horse rides (Ikr4500) are also a possibility, as is a visit to the 'Viking pool' tucked into the nearby lava field.

With its dramatic volcanic backdrop and proximity to the highlands, the area is also famous for its **horse farms**. Most of the region's stables offer multiday trips rather than short rides. The best options include the following.

TOP CHOICE Hekluhestar   HORSE RIDING

(☑869 8953; www.hekluhestar.is; Austvaðsholt) Hidden away along Rtes 271 and 272, 9km northeast of Hella. Run by a friendly French-Icelandic family who specialise in six- to eight-day trots through the Highlands. Sleeping-bag accommodation is offered in an unusual cross-shaped cabin.

Herríðarhóll   HORSE RIDING

(☑487 5252; www.herridarholl.is) Off Rte 284, 6km from the Ring Road, west of Hella. There are horse tours galore and a heartfelt welcome to guests who simply want a farm-stay experience.

Hestheimar   HORSE RIDING

(☑487 6666; www.hestheimar.is) Near Rte 281, 7km northwest of Hella. Family-run horse tours, shows and a variety of comfortable accommodation suited to budget and mid-range travellers.

Kálfholt   HORSE RIDING

(☑487 5176; www.kalfholt.is; Ásahreppi) On Rte 288, 17km west of Hella (eastern bank of the Þjórsá). Family-run farm with comfy accommodation in two green cabins, offering four-day or week-long horse tours, hands-on weekend farmstay experiences, and shorter day trips in summer.

🛏 Sleeping & Eating
TOWN CENTRE

Lacking the rural splendour of the accommodation further afield, the lodging and eating options in Hella are efficient and cheap.

There's a **Kjarval supermarket** (Suðurlands-vegur 1) with a small bakery next door for self-caterers; the best place to eat in town is Árhús.

Guesthouse Nonni   GUESTHOUSE €€

(☑894 9953; www.bbiceland.com; Arnarsandur 3; s/d incl breakfast €65/75; 🖭) Run by friendly Nonni, who loves cooking a large breakfast for his guests (fresh bread and flower-shaped waffles!), this small guesthouse has five wooden-walled rooms tucked up a cork stairwell.

Gistiheimilið Brenna   GUESTHOUSE €

(☑487 5532; www.mmedia.is/toppbrenna; Þróðvan-gur 37; dm Ikr4000) A spunky older lady runs this absolutely adorable tin house with eight beds, a little kitchen and a comfy sitting room. Guests must stay for a minimum of two nights. Linen costs Ikr1000.

Árhús   CAMPGROUND €

(☑487 5577; www.arhus.is; Rangárbakkar 6; sites per tent Ikr2000, cabin Ikr9000-14,300) Like some kind of Icelandic summercamp colony set along the trickling stream, Árhús has a cluster of cottages, ample camping space, a guest kitchen block, and a restaurant (mains Ikr1890 to Ikr3100; open noon to 10pm) serving the best food in town.

Fosshótel Mosfell   HOTEL €€

(☑487 5828; www.fosshotel.is; Þróðvangur 6; d with/without bathroom Ikr26,500/14,100; 🖭🖭) A rather faded option, this hotel has small rooms with two single beds each; the staff, however, is very friendly.

RTE 26 (TO HELKA)

Most of the horse farms in the highland plains behind Hella have accommodation for their riders, but many open their doors to other travellers as well. Campers can pitch a tent at **Laugaland** (www.tjalda.is/lau galand; sites per person Ikr850).

Hótel Leirubakki   HOTEL €€

(☑487 8700; www.leirubakki.is; Holta og Landveit; sites per person Ikr1100, s/d Ikr22,900/27,900; 🖭) A large farming estate with a charming brown house and a more modern hotel block decked out in all white, Leirubakki is a good base for Hekla enthusiasts. The on-site restaurant (mains Ikr1890 to Ikr5690) serves an assortment of Icelandic faves like horse, lamb, and trout from a stream 15km away. The hotel also runs Heklusetrið.

RTE 1 (RING ROAD)

Back on the Ring Road, the drive from Hella east to Hvolsvöllur is rather quiet, with a few reasons to lure you off the road, including rural Iceland's most upscale lodging option.

Hótel Rangá   HOTEL €€€

(☑487 5700; www.hotelranga.is; Suðurlandsvegur; d from €259; @ 🛜) Situated just off the Ring Road midway between Hella and Hvolsvöllur, Hótel Rangá looks like a luxurious horse ranch catering to the island's high-end travellers. Service is top-notch, both in the cosy wood-panelled rooms, and at the in-house restaurant flanked by long sheets of glass. If you really want to splash out, go for one of the seven 'World Pavilion' suites (€549 to €829), each decorated as a different continent. They're so distinctive that it's hard to choose a favourite, although understated 'Asia' – which looks like a Japanese ryokan – is our favourite (and apparently it's Charlize Theron's pick, too!).

❶ Getting There & Away

Hella

Reykjavik Excursions and Trex both operate buses from Reykjavík up into the Þórsmörk and Landmannalaugar; all of these buses stop in Hella on the way. The Trex bus stops at Árhús; all of the Reykjavik Excursions buses stop at the Ólis petrol station.

Reykjavík Excursions (☑580 5400; www.re.is) Runs bus 20/20a from Reykjavík (departing at 8am) through to Skaftafell stopping here once daily from June to mid-September.

Sterna (☑551 1166; www.sterna.is) Runs bus 12b/12c from Reykjavík to Vík stopping in Hella twice daily from mid-May to mid-September.

Strætó (☑540 2700; www.straeto.is) Buses 51 and 52 stop here twice daily on the Reykjavík–Vík/Höfn route and the Reykjavík–Landeyjahöfn route.

Rte 26 (to Hekla)

From mid-June to mid-September, **Reykjavík Excursions** (☑580 5400; www.re.is) has a daily bus at 8.30am from Reykjavík to Landmannalaugar, which passes Leirubakki (2¼ hours) at 10.45am. The return trip passes Leirubakki at 4.45pm.

Hvolsvöllur & Around

POP 850

The countryside surrounding Hvolsvöllur is soaked with history. Its farms were the setting for the bloody events of *Njál's Saga* (see the boxed text, p112), one of Iceland's favourites; today, though, the saga sites exist mainly as place names, peaceful grassed-over ruins or modern agricultural buildings. Hvolsvöllur itself is a small, and rather uninspiring, village dominated by two petrol stations – one at either end of town.

◉ Sights & Activities

Sögusetriðis   MUSEUM

(Saga Centre; ☑487 8781; www.njala.is; Hliðarvegur 14; adult/child lkr750/free; ⊙9am-6pm May-Sep, 10am-5pm Sat & Sun Oct-Apr) As you might expect, the so-called Saga Centre is devoted to the events of *Njál's Saga*, which took place in the surrounding hills. Written boards explain the most dramatic parts of the story (in Icelandic, English and German). The centre also doubles as the area's information point, stocking plenty of brochures; staff can answer tourist questions too.

Keldur   RUIN

(☑487 8452; ⊙hours variable) About 5km west of Hvolsvöllur, unsurfaced Rte 264 winds around 8km north along the Rangárvellir valley to the medieval turf-roofed farm at Keldur. This historic settlement once belonged to Ingjaldur Höskuldsson, a character in *Njál's Saga*. The structure is owned by the National Museum Trust, and hours are frustratingly variable, but it's still worth visiting to see the Saga Age foundation of the main hall (yes, you read that correctly, the structure was actually built during saga times). There's no public transport along Rte 264.

Bergþórshvoll   FARM

Down by the coast, Bergþórshvoll was Njál's farm (although there's nothing to see today besides a working farm). *Njál's Saga* relates that this is where he and his wife and grandchild were burnt to death in their bed in 1011. About 4km east of Hvolsvöllur, Rtes 255 and then 252 will take you there (21km).

Swimming Pool   SWIMMING POOL

(Vallarbraut 16; admission lkr500) The town has a modern outdoor swimming pool with a baby pool and two hot-pots.

☞ Tours

South Iceland Adventures   ADVENTURE TOUR

(☑770 2030; www.siadv.is) Hvolsvöllur is home to the headquarters of one of Iceland's best bespoke adventure operators, South Iceland Adventures. The founder, Siggi Bjarni, is

SOUTHWEST ICELAND & THE GOLDEN CIRCLE HVOLSVÖLLUR & AROUND

a wilderness prodigy who grew up in the region and knows every hidden trail that winds through the Icelandic Outback. If you're contemplating a guided hike along Fimmvörðuháls or Laugavegurinn, then Siggi's your guy. He also organises lesser-known walks through the mystical recesses of Þórsmörk and Tindafjöll (half-day from Ikr25,900). In addition to leading treks, South Iceland Adventures also offers a spate of blood-pumping activities, like canyoning, super-Jeep safaris and ice climbing.

You don't need to be based in Hvolsvöllur to benefit from Siggi's savviness – he and his team can meet you anywhere in the southwest.

🛏 Sleeping & Eating

The sleeping and eating options in town aren't brilliant. Both petrol stations have grills if you're looking for a quick bite, or you can hit up the **farmers market** (⊘noon-6pm Jun-Aug) beside the post office.

Vestri-Garðsauki   GUESTHOUSE €

(📞487 8078; www.gardsauki.is; s/d Ikr7000/ 10,000; 🖥) Located just off Rte 1, this friendly Icelandic-German farming family has a small aeroplane parked out the front, and tends to four tidy rooms that – while located in the basement – receive plenty of summer sunlight. The owners offer informal walking trips in the area.

Hótel Hvolsvöllur   HOTEL €€

(📞487 8050; www.hotelhvolsvollur.is; Hlíðarvegur 7; s/d incl breakfast Ikr23,500/28,300; @🖥) This large business-style hotel has 64 rooms and a parking lot full of tour-group buses. Try for a newer room with green carpets and generic, dark-wood furniture. The wind-beaten facade doesn't provide the warmest welcome, but inside you'll find soothing hot-pots and a buffet dinner (Ikr5900) in summer.

Gallerí Pizza   FAST FOOD €€

(Hvolsvegur 29; meals Ikr1300-2300; ⊘noon-9pm Sun-Thu, noon-10pm Fri & Sat) The town pizzeria, one street back from the main road, is a busy, beery place despite the design aesthetic,

---

NJÁL'S SAGA

One of Iceland's best-loved sagas is also one of the most complicated and nuanced. The crux of the story involves two friends, Gunnar Hámundarson and Njál Þorgeirsson, and a petty squabble between their wives acts as a prelude to the feuds and battles later on that ultimately leave almost every character dead. Written in the 13th century, it recounts 10th-century events that took place in the hills around Hvolsvöllur.

The saga's doomed hero is Gunnar of Hlíðarendi (near Fljótsdalur), who falls for and marries the beautiful, hot-tempered Hallgerður, who has long legs but – ominously – a 'thief's eyes'. Hallgerður has a falling-out with Bergþóra, wife of Njál. Things become increasingly strained between Gunnar and Njál as Hallgerður and Bergþóra begin murdering each other's servants.

In one important episode, Hallgerður sends a servant to burgle food from a man named Otkell. When Gunnar comes home and sees Hallgerður's stolen feast, his temper snaps. 'It's bad news indeed if I've become a thief's accomplice', he says, and slaps his wife – an act that later comes back to haunt him.

Through more unfortunate circumstances, Gunnar ends up killing Otkell and is eventually sentenced to exile. As he rides away from home, his horse stumbles. Fatally, he takes one last glance back at his beloved farm Hlíðarendi and is unable to leave the valley. His enemies gather their forces and lay siege to the farm, but Gunnar manages to hold off the attackers until his bowstring breaks. When he asks Hallgerður for a lock of her hair to repair it, she refuses, reminding him of the slap she received years earlier – and Gunnar is killed.

The feud continues as Gunnar and Njál's clan members try to avenge their slaughtered kin. Njál himself acts as a peace broker, forming treaties between the two families, but in the end, the complicated peacemaking is all for naught. Njál and his wife are besieged in their farm. Tucking themselves up in bed with their little grandson between them, the couple allow themselves to be burnt alive.

The only survivor of the fire is Njál's son-in-law Kári, who launches a legal case against the arsonists, commits a bit of extrajudicial killing himself and is finally reconciled with his arch-enemy, Flosi, who ordered the burning of the Njál family.

which feels like a public bathroom at an airport. Go for the Bearnaise burger – a local favourite.

Eldstó Art Café INTERNATIONAL €€
(http://en.eldsto.is; Austurvegur 2; mains Ikr1500-3000) Eldstó has the attitude of a cafe from the capital – there's fresh-brewed coffee, home-made Chilean empanadas, brusque service and outdoor seating on iron-wrought furniture (though the tables sit right along the Ring Road). The cafe also offers accommodation upstairs.

❶ Getting There & Away

Buses headed to Þórsmörk stop in Hvolsvöllur before venturing inland; for more details, see p128. If you're heading to Vestmannaeyjar, you must continue east and take Rte 254 to Landeyjahöfn (which is also serviced by buses).

Sterna (☑551 1166; www.sterna.is) Runs bus 12b/12c from Reykjavík to Vík stopping in Hvolsvöllur twice daily from mid-May to mid-September.

Reykjavík Excursions (☑580 5400; www.re.is) Runs bus 20/20a from Reykjavík (departing at 8am) through to Skaftafell stopping here once daily from June to mid-September.

Strætó (☑540 2700; www.straeto.is) Buses 51 and 52 stop here twice daily on the Reykjavík–Vík/Höfn route and the Reykjavík–Landeyjahöfn route. Buses run twice daily.

Hvolsvöllur to Skógar

After Hvolsvöllur, the Ring Road chugs along towards Skógar with three important sideroads. The first is Fljótshlíð (Rte 261), right at the eastern end of Hvolsvöllur; the second is Rte 254, which shoots 12km towards Landeyjahöfn along the coast linking travellers to the ferry bound for Vestmannaeyjar (p133); and the third is Rte 249 headed for Þórsmörk. Staying straight on the Ring Road, you'll pass under hulking Eyjafjallajökull, made famous during the ash-ridden explosion in 2010.

FLJÓTSHLÍÐ

At the edge of Hvolsvöllur (right near the N1 petrol station), Rte 261 turns northeast off the Ring Road. It follows the edge of the Fljótshlíð hills, offering great views over the flood plain of the Markarfljót river and the Eyjafjallajökull glacier.

There are several B&Bs along the surfaced section of the road, which ends near the farm and church at Hlíðarendi, once the

home of Gunnar Hámundarson from *Njál's Saga*. Although it seems tantalisingly close, Þórsmörk can only be reached via mountain road F249. With a 4WD you can continue along mountain road F261 towards Landmannalaugar and the unexplored Tindafjöll – a hiker's paradise. South Iceland Adventures runs hiking and canyoning tours in the region (p111).

🛏 Sleeping & Eating

Hótel Fljótshlíð HOTEL €€
(Smáratún; ☑487 1416; www.smaratun.is; sites per person Ikr900, d Ikr20,950, cottage Ikr14,500; ☎) This attractive white farm with a blue tin roof has four- to six-person summerhouses for hire. There are also smart hotel-style rooms, cheaper guesthouse rooms (with shared facilities), sleeping-bag places, and spaces to pitch a tent. We just adore the owners – the husband runs the restaurant's kitchen, and the affable wife loves to take her guests on evening strolls through the flood plains while telling stories about the 2010 eruption. It's about 13km from Hvolsvöllur. Linen costs Ikr1500 per person.

Fljótsdalur Youth Hostel HOSTEL €
(☑487 8498; www.hostel.is; Fljótshlíð; dm Ikr3800; ☺mid-March–Oct) It's very basic and not to everyone's taste, but if you're looking for a peaceful base for highland walks, with a beautiful garden, homey kitchen, cosy sitting room, and mountain views that make your knees tremble, then you'll find it here. Advance booking is recommended, as space is limited – there are seven mattresses in the attic and two four-bed rooms on the main floor. The nearest shop is 27km away at Hvolsvöllur, so bring in all supplies.

RTE 249/F249 (TO ÞÓRSMÖRK)

The road to Þórsmörk (Rte 249/F249) begins just east of the Markarfljót river on the Ring Road (Rte 1). Although it quickly turns into a 4WD-only road, there are some interesting sights at the start of the road that can be reached by car.

From the highway you can see the beautiful high falls at Seljalandsfoss, which tumble over a rocky scarp into a deep, green pool. It's perfect for romantics who dream of walking behind waterfalls – a (slippery) path runs around the back. A few hundred metres further down the Þórsmörk road is the spooky waterfall Gljúfurárbui, which gushes into a hidden canyon.

Seljalandsfoss is the pick-up point for Ring Road travellers who want to reach Þórsmörk by bus (it is impossible to reach by private vehicle). You'll see dozens of vehicles parked in front of the falls.

If you want to spend the night in the area, you can camp at Hamragarðar (☑867 3535; sites per person Ikr1000), just after Gljúfurárbui – it's open all year. There's a small on-site cafe (☺9am-11pm Jun-Aug) selling cake and coffee. Go for the heavenly carrot and apple cake. The cafe also functions as the information desk for South Coast Adventure (☑867 3535; www.southadventure. is) – you can book tailormade tours, and get important information about hiking in Þórsmörk and beyond. South Coast Adventure is a small tour operator comprised of a group of enthusiastic locals. They offer snowmobiling tours, super-Jeep day trips, volcano tours and glacier walks.

About 5km beyond the cluster of traffic at the falls (still on Rte 249), a dirt track leads to the historical Stóra-Mörk III (☑487 8903; www.storamork.com; s Ikr3000) farmhouse (mentioned, of course, in *Njál's Saga*), which offers rooms spread across two houses with shared facilities and a main house (where you'll find reception) with private bathroom. Linen costs an extra Ikr1000.

RTE 1 (UNDER EYJAFJALLAJÖKULL)

If you follow the Ring Road (Rte 1), ignoring the detours into the interior, you'll pass a loose string of accommodation options as you go directly through the flood zone that was littered with muddy ash during the infamous Eyjafjallajökull (*ay-ya-fiat-la-yo-gootl*) eruption in 2010. Stop at the clearly marked Eyjafjallajökull Visitors Centre (Iceland Erupts; ☑487 8815; www.icelanderupts.is; Þorvaldseyri; admission Ikr750; ☺9am-6pm Jun-Aug, 10am-5pm May & Sep) about 7km before Skógar to learn about the devastating effects of the eruption first hand. A 20-minute film runs continuously (usually in English) telling the story of the family farm across the street, as they dealt with the ominous warnings about the eruption and, eventually, the devastating aftermath of the flooding ash afterwards. Movie snippets include tender family moments and highlights from the team of local rescuers that dug the farm out of the muddy ash. You can ask here about 20-minute helicopter tours of the eruption site (Ikr30,000 per person).

Also worth a look is Seljavallalaug, a historical old concrete pool filled by a natural hot spring. It's about a five-minute drive beyond Edinborg (7km west of Skógar); park by the farm, and follow the river upwards for about a 10-minute walk.

🛏 Sleeping & Eating

Drangshlíð HOTEL €€
(☑487 8868; drangshlid@drangshlid.is; s/d Ikr14,300/21,900; @☎; ☺May-Sep) A bolthole during the Eyjafjallajökull eruption, the friendly, 200-year-old farm at Drangshlíð has a smattering of comfortable if somewhat plain accommodation in three separate buildings. Check out the haunting photos from the 2010 eruption in the dining room while enjoying the evening set menu (Ikr5850). Several structures on the property are built right into the bluffs – ask the owner where they used to store their potatoes, we guarantee you'll be surprised.

Country Hotel Anna INN €€
(☑487 8950; www.hotelanna.is; Moldnúpur; s/d incl breakfast Ikr17,300/24,900; ☎) Anna, the inn's namesake, wrote many books about her voyages around the world – and her descendants' country hotel upholds her passion for travellers with seven rooms furnished with found antiques and embroidered bedspreads that settle over big, comfy beds. Meals are served in the adorable restaurant (open 11am to 9pm May to mid-September) bedecked with off-white stones and wooden beams.

Edinborg GUESTHOUSE €€
(☑846 1384; www.islandia.is/thorn; Lambafell; s/d incl breakfast €129/149; @☎; ☺Apr-Sep) Formerly named Hotel Edinborg (and still signposted as such from the main road), this is actually a small abode on a farm with limited facilities. The tall, tin-clad house has inviting wood-floored rooms with comfy beds and private bathroom, and an attic seating area with glacier views. The nearest place for an evening meal is 5km away.

TOP CHOICE Gamla Fjósið ICELANDIC €€
(www.gamlafjosid.is; Steinar; mains Ikr1300-5790; ☺Jun-Aug) Built in a former cowshed that was very much in use until 1999, this charming eatery's focus is on meaty mains. The burger is great value – the ground steak comes from the farm just behind; or go for the Volcano Soup, a spicy meat stew. The stone floor and creaky beams are cheered with polished dining tables, mismatched chairs and large wooden hutches. For low-season travellers

there's a buffet (Ikr5000 to Ikr7000) of Icelandic treats every third weekend from September to January.

Skógar

POP 20

You begin to enter the south coast's realm of ice at Skógar, which nestles under the Eyjafjallajökull ice cap about 1km off the Ring Road. This tiny settlement offers two excellent attractions. At its western edge, the dizzyingly high Skógafoss waterfall tumbles down a mossy cliff. On the eastern side you'll find the fantastic folk museum, open year-round for your delectation.

The village is also the start (or sometimes the end) of the hike over the Fimmvörðuháls Pass to Þórsmörk (see the boxed text, p116), and is primed to be an activities centre in the southwest.

◉ Sights

Skógar Folk Museum MUSEUM
(☑487 8845; www.skogasafn.is; adult/child Ikr1500/500; ☉ 9am-6pm Jun-Aug, 10am-5pm May & Sep, 11am-4pm Oct-Apr) The highlight of little Skógar is the wonderful Skógar Folk Museum, which covers all aspects of Icelandic life. The vast collection was put together by 91-year-old Þórður Tómasson, who has been amassing items for well over 75 years. You might be lucky enough to meet Þórður in person – he often comes in to play traditional songs for visitors on an old church organ. There are also various restored buildings (church, turf-roofed farmhouse, cowsheds etc) in the grounds, and a hangar-like building at the back houses an interesting transport museum, plus a cafe – Skogakaffi (soup Ikr1000) – and souvenir shop.

Skógafoss WATERFALL
The 62m-high waterfall of Skógafoss topples over a rocky cliff at the western edge of Skógar in dramatic style. Climb the steep staircase alongside for giddying views downwards, or walk to the foot of the falls, shrouded in sheets of mist and rainbows. Legend has it that a settler named Þrasi hid a chest of gold behind Skógafoss – sometimes you can almost see it glittering...

☞ Tours

Skógar is poised to be your activity and tour base during your visit to Iceland's southwest. Several major operators have their base in or around the tiny township offering tours to the geological wonders – like glaciers and volcanoes – just beyond.

Icelandic Mountain Guides ADVENTURE TOUR
(☑587 9999; www.mountainguide.is) One of the largest and finest operators in the country, Icelandic Mountain Guides has a large office in downtown Reykjavík and a second branch in Skógar. The main tour on offer is the short glacier walk on Sólheimajökull, which runs five times a day from June to August (and two or three times a day in low season). It also runs guiding services for the Fimmvörðuháls hike. Its base camp in Skógar is the **Icelandic Travel Market** (☑894 2956; www.icelandictravelmarket.is; ☉8.30am-6pm mid-Jun–Aug), a prim bungalow just beyond Hótel Skógar that acts as a veritable tourist information centre. The friendly staff offer excellent information about the region and are happy to book visitors on a variety of tours in the area. Ask here about horse riding – they partner with several stables nearby, like **Skálakot** (☑487 8953; www.skalakot.com).

Arcanum ADVENTURE TOUR
(☑487 1500; www.arcanum.is) This popular tour operator is geared towards all ages; it has a small information and booking table at Fossbúð, but is based on a farm towards Vík (p117).

South Iceland Adventure ADVENTURE TOUR
(☑770 2030; www.siadv.is) A fantastic operator run by young local adventurers, based in Hvolsvöllur and running tours and excursions all throughout the southwest. This is the best choice for private guiding, especially for hikes in Þórsmörk, Landmannalaugar and Fimmvörðuháls. Pick-ups are easily arranged from Skógar; see p111 for more.

South Coast Adventure ADVENTURE TOUR
(☑867 3535; www.southadventure.is) An operator with an excellent reputation, South Coast Adventure is located on the 2WD-friendly Rte 249 – the road to Þórsmörk (p113).

⌚ Sleeping & Eating

Although Skógar is very small, there are some solid places to stay. Campers can pitch a tent at the **campsite** (sites per person Ikr1000; ☉Jun–mid-Sep) beside the waterfall (pay at the hostel nearby); the sound of falling water makes a soothing lullaby. As for food, however, the choice is quite limited. Hótel Skógar is the best option, but you'll

SOUTHWEST ICELAND & THE GOLDEN CIRCLE SKÓGAR

FIMMVÖRÐUHÁLS

If you aren't planning to tackle the famous 55km-long Laugavegurinn hike (see p123) from Landmannalaugar to Þórsmörk, then Fimmvörðuháls – named for a pass between two brooding glaciers – will dazzle the eye with a shorter parade of wild inland vistas.

Linking Skógar and Þórsmörk, the awesome Fimmvörðuháls hike is 23.4km long, and can be divided into three distinct sections of somewhat equal length. Figure around 10 hours to complete the hike, which includes stops to rest, and to check out the steaming remnants of the Eyjafjallajökull eruption. It's best to tackle the hike from July to mid-September. See p34 for important packing information; you can experience all four seasons over the course of this hike.

» **Part 1: Waterfall Way** From Skógafoss to the 'bridge'. Starting on the right side of splashy Skógafoss, the path zooms up and over falls quickly, revealing a series of waterfalls just behind. Stay close to the tumbling water as you climb over small stones and twisting trees – there are 22 chutes in all, each one possibly more magnificent than the next. The path flattens out as the trees turn to windswept shrubs. Then, set your sights on the 'bridge', which is a crude walkway over the gushing river below. It's imperative that you make the crossing on the manmade walkway otherwise you won't make it over and down into Þórsmörk later on.

» **Part 2: The Ashtray** From the 'bridge' to the eruption site. After crossing the crude bridge onto the left side of the moving water you start to enter the gloomy heart of the pass between two glaciers: Eyjafjallajökull and Mýrdalsjökull. The weather can be quite variable here – it could be raining in the pass when there is sunshine in Skógar. Expect to bundle up at this point as you move through icy rifts in the earlier parts of summer; from August on the region feels like some kind of giant ashtray. If you want to break up the hike into two sections to complete over two days, there's a 23-person hut positioned 600m away from the main trail about halfway through this section of the walk (not to be confused with the easily noticeable emergency hut). It's called Fimmvörðuskáli (www.utivist.is; N 63°37.320', W 19°27.093'), and it's run by Útivist. Unfortunately, in bad weather it can be difficult to find. There's no campsite. Continuing on, the initial eruption site from the famed Eyjafjallajökull eruption reveals itself; here you'll find steaming earths and the world's newest mountains – Magni and Móði. Climb up to the top of Magni and roast some wieners over one of the sizzling vents.

» **Part 3: Goðaland** From the eruption site down into Þórsmörk. After climbing down from Magni, the last part of the hike begins. The barren ashiness continues for a while, then an otherworldly kingdom reveals itself – a place ripped straight from the pages of a fairy tale. Here in Goðaland – the aptly named 'Land of the Gods' – wild Arctic flowers bloom as stone cathedrals emerge in the distance, with their flying buttresses stacking one after the next like some king of celestial zipper. Vistas of endless green continue as you descend down into Þórsmörk to complete the journey.

Although the hike is relatively short when compared to some of Iceland's famous multi-day treks, it's important to bring a GPS along – especially for the second portion of the hike when the way isn't always obvious. Guided tours are quite popular; see p115. We've provided the following nine GPS markers to keep DIYers on track:

1. N 63°31.765, W19°30.756 (start)
2. N 63°32.693, W19°30.015
3. N 63°33.741, W19°29.223
4. N 63°34.623, W19°26.794 (the 'bridge')
5. N 63°36.105, W19°26.095
6. N 63°38.208, W19°26.616 (beginning of eruption site)
7. N 63°39.118, W19°25.747
8. N 63°40.561, W19°27.631
9. N 63°40.721, W19°28.323 (terminus at Básar)

be paying a premium price – budgetarians should self-cater or else grab food at the museum.

Hótel Skógar   HOTEL €€€

(☑487 4880; www.hotelskogar.is; s/d incl breakfast €194/224; ☎) Breaking the IKEA mould, this architecturally interesting hotel has unusual but quite romantic rooms, all with private bathroom, embroidered curtains and bedspreads, finely polished floors and carefully chosen antiques. There's a good restaurant, a hot tub, and a sauna in the garden.

Skógar Youth Hostel   HOSTEL €

(☑487 8801; skogar@hostel.is; dm/d Ikr3500/ 9200; ☺late May–mid-Sep) An excellent link in the HI chain, this spot is located a stone's throw from Skógafoss in an old school. In fact, six rooms have views of the spilling chute. There's a guest kitchen and a laundry (Ikr800).

Hótel Edda   HOTEL €

(☑444 4000; www.hoteledda.is; s/d Ikr9500/ 11,800; ☺early Jun-late Aug; ☎) Perfectly serviceable with a few less bumps and scratches than the other Edda hotels, this summer inn close to the museum is split over two buildings. Sleeping-bag spaces (Ikr4000 per person) are in the gym, and all rooms have shared bathroom. The dinner buffet costs Ikr5200.

Fossbúd   FAST FOOD €

(☺7am-9pm Jun-Aug) Advertised as a restaurant, Fossbúd is really more a convenience store or place for quick snacks – soup, hamburgers, bagged chips and chocolate bars. We'd rather eat at the museum when it's open. Arcanum has a small tour table at the entrance.

❶ Getting There & Away

Reykjavík Excursions (☑580 5400; www.re.is) Run bus 20/20a from Reykjavík (departing at 8am) to Skaftafell stopping here once daily from June to mid-September.

Sterna (☑551 1166; www.sterna.is) Run bus 12b/12c from Reykjavík to Vík stopping in Skógar twice daily from mid-May to mid-September.

Skógar to Vík

Flanked by looming glaciers and punctuated by strange rock formations, the sweeping landscape between Skógar to Vík may not seem the most captivating area from the Ring Road, but once you leave the highway you'll discover an outdoor adventure wonderland that's easily explorable when you team up with a local tour operator.

◉ Sights & Activities

Sólheimajökull   GLACIER

One of the easiest glacial tongues to reach is Sólheimajökull, a favourite spot for glacial walks and treks. This icy tongue unfurls from the main Mýrdalsjökull ice cap in a gentle fashion, making it easy to mount. A 5km bumpy dirt track (Rte 222) leads off the Ring Road to a small car park punctuated by a small cafe; from there, the ice is approximately 800m away. Almost all operators in the area run trips up onto this glacial tongue – they depart from Cafe Solheimajökull (www.solheimajokull.is; snacks Ikr480-1200; ☺10.30am-6pm Jun-Aug, daylight Sep-Apr) set up in a series of conjoined prefab portables.

Mýrdalsjökull   ICE CAP

The gorgeous glacier Mýrdalsjökull is Iceland's fourth-largest ice cap, covering 700 sq km and reaching a thickness of almost 750m in places. The volcano Katla snoozes beneath, periodically blasting up through the ice to drown the coastal plain in a deluge of meltwater, sand and tephra – see the boxed text, p119. Several tours run up along the glacial crown as part of a longer trip that explores the 2010 eruption site and Fimmvörðuháls Pass. Do not attempt to explore the area on your own; the ice can be unstable and the track to the caldera can be near impossible to navigate.

Dyrhólaey   LANDMARK

One of the south coast's most recognisable natural formations is the rocky plateau and huge stone sea arch at Dyrhólaey (*deer*-lay; 10km west of Vík), which rises dramatically from the surrounding plain. The promontory is a nature reserve and is particularly rich in bird life, including puffins; however, it's closed to visitors during the nesting season. At other times you can visit its crashing black beaches and get the most awesome views from the top of the archway (best seen in its entirety from Reynisfjara). According to *Njál's Saga*, Kári – the only survivor of the fire that wiped out Njál's clan – had his farm here. Another Viking Age connection is the cave Loftsalahellir, reached by a track just before the causeway to Dyrhólaey, which was used for council meetings in saga times. Note that the area closes for nesting birds for around 10 days in early May and 10 days in the middle of June.

Reynisfjara   LANDMARK
On the west side of Reynisfjall, the high ridge above Vík, Rte 215 leads 5km down to the black-sand beach at Reynisfjara, backed by an incredible stack of basalt columns that look like a giant church organ. The surrounding cliffs are full of caves formed from twisted basalt, and puffin chicks bellyflop from here every summer. Immediately offshore are the sea stacks of Reynisdrangur, and there are outstanding views west to Dyrhólaey.

☞ Tours
Besides the following tour operators, other operators in and around Skógar (p115) offer a variety of tours in this area.

Arcanum   ADVENTURE TOUR
(☑487 1500; www.arcanum.is) Although Arcanum has a small booking table in Skógar and Vík, its headquarters are located on a well-marked farmstead in between. The operator's speciality is two-hour tours of the local wonders, be it ice climbing (from Ikr5990), glacier trekking, snowmobiling on Mýrdalsjökull (from Ikr18,900), or super-Jeep excursions into the interior. Arcanum runs the popular 'Volcano Tour' (Ikr24,900), a half-day trip via super-Jeep that follows the Katla caldera up to one of the Eyjafjallajökull eruption sites, where you can walk to the top of Magni, much like the middle portion of the Fimmvörðuháls hike (see the boxed text, p116).

Mountain Excursions   ADVENTURE TOUR
(☑486 1200; www.volcanohotel.is) A small outfit run by two brothers offering two-hour glacier hikes (Ikr9000), interesting local excursions that take you off the tourist trail, and super-Jeep tours that vaguely follow a portion of the Fimmvörðuháls route (from Ikr22,000). It's based at Volcano Hotel.

🛏 Sleeping & Eating
Camping is prohibited on Dyrhólaey.

⬛TOP Garðar   GUESTHOUSE €€
CHOICE
(☑487 160; http://reynisfjara-guesthouses.com; cottages Ikr12,000-16,000) Garðar, at the end of Rte 215, is a magical, view-blessed place. Friendly farmer Ragnar rents out self-contained beachside huts: one snug stone

cottage sleeps two (in a bunk bed), two roomier timber cottages sleep up to four. Linen costs Ikr1000 per person.

Volcano Hotel   HOTEL €€
(☑486 1200; www.volcanohotel.is; s/d Ikr16,900/24,900; 🐾) A newer additional to the pool of accommodation within Vík's reach, this seven-room hotel plays with a volcano motif in its decor. The floors are made from a mosaic of pebbles, candles glow throughout and extra cushions give the space a fiery *coupe de rouge*. Mountain Excursions, a small tour operator, is based at the hotel.

Vellir   GUESTHOUSE €€
(d with/without bath incl breakfast Ikr20,000/17,000; 🐾) Located in a renovated dairy, the farmstay at Vellir sits near a massive earthen mound that was once an island many eons ago. The owner – who looks as though she could be a saga character – likes to point out that you can see the ice on Mýrdalsjökull and the Atlantic Ocean from the same chair in the dining room.

Hótel Dyrhólaey   HOTEL €€
(☑487 1333; www.dyrholaey.is; s/d €125/160; 🐾🐾) About 9km west of Vík, this large hotel (by Icelandic standards) is wildly popular with groups. Large rooms with all the mod cons sprout off three wings with wide, carpeted hallways. The on-site restaurant is open from 6pm to 9pm nightly from May to October.

Vík (Vík í Mýrdal)
POP 300
The welcoming little community of Vík has three distinctions. One, it's Iceland's southernmost town. Two, it's the rainiest place on the island. And three, it has one of the most beautiful beaches in the world (according to an American magazine in the 1990s). White waves wash up on black sands, like a beach seen in negative exposure, and the cliffs above glow green from all that rain. Put simply, it's beautiful.

◉ Sights & Activities
Reynisdrangur   LANDMARK
Vík's most famous sight is the cluster of sea stacks known as Reynisdrangur, which rise from the ocean at the western end of the black-sand beach like sinister fingers. They're traditionally believed to be ill-fated trolls that got caught out in the sun. The

KATLA GEOPARK

In 2011, following a sudden surge in interest after the headline-making eruptions of 2010, Iceland formed its first 'geopark' to protect a region of great geological importance and educate interested visitors. The Katla Geopark extends from Hvolsvöllur northeast to the great Vatnajökull; it includes the namesake Katla volcano, the infamous Eyjafjallajökull and the tortured earth at Lakagígar.

Of all the volcanoes in Iceland, it will probably be Katla that causes the most trouble to Icelanders over the next few years. This highly active 30km-long volcano, buried deep under the Mýrdalsjökull glacier, has erupted roughly twice per century in the past. Since the last eruption was in 1918, it's now several decades overdue.

It's expected that when Katla does blow, days of poisonous ashfall, tephra clouds and lightning strikes will follow the initial explosion, with flash floods caused by the sudden melting of glacial ice. The geological record shows that past eruptions have created tidal waves, which have boomeranged off the Vestmannaeyjar and deluged the area where the town of Vík stands today.

Local residents receive regular evacuation training for the day when Katla erupts. After receiving mobile phone alerts, farmers must hang a notice on their front doors to show that they have evacuated, before unplugging their electric fences, opening cattle sheds so that their animals can flee to higher ground, and heading for one of the evacuation centres in Hella, Hvolsvöllur or Skógar.

The national TV station RÚV has a webcam close to Vík, set up to film the floods when Katla erupts (see www.ruv.is/katla).

nearby cliffs are good for puffin watching. A recommended walk (upwards from the western end of Vík) takes you to the top of the ridge Reynisfjall (340m), offering superb views along the coast.

Brydebúð
MUSEUM

(Víkurbraut 28) In town, the tin-clad house Brydebúð was built in Vestmannaeyjar in 1831 and moved to Vík in 1895. Today it houses the tourist office, Halldórskaffi and a small museum (adult/child Ikr500/free), with displays on local fishing, and explanations of what it's like to live under the volcano Katla.

Church
CHURCH

(Hátún) High above town, Vík's 1930s church has stained-glass windows in spiky geometrical shapes, but we like it more for its village views.

Víkurprjón
SHOP

(Austurvegur 20; ⊙8am-10pm Mon-Fri, 9am-10pm Sat & Sun Jun-Aug, shorter hours rest of year) The big souvenir and knitwear shop next door to the N1 is a coach-tour hit – you can watch woolly jumpers being made here.

☞ Tours

Skógar (33km west of Vík) is the hub for activity tours on the south coast – see p115 for more details, as well as opposite for more local operators.

In Vík, the hostel arranges 2½-hour tours to Mýrdalsjökull, or you can contact Katla Track (☑ 849 4404; www.katlatrack.is), which runs six-hour 'Under the Volcano' tours (Ikr19,990) from July to mid-August that take in local landmarks as well as exploring Mýrdalsjökull.

☰ Sleeping

Note that there are plenty of additional lodging options orbiting Vík on private farmsteads – see opposite.

Norður-Vík Youth Hostel
HOSTEL €

(☑487 1106; www.hostel.is; Suðurvíkurvegur; dm/d Ikr3800/10,000; ⬚) Vík's small, homey, year-round hostel lives in the beige house on the hill behind the village. Good facilities include guest kitchen, lunch packs (Ikr1500) and bike hire (per half-/full day Ikr2000/3000). Staff also arrange 2½-hour glacier tours to Mýrdalsjökull (Ikr7000). There's a Ikr600 discount per person for members. Linen costs Ikr1250.

Heimagisting Erika
B&B €€

(☑487 1117; www.erika.is; Sigtún 5; B&B per person without bathroom Ikr9000) German Erika is a warm hostess with a lovely panorama-filled house. Her highly praised breakfasts feature home-made jams, syrups and herbal teas (many for sale). There is a cheaper sleeping-bag option (per person Ikr6000). Bookings essential.

Hótel Lundi   HOTEL €€

(☑487 1212; www.hotelpuffin.is; Víkurbraut 24-26; s/d incl breakfast Ikr25,000/28,000; @🛜) A new wing of bright, pebble-floored rooms is a recent expansion at this friendly, family-run hotel. All rooms have tea/coffee-making facilities. There's also a good restaurant here, with summer chefs proffering langoustine and lamb dishes (dinner mains Ikr3000 to Ikr4000).

Gistihúsið Lundi   GUESTHOUSE €

(☑487 1212; www.hotelpuffin.is; Víkurbraut 24a; per person Ikr6500) There's loads of character at this century-old abode, a guesthouse operated by Hótel Lundi. Sure, walls are thin, but check out the guest kitchen's antique fridge and the diagonally opening draws. Linen costs Ikr2000.

Edda Hótel Vík í Mýrdal   HOTEL €€

(☑444 4000; www.hoteledda.is; s/d Ikr17,500/21,900; ☉mid-May–Sep; @🛜) With a lengthier opening season than most Edda hotels, this modern place has unmemorable but decent rooms with phone, TV and bathroom. The on-site restaurant is only for groups.

Vík campsite   CAMPGROUND €

(☑487 1345; sites per person Ikr1100, cottages Ikr8000; ☉Jun-Aug) The campsite sits under a grassy ridge at the eastern end of town, just beyond the Edda Hótel. An octagonal building houses cooking facilities, washing machine, toilets and free showers.

✖ Eating

✱ Halldórskaffi   INTERNATIONAL €€

(Víkurbraut 28; mains Ikr3300-5000; ☉11am-10pm Sun-Thu, 11am-2am Fri & Sat Jun-Aug, shorter hours Sep-May) Inside Brydebúð, this timber-lined all-rounder has a popular lunchtime soup buffet and serves a crowd-pleasing menu into the evening (from pizzas to lamb fillet). The coffee (Lavazza) is a decent brew.

Ströndin Bistro   INTERNATIONAL €€

(Austurvegur 18; mains Ikr1400-4350; ☉6-10pm Jun-Aug) Behind the N1 petrol station is this semi-smart option enjoying sea-stack vistas. Go local with lamb soup or fish stew, or global with pizzas and burgers. At lunchtime, or for something more casual, grab a booth

and a burger at the old-school grill, Víkur-skáli, inside the N1 (open year-round).

Kjarval   SUPERMARKET €

(Víkurbraut 4; ☉9am-8pm Jun-Aug, 10am-6pm Mon-Fri, 10am-2pm Sat Sep-May) A good option for self-caterers.

ℹ Information

Post office (Austurvegur 1; ☉9am-noon & 1-4pm Mon-Fri) Has a computer for internet access (per 30/60 minutes Ikr400/600).

Tourist information centre (☑487 1395; www. visitvik.is; Víkurbraut 28; ☉8am-6pm Mon-Fri, 11am-5pm Sat & Sun Jun-Aug, shorter hours May & Sep; 🛜) Inside Brydebúð; free wi-fi.

ℹ Getting There & Away

Vík is a major stop for all Reykjavík–Höfn bus routes; buses stop at the N1 petrol station.

Reykjavík Excursions (☑580 5400; www.re.is) Runs bus 20/20a from Reykjavík to Skaftafell, stopping here once daily from June to mid-September. Departs Reykjavík at 8am, stopping at southwest places of interest (including Reynisfjara beach), arriving at Vík at 1.20pm (Ikr6100).

Sterna (☑551 1166; www.sterna.is) Runs bus 12b/12c from Reykjavík to Vík, stopping twice daily from mid-May to mid-September. Departs Reykjavík at 8.30am and 5pm; the evening service is faster, taking 3¼ hours (Ikr5900). Onward travel once daily to Höfn on bus 12/12a.

Strætó (☑540 2700; www.straeto.is) Runs bus 51 from Reykjavík to Vík (Ikr4900) once or twice daily year-round. Has daily summer connections east to Höfn; however, from September to May this service drops to three times a week (with a need to prebook).

East of Vík

MÆLIFELL

On the edge of the Mýrdalsjökull glacier, this 642m-high ridge and the countryside around it are spectacular. The simple, idyllic campsite at Þakgil (☑853 4889; www.thakgil.is; sites per person Ikr1100, cabins Ikr15,000; ☉Jun-Aug), a green bowl among stark mountains, makes a convenient base for explorations. You can walk up Mælifell, or even get onto the glacier – a path leads to the nunatak (hill or mountain completely surrounded by a glacier) Huldufjöll. You can drive to Þakgil, 14km along a rough dirt road (Rte 214) that branches off Rte 1 about 5km east of Vík, or there is a hiking trail from Vík.

At the start of Rte 214, Hótel Höfða-brekka (☎487 1208; www.hofdabrekka.is; s/d incl breakfast €135/165; ☉Mar-Oct; @🛜) is a large country hotel with comfy wood-panelled rooms in annexes of varying vintage, plus four hot-pots, a guest kitchen and restaurant (buffet dinner Ikr4900).

MÝRDALSSANDUR
The vast black-lava sand flats of Mýrdalssan-dur, east of Vík, are formed from material washed out from underneath Mýrdalsjökull during Katla eruptions. This 700-sq-km desert is bleak and desolate (some say haunted). It looks to be lifeless, but arctic foxes and seabirds are common sights.

South of Rte 1, the small peak of Hjör-leifshöfði (221m) rises above the sands and offers good views towards Vestmannaeyjar. On the other side of Rte 1, the green hill of Hafursey (582m) is another option for walks from Vík.

LANDMANNALAUGAR & ÞÓRSMÖRK

Southwest Iceland's interior wonders take the form of two wildly different domains – one is Landmannalaugar, a bubbling wonderland with caramel-coloured peaks, the other is Þórsmörk, a verdant valley tucked safely away from the brutal northern elements under a series of wind-shattering ice caps.

Landmannalaugar

Multicoloured mountains, soothing hot springs, rambling lava flows and clear blue lakes make Landmannalaugar one of Iceland's most unique destinations, and a must for explorers of the interior. It's a favourite with Icelanders and visitors alike...as long as the weather cooperates.

Landmannalaugar (600m above sea level) includes the largest geothermal field in Iceland outside the Grímsvötn caldera in Vatnajökull. Its weird peaks are made of rhyolite – a mineral-filled lava that cooled unusually slowly, causing those amazing colours.

The area is the official starting point for the famous Laugavegurinn hike (see p123), and there's some excellent day hiking amid the caramel hills as well.

🏃 Activities

There's plenty to do in and around Land-mannalaugar, though many hikers skip the area's wonders in favour of setting off right away for their multiday hike to Þórsmörk. If you plan to stick around you'll be happy to know that the crowds dwindle in the evenings, and despite the base's chaotic appearance, you'll find peace in the hills above.

Hot Springs
Follow the wooden planks just 200m from the Landmannalaugar hut, to find a steaming river filled with bathers. Both hot and cold water flow out from beneath Laugahraun and combine in a natural pool to form the most ideal hot bath imaginable. There are no facilities at the wading area itself so bathers change at the hut, or simply drop trow in front of the other bathers.

Horse Riding
Landmannalaugar has on-site horse-riding tours (☎868 5577; www.hnakkur.com) from July to mid-August. Trots are led by a woman who makes saddles; you ride up to beautiful Brandsgil. A one-hour tour costs Ikr6500 per person. The stables in the plains around Hella also offer riding (usually longer trips) in and around the Landmannalaugar area – see p109 for more.

Hiking
If you're planning on doing some day hiking in the Landmannalaugar area, stop by the warden's house to purchase the useful daytrip map (Ikr300), which details all of the best hikes in the region.

On cloudier days try the day-hike to the ill-named Ljótipollur (Ugly Puddle), an incredible red crater filled with bright-blue water. The intense, fiery red comes from iron-ore deposits. Oddly enough, although it was formed by a volcanic explosion, the lake is rich in trout. The walk to the Puddle offers plenty of eye candy, from tephra desert and lava flow to marsh and braided glacial valleys. To get there you can climb over the 786m-high peak Norðurnámur or just traverse its western base to emerge on the Ljótipollur road (a 10km to 13.3km return trip, depending on the route).

When the weather is clear, try a walk that takes in the region's spectacular views. Climb to the summit of rainbow-streaked Brennisteinsalda – covered in steaming vents and sulphur deposits – for a good view across the rugged and variegated landscape (it's a 6.5km round-trip from Landmannalaugar). From Brennisteinsalda it's another 90 minutes along the Þórsmörk route to the impressive **Stórihver** geothermal field.

The blue lake **Frostastaðavatn** lies behind the rhyolite ridge immediately north of the Landmannalaugar hut. Walk over the ridge and you'll be rewarded with far-ranging views as well as close-ups of the interesting rock formations and moss-covered lava flows flanking the lake. If you walk at least one way on the road and spend some time exploring around the lake, the return trip takes two to three hours.

Guided hikes can also be a great way to explore the area – see p115 for more info.

🛏 Sleeping

Landmannalaugar has a large base with camping and hut facilities that, in the middle of summer, unfortunately looks like a refugee camp with hundreds of tents, several structures inundated with dirty hikers, and drying laundry dangling throughout. The base – simply known as **Landmannalaugar** (☎ 863 1175; N 63°59.600', W 19°03.660'; per person Ikr5000; ☉ early Jun-Sep) is operated by Ferðafélag Íslands, much like the huts on the Laugavegurinn hike (p125). It accommodates 85 people in closed (and close) quarters. There's a kitchen area, showers (Ikr500 for five minutes of hot water), and several wardens on-site. Campers can pitch a tent in the designated areas (Ikr1100 per person) – they have access to the toilet and shower facilities as well. Wild camping is strictly prohibited, as the entire area is a protected reserve.

🛈 Information

The Landmannalaugar hut wardens run a small **tourist information centre** (☉ 8am-10pm Jun-Sep) and can help with specific questions, including directions and advice on hiking routes. They also sell a sheet with day-hike info (Ikr300). Note that wardens do not know if it will rain (yes, this is the most frequently asked question here).

Also on the Landmannalaugar grounds is the **Mountain Mall** (☉ 8am-8pm Jun-Aug, 10am-6pm Sep), set up inside two buses, selling everything from hats, hot tea and maps, to fresh fish from the neighbouring mountain lakes.

The start to the Laugavegurinn hike can be found behind the Landmannalaugar hut – it's marked in red.

Getting There & Away

Bus

Landmannalaugar can be reached by bus from three different directions. **Reykjavík Excursions** (www.re.is) runs buses from around mid-June to mid-September. It's possible to travel from Reykjavík straight through to Skaftafell along the Fjallabak Route (see the boxed text, p125) with about a two-hour layover in Landmannalaugar, which is about enough time to take a dip in the springs and not much else.

FROM REYKJAVÍK Buses travel along the western part of the Fjallabak Rte, which first follows Rte 26 east of the Þjorsá. Departure is at 8am, arriving in Landmannalaugar around 12.30pm.

FROM SKAFTAFELL Buses leave Skaftafell at 8am arriving in Landmannalaugar around 1pm. The bus follows the Fjallabak Rte (F208).

Car

There are three routes to Landmannalaugar from the Ring Road. If you have a small 4WD, you will have to leave your vehicle about 1km before Landmannalaugar as the river crossing here is just too perilous for little cars. Two-wheel drive rentals are not allowed to drive on F roads, but we've seen a few private vehicles (we're going to assume that they're not rental cars) parked at the edge of the gushing river crossing as well.

You can hire a super-Jeep service; see Tours, p115 for more.

There's no petrol at Landmannalaugar. The nearest petrol pumps are 40km north at Hrauneyjar (close to the beginning of the F208), and 90km southeast at Kirkjubæjarklaustur, but to be on the safe side you should fill up along the Ring Road if approaching from the west or the north.

F208 NORTHWEST You can follow the west side of the Þjorsá (Rte 32), passing Árnes, then take Rte F208 down into Landmannalaugar from the north. This is the easiest path to follow for small 4WDs. After passing the power plant, the road from Hrauneyjar becomes horribly bumpy and swerves in between the power lines all the way to the 'Ugly Puddle'.

F225 On the east side of the Þjorsá, follow Rte 26 inland, pass through the low plains behind Hella, loop around Hekla, then take Rte F225 in a westerly direction until you reach the base. This route is harder to tackle (rougher roads) if you're driving on your own.

F208 SOUTHEAST The hardest route to tackle comes from the Ring Road between Vík and Kirkjubæjarklaustur. This is the Skaftafell–Landmannalaugar bus route.

FROM MÝVATN It takes all day to make the journey between Landmannalaugar and Mývatn along the Sprengisandur Rte. Buses leave from Mývatn at 8am; see p290 for more information.

Landmannalaugar to Þórsmörk

The hike from Landmannalaugar to Þórsmörk – commonly known as Laugavegurinn – is where hikers earn their stripes in Iceland. The harsh, otherwordly beauty of the landscape morphs in myriad ways as you trudge straight through the island's interior. As it is the most popular hike, the infrastructure is sound – there are carefully positioned huts along the zigzagging route that must be booked in advance.

🏃 Activities

Laugavegurinn (55km) is the name of the hike from Landmannalaugar to Þórsmörk – it means 'Hot Spring Road', and it's easy to understand why. The popular hike winds its way through myriad lunar landscapes, many steaming and bubbling from the intense activity below the earth's surface.

Ferðafélag Íslands (www.fi.is) runs the facilities in the area and publishes a small book about the hike offering detailed information about the landscape, sights and path. We recommend bringing along a map and a GPS if you plan on tackling the walk without a guide.

The track is almost always passable for hiking from early July through to mid-September. Early in the season (mid-June to early July) there can be icy patches that are difficult to manoeuvre – projected hut openings offer a good gauge of conditions.

At any time of year the Landmannalaugar to Þórsmörk hike is not to be undertaken lightly. It is imperative that you pack appropriate clothing, as weather conditions can change with the snap of a finger – see p34 for details. You'll also need to carry sufficient food and water. Most hikers walk from north to south to take advantage of the net altitude loss and the facilities at Þórsmörk. From there you can continue on to Skógar, which takes an extra day or two (about additional 22km).

Laugavegurinn in Four Days

Ferðafélag Íslands breaks Laugavegurinn into four sections, and many hikers opt to tackle one section each day for four days, as carefully positioned sleeping huts (and adjoining campsites) punctuate the start and end point of each leg.

Part 1: Landmannalaugar to Hrafntinnusker (12km; 3–5 hours) A relatively easy start to your adventure, the walk to the first hut passes the boiling earth at Stórihver and sweeping fields of glittering obsidian. If you want to extend the walk, start at Landmannalaugar and hike to Hrafntinnusker via Skalli – the warden's office in Landmannalaugar has a handout (Ikr300) that details this quieter route. You'll need to fill up on fresh water before you depart as there's no source until you reach the first hut. About 2km before Hrafntinnusker there's a memorial to a solo Israeli hiker who died on the trail in 2005 after ignoring a warden's warning – a reminder to properly prepare for your hike and always keep your ear to the ground.

Part 2: Hrafntinnusker to Álftavatn (12km; 4–5 hours) At Hrafntinnusker you can try a couple of short local hikes without your pack before setting off – there are views at Söðull (20 minutes return) and Reykjafjöll (one hour return), and a hidden geothermal area behind the ice caves (three hours return) – ask the warden for walking tips. Views aplenty are found on the walk to Álftavatn as well – hike across the northern spur of the Kaldaklofsfjöll ice cap for vistas from the summit. Walking into Álftavatn you'll see looming Tindfjallajökull, Mýrdalsjökull and the infamous Eyjafjallajökull before reaching the serenely beautiful lake where you'll spend the night.

Part 3: Álftavatn to Emstur (16km; 6–7 hours) To reach Emstur you'll need to ford at least one large stream – you can take your shoes off and get wet or wait at the edge of the river for any 4WD to give you a lift over. Not to be missed is the detour to Markarfljótsgljúfur – a gaping green canyon. It's well marked from Emstur, and takes about an hour to reach (you come back the same way).

Part 4: Emstur to Þórsmörk (15km; 6–7 hours) Bleakness and barrenness quickly turn to the lush Arctic flowers of a brilliantly verdant kingdom. If you're not planning on staying in Þórsmörk, you should aim to arrive by 3.30pm, as the amphibious bus departs for the Ring Road and Reykjavík at 4pm sharp.

Laugavegurinn in Three Days

If you're fit, it is well within your reach to complete the hike in three days instead of four – in fact, many people prefer to complete Laugavegurinn in three days. If you're starting from Reykjavík, take the first bus to Landmannalaugar, which arrives at noon,

Laugavegurinn Hike

0   10 km
0   5 miles

Stóra-Melfell ▲
(620m)

To Reykjavik

Skyggnisvatn

Litla-
Melfell

F208

Löðmundur
▲ (1074m)

Fjallabak
Route

Tjörvafell
Svartikrókur

Krókadiljabrún

Langasáta
▲ (792m)

Landmannale

Fitjafell

Frostastaðavatn

Ljótipollur   Austurbjallar

Norðurnámur
▲ (786m)

Stútur

Fjallabak Nature
Reserve

Suðurnámur

Landmannalaugar
Hut

START

Landmannalaugar

Jökuldalur

Vestur-Reykjadalir

Brennisteinsalda
Dalamót (880m)

Bláhnúkur
▲ (943m)

Kirkjufell

F208

Norður
Barmur

To Eldgjá (19km);
Kirkjubæjarklaustur (79km)

Austur-Reykjadalir

Stórihver   Skalli

Laufafell
(1164m) ▲

Hrafntinnusker
Hut

Reykjafjöll

Kaldaklofsjökull

Torfajökull

4WDs Only

F210

Álftaskarð

Háskerðingur
(1278m)

Torfahlaup

Álftavatn
Huts

Bratthálskvísl

Hvanngil Hut

Blessárjökull

Tindfjallajökull

Stóra Grænafell
(850m)

Mælifellssanður

F210

Mosar

Innri-Emstruá

Sléttjökull

Markarfljótsgljúfur

Tindfjöll
(1251m) ▲

F261

Emstrur
Huts

Markarfljót

Slyppugil

Ljósá

Entujökull

To Ring Road
(Amphibious Bus)

Langidalur
Valahnúkur Hut

END

Prongá

Húsadalur
Hut

Þórsmörk

Básar Hut

Krossá

Merkurjökull

Krossárjökull

MÝRDALSJÖKULL

Stakksholtsgjá

Goðaland

2010 Eruption Site

Fimmvörðuháls
Hike

Fimmvörðuháls
Hut

Goðalandsjökull

Eyjafjallajökull

Fimmvörðuháls

Emergency
Hut

Skógaheiði

Skógá

Háabunga
(1450m)

Fimmvörðuháls
Hike

Skógafoss

1

Skógar

FJALLABAK ROUTE

In summer, the Fjallabak Rte (F208) makes a spectacular alternative to the coast road between Hella, in southwest Iceland, and Kirkjubæjarklaustur. Its name translates as 'Behind the Mountains', and that's exactly where it goes.

Leave the Ring Road from Hella on Rte 26 (the east side of the Þjorsá), then take Rte F208 from near the Sigölduvirkjun power plant until you reach **Landmannalaugar**. From there, F208 continues east past the **Kirkjufell** marshes and beyond **Jökuldalur**, before coursing through the icy veins of a riverbed for 10km, climbing up to the **Hörðu-breið lookout**, then descending down into **Eldgjá**. The 40km stretch from Eldgjá to **Búland** is in reasonable shape, but there are some rivers to fond before the road turns into Rte 208 and emerges back along the Ring Road southwest of Kirkjubæjarklaustur.

A 2WD vehicle wouldn't have a hope of completing even a small portion of the route. In summer, if the rivers are low, a conventional vehicle can get within 1km of Landmannalaugar from the west (F208 only). Note that car-hire companies prohibit taking 2WD vehicles on any F roads, so if something should go wrong on this route, your insurance will be void.

Since much of the Fjallabak Rte is along rivers (or rather, in rivers!), it's not ideally suited to mountain bikes either. Lots of people attempt it, but it's not casual cycling by any stretch.

You can tackle the entire route by bus with **Reykjavík Excursions** (☑580 5400; www.re.is) by leaving Reykjavík at 8am and switching to the Skaftafell-bound bus in Landmannalaugar. The journey takes about 11 hours. You can break up the journey in Landmannalaugar, spending a few nights at the base exploring the area before taking the second bus leg of the journey.

and set off immediately for your hike. Alternatively you can spend a night in Landmannalaugar exploring the area and then set off in the morning of the next day. You'll be full of energy and excitement, so capitalise on that adrenaline and complete Part 1 and Part 2 (previously outlined) in one day, arriving at Álftavatn after a full eight to 10 hours of hiking. Hike to Emstur on your second day, and you'll arrive in Þórsmörk in the evening of your third.

Laugavegurinn in Two Days

If you're tight on time, or an avid hiker, you can complete all 55km of the hike in two full days. On your first day hike all the way to Álftavatn – or better yet, continue an additional 5km to reach Hvanngil. Making it all the way to Hvanngil will shave off some trekking during your second day. It's possible to combine Part 3 and Part 4 on your second day, as these 30km are relatively flat. There's an overall 100m decline, making the hike well suited to endurance walkers.

Laugavegurinn Extended

If you love the outdoors and the weather conditions are favourable, there's no reason to rush your experience in the region. You can use any of the huts as hiking bases, and explore some of the paths that veer away

from the main Laugavegurinn trail. You can also spend a couple of days based in Landmannalaugar before setting off, though we prefer to stick around Þórsmörk on the flip side. Alternatively, you can hike some kind of Laugavegurinn remix with a local guide who can get off the beaten track (literally), taking you to hiker-free mountain passes that run parallel to the main trail – see p115 for more info.

🛏 Sleeping

As the route is very well travelled, you'll find a constellation of carefully positioned huts along the way – all are owned and maintained by **Ferðafélag Íslands** (☑568 2533; www.fi.is). These huts sleep dozens of people and must be booked well in advance – the wardens recommend booking in early spring even if you plan on travelling at the end of summer. We cannot stress enough the fact that these beds go quickly. It's also important to note that bunk beds at most of the huts sleep four people each – two (side by side) on each level. If you are travelling alone, expect to be paired with a stranger.

You can also camp in the designated areas around the huts, although these spaces tend to be open to the elements making it difficult to steady your tent – do as the other travellers do and streamline your tent with the wind, then pin down your tent with extra boulders. All camping costs Ikr1100 per person.

The following huts are listed from north to south; they all accept credit cards.

Hrafntinnusker   HUT
(Höskuldsskáli; N 63°56.014', W 19°10.109'; hut per person Ikr5000) Open from mid-June to early September, this hut holds 52 people (around 22 of whom sleep on mattresses on the floor in a converted attic space). The hut is at 1000m elevation – be prepared for some particularly inhospitable conditions if you are planning on camping here. There's no electricity, no refuse facilities and no showers at this site – you must carry your rubbish to Álftavatn. The kitchen can be used by campers for an additional Ikr400. Some campers cook their food on the natural steam vents nearby – ask the warden to point you in the right direction.

Álftavatn   HUT
(N 63°51.470', W 19°13.640'; hut per person Ikr5000) Opening coincides with the opening of the local F roads, which can be anywhere from early to late June depending on weather. The site closes in mid-September (coinciding with the season's final bus to Landmannalaugar). There are two huts holding 72 people total; both have drinking water, mattresses and outhouse facilities. There's no electricity; you'll need a torch if you're hiking in August or September. Kitchen facilities have gas stoves, but no refrigerator – campers are not allowed to use the kitchen. Strict quiet hours are from midnight to 7am. You can continue on past Álftavatn for five additional kilometres and follow a small detour that leads you to Hvanngil (N 64°50.026', W 19°12.507'; hut per person Ikr5000). It holds 60 people, and has a kitchen and shower. It's a good choice for people tackling Laugavegurinn in two days. It tends to be much less busy than Álftavatn, but you'll be missing out on a great backpackers vibe.

Emstrur   HUT
(Botnar; N 63°45.980', W 19°22.480'; hut per person Ikr5000) Opens in early June and closes in mid-September. It has 60 beds divided into three huts. There are two showers (Ikr100 for five minutes of hot water) and eight toilets. Campers can use the kitchen for an additional Ikr400. There are no garbage facilities or power outlets. Inga, the warden, likes to do a little matchmaking when setting up her sleeping arrangement – her pancakes

are legendary. Although it's located under the glacier, the other huts have a more striking position along the trail. Note that mobile phone reception is particularly spotty here.

Þórsmörk

A hidden valley deep in the Icelandic Outback, Þórsmörk is a verdant realm filled with curling gorges, flower-filled leas, icy streams, and views to three looming glaciers (Tindfjallajökull, Eyjafjallajökull and Mýrdalsjökull) that guard the quiet hamlet from harsher weather. Be warned, though: Þórsmörk's ravishing appearance and proximity to Reykjavík (130km) make it a popular spot in summer, and although it seems relatively close to the Ring Road on a map, you'll need to hike or take a high-clearance 4WD to reach the reserve.

The higher reaches of the valley are known as Goðaland (Land of the Gods), which is – as the name suggests – divine. Rock formations twist and twirl skyward like some stone arches of an ancient, ethereal cathedral. Fluorescent Arctic flowers burst forth from the spongy moss adding brilliant slashes of colour to the quiet interior landscapes. Goðaland is the endpoint for the glorious Fimmvörðuháls hike, which starts in Skógar (see the boxed text, p116). The main camping area in Goðaland is Básar; to reach the area from Þórsmörk you must cross the dangerous Krossá river using the bridge near Langidalur. Regular 4WDs cannot make the crossing.

Check the bus schedules to see when Þórsmörk is open for exploring – it's usually from May to September.

🏃 Activities

Although Þórsmörk is the terminus for the uber-popular Laugavegurinn hike, many tired travellers opt to catch the 4pm bus out of the reserve, missing some spectacular day hiking (sans backpack) in the area. We highly recommend staying on for an extra day or two to check out some of the beautiful trails in the area. Some travellers continue on along the Fimmvörðuháls hike down into Skógar, which is a truly incredible walk, but better tackled in the opposite direction (depart from Skógar).

If you plan to explore Þórsmörk on several short hikes, we recommend staying at Húsadalur (Volcano Huts Thorsmork), as the staff can offer detailed information on which walks to try. You can also trek through the area on a guided hike with many of the operators positioned closer to the easily accessible Ring Road – see p115.

Following are three of the most popular hikes in Þórsmörk.

STAKKSHOLTSGJÁ

Take the 12.30pm bus from Húsadalur bound for Langidalur and Básar, and ask the bus driver to let you off at Stakksholtsgjá (about a 15-minute ride), a beautiful gorge. Walk along the river bed, hop across the river, and when it splits in two veer left down a narrower canyon. Scamper over a few boulders and you'll spot a scenic waterfall. If you time it correctly you can catch the bus returning to Húsadalur at around 3.35pm, which will pick up at the gorge. You'll have plenty of time, as the walk only takes around 90 minutes.

VALAHNÚKUR CIRCLE

A 2½-hour loop that takes you up to the brilliant viewpoint at Valahnúkur. From Húsadalur, follow the trail up to the viewpoint then down into Langidalur. From there pass along the ridge between the valleys to make it back to your starting point. If you want to use the buses to your advantage, hop on the bus bound for Langidalur and walk back to Húsadalur taking in the viewpoint from the opposite direction.

TINDFJÖLL CIRCLE

The longest of the most popular 'short hikes' in the valley takes around 4½ hours from Langidalur and around six hours from Húsadalur. Wander through the Slyppugil Valley (or follow the like-named ridge), then you'll have to hike across some moraine along the side of a second ridge. Although there are a lot of loose stones, it is not as dangerous as it might look. You'll then pass through Tröllakirkja – the trolls' church – which has the sweeping stone arches similar to the Fimmvörðuháls hike. A lush green field appears next before revealing a postcard-worthy viewpoint to the Þórsmörk valley. Follow the top of the sandstone ridge until you find yourself at the twisting Krossá, which takes you back to Langidalur, or Húsadalur further on.

☞ Tours

Many tour operators in the region offer hiking trips through Þórsmörk and beyond. Ask the managers at Húsadalur for assistance, though it's best to book in advance with one of the companies based closer to the Ring Road – see p115 for more information.

🛏 Sleeping

There are three lodging areas in the Þórsmörk area: Langidalur (sometimes referred as Þórsmörk), Básar (technically in Goðaland) and Húsadalur (also called Volcano Huts Thormsork). All have huts and campsites, cooking facilities and running water. They get rammed during the summer months, so it's crucial to book space in the huts in advance. We recommend bringing a sleeping bag and your own food. Note that wild camping is frowned upon in the area.

Húsadalur   HOSTEL, CAMPING €
(Volcano Huts Thorsmork; ☎552 8300; http://volcanohuts.com; sites per person Ikr1100, dm/d Ikr6000/7000 ☙May-Sep) The Húsadalur area is often called Volcano Huts Thorsmork, and feels decidedly more like a hostel. There are dorm rooms and double rooms aplenty – enough for 130 guests, and cottages for small groups are also available for Ikr20,000. Linen costs an extra Ikr3000. The Volcano Huts is a great place to stay if you want catered meals – buffet dinner costs Ikr3500.

Langidalur   HUT, CAMPING €
(Þórsmörk; ☎893 1191; www.fi.is; N 63°40.960', W 19°30.890'; sites/huts per person Ikr1100/5000; ☙mid-May–Sep) Langidalur – also referred to simply as Þórsmörk, or Skagfjörðsskáli – is the oldest and most rustic option of the three huts. It can sleep 75, and there's well-tended camping space all around the hut. You can book through Ferðafélag Íslands, the same organisation that takes bookings for huts along the Landmannalaugar–Þórsmörk track.

At the time of research a neighbouring campsite called **Slyppugil** was getting remodelled by the **Hostelling International** (www.hostel.is) consortium to handle the ever-increasing number of campers in the area. It is located three minutes' away from Langidalur by foot.

Básar   HUT, CAMPING €
(☎562 1000; www.utivist.is; sites per person Ikr1100, hut per person Ikr3600) Básar is the choice base for Icelanders, largely due to the beautiful positioning in the trees. Space is very cramped, but there's hut accommodation for 80 people, which can be booked through Útivist. Grass and wooden planks

lead around the private camping space, which gets extremely crowded on summer weekends.

🛈 Getting There & Away

Bus

Reykjavík Excursions (☑580 5400; www.re.is) bus service from Reykjavík to Þórsmörk departs Reykjavík at 8am, arriving at Húsadalur at noon. At 12.30pm it departs for Básar, arriving at 1pm. At 3pm the bus continues to Langidalur, and at 3.15pm it leaves Langidalur returning back to Húsadalur at 3.30pm before continuing on to Reykjavík at 4pm. There's a second bus that leaves Reykjavík at 4.30pm, arriving in Húsadalur around 8pm – it makes no other stops. The same bus leaves from Húsadalur at 8.15am heading back towards Reykjavík; if you want the bus to make a stop at Básar or Langidalur, you must request a pick-up (or drop off) the night before.

TREX (☑587 6000; www.trex.is) runs a daily bus from Reykjavík (with pick-ups in Selfoss, Hella, Hvolsvöllur and Seljalandsfoss) to Langidalur – it makes no other stops. The bus leaves Reykjavík at 7.30am and arrives in Þórsmörk around 11.30am, returning in the other direction at 2.30pm.

Many tourists opt to board and disembark the Þórsmörk buses in Seljalandsfoss, located back on the Ring Road – a one-way ticket costs Ikr3700. Buses run from early June to 31 August.

Car

You cannot drive all the way into Þórsmörk with your private vehicle. End of story. If you have your own 4WD with excellent clearance, you can plough down Rtes 249 and F249 until you reach the crossroads for Húsadalur and Básar. It's there that you must leave your car – you will not be able to ford the gushing river. The bus that takes passengers is a special amphibious vehicle that has been outfitted to pass the deep ravine littered with boulders. If you want to drive all the way until the crossroads, the bus makes the river crossing around 11.45am, 3.30pm and 7.30pm, and you can jump on board for Ikr1000 per person. Alternatively you can call ahead to Húsadalur and staff can take you over for the same price when they have a car available.

Hiking

Þórsmörk is the terminus of the popular Laugavegurinn hike (p123), which begins in Landmannalaugar; it's also popular to reach Þórsmörk from Skógar on the beautiful Fimmvörðuháls hike (p116). If you are planning to reach Þórsmörk by foot we recommend one of the aforementioned options; walking along Rtes 249 and F249 from Seljaland is far less scenic.

Note that it takes around 20 to 30 minutes to walk between Langidalur and Húsadalur.

VESTMANNAEYJAR

Black and brooding, the Vestmannaeyjar form 15 eye-catching silhouettes off the southern shore. The islands were formed by submarine volcanoes around 11,000 years ago, except for sulky-looking Surtsey, the archipelago's newest addition, which rose from the waves in 1963. Surtsey was made a Unesco World Heritage Site in 2008, but its unique scientific status means that it is not possible to land there.

Heimaey is the only inhabited island. Its little town and sheltered harbour lie between dramatic *klettur* (escarpments) and two ominous volcanoes – blood-red Eldfell and conical Helgafell. These days Heimaey is famous for two things: its puffins (around 10 million birds come here to breed) and Þjóðhátíð, Iceland's biggest outdoor festival, held in August.

Heimaey

POP 4135

The small town of Heimaey (*hey*-my) is encased in a fortress of jagged lava; its port sits at the end of a convoluted waterway that carves a path between towering cliffs and jagged dunes riddled with bird nests. Although only a few kilometres from the mainland, Heimaey feels like a million miles away, lost amid the frigid waters of the north Atlantic.

Over the centuries the island was a marauders' favourite. The English raided Heimaey throughout the 15th century, building the stone fort Skansinn as their HQ. In 1627 Heimaey suffered the most awful attack by Algerian pirates, who went on a killing spree around the island, murdering 36 islanders and kidnapping 242 more (almost three-quarters of the population). The rest managed to escape by abseiling down cliffs or hiding in caves along the west coast. Those who were kidnapped were taken as slaves to north Africa; years later, 27 islanders had their freedom bought for them...and had a long walk home.

The volcanoes that formed Heimaey have come close to destroying the island on several occasions. The most famous eruption in modern times began unexpectedly at 1.45am on 23 January 1973, when a vast fissure burst open, gradually mutating into the volcano Eldfell, and prompting the island's evacuation (see the boxed text, p130).

Heimaey

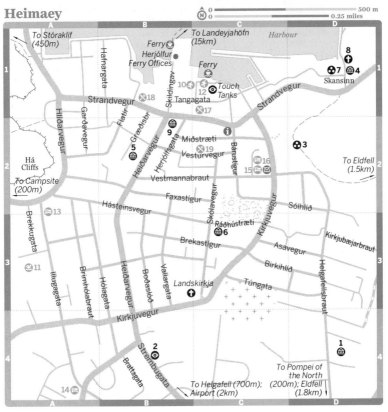

Heimaey

◉ Sights

TOWN CENTRE

If you're interested in visiting several of the island's museums, you can ask at any of the ticketing offices about the latest museum pass scheme – every summer the different establishments unite to offer discounts on admission. Videos on the famous eruptions in 1969 and 1979 play in several locations during summer; at the time of research there was a showing at Höllin (Strembugata; ☺4pm), footage at Surtseyjarstofa, and a film at Café Kró (p133).

Sæheimar

MUSEUM

(Náttúrugripasafn Vestmannaeyja; ☑481 1997; Heiðarvegur 12; adult/child Ikr1000/free; ☺11am-5pm mid-May–mid-Sep, 1-4pm Sat mid-Sep–mid-May) The Aquarium and Natural History Museum has an interesting collection of stuffed birds and animals, plus fish tanks of hideous Icelandic fish. It's great fun for the family, and there's often a baby puffin wobbling about – the museum is an informal bird hospital as well.

Surtseyjarstofa

MUSEUM

(Surtsey Visitors Centre; ☑591 2140; www.ust.is/surtsey; Heiðarvegur 1; adult/child Ikr1000/free; ☺11am-5pm Jun-Aug, 1-4pm Sep-May) A beautiful space dedicated to all things Surtsey, this museum offers interactive insight into the formation of one of the world's newest islands. Today Surtsey is shaped like a stingray, but scientists believe that the island will look more like a lima bean by 2052.

Sagnheimar Byggðasafn

MUSEUM

(Folk Museum; ☑488 2040; Raðhústræti; adult/child Ikr1000/600; ☺11am-7pm mid-May–mid-Sep, 1-4pm Sat mid-Sep–mid-May) Housed in the city library, this interactive folk museum tells the story of Heimaey from the era of marauding pirates up to the 1979 eruptions and beyond. Displays also shed light on local sports heroes and native bird life; there's even rumoured to be a stash of Nazi regalia, though it's currently not on display.

Stóraklif

VIEWPOINT

The top of the craggy precipice Stóraklif is a treacherous 30-minute climb from behind the petrol station at the harbour. The trail starts on the obvious 4WD track; as it gets steeper you're 'assisted' by ropes and chains (don't trust them completely), but it's worth the terror for the outstanding views.

SKANSINN

The oldest structure on the island was Skansinn, a 15th-century fort built to defend the harbour (not too successfully – when Algerian pirates arrived in 1627, they simply landed on the other side of the island). Its walls were swallowed up by the 1973 lava, but some have been rebuilt. Above them, you can see the remains of the town's old water tanks, also crushed by molten rock.

Across from the half-covered tanks is the tiny wooden house Landlyst (admission free; ☺11am-5pm mid-May–mid-Sep). It was once a maternity hospital, and today contains a small display about a local woman, Sólveig, who was sent abroad to be trained as a midwife when the island's infant mortality rate was a tragic 80%.

THE 1973 ERUPTION

Without warning, at 1.45am on 23 January 1973 a mighty explosion blasted through the winter's night as a 1.5km-long volcanic fissure split the eastern side of the island. The eruption area gradually became concentrated into a growing crater cone, which fountained lava and ash into the sky.

Normally the island's fishing boats would have been out at sea, but a force-12 gale had prevented them from sailing the previous afternoon. Now calm weather and a harbourful of boats allowed the island's 5200 inhabitants to be evacuated to the mainland. Incredibly, there was just a single fatality.

Over the next five months more than 30 million tonnes of lava poured over Heimaey, destroying 360 houses and creating a brand-new mountain, the red cinder cone Eldfell. One-third of the town was buried beneath the lava flow, and the island increased in size by 2.5 sq km.

As the eruption continued, advancing lava threatened to close the harbour and make the evacuation permanent – without a fishing industry, there would have been no point in returning. In an attempt to slow down the inexorable flow of molten rock, firefighters hosed the lava with over six million tonnes of cold sea water. The lava halted just 175m short of the harbour mouth – actually improving the harbour by creating extra shelter!

The islanders were billeted with friends and family on the mainland, watching the fireworks and waiting to see if they could ever go home. Finally, the eruption finished, five months after it started, at the end of June. Two-thirds of the islanders returned to face the mighty clean-up operation.

The bitumen-coated Stafkirkjan (admission free; ⊘11am-5pm mid-May–mid-Sep) is a reconstruction of a medieval wooden stave church. It was presented by the Norwegian government in 2000 to celebrate 1000 years of Christianity.

House Graveyard & Pompei of the North   LANDMARK
(www.pompeinordursins.is) Four hundred buildings lie buried under the lava from the 1973 eruption. On the edge of the flow is a strange graveyard where beloved homes rest in peace. 'Pompei of the North' is a modern 'archaeological' excavation in which 10 houses are being dug up. So far, the crumpled concrete remains of a handful of houses have been unearthed along what was formerly Suðurvegur. Plans are underway to create a museum called Eldheimar about the eruption and the subsequent excavations.

Eldfellshraun   LANDMARK
Known as Eldfellshraun, the new land created by the 1973 lava flow is now criss-crossed with a maze of hiking tracks that run down to the fort at Skansinn and the house graveyard, and all around the bulge of the raw, red eastern coast. Here you'll find small black-stone beaches, a lava garden (Gaujulundur) and a lighthouse.

OUT OF TOWN
Eldfell & Helgafell   VOLCANO
The 221m-high volcanic cone Eldfell appeared from nowhere in the early hours of 23 January 1973. Once the fireworks finished, heat from the volcano provided Heimaey with geothermal energy from 1976 to 1985. Today the ground is still hot enough in places to bake bread or char wood. Eldfell is an easy climb from town, up the collapsed northern wall of the crater; stick to the path, as the islanders are trying to save their latest volcano from erosion.

Neighbouring volcano Helgafell (226m) erupted 5000 years ago. Its cinders are grassed over today, and you can scramble up here without much difficulty from the football pitch on the road to the airport.

Herjólfsdalur & the West Coast   LANDMARK
Sheltered by an extinct volcano, green and grassy Herjólfsdalur was the home of Vestmannaeyjar first settler, Herjólfur Barðursson. Excavations have revealed remains of a Norse house where a replica now stands. The island's campsite is also here.

On the cliffs west of the golf course, there's a little monument to the 200 people who converted to Mormonism and departed for Utah in the 19th century.

Several perilous tracks climb the steep slopes around Herjólfsdalur, running along the top of Norðklettur to Stafnsnes. The ascent is exhilarating, but there are some sheer drops. A gentler walk runs south along the western coast of the island, passing above numerous lava caves where local people hid from the pirates in 1627. At Ofanleitishamar, hundreds of puffins nest in the cliffs, and you can often get within metres for close-up photos.

Stórhöfði   LANDMARK
A windy meteorological station has been built on Stórhöfði, the rocky peninsula at the southern end of Heimaey. It's linked to the main island by a narrow isthmus (created by lava from Helgafell's eruption 5000 years ago), and there are good views from the summit. It's possible to scramble down to the boulder beach at Brimurð and continue along the cliffs on the east coast, returning by the main road just before the airport. From June to August the sea cliffs at Litlihöfði are a good place to watch puffins.

✗ Activities

Pick up a copy of *Hiking High in Vermannaeyjar* for a detailed walking map focused on Heimaey; try the scenic walks on the island's western shores. There's a saltwater swimming pool (adult/child Ikr450/160; ⊘6.15am-9pm Mon-Fri, 9am-6pm Sat & Sun Jun-Aug, 6.15am-9pm Sep-May), with hot-pots, a water slide and a gym. Contact Lyngfell (☑898 1809; http://lyngfell.123.is) to enquire about horse riding (one hour Ikr5000).

☞ Tours

Rib Safari   BOAT TOUR
(☑661 1810, 846 2798; www.ribsafari.is; ⊘May–mid-Oct) One-hour tours (Ikr7000) run everyday at 2pm in a rubber zodiac that bounces on the waves as it jets through the archipelago. The small size of the boat means that the captain can navigate through small caves and between rocky outcrops for up-close views of the area's bird colonies and world's biggest elephant (you'll see!). Charter trips to Surtsey (note: you cannot get off the boat) cost Ikr15,500 per person and require a minimum of 10 people; you can circumnavigate the entire cluster of islands for Ikr10,500 (100 minutes).

Viking Tours
BOAT TOUR

(☑488 4884; www.vikingtours.is; Harbour; adult/child Ikr4900/3900; ⊘mid-May–mid-Sep) Stop by Cafe Kró to sign up for boat or bus trips with the friendly folks at Viking Tours. Leaving at 11am and 3.30pm everyday, they zip right around the island, slowing for the big bird-nesting sites on the south coast, and sailing into the sea cave Klettshellir, where the boat driver gets to show off his saxophone skills! His wife, Unnur, often runs 1½-hour bus tours at 1.30pm. Boat-lunch-bus combos are available for a cool Ikr9720. Trips coincide with ferry departure times for the mainland, making it a convenient option for day-trippers.

✷ Festivals & Events

Þjóðhátíð
OUTDOOR

(National Festival; www.dalurinn.is; admission Ikr18,900) The country's biggest outdoor festival is the three-day Þjóðhátíð, held at the festival ground at Herjólfsdalur over the first weekend in August. It involves music, dancing, fireworks, a big bonfire, gallons of alcohol and, as the night progresses, lots of drunken sex (it's something of a teen rite of passage), with upwards of 15,000 people attending. Extra flights are laid on from Reykjavík, but you should book transport and accommodation far in advance.

Historically, the festival was first celebrated when bad weather prevented Vestmannaeyjar people from joining the mainland celebrations of Iceland's first constitution (1 July 1874). The islanders held their own festival a month later, and it's been an annual tradition ever since.

🛌 Sleeping

The 30-minute ferry ride from the mainland means that a trip to Vestmannaeyjar can be easily done as a day trip. If you choose to spend the night (which we highly recommend), you'll have the choice of many accommodation options, several listed here. Cautious travellers should book in advance, but usually there are plenty of sleeping options due to Heimaey's day-tripping popularity. Check out www.vestmannaeyjar.is for a full list of accommodation.

Hótel Vestmannaeyjar
HOTEL €€

(☑481 2900; www.hotelvestmannaeyjar.is; Vestmannabraut 28; d Ikr21,500) Iceland's first cinema is now a pleasant hotel, with freshly redone rooms and the friendliest staff in town.

Sunnuhöll HI Hostel
HOSTEL €

(☑481 2900; www.hotelvestmannaeyjar.is; Vestmannabraut 26; dm Ikr3800) We have a soft spot for homey Sunnuhöll hostel, with its handful of prim rooms. The recent surge in day-trippers means that dorms are rarely full, and there's generally a quiet and laidback vibe. Reception is at Hótel Vestmannaeyjar.

Campsite
CAMPING €

(sites per person Ikr1200; ⊘Jun-Aug) Cupped in the bowl of an extinct volcano, this campsite has hot showers, a laundry room and cooking facilities. You can also pitch a tent across the street – this second spot is a bit less windy.

Gistiheimilið Hvíld
GUESTHOUSE €€

(☑481 1230; www.simnet.is/hvild; Höfðavegur 16; d Ikr10,000) A friendly family owns this large green house, which has smallish guest rooms with shared bathroom, a TV lounge and a peaceful garden. There's no breakfast, but there is a guest kitchen where you can prepare your own.

Gistiheimilið Árný
GUESTHOUSE €

(☑481 2082; Illugagata 7; d Ikr11,800) A charming couple runs this neat suburban house, which also offers guests a kitchen and washing machine, and packed lunches by arrangement. Upstairs rooms have epic views, and the owner prays for a sound sleep for all her guests!

🍴 Eating

Heimaey has several cheap petrol-station snack bars where you can get fast food. For self-catering, there's the igloo-like **Vöruval supermarket** (Vesturvegur 18; ⊘9am-7pm), and two streets away is **Krónan supermarket** (Strandvegur; ⊘11am-7pm Mon-Fri, 11am-6pm Sat, 11am-4pm Sun). There are several dining options in town; the following options are your best bets.

TOP CHOICE Slippurinn
ICELANDIC €€

(Strandvegur 76; mains Ikr1790-3690; ⊘11am-11pm Tue-Fri, 11.30am-midnight Sat & Sun mid-Apr–Sep) Family owned and operated, Slippurinn sits inside an old machine workshop that once serviced the lonely ships in the harbour at the back. The tool shelves and many of the old apparatuses are still in their original positions, with tables – made from old boat scraps – gently sprinkled around. The food is decidedly Icelandic with a pinch of bright

SURTSEY

In November 1963 the crew on the fishing boat *Ísleifur II* noticed something odd – the sea south of Heimaey appeared to be on fire. Rather than flee, the boat drew up for a closer look – and its crew were the first to set eyes on the world's newest island.

The incredible subsea eruption lasted for 4½ years, throwing up cinders and ash to form a 2.7 sq km piece of real estate (since eroded to 1.4 sq km). What else could it be called but Surtsey (Surtur's Island), after the Norse fire giant who will burn the world to ashes at Ragnarök.

It was decided that the sterile island would make a perfect laboratory, giving a unique insight into how plants and animals colonise new territory. Surtsey is therefore totally off-limits to visitors (unless you're a scientist specialising in biocolonisation). Just so you know, though, in the race for the new land, the blue-green algae *Anabaena variabilis* got there first.

You can get a vicarious view of Surtsey's thunderous birth by visiting the Surtsey-jarstofa on Heimaey (p130). Both Rib Safari and Viking Tours run boat trips around the island if there's enough interest.

And here's a little conundrum for you: what are fossils doing on this newly minted island?

flavours from the Med. A fresh, three-/five-course dinner costs Ikr5490/7490.

Einsi Kaldi SEAFOOD €€€
(www.einsikaldi.is; Vestmannabraut 28; mains Ikr3700-5200; ⏱10am-10pm mid-May–mid-Aug, 5-10pm mid-Aug–mid-May) On the ground floor of Hótel Vestmannaeyjar, Einsi Kaldi serves well-crafted seafood recipes amid dimly lit surrounds that look a bit like a Vegas disco.

Café Kró INTERNATIONAL €€
(Harbour; mains Ikr1200-2300; ⏱9.30am-5.30pm mid-May–mid-Sep; 🛜) A good choice for day-trippers, Café Kró is run by the friendly folk from Viking Tours. While nibbling on a selection of international staples (think burgers and pizza) you can collect information about the island and watch an interesting film about the '73 eruption (which airs at 4pm daily).

❶ Information

Library (Ráðhústræti; ⏱10am-5pm Mon-Fri Jun-Aug, 11am-2pm Sat Sep-May) Internet access is available for Ikr100 per 30 minutes.

Tourist information centre (www.vestman naeyjar.is; Strandvegur; ⏱9am-6pm Mon-Fri, 10am-5pm Sat, 1-5pm Sun Jun-Aug) The summer tourist office is staffed by local teens. Consider it more of a place to pick up pamphlets.

❶ Getting There & Around

Air

The airport for Vestmannaeyjar is about 3km from Heimaey – a **taxi** (☎897 1190) will cost about Ikr2000, or you could walk it in 15 min-

utes. At the time of research there were no scheduled flights from Bakki (near the ferry port at Landeyjahöfn); however, a charter flight with **Air Arctic** (☎571 4500, 662 4500; www. airarctic.is) could be arranged (six person minimum) for Ikr4500 each way per person. Or you can take an aerial trip that starts and finishes in Bakki; a 30-minute flight costs €120. There are two daily flights between Reykjavík's domestic airport and Vestmannaeyjar on **Eagle Air** (☎562 4200; www.eagleair.is) for Ikr25,000 round trip.

Boat

Eimskip's ferry **Herjólfur** (☎481 2800; www. herjolfur.is) sails from Landeyjahöfn (about 12km off the Ring Road between Hvolsvöllur and Skógar) to Heimaey year-round. The journey takes about 30 minutes. From 15 May to 14 September boats depart Vestmannaeyjar daily at 8.30am, 11.30am, 2.30pm, 5.30pm and 8.30pm (on Tuesdays there's no 2.30pm boat); from Landeyjahöfn the boats depart at 10am, 1pm, 4pm, 7pm and 10pm (again, no 4pm boat on Tuesdays).

Low-season boats leave Vestmannaeyjar daily at 8am, 11.30pm, 5.30pm and 8.30pm; they depart Landeyjahöfn at 10am, 1pm, 7pm and 9.30pm. In bad weather, the port at Landeyjahöfn can fill with sand, in which case the ferry will sail for Þorlákshöfn (p104) instead. Note that the harbour landing can switch in bad summer weather as well – boat officials take your mobile phone number when you book so they can reach you if the port of call changes. It takes roughly two hours to drive from Landeyjahöfn west to Þorlákshöfn.

South Iceland's bus infrastructure offers convenient links to the port from various points along the Ring Road all the way to Reykjavík.

SOUTHWEST ICELAND & THE GOLDEN CIRCLE HEIMAEY

West Iceland

Best Places to Eat

» Narfeyrarstofa (p146)
» Settlement Centre Restaurant (p140)
» Erpsstaðir (p156)
» Gamla Rif (p151)
» Fish Buffet at Hótel Brú (p140)

Best Places to Stay

» Hótel Egilsen (p145)
» Hótel Flatey (p148)
» Hótel Hellnar (p153)
» Fljótstunga (p142)
» Hótel Edda (p156)

Why Go?

Geographically close to Reykjavík yet miles and miles away in sentiment, west Iceland is in many ways a splendid microcosm of what the country has to offer beyond the capital. Yet, surprisingly, most tourists have somehow missed the memo, preferring instead to zoom around the Ring Road in search of other wonders. It's good news for you though – you're likely to have much of this under-appreciated region to yourself.

The long arm of the Snæfellsnes is a favourite among tourists. Capped by a glacial fist, the peninsula is a veritable artist's palette of sulphuric yellows, snowy whites, mossy greens, scorched charcoals and Caribbean blues.

Icelanders, on the other hand, hold west Iceland in high regard for its canon of local sagas. Two of Iceland's best-known tales, the *Laxdæla* and *Egil's Sagas,* took place along the region's brooding waters, marked today by haunting cairns and ruins.

Road Distances (km)

	Borgarnes	Húsafell	Stykkishólmur	Hellnar	Búðardalur
Húsafell	65				
Stykkishólmur	99	158			
Hellnar	122	179	90		
Búðardalur	79	103	86	145	
Reykjavík	74	129	173	194	152

BORGARBYGGÐ

Decidedly positioned beyond Reyjavík's suburban sprawl, Borgarbyggð and the surrounding area feels suddenly pastoral despite being a mere 30-minute drive from the capital. Although lacking the mystique and majesty of the Snæfellsnes Peninsula further on, the region's finger-like fjords and stone-strewn highlands offer plenty of day-trip fodder for those who need a quick fix of country living.

Hvalfjörður

If you have plenty of time (and a private vehicle), follow Rte 47 along the scenic 80km road around Hvalfjörður. Those with a need for speed should instead head straight through the 5.7km-long tunnel (Ikr1000) that runs beneath its waters. Cyclists aren't permitted to use the tunnel.

On the southern side of the fjord you'll find dramatic Esja (914m), a great spot for wilderness hiking. The trail to the summit begins at Esjuberg, just north of Mosfellsbær, and ascends via Krehólakambur (850m) and Kistufell (830m).

At the head of the fjord, Glymur, Iceland's highest waterfall (198m), can be reached by following the turn-off to Botnsdalur until you reach the end of the road. From there, it'll take a couple of hours to reach the chute. Try to visit after heavy rain or snowmelt – in a dry period it can be a little underwhelming.

The church at the Saurbær (☑433 8952) farmstead, further along, is worth a look for its beautiful stained-glass work. Built in memory of Hallgrímur Pétursson, who composed Iceland's most widely known religious work, *50 Passion Hymns,* the church is only slightly more modest than Reykjavík's Hallgrímskirkja, also named after the composer.

Hvalfjörður has several places to spend the night, including Hótel Glymur (☑430 3100; www.hotelglymur.is; s/d/ste from €209/269/329; @☎), on the northern side of the fjord near Saurbær. Most guests enjoy the quirky clash of modern and antique knick-knacks (it's all a bit East-meets-West); to us, the hotel feels a bit like an orphanage for unwanted objets d'art. Contemporary amenities abound: brand-new villas with private plunge pools, giant picture windows and heated floors. It's worth stopping by for some homemade cake while learning about the fjord's surprising history (over 20,000 American and British soldiers parked their submarines here during WWII).

Akranes

POP 5600

Set under the imposing concave plateau Akrafjall (572m), the pleasant town of Akranes lies at the tip of the peninsula separating Hvalfjörður from Borgarfjörður. According to the Icelandic history text the *Landnámabók,* the area was once controlled by a group of Irish hermits, but today it's the factory towers of the fish and cement plants that dominate.

The town's main attraction is the engaging Museum Centre (☑431 5566; www.museum.is; adult/child Ikr500/free; ☉10am-5pm Jun-Aug, 1-5pm Sep-May), which is full of nautical relics, crystals, fossils and tales of local sporting heroes. The folk museum wing – housed in the '70s-style building – displays semi-interesting antiques like an old car and fishing apparel. Outside, there's a restored boathouse, a drying shed, a church and several fishing boats, including the cutter *Sigurfari.* The museum is about 1km east of the centre, just off Garðagrund.

🛏 Sleeping

TOP CHOICE Little Guest House by the Ocean   GUESTHOUSE €
(☑695 6255; www.leopold.is/gist ing; Bakkatún 20; s/d Ikr7500/11,000; ☎) We just adore the friendly couple who run this lovely B&B. The living room is cluttered with quilts, watercolours and various works-in-progress (the owners are part-time artists), while three antique-clad guest rooms are tucked away in the basement below. Learn to make traditional Icelandic pancakes, then savour the end result in the inviting garden out back. Sleeping-bag accommodation costs Ikr4300.

Akranes HI Hostel   HOSTEL €
(☑868 3332; www.hostel.is; Suðurgata 32; dm/d Ikr3500/9200; @☎) This beautiful hostel sits along a quiet residential lane near the port. Look for the white house with 'Apotek' written across the facade – the building was once the local drugstore. Members receive a Ikr600 discount.

🍴 Eating

Despite its location in a completely nondescript commercial block, Galito (Stillholt 16-18; mains Ikr1800-3400; ☉11.30am-9pm Mon-Thu,

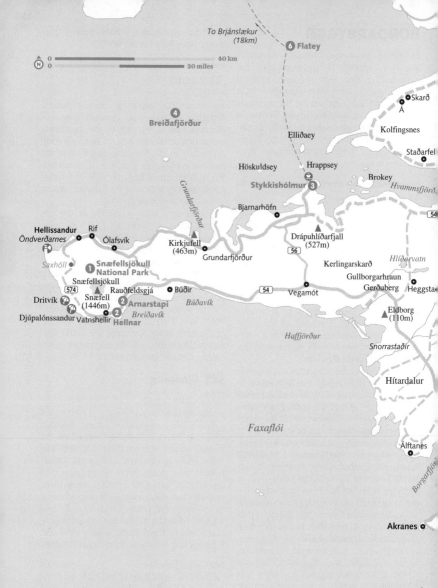

To Brjánslækur
(18km)
6 Flatey

0 ──────── 40 km
0 ──────── 20 miles

4
Breiðafjörður

Skarð
Á
Kolfingsnes
Elliðaey
Staðarfel
Höskuldsey   Hrappsey
Stykkishólmur 3   Brokey   Hvammsfjörð
Bjarnarhöfn
54
Grundarfjörður
Hellissandur Rif
Öndverðarnes
Ólafsvík
Kirkjufell   Drápuhlíðarfjall
(463m)   (527m)
Grundarfjörður   56
Kerlingarskarð   Hlíðarvatn
Saxhöll   **Snæfellsjökull**
National Park   Gullborgarhraun
Snæfellsjökull   Gerðuberg Heggsta
574   Rauðfeldsgjá   Búðir
Dritvík   Snæfell   **2 Arnarstapi**   54   Vegamót
(1446m)   Búðavík   Eldborg
Djúpalónssandur Vatnshellir   **2**   (110m)
Hellnar   Breiðavík
Haffjörður   Snorrastaðir

Hítardalur

Faxaflói
Álftanes
Borgarfjör

Akranes

REYKJAVÍK

West Iceland Highlights

1 Tramp through crunchy lava fields, then zip across windswept Snæfellsjökull, the icy heart of the magical **Snæfellsjökull National Park** (p151)

2 Follow the green carpet of velvety moss through the striking crags between **Hellnar** (p153) and **Arnarstapi** (p153)

3 Wander around charming chocolate-box houses in the harbour town of **Stykkishólmur** (p143)

Króksfjarðarnes
Efri-Brú
To Akureyri (85km)
Hvammstangi
Hrútafjörður
1

Laugar
Hvammur
Dalir
Laxá
Laxárdalur
Hjarðarholt
Búðardalur
Höskuldsstaðir
Staðarskáli
586
Stóra-Vatnshorn
Eiríksstaðir
Haukadalsá
Erpsstaðir
Haukadalur
60
Árnarvatnsheiði
Arnarvatnsheiði
Hítarvatn
Baula (934m)
1
Tvídægra
F578
Grábrók
Hraunsnef
Bifröst
Surtshellir & Stefánshellir
Viðgelmir 7
Hallmundarhraun
Munaðarnes
Fossatún
Hraunfossar
Barnafoss
50
Reykholt
518
Húsafell
Svignaskarð
Hvítá
Deildartunguhver
Ok (1190m)
Langjökull
rg á Mýrum
Kleppjárnsreykir
Borgarbyggð
Flókadalur
Kaldá
Kaldidalur
garnes
5
Hvanneyri
Þórisjökull
Hafnarfjall (666m)
50
508
52
F550
Miðsandur
F338
Akrafjall (572m)
Saurbær
Whaling Station
Grundartangi
Botnsdalur
Glymur
36
Geysir
Gulfoss
Hvalfjörður Tunnel
Múlafjall
Esja (914m)
1
Kistufell (830m)
36
37
Esjuberg
Laugarvatn
Mosfellsbær
Þingvallavatn

④ Sail past swooping puffins and ancient Viking hideouts on a breezy boat ride through the innumerable islands of **Breiðafjörður** (p143)

⑤ Step back into Saga times at the impressive Settlement Centre in **Borgarnes** (p139)

⑥ Cast away all of your cares and spend a night (or six) on the island of **Flatey** (p148)

⑦ Explore the fascinating subterranean remains of a hellish volcanic eruption at **Viðgelmir** (p142)

to 10pm Fri, 5-10pm Sat & Sun) is undoubtedly top dog if you're looking to upgrade from a petrol station wiener. Self-caterers can hit up the **Krónan** (Stillholt).

ℹ️ Information

Ask at the **tourist information centre** (www. visitakranes.is; Akratorg; ⏰10am-5pm mid-May–Aug) about the sandy beach nearby, and the rotating art exhibits in the lighthouse.

ℹ️ Getting There & Away

Akranes is part of the Reykjavík city transport area (www.straeto.is); bus 27 runs every two hours to Háholt, from where bus 57 runs to the city centre.

Borgarnes

POP 1780

Unassuming Borgarnes guards its convenient position on the Ring Road near the brooding waters of Borgarfjörður. The buzzing petrol station signs may trick you into zooming straight through, but a quick trip into the old town will reveal a lovely bucolic vibe and one of Iceland's best museums.

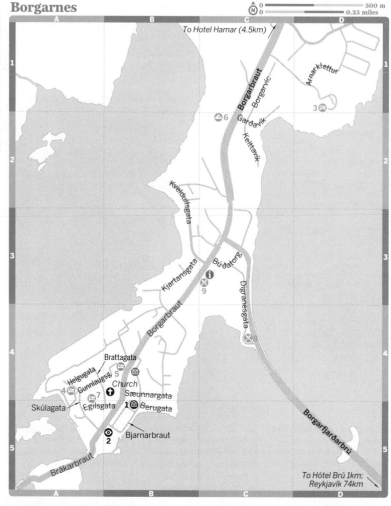

Borgarnes

0 — 500 m
0 — 0.25 miles

To Hotel Hamar (4.5km)

Borgarbraut
Borgarvík
Arnarklettur
3
Garðavík
Keldhavík
Kveldúlfsgata
Kjartansgata
Búðatorg
ℹ️ 9
Digranesgata
8
Borgarbraut
Brattagata
Helgugata 5
Gunnlaugsg 7
4
Church
Sæunnargata
Skúlagata
Egilsgata
1 Berugata
Bjarnarbraut
2
Brákarbraut

To Hótel Brú 1km;
Reykjavík 74km

◉ Sights

TOP CHOICE **Settlement Centre** MUSEUM
(Landnáms-setur Íslands; ☑437 1600; www.
landnam.is; Brákarbraut 13-15; 1 exhibition adult/
child Ikr1900/1500, 2 exhibitions Ikr2500/1900;
⊙10am-9pm Jun-Sep, 11am-5pm Oct-May)
Housed in a wonderfully restored warehouse by the harbour, the must-see Settlement Centre offers a fascinating insight into
the history of Icelandic settlement and the
Saga era. The museum is divided into two
exhibitions, one covering the discovery
and settlement of the island and the other
recounting the adventures and tales of the
man behind *Egil's Saga*. This is not your
run-of-the-mill Icelandic folk museum – the
Settlement Centre offers excellent insight
into Iceland's history and a firm context in
which to place your Icelandic visit. Included
in the price is an audio guide in a multitude
of languages; ask at the reception about discounts for families.

After visiting the museum and eating
at its top-notch restaurant, visit the large
rock *(borg)* at **Borg á Mýrum** (Rock in the
Marshes), the core location in *Egil's Saga*,
which lies just north of town on Rte 54.
The saga recounts the tale of Kveldúlfur,
grandfather of the warrior-poet Egill Skallagrímsson, who fled to Iceland during
the 9th century after a falling out with the
king of Norway. Kveldúlfur grew gravely ill
on the journey, however, and instructed his
son, Skallagrímur Kveldúlfsson, to throw his
coffin overboard after he died and build the
family farm wherever it washed ashore –
this just happened to be at Borg. Egill Skallagrímsson grew up to be a bloodthirsty

individual who killed his first adversary at
the age of seven and went on to carry out
numerous raids on the coast of England.

The Settlement Centre has marked eight
additional sites featured in *Egil's Saga*,
including **Skallagrímsgarður**, the burial
mound of the father and son of saga hero
Egill Skallagrímsson. Check out the website
for more information – or ask at the ticket
counter about the free iPad apps.

TOP CHOICE **Borgarfjördur Museum** MUSEUM
(☑430 7200; www.safnahus.is; Bjarnarbraut 4-6;
adult/child Ikr800/free; ⊙1-5pm Jun-Aug, reduced
hours Sep-May) This small municipal museum
has one exhibit: the story of children in Iceland over the last 100 years as told through
myriad photographs and found items. We
don't want to give too much away, but don't
be shy about having someone from the museum show you through – the story behind
each photograph is captivating and the cura-
tion sublime. You'll be thinking about this
exhibit long after your trip to Iceland, we
guarantee it.

🛏 Sleeping

The following options represent but a smattering of choices in the area. Stop by the
information centre for a supplemental list,
or try browsing the ubiquitous *Áning* guide.
There's a **campsite** (sites per person Ikr750)
on the main road, though there are enough
budget options in the area that it's worth
making the price jump to accommodation
with walls.

Bjarg GUESTHOUSE €
(☑437 1925; bjarg@simnet.is; d Ikr13,300) One of
the nicer places to stay in the area, this attractive farmhouse overlooking the fjord has
warm, cosy rooms with tasteful wood panel-
ling and crisp white linens. There's a shared
guest kitchen, a BBQ, spotless bathrooms
and a turf-roofed cottage that sleeps four
(Ikr28,900; our favourite!).

Borgarnes B&B B&B €
(☑842 5866; www.borgarnesbb.is; Skúlagata 21;
s/d incl breakfast Ikr11,300/14,900; @⍟) Antique
wooden doors, modern fixtures and generous coats of white paint put this charming
guesthouse near the top of our list. Go for
one of the two rooms on the ground floor
(the rest are in the basement) that have fab
views of the bay out back. Included in the
price is a gut-busting buffet-style breakfast
of Icelandic faves.

WEST ICELAND BORGARNES

Ensku Húsin
GUESTHOUSE €€

(☎437 1826; www.enskuhusin.is; d with/without bathroom Ikr18,900/15,500; ☎) Located 8km north of central Borgarnes, this old lodge has been stripped to its original paint and refitted with generous coats of old-school charm. The upstairs rooms retain much of the long-ago feel, while a new motel block extending from the cosy den is much more '70s-retro. Additional accommodation is in a restored farmhouse about 2km down the road. The friendly owners are ready at a moment's notice to attend to any whim.

Hotel Hamar
HOTEL €€

(☎433 6600; www.icehotels.is; Golfvöllurinn; d May-Sep Ikr27,600, Oct-Apr Ikr11,000-14,700; @☎) We found the prefab exterior to be slightly off-putting, but surprisingly sleek decor and a cache of mod cons hide within. Hamar sits on a well-maintained golf course flanked by snowy peaks in the distance.

Hótel Brú
HOTEL €

(☎437 2345; www.hotelbru.is; d incl breakfast Ikr10,500; ☎) What happens when an eager entrepreneur takes over a rather forlorn-looking property? He turns it into the little hotel that could – friendly staff, a great dinner buffet, Northern Lights wake-up calls and a price point that undercuts the competition is the secret recipe that makes Hótel Brú a worthy option in our book.

Hótel Borgarnes
HOTEL €€

(☎437 1117; www.hotelborgarnes.is; Egilsgata 12-14; s/d incl breakfast Ikr18,900/28,700; ☺Apr-Nov; @☎) Large and characterless, Hótel Borgarnes has boring business-style rooms that are largely the domain of package tourists.

Borgarnes HI Hostel
HOSTEL €

(☎695 3366; www.hostel.is; Borgarbraut 9-13; dm/d Ikr3500/9000; @☎) This no-frills sleeping spot across from the post office gets the job done; despite the Lissitzky-esque murals and African masks on the cinder-block walls, it all feels very much like a high school dorm. Members receive a Ikr600 discount.

✗ Eating

For the usual array of burgers, fried chicken and doughy pizza, try the grill bar at the N1 petrol station. Self-caterers should head to the **Bónus supermarket** (Borgarbraut 57) at the edge of the fjord bridge coming into town. There's a branch of **Vín Búð** (Hyrnu Torg centre) on the main road.

TOP CHOICE Settlement
Centre Restaurant
INTERNATIONAL €€

(☎437 1600; Brákarbraut 13; mains Ikr2200-4500; ☺10am-9pm Jun-Sep, 11am-9pm Oct-May) After reliving Egil's adventures, continue the sensorial journey back through time at the Settlement Centre's restaurant – one of Borgarnes' best bets for food. Choose from an assortment of traditional Icelandic and international eats (lamb, fish stew etc) then flip to the back of the menu and read up on the history of the town's oldest buildings (including the one you're sitting in!). The lunch buffet (Ikr1890) is very popular with museum visitors; it's best to call ahead and reserve a table for dinner.

TOP CHOICE Fish Buffet at Hótel Brú
SEAFOOD €€

(buffet Ikr2900; ☺7-10pm) Been in Iceland for a while, but still have several fish to check off your tasting list? Hótel Brú's tasty buffet offers up the best of Iceland with handy photographic cue cards so you know what you're eating. Reasonable prices and succulent marinades make it a healthy rival for the Settlement Centre's restaurant.

❶ Getting There & Away

All buses between Reykjavík and Akureyri, Snæfellsnes and the Westfjords stop near the cluster of petrol stations at the fjord bridge. In winter, high winds rolling in off the Atlantic can close the southern approach to town. Borgarnes is one hour from Reykjavík.

Upper Borgarfjörður
REYKHOLT

Laid-back, postcard pretty and incredibly unassuming, Reykholt is a sleepy kind of place that on first glance offers few clues to its bustling past as one of the most important medieval settlements in Iceland.

To get some insight into the significance of the area, visit the fascinating medieval study centre **Snorrastofa** (☎433 8000; www.reykholt.is, www.snorrastofa.is; admission Ikr1000; ☺10am-6pm May-Aug, to 5pm Mon-Fri Sep-Apr), devoted to the celebrated medieval historian Snorri Sturluson. The displays here explain the laws, literature, society and way of life in medieval Iceland. The main exhibit features information about the life of Snorri and the times in which he lived. Information about the excavations in the region during the 1990s is also available. Ask to see the beautiful reading room upstairs if you're interested in thumbing through a complete collection of academic works on the sagas.

The on-site church features beautiful stained glass, an early Lutheran baptismal font and an organ that was originally built for Reykjavík's modernist cathedral – it was moved here in 1984. If you're visiting in late July, look out for information on the annual classical-music festival – the acoustics in the church are brilliant.

Further on, you'll come to Snorralaug (Snorri's Pool), a circular, stone-lined pool fed by a hot spring. The stones at the base of the pool are original, and it is believed that this is where Snorri came to bathe. The wood-panelled tunnel beside the spring leads to the old farmhouse – the site of Snorri's gruesome murder. The pool is apparently the oldest manmade structure in Iceland.

The Reykholt area (about 5km before Snorrastofa) is also home to Europe's biggest hot spring, Deildartunguhver, where billowing clouds of steam rise up as scalding water bubbles up from the ground (180L per second!) A take-and-pay tomato stall is usually set up in the parking lot – the tomatoes are grown in a nearby greenhouse that harnesses the spring's natural power.

The only accommodation in Reykholt proper is Fosshótel Reykholt (☑435 1260, 562 4000; www.fosshotel.is; s/d incl breakfast Ikr24,900/26,500; ☎). Housed in a modern block behind the old church, this well-equipped link in the Fosshótel chain has businesslike rooms and a couple of 'wellness' hot-pots (which were out of order when we stayed here). The hotel's mediocre restaurant (mains Ikr2990 to Ikr4190) is the only one around, although the nearby petrol station sells sandwiches in summer.

Refer to the handy *The Ideal Holiday* farmstay brochure for sleeping options scattered across the arable lands further afield, or try Fossatún (☑433 5800; www.fossatun.is; sites per person Ikr1000, d incl breakfast Ikr12,900; ☺Jun-Aug; @☎) located on Rte 50 between Borgarnes and Reykholt. This family-friendly spot has camping grounds aplenty next to a beautiful waterfall, and a small guesthouse to rest your head. Minigolf and a playground keep things kid-focused (the owner is a well-known children's book author), while the on-site cafe (mains from Ikr1400) features an amazing record collection (3000 and counting; you can play 'em) geared towards adults.

Reykholt is 40km northeast of Borgarnes along Rte 518. Buses from Reykjavík leave at 5pm on Friday and Sunday. In the opposite direction, the bus leaves Reykholt at 7.10pm.

HÚSAFELL

Tucked between the river Kaldá and a desolate lava field, the campus of cottages at Húsafell is a popular outdoor retreat for Reykjavík residents. The leisure complex Ferðaþjónustan Húsafelli (☑435 1550; www.husafell.is; site/hut per person Ikr1200/3000) is a one-stop shop, with campsite, cabin

WEST ICELAND UPPER BORGARFJÖRÐUR

SNORRI STURLUSON

The chieftain and historian Snorri Sturluson is one of the most important figures in medieval Norse history – partly because he wrote a lot of it down himself. Snorri was born at Hvammur near Búðardalur (further north), but he was raised and educated at the theological centre of Oddi near Hella and later married the heir to the farm Borg near Borgarnes. For reasons not fully revealed, he abandoned his family at Borg and retreated to the wealthy church estate at Reykholt. At the time, Reykholt was home to 60,000 to 80,000 people and was an important trade centre at the crossroads of major routes across the country. Snorri composed many of his most famous works at Reykholt, including *Prose Edda* (a textbook to medieval Norse poetry) and *Heimskringla* (a history of the kings of Norway). Snorri is also widely believed to be the hand behind *Egil's Saga*, a family history of Viking *skald* (court poet) Egill Skallagrímsson (see p139).

At the age of 36 Snorri was appointed *lögsögumaður* (law speaker) of the Alþing (Icelandic parliament), but he endured heavy pressure from the Norwegian king to promote the king's private interests at the parliament. Instead, Snorri busied himself with his writing and the unhappy Norwegian king Hákon issued a warrant for his capture – dead or alive. Snorri's political rival and former son-in-law Gissur Þorvaldsson saw his chance to impress the king and possibly snag the position of governor of Iceland in return. He arrived in Reykholt with 70 armed men on the night of 23 September 1241 and hacked the historian to death in the basement of his home.

accommodation, restaurant and outdoor geothermal swimming pool.

Icelandic artist Páll Guðmundsson – best known for collaborating with Sigur Rós – has a sculpture studio in Húsafell. Keep an eye out for his striking black silo and odd hobbit-house-like storage shed. There's a small **sculpture garden** to peruse when the reclusive artist is not in the studio.

Once based near Mýrdalsjökull in the southwest, **Dogsledding.is** (☑487 7747; www.dogsledding.is) now runs tours on nearby Langjökull.

There's no public transport to Húsafell, but twice a week you can get as far as Reykholt from Reykjavík. Hitch or organise a car share in advance on www.semferda.net from there to Húsafell.

AROUND HÚSAFELL

HALLMUNDARHRAUN (FLJÓTSTUNGA)

East of Húsafell, along Rte 518, the vast, barren lava flows of Hallmundarhraun make up an eerie landscape dotted with gigantic lava tubes. These long, tunnel-like caves are formed by flows of molten lava beneath a solid lava crust, and they look as though they've been burrowed out by some hellish giant worm.

[TOP CHOICE] **Fljótstunga** (☺865 4060; www.fljot stunga.is; admission Ikr2500; ☺May-Sep) offers 90-minute tours of the easiest lava tube to visit, the 1.5km-long **Viðgelmir**, located on private property near the farmstead (follow the signs for Fljótstunga). The owner and his friendly family run the tours four times a day during the peak season (10am, noon, 3pm and 5pm); all caving gear is included in the price, and extended tours are available for real geological enthusiasts. Accommodation is available at the farm in a series of lovely little cabins (Ikr5000 to Ikr17,000 depending on occupancy). They are exceptional value considering the wild location and rustic charm. Camping on the property is also permitted (Ikr1000 per person; hot showers included).

As Rte 518 begins to loop back around, a bright yellow sign marks the turn-off to Arnarvatnsheiði along Rte F578. Make the turn (2WDs can do it too – just take it slow) and follow the bumpy track for 7km until you reach **Surtshellir**, a dramatic, 2km-long lava tube connected to **Stefánshellir**, a second tunnel about half the size. It is possible to explore Surtshellir on your own – you'll need good shoes, a torch and (prefer-

ably) a hard hat. You can rent any necessary caving equipment (Ikr1000) from the folks at Fljótstunga.

Keep an eye out for the cairn markings, or try the **travel service** (☑435 1550) at Húsafell for updates on possible tours. If you've got a 4WD, it's possible to continue beyond Surtshellir along the 'L-shaped Rte F578 through the lakes at **Arnarvatnsheiði** and on to Hvammstangi. Note that Rte F578 is usually only open for seven weeks each year; see www.vegagerdin.

KALDIDALUR CORRIDOR

Southeast of Húsafell, the Kaldidalur valley skirts the edge of a series of glaciers offering incredible views of the Langjökull ice cap and, in clear weather, the snows of Eiríksjökull, Okjökull and Þórisjökull. The Kaldidalur corridor, also known as the unsurfaced Rte 550, links to the Golden Circle (p95), offering tourists the option to create an extended day trip from Reykjavík. Access to Rte 550 is limited to sanctioned vehicles – ask at your rental outfit before setting off.

SNÆFELLSNES PENINSULA

Lush fjords, haunting volcanic peaks, dramatic sea cliffs, sweeping golden beaches and crooked crunchy lava flows make up the diverse and fascinating landscape of the 100km-long Snæfellsnes Peninsula. The area is crowned by the glistening ice cap Snæfellsjökull, immortalised in Jules Verne's fantasy tale *Journey to the Centre of the Earth*. Good roads and regular buses mean that it's an easy trip from Reykjavík and ideal for a short break, offering a cross-section of the best Iceland has to offer in a very compact region.

Our Snæfellsnes section begins in Stykkishólmur on the populated northern coast. It's the region's largest town and a logical base for exploring the peninsula. From there we move west along the northern shoreline, passing several smaller townships before circling around the glacier (the heart of Snæfellsjökull National Park) and returning along the quieter southern coast. The peninsula is best explored by private vehicle, though buses do pass through during summer; day trips from Reykjavík (see the boxed text, p58) are a possibility for those who are short on time.

Stykkishólmur

POP 1100

The charming town of Stykkishólmur, the largest on the Snæfellsnes Peninsula, is built up around a natural harbour protected by a dramatic basalt island. It's a picturesque place with a laid-back attitude and a sprinkling of brightly coloured buildings from the late 19th century. With a comparatively good choice of accommodation and restaurants, and convenient transport links, quaint Stykkishólmur makes an excellent base for exploring the region.

Sights & Activities

TOP CHOICE Breiðafjörður   BAY

Stykkishólmur's jagged peninsula pushes north into stunning Breiðafjörður, a gaping waterway (*breiðafjörður* means 'broad fjord') separating the torpedo-shaped Snæfellsnes from the looming cliffs of the distant Westfjords. According to local legend, there are only two things in the world that cannot be counted: the stars in the night sky and the craggy islets in the bay. Despite the numerical setback, those who visit beautiful Breiðafjörður *can* count on epic vistas – idyllic tapestries of greens and blues – and its menagerie of wild birds (puffins, eagles, guillemots etc). See p144 for information on tours of the bay; Hótel Framnes (☑438 6893; www.hotelframnes.is) in Grundarfjörður also runs boat trips, as do outfitters such as Eyjasigling (☑849 6748; www.eyjasigling.is) in Reykhólar in the Westfjords.

Try mounting the basalt island of Súgandisey, which features a scenic lighthouse and offers grand views across Breiðafjörður. You can get to the island by walking across the stone causeway from the harbour. If you have your own wheels, the broad fjord is best appreciated from the south coast of the Westfjords or between the two lonely churches on Rte 54 that heads west into town.

Eldfjallasafn   MUSEUM

(Volcano Museum; ☑433 8154; www.eldfjallasafn.is; Aðalgata 6; admission Ikr800; ⊙11am-5pm May-Sep) Get the backstory on the neighbouring lava flows at the Volcano Museum, housed in the town's old cinema. The brainchild of vulcanologist Haraldur Sigurðsson, the museum features art and artefacts relating to the study of eruptions and their devastating effects – including 'magma bombs' from the Eyjafjallajökull eruption in 2010. Haraldur himself is sometimes hangin' around offering additional titbits from his 40 years in the field. Ask about the geologically themed day trips (eight hours; Ikr20,000), which circle the peninsula.

Norska Húsið   MUSEUM

(Norwegian House; ☑433 8114; www.norkshusid.is; Hafnargata 5; admission Ikr800; ⊙noon-5pm Jun-Aug) Stykkishólmur's quaint maritime charm comes from the cluster of wooden warehouses, stores and homes orbiting the town's harbour. Most date back about 150 years and many are still in use. One of the most interesting buildings (and the oldest) is the Norska Húsið, now the municipal museum. Built by trader Árni Thorlacius in 1832, the house has been skilfully restored and displays a wonderfully eclectic selection of local antiques. On the 2nd floor you can see the typical layout of an upper-class home in 19th-century Iceland – it was Árni's home, and is decked out in his original wares.

Stykkishólmskirkja   CHURCH

(☑438 1288; ⊙10am-5pm) Looking decidedly out of place among the clutter of quaint houses, Stykkishólmur's futuristic church is a striking white structure with a sweeping bell tower that looks like a ship's vent or a giant vertebra – it's most striking from the side vantage point. The interior features hundreds of suspended lights and a large painting of the Mother and Child floating in the night sky. Enthusiasts of oddball architecture will be glad to know that there are heaps of funky churches throughout Iceland (see p19).

Library of Water   MUSEUM

(Vatnasafn; ☑857 1221; www.libraryofwater.is; Bókhlöðustígur 17; admission Ikr500; ⊙1-6pm Jun-Aug) For relaxing views of the town and the bay, head up the hill to the Library of Water. Housed in the old municipal library, this hallowed space flooded by natural light features a permanent exhibit by noted American artist Roni Horn. Twenty-four glass pillars are scattered throughout the room, each one filled to the brim with locally sourced glacier water. Light is reflected and refracted through the aqueous tubes, and adjectives in both English and Icelandic are inscribed into the delicate floor. It's the perfect place to curl up with your journal or play a game of chess (provided); just don't forget to take off your shoes. Although the space is closed during

WEST ICELAND STYKKISHÓLMUR

Snæfellsnes Peninsula

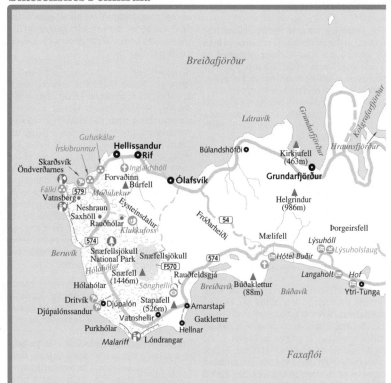

Breiðafjörður

Látravík

Grundarfjörður

Kolgrafarfjörður

Gufuskálar

Hellissandur
Rif

Búlandshöfði

Kirkjufell
(463m)

Hraunsfjörður

Írskibrunnur

Skarðsvík
Öndverðarnes

Forvaðinn
Ingjaldshóll

Ólafsvík

Grundarfjörður

Fálkí 579
Vatnsborg

Búrfell

Helgrindur
(986m)

Móðulækur

Neshraun
Saxhóll
Rauðhólar

Eysteinsdalur

Fróðárheiði

54

Þorgeirsfell

Mælifell

Lýsuhóll

Lýsuhólslaug

Klukkufoss

Beruvík 574

Snæfellsjökull
National Park

Snæfellsjökull

574

Hótel Búðir

Hólahólar

Snæfell ▲
(1446m)

F570

Rauðfeldsgjá

Langaholt

Hof

Hólahólar

Sönghellir

Breiðavík

Búðaklettur
(88m)

Búðavík

Ytri-Tunga

Dritvík
Djúpalónssandur

Djúpalón

Stapafell
(526m)

Arnarstapi

Vatnshellir

Gatklettur

Purkhólar

Hellnar

Malarif

Lóndrangar

Faxaflói

---

the colder months, travellers can arrange a visit via email or phone.

Sundlaug Stykkishóms GEOTHERMAL POOL
(adult/child Ikr500/180; ⏰7.05am-10pm Mon-Thu, to 7pm Fri, to 6pm Sat & Sun Jun-Aug, reduced hours Sep-May) Try the tangle of water slides or one of the soothing hot-pots at the town's geothermal swimming pool located in the municipal sports complex. If you're lucky, you might catch the local basketball team (Iceland's best) practising their tricks.

🐾 Tours

Seatours BOAT TOUR
(Sæferðir; ☑438 2254; www.seatours.is; Smiðjustígur 3; ⏰8am-8pm mid-May–mid-Sep, 9am-5pm mid-Sep–mid-May) Seatours runs a variety of boat tours, its main trip being the 'Unique Tour' – a 2¼-hour boat ride (adult/child Ikr6690/free), which takes in postcard-worthy views of the bay and its myriad islands. Kodak moments abound as the boat

passes colonies of puffins and eagles, and haunting basalt formations (listen out for the gruesome legend of 'hanging rock'!). Towards the end of the trip a net is lowered into the sea, and up comes wiggly shellfish ready to be devoured raw (absolutely delish – we promise). There's an abridged version targeted to children that departs once daily in the warmer months, and three times a week there's a 'taste of Iceland' dinner cruise (Ikr8750).

Seatours also runs the *Baldur* ferry to Flatey, which makes an excellent excursion in itself. See p148 for more information; the ride takes 1.5 hours to reach the small island.

Ocean Safari BOAT TOUR
(☑820 0350; www.oceansafari.is; tour Ikr8900; ⏰Apr-Sep) Joining the Zodiac craze that has taken Iceland's adventure scene by storm, Ocean Safari offers RIB (rigid inflatable boat) tours of the beautiful bay. As the boats are quite small, it is possible to zoom up close to

the fjord's islets to check out the local colonies of birds and seals. Tours are around two hours and depart at 10am and 2pm; from June to August there's a third trip at 8pm as well. Custom tours are also available for those who want to disembark on one of the small islands for some serious birding (prices start at Ikr50,000 for the captained boat).

★ Festivals & Events

If you're passing through the area during the third weekend in August, you'll be treated to festive bridge dancing and a bevy of live bands during Stykkishólmur's annual **Danish Days** ('Danskir dagar' in Icelandic) – an event that pays tribute to the town's Danish roots.

🛌 Sleeping

Stykkishólmur could fill a phonebook with the names of locals renting out rooms during summer – either as a guesthouse or apartment stay. This is a good time to make use of those accommodation brochures – like *Áning* or *The Ideal Holiday* farmstay booklet – that you've been carrying around; the *Stykkishólmur Simply Spectacular* brochure has a lengthy list of sleeping options as well. Camping is available at the golf course; however, our readers have reviewed it negatively. Travellers also love to comment about Stykkishólmur's B&B scene on Tripadvisor (www.tripadvisor.com), making it another reasonable resource.

TOP
CHOICE **Hótel Egilsen**   BOUTIQUE HOTEL €€

(☑554 7700; www.egilsen.is; Aðalgata 2; s/d Ikr19,000/25,000; @🛜) Bold statement alert: this might just be our favourite little inn in all of Iceland. The boutique-iest boutique hotel around, Hótel Egilsen lives inside a lovingly restored timber house that creeks in the most charming way when the fjord winds come howling off the bay. Follow the yellow stairwell up to find cosy (tiny!) rooms outfitted in adorable accoutrements that would have Martha Stewart giving jealous glares. Complimentary iPads and a locally sourced breakfast sweeten the already-sweet deal.

Bænir og Brauð   B&B €

(☑820 5408; www.baenirogbraud.is; Laufásvegur 1; d Ikr14,200-16,200; @🛜) A fine example of Stykkishólmur's quality B&B scene, this homely spot sits along the fjord waters with lovely views of the modernist church. Greta, the kindly owner, keeps herself extra busy with many pet projects, including the gorgeous Hótel Egilsen down the road.

Hótel Stykkishólmur   HOTEL €

(☑430 2100; www.hringhotels.is; Borgarbraut 8; s/d incl breakfast Ikr21,000/24,000; ⊙Apr-Sep; @🛜) Set away from the harbour up on a hill, this boxy hotel feels almost as out of place as the modern church nearby. Rooms are spread across two wings – the old hall has the views, but the newer annexe has modern furnishings. The 'old wing' was under renovation at the time of research, promising a fresher face for future guests.

Hótel Breiðafjörður   HOTEL €€

(☑433 2200; www.hotelbreidafjordur.is; Aðalgata 8; s/d €90/140; ⊙May-Sep; @🛜) Lacking any discernible character whatsoever, this is where you'll end up if all of the two-room guesthouses are full. Rooms are clean with faux-wood finishes; the hotel also manages

Stykkishólmur

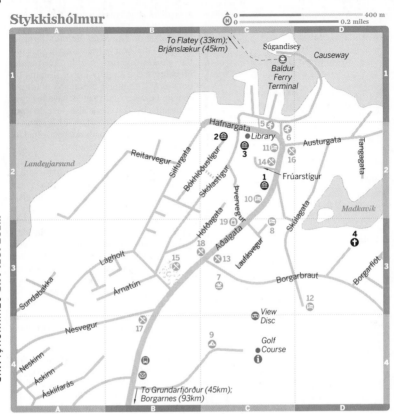

a ramshackle house with dorm rooms a couple of blocks away.

✖ Eating

You'll be spoilt for choice in Stykkishólmur; self-caterers can make full use of the Bónus supermarket near the swimming pool. The local Vín Búð is across the main road from the Bónus.

TOP
CHOICE **Narfeyrarstofa** ICELANDIC €€€
(☑438 1119; Aðalgata 3; mains Ikr1990-4250; ⊙11.30am-10pm Apr–mid-Oct, 6pm-10pm Sat & Sun mid-Oct–Mar) If we handed out prizes for the best fish soup and the top lamb stew, this charming restaurant would win both. Run by an award-winning chef (famous in Denmark for his superlative desserts – the caramel ice cream is for fainting), Narfeyrarstofa is the Snæfellsnes' darling dining destination and the undoubted favourite of visiting tour groups. Book a table on the 2nd

floor and dine under gentle eaves and the romantic lighting of antique lamps. Don't forget to ask your waiter about the portraits on the wall – the building has quite an interesting history.

Sjávarpakkhúsið ICELANDIC €€
(Hafnargata 2; mains Ikr1890-2950; ⊙noon-10pm Jun-Aug, reduced hours Sep-May) Owned by the folks at Ocean Safari (and used as their ticketing office), this old fishing packinghouse has been transformed into a harbourside restaurant with appealing outdoor seating in warmer weather. The speciality here is the blue shell mussels straight from the bay out back. In the evenings it's popular with locals who come to pound out tunes on the in-house piano – search for the restaurant on Facebook to find a crude calendar of events.

Meistarinn FAST FOOD €
(Aðalgata; mains from Ikr800 ⊙noon-8pm Jun-Aug) Skip the greasy grill at the local petrol

Stykkishólmur

station and swing by this friendly *pýlsuvagninn* (wiener wagon) for the best hot dogs in town. It's a great spot to up your caloric intake, especially if you missed the ubiquitous *pýlsur* stands in Reykjavík. Fun fact: each item on the menu is named after a person in town – especially the local sports stars.

Nesbraud BAKERY €
(☏438 1830; Nesvegur 1; snacks from Ikr195; ☺8am-6pm) At the crossroads on the way out of town, this small bakery is a good choice for a budget-friendly breakfast or lunch. Stock up on sugary confections like *kleinur* (traditional twisty doughnuts) or *ástar pungur* (literally 'love balls'; fried balls of dough and raisins).

Fimm Fiskar ICELANDIC €€€
(Frúarstígur 1; mains Ikr1800-5000; ☺11am-11pm) The Five Fishes is housed in a chalet-style abode just up the street from Narfeyrarstofa, its main competition. Fresh seafood is the headliner – overall it's a solid choice if the 'N-word' is full.

🛍 Shopping

In the last few years, Stykkishólmur has attracted several artists who have set up small galleries along the harbourside streets. It's well worth checking out **Leir 7** (www.leir7.is; ☺2-5pm), a working pottery studio in the heart of town where artist Sigríður Erla produces tableware from the dark clay in the nearby fjord.

ℹ Information

The town's **tourist information centre** (☺8am-10pm Jun-Aug; 🛜) changes location every summer depending on municipal funding. At the time of research it was located at the golf course, though in years past it has also been found at the swimming pool. Wherever it may be located during your visit, expect a plethora of brochures and assistance with guesthouse accommodation bookings in the area.

ℹ Getting There & Away

Boat
The car ferry **Baldur** (☏438 1450; www.seatours.is) operates between Stykkishólmur and Brjánslækur in the Westfjords (three hours), via Flatey. From the second weekend in June to the fourth weekend in August there are daily departures from Stykkishólmur at 9am and 3.15pm, returning from Brjánslækur at 12.15pm and 7pm. During the rest of the year there is only one ferry per day, leaving Stykkishólmur at 3pm (no boats on Saturdays), returning at 6pm, and often not stopping in Flatey at all. Adult fares to Brjánslækur are Ikr4950 (Ikr3640 low season), vehicles cost an additional Ikr4950. A round-trip ticket from Stykkishólmur to Flatey costs Ikr6760. Check the website for complicated concession fares.

Bus
There are at least two daily buses running to/from Reykjavík (2½ hours) from mid-June to August. One daily bus continues out of season except on Wednesday and Saturday. To reach town, you must get off at the Vatnaleið stop and switch to reach Stykkishólmur. Buses also link Vatnaleið to Grundarfjörður, Ólafsvík and Hellissandur. Services from Vatnaleið don't always link well with the *Baldur* ferry.

Stykkishólmur to Grundarfjörður

The scenic stretch of land between Stykkishólmur and Grundarfjörður is filled with myth and mystique. About 5km south of Stykkishólmur is the holy mountain

WORTH A TRIP

FLATEY

Of Breiðafjörður's innumerable islands, Flatey (literally 'flat island') is the only one with year-round inhabitants: two families embroiled in an age-old feud that rivals the Capulets and Montagues. In the 11th century, Flatey was home to a literary monastery, and today the charming island is a popular layover for travellers heading to (or from) the West-fjords. Push the slo-mo button on life, and enjoy a windswept afternoon amid brightly coloured catalogue houses and swooping Arctic terns.

If you are crossing Breiðafjörður aboard the *Baldur* ferry and would like to have a look around the island, you must take the first ferry of the day, disembark, and board the second daily ferry to your final destination (boats only pause on the island for around five minutes as they cross the fjord). For those travelling by car, it is possible to send your vehicle across the bay (at no additional charge) while staying behind in Flatey. If you want to visit Flatey as a mini day trip from Stykkishólmur, you can take either boat during summer, disembark at Flatey for around two hours and catch the ferry on the flip side as it returns to Stykkishómur after dropping off passengers in the Westfjords. Note that the twice-per-day ferry service only runs from the second weekend in June to the fourth weekend in August (boats only run once a day out of season; note that there is no service on Saturdays).

Hótel Flatey (☑555 7788; www.hotelflatey.is; s/d Ikr19,900/23,900; ☺Jun–late-Aug) has some of the most charming nooklike rooms in all of Iceland, and the on-site **restaurant** (3-course menu Ikr7500-8500; ☺10.30am-9pm) is fantastic as well. On weekends, slip down into the basement for live evening jam sessions with some of the locals. Penny-pinchers can pitch a tent at **Krákuvör** (☑438 1451; sites per person Ikr1000, apt Ikr12,000-14,000) or stay at **Læknishús** (☑438 1476; s/apt Ikr4000/18,000) in summer – both are within 400m of the pier on the way to Hótel Flatey.

Helgafell (73m), once venerated by worshippers of the god Þór. Although quite small, the mountain was so sacred in Saga times that elderly Icelanders would seek out the hill near the time of their death. Today, locals believe that wishes are granted to those who climb the mount. In the late 10th century, Snorri Goði, a prominent Þor worshipper, converted to Christianity and built a church at the top of the hill. The church ruins are still prominent in the terrain. The nearby farm of the same name was where the conniving Guðrun Ósvífursdóttir of the *Laxdæla Saga* lived out her later years in isolation. Her grave marks the base of the mount.

About 15km west of the intersection of Rte 54 and Rte 58 (the road to Stykkishólmur) lies the extra-spiky lava field at **Berserkjahraun** (Berserkers' lava field). Crowned by looming mountains, this lunar landscape gets its name from the *Eyrbyggja Saga*. Those with a little extra time on their hands will enjoy the winding drive along the 2WD-friendly Rte 558. Known as **Bersekjahraunsvegur** (try saying that three times fast!), this scenic stretch ambles through an endless expanse of charcoal blacks, sulphur yellows and mossy greens. Pick a flat patch and pitch a tent – not only is this a prime spot for **wilderness camping**, it's one of the region's best-kept secrets (until now!). If you're looking for a bit of comfort, there are a few lodging options in the area as well.

On the northeastern edge of Berserkjahraun is the farmstead at **Bjarnarhöfn** (☑438 1581; www.bjarnarhofn.is; museum admission Ikr800; ☺9am-8pm) – a must for every traveller with a taste for adventure (literally). Smell that? Yup, it's rotting shark flesh – the farm is the region's leading producer of *hákarl* (putrid shark meat), a traditional Icelandic dish. The on-site museum details the fragrant history of this culinary curiosity by displaying restored shark fishing boats and harpooning tools, and explaining the fermenting process. Each visit to the museum comes with a complimentary nibble of the delicacy in question, along with a piece of rye bread to wash it down. Some say it tastes like a sponge dipped in ammonia; we thought it was somewhat similar to old cheese. Before you leave, ask about the drying house out back. If you're lucky, you'll see hundreds of dangling shark slices being attacked by zealous flies (you'll be glad you tried the shark meat *before* visiting the drying house!). To reach the farm, follow the signposts down a series of paved and gravel roads leading away from Rte 54. You'll see a large iron shark marking the turn-off.

Grundarfjörður

POP 910

Spectacularly set on a dramatic bay, little Grundarfjörður is surrounded by sugar-loaf peaks often shrouded in wispy, cotton-puff fog. Preferring prefab to wooden construction, the town feels like a typical Icelandic fishing community, but the tourist facilities are good and the surrounding landscape can't be beat.

A tourist information office, cafe, internet point and heritage museum all rolled into one, the Saga Centre (Eyrbyggja Heritage Centre; ✆438 1881; www.grundarfjordur.is; Grundargata 35; ⊙10am-6pm mid-May–mid-Sep; @☎) is a must for every visitor. Sip a fresh double latte while chatting with the friendly employees, update your blog (internet Ikr200 for 15 minutes), and check out the museum's detailed exhibits (free admission) about the town's French-influenced history and the advent of the boat engine. The museum also features a life-sized model of a turn-of-the-century Icelandic home. You'll be shocked to learn that this bite-size abode would sleep around eight people. Icelandic films and photo slideshows often play in the on-site screening room.

In summer, it'll be hard to tear yourself away from Grundarfjörður without ascending the majestic Kirkjufell (463m), guardian of the town's northern vista. Ask the Saga Centre to hook you up with a guide (around €30 per guide) – three spots involving a rope climb make it dangerous to scale the mountain without assistance. The whole adventure should take no more than four hours.

☞ Tours

Láki Tours   WILDLIFE TOUR
(✆438 6893; www.lakitours.com) Run by the owners of Hótel Framnes, Láki Tours specialises in '3-in-1' trips (whale spotting, birdwatching and fishing) during summer. Tours last for around three hours and run at 10am, 2pm and 8pm with a minimum of four people (Ikr6900). We highly recommend its two-hour orca-viewing trip from January to mid-March (Ikr6500) – dress warmly!

🛏 Sleeping

Refer to the handy *Ideal Holiday* brochure for sleeping options sca the nearby headlands. The following are the most viable options in town.

Hótel Framnes   HOTEL €€
(✆438 6893; www.hotelframnes.is; Nesvegur 8; s/d incl breakfast €100/139; @☎) This comfy dockside inn has a spacious lobby and top-floor rooms nestled under eaved roofs. The owners run a small tour company as well as the in-house restaurant (mains Ikr3900 to Ikr4800) that opens every evening to serve the daily catch.

Grundarfjörður HI Hostel   HOSTEL €
(✆562 6533; grundarfjordur@hostel.is; www.hostel.is; Hlíðarvegur 15; dm/d Ikr4000/9500; @☎) Not just a hostel, Grundarfjörður's contribution to the budget category features everything from prim dorm rooms to smart, apartment-style lodging. Reception is in the red house, at the listed address – accommodation is spread across several buildings in town. Members get a Ikr600 discount.

🍴 Eating

Compared to Stykkishólmur's many options, Grundarfjörður's eating scene is in a sad state of affairs. Your best bet is to eat at Hótel Framnes, or try Kaffi 59 (Grundargata

WORTH A TRIP

WISHING AT HELGAFELL

It is commonly believed that those who ascend humble Helgafell (p147) will be granted three wishes, provided that the requests are made with a pure heart. However, it isn't as simple as merely climbing the hill and thinking happy thoughts. You must follow three important steps in order to make your wishes come true:

Step 1: Start at the marked grave of Guðrún Ósvífursdóttir, heroine of an ancient local saga.

Step 2: Walk up to the Tótt (the chapel ruins) never uttering a single word, and (like Orpheus leaving Hades), never looking back along the way.

Step 3: Once at the chapel ruins, you must turn and face east while wishing. And remember – never tell your wishes to anyone or they won't come true.

≈; mains Ikr1800-3100; ⊙10am-11pm Mon-Thu, to 1am Fri, 11am-1am Sat, 11am-11pm Sun; 🛜) – a well-worn joint with pizza, sandwiches, ice-cream sundaes and beer, served up in a crumby (both meanings) diner-style building by the main road through town. There's also a Meistarinn hot dog wagon, where the menu items are named after members of the Danish royal family. There's a small **supermarket** (⊙9am-10pm Jun-Aug, reduced hours Sep-May) within eyeshot of the Saga Centre.

❶ Getting There & Away

The Reykjavík–Hellissandur bus stops here once or twice a day in summer. A bus runs every day except Wednesday and Saturday out of season. The trip from Reykjavík takes 2¾ hours.

Ólafsvík

POP 990

Quiet, unassuming and well kept, workaday Ólafsvík won't win any hearts, but it's a pleasant place to pause and regroup after negotiating a few too many bumps in the road. Although it's the oldest trading town in the country (it was granted a trading licence in 1687), few of the original buildings survive – we much prefer spending the night in Stykkishólmur nearby.

◉ Sights

Perhaps more interesting than the town's designated sights is the local **church** (⊙8am-6pm Jun-Aug), made entirely of triangular pieces – it looks like the baby brother of the house of worship in Stykkishólmur.

Sjávarsafnið Ólafsvík MUSEUM
(☑436 6926; admission Ikr500; ⊙2-8pm Jun-Aug) Towards the harbour, the small aquarium and maritime museum contains tanks with crabs and fish, as well as a lovely collection of old fishing boats. During summer there's a small fish market at the entrance where you can purchase the daily catch of the local fishermen.

Gamla Pakkhúsið MUSEUM
(Old Packinghouse; ☑436 1543; Ólafsbraut; adult/child Ikr500/free; ⊙11am-5pm Jun–mid-Sep) A mildly interesting folk museum telling the story of the town's development as a trading centre.

🛏 Sleeping & Eating

You can pitch a tent at the local **campsite** (Dalbraut; sites per person Ikr500) – pay at the tourist information centre – though we prefer the camping grounds in Hellissandur nearby.

Hótel Ólafsvík HOTEL €
(☑436 1650; www.hotelolafsvik.is; Ólafsbraut 20; d with/without bath incl breakfast €79/148; ⊙mid-May–mid-Sep; @🛜) This large hotel has spacious, functional rooms with tiled floors, neutral decor and very little character. Rooms with shared bathroom are in the 'old wing' annexe called the 'guesthouse' (note: it feels nothing like a guesthouse). Additional rooms are in a second annexe across the street (we liked these the most). The on-site restaurant (mains Ikr3800 to Ikr5200), much like the entire hotel, is popular with tour groups.

GONE BERSERK

Long ago, according to the *Eyrbyggja Saga,* a farmer from Hraun grew weary from having to walk around the jagged lava flows to visit his brother at the farm in Bjarnarhöfn. Returning from a voyage to Norway, he brought back two berserkers – insanely violent fighters who were employed as hired thugs in Viking times – to work on his farm, but to his dismay one of the berserkers took a liking to his daughter. He turned to the local chieftain, Snorri Goði, for advice, but Snorri had his eye on the farmer's daughter as well and he recommended setting the berserker an impossible task. The farmer decided to promise the amorous berserker his daughter's hand in marriage if he was able to clear a passage through the troublesome lava field – surely impossible for a normal man.

To the shock and horror of both Snorri and the farmer, the two berserkers quickly set to work and managed to rip a passage straight through the treacherous moonscape. Rather than honouring his promise, the farmer trapped the berserkers in a sauna and murdered them, allowing Snorri to marry his daughter.

Today, a path through the 'Berserkjahraun' can still be seen, and recently a grave was discovered in the vicinity containing the remains of two large men.

Hobbitinn FAST FOOD €
(Ólafsbraut; mains Ikr290-2140; ⊙10am-11pm Jun-Aug, reduced hours Sep-May) Dressed up with a shop-window facade, Hobbitinn is merely a fast-food joint specialising in burgers, pizzas, hot dogs and fish dishes. Apparently the owner is quite small and hobbit-like.

❶ Information

Ólafsvík is the largest settlement in Snæfellsbær district – the region's **tourist information centre** (Kirkjutún 2; ⊙8am-6pm Mon-Fri, 10am-3pm Sat & Sun Jun-Aug, reduced hours Sep-May) is located in a drab white building behind the Old Packinghouse.

❶ Getting There & Away

In summer, there are one or two daily links (bus 350/350a) between Reykjavík and Ólafsvík, passing through Vegamót (2¾ hours) and continuing on to Hellissandur (15 minutes). There is a bus every day except Wednesday and Saturday in winter. The buses drop off and pick up at the petrol station.

Rif & Hellissandur

POP 140 & 390

A mere 6km after Ólafsvík is blink-and-you'll-miss-it Rif, a harbour village that makes Ólafsvík look like the big city.

TOP CHOICE ❯ **Gamla Rif** (☑436 1001; Háarifi 3; cakes from Ikr750, fish soup Ikr1700; ⊙noon-8pm Jun-Aug), run by two fishermen's wives who have perfected a variety of traditional snacks and dispense local travel tips with a smile, serves tasty coffee and cakes. They make a mean fish soup (from their husbands' daily catch) with notes of curry and tomato if you're feeling extra peckish. Scenic **Svöðufoss**, with its trickling chutes and dramatic hexagonal basalt, can be seen in the distance.

After Rif, there is the lonely church at **Ingjaldshóll**, the first concrete church in the world (built in 1903). Ingjaldshóll was the setting of the *Víglundar Saga*. If the church doors are open, you can see a painting depicting Christopher Columbus' apparent visit to Iceland in 1477 (see p153).

Hellissandur, next door, is the original fishing village in the area. Snæfellsjökull National Park has a ranger office here, but the opening hours are infrequent and limited; tourists should head to Hellnar for park information, or download a trail brochure from www.ust.is.

Kids will enjoy **Sjómannagarður** (☑436 6619; Útnesvegur; adult/child Ikr250/free; ⊙9am-6pm Jun-Jul, noon-6pm Aug–mid-Sep), a small maritime museum with an adorable turf house, loads of old photos and plenty of local memorabilia, including a set of lifting stones once used to test the strength of prospective fishermen.

The full-service **campsite** (sites per person Ikr500) in Hellissandur is one of our favourites – it's set right in the middle of a spiky lava field.

All buses from Reykjavík to Ólafsvík continue to Hellissandur, stopping at the N1 petrol station.

Snæfellsjökull National Park

Continuing west from Hellissandur, the scenic Rte 574 skirts the rugged slopes of Snæfellsjökull – the icy fist at the end of the long Snæfellsnes arm. Known as Undir-Jökli, this desolate area offers eerie views of lava spurs sticking straight up through the scree; on misty days, when the fog swirls among the peaks, you can easily see how the legends of cantankerous trolls came to life.

As haunting and isolated as this ethereal realm may feel, the looming ice cap was famous worldwide long before it was protected under a national park mandate in June 2001 – Jules Verne used the glacier as the setting for his famous *Journey to the Centre of the Earth*. In his book, a German geologist and his nephew embark on an epic journey into the crater of Snæfells, guided by a 16th-century Icelandic text with the following advice:

> Descend into the crater of Yocul of Sneffels, Which the shade of Scartaris caresses, Before the kalends of July, audacious traveller, And you will reach the centre of the earth. I did it.
>
> *Arne Saknussemm*

SNÆFELLSJÖKULL

It's easy to see why Jules Verne selected Snæfell – the dramatic peak was torn apart when the volcano beneath the ice cap exploded and the volcano subsequently collapsed into its own magma chamber, forming a huge caldera. Among certain New Age groups, Snæfellsjökull is considered one of the world's great 'power centres', and it definitely has a brooding presence.

WEST ICELAND RIF & HELLISSANDUR

Today the crater is filled in with ice and makes a popular hiking destination in summer. The best way to reach the glacial summit is to approach the peak from the south side of Rte F570 and link up with a snowmobile tour in Arnarstapi. Route F570's northern approach (near Ólafsvík) is frustratingly rutty (4WD needed) and frequently closed due to weather-inflicted damage.

Do not attempt an ascent without a proper briefing about road conditions and weather forecasts; contact the Gestastofa in Hellnar for more information. Note that there is no mobile phone reception from Hellissandur to Lóndrangar.

ÖNDVERÐARNES

At the westernmost tip of Snæfellsnes, Rte 574 cuts south, while a tiny gravel track heads further west across an ancient lava flow to the tip of the Öndverðarnes peninsula. As the road winds through charcoal lava cliffs you'll pass Skarðsvík, a perfect golden beach lapped by Caribbean blue waters. A Viking grave was discovered here in the 1960s and it's easy to understand why this stunning spot in the middle of an otherwise desolate area would have been favoured as a final resting place.

After Skarðsvík the track gets much bumpier (still manageable for a 2WD though). Follow the turn-off (left side) through the craggy lava flows to the imposing volcanic crater Vatnsborg, or continue straight on until you hit the dramatic Svörtuloft bird cliffs at the end of the road. A bumpy track runs parallel to the sea connecting the area's two squat lighthouses. To reach the very tip of the peninsula, go right (north) until you reach the yellow lighthouse. From the informal parking area near the lighthouse, it's a mere 200m stroll to Fálki, an abandoned stone well which used to be the only source of fresh water in the area.

SAXHÖLL

Back on Rte 54, southwest of the Öndverðarnes area, follow the marked turn-off to the roadside scoria crater Saxhóll. There's a driveable track leading straight to the base, from where it's a quick 300m climb for magnificent views over the Neshraun lava flows.

DRITVÍK & DJÚPALÓN

Further along, Rte 572 leads down to the wild black-sand beach at Djúpalónssandur. It's a dramatic place to walk, with a series of rocky stacks emerging from the ocean. You can still see four 'lifting stones' on the beach where fishing-boat crews would test the strength of aspiring fishermen. The smallest stone is Amloði (Bungler) at 23kg, followed by Hálfdrættingur (Weak) at 54kg, Hálfsterkur (Half-Strong) at 100kg, and the largest, Fullsterker (Fully Strong), at 154kg. Hálfdrættingur marked the frontier of wimphood, and any man who couldn't heft it was deemed unsuitable for a life at sea. Mysteriously, there now appear to be five stones. A bitumen car park and public toilets (in summer) have made the area a bit more accessible as of late.

If you tramp up over the craggy headland you'll reach the similar black-sand beach at Dritvík, where around 60 fishing boats were stationed from the 16th to the 19th century. The black sands are covered in pieces of rusted metal from the English trawler *Eding,* which was wrecked here in 1948. Several freshwater pools and the rocky arch Gatklettur are close to the car park.

About 2km south of Djúpalón, a track leads down to the rocket-shaped lighthouse at Malariff, from where you can walk along the cliffs to the rock pillars at Lóndrangar, which surge up into the air like a frozen splash of lava. Locals say that elves use the lava formations as a church.

VATNSHELLIR

The national park's newest offering are the much-loved ranger tours of the Vatnshellir (water caves; ☑665 2818; tours Ikr2000). Tours run from 10 June to 22 August four times per day (at 10am, 11.30am, 2pm and 3.30pm) and last approximately one hour. During your visit you will have a chance to explore an intact lava tube located 32m below the earth's surface. After entering the first chasm, you are guided through a corridor – much like the central aisle of a cathedral – until you reach a second chasm further inside. Guides shed light on the fascinating geological phenomena at play, while also giving some background on the region's troll-filled lore. We strongly advise booking in advance at the Gestastofa in Hellnar – groups max out at 20 people.

Southern Snæfellsnes

Beyond the glacier's frosty grip, the road smooths out to the south, passing the interesting sea-sculpted rock formations at

Hellnar and Arnarstapi, then continuing east along the broad southern coastal plain, hugging the huge sandy bays at Breiðavík and Búðavík.

HELLNAR

Bárður, the guardian spirit of Snæfell, chose Hellnar, a picturesque spot overlooking a rocky bay, as his home. Today Hellnar is a tiny fishing village where the shriek of seabirds fills the air and whales are regularly sighted. Down on the shore, the cave Baðstofa is chock-a-block with nesting birds, and Bárðarlaug, up near the main road, was supposedly Bárður's bathing pool (sadly, the pond is no longer hot). Ancient, velvety moss-cloaked lava flows tumble east, spilling down the nearby mountains and into the churning sea.

Travellers seeking information about the Snæfellsjökull National Park should stop at Gestastofa (☎436 6888, 665 2818; admission free; ☺10am-5pm 20 May-10 Sep). The building functions as an info office, cafe (a cute spot called Primus Kaffi; soup Ikr1090) and museum, featuring displays on the local geology, history, people, customs and wildlife. Ranger-led tours of Vatnshellir within in the park boundaries can be arranged from here.

TOP
CHOICE Hótel Hellnar (☎435 6820; www. hellnar.is; s/d incl breakfast from €130/140; ☺May-Sep; ☎) is the area's choice sleeping option. Recently, the comfortable inn has shifted away from its yogic reputation, proffering comfortable sun-filled rooms at reasonable prices instead. At the time of research, a new wing was under construction – it all looked very promising. If you're addicted to your iPhone, this is not the hotel for you – mobile phone reception is very limited h. the staff charge a pretty penny for acc. wi-fi.

Even if you're not spending the night, we highly recommend having dinner at the onsite restaurant (mains Ikr4000-5000; ☺6.30-9.30pm May-Sep). The black cod and the lamb are both winners – don't miss the heavenly skyr cake for dessert.

Follow the rickety stone path down to the ocean's edge for some fish soup at quaint Fjöruhúsið (fish soup Ikr1950; ☺10am-10pm Jun-Aug, reduced hours Apr-May & Sep-Oct). It's located at the trailhead of the scenic Hellnar–Arnarstapi path.

ARNARSTAPI

Linked to Hellnar by both the main road and a must-do coastal hike, this hamlet of summer cottages is nestled between the churning Arctic waters and the gnarled pillars of a neighbouring lava field. A recently erected monument pays tribute to Jules Verne with a wooden information panel and comical signpost measuring distances to major cities through the core of the earth. A second, troll-like monument also stands in Arnarstapi as a tribute to Bárður, the region's guardian spirit.

Arnarstapi is the best place to organise an ascent to the glacial crown. Snowmobile tours on the glacier are run by Snjófell (☎435 6783; www.snjofell.is). In summer, snowcat (truck with chain wheels) tours of the glacier cost Ikr8500 per person (minimum of six people); there's also a snowmobile tour for Ikr21,900 per person or a solo skidoo (minimum of two people) for Ikr25,500. Trips run from mid-April to early September

HEY COLUMBUS, EAT YOUR HEART OUT!

Icelanders are very quick to point out that Christopher Columbus did not 'discover' America. In fact, it is commonly believed that Columbus visited the Snæfellsnes Peninsula in 1477 to learn about the earlier Viking conquests in the New World.

During his Icelandic foray, Columbus was surprised to discover that a woman, Guðríður Þorbjarnardóttir, was among Iceland's pantheon of celebrated explorers. Born in Hellnar before the year 1000 (a beautiful sculpture marks the site of her family's farm at Laugabrekka), Guðríður had a serious case of wanderlust. Not only was she one of the first Europeans to reach Vinland (most likely Canada's Newfoundland), she bore a child while visiting (the first European child born in North America)! After her son, Snorri, married and moved to Glaumbær, Guðríður converted to Christianity and embarked on an epic pilgrimage to Rome. Upon arrival, she met with the pope and recounted her experiences at the edge of the earth.

For more information about Guðríður, read *The Far Traveler* by Nancy Marie Brown, or *The Sea Road* by Margaret Elphinstone.

OR A RAINY DAY!

n Iceland? Oh yes, there are many. But don't let the drizzle make your holi-
zzle – there are several stunning landscapes that are even more dramatic
including the scenic 2.5km walk (around 40 minutes) between Hellnar and
. This slender trail follows the jagged coastline, passing frozen lava flows and
one caves. During bouts of tumultuous weather, the waves pound through
the rocky arches like water spraying out of a blowhole. After your jaunt, reward yourself with a hearty repast at one of the cleverly positioned restaurants plonked on either side of the trail. If you finish in Hellnar, savour fish soup at Fjöruhúsið or heavenly *skyr* (yoghurt-like dessert) cake at Hótel Hellnar, while those who end up in Arnarstapi can treat themselves to the daily catch at Ferðaþjónustan Snjófell.

Don't get us wrong, however; this short walk is absolutely stunning on a sunny day as well!

every two hours until midnight and last for around 1½ hours.

The tours start at the edge of the snow-field, so you'll have to drive along the bumpy Rte F570 towards the summit. Road conditions can be uncertain, so it's best to ask at Snjófell for details when purchasing your tour ticket. Minivans (Ikr2000 per person) to the top can be negotiated if you don't have your own wheels or if the roads are damaged. Note that the summit should always be approached from the south (from Arnarstapi). The northern part of Rte F570 (near Ólafsvík) is often closed and never suitable for a 2WD (see p348 for vital information about F roads).

As you drive up from Arnarstapi, you'll pass **Stapafell** (526m), the supposed home to the local little people – you'll see miniature house gables painted onto rocks in their honour. Further along you'll pass a collapsed crater, which has created a series of strange lava caves about 1.5km from the main road. The largest cave is **Sönghellir** (Song Cave), which is full of 18th-century graffiti and is rumoured to resound with the songs of dwarfs. Bring a torch or use the flash of your camera to read the various markings of passers-by and don't be shy about belting out your favourite melody.

Snjófell offers accommodation and dining at **Ferðaþjónustan Snjófell** (☎435 6783; www.snjofell.is, www.hringhotels.is; sites per tent Ikr1500, d €85; ⏰mid-Apr–mid-Sep) in Arnarstapi. Travellers can pitch a tent on a grassy patch outside (sorry, no showers) or plop their sleeping bag down in the prefab guesthouse. The menu in the turf-roofed restaurant (meals Ikr1200 to Ikr4200) focuses on the delicious assortment of fish brought to shore at the harbour down the street.

RAUÐFELDSGJÁ

Past Stapafell, a small track branches east off Rte 574 to Rauðfeldsgjá, a steep and narrow cleft that mysteriously disappears into the cliff wall. A stream runs along the bottom of the gorge, and you can slink between the sheer walls for quite a distance.

BREIÐAVÍK & BÚÐAVÍK

East of Hellnar and Arnarstapi, Rte 574 skirts the edges of the long sandy bays at Breiðavík and Búðavík. These windswept beaches are covered in yellow-grey sand and are wonderfully peaceful places to walk. In fact, the region is considered one of the best places for horse riding, and there are several stables in the area of international repute.

At Búðavík the abandoned fishing village of Búðir has a stunningly lonely church, and is home to one of Iceland's first 'luxury' country inns. From the hotel, a walking trail leads across the elf-infested Buðahraun lava field to the crater **Búðaklettur**. According to local legend, a lava tube beneath Buðahraun, paved with gold and precious stones, leads all the way to Surtshellir in upper Borgarfjörður. It takes about three hours to walk to the crater and back.

TOP CHOICE **Lýsuhólslaug** (admission Ikr550; ⏰1-8pm Jun–mid-Aug), just beyond the horse ranch at Lýsuhóll, offers the opportunity to have a dip in mineral-filled waters. The geothermal source is very close by and pumps in the carbonated liquid at a perfect 37°C to 39°C. Don't be alarmed that the pool is a murky green – the iron-rich water attracts some serious algae; after a 30-minute dip, your skin will be soft like the back of a seal.

Sleeping & Eating

The following options are arranged in geographic order from west to east. There are several other accommodation options in the area – check out *The Ideal Holiday* farmstay booklet – though these are our favourite.

Hótel Buðir   BOUTIQUE HOTEL €€€

(☑435 6700; www.budir.is; d incl breakfast Ikr30,500-42,500; @🛜) Windswept, lonely and very romantic, Hótel Buðir is a stylish spot with an understated-yet-regal design and not a hint of pretension. Expect elegant furnishings, DVD players and plasma TVs, and – if you're lucky enough to bag No 23 – a freestanding bath separated from the bedroom by a wooden screen. No 28 has the best views (and a teeny tiny balcony). Try the five-course kitchen special (Ikr10,100) or go for one of the perfected fish dishes.

Lýsuhóll   HORSE FARM €€

(☑435 6716; www.lysuholl.is; d Ikr17,000; 🛜) Equine enthusiasts should look no further than this friendly horse farm. The affable owner proudly displays her awards at the breakfast table and reminds guests that the southern Snæfellsnes is one of the best places in Iceland to go for a trot. Even if you're not on a riding trip, the farm is still a fun place to spend the night – the guides will gladly show you around the stables, or take you on a short excursion (two hours Ikr8700). Don't miss the swimming pool nearby, which is fed by a gurgling geothermal source.

Gistihúsið Langaholt   GUESTHOUSE €€

(☑435 6789; www.langaholt.is; Görðum; sites per person Ikr900, d Ikr21,000; 🛜) One of the most curious spots to rest your head, Langaholt is a golfing haven, guesthouse and gastronomic pit stop captained by a quirky fellow who dresses entirely in black (hat and shoes included). Rooms are arranged motel-style (go for No 120, which has views of both the glacier and the sea) and the restaurant serves up some tasty seafood mains (Ikr1850 to Ikr5800). Nine holes of golf costs Ikr2500 (clubs available for rent). Book ahead.

Gistiheimilið Hof   GUESTHOUSE €€

(☑435 6802; www.gistihof.is; d incl breakfast Ikr17,200) Further along, friendly Hof has a selection of turf-roofed apartment-style accommodation with shared kitchens, living rooms and bathrooms, as well as a small cluster of newly finished darkwood cabins. Ask the owners about the local colony of barking seals at Ytri-Tunga and don't forget to take a dip in the relaxing hot-pots.

DALIR

The scenic corridor between west Iceland and the Westfjords served as the setting for the *Laxdæla Saga,* the most popular of the Icelandic sagas. The story revolves around a love triangle between Guðrun Ósvífursdóttir, said to be the most beautiful woman in Iceland, and the foster brothers Kjartan Ólafsson and Bolli Þorleiksson. In typical saga fashion, Guðrun had both men wrapped around her little finger and schemed and connived until both of them were dead – Kjartan at the hands of Bolli, and Bolli at the hands of Kjartan's brothers. Most Icelanders know the stories and characters by heart and hold the area in which the story took place in great historic esteem.

It's worth picking up a free copy of the excellent *Dalasýsla Heritage Map,* available at the tourist information centre in Búðardalur or at the hotel in Laugar. Hikers should invest in the *Vestfirðir & Dalir 6 & 7* maps (available at most regional information centres for around Ikr1200 to Ikr1500).

Eiríksstaðir

The farm Eiríksstaðir, down the Haukadalsá from Stóra-Vatnshorn's church, was the

---

DETOUR: RTE 590

This 100km track (doable in a 2WD) follows the dramatic coastline of the oft-forgotten peninsula between the Snæfellsnes and Westfjords (look for the turn-off at Fellströnd along Rte 60). Windswept farmsteads lie frozen in time, and boulder-strewn hills roll skyward turning into flattened granite crowns – in the mist and midnight sun they look like impenetrable walls of a stone fortress. If you want to spend the night, you can shack up at Vogur (☑894 4396; www.vogur.org; d incl breakfast €154); there's also a campsite at Á (☑434 1420), just before Skarð – a lonely farm that has remained in the hands of the same family for over 1000 years.

WORTH A TRIP

ERPSSTAÐIR

When the peanut gallery starts moaning, 'Are we there yet?', you know it's time to pull off the road. **Erpsstaðir** (☎843 0357; www.erpsstadir.is; admission to cowshed Ikr800; ☺1-5pm Jun–mid-Sep) is the perfect place to stretch your legs – especially if you've got the brats in tow. Like a mirage for sweet-toothed wanderers, this dairy farm on Rte 60 between Búðardalur and the Ring Road specialises in delicious homemade ice cream. Park at the grey barn, and you can tour the farm, greet the buxom bovines, then gorge on a signature scoop of '*kjaftæði*' (which literally means 'mouth watering', but is best known as a euphemism for 'bullshit'). The farm also sells *skyr* and cheese – try the oddly shaped *skyr-konfekt* (which is meant to look like an udder, but we think it bears more resemblance to a suppository), a delicious dessert made from a hard white chocolate shell that encases thick yoghurt-y *skyr* in the middle. It'll blow your taste buds away.

Erpsstaðir also offers cottage accommodation (from Ikr17,000) if you're contemplating ice cream for breakfast...

home of Eiríkur Rauðe (Erik the Red), father of Leifur Eiríksson, believed to be the first European to visit America. Although only a faint outline of the original farm remains, an impressive **reconstruction** (☎434 1118; www.leif.is; adult/child Ikr1000/free; ☺9am-6pm Jun-Aug) – which looks more like a crude turf house – has been built using only the tools and materials available at the time. Enthusiastic period-dressed guides show visitors around, brandish weapons and tell the story of Erik the Red, who went on to found the first European settlement in Greenland.

Búðardalur

POP 230

Founded as a cargo depot in Saga times, the pin-sized town now survives by dairy farming and station services; it occupies a pleasant position looking out over Hvammsfjörður, at the mouth of the Laxá river.

There's a Viking exhibit, tourist information centre and cafe all rolled into one at **Leifsbúð** (☎434 1441; www.dalir.is; ☺10.30am-6pm Mon-Fri, 11am-4pm Sat & Sun Jun-Aug) down by the harbour. Ask here about staying at the local **campsite** (sites per person Ikr750; ☺Jun-Aug). Alternatively, guesthouse **Bjarg** (☎434 1644; www.aknet.is/bjarg; Dalbraut 2; d Ikr10,000; ☎) has simple rooms. The attached restaurant, **Villapizza** (mains Ikr1150-2500; ☺11am-10pm), serves grilled meat, fish and pizzas from the Bootland.

Bus 37/37a runs between Reykjavík and Búðardalur (2¾ hours) daily except on Wednesday and Saturday. Service continues to Bjarkalundur in the Westfjords. The bus stops at the N1 petrol station.

Hjarðarholt

Although the region is central to many of the best-loved Icelandic sagas, little remains of the original farms from Saga times, so you will need to use your imagination to make the connection.

Hjarðarholt is the main attraction in the area – it's the one-time home of Kjartan and his father, Ólafur Peacock. Their Viking farm was said to be one of the wonders of the Norse world, with scenes from the sagas carved into the walls and a huge dining hall that could seat 1100 guests. No trace of it remains today. There is, however, a beautiful **church** on the premises and great views of the valley below where the region's history unfurled.

Nearby, also on the Laxá river, **Höskuldsstaðir** was the birthplace of Hallgerður Longlegs (also called Longtresses), wife of Gunnar of Hlíðarendi, who starred in *Njál's Saga*. Other important descendants of the farm include Bolli and his foster brother Kjartan from *Laxdæla Saga*.

Laugar & Around

Further north, follow the turn at Rte 590 to find the farm at **Hvammur**, which produced a whole line of prominent Icelanders, including Snorri Sturluson of *Prose Edda* fame. It was settled in around 895 by Auður the Deep-Minded, the wife of the Irish king Olaf Godfraidh, who has a bit part in the *Laxdæla Saga*. By coincidence, Árni Magnússon, who rescued most of the Icelandic sagas from the 1728 fire in Copenhagen, was also raised at Hvammur.

Head past the turn-off for Rte 590 to find the geothermal village of Laugar, known throughout Iceland as the birthplace of *Laxdæla Saga* beauty Guðrun Ósvífursdóttir. Base yourself at the friendly Hótel Edda ([icon]444 4930; www.hoteledda.is; Sælingsdalur; sites per person Ikr900, d with/without bathroom Ikr21,900/11,800; [icons]). There's a newer wing with surprisingly modern rooms, an older hospital-style annexe with shared bathrooms, and sleeping-bag space (Ikr2400 per person) in converted classrooms. During the rest of the year, the complex is used as a boarding retreat for Icelandic teens. The restaurant (mains Ikr2600-4100; [icon]6-9pm) gets good reviews for its local angelica-fed lamb – it also serves the delicious ice cream from Erpsstaðir, and there's a fascinating on-site museum ([icon]admission free; 1-6pm Jun-Aug) in the basement that details the region's history. The curator is a memorable character who knows a great deal about Dalir's brilliant Viking history. Local historians believe that they've found Guðrun's bathing pool; it is well marked near the entrance to the hotel. Ask about Tungustapi – one of the largest elf cathedrals in Iceland, located in the distance.

WEST ICELAND LAUGAR & AROUND

The Westfjords

Includes »

Why Go?

Like giant lobster claws snipping away at the Arctic Circle, the Westfjords is where Iceland's dramatic landscapes come to a riveting climax. Jagged cliffs and broad sweeping beaches flank the south, while dirt roads snake along the tortuous coastline dotted with tiny fishing villages clinging doggedly to a traditional way of life. Further on, stone towers rise from the deep, hoisting tundra-ridden buffs up towards the northern elements. The Hornstrandir hiking reserve crowns the quiet region; it is, undoubtedly, the island's most scenic terrain, with countless fjords and cairn-marked walking paths.

Give yourself plenty of time for a trip to the Westfjords. The roads around the coast weave in and out of fjords and over unpaved mountain passes pitted with giant potholes. The going is frustratingly slow at times, but the scenery is never short of breathtaking.

Best Places to Eat

» Heydalur (p172)
» Simbahöllin (p164)
» Tjöruhúsið (p169)
» Bræðraborg (p169)

Best Places to Stay

» Hótel Djúpavík (p177)
» Hótel Laugarhóll (p177)
» Einarshúsið (p170)
» Camping in Hornstrandir (p173)

Road Distances (km)

	Patreksfjörður	Þingeyri	Ísafjörður	Hólmavík	Norðurfjörður
Þingeyri	129				
Ísafjörður	175	47			
Hólmavík	234	265	221		
Norðurfjörður	333	348	303	105	
Reykjavík	397	405	450	230	334

SOUTH COAST

The sparsely populated south coast of the Westfjords is the least dramatic of the region, and it's nowhere near as wild and wonderful as the peninsulas further north. However, the ferry connection to Stykkishólmur on the Snæfellsnes Peninsula is a handy route to the area.

Travellers who don't take the *Baldur* ferry will enter the Westfjords from the historic Dalir region in west Iceland. If you have your sights set on the Strandir coast, follow the bitumen road to Hólmavík.

Reykhólar

Reykhólar sits on the tip of the kidney-shaped Reykjanes Peninsula, a minor geothermal area. The little town is poised to become a stop for tourists, and in the last couple of years a few tour operators and attractions have sprouted up, including Eyjasigling (☑849 6748; www.eyjasigling.is), which specialises in tours around the islets of Breiðafjörður. Skip the geothermal pool and try a soak in the local seaweed baths (☑577 4800; www.sjavarsmidjan.is) instead.

Ask at the tourist information centre (www.visitreyholarhreppur.is; ◷11am-5pm Mon-Fri, to 6pm Sat & Sun Jun-Aug) about the new eagle museum that was being constructed during the research of this guide. The info centre also has a little museum (admission Ikr500) with antique boats and stuffed birds.

Gistiheimilið Álftaland (Reykhólar HI Hostel; ☑434 7878; www.alftaland.is; s Ikr5200; 🛜) meets all accommodation needs, with no-frills rooms prepped for sleeping bags, two soothing hot-pots out back, and a kitchen available for guests' use.

BJARKALUNDUR

On Rte 60, just beyond the turn-off to Reykhólar, Hótel Bjarkalundur (☑434 7762/7863; www.bjarkalundur.is; s/d incl breakfast Ikr8500/13,500; ◷May-Oct) is a large farmhouse with a petrol station and a restaurant serving Icelandic grub (mains Ikr1550 to Ikr4000). It's the oldest summer hotel in Iceland and the unofficial gateway to Vaðalfjöll, the largest elf palace in the Westfjords (or so says the hotel owner).

Buses run between Reykjavík and Bjarkalundur (3¾ hours), via Króksfjarðarnes in Dalir, every day except Wednesday and Saturday. There's no bus service between Bjarkalundur and Flókalundur or Brjánslækur.

Djúpadalur

Heading west, you'll come across the steaming waterfalls in the Djúpadalur geothermal field, 20km west of Bjarkalundur. There's an indoor geothermal swimming pool (☑434 7853; adult/child Ikr350/100; ◷8am-11pm) here and good accommodation at the welcoming nine-bed Guesthouse Djúpadalur (☑434 7853), where sleeping bag-ers can stay for Ikr4000.

Flókalundur

After driving over 100km along a series of stunningly desolate fjords, you'll reach Flókalundur, the junction point between the road up to Ísafjörður and the bumpy route to the southwestern peninsulas. The two-house 'town' of Flókalundur was named after the Viking explorer Hrafna-Flóki Vilgerðarson, who gave Iceland its name in AD 860.

Today, the most interesting thing in the area is the Vatnsfjörður Nature Reserve, established to protect the area around Lake Vatnsdalsvatn, a nesting site for harlequin ducks and great northern divers (loons). Various hiking trails run around the lake and into the hills beyond.

Pick up a Vatnsfjörður hiking brochure at Hótel Flókalundur (☑456 2011; www.flokalundur.is; sites per person Ikr1100, s/d incl breakfast Ikr15,200/19,500; ◷mid-May–mid-Sep), an ageing bungalow-style hotel with small wood-panelled rooms and a decent restaurant serving all three meals of the day. You'll have the choice of a manmade swimming pool owned by the hotel, or a natural hot-pot called Hellulaug, nearby. At high tide, do as the locals do and jump in the frigid sea, then run back to the pool to warm up.

Brjánslækur to Patreksfjörður

Brjánslækur is nothing more than the terminus for the *Baldur* ferry from Stykkishólmur. Bus schedules are loosely timed to connect with the ferry. After the ferry terminal, Rte 62 follows the sandy coast until it reaches the top of scenic Patreksfjörður, marking the beginning of the southwest peninsulas.

DENMARK
STRAIT

Aðalvík
Hesteyri
Grænahlíð

Grunnavík

Grunna

Skálavík

Súgandafjörður

Hnífsdalur–
Bolungarvík Tunnel

Bolungarvík

Sandey

Suðureyri

Syðridalsvatn

Ísafjarðardj

3

65

Tungudalur

Hnífsdalur

Önundarfjörður

Flateyri

4 Ísafjörður

Vig

Ingjaldsandur

Höll

Breiðafell

Suðavík

Skutulsfjörður

Ísafjörður–
Suðureyri–
Flateyri Tunnel

Langeyri

Litlibæ

60

61

Dýrafjörður

Svalvogar

622

Skrúður

Haukadalur

Þingeyri

Þingeyri
Peninsula

Meðaldalur

Sandfell

5

Kaldbakur
(998m)

Selárdalur

Hrafnseyri

Sjónfríð
(920m)

Arnarfjörður

Grænahlíð

Borgarfjörður

Gláma

Ketildalir

619

Dynjandi

Bíldudalur

60

Kollsvík

Patreksfjörður

Tálknafjörður

Suðurfjörður

Vatnsfjörður
Nature Reserve

Hænuvík

Breiðavík

615

63

Patreksfjörður

Foss

Hvallátur

Fossdalur

Fossdalur

Flókalundur

Fossá

Brunnar

Bjargtangar

Hnjótur

62

Krossholt

62

Keflavík

Sauðlauksdalur

Látrabjarg

6

Tungamúli

Brjánslækur

Rauðasandur

614

612

Kleifaheiði

Vatnsfjörður

Barðaströnd

Stálfjall

Breiðafjörðu

To Flatey (5km);
Stykkishólmur (25km)

The Westfjords Highlights

1 Feel the breeze kiss your face as you rove around saw-toothed cliffs and lonely coves during a life-changing hike across **Hornstrandir** (p174)

2 Take in the wild serenity of the **Strandir coast** (p175), stopping at strangely seductive Djúpavík before soaking in the waters at Krossneslaug

3 Duel with an Arctic tern on offshore Vigur, learn about the elusive Arctic fox or slink across silent fjordlings throughout beautiful **Ísafjarðardjúp** (p170)

Hornbjarg

Arctic Fox Research
Station (Private)

Hornvík

nstrandir
❶

ulfirðir

Bolungarvík

Furufjörður

Reykjarfjörður *Reykjarfjörður*

Bjarnarfjörður

fjallaströnd

Drangar *Drangavík*

Drangajökull

ðey Unaðsdalur

Dalbær

Ófeigsfjörður

Ögur Melgraseyri

Kaldalón

Lóndjúp Ófeigsfjörður
Norðurfjörður
Strandir
Vatnsfjörður Árnes **Coast** Reykjaneshyrna
635 Göngumannaskarð ❷ Reykjanes
Pass Gjögur
insfjörður Reykjarfjörðardalur Naustavík *Reykjarfjörður*
kjarfjörður
Djúpavík **Strandir**
ðifjörður **Coast**
Ísafjörður Lambatindur **643**
(854m) *Kaldbaksvík*

Hólsfjall
(469m)

Laugarhóll

61 Staður Bjarnarfj-
arðarháls *Bjarnarfjörður*

Ós
60 Stakkar **Hólmavík** Bær
Drangsnes *Grímsey*

Þiðriksvallavatn *Steingrímsfjörður*

Djúpadalur **61**

Djúpafjörður Vaðalfjöll
(508m) *Húnaflói*
Bjarkalundur

Reykjanes
Bær

Reykhólar Króksfjarðarnes *Bitrufjörður*
To Staðarskáli (40km);
To Búðardalur (25km); *Akureyri (110km);*
Reykjavík (95km) *Reykjavík (110km)*

❹ Pick wild rhubarb on the side of the highway, then gorge on piles of salted fish in **Ísafjörður** (p166), the Westfjords' surprisingly cosmopolitan capital

❺ Hop on a mountain bike and swerve around the lonely peninsula that wraps around **Þingeyri** (p165)

❻ Watch chatty seabirds and clumsy puffins swoop around the crowded cliffs at **Látrabjarg** (p162), then take in the sweeping, desolate beachscapes just beyond

SOUTHWEST PENINSULAS

The trident-shaped peninsulas in the southwest of the Westfjords are spectacularly scenic. Sand beaches as fine as you'll find in Iceland, shimmering blue water, towering cliffs and stunning mountains weave between the fjords, providing a fantastic retreat for hikers. The region's most popular destination is Látrabjarg, a 12km stretch of cliffs that is home to thousands of nesting seabirds in summer. The roads in this sparsely populated region are rough and driving is slow – take a deep breath, you'll get there!

Látrabjarg Peninsula

Best known for its dramatic cliffs and abundant bird life, the Látrabjarg Peninsula also has wonderful deserted beaches and plenty of opportunities for long, leisurely walks.

Joining Rte 612 from Rte 62, you'll pass the rusting hulk of the fishing boat *Garðar* near the head of the fjord before passing the empty, golden beaches around the airstrip at Sauðlauksdalur. In Hnjótur, about 10km further on, it's worth stopping at the entertaining museum (☑456 1511; www.hnjotur.is; admission Ikr1000; ☺10am-6pm mid-May–mid-Sep). The eclectic collection includes salvaged fishing boats and displays on the history of the region. There's an on-site cafe (sandwiches Ikr650) that specialises in local food (including razorbill eggs plucked from the cliffs) during the earlier parts of the summer.

At Breiðavík, a stunning golden-sand beach is framed by rocky cliffs and the turquoise waters of the bay. It's an idyllic spot, certainly one of Iceland's best beaches and usually deserted – there's a spot for wild-camping at Melanes. Should you find yourself with more company than you'd hoped for, head further on to Hvallátur, where there's another gorgeous golden-sand beach and excellent opportunities for camping at Brunnar next door.

Soon the Bjargtangar lighthouse, Europe's westernmost point (if you don't count the Azores), comes into view and nearby the renowned Látrabjarg bird cliffs. Extending for 12km along the coast and ranging from 40m to 400m, the dramatic cliffs are mobbed by nesting seabirds in early summer and it's a fascinating place even for the most reluctant of twitchers. Unbelievable numbers of puffins, razorbills, guillemots, cormorants, fulmars, gulls and kittiwakes nest here from June to mid-August. The puffins in particular are incredibly tame, and you can often get within a few feet of the birds. On calm days, seals are often seen basking on the skerries around the lighthouse.

East of the cliffs (about a 20km walk along the coast path from the lighthouse), the stunning Rauðasandur beach stretches out in shades of deep pink and red sands. Pounded by the surf and backed by a huge lagoon, it is an exceptionally beautiful and serene place. To get here by road you'll have to backtrack on Rte 612 towards the head of the fjord. Take a right turn onto Rte 614 soon after the airfield at Sauðlauksdalur and follow the bumpy track for about 10km.

☞ Tours

Birdwatching and hiking tours can be arranged with Umfar (☑892 9227; www.umfar.is). Although based in nearby Patreksfjörður, the knowledgeable guides can meet you in or near the cliffs.

🛏 Sleeping & Eating

Breiðavík   GUESTHOUSE €€
(☑456 1575; www.breidavik.is; sites per person Ikr1700, d with/without bathroom incl breakfast Ikr25,500/17,500; ☺May-Sep) Besides some wonderful wild-camping at Melanes, the best place to stay in the area is Breiðavík, located near an incredible cream-coloured beach of the same name. The large guesthouse offers homey rooms with patchwork quilts and wobbly furniture. Sleeping-bag accommodation costs Ikr4750 per person. The hotel can arrange guided ATV tours along the desolate beach (Ikr10,000 per person).

Kirkjuvammur   CAFE €
(☺1-6pm mid-Jun–Aug) There's a small cafe on the sands of Rauðasandur called Kirkjuvammur, though locals like to call it the 'French cafe' due to the charming collection of imported furniture within. At low tide you can walk right down to the reef.

❶ Getting There & Away

South of Patreksfjörður, Rte 62 cuts across the ridge at Kleifaheiði to the south coast, while Rte 612 runs west to the end of the Látrabjarg Peninsula.

On Monday, Wednesday and Saturday from June to August, buses from Ísafjörður route through Látrabjarg on their way to Brjánslækur, where you can pick up the *Baldur* ferry to Stykkishólmur. The buses stop at the cliffs for two hours, leaving you plenty of time to explore.

Patreksfjörður

POP 620

Although it's the largest village in this part of the Westfjords, unattractive Patreksfjörður is of very little interest to tourists besides being a reasonably convenient jumping-off point for visits to the Látrabjarg peninsula. The town was named after St Patrick of Ireland, who was the spiritual guide of Örlygur Hrappson, the first settler in the area.

At the time of research, a new branch of the Foss hotel chain was under construction in the village's old butchery; freshly refinished camping grounds at the town's entrance have also been promised to future visitors. The town has two memorable cafes, should you want to break up the journey. The Pirates' House (Sjóræningjahúsið; www.sjoraeningjar.is; Vatneyri; ⊙11am-6pm Jun-Aug) is set up in an old ship machinery factory – numbered shelves once full of bolts and screws are now lined with bottles of spirits and books. Boxes full of dress-up clothes and board games will keep the kids busy while you swig a coffee and down a bowl of tasty soup (Ikr950). Check out the posters on the walls detailing famous pirate expeditions in colourful detail. At Stúkurhúsið (www.stukurhusid.is; panini Ikr980; ⊙11am-11pm Jun-Aug, reduced hours May & Sep) expect to find simple sandwiches and pastries being dished out in an adorable little house that has benefited from a recent renovation.

Buses connect Patreksfjörður to Brjánslækur (1¼ hours), Látrabjarg (two hours) and Ísafjörður (two hours). An 'airbus' runs by request from Patreksfjörður to meet flights into Bíldudalur.

Tálknafjörður

POP 290

Set amid rolling green hills, rocky peaks and a wide fjord, friendly Tálknafjörður is another soporific village surrounded by magnificent scenery. Fed by the geothermal field nearby, the Tálknafjörður Swimming Pool (adult/child Ikr370/250; ⊙10am-9pm Jun-Aug, 8am-noon & 4-9pm Mon-Fri, 1-6pm Sat & Sun Sep-May) is the main hang-out spot in town.

In summer, a laid-back tourist office operates at the pool and its staffers are always happy to lend a hand. Ask here for a detailed hiking map of the area, *Vestfirðir & Dalir 4* (and try the gorgeous 10km cairn-marked hike to Bíldudalur). Completely unknown to tourists is the cement-lined natural bathing pool at Pollurinn, 3.8km beyond the swimming pool along Rte 617. The spring is marked by a tiny white sign with black lettering.

Pay for the campsite (sites per person Ikr1000; ⊙Jun-Aug) at the swimming pool next door. Amenities include laundry, cooking facilities and showers. Spotless accommodation awaits the weary traveller at Bjarmaland (☑891 8038; www.facebook.com/GuesthouseBjarmaland; Bugatún 8; ☎), where sleeping-bag space will set you back Ikr3000 per person.

The Patreksfjörður–Bíldudalur 'airbus' stops in Tálknafjörður along the way; ask at the swimming pool for details. The bus only runs in conjunction with the arriving and departing flights.

Bíldudalur

POP 180

Set on a gloriously calm bay surrounded by towering peaks, the sleepy fishing village of Bíldudalur (www.bildudalur.is) has one of the finest fjordside positions in the region. Arriving by road from either direction, you're treated to some spectacular outlooks.

Bíldudalur was founded in the 16th century and today is a major supplier of prawns (hence the slight smell when the wind blows the wrong way). For tourists, the town's most promising attraction is the Skrímslasetur Sea Monster Museum (admission Ikr700; ⊙11am-6pm) across from the church. The multimedia exhibits about local and foreign monster legends are quite impressive for such a small town.

Jón, Bíldudalur's premier entrepreneur, runs Eagle Fjord Tours (☑894 1684; per group tour from Ikr35,000), a small outfitter specialising in private tours. Trips run to Selárdalur, Hringsdalur (a Viking grave site from AD 900), Látrabjarg and Dynjandi. Sea-angling excursions and boat outings are also on offer. Eagle Fjord can arrange accommodation in comfortable apartments (s/d Ikr11,000/16,000; ☎) upon request; three-course dinners can also be arranged at

WORTH A TRIP

SELÁRDALUR

Hidden beyond Bíldudalur along Rte 619 is beautiful Ketildalir (Kettle Valley) and a strange museum at the tip of the fjord. Local artist Samúel Jónsson lived out his remaining years at a remote farm in Selárdalur, and filled his days by creating a series of 'naïve', cartoon-like sculptures. Visitors can stop by and check out what remains. There are four parts to the exhibition: a flamboyant house that looks somewhat like a birthday cake, a circle of lions (created from a postcard Samúel saw of the Alhambra), a church and Samúel's home. Of particular note, however, is the sculpture of a man and seal. If you look at them from the right (or wrong) angles, they're placed in a rather unflattering pose...

Galeri Dynjandi (meals in town are otherwise limited to fast food).

Accommodation for penny pinchers can be found at **Bíldudalur HI Hostel** (Gistiheimilið Kaupfélagið; ☑456 2100, 860 2100; www.hostel.is; Hafnarbraut 2; s/d Ikr3650/9350), which was a harbour-front supermarket during the 1950s. Today, a dedicated renovation has turned the building into an inviting little spot with basic but squeaky-clean rooms. Members get a Ikr600 discount per person.

Campers with their own wheels should skip the free site beside the golf course and venture 23km away (in the direction of Rte 60) to find a designated **wild-camping zone** easily distinguishable by the welcoming hotpot filled with soothing geothermal water – we can't think of a better place to hunker down in the region.

Eagle Air (☑562 4200; www.ernir.is; Reykjavík Domestic Airport, IS-101 Reykjavík) provides flights to/from Reykjavík (45 minutes). **Buses** (☑893 2636) run on request to/from Patreksfjörður via Tálknafjörður to connect with flights. It is possible to rent a car from **Bílaleiga Akureyrar** (www.holdur.is) from the small satellite bureau here.

CENTRAL PENINSULAS

Dynjandi

Tumbling in a broad sweep over a 100m-rocky scarp at the head of Dynjandivogur bay, Dynjandi (Fjallfoss) is the most dramatic **waterfall** in the Westfjords, and the perfect doormat to its central peninsulas. Coming from the car park you'll pass a series of smaller falls at the base of the main chute, but it's well worth following the path up to the bottom of the massive cascade that plunges over the mountain side. The thundering water and views out over the broad fjord below are spectacular.

The surrounding area is protected as a nature reserve, but there's a free (albeit noisy) campsite right by the falls. Dynjandi is well signposted off Rte 60 – after the falls, the roads get even more jaw-clenchingly bumpy as you wander up into the towering peninsulas.

Þingeyri

POP 300

This tiny village, on the north side of the peninsula, was the first trading station in the Westfjords, but these days the world seems to have passed Þingeyri by. Although there's little to see here, the town is a great jumping-off point for hikes, bike riding and trots on horseback through the surrounding peninsula.

TOP CHOICE **Simbahöllin** (www.simbahollin.is; mains Ikr750-2900; ☺10am-10pm mid-Jun–mid-Aug, reduced hours early Jun & late Aug) is that homey cafe you've been longing for ever since you left Reykjavík for wilder landscapes. The friendly baristas dote on the customers with tasty Belgian waffles during the day and hearty lamb tagines in the evening when fjord winds blow through. The welcoming bolthole is also ground zero for an active adventure on the peninsula – high-quality mountain bikes are available for rent (Ikr10,000 per day), and horse-riding tours (Ikr8500 for two hours) set off whenever a small group is interested.

If you're visiting on the first weekend in July, it's worth checking out the local **Dýrafjarðardagar Viking festival** (www.westvikings.info). The festival celebrates the area's Viking heritage and the saga of local man Gísli Súrsson.

If you'd like to stay, you'll find the camp-site (sites per tent Ikr1200) behind the swimming pool. The most viable lodging option is Við Fjörðinn (☎456 8172; www.vidfjordinn. is; Aðalstræti 26; d Ikr11,000), where bathrooms are shared among simple rooms with mismatched furniture; there's a good guest kitchen and a TV lounge as well.

Local buses (☎456 4258) run twice every weekday between Þingeyri and Ísafjörður (30 minutes). From June to August a daily bus runs to Brjánslækur, where you'll be able to catch the *Baldur* ferry to Stykkishólmur.

ÞINGEYRI PENINSULA

Ringing around the quaint township of Þingeyri, the Þingeyri Peninsula's dramatic northern peaks have been dubbed the 'Northwestern Alps', and the region offers – unsurprisingly – some spectacular hiking.

Grab a mountain bike and follow the dirt road that runs northwest along the eastern edge of the peninsula to the scenic valley at Haukadalur, an important Viking site. If landslides don't block the road, you can continue right around the peninsula, passing cliffs where birds perch and the remote lighthouse at Svalvogar. Do not attempt this track with a 2WD car – you will not make it.

Inland, the Westfjords' highest peak Kaldbakur (998m) is a good hiking spot. The steep trail to the summit begins from the road about 2km west of Þingeyri town.

Over on the southern side of the Þingeyri peninsula, Hrafnseyri was the birthplace of Jón Sigurðsson, the architect of Iceland's independence, which took place on 17 June 1811. The fully renovated museum (☎456 8260; www.hrafnseyri.is; adult/child Ikr500/free; ⊙10am-8pm mid-Jun–Aug) outlines aspects of his life – there's also a charming turf house out back.

Dýrafjörður & Önundarfjörður

North from Þingeyri, on the northern shore of Dýrafjörður, are a series of gorgeous broad valleys. At the head of the valleys is a lovely weatherboard church and one of Iceland's oldest botanic gardens, Skrúður (admission free; ⊙24hr), which was established as a teaching garden in 1905.

Beyond Skrúður, about 7km from Rte 60, is Hótel Núpur (☎456 8235; www.hotelnupur. is; sites per tent Ikr2500, s/d without bathroom

incl breakfast Ikr11,500/16,000). The owners have done their darnedest to turn this former schooling complex into desirable digs, though the dormlike design remains. Sleeping-bag accommodation costs Ikr4500 per person; at the time of research, en-suite rooms were being created to lure midrange travellers.

After Hótel Núpur, the road passes an abandoned farmhouse before swerving inland to head over the top of the rugged peninsula. It takes about 20 minutes to reach Ingjaldsandur at the mouth of Önundarfjörður. Set in a picturesque valley, this isolated beach is a fantastic spot to watch the midnight sun as it flirts with the sea before rising back up into the sky.

Back on Rte 60, near upper Önundarfjörður, you'll pass a marked turn-off for Kirkjubó (☎456 7679; www.kirkjubol.is; s/d from Ikr6400/10,400; ⊙Jun-Aug). The white-and-green exterior could use a little paint job, but the inside is squeaky clean, sporting several well-chosen antiques mixed in with a few mod cons.

A second turn-off further north (also marked Kirkjubó!) leads to the popular Korpudalur HI Hostel (Korpudalur Kirkjubó; ☎456 7808, 892 2030; www.korpudalur.is, www. hostel.is; sites per tent Ikr1000, dm Ikr4200; ⊙mid-May–mid-Sep; ☎). The quirky owners, stunning location, home-made breakfast bread and brand-new cottages out back make this 100-year-old farmhouse well worth visiting. Hikers will find plenty of scenic spots to stomp around in the surrounding hills. Pick-ups can be arranged from Ísafjörður for Ikr1500. Members get Ikr600 discount.

Flateyri

POP 300

Once a giant support base for Norwegian whalers, Flateyri is now a sleepy little place set on a striking gravel spit sticking out into broad Önundarfjörður. There is very little of interest to tourists besides the beautiful views and the so-called Nonsense Museum (☎894 8836; dellusafnid@simnet.is; admission Ikr700; ⊙11am-5pm Jun-Aug), which contains the private collections of several locals. You'll find hundreds of pens, matchboxes and model ships showcased in pathologically organised displays.

On weekdays there are three daily buses (☑456 4258) between Ísafjörður and Flateyri (30 minutes). To be picked up in Flateyri, call ahead – otherwise the bus might not drive into the village.

Suðureyri

POP 350

Perched on the tip of 13km-long Súgandafjörður, the fishing community of Suðureyri was isolated for years by the forbidding mountains. Now connected with Ísafjörður by a 5km tunnel, the village has a new lease of life and warmly welcomes tourists into the community.

In many ways the village is staunchly traditional – all fishing is done by rod and hook, and the grand tourism plans being developed are all about preserving nature and sharing rather than changing this traditional way of life. It's the best place in Iceland to catch halibut, making the town a natural haven for angling.

There's no formal information centre; however, there are informative billboard-like posters near the hotel that offer insights into the town's history and recent attempts at creating an infrastructure for sustainable tourism.

Sights & Activities

Locals congregate at the excellent geothermal swimming pool (Túngata 8; adult/child Ikr510/260; ⊙10am-8pm Mon-Fri, to 6pm Sat & Sun Jun-Aug, reduced hours Sep-May).

Fisherman FISHING
(☑450 9000; www.fisherman.is) The Fisherman project allows visitors to join in the regular life of the village in order to understand the lifestyle of fishing families in rural Iceland. You can visit the local fish factory at 11am and 2pm (Ikr1500), join a sea-angling tour (two hours; Ikr6900) or request to go out on a working fishing boat (Ikr24,900 per group for an afternoon). Activities can be booked online or at the hotel. You can also feed the cod in the nearby lagoon. The trick is to first bounce a stone in the lagoon, which sends the cod jumping out of the water to grab a bite!

Those without the time (or money) for a seafaring adventure can swing by the harbour between 3pm and 5pm to watch the local fisherfolk bring in the daily catch.

🛏 Sleeping & Eating

Fisherman Hotel HOTEL €€
(☑450 9000; www.fisherman.is; Aðalgata 14; s/d Ikr13,900/17,600; @🖥) Customer focused, thoroughly modern and really comfy, this friendly hotel – which feels more like a guesthouse – has bright rooms, crisp linens, pine furniture and informative cards about the area's fish. Sleeping-bag accommodation costs Ikr4000 per person.

Talisman SEAFOOD €€
(mains Ikr1900-3900; ⊙6-9pm mid-May–mid-Sep) The Fisherman Hotel's on-site restaurant has moleskin chairs, large windows, and place mats and menu covers made from fish skins. The menu features a wonderful array of locally sourced food – from sea creatures to lamb.

🔒 Shopping

Fun fact: the founder of 66° North was born in Suðureyri – conveniently located along the 66th parallel.

Á Milli Fjalla HANDICRAFTS
(Aðalgata; ⊙1-6pm Mon-Fri, 1-4pm Sat & Sun Jul-Aug) Á Milli Fjalla is an intriguing boutique selling a variety of locally crafted items like knits, ceramics, and unique trinkets made from human hair. Apparently Björk likes to shop here.

Getting There & Away

From Monday to Friday there are three daily local buses between Ísafjörður and Suðureyri (20 minutes).

Ísafjörður

POP 2540

Hub of activity in the Westfjords and by far the area's largest town, Ísafjörður is a pleasant and prosperous place and an excellent base for travellers. The town is set on a gravel spit that extends out into Skutulsfjörður, and is hemmed in on all sides by towering peaks and the eerily dark waters of the fjord.

The centre of Ísafjörður is littered with old timber and tin-clad buildings, many unchanged since the 18th century, when the harbour was full of tall ships and Norwegian whaling crews. Today it is a surprisingly cosmopolitan place, and after some time spent travelling in the Westfjords, it'll feel like a bustling metropolis with its tempting cafes and fine choice of restaurants.

VIGUR

With one farm and zillions of puffins, charming Vigur is a popular destination for day-trippers from Ísafjörður. The tiny island sits at the mouth of Hestfjörður, offering sweeping fjord views in every direction. There's not much to do on the island besides taking a stroll (grab a stick from the windmill and hold it over your head – the Arctic terns are fierce here!), visiting the eider ducks and savouring cakes at the cafe. Try 'marital bliss', a marzipan confection – it was either the most delicious thing we've ever eaten, or we were just insanely hungry, having worked up a monstrous appetite while kayaking all the way to the island. While you're sending some snail mail in the tiny post office, don't forget to have a look at the interesting egg collection inside.

West Tours (☑456 5111; www.vesturferdir.is) in Ísafjörður and Ögur Travel (☑857 1840; www.ogurtravel.com) in Ögur run tours to the island.

There's good hiking in the hills around the town, skiing in winter and regular summer boats to ferry hikers across to the remote Hornstrandir Peninsula. In fact, Ísafjörður's only downside is the long journey to get here. You'll either have to wind in and out of numerous fjords on bumpy roads or take a hair-raising flight into the tiny airstrip. Then again, it's the town's remote location and surprisingly urbane attitude that really give it its wonderful character.

⊙ Sights

Apart from the museum, Ísafjörður's formal attractions are pretty thin on the ground. The Faktorhúsið is one of the oldest catalogue buildings (an edifice made using IKEA-like instructions) in Iceland – sometimes there's a makeshift cafe inside. Of minor interest is the whalebone arch made from a whale's jawbone in the park in the centre of town. Nearby are Ísafjörður's interesting seamen's monument and the modernist town church, which looks a lot like an old-fashioned press camera with a flash on top. The altarpiece has over 100 doves, each one made by a local during a group art-making project.

Westfjords Folk Museum   MUSEUM
(☑456 3293; Neðstíkaupstaður; adult/child Ikr500/free; ☺10am-5pm Mon-Fri, 1-5pm Sat & Sun Jun, 10am-5pm daily Jul & Aug) Housed in a cluster of ancient wooden buildings by the harbour, 400m south of the tourist information centre on the spit of land in the middle of the fjord, the Westfjords Folk Museum is an atmospheric place full of relics. The dimly lit main building, the Turnhús, dates from 1784 and was originally used as a warehouse. Inside it's like stepping back in time, with

every available surface covered by fishing and nautical exhibits, tools and equipment from the whaling days, and fascinating old photos depicting life in the town over the centuries. To the right of this building is the wooden Tjöruhús (1781), which now operates as a very pleasant cafe and seafood restaurant. Two other buildings on the site, the Faktorhús, built in 1765 to house the manager of the village shop, and the Krambúd (1757), originally a storehouse, are now private residences.

↪ Tours

Tours from Ísafjörður are largely focused around the Hornstrandir reserve nearby; both West Tours and Borea run regular ferry services into the park.

Borea   BOAT TOUR
(☑456 3322; www.borea.is; Aðalstræti 22b) Borea is an adventure outfitter par excellence, offering a variety of mind-blowing experiences that could have you coming back to the Westfjords for years. High-quality tours often involve multiday trips aboard *Aurora*, a yacht built for the Clipper Round the World Race. The boat is beautifully outfitted and meals aboard will be some of the best you'll have during your visit to Iceland. A yearly voyage schedule is posted on the website and includes exhilarating journeys to Greenland. These days Borea is really upping the ante on adventures in Hornstrandir; besides running regular ferry services from Bolungarvík, it also offers a variety of trips like multiday kayaking excursions, springtime skiing and guided day-long hiking. It also makes full use of Kviar, a private cabin tucked away in the

Ísafjörður

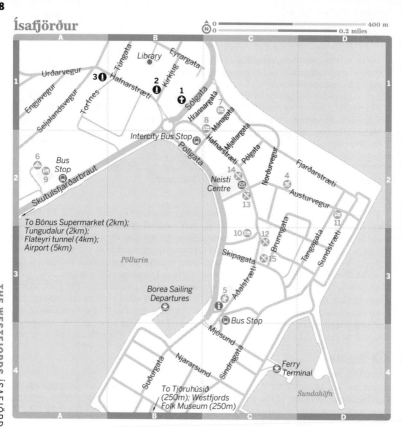

silent hills of the reserve. Check out the website for details.

West Tours
BOAT TOUR

(Vesturferðir; ☑456 5111; www.vesturferdir.is) Housed in the same building as the tourist information centre, the popular and professional West Tours organises a mind-boggling array of trips in the area. There are tours of Vigur and kayaking excursions all year. You can visit the abandoned village at Hesteyri on a day trip, or organise an extended tour package to explore Hornstrandir over several days. Biking, birdwatching and cultural excursions are but a few of the other activities on offer. Visit the office when you're in town to learn more; check the website for specifics.

🛏 Sleeping

Campers can pitch a tent at Hótel Edda's **campsite** (sites per person lkr1000; ⊗Jun-Aug) or at the **campsite** (☑444 4960; Skutulsfjarðarbraut; sites per person lkr1000; ⊗mid-Jun–mid-Aug) further out of town near the scenic waterfall in Tungudalur. The last stop on the local town bus will take you to within 1km of the site.

Immaculate and fully equipped apartments in the city centre can be rented from **Gentle Space** (☑892 9282; www.gentlespace.is; apt lkr17,700-19,900).

Gamla Gistihúsið
GUESTHOUSE **€**

(Old Guest House; ☑456 4146; www.gisti hus.is; Mánagata 5; dm/d incl breakfast from lkr4800/13,000; @🤶) Bright, cheerful and immaculately kept, this excellent guesthouse has simple but comfortable rooms with plenty of homey touches. The bathrooms are shared, but each double room has telephone, washbasin and bathrobes. An annexe just down the road has a guest kitchen and more modern, functional rooms.

Ísafjörður

Litla Guesthouse GUESTHOUSE €
(☑474 1455; www.guesthouselitla.is; Sundstræti 43; s/d Ikr12,000/14,000; ⊕) Wooden floors, crisp white linen, fluffy towels and TVs are available in the high-quality rooms of Litla, another cosy guesthouse with tasteful decor. Two rooms share each bathroom, and there's a guest kitchen. Check out the jungle mural painted along the stairwell.

Hótel Ísafjörður HOTEL €€
(☑456 4111; www.hotelisafjordur.is; Silfurtorg 2; s/d incl breakfast from Ikr22,500/27,500; @⊕) Look up 'business hotel' in the dictionary and you'll define this place, slap bang in the centre of town. Rooms on the higher floors have great views over the tin-roofed town and the waters beyond.

Hótel Edda HOTEL €€
(☑444 4960; www.hoteledda.is; d with/without bathroom from Ikr22,900/14,200; ⊙Jun-Aug; @⊕) No-frills summer accommodation is available at the town's secondary school. You can choose from basic sleeping-bag accommodation (Ikr5000) in the classrooms, private rooms with shared bathrooms and doubles with private bathrooms. We actually liked the shared bathrooms more – the

rooms with private facilities all had twin beds and felt a bit too like a hospital. On-site camping is available – with showers.

✕ Eating

There's a **Samkaup supermarket** (⊙10am-8pm Mon-Sat, noon-8pm Sun) in the Neisti Centre on Hafnarstræti and a cheaper **Bónus supermarket** (⊙9am-6pm) on the main road into town (expect long lines – it's the only Bónus in the Westfjords), though you can't go wrong with the multitude of bakeries around town. For alcohol, there's a **Vín Búð** (Aðalstræti 20).

Tjöruhúsið ICELANDIC €€
(Tar House; Hólgata 10; mains Ikr2000-5000; ⊙Jun-Sep) The faux-rustic summer restaurant at the folk museum offers some of the best fish and seafood dishes in town, and at very reasonable prices! Go for the *plokk-fiskur* – flaked fish, potatoes and onions – or try the catch of the day fresh off the boat from the harbour up the street.

Bræðraborg CAFE €
(www.borea.is; Aðalstræti; mains Ikr550-1190; ⊙8am-10pm Mon-Fri, to 1am Sat & Sun Jun-Aug, reduced hours Sep-May; ⊕) Fancying itself as a travellers cafe, Bræðraborg is a comfy spot to update your blog while munching on healthy snacks and chatting with other visitors who have gathered to earn their Hornstrandir stripes. The cafe doubles as the headquarters for Borea – a friendly outfitter specialising in Arctic adventures.

Hamraborg FAST FOOD €
(Aðalstræti; Hafnarstræti 7; mains Ikr1099-1499; ⊙9am-11.30pm) Voted Iceland's best kiosk by national radio polls, this fast-food outpost attracts all the locals who crowd around to gossip over Béarnaise burgers. Sports frequently play on the TV, and hikers like to swing by after completing their Hornstrandir mission.

Edinborg ICELANDIC €€
(Aðalstræti 7; mains Ikr1800-3000) In the same building as the info centre, this social space sees lots of tourist traffic and makes a convenient spot to try some local fish and lamb. The house bread is made with the yeast from discarded beer. The owners also run Hótel Núpur (p165).

Við Pollinn ICELANDIC €€
(Silfurtorg 2; mains Ikr2300-4600) Although the decor feels a bit IKEA-ish, Hótel Ísafjörður's

restaurant has an excellent selection of local cuisine. The windows offer great views over the fjord – you might even see your next meal getting hauled into the harbour.

Thai Koon ASIAN €€
(Neisti Centre, Hafnarstræti 9; mains Ikr1590-1790; ⏱11.30am-9pm Mon-Sat, 5-9pm Sun) After a few weeks of limited choice for meals, this small Thai canteen seems decidedly exotic. Although there's no atmosphere here whatsoever, the food is reliable and served up in heaping portions.

❶ Information

The friendly **tourist information centre** (www.isafjordur.is; Aðalstræti 7; ⏱8am-6pm Mon-Fri, 8.30am-2pm Sat, 11am-2pm Sun Jun-Aug, reduced hours Sep-May) is down by the harbour in the Edinborgarhús, built in 1907. The tourist office also has a single internet terminal that travellers can use for a free 10-minute session. Luggage storage is available for Ikr200 a day.

❶ Getting There & Away

Air

Air Iceland (☑456 3000; www.airiceland.is) is based at the airport and flies to/from Reykjavík two or three times daily. Flights to Akureyri connect through Reykjavík.

A special bus service runs to the airport about 45 minutes before departures. It starts in Bolungarvík and stops near the Hótel Ísafjörður.

Boat

In summer, ferries to Hornstrandir depart from the Sundahöfn docks on the eastern side of the isthmus; ferries to Hornstrandir also depart from Bolungarvík.

Bus

All buses circling through the Westfjords stop in Ísafjörður. Buses stop at the N1 petrol station on Hafnarstræti. **Local council buses** (☑456 4258) run twice daily Monday to Friday from Ísafjörður to Flateyri and Þingeyri, and three times daily to Suðureyri and Bolungarvík.

As the hub of activity in the region, it might be worth trying out ridesharing if you're a bit tight on cash. Check out www.bilfar.is.

❶ Getting Around

City buses operate from 7.30am to 6.30pm on weekdays (until 10.30pm in winter) and connect the town centre with Hnífsdalur and Tungudalur. Contact **West Tours** (☑456 5111; www.vesturferdir.is) for bike rentals.

Bolungarvík

POP 920

Despite its stunningly dramatic position at the fjordhead, Bolungarvík is sleepy and rundown. For hikers, however, it's a great place to launch oneself into the wild Hornstrandir reserve; there's a good lodging and eating option for those who need to spend the night in town.

Housed in a series of old turf-and-stone fishing shacks, located down a turn-off just after the tunnel into town, the open-air Ósvör Maritime Museum (☑892 1616; adult/child Ikr900/600; ⏱10am-5pm Jun-Aug) is well worth a visit. A guide in a typical sheepskin fisherman's outfit shows you round (warning: his English isn't tops), explaining the history of the area and the traditional methods for salting fish. The cramped fishermen's hut is full of interesting relics. A traditional rowing boat is also on display.

In the town's main shopping arcade, the Natural History Museum (www.nabo.is; Vitastíg 3; adult/child Ikr600/free; ⏱9am-5pm Mon-Fri, 1-5pm Sat & Sun Jun-Aug) has a comprehensive collection of minerals and stuffed animals – including a polar bear shot by local fishermen while swimming off the Hornstrandir coast.

TOP
CHOICE Einarshúsið (☑456 7901; www.einarshusid.is; Hafnargata 41; d incl breakfast Ikr16,500) is a turn-of-the-century heritage home along the harbour, and the best place to eat and sleep rolled up in one bundle. The super-friendly owners dote on their guests, who gorge on tasty seafood mains after returning from a multiday adventure in the Hornstrandir reserve. You can't go wrong with the hearty seafood soup – each bowl is made fresh. Should you want to spend the night, you'll find five lovely rooms upstairs, decorated in the style from when the house was originally built (1902).

From June to August there are three buses from Ísafjörður to Bolungarvík from Monday to Friday, and two in the opposite direction. Borea's ferry service to Hornstrandir departs from here.

Ísafjarðardjúp

The largest of the fjords in the region, 75km-long Ísafjarðardjúp takes a massive swath out of the Westfjords' landmass. Circuitous Rte 61 winds in and out of a series of smaller fjords on the southern side, making the drive from Ísafjörður to Hólmavík like sliding along each tooth of a fine comb.

SÚÐAVÍK
POP 200

Just east of Ísafjörður, the small fishing community of Súðavík commands an imposing view across the fjord to Hornstrandir. Although the township is nothing more than a string of bright, box-shaped houses, it is definitely worth stopping by to visit the Arctic Fox Center (☎862 8219; www. arcticfoxcenter.com; admission Ikr800; ☺10am-10pm; ☎). The study of the Arctic fox has been under way on nearby Hornstrandir for several years, but the locally loved exhibition centre has taken things to the next level. Interesting displays detail the life of the local Arctic fox and its relationship with humans and the surrounding nature. Don't forget to sign the beautiful fish-skin guestbook and play with the orphaned foxes in the pen outside.

The centre sits inside the renovated farmstead of Eyrardalur – one of the oldest buildings in the area. Even if foxes aren't your bag, the on-site Fox Cafe (soup Ikr900) is a great place to break up the journey and hang out with welcoming locals – try the filling Hornstrandir soup, which comes with home-made bread.

The centre's friendly managers are always looking for enthusiastic volunteers to work in Súðavík and/or go on surveying missions in Hornstrandir.

Daily from Monday to Saturday there's a private bus from Ísafjörður to Súðavík (20 minutes). The buses between Ísafjörður and Hólmavík also pass through town on Sunday, Tuesday and Friday.

LITLIBÆR

Litlibær (☎456 4809; hvitanes@isl.is; admission free; ☺Jun-Aug) is a wee museum and cafe set up on a lonely farmstead. The owner was born and raised on the land, and these days he dotes on weary tourists with tasty pancakes and tips on seeing the seals and Celtic ruins nearby. After filling your belly, scout out the picnic table about 200m away – here you'll find a small box with binoculars to help view the blubbery beasts.

ÖGUR

Run by seven siblings, Ögur Travel (☎857 1840; www.ogurtravel.com; ☺May-Sep) offers personal kayaking trips in the region. The

---

VOLUNTEERING AT THE ARCTIC FOX RESEARCH STATION

Trying to find an excuse to extend your Icelandic vacation? Look no further than the Arctic Fox Research Station, situated on the northern cliffs of the jaw-dropping Hornstrandir Peninsula – a photographer's Eden and naturalist's dream.

Although it's a private facility, the research station at Hornbjarg is quite informal – just a cluster of tents and a charming outhouse a few kilometres away. Each day, the team of researchers/volunteers sets off for an eight-hour viewing session during which they monitor fox behaviours, interactions and changes in location. There's a lot of sitting and looking involved, but we can't think of a more stunning location to take in the views and the nature. In fact, we took a bit of time off from our research to hunker down on the mossy cliffs and help out. We lucked out with T-shirt weather – the temperatures are usually a bit more shivery...

There are no requirements for becoming a volunteer – just a love of the great outdoors! However, preference is given to those studying biology, conservation or tourism. Volunteers are asked to give at least one week of their time and should keep their departure date somewhat flexible (ferry service can be delayed by a day or two when the seas around Hornstrandir are particularly rough). You'll also need to have the usual trappings of an outdoor adventure: a tent, hiking boots, thermal sleeping bag and clothing appropriate for negative temperatures. The research centre will handle everything else (food, transport, additional equipment etc).

If the windswept wilderness isn't your cup of tea, you can also volunteer at the headquarters in cosy Súðavík, near Ísafjörður. The Arctic Fox Center (www.arcticfoxcenter. com) is affiliated with the University of Iceland in Reykjavík and features an exhibition space telling the story of the Arctic fox's lifestyle, biology, history and tumultuous relationship with fur-hunting humans. Staff working here may even have the opportunity to help train rescue dogs. Volunteers are offered free spaces to camp on the premises.

most popular option is the six- to seven-hour tour of Vigur (Ikr15,000), which takes in the incredible scenery and much of the local bird life. Multiday trips are also on offer with plenty of advance booking. Tours run from the small **cafe** (mains Ikr900-2300; ☺Jun-Aug) – if you're coming from Ísafjörður and you hit the field of parked abandoned cars, then you've gone too far.

MJÓIFJÖRÐUR & VATNSFJÖRÐUR

TOP CHOICE **Heydalur** (☎456 4824; www.heydalur.is; sites per person Ikr1000, s/d Ikr10,650/14,850; ☜) is a fantastic place to break up the journey following Rte 61 as it wiggles its way along the undulating, fjord-ridden coast from Suðavík. At the head of Mjóifjörður, 11km from the main road, the farm is run by the affable Stella, who spends most of her time cooking up delicious treats in the on-site restaurant. Her son always has a multitude of construction projects under way – when we stayed he was building an additional 10 rooms. Activities abound, including guided horse riding (Ikr4500 per hour) and kayaking (Ikr5000 for 2½ hours).

Even if you don't have plans to stop for the night, Heydalur's **restaurant** (mains Ikr1500-3300; ☺8am-10pm) is a great place to unwind and stretch your legs. Say hello to the parrot (he'll say hello back!) while savouring excellent soups, home-made breads, organic vegies from the local garden, and the popular lamb curry and fillets. The restaurant itself sits inside a restored barn. Don't forget to look up – the beautiful chandelier overhead is made from green glass buoy balls once used to steady fishing traps.

REYKJARFJÖRÐUR

At the end of tiny Reykjarfjörður is the friendly but well-weathered **Hótel Reykjanes** (☎456 4844; www.hotelreykjanes.is; sites per tent Ikr2100, s/d Ikr8900/12,000; @☜), housed in the huge white complex that was once the district's school. The rooms are compact and functional (most bathrooms are shared), but there's a randomly gigantic (50m) outdoor **geothermal pool** here, which is fed by a steamy spring just beyond. Meals can be purchased (mains Ikr1500 to Ikr3900) if you're not self-catering. Ask about **Saltverk Reykjanes**, the salt-producing atelier 200m away; there's also a second massive pool that's hidden up on a hill and was apparently built over 300 years ago.

SNÆFJALLASTRÖND

On the eastern shore of Ísafjarðardjúp, the unsurfaced Rte 635 leads north to **Kaldalón**, a beautiful green valley running

Hornstrandir

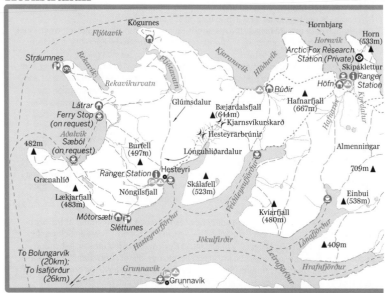

up to the receding Drangajökull ice cap. It's an easy walk up to the snow line, but watch out for dangerous crevasses if you venture out onto the ice. Further north, Snæfjallaströnd was abandoned in 1995, but adventurous hikers can walk along the 'Postal Road' from the church at Unaðsdalur along the coast to the bunkhouse at Grunnavík, from where you can catch boats to Ísafjörður and Hesteyri.

Just before the church at Unaðsdalur, **Dalbær** (☑ 898 9300; www.snjafjallasetur.is/tour ism.html; ☺mid-Jun–Aug) is a great wilderness outpost on the edge of Hornstrandir. The owner has a flower shop in Reykjavík during the rest of the year and is known in the region for cooking up a mean reindeer. Pricing wasn't available at the time of writing, so call or check the website for details.

HORNSTRANDIR

Craggy mountains, precarious sea cliffs and plunging waterfalls ring the wonderful uninhabited Hornstrandir Peninsula at the northern end of the Westfjords. This is one of Europe's last true wilderness areas, covering some of the most extreme and inhospitable parts of the country. It's a fantastic destination for hiking, with challenging

terrain and excellent opportunities for spotting Arctic foxes, seals, whales and teeming bird life.

A handful of hardy farmers lived in Hornstrandir until the 1950s, but since 1975 the 580 sq km of tundra, fjord, glacier and alpine upland have been protected as a national monument and nature reserve. The area has some of the strictest preservation rules in Iceland, thanks to its incredibly rich, but fragile, vegetation.

There are no services available in Hornstrandir and hikers must be fully prepared to tackle all eventualities. The passes here are steep and you'll need to carry all your gear, so hiking can be slower than you might expect. In addition, most trails are unmarked, so it's essential to carry a good map (try *Vestfirðir & Dalir* #3) and a GPS.

The best time to visit is in July. Outside the summer season (from late June to mid-August) there are few people around and the weather is unpredictable. If travelling in the off season, it is essential to plan ahead and get local advice, as vast snow drifts with near-vertical faces can develop on the mountain passes. There are emergency huts with radios and heaters at various points in the park for use in case of sudden blizzards or storms. Don't let the fickle forces of nature deter you from exploring – ask some of the local operators about current conditions before setting off. Guided trips can also be easily arranged.

☞ Tours

The two main operators running tours (boating, hiking, kayaking, skiing etc) into the wilds of Hornstrandir are West Tours and Borea, both based in Ísafjörður (see p167).

🛏 Sleeping

Wild-camping in Hornstrandir is free (make sure to take all of your rubbish with you). Staying on private grounds with facilities costs around Ikr1000. Expect to pay upwards of Ikr2000 for sleeping-bag space. There are three options for sleeping-bag accommodation in the main part of the Hornstrandir reserve: **Hesteyri** (☑456 1123), which has accommodation for 18 people in the old doctor's house, with coffee and pancakes available; **Hornbjargsviti** (☑566 6762; www.fi.is), run by Ferðafélag Íslands (FI), and attached to the lighthouse; and **Grunnavík** (☑852 4819; www.grunnavik.is), which has space for around 20 people – the owner

HIKING IN HORNSTRANDIR

The word 'Hornstrandir' is synonymous with stunning subarctic hiking, so how is one ever supposed to choose from the array of trails that zigzag across the peninsula like tangled shoelaces? Locals and tourists agree: the Royal Horn (or 'Hornsleið') is, hands down, your best option to take in all of what the reserve has to offer. Follow this four-to-five-day hike from Veiðileysufjörður to Hesteyri and you'll get a good picture of the region; the itinerary can also be easily modified if you run into bad weather. The trails on this route are clearly marked, but at the same time there are very few tourists, so it's a great opportunity to experience the desolate landscape.

The Royal Horn

Day 1: Sail from Bolungarvík or Ísafjörður to Veiðileysufjörður, one of the local *jökulfirðir* (glacier fjords). The hike begins on a street near the bottom of the fjord and follows a cairn-marked trail up the slope and through the mountain pass. From the pass you can descend the mountain on either side until you reach the campsite at Höfn in Hornvík. The hike from Veiðileysufjörður to Hornvík can take anywhere between four and eight hours. There's a ranger station at the campsite here, so feel free to stop by to get the latest weather forecast and information about trail conditions.

Day 2: Stay in Hornvík for a second night and use your second day to visit Hornbjarg, one of Iceland's most beautiful bird cliffs with diverse flora and fauna. Alternatively, you could spend the second day exploring the area around the lighthouse, Hornbjargsviti.

Day 3: Hike from Hornvík to Hlöðuvík. The partly marked trail goes through a mountain pass and is relatively easy to find. Camping in Hlöðuvík is best by the Hlöðuvíkurós (the mouth of the Hlöðuvík river). Like Hornvík, Hlöðuvík faces north – it's the perfect place to watch the spectacular midnight sun. Figure around six hours to reach Hlöðuvík.

Day 4: Hike through Kjarnsvíkurskarð (a mountain pass) and Hesteyrarbrúnir to Hesteyri (figure around eight hours). Hesteyri is an old village that was abandoned around the middle of the 20th century. There are still several well-kept houses here, amid the fields of angelica. Ruins of a turn-of-the-century whaling station are found near the village. The coffee shop in Hesteyri is a good place to visit at the end of your hike – you can wait here for the ferry back to Bolungarvík or Ísafjörður.

Day 5: If the ferry isn't running that day, enjoy a night in Heysteri and spend one more day walking in the area before catching the boat. Pitch your tent at the campsite just south of the village.

Abridged

If you don't have the time, or the gumption, to tackle the Royal Horn, you can take the ferry to Veiðileysufjörður, hike up to Hornvík, spend the night (or two) there, and walk down to Lónafjörður to link back up with a boat, which stops here for passengers around 7pm. The walk from Hornvík to Lónafjörður takes around six to seven hours.

heats a hot-pot by fire and stirs it like human soup.

There are two additional sleeping-bag options in the far-eastern part of the reserve: Reykjarfjörður (☑456 7215) and Bolungarvík (☑456 7192). Consider using these if you're trekking overland between Hornstrandir and Norðurfjörður. If you're coming from Norðurfjörður it'll take three days by foot to reach Reykjarfjörður; Bolungarvík is one more day beyond. On days one and two you can wild-camp at Ófeigsfjörður and Drangar.

🛈 Getting There & Away

Getting to Hornstrandir requires a boat trip from Ísafjörður or Bolungarvík, from where there are regular ferry services from June to mid-August. Typically a one-way ride costs Ikr6000 to Ikr7500, depending on your destination.

West Tours runs **Sjóferðir** (☑456 3879; www.sjoferdir.is) from Ísafjörður. Boats run to Hornvík four times a week, to Hesteyri five times a week, and Aðalvík twice a week, among other destinations. See www.vesturferdir.is for more information.

Borea runs **Bjarnarnes** (☑696 6565; www. bjarnarnes.is), which departs from Bolungarvík. Expect transfers to Veiðileysufjörður and Hesteyri four days a week. Check out www. borea.is/Ferry for the schedule and pricing.

There is no boat service from the Strandir coast, though it is possible to hike into the reserve – it takes three full days if you walk through Fossadalsheiði instead of following the coast.

STRANDIR COAST

Sparsely populated, magnificently peaceful and all but deserted by other travellers, the Westfjords' eastern spine is one of the most dramatic places in all of Iceland. Indented by a series of bristle-like fjords and lined with towering crags, the drive north of Hólmavík, the region's only sizeable settlement, is rough, wild and incredibly rewarding. South of here, gently rolling hills stretch along the isolated coastline as far as Staðarskáli, where the sudden rush of traffic tells you that you've returned to the Ring Road and the travelling masses.

There are buses along the coast as far as Hólmavík and Drangsnes, but you'll need your own vehicle and a sense of adventure to get further.

Staðarskáli to Hólmavík

Although lacking the natural drama further north, the long drive along Rte 68 from Staðarskáli (formerly Brú) to Hólmavík is pleasantly pastoral, with rolling hills dotted by small farmhouses and lonely churches. If counting sheep doesn't make you fall asleep, then stop by the small **Sheep Farming Museum** (☑451 3324; www.strandir.is/saudfjarsetur;

adult/child Ikr700/free; ☺10am-6pm Jun-Aug), which details the region's farming history through photos and artefacts. Chessboards and home-made rhubarb pie may keep you around longer than expected. For accommodation, try the retro starship-styled **Broddanes HI Hostel** (☑618 1830; www.broddanes. is; dm/d from Ikr4000/10,000; ☎), positioned closer to Bitrufjörður along Rte 68.

Hólmavík

POP 420

The fishing village and service centre of Hólmavík offers sweeping views over the still waters of Steingrímsfjörður and has a quirky witchcraft museum. The town is a good place to stock up on supplies before venturing off into more rugged territory further north.

◉ Sights

Museum of Icelandic Sorcery & Witchcraft   MUSEUM
(☑451 3525; www.galdrasyning.is; Höfðagata 8-10; adult/child Ikr800/free; ☺9am-6pm) Hólmavík's main tourist attraction is the award-winning Museum of Icelandic Sorcery & Witchcraft, by the central harbour. Unlike the widely known Salem witch trials in New England, almost all of Iceland's convicted witches were men. Most of their occult practices were simply old Viking traditions, but hidden *grimoires* (magic books) full of puzzling runic designs were proof enough for the local witch-hunters to burn around 20 souls at the stake. Several *grimoires* (some even used in the early 20th century!) are on display, as are kookier exhibits like 'the invisible boy' (you'll see), and the 'necropants'.

NECROPANTS...

Of all the strange displays at the Museum of Icelandic Sorcery & Witchcraft, perhaps the most bizarre is a plastic replica of the legendary 'necropants' – trousers made from the skin of a dead man's legs and groin. It was commonly believed that the necropants would spontaneously produce money when worn, so long as the donor made an honest verbal agreement that his corpse could be skinned upon his death. Once dead and buried, the donor corpse had to be unearthed at the dead of night, then a magic rune and a coin from a poor widow (the penniless widows *always* got picked on in Icelandic lore!) were placed in the dead man's scrotum.

The necropants brought incredible wealth to its wearer – anytime money was needed, one could reach down into the scrotal area and...voila! There was a catch, however; if you were to die wearing the necropants, your soul would be condemned to roam the earth until the end of time.

Additional displays can be found on the 2nd floor.

There is another section of the museum along the Strandir coast – a turf-roofed 'sorcerer's cottage' in Bjarnarfjörður.

🛏 Sleeping & Eating

As always, there's a small grocery, campsite (sites per person Ikr900), swimming pool, and cheap eats at the petrol station.

Finna Hótel   GUESTHOUSE **€**
(📞451 3136; www.finnahotel.is; Borgarbraut 4; d without bathroom Ikr10,600; @🛜) Friendly Finna is split between two locations – a second building called Steinhúsið sits near the witch museum. Rooms are basic, but everything is kept clean and fresh. Sleeping-bag accommodation costs Ikr4200 per person.

Sorcery Cafe   CAFE **€€**
(www.galdrasyning.is; Höfðagata 10; mains Ikr1900-2350; ⊗9am-6pm) About as 'local' as things get in the region – the menu changes daily at this friendly museum cafe. Expect mussels fresh from the fjord and wild berries for dessert.

Café Riis   INTERNATIONAL **€€**
(Hafnarbraut 39; mains Ikr1550-3990; ⊗11.30am-9pm) The town's pub and restaurant is a popular place set in a historic wooden building with stripped floors and carved magic symbols on the bar. Roasted chicken breast, puffin and trout are the menu's biggest hits.

ℹ Information

The **tourist information centre** (📞451 3111; www.holmavik.is/info; Norðurtún 1; ⊗9am-6pm) is beside the new swimming complex in the modern community centre – the N1 petrol station is across the street. You can access the internet here (free) and pick up copies of the useful *Vestfirðir & Dalir* #3 and #6 hiking maps for Ikr1200. Ask here about horse riding for all levels with **Strandhestar** (www.strandhestar.is).

ℹ Getting There & Away

From June to August, buses run between Staðarskáli and Hólmavík (two hours) on Tuesday, Friday and Sunday only. The same service continues from Hólmavík on to Drangsnes (30 minutes) on Friday. Buses from Ísafjörður to Hólmavík (Sunday, Tuesday and Friday from June to August, four hours) are timed to connect with the service to Staðarskáli. You can connect to services to Reykjavík and Akureyri from Staðarskáli. During winter there is one bus a week (on Friday) from Reykjavík to Hólmavík via Staðarskáli.

Drangsnes

POP 80

Across the fjord from Hólmavík, Drangsnes (pronounced *drowngs*-ness) is a remote little village with views across to north Iceland and the small uninhabited island of Grímsey. Guarding the shoreline is ominous rocky stack Kerling, the supposed remains of a petrified troll. Uxi, her bull, is the formation out at sea near Grímsey.

As haunting as the bizarre sea stacks may be, a favourite attraction is the secreted set of free geothermal hot-pots built into the sea wall along the main road. Eagle eyes will have to spot a small swimming sign pointing to a shower and the three geometric Jacuzzis; keep an eye out for the town's modern church instead – the little pools are directly across the street. During the colder months you'll often see bathrobe-clad locals driving up for a quick soak after work (remember – everyone has to shower before jumping in!). There's also the town's swimming pool, Drangsnes sundlaug (adult/child Ikr500/free; ⊗10am-9pm mid-Jun–mid-Aug, 11am-6pm mid-Aug–mid-Jun), with two sparkling hot-pots for when the weather's too tumultuous by the sea.

Located next to the Kerling, Malarhorn (📞451 3238; www.malarhorn.is; Grundargata 17;

THE GRÍMSEY TROLLS

According to legend the island of Grímsey, off the coast of Drangsnes, was created by evil trolls, now petrified into the stone stacks at Drangsnes. Intent on severing the Westfjords from the mainland, the trolls decided to dig a trench right across the peninsula. Unfortunately, they were so wrapped up in the job that they failed to notice the rising sun. As the first rays broke over the horizon, the two trolls at the trench's western end were transformed into standing stones at Kollafjörður. The female troll on the east side nearly escaped, but as she was turning to flee she realised that she had marooned her bull on the newly created island of Grímsey. Suddenly the sunbeams struck – she was promptly turned to stone forever, gazing back at her lost bull.

d Ikr12,300; 🐾) has a variety of accommodation including a peaceful row of crisp pine cabins that feel thoroughly modern yet remarkably cosy. Additional lodging options take the form of a large wooden house with several apartments inside. Malarhorn runs a variety of sailing, sea-angling and fishing trips (Ikr2000). Three-hour tours of the puffin-infested Grímsey (adult/child Ikr4600/2000) are on offer at 1.30pm every day (four person minimum).

Malarkaffi (www.malarhorn.is; Grundargata 17; mains Ikr1800-4000; ⏰11.30am-9pm) serves an array of fish, lobster and lamb on its 2nd-storey verandah overlooking the fjord.

The Friday bus from Staðarskáli to Hólmavík continues to Drangsnes (30 minutes), returning the same day. No buses run north of Drangsnes, so you'll need a vehicle to reach Laugarhóll or anywhere further north.

Bjarnarfjörður

North of Drangsnes, a rough road winds around a series of gorgeous crumbling escarpments and dramatic fjords. There's no public transport and few services on this route, but if you've got your own vehicle, the utter tranquillity, incredible views and sheer sense of isolation are truly remarkable. For those interested in the sagas, you'll be keen to know that *Njál's Saga* (p112) starts here.

TOP CHOICE Hótel Laugarhóll (☑451 3380; www.laugarholl.is; d with/without bath incl breakfast Ikr20,600/16,000; @🐾), in the first indent along the coast, is run by perhaps the friendliest people you'll meet during your time in Iceland. The owners are former school teachers – in fact they once taught in this very building, which has now been turned into a hotel of modest proportions. Crisp white duvets lie neatly folded on every bed, some with original artwork hanging just above. There's a small on-site gallery, and the owners also run the toasty **geothermal pool** (admission Ikr350; ⏰8am-10pm Jun-Aug, 24hr Sep-May) next door, which has some of the warmest water in Iceland.

Near the hotel is an ancient **artificial pool** that was blessed by a bishop in the 11th century and is now a national monument. The consecrated pool feeds the lovely geothermal pool nearby, so if you stop by for a dip you're essentially bathing in holy water (or so the locals say). Just a few steps away is

the turf-roofed **Sorcerer's Cottage** (admission free; ⏰8am-10pm Jun-Aug), which is part of the witchcraft museum in Hólmavík. A collection of *grimoire* translations and a brochure about the cottage can be purchased at the hotel – the author lives in the yellow house on the far side of the road.

North of Bjarnarfjörður the scenery becomes more rugged and there are fine views across to the Skagi Peninsula in north Iceland. This road often closes with the first snows in autumn and may not reopen until spring. If you're travelling late in the season, ask locally for up-to-date information on conditions.

At **Kaldbaksvík** the steep sides of a broad fjord sweep down to a small fishing lake that serenely reflects the surrounding mountains. Just beyond the lake, a 4km trail runs up to the summit of craggy Lambatindur (854m). You'll notice copious amounts of driftwood piled up along the shore on this coast – most of it has arrived from Siberia across the Arctic Ocean.

Reykjarfjörður

Tucked in beneath a looming rock wall at Reykjarfjörður is the strangely enchanting factory at Djúpavík. Once a thriving centre for herring processing, the area was all but abandoned when the plant closed in 1950. The looming bulk of the deserted factory dominates the village, but for those travellers who make it here it's one of the most memorable locations of their trip.

🍴 Sleeping & Eating

TOP CHOICE Hótel Djúpavík   GUESTHOUSE €
(☑451 4037; www.djupavik.com; d from Ikr6200; 🐾) A charming bolthole swathed in antiques and set in the former factory accommodation block, Djúpavík's understated charm lies in its ability to calm the most angst-ridden soul. There's something truly magical about its sprinkling of cabins and cottages positioned next to a decaying factory on one of the most stunning bays in all of Iceland. If only the staff's demeanour matched the pleasant surrounds...

The hotel has an OK in-house restaurant serving fish from the fjord, there's a self-service kitchen for those who are so inclined, and a section of the abandoned factory has been turned into an art exhibition space by **Claus** (www.clausiniceland.com).

Norðurfjörður

North of Djúpavík, there are two interesting churches at **Árnes** – one is a traditional wooden structure, and the other (virtually across the street) is strangely and dramatically futuristic. Also worth a look is the small museum, **Kört** (www.trekyllisvik.is; Árnes 2; admission Ikr750; ☉10am-6pm Jun-Aug), which sells handicrafts, offers info about the area, and has displays on fishing, farming and collected knick-knacks. Check out **Kistan** (meaning 'the coffin'), an area of craggy, waterlogged rocks that served as the region's main site for witch executions. Iceland's last documented case of witch burning took place here. It's marked on the main road, but easier to find if you ask for directions.

Clinging onto life at the end of the long bumpy road up the Strandir coast is the little fishing village of **Norðurfjörður**. The township has a cafe, a petrol station and a few guesthouses, and it's the last place to stock up and indulge in some home comforts before heading off to Hornstrandir by foot.

TOP CHOICE **Krossneslaug** (admission Ikr450) is a geothermal swimming pool, up a dirt track about 3km beyond Norðurfjörður. Sitting at the edge of the universe on a wild black-pebble beach, it's an incredible place to watch the midnight sun flirt with the lapping waves.

🛏 Sleeping & Eating

Urðartindur   GUESTHOUSE €
(☎843 8110; www.urdartindur.is; d Ikr14,000; ☉May-Sep) Blessed with unobstructed fjord views along a black-sand beach, this small collection of accommodation features four guest rooms and two cottages (Ikr17,000 each) that can sleep up to four people. Ask

Arinbjörn, the kindly owner, about a secret hiking path that leads to a hidden lake. Sleeping-bag accommodation costs Ikr5000 per person; guest kitchen facilities are also available.

Bergistangi   HOSTEL €
(☎451 4003; gunnsteinn@simnet.is; d Ikr8600) On the hill overlooking the harbour, this friendly guesthouse has good sleeping-bag accommodation (Ikr3000 per person) and a guest kitchen. The owners have recently converted the old slaughterhouse into a prim batch of additional dorm rooms.

Kaffi Norðurfjörður   NORDIC €€
(Gamla Verbúðin; mains Ikr1500-3000; ☉11am-9pm; ☉late May-late Aug; 🖥) The food isn't anything to write home about, but the fjord views are lovely, the owners are very chatty, and you can play old vinyl records in the corner.

❶ Getting There & Away

Air

No buses run to Norðurfjörður, but **Eagle Air** (☎562 4200; www.ernir.is; Reykjavík Domestic Airport) pilots charter flights on Mondays in summer and on Mondays and Thursdays in winter between Reykjavík and the airstrip at Gjögur, 16km southeast of Norðurfjörður. The trip takes 50 minutes.

Boat

Ferries no longer run from Norðurfjörður to the Hornstrandir reserve. You can try offering some cash (Ikr6000 should do it) to hitch a ride north on one of the local fishing ships; your best chance of success is from Monday to Thursday during the earlier part of the month in summer when the monthly fishing quotas haven't been filled and locals stop sending out ships.

Iceland: Nature's Wonderland

Fire & Ice »
Wildlife Watching »
The Hot-Pot Hop »
Hiking »

Northern Lights (aurora borealis; p37) over Hveragerði

SILVIA OTTE / GETTY IMAGES ©

Fire & Ice

Like a real-life version of *Game of Thrones*, Iceland's volatile landscape is an unholy – and ever-quaking – realm of windswept glaciers and ominous volcanic peaks threatening to unleash their fire-breathing fury on the quiet plains below.

Vatnajökull

1 The island's ice queen is Europe's largest ice cap and the namesake for its largest national park (p282). Don't miss the chance to explore this endless kingdom of white aboard a snowmobile.

Eyjafjallajökull

2 We've all heard the name (or at least heard people try to pronounce the name) of the treacherous eruption that spewed impenetrable tufts of ash over Europe in 2010, causing the cancellation of thousands of flights (p114).

Hekla & Katla

3 Like wicked stepsisters from some Icelandic fairytale, Hekla and Katla (p109) are volatile beasts that dominate many of the southern vistas, threatening to belch forth steam, smoke and oozing lava that melts the nearby glaciers and floods the southern plains.

Snæfellsjökull

4 Jules Verne's famous journey to the centre of the earth starts here – the Snæfellsnes Peninsula's prominent glacial fist (p151) that can be easily glimpsed from Reykjavík on clear days.

Magni & Móði

5 Iceland's newest mountains (p116) were formed during the eruptions of 2010. Bring a pack of *pylsur* (hot dogs) with you as you mount Magni – the still-steaming earth will cook them in no time flat.

Clockwise from top left
1 Svínafellsjökull glacier (p275), Vatnajökull 2 Ash clouds from Eyjafjallajökull (p114) eruption 3 Hekla (p109)
4 Snæfellsjökull (p151)

Wildlife Watching

Iceland's magical natural realm is the playground for some particularly curious creatures, including whales, puffins, Arctic foxes and seals. And although casual roadside sightings of animals are usually limited to sheep, cows and horses, it's quite simple to orchestrate a wildlife-watching expedition on your own terms.

The bird life in Iceland is abundant, especially during the warmest months when migrating species arrive to nest. On coastal cliffs and islands around the country, you can see a mind-boggling array of seabirds. Posted coastal hikes offer access to some of the most populous bird cliffs in the world – don't miss a chance to cavort with puffins (see p37 for info on how to find them).

Whale watching has become one of Iceland's most cherished pastimes – boats depart throughout the year (limited service in the colder months) to catch a glimpse of these lurking beasts as they wave their fins and spray the air. The northern waters around Húsavík and Akureyri are a haven for feeding creatures (usually minke and fin species); travellers who are short on time can hop on a boat that departs directly from downtown Reykjavík. In winter, it's possible to see orcas crash through the frigid waters – the best point of departure is the Snæfellsnes Peninsula.

BEST WILDLIFE-WATCHING SPOTS

» **Vestmannaeyjar** (p128) Zoom between islets as you snap photos of a Peterson Field Guide's worth of bird life.

» **Borgarfjörður Eystri** (p247) It's like you've died and gone to puffin heaven, where encounters with these clumsy birds are up close and personal.

» **Húsavík** (p225) Sample Iceland's original flavour of whale watching at this charming fishing village. There are tours aplenty, especially in summer.

Clockwise from top left
1 Humpback whale, Húsavík (p225) 2 Seal swimming in glacier lagoon, Jökulsárlón (p277) 3 Meadow pipit, Vestmannaeyjar (p128)

The Hot-Pot Hop

A Two-Week Itinerary

Slap on those swim trunks and enjoy Iceland's favourite pastime: wading in warm, mineral-rich hot springs that soothe the mind and soul. Hop across this geothermic kingdom, dipping your toes in each source.

» Start in **Reykjavík** (p44) and do as the locals – bring your backstroke and some gossip to share at the public pools.

» Next, try **Blue Lagoon** (p88), the Disneyland of swimming spots, and spread gobs of rich silica on your face.

» Pause in **Hveragerði** (p102), one of Iceland's most geothermally active areas – bubbling water abounds.

» Head to **Landmannalaugar** (p121), where a steaming stream is the perfect cure-all after some serious hiking.

» Swing through mod Fontana, in **Laugarvatn** (p97), with its naturally occurring geyser-sauna (you'll see!).

» Soak in **Lýsuholslaug** (p154) and emerge from the algae soup with dolphin-like skin.

» Scout out **Pollurinn** (p163), just outside of Tálknafjörður – a favourite local hang-out.

» Blink and you'll miss the roadside hot-pot in **Drangsnes** (p176), built into a sea wall.

» Bask in the otherworldly beauty at **Krossneslaug** (p178), set along the wild, pebble-strewn shore.

» Check out **Hofsós** (p197) – from within the new pool it feels as though you're swimming in the sea.

» The north's mellower version of Blue Lagoon is found at **Mývatn Nature Baths** (p216).

» Finish up at **Selárdalslaug** (p236), tucked between two hillocks near Vopnafjörður, then fly back to Reykjavík from **Egilsstaðir** (p239).

Clockwise from top left
1 Pool in Laugardalur (p51), Reykjavík 2 Mývatn Nature Baths (p216) 3 Krossneslaug (p178) 4 Hot-spring relaxation, Landmannalaugar (p121)

2

IMAGEBROKER / ALAMY ©

3

BRANDON PRESSER ©

Hiking

In a land where each stone has a story and each pass a name, nothing beats the intimacy of exploring Iceland's magical landscapes by foot. The possibilities are endless, though the following options are the island's tried-and-true favourites.

Laugavegurinn

1 Iceland's classic rite of passage takes you through kingdoms of caramel-coloured dunes, smoking earth and devastating desert (p123); duration two to five days.

Ásbyrgi to Dettifoss

2 A veritable sampler of Iceland's geological phenomena starts at the northern end of Jökulsárgljúfur (in Vatnajökull National Park) and works its way down the gorge, ending with the rumbling of Europe's largest waterfall; duration two days (p232).

The Royal Horn

3 Words cannot do justice to the views of lonely fjords, Ireland-green bluffs, swooping gulls and roving foxes. Hornstrandir's fan-favourite route (p174) is a circuit through the reserve's superlative moments; duration four to six days.

Fimmvörðuháls

4 A parade of waterfalls turns into a blustery desert as you pass between two brooding glaciers. Then, the steaming stones from the 2010 eruption appear before the path leads down into flower-filled Þórsmörk; duration one to two days (p116).

The Kerlingarfjöll Loop

5 Largely untouched and yet to be explored by most hikers, this interior circuit unveils postcard-worthy vistas that rival those of well-trodden Laugavegurinn; duration two to three days (p289).

Clockwise from top left
1 Crossing a crevasse on the Laugavegurinn hike (p123)
2 Dettifoss (p234), Jökulsárgljúfur

North Iceland

Why Go?

Iceland's mammoth and magnificent north is a geologist's heaven. A wonderland of moonlike lava fields, belching mudpots, epic waterfalls, snow-capped peaks and whale-filled bays – this is Iceland at its best. The region's top sights are variations on one theme: a grumbling, volcanically active earth.

There are endless treats to uncover: little Akureyri, with its surprising moments of big-city living; windy fjordside pastures full of stout Viking horses; fishing villages clinging tenaciously to life at the end of unsealed roads. Prepare to be lured by offshore islands populated by roaring colonies of seabirds and a few hardy locals; lonely peninsulas stretching out towards the Arctic Circle; white-water rapids ready to deliver an adrenalin kick; national-park walking trails to reach unparalleled views; unhyped and underpopulated ski fields; and underwater marvels that woo divers into frigid depths.

Best Places to Eat

» Pallurinn (p228)
» Geitafell (p190)
» Hannes Boy (p199)
» Vogafjós (p220)
» Lónkot (p197)

Best Places to Stay

» Skjaldarvík (p210)
» Dalvík HI Hostel (p201)
» Ytra Lón HI Hostel (p235)
» Sæluhús (p210)
» Gamla Pósthúsið (p195)

Road Distances (km)

	Reykjavík	Akureyri	Siglufjörður	Húsavík	Reykjahlíð (Mývatn)
Akureyri	389				
Siglufjörður	384	76			
Húsavík	476	92	168		
Reykjahlíð (Mývatn)	478	100	176	54	
Þórshöfn	613	235	311	142	172

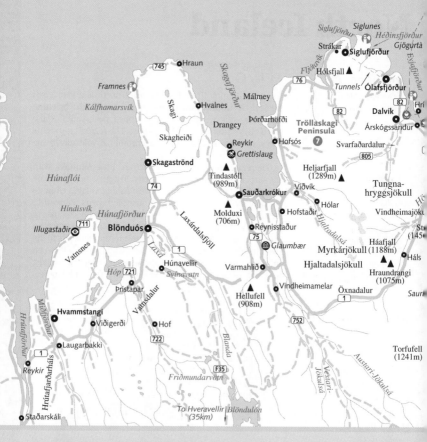

North Iceland Highlights

① Discover northern Iceland's version of city living in **Akureyri** (p203)

② Cross Iceland's only true slice of the Arctic Circle – the tern-filled and troll-infested island of **Grímsey** (p202)

③ Wander around lava castles, pseudocraters and hidden fissures at otherworldly **Mývatn** (p215)

④ Hold your breath as gentle giants emerge from the deep on a whale-watching trip from **Húsavík** (p225)

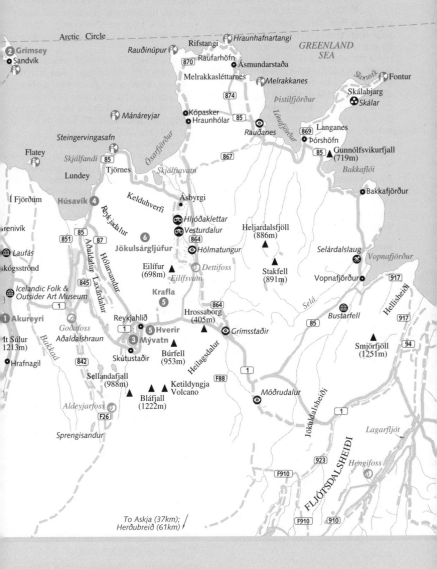

Arctic Circle

② **Grímsey**
Sandvík

GREENLAND
SEA

Rauðinúpur ⛽ Rifstangi ⛽ Hraunhafnartangi
Raufarhöfn
(870)
Ásmundarstaða
Melrakkaslétta ⛽ Melrakkanes
Skoruvík ⛽ Fontur
(874)
Þistilfjörður
Skálabjarg
⛽ Skálar

Mánáreyjar
Kópasker
Hraunhólar (85)
Rauðanes
(869) Langanes
Þórshöfn
(85) ▲ Gunnólfsvíkurfjall
(719m)

Steingervingasafn
Öxarfjörður
Flatey
Skjálfandi (85)
Lundey
Tjörnes
Skjálftavatn
(867)
Bakkaflói

Í Fjörðum
Húsavík **④**
Kelduhverfi
Ásbyrgi
Bakkafjörður

renivík
Reykjadalur
(851)(85)(87)
Hljóðaklettar 🚻
Laufás
(6)
Vesturdalur
(864)
Heljardalsfjöll
(886m)
Selárdalslaug
Vopnafjörður
skógsströnd
(845)
Jökulsárgljúfur
Hólmatungur
▲ Stakfell
(891m)
Vopnafjörður
(917)
Icelandic Folk &
Outsider Art Museum
(1)
Eilífur
(698m) ▲ Dettifoss
Eilífsvatn
Krafla
Hellisheiði
① **Akureyri**
(5)
(864)
(917)
Goðafoss
Hrossaborg
(405m)
Bustarfell 🏛
4t Súlur
1213m
Reykjahlíð
▲ Grímsstaðir
(85)
(1) (5) **Hverir**
Hrafnagil
(842)
③ **Mývatn**
Skútustaðir
Búrfell
(953m)
Heiðagsdalur
Smjörfjöll
(1251m)
(94)
Sellandafjall
(988m)
Ketildyngja
Volcano
(F88)
(1)
Móðrudalur
Bláfjall
(1222m)
Aldeyjarfoss
Jökuldalsheiði
(F26)
(923)
Lagarfljót
Sprengisandur
Hengifoss
FLJÓTSDALSHEIÐI
(F910)
To Askja (37km);
Herðubreið (61km)
(F910) (910)

⑤ Step gingerly through the rust-coloured world at **Hverir** (p224), then crunch shattered lava underfoot at **Krafla** (p224)

⑥ Savour thundering chutes, hypnotic rock forms and a storied canyon at **Jökulsárgljúfur** (p230)

⑦ Tour the **Tröllaskagi Peninsula** (p196), eyeballing vast vistas and rugged mountainscapes between perfect pit stops

EASTERN HÚNAFLÓI

Although sparsely populated and scattered with only a handful of tiny settlements, the bay of Húnaflói is rich in wildlife. It's also known as Bear Bay, named after the many polar bears that have drifted on sea ice from Greenland and come ashore here. The scenery of the area is far gentler than that of the Westfjords, and the low, treeless hills provide nesting sites for wild swans, ptarmigans, divers and golden plovers. Add some neatly manicured towns, some barking seals and a cluster of good museums, and there's plenty to keep you occupied en route to Akureyri.

It's worth stopping at an information point to pick up the *Húnaþing vestra* booklet, which offers detailed tourist info about Hvammstangi and surrounds. Try *The Ideal Holiday* (www.farmholidays.is) guide too – there are heaps of homey farmstays in this neck of the woods. The website www.north west.is is excellent for planning.

Hrútafjörður

Little Hrútafjörður marks the divide between northwest Iceland and the Westfjords.

No more than a road junction with a big, busy N1 petrol station and cafeteria, **Staðarskáli** (once known as Brú) acts as a popular leg-stretching spot for motorists.

At **Reykir**, 13km north of Staðarskáli, you'll find the **Byggðasafn** (adult/child Ikr800/ free; ⊙10am-6pm). Highlights of this regional museum include the well-reconstructed interior of a 19th-century homestead and the fantastic shark-fishing boat *Ófeigur*, built from driftwood in 1875.

Not far from the museum, **Sæberg HI Hostel** (☑894 5504; www.hostel.is; dm/d without bathroom Ikr3800/10,000; ⊙Mar-Oct; ☜) is a good place to break up a Reykjavík–Akureyri trip. It's a cosy, peaceful little hostel with two geothermally heated hot-pots, two self-contained cottages and sprawling views. HI members get a discount of Ikr600 per person; linen hire costs Ikr1250. Campers are welcome; bring supplies, as the nearest shop is 15km away.

Hvammstangi

POP 580

Six kilometres north of the Ring Road, sweet, slow-paced Hvammstangi's biggest (and pretty much only) attraction is the harbourfront **Icelandic Seal Centre** (☑451 2345; www.selasetur.is; adult/child Ikr900/650; ⊙9am-6pm Jun–mid-Sep, to 9pm mid-Jun–mid-Aug), where you can learn about conservation of seals, historic seal products and traditional folk tales involving seals. There's also a helpful **tourist information point** located here.

Selasigling (☑897 9900; www.sealwatch ing.is) operates regular seal- and nature-watching boat trips from the harbour, plus angling and midnight-sun sailings by arrangement. Scheduled 1¾-hour tours (adult/child Ikr7500/3500) leave at 10am, 1pm and 4pm daily June to August.

The harbour is the hub of the town's tourist action, with cute-as-a-button **Hlaðan Kaffihús** (Brekkugata 2; ⊙9am-9pm Mon-Sat mid-May–Aug; ☜) luring customers with soups, sandwiches and cakes. There's a gallery-handicrafts store, **Bardúsa**, next door, and a well-stocked **KVH supermarket** (⊙9am-6pm Mon-Thu, 9am-7pm Fri, 11am-6pm Sat, noon-4pm Sun Jun-Aug, shorter hours Sep-May) in the neighbourhood.

An excellent choice for an overnight stay, **Guesthouse Hanna Sigga** (☑451 2407; www. simnet.is/gistihs; Garðavegur 26; s/d without bathroom Ikr7400/12,500) is on a residential street in the centre of town. Rooms are well kept, and there's a guest lounge, but the real draw is the homemade breakfast (Ikr1600) served in a beautiful nook overlooking the water. Sleeping-bag accommodation costs Ikr3900.

Pricier rooms can be found behind the black timber walls of the bright new **Welcome Hotel Hvammstangi** (☑566 7979; www.greatnorth.is; Norðurbraut 1; r incl breakfast €139; ⊙May-Sep; ☜), or try the large, well-maintained **Kirkjuhvammur campsite** (☑899 0008; sites per person Ikr1000; ⊙mid-May–mid-Sep) up the hill near the old church. It has cabins available too. Find the turn-off near the town pool.

Sterna (☑551 1166; www.sterna.is) bus service 60/60a between Reykjavík and Akureyri (daily, year-round) calls at Hvammstangi.

Vatnsnes Peninsula

Poking out into Húnaflói, stubby Vatnsnes Peninsula is a starkly beautiful place with wheat-strewn shores and a ridge of craggy hills marching down its spine. Rte 711, a rough gravel road, weaves along the coast and makes a great detour off the Ring Road. Without your own wheels, ask at the info centre in Hvammstangi about an infrequent summer bus around the peninsula.

On the west side there's a lonely cafe (⊙2-6pm mid-Jun–Aug) and simple campsite (sites per person lkr800) at Illugastaðir, with wonderful views of peaks along the Strandir coast in the Westfjords. The storied farm is the site of the crime leading to the last execution in Iceland (1830). There are lovely walks through bird-filled fields to a popular site for sunbaking seals; note that the farm is closed from 1 May to 20 June due to eider duck nesting.

Three kilometres past Illugastaðir (roughly 25km from Hvammstangi) is the wonderfully unique Geitafell (www.geitafell.is; fish soup lkr2700; ⊙11am-10pm Jun-Aug), a new restaurant in a converted barn where fish soup is the star (skyr tart is another highlight on the short menu). The property owners, Sigrún and Robert, are long-time locals with fascinating stories. Robert's father was a Scottish minister who came to preach (and teach football skills) in Iceland; Robert has a small history exhibition next to the restaurant, in his 'Scottish castle'.

In the east you'll happen upon one of Iceland's largest seal colonies at Hindisvík (although this was closed to the public at the time of research). Ten kilometres south is a signed path leading to the 15m-high sea stack Hvítserkur. Legend has it that Hvítserkur was a troll caught by the sunrise while attempting to destroy the monastery at Þingeyrar; we think he looks like a huge stone beast drinking from the water.

Just south of Hvítserkur (or 30km north of the Ring Road), to the east is a trail to a seal-watching spot, inland is the charming Ósar HI Hostel (☑862 2778; www.hostel. is; dm/d without bathroom lkr3800/10,000; ⊙May-Sep), one of Iceland's nicest hostels thanks to friendly management, good views and the nearby wildlife. The hostel is on a working dairy farm, and the owner indulges his hobby of building more rooms and cottages each year (breakfast is served in a Mongolian yurt!). Bring your own food as there are no shops nearby. Members get a discount of lkr600 per person; linen hire costs lkr1250.

Hvammstangi to Blönduós

Horse-lovers will be in heaven at Gauksmýri (☑451 2927; www.gauksmyri.is; d with/without bathroom incl breakfast €140/96; @🛜), a highly regarded horse farm and lodge on the Ring

Road just east of the turn-off to Hvammstangi. Two-hour horse rides (lkr10,000) leave four times a day from June to mid-September. The restaurant (buffet Ikr4700; open mid-May to mid-September) does a full dinner buffet (bookings advised) where the variety of meats may rankle (it includes whale and foal, but also local salmon, lamb and trout). Snacks and coffee are served from 11am to 6pm.

If two hours on horseback aren't enough, serious horse riders should book ahead with Brekkulækur (☑451 2938; www.abbi-island. is), which offers adventurous and highly acclaimed multiday trips (€1290 to €2960 for eight to 15 days). The farm is 8km south of the Hvammstangi turn-off on Rte 704.

Travelling east past Gauksmýri, take Rte 715 south for 6km to reach the scenic waterfalls at Kolugljúfur, an enchanting canyon that was once home to a beautiful trolless.

Around 19km before you reach Blönduós, another quick 6km detour (this time along Rte 721) leads you to a precious stone church, Þingeyrar (adult/child lkr500/free; ⊙10am-5pm), sitting quietly and photogenically on Hóp lagoon. The current structure was erected in the 1860s, but 800 years earlier the site hosted a district þing (assembly) and a Benedictine monastery.

Blönduós

POP 850

A couple of museums and an unusual modern church – the underwhelming service town Blönduós is about as simple as that. There isn't much to woo you off the road, but it's an OK place to break the journey and refuel.

The churning Blanda river sharply separates the town in half. The N1 station marks the northern entrance to town, the Olís station sits at the southern approach. The islet of Hrútey, just upstream from the Blanda Bridge, is a nature reserve and the site of a reforestation project. Access is via a footbridge 200m north of the campground.

◎ Sights & Activities

Textile Museum   MUSEUM
(Heimilisiðnaðarsafnið; www.textile.is; Árbraut 29; adult/child lkr900/free; ⊙10am-5pm Jun-Aug) Set in an intriguing building (think 'turf-roof chic') on the north bank of the Blanda, this small but beguiling museum displays local

handicrafts, painstakingly intricate embroideries and early Icelandic costumes.

Sea Ice Exhibition Centre   MUSEUM
(Hafíssetrið; www.blonduos.is/hafis; Blöndubyggð 2; adult/child Ikr500/free; ☺11am-5pm Jun-Aug) Housed in an antique merchant's house (dating from 1733), the centre's small but informative exhibits look at the formation and types of sea ice, weather patterns and early Icelandic settlers. You'll also come face to face with the polar bear that wreaked havoc in the region during the summer of 2008 (don't worry, he's been stuffed).

Icelandic Salmon Centre   MUSEUM
(Laxasetur Íslands; www.laxasetur.is; Efstubraut 1; adult/child Ikr900/300; ☺10am-6pm Jun-Aug) The Blönduós area is a mecca for fly-fishing (Eric Clapton makes an annual pilgrimage) and this new museum has information on the activity, plus live samples of the prize (salmon, brown trout, Arctic char) in tanks. Labelling is only in Icelandic.

🛏 Sleeping & Eating

Glaðheimar   CAMPGROUND, COTTAGES €
(☎820 1300; www.gladheimar.is; tent site per person Ikr900, campervan site Ikr2200, cottages Ikr13,000-21,000) In a lovely setting near the river (off the Ring Road), Glaðheimar has camping and an assortment of self-contained cottages sleeping up to six people (larger cottages have the bonus of a hot tub, a few also have sauna). Linen costs Ikr1800 per person. There are also sleeping-bag beds available (Ikr5000). The reception building doubles as the town's tourist info centre.

Hótel Blönduós   HOTEL €€
(☎452 4205; www.hotelblonduos.is; Aðalgata 6; s/d incl breakfast Ikr18,700/22,400; @🛜) The town's only hotel has dated decor and a slightly neglected air, but will do in a pinch. It's popular with visiting anglers. Nearby is the hotel's cheaper annexe, the Old Post House (s/d Ikr12,500/15,500), with shared facilities.

Potturinn   INTERNATIONAL €€
(Nordurlandsvegur 4; mains Ikr1690-6000; ☺11am-10pm) A surprisingly international menu greets diners at this modern restaurant neighbouring the N1. There's soup and salad all day, fantastic burgers, and oddities like grilled seal steak and tandoori-spiced lamb.

Við Árbakkann   CAFE €
(Húnabraut 2; mains Ikr550-1890; ☺11am-8pm Jun-Aug) In a big blue house by the swimming pool and supermarket, this country cafe serves up soups, salads and grilled bagels and paninis.

Samkaup-Úrval   SUPERMARKET €
(Húnabraut 4; ☺9am-7pm Mon-Fri, 10am-6pm Sat, 1-5pm Sun) Fulfils self-catering needs. There's an early-opening bakery-cafe next door.

❶ Information

The reception of Glaðheimar doubles as the tourist information centre (☎820 1300; ☺8am-8pm Jun-Aug) but its adherence to opening hours can be erratic. A good online resource for the town and region is www.northwest.is.

❶ Getting There & Away

The Sterna (☎551 1166; www.sterna.is) bus service 60/60a between Reykjavík and Akureyri (daily, year-round) calls at Blönduós. To Reykjavík is four hours (Ikr7600), to Akureyri two hours (Ikr4700).

WESTERN SKAGAFJÖRÐUR

Renowned for horse breeding and wild landscapes, Skagafjörður is a little-visited region in Iceland's quiet northwest. The at-times bleak landscapes, historic remains, abundant bird life and adrenalin-infused activities make it a rewarding destination. Look out, too, for the growing emphasis on culinary tourism in the area, and the red stamps on menus highlighting local produce. For more information, see www.visit skagafjordur.is.

Varmahlíð
POP 90

This bustling Ring Road service centre is slightly more than a road junction and yet not quite a town, and it's a great base for rafting and horse riding.

🜚 Activities

White-Water Rafting

Between May and September the area around Varmahlíð offers the best white-water rafting in northern Iceland. Note that prices listed are for summer 2012.

Arctic Rafting   WHITE-WATER RAFTING
(☎571 2200; www.arcticrafting.com) Specialises in rafting trips on local rivers. Options include an easy, family-friendly four-hour trip

on the more-placid Vestari-Jökulsá (West Glacial River; Ikr9900); a challenging seven-hour adventure on the Austari-Jökulsá (East Glacial River; Ikr19,990); and the ultimate rafting adventure, the three-day 'River Rush' (Ikr69,990), which starts from the Sprengisandur highlands. See the website for more details. The company's basecamp is at Hafgrímsstaðir, 15km south of Varmahlið on Rte 752. Pick-ups can be arranged from Akureyri.

Bakkaflöt   WHITE-WATER RAFTING
(☑453 8245; www.riverrafting.is) South along Rte 752 (11km from the Ring Road), the farm Bakkaflöt offers cheaper rafting excursions: three hours on the Vestari-Jökulsá (Ikr8600), and six hours on the Austari-Jökulsá (Ikr13,800). The centre also has good accommodation.

Horse Riding

Hestasport   HORSE RIDING
(☑453 8383; www.riding.is; ☺May-Sep) One of Iceland's most respected riding outfits, with its helpful office just off the Ring Road on Rte 752. It offers one-/two-hour tours along the Svartá river for €40/65, and full-day rides for €120. Longer trips are also available (book well in advance), including eight-day trips (five days in the saddle) along lesser-known routes through the highlands (€1870). Ask here for directions to the hidden waterfall Reykjafoss.

Lýtingsstaðir   HORSE RIDING
(☑453 8064; www.lythorse.com) The farm Lýtingsstaðir, 19km south of Varmahlíð on Rte 752, offers a program of hourly riding or longer multiday trips. It also features a 'stop and ride' package that includes one night in a self-contained cottage and a two-hour ride for €170 (two people, linen excluded). Longer tours (from €930) are also available.

Horse Shows

Regular hour-long horse shows are hosted by **Flugumýri** (☑453 8814; www.flugumyri.is) and **Varmilækur** (☑898 7756; www.varmilaekur.is). They showcase the five gaits of the Icelandic horse, and detail the breed's history. Both ranches are within 10km of Varmahlíð; they usually schedule shows for groups, and individuals can then attend. Ask at the tourist office for a schedule, or contact the farms direct.

🍽 Sleeping & Eating

There are plenty of rural places to crash in the area; ask at the information centre or use the handy Icelandic Farm Holidays booklet, *The Ideal Holiday* (www.farmholidays.is).

For self-caterers, the supermarket by the N1 is open until late in summer (closing hours between 10pm and 11.30pm).

Hestasport Cottages   COTTAGES €€
(☑453 8383; www.riding.is/cottages; d cottages €150) Perched on the hill above Varmahlíð (follow the road past the town hotel), this cluster of seven high-quality self-contained timber cottages has good views, comfy rooms and a very inviting stone hot-pot. There are photos of the interior of each cottage on Hestasport's website; some sleep up to six.

NORTH ICELAND VARMAHLÍÐ

WORTH A TRIP

ICELAND'S COUNTRY-MUSIC CAPITAL

The main reason to bootscoot the 22km north of the Ring Road to Skagaströnd (population 530) is to visit **Kántrýbær** (www.kantry.is; Holanesvegur; mains Ikr1190-3990; ☺11.30am-10pm Jun-Aug, shorter hours Sep-May), Iceland's only country-music saloon. With its Wild West log-cabin atmosphere, bright murals and the constant twang of country music, this place is truly a unique Icelandic experience. Upstairs is a small museum of country-music memorabilia and a working radio station playing (you guessed it) country tunes.

You're no doubt wondering how, and why? Hallbjörn Hjartarson, the 'Icelandic Cowboy' who owns Kántrýbær, fell in love with country-and-western music while working on the American base at Keflavík in the 1960s. Even after moving back to Skagaströnd, he continued to indulge his passion for playing and recording. He released his first record in 1975 (he's released 11 all up), and organised Iceland's first country-music festival, Kántrý Dagar (Country Days), in Skagaströnd in 1984. The event is held annually, on the third weekend in August.

Campsite
CAMPGROUND €

(sites per person Ikr1000; ⊙mid-May–mid-Sep) Follow the signs from the hotel to reach this secluded, sheltered spot above the town.

Hótel Varmahlíð
HOTEL €€

(☑453 8170; www.hotelvarmahlid.is; s/d incl breakfast Ikr19,600/24,900; @🛜) Freshly modernised rooms are found at this small hotel. Its restaurant (mains Ikr1750 to Ikr5100; open lunch and dinner mid-May through to mid-September) is one of the best places in the region to try the local delicacy, foal, and the scrumptious lamb comes from the manager's own flock.

Bakkaflöt
GUESTHOUSE €€

(☑453 8245; www.riverrafting.is; d with/without bathroom incl breakfast Ikr23,550/17,420; @🛜📶) South along Rte 752 (11km from the Ring Road), at its rafting HQ, Bakkaflöt mini resort includes restaurant-bar, guesthouse, camping area, small swimming pool, hot-pots, motel-style cabins with bathroom, and family-sized houses. There's also sleeping-bag accommodation for Ikr5400.

❶ Information

Inside the N1 petrol station, the **tourist information centre** (☑455 6161; www.visitskagafjordur. is; ⊙10am-6pm Jun-Aug, 9am-4pm Mon-Fri Sep-May; @) is a room of brochures and maps, with a staffed info desk.

❶ Getting There & Away

Sterna (☑551 1166; www.sterna.is) bus service 60/60a between Reykjavík and Akureyri (daily, year-round) calls at Varmahlíð, stopping at the N1. Reykjavík–Varmahlíð is four hours (Ikr9100), Varmahlíð–Akureyri takes one hour (Ikr3100).

In summer, buses trundling along the highland Kjölur route between Reykjavík and Akureyri also stop here (for more on these buses, see p290).

From June to August, Sterna bus service 580/580a runs twice daily between Varmahlíð and Sauðárkrókur. Three times a week it continues north to Hólar, Hofsós and Siglufjörður.

Öxnadalur

If you haven't the time to explore scenic Skagafjörður or magnificent Tröllaskagi, never fear: you'll still be treated to some incredible vistas courtesy of Öxnadalur, a narrow, 30km-long valley on the Ring Road between Varmahlíð and Akureyri. Stunning peaks and thin pinnacles of rock flank the mountain pass; the imposing 1075m spire of Hraun-drangi and the surrounding peaks of Háafjall are among the most dramatic in Iceland.

Engimýri Guesthouse (☑462 7518; www. engimyri.is; d with/without bathroom Ikr16,900/ 13,900; @🛜) has a plumb location in the middle of this splendour, some 35km west of Akureyri. There's a smart restaurant, hot-pot, hiking trails, and the chance to take quad-bike tours through the valley (Ikr12,000 for one hour).

Glaumbær

Following Rte 75 north from Varmahlíð towards Skagafjörður's marshy delta leads to the 18th-century turf farm museum (www. glaumbaer.is; adult/child Ikr900/free; ⊙9am-6pm Jun–mid-Sep) at Glaumbær. It's the best museum of its type in northern Iceland and well worth the easy 8km detour off the Ring Road.

The traditional Icelandic turf farm was a complex of small separate buildings, connected by a central passageway. At Glaumbær you can see this style of construction, with some building compartments stuffed full of period furniture, equipment and utensils. It gives a fascinating insight into the cramped living conditions of the era.

Also on the site are two 19th-century houses – one is home to Áskaffi (cake Ikr200-890), an impossibly quaint tearoom with old-world atmosphere and dollhouse dishware. Peruse the brochure explaining the history behind its delicious traditional Icelandic cakes and pancakes.

Snorri Þorfinnsson, the first European born in North America (in 1004; see the boxed text, p153), is buried near the church at Glaumbær.

Buses between Varmahlíð and Sauðárkrókur pass Glaumbær daily in summer.

Sauðárkrókur
POP 2640

As the winding Jökulsá river collides with the marshy delta of upper Skagafjörður, you'll find scenic Sauðárkrókur sitting quietly at the edge of the windy waterway.

Economically, Sauðárkrókur is doing quite nicely, thank you, with fishing, tanning and trading keeping the community afloat and the population young and energetic. The town has all the services you'll need, plus excellent sleeping and eating options; tourist information is dispensed by the town museum.

◉ Sights

Minjahúsið   MUSEUM
(Aðalgata 16b; adult/child Ikr500/free; ⊙1-7pm Jun-Aug) There's a quirky ensemble of exhibits at the excellent town museum, including a series of restored craftsmens' workshops, a pristine A-model Ford from 1930, and a stuffed polar bear caught locally in 2008.

FREE Tannery Visitor Centre   MUSEUM
(Gestastofa Sútarans; www.sutarinn.is; Borgamýri 5; ⊙10am-5pm Mon-Fri, 11am-3pm Sat Jun–mid-Sep, 1-5pm Wed & Fri mid-Sep–May) At 2pm weekdays you can tour Iceland's only tannery (Ikr1000), or stop by the visitor centre anytime to admire (and purchase) the products: gorgeous sheepskins, leather goods, and unique products made from fishskin processed at the tannery.

🛏 Sleeping

TOP CHOICE Gamla Posthúsið   APARTMENT €€
(📞892 3375; www.ausis.is; Kirkjutorg 5; apt €135-145; 🛜) Australian Vicki moved to town in 2010 and took it upon herself to restore the old post office opposite the church. The two resulting one-bedroom apartments make a superb home-from-home. Each boasts a full modern kitchen, a welcome pack of food, oodles of room and Scandi-chic decor. Winter prices are almost halved, making them a steal.

Guesthouse Mikligarður   GUESTHOUSE €€
(📞453 6880; www.mikligardur.is; Kirkjutorg 3; d with/without bathroom incl breakfast Ikr20,800/16,200; 🛜) This adorable, welcoming spot near the church has comfortable, modern rooms with TV and tasteful decor. There's also a spacious guest kitchen and TV lounge.

Hótel Tindastóll   HOTEL €€
(📞453 5002; www.hoteltindastoll.com; Lindargata 3; s/d incl breakfast Ikr19,800/27,400; @🛜) Legend has it that Marlene Dietrich once stayed at this charming boutique hotel, which dates from 1884. The individually decorated rooms blend period furniture and modern style. Outside there is an irresistible stone hot-pot, and in the basement there's a cosy bar. There is also a new annexe of modern rooms, but the period rooms have loads more character.

Hótel Mikligarður   HOTEL €€
(📞453 6330; www.mikligardur.is; s/d incl breakfast Ikr15,400/19,800; ⊙Jun-late Aug; @🛜) The district boarding school becomes a basic but rather characterless hotel in summer. It's a big orange building about 1km southwest of the church; rooms are being renovated to add some personality. Sleeping-bag accommodation is available for Ikr5500.

Campsite   CAMPGROUND €
(sites per person Ikr1000; ⊙mid-May–mid-Sep) The campsite beside the swimming pool is a bit barren, but has decent facilities. Showers cost Ikr250.

🍴 Eating

Ólafshús   ICELANDIC €€
(Aðalgata 15; lunch Ikr1350-1690, dinner mains Ikr1350-5590; ⊙11am-10pm or 11pm) A bold blue paint-job announces this quality year-round option, where you can go radical with pan-fried puffin breast, fancy-pants with lobster tails, or safe with pizza and pasta. Try Gæðingur, the locally microbrewed beer.

Kaffi Krókur   ICELANDIC €€
(Aðalgata 16; mains Ikr1290-2690; ⊙11.30am-11pm Mon-Thu & Sun, 11.30am-3am Fri & Sat Jun-Aug; 🛜) Across from Ólafshús (and with the same owner), this cafe has a more understated beige exterior and a crowd-pleasing menu dedicated to Icelandic pop stars. It's known for its lobster and shrimp sandwich, filled crepes and warm rhubarb cake. In winter it's the local pub (with live music), open only on Thursday, Friday and Saturday nights.

Skagfirðingabúð   SUPERMARKET €
(Ástorg; ⊙9am-7pm Mon-Fri, 10am-4pm Sat) South of town, close to the N1.

❶ Getting There & Away
From June to August, **Sterna** (📞551 1166; www.sterna.is) bus service 580/580a runs twice daily between Varmahlíð and Sauðárkrókur, connecting with Ring Road buses to/from Reykjavík and Akureyri. Northbound, there are three buses a week connecting Sauðárkrókur with Hólar, Hofsós and Siglufjörður. The bus stop is at the N1.

Around Sauðárkrókur

North of Sauðárkrókur, Skagafjörður's western coast is a stunningly silent place capped by scenic mountains. Guarding the mouth of Skagafjörður are the uninhabited islands

WORTH A TRIP

DRANGEY

The tiny rocky islet of Drangey (*drown*-gay), in the middle of Skagafjörður, is a dramatic flat-topped mass of volcanic tuff with 180m-high sheer cliffsides rising abruptly from the water. The cliffs serve as nesting sites for around a million seabirds (lots of puffins), and have been used throughout Iceland's history as 'nature's grocery store'. *Grettir's Saga* recounts that both Grettir and his brother Illugi lived on the island for three years and were slain there. Brave (foolhardy?) saga fans come to the area to recreate Grettir's feat, swimming the 7km between Drangey and Reykir.

Drangeyjarferðir (☑821 0090; www.drangeyjarferdir.is; tours Ikr8800) offers four-hour boat trips to Drangey, departing from Reykir (near Grettislaug) at 11am daily from June to mid-August; call the day beforehand to book. One-hour sea-angling trips can also be arranged.

of Drangey and Málmey, tranquil havens for nesting seabirds.

Tindastóll (989m) is a prominent Skagafjörður landmark, extending for 18km along the coast. The mountain and its caves are believed to be inhabited by an array of sea monsters, trolls and giants. The summit of Tindastóll affords a spectacular view across all of Skagafjörður. The easiest way to the top is along the marked trail that starts from the high ground along Rte 745 west of the mountain.

At Tindastóll's northern end is a geothermal area, **Reykir**, that was mentioned in *Grettir's Saga*. Grettir supposedly swam ashore from the island of Drangey and soothed his aching bones in an inviting spring. Today, **Grettislaug** (Grettir's Bath; (☑821 0090; www.drangeyjarferdir.is; adult/child Ikr700/350; ◎morning-midnight) is a popular bathing hole, alongside a second hot-pot.

In the immediate vicinity of Grettislaug are a small cafe, well-equipped **campground** (per person Ikr1000) and **guesthouse** (s/d Ikr7000/13,000) with sleeping-bag beds for Ikr4400. Boats to Drangey leave from here, and there are great walks in the area. Drivers beware: it's a rough, skiddy 15km on gravel from Sauðárkrókur to Grettislaug.

TRÖLLASKAGI PENINSULA

The Tröllaskagi Peninsula rests its mountainous bulk between Skagafjörður and Eyjafjörður. Here, the craggy mountains, deep valleys and gushing rivers are more reminiscent of the Westfjords than the gentle hills that roll through most of northern Iceland. In great news for travellers seeking spectacular road trips, tunnels now link the northern Tröllaskagi townships of Siglufjörður and Olafsfjörður, once dead-end towns that saw little tourist traffic.

The journey from Varmahlið to Akureyri along the Ring Road (Rte 1) measures 95 very scenic kilometres, but if you have some time up your sleeve and a penchant for getting off the beaten track, the 186km journey between those two towns following the Tröllaskagi coastline (Rtes 76 and 82) conjures up some magical scenery, and plenty of excuses to pull over and explore.

Hólar í Hjaltadalur

With its prominent church dwarfed by the looming mountains, tiny **Hólar** (www.holar.is) makes an interesting historical detour. The bishopric of Hólar was the ecumenical and educational capital of northern Iceland between 1106 and the Reformation, and it continued as a religious centre and the home of the northern bishops until 1798, when the bishop's seat was abolished.

Hólar then became a vicarage until 1861, when the vicarage was shifted west to Viðvík. In 1882 the present agricultural college was established, and in 1952 the vicarage returned to Hólar.

◉ Sights

An informative historical-trail brochure (available at the accommodation info desk) guides you round some of the buildings at Hólar. **Nýibær** is a historical turf farm dating from the mid-19th century and inhabited until 1945. Also worth seeing is **Auðunarstofa**, a replica of the 14th-century bishop's residence, built using traditional tools and methods.

Cathedral
CHURCH

(⊙10am-6pm Jun–mid-Sep, Sun services 11am, evening prayer 6pm Mon-Sat) Completed in 1763, Hólar's red-sandstone cathedral is the oldest stone church in Iceland and brimming with historical works of art, including a 1674 baptismal font carved from a piece of soapstone that washed in from Greenland on an ice floe. The extraordinary carved altarpiece was donated by the last Catholic bishop of Hólar, Jón Arason, around 1520. After he and his sons were executed at Skálholt for opposition to the Danish Reformation, his remains were brought to Hólar and entombed in the bell tower. The present **church tower** was built in 1950 as a memorial. It contains a mosaic of the good reverend, and his tomb.

Icelandic Horse History Centre
MUSEUM

(www.sogusetur.is; adult/child Ikr900/450; ⊙1-7pm Jun–mid-Sep) The price of admission gets you a personalised tour around this comprehensive exhibit on Iceland's unique breed and its role in Iceland's history. It's fittingly located in an old stable at the heart of the Hólar estate.

🛏 Sleeping & Eating

Ferðaþjónustan Holum Hjaltadal
GUESTHOUSE, COTTAGES

(☑455 6333; www.holar.is; d with/without bathroom Ikr14,900/11,900, d apt Ikr20,300; ⊙Jun-Aug; @🐾) The college accommodation block offers summer stays in vacant student rooms and apartments. Alternatively, wooden cabins in the grounds sleep up to six. Reception is open from 8am to 10pm, and there's a restaurant and swimming pool.

Hofsós

POP 190

The sleepy fishing village of Hofsós has been a trading centre since the 1500s. Today, several restored buildings along the harbour have been turned into the **Icelandic Emigration Center** (Vesturfarasetrið; www.hofsos.is; admission Ikr700-1500, children free; ⊙11am-6pm Jun-Aug), which explores the reasons behind Icelanders' emigration to the New World, their hopes for a new life and the reality of conditions when they arrived. The main exhibition, 'New Land, New Life', follows the lives of emigrating Icelanders through carefully curated photographs, letters and displays. It's fascinating to note that this small country lost 16,000

emigrants from 1870 to 1914, leaving behind a 1914 population of only 88,000. The centre provides an absorbing history lesson, even if you're not of Icelandic descent, and it's a fine place to start if you're tracing roots.

TOP
CHOICE **Sundlaugin á Hofsós** (adult/child Ikr500/200; ⊙9am-9pm Jun-Aug, 7am-1pm & 5.15-8.15pm Mon-Fri, 10am-4pm Sat & Sun Sep-May), the town's magnificent new outdoor swimming pool, has placed Hofsós firmly in the country's collective conscience. It was opened in 2010 thanks to donations from two local women, and its fjordside design, integrated into the landscape and offering almost-infinity views, is close to perfect.

If you want to spend the night, the emigration centre can help. It arranges sleeping-bag space (Ikr3900) at the simple Prestbakki cottage, and cosier rooms with bathroom at homey **Sunnuberg** (☑893 0220, 861 3474; gisting@hofsos.is; Suðurbraut 8; s/d Ikr8900/11,900), 200m past the pool, opposite the petrol pump.

Down at the small harbour among the museum buildings, **Sólvík** (dinner mains Ikr1600-2800; ⊙11am-10pm Jun-Aug) is a sweet country-style restaurant with a short, simple menu of local classics (cod, lamb, burgers).

There are services in town, and a small campground. The thrice-weekly summer Varmahlíð–Siglufjörður bus stops in Hofsós.

Hofsós to Siglufjörður

Wonderfully blustery, **Lónkot** (☑453 7432; www.lonkot.com; d with/without bathroom incl breakfast Ikr24,900/19,900; ⊙Jun-Sep) is a gourmet pit stop along the rugged coast, 13km north of Hofsós. The owners bill it as a 'bucolic resort', and great things are done in the kitchen with local produce and slow-cooking principles (dinner mains around Ikr3600). Lónkot also has boutique accommodation (including big family suites and a campground) with super sea views across to the island of Málmey and the bizarre promontory Þórðarhöfði, which is tethered to the mainland by a delicate spit.

Further around the peninsula, halfway between Lónkot (24km) and Siglufjörður (25km) is **Bjarnagil** (☑467 1030; www.bjarnagil.is; r without bathroom incl breakfast Ikr6000; ⊙mid-Jun–mid-Sep), a very homey farmstay with Sibba and Trausti, a welcoming older couple with plenty of local knowledge to share. Meals, walks and guiding in the area can be arranged with notice (including winter cross-country skiing – Trausti was a Winter Olympian in the 1970s).

Siglufjörður

POP 1360

Sigló (as the locals call it) sits precariously at the foot of a steep slope overlooking a beautiful fjord. Once one of Iceland's boom towns, it's now a quiet but endearing place with a dramatic setting, photogenic marina and a wonderful museum detailing the town's former glory as the herring-fishing capital of Iceland.

In its heyday Siglufjörður was home to 10,000 workers, and fishing boats crammed into the small harbour to unload their catch for the waiting women to gut and salt. After the herring abruptly disappeared from Iceland's north coast in the late 1960s, Siglufjörður declined and never fully recovered. The recent opening of tunnels linking it with Olafsfjörður have seen a new spring in the town's step, and it won't be long until travellers start paying it more attention.

◉ Sights

TOP CHOICE Herring Era Museum   MUSEUM

(Síldarminjasafnið; www.sild.is; Snorragata 15; adult/child Ikr1200/free; ⊙10am-6pm Jun-Aug, 1-5pm Mar-May & Sep-Nov, by appointment in winter) Lovingly created over 16 years, this award-winning museum does a stunning job of recreating Siglufjörður's boom days between 1903 and 1968. Set in three buildings that were part of an old Norwegian herring station, the museum brings the work and lives of the town's inhabitants vividly to life.

Start at the red building on the left, and move right. In the first building, photographs, displays and a 1930s English film show the fishing and salting process, while upstairs the accommodation block looks as though the workers have just left. Next door is a recreated reducing plant, where herrings were separated into oil (a valuable commodity) and meal (used for fertiliser). The third building is a recreation of harbour life, with actual trawler boats and equipment based on life on the busy pier during the boom days.

If you're travelling in July, visit on a Saturday when herring-salting demonstrations are held, accompanied by lively music and theatrical performances.

Icelandic Folk Music Centre   MUSEUM

(www.folkmusic.is; Norðurgata 1; adult/child Ikr800/free; ⊙noon-6pm Jun-Aug) Traditional-music enthusiasts may be interested in this sweet little museum, which displays 19th-century instruments and offers recordings of Icelandic songs and chants.

Activities

Siglufjörður is a great base for hikers, with a series of interesting walks in the area. Some 19km of paths are marked along the avalanche-repelling fence above town, with numerous access points. There's a worthwhile information panel on the northern outskirts of town, beside a parking area, detailing these avalanche defences.

Another popular option is over the passes of Hólsskarð and Hestsskarð into the beautiful, uninhabited Héðinsfjörður, the next fjord to the east. This is where the tunnels connecting Siglufjörður and Olafsfjörður see the light, and it's breathtaking to come across when you're driving. Pull over and enjoy the scenery.

In winter, three ski lifts operate in Skarðsdalur above the head of the fjord, with some of Iceland's best skiing (☑878 3399; http://skard.fjallabyggd.is, in Icelandic). In summer you can opt for an ultrascenic nine-hole round of golf at the Hóll sports centre.

✦ Festivals & Events

Folk Music Festival   MUSIC

(www.folkmusic.is) Folk-music aficionados will enjoy this festival, a delightfully relaxed five-day affair in early July.

Herring Festival   CULTURAL

Despite the demise of the herring industry, Siglufjörður remains nostalgic about the good old days. Its biggest shindig takes place on the bank-holiday weekend in early August and recreates the gold-rush atmosphere of the town's glory days. It's one of Iceland's most enjoyable local festivals, with much singing, dancing, drinking, feasting and fish cleaning.

⌂ Sleeping

Most sleeping and eating options can be scouted on Aðalgata – turn away from the church when you reach the town square.

The town's 'patron', a local man made good in the US, is behind the marina development and has turned his attention to building an upmarket harbourside hotel by 2015.

TOP CHOICE **Herring Guesthouse** GUESTHOUSE €

(☑868 4200; www.theherringhouse.com; Håve-gur 5; s/d without bathroom Ikr11,000/15,000, apt Ikr40,000) Þorir is a charming, knowledge-able host (he's a former town mayor) at this comfy new four-room guesthouse, with guest kitchen. He also offers a two-bedroom apart-ment, plus a nearby five-bedroom house that sleeps nine (check it out on www.580.is).

Gistiheimilið Tröllaskagi GUESTHOUSE €

(☑467 2100; www.northhotels.is; Lækjargata 10; s/d without bathroom incl breakfast Ikr8900/14,900) Another affordable guesthouse option, with clean and simple rooms a couple of blocks back from the marina.

Siglufjörður HI Hostel HOSTEL €

(Gistihhúsið Hvanneyri; ☑467 1506; www.hvan neyri.com; Aðalgata 10; dm/d without bathroom Ikr3800/10,000; ☎) Chipped cherubs and faded gilt make up the dated decor of this quirky 1930s hotel, whose stately propor-tions hint at wealthier times. There are 19 rooms with kitsch furnishings, a couple of TV lounges, a mighty dining room and a guest kitchen. HI members get a discount of Ikr600 per person; linen hire costs Ikr1250.

Campsite CAMPGROUND €

(sites per person Ikr800; ☼Jun-Aug) Oddly placed right in the middle of town near the harbour and town square, this municipal campsite has showers and a laundry. You'll find a second patch of grass beyond the city limits – follow Suðurgata out of town to-wards the tunnel to Ólafsfjörður.

✖ Eating

Aðalgata is home to a busy bakery and good pizzeria, but come mealtime most appetites are focused on the primary-coloured marina, where old warehouses have been reborn as photogenic eateries.

TOP CHOICE **Hannes Boy** ICELANDIC €€

(☑461 7730; www.raudka.is; mains Ikr2350-5390; ☼6-10pm daily plus noon-2pm Sat & Sun Jun-Aug, 6pm-midnight Fri & Sat Sep-May) Dressed in sunny yellow, this stylish, light-filled space is furnished with funky seats made from old herring barrels. The upmarket menu is fish-focused (naturally), with lobster soup and catch of the day fresh from the boats out-side. Reservations recommended.

Kaffi Rauðka ICELANDIC €€

(mains Ikr590-1690; ☼10am-8pm or later Jun-Aug, noon-6pm Sep-May; ☎) The counterpoint to neighbouring Hannes Boy, ruby-red Rauðka has a more informal air, with an all-day menu of sandwiches, salads and crepes, plus good-value meal/soup of the day (Ikr1390/1050). At weekends, it often stages live music.

Samkaup-Úrval SUPERMARKET €

(Aðalgata; ☼10am-7pm Mon-Fri, 11am-7pm Sat, 1-5pm Sun) Well stocked for self-caterers.

Vín Búð ALCOHOL €

(Eyrargata 25; ☼2-6pm Mon-Thu, 1-7pm Fri, 11am-2pm Sat Jun-Aug, shorter hours Sep-May) The government-run liquor store.

❶ Information

The town has all the services you might require (bank, pharmacy, post office etc). The herring museum offers some town info, as does the **information desk** (☼1.30-4.30pm Jun-Aug) inside the Ráðhús (town hall) on Gránugata.

❶ Getting There & Away

Bus

From June to August, **Sterna** (☑551 1166; www.sterna.is) bus 580/580a runs three times a week between Varmahlíð and Siglufjörður, call-ing at Sauðárkrókur, Hólar and Hofsós.

Hópferðabílar Akureyrar (☑898 5156; www.hba.is) runs bus 620/620a (also listed under the Sterna umbrella of bus services) year-round be-tween Akureyri and Ólafsfjörður, running three times daily on weekdays only, stopping at Dalvík and Árskógsströnd. In winter 2012, the service was continuing to Siglufjörður twice a day (from Akureyri Ikr2100, 80 minutes); hopefully, this will continue in summer 2013.

Car

Prior to the tunnels opening in 2010, Siglufjörður and Ólafsfjörður were joined by the 62km moun-tain road over Lágheiði (the old Rte 82). This road was only accessible in summer; in winter the towns were 234km apart. Thanks to the new tunnels through the mountains, that connection now measures 16km.

Travelling east, there's a 4km tunnel that opens into beautiful Héðinsfjörður, before a second tun-nel travels the remaining 7km to Ólafsfjörður.

Ólafsfjörður

POP 920

Beautifully locked between the sheer moun-tain slopes and the dark fjord waters, on-the-up fishing town Ólafsfjörður still

NORTH ICELAND ÓLAFSFJÖRÐUR

retains a sense of rural isolation, even with tunnels now linking it with Siglufjörður, its sister settlement further north.

From Akureyri, you have to pass through a thin 3km tunnel just to make your way into town, which makes for a cinematic entrance.

◉ Sights & Activities

Nátúrrugripasafnið (Aðalgata 14; admission Ikr500; ⏱2-5pm Jun-Aug) is a small bird-oriented museum; it's Ólafsfjörður's only formal sight and a source of local information. Far more interesting is the chance to get out among the natural splendour on a three-hour whale-watching tour with North Sailing (☏464 7272; www.northsail ing.is; adult/child €49/18), a major player in Húsavík whale watching and with a new base in Tröllaskagi from 2011. Tours depart on old oak boats two or three times daily from June to August; the trips are less crowded than those from Húsavík, the scenery just as spectacular, and the whales as compliant.

Ólafsfjörður receives good snow coverage in winter, when the downhill ski slopes above town lurch into action. There's also an excellent swimming pool, and nine-hole golf course. Hótel Brimnes offers rental of boats, kayaks and bikes for exploration; check the hotel's website for a rundown of possible activities in the area.

🛏 Sleeping & Eating

At mealtimes, consider a jaunt up the road to Siglufjöður.

Gistihús Jóa   GUESTHOUSE €
(Joe's Guesthouse; ☏847 4331; gistihusjoa@gmail.com; Strandgata 2; d without bathroom Ikr10,000-12,000) Finishing touches were going on here when we dropped by, and it's shaping up as an excellent choice. Joe's is in a restored old post office next to the supermarket; there are plans for a cafe and info centre downstairs. Compact rooms have handbasins, quirky flooring and modern chocolate-brown decor.

Brimnes Hotel
& Bungalows   HOTEL, COTTAGES €€
(☏466 2400; www.brimnes.is; Bylgjubyggð 2; s/d incl breakfast Ikr12,600/18,000, cottages from Ikr23,400; 🖵) The real draws at the town's primary accommodation are the cosy lakeshore log cabins (varying sizes, sleeping up to seven), with hot tubs built into the verandah and

views over the water. There are also 11 cosy en-suite rooms, plus a simple restaurant.

Campsite   CAMPGROUND €
(per person Ikr800) Toilets, water and electricity are available; guests use the showers inside the neighbouring pool complex.

Höllin   ICELANDIC €€
(Hafnargötu 16; mains Ikr900-3500; ⏱11.30am-10pm) This locals' haunt is signposted from the main road and offers a few dishes beyond the pizza-and-burger brigade (salads, lamb etc).

Samkaup-Úrval   SUPERMARKET €
(Aðalgata; ⏱10am-7pm Mon-Fri, 11am-6pm Sat, 1-5pm Sun) For self-catering.

❶ Getting There & Away

Hópferðabílar Akureyrar (☏898 5156; www.hba.is) runs bus 620/620a (also listed under the Sterna umbrella of bus services) year-round between Akureyri and Olafsfjörður (one hour, Ikr1700), running three times daily on weekdays only, stopping at Dalvík and Árskógsströnd. In winter 2012, the service was continuing to Siglufjörður twice a day.

Dalvík

POP 1400

Sleepy Dalvík found a snug spot between breezy Eyjafjörður and the rolling hills of Svarfaðardalur. Most tourists come here to catch the Grímsey ferry, but if you've got some time there's good hiking, interesting museums and superb accommodation.

There's a tourist information point (☏460 4000; www.dalvik.is; ⏱11am-6pm Mon-Fri, noon-5pm Sat & Sun) at Menningarhúsið Berg, the shiny new cultural centre that houses the library and an appealing cafe. The town's excellent swimming pool is in the neighbourhood, and the region offers activities such as horse riding, skiing, golf, guided hiking and birdwatching.

◉ Sights & Activities

Byggðasafnið Hvoll   MUSEUM
(www.dalvik.is/byggdasafn; Karlsbraut; adult/child Ikr500/free; ⏱11am-6pm Jun-Aug) Dalvík's folk museum is high on oddball factor. Skip the usual taxidermic characters (yes, another polar bear!) and find the rooms dedicated to local giant Jóhan Pétursson who, at 2.34m (almost 7ft 7in), was Iceland's tallest man.

Birdland Exhibition MUSEUM
(www.birdland.is; adult/child Ikr800/400; ⊙noon-5pm Jun-Aug) Outside town, 5km on Rte 805, this sweet-natured, kid-friendly museum showcases quirky avian facts beside a wetland reserve beloved by birdwatchers.

Arctic Sea Tours WHALE WATCHING
(www.arcticseatours.is; adult/child Ikr8000/4000; ⊙mid-May–Sep) More whale-watching companies are setting up in the towns along Eyjafjörður, offering an alternative to Húsavík. This company operates three-hour tours a couple of times a day in high summer, including a midnight sailing in June. All tours include a short sea-angling stint; pick-up from Akureyri is available (Ikr4000).

🛏 Sleeping & Eating

There's a campground (per campervan/tent Ikr2000/1500) by the swimming pool, and simple yet tasteful rooms behind the boxy facade of Fosshótel Dalvík (📋466 3395; www. fosshotel.is; Skíðabraut 18; d with/without bathroom incl breakfast Ikr25,000/13,200; ⊙May-Sep; @ 🛜).

A central Samkaup-Úrval (⊙10am-7pm Mon-Fri, to 6pm Sat, 1-5pm Sun) supermarket is by the N1, plus there are grill-bars and petrol stations, and a solitary restaurant, Við höfnina (Hafnarbraut 5; mains Ikr2000-4000; ⊙noon-1.30pm & 6-9pm), by the harbour.

[TOP CHOICE] **Dalvík HI Hostel** HOSTEL €
(Vegamót; 📋466 1060, 865 8391; www.vega mot.net; Hafnarbraut 4; dm/d without bathroom Ikr4500/10,200) This is, for our money, one of Iceland's best hostels, and certainly its prettiest – it's more like a boutique guesthouse than a budgeteer's bunkhouse. Heiða, the friendly owner, has a creative streak put to good use in quirky, vintage-inspired decor. The seven-room hostel is in the centre of town, in a white building called Gimli, but the owners also have three wooden cabins (Ikr12,800) and hot-pot beside their house (close to the swimming pool), and Gamli Bærinn (the 'Old House'), a gorgeously romantic self-contained cottage (Ikr19,800). At the hostel, HI members get a discount of Ikr600 per person; all the prices listed here exclude linen, which can be hired for Ikr1400 per person.

❶ Getting There & Away

Dalvík is the jumping-off point for ferries to Grímsey.

Hópferðabílar Akureyrar (📋898 5156; www. hba.is) runs bus 620/620a (also listed under

the Sterna umbrella of bus services) year-round between Akureyri and Olafsfjörður (weekdays only); the buses stop at Dalvík en route (Akureyri–Dalvík is 45 minutes, Ikr1300).

Árskógsströnd

The rich agricultural region known as Árskógsströnd runs north along the western shore of Eyjafjörður, from where there are dramatic views across the water to the mountains opposite. It's the main jumping-off point for those who want to explore little Hrísey offshore. It's also the home of Bruggsmiðjan (www.bruggsmidjan.is) microbrewery; tours are available by appointment, or join a food-focused tour from Akureyri-based Saga Travel. Alternatively, sample Bruggsmiðjan's fine Kaldi beers at Brugghúsbarinn in Akureyri.

Consider detouring to the village of Hauganes to climb aboard the former fishing boat Niels Jónsson (📋867 0000; www.niels. is; 3hr tour adult/child Ikr7000/3500; ⊙Jun-Aug) for an adventure that includes fishing and whale watching. Hauganes is 2km off Rte 82, about 14km south of Dalvík (35km north of Akureyri).

Hrísey

POP 180
Iceland's second-largest offshore island (after Heimaey) is the peaceful, low-lying Hrísey, a thriving community easily reached from the mainland. Thrust out into the middle of Eyjafjörður, the island is especially noted as a breeding ground and protected area for ptarmigan, as well as being home to a flourishing population of eider duck and an enormous colony of Arctic terns.

There's a small information office (⊙1-5pm Jun-Aug) inside Hús Hákarla Jörunder, a small museum (admission Ikr500) on shark-fishing beside the church in the picturesque village where the boat docks. You can pick up the handy Hrísey brochure here or in Akureyri, or check out two competing websites: www.hrisey.net and www.visithrisey.is. The latter outlines some houses for rent on the island.

Incredibly tame ptarmigan frequent the village streets. From here, three marked nature trails loop around the southeastern part of the island and lead to some good clifftop viewpoints. Not to be missed are the tons-of-fun 40-minute tractor trips

GRÍMSEY

Best known as Iceland's only true piece of the Arctic Circle, the remote island of Grímsey (population 90), 41km from the mainland, is a lonely little place where birds outnumber people by about 1000 to one. Believe it or not, Grímsey has been inhabited by humans since the year 1200. According to legend, it was a Norse fisherman named Grimur who first arrived on the island after falling in love with the daughter of a local troll. Sadly, the troll swiftly met her maker after an accidental encounter with the midnight sun – her petrified remains lie frozen near the island's pencil-thin church.

Today, much of Grímsey's appeal remains mythic in nature. Tourists flock here to snap up their 'I visited the Arctic Circle' certificate and pose for a photo with the 'you're standing on the Arctic Circle' monument (which is actually around 20m south of the 'real' line). Afterwards, there's plenty of time to appreciate the windswept setting. Scenic coastal cliffs and dramatic basalt formations make a popular home for 36 different species of seabirds, including the kamikaze Arctic tern. We're particularly fond of the anecdote that the airport runway has to be cleared of the terns a few minutes before aircraft are scheduled to arrive.

If sleeping inside the Arctic Circle sounds too adventurous to pass up, two places offer accommodation. Follow the stairs up through the trapdoor at cosy **Gullsól** (☏467 3190; gullsol@visir.is; r without bathroom adult/child Ikr4500/2500) to find teeny-tiny rooms perched above the island's gift shop (which opens in conjunction with ferry arrivals and sells coffee/tea and waffles). The full kitchen is handy for self-caterers; sleeping-bag beds are Ikr3000.

Things are more upmarket at **Básar** (☏467 3103; www.gistiheimilidbasar.is; s/d without bathroom Ikr5000/9000), right next to the airport. Sleeping-bag accommodation here is Ikr3000. There is a guest kitchen and meals are available, and sailing and sea-angling trips can be arranged.

There's a small campground by the community centre. The only restaurant is **Krían**, open daily in summer (definitely on days when the ferry docks, less reliably on other days). A general store is attached.

Getting There & Away

Despite its isolated location, getting to Grímsey is a cinch.

Air From mid-June to mid-August, **Air Iceland** (www.airiceland.is) flies daily to/from Akureyri; flights operate three times weekly the rest of the year. The bumpy 25-minute journey takes in the full length of Eyjafjörður and is an experience in itself. One-way online fares cost from around €60.

Air Excursion From mid-June to mid-August, Air Iceland offers half-day excursions from Akureyri (€144) or from Reykjavík (€236) that include flights and a couple of hours on the island (including a guided walk).

Ferry From mid-May to August, the **Sæfari ferry** (☏458 8970; www.saefari.is) departs from Dalvík at 9am Monday, Wednesday and Friday, returning from Grímsey at 4pm (giving you four hours on the island if you're not overnighting). The journey takes three hours and costs adult/child Ikr4000/free one way. If coming from Akureyri, the morning bus 620 at 7.45am should get you to Dalvík in time for the boat's departure. In winter, the ferry departure service remains the same; however, the ship immediately returns to Dalvík once cargo has been discharged and loaded.

Sailing Excursion **North Sailing** (☏464 7272; www.northsailing.is) offers two-day sailing expeditions out of Húsavík, which moor overnight at Grímsey. Trips depart weekly from May to mid-July (€590).

(adult/child Ikr1000/500), which plough across the island, passing all the important sights. They leave regularly from the boat dock, generally at 10am, noon, 2pm and 4pm daily in summer.

While a leisurely half-day is enough to explore the island, it's worth staying overnight for a more authentic glimpse of island life. Try **Brekka** (☑466 1751; www.brekkahrisey.is; s without bathroom Ikr7000, d without bathroom Ikr10,000-12,000; ☺mid-May–mid-Sep), Hrísey's one-stop shop for food and accommodation. Its menu is a treat: local mussels, lobster salad, Galloway steak.

There's a **campground** (per person Ikr1000) with its reception and amenities at the shiny new swimming-pool complex. The village store **Júllabúð** (☺11.30am-6.30pm Mon-Thu, to 10pm Fri, noon-6pm Sat & Sun) has supplies.

The passenger ferry **Sævar** (☑695 5544; adult/child Ikr1200/600) runs between Árskógssandur and Hrísey (15 minutes) at least seven times daily year-round; see www.hrisey.net for schedules. Bus 620 from Akureyri (three times daily, weekdays only) stops at Árskógssandur.

On Tuesday and Thursday year-round, the **Sæfari ferry** (☑458 8970; www.saefari.is; adult/child Ikr1015/free) runs from Dalvík to Hrísey at 1.15pm (30 minutes), returning immediately after passengers and cargo are discharged and loaded.

AKUREYRI

POP 17,300

Akureyri stands strong as Iceland's second city, but a Melbourne, Manchester or Montreal it is not. And how could it be? There are only just over 17,000 residents! It's a wonder the city (which would be a 'town' in any other country) generates this much buzz. Expect cool cafes, gourmet restaurants and something of a late-night bustle – a far cry from other towns in rural Iceland.

Akureyri nestles at the head of Iceland's greatest fjord, at the base of snowcapped peaks, and across the city flowerboxes, trees and well-tended gardens belie the location, just a stone's throw from the Arctic Circle. With a lively summer festival season, some of Iceland's best winter skiing, and a relaxed and easy attitude, it's the natural base for exploring Eyjafjörður.

History

The first permanent inhabitant of Eyjafjörður was Norse-Irish settler Helgi Magri (Helgi the Lean), who arrived in about 890. By 1602 a trading post had been established at present-day Akureyri. There were still no permanent dwellings though, as all the settlers maintained rural farms and homesteads. By the late 18th century the town had accumulated a whopping 10 residents, all Danish traders, and was granted municipal status. The town soon began to prosper and by 1900 Akureyri's population numbered 1370.

Today Akureyri is thriving. Its fishing company and shipyard are the largest in the country, and the city's university (established in 1987) gives the town a youthful exuberance.

◉ Sights

Akureyri has several museums, and while it's laudable that the town celebrates its artists and authors, many of these institutions are of limited interest unless you have a particular admiration for a specific artist's work. There are also museums dedicated to local industry, antique toys and motorbikes.

Akureyrarkirkja   CHURCH
(Eyrarlandsvegur) Dominating the town from high on a hill, Akureyri's landmark church was designed by Guðjón Samúelsson, the architect responsible for Reykjavík's Hallgrímskirkja. Although the basalt theme connects

---

THE AKUREYRI RUNTUR

Bored, restless and keen to be seen, Akureyri's teenagers have developed their own brand of *runtur* (literally 'round tour'). While Reykjavík's world-famous equivalent demands a hard stomach and a disco nap, in Akureyri you just need to be old enough to borrow a car. From about 8pm on any night of the week (though usually Friday and Saturday), you'll see a procession of cars, bumper to bumper, driving round and round in circles along Skipagata, Strandgata and Glerárgata. The speed rarely rises above 5km/h, but horns blare and teenagers scream out to each other until the wee hours.

Runtur rowdiness is inversely proportional to a city's size, so if you think Akureyri's honk-fest is irksome then don't go to Húsavík – that town only has three streets!

Akureyri

0.25 miles
500 m

Eyjafjörður

Akureyrarkirkja

Hof

Glerárgata
Strandgata
Hjalteyrargata
Hríseyjar
Norðurgata
Eiðsvallagata
Lundargata
Grænagata
Glerárgata
Eyrarvegur

Hofsbót
Skipagata
Gránufé lagsgata
Laxagata
Hólabraut
Brekkugata
Library
Klappargata
Munkaþverárstræti
Þórunnarstræti
Ásvegur
Byggðavegur
Eyrarvegur

Sports
Stadium

Glerártorg
Shopping Mall

Borgarbraut

Glerá

Lookout
Helgi
the Lean
Statue

To Akureyri HI Hostel (450m);
Bónus Supermarket (600m)

Oddeyrargata
Oddeyri
Bjarmastígur
Ráðhústorg
Helgamagrastræti
Bjarkarstígur
Hamarstígur
Þingvallastræti
Lögbergsgata
Laugargata
Grísabakkavegur
Eyrarlandsvegur
Kaupvangsstræti
Hafnarstræti

27
23
2
37
41
34
25
14
38
8
24
31
32
36
16
10
3
5
35
20
42
29
1
33
15
19
26
4
11
6
17

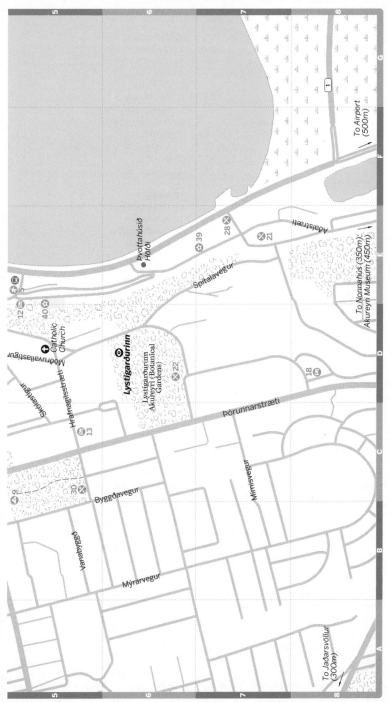

Akureyri

them, Akureyrarkirkja looks more like a stylised 1920s US skyscraper than its big-city brother. Built in 1940, the church contains a large 3200-pipe organ and a series of rather untraditional reliefs of the life of Christ. There's also a suspended ship hanging from the ceiling, reflecting an old Nordic tradition of votive offerings for the protection of loved ones at sea. Perhaps the most striking feature, however, is the beautiful central window in the chancel, which originally graced Coventry Cathedral in England. The church admits visitors; check the board outside for opening times, as they change frequently.

Akureyri Museum
MUSEUM

(Minjasafnið á Akureyri; www.akmus.is; Aðalstræti 58; adult/child Ikr800/free; ◎10am-5pm Jun–mid-Sep, 2-4pm Sat & Sun mid-Sep–May) This museum houses art and historical items from the Settlement Era to the present. There are photos, farming tools and recreations of early Icelandic homes. The **museum garden** became the first place in Iceland to cultivate trees when a nursery was established here in 1899.

FREE **Centre for Visual Arts**
MUSEUM

(Sjónlistamiðstöðin; www.sjonlist.is; Kaupvangsstræti 8-12; ◎noon-5pm Tue-Sun) Escape bad weather with a browse at this newly formed centre, which combines the Akureyri Art Museum with a handful of local galleries and hosts eclectic, innovative exhibitions.

Icelandic Aviation Museum
MUSEUM

(Flugsafn Íslands; www.flugsafn.is; adult/child Ikr1000/free; ◎11am-5pm Jun-Aug, 2-5pm Sat Sep-May) In a hangar at Akureyri airport, this museum charts the history of aviation in Iceland, from the first flight in 1919 to the present. Several restored aircraft fill the exhibition space, including a coast-guard

DIVING IN EYJAFJÖRÐUR — BRANDON PRESSER

Thoughts of scuba diving usually involve sun-kissed beaches and neon tropical fish, so perhaps it's surprising that some of the world's most fascinating diving lies within Iceland's frigid waters. Most bubble-blowers flock to crystalline Silfra, but the real diving dynamo, known as 'strýtan', lurks beneath Eyjafjörður. Strýtan, a giant cone (55m) soaring up from the ocean floor, commands a striking presence as it spews out gushing hot water. This conical structure – made from deposits of magnesium-silicate – is truly an anomaly. You see, the only other strýtan-like structures ever discovered were found at depths of 3000m or deeper; strýtan's peak is a mere 15m below the surface.

We had the opportunity to grab a meal with the man who discovered strýtan – Erlendur Bogason – and over a hearty plate of home-cooked reindeer, he told us all about Eyjafjörður's other scuba superlatives.

In addition to majestic strýtan, there are smaller steam cones on the other side of the fjord. Known as Artnanesstrýtur (also dubbed 'French Gardens'), these smaller formations aren't as spectacular, but it's fun to bring down guillemot eggs and cook them over the vents. Actually, the water that bubbles up is completely devoid of salt, so you can put a thermos over any of the vents, bottle the boiling water, and use it to make hot chocolate when you get back to the surface!

Diving around the island of Grímsey is also a very memorable experience – it's one of the only places in the Arctic Circle where you can dive recreationally. The water is surprisingly clear here, but the main draw is the bird life. (Yes, you read that correctly.) Bazaars of guillemots swoop down deep as they search for food. Swimming with birds is definitely a strange experience – when the visibility is particularly good it can feel like you're flying!

Interested in checking out these marvels and more? Drop Erlendur a line at his diving outfit, **Strytan Divecentre** (☎862 2949; www.strytan.is; 2-dive day trips from Ikr30,000). **Dive the North** (www.divethenorth.is) is an Akureyri-based dive company also diving in northern hotspots. Note that Reykjavík-based dive operators also offer diving tours to the area; check the websites of **Dive.is** (www.dive.is), **Diveiceland.com** (www.diveiceland.com) and **Scuba Iceland** (www.scubaiceland.is).

helicopter and the remains of a British war craft that crashed near Akureyri during WWII.

Nonnahús — MUSEUM
(www.nonni.is; Aðalstræti 54; adult/child Ikr700/free; ⊙10am-5pm Jun-Aug) The most interesting of the artists' homes, Nonnahús was the childhood home of renowned children's writer Reverend Jón Sveinsson (1857–1944), known to most as Nonni. His old-fashioned tales of derring-do have a rich local flavour. The house dates from 1850; its cramped rooms and simple furnishings provide a poignant insight into life in 19th-century Iceland.

FREE Lystigarðurinn — GARDENS
(Eyrarlandsholt; ⊙8am-10pm Mon-Fri, 9am-10pm Sat & Sun Jun-Sep) The most northerly botanical garden in the world makes a delightful picnic spot on sunny days. The wealth of plant life on display is truly astonishing considering the gardens' proximity to the Arctic Circle. You'll find examples of every species native to Iceland, as well as a host of high-latitude and high-altitude plants from around the world. While you're here, stop in at Cafe Björk for a cuppa.

Kjarnaskógur — GARDENS
About 3km south of town is Iceland's most visited 'forest', the Kjarnaskógur woods. This bushland area has a 2km-long athletic course, walking tracks, picnic tables, an amusing children's playground and some novel fitness-testing devices.

🏃 Activities

Akureyri has plenty of options to keep the blood flowing. In winter, skiing is the biggest draw, while summertime activities include golf, horse riding and hiking. For an experience you won't forget, there's world-class diving in Akureyri's fjord, Eyjafjörður.

Swimming
Sundlaug AkureyrarSundlaug Akureyrar — SWIMMING POOL
(Þingvallastræti 21; adult/child Ik470/150, sauna Ikr750; ⊙6.45am-9pm Mon-Fri, 8am-7.30pm Sat &

Sun) The outdoor swimming pool, near the campground, is one of Iceland's finest. It has three heated pools, hot-pots, waterslides, saunas and steamrooms – perfect for a relaxing afternoon.

Horse Riding

Horse tours are available from a range of outlying farms. Most can arrange town pick-up if needed.

Pólar Hestar HORSE RIDING
(☑463 3179; www.polarhestar.is) Offers by-the-hour trots and week-long wilderness trips.

Skjaldarvík HORSE RIDING
(☑552 5200; www.skjaldarvik.is) With a superb guesthouse and restaurant, 6km north of town, Skjaldarvík offers 1½-hour tours along the fjord and into the surrounding hills for Ikr6900, departing at 10am, 2pm and 5pm daily in summer. It also offers the good-value 'Ride & Bite', where for Ikr9900 you get the 5pm horse ride followed by access to an outdoor hot-pot and a two-course dinner.

Kátur HORSE RIDING
(☑695 7218; www.hestaleiga.is; Kaupangur; 1/3hr ride Ikr5000/9000; ☺Jun-Aug) A few minutes southeast of Akureyri off Rte 829, Kátur is another respected outfit offering daily rides of one to three hours.

Hiking

For information on hiking in the area, contact **Ferðafélag Akureyrar** (Touring Club of Akureyri; www.ffa.is; Strandgata 23; ☺3-6pm Mon-Fri Jun-Aug) and check out its helpful website detailing the huts it operates in northern Iceland and the highlands, plus notes on the Askja Trail (p292), and its program of hiking tours that travellers are welcome to join.

Another helpful resource is the collection of Útivist & afþreying hiking maps (there are seven in the series – #1 and #2 focus on the

---

LONG WEEKEND REMIX: THE NORTHERN TRIANGLE

Perfectly positioned in the chilly Atlantic waters between North America and Europe, Iceland has become the *it* destination for a cool weekend getaway. The constant stream of tourists has turned the three-day Reykjavík–Ring Road–Blue Lagoon trip into a well-worn circuit, so why not blaze a new trail and tackle Iceland's northern triangle of stunning attractions: Mývatn, Húsavík and Akureyri. It's a lot less legwork than you think – when you land at Keflavík airport, catch a connecting flight to Akureyri (you may need to travel to the capital's domestic airport). And to make things even simpler, here's a handy li'l planner.

Day 1: Akureyri

Jump-start your visit to the north with something quintessentially Icelandic: horse riding. Trust us: these aren't your usual horses. Then, a half-day is plenty of time to bop around the streets of the city centre. Or for those who can withstand another plane ride, spend the afternoon on Grímsey, Iceland's only slice of the Arctic Circle. For dinner, a good option is Strikið or RUB23, followed by a spirited night out on the town.

Day 2: Húsavík & Around

In the morning, head to Húsavík. First, swing by the Húsavík Whale Museum for a bit of background info, then hop aboard a whale-watching tour. Consider heading east for a walk among the canyon walls of Ásbyrgi, check out the roar of thunderous Dettifoss, then recount your whale tales over dinner back at Húsavík's Pallurinn.

Day 3: Mývatn

For those of you who have been drooling over the tantalising photos of Iceland's turquoise-tinted spa springs, fret not. Mývatn has its very own version of the Blue Lagoon. Known as the Mývatn Nature Baths, it's smaller than its southern brother, but noticeably less touristy. After a leisurely soak, it's time to get the blood flowing again. A three-hour hike around eastern Mývatn takes in a smorgasbord of geological anomalies. A stop at stinky Hverir is a must, and, if time permits, have a wander around the steam vents at Krafla. Then make your way back to Akureyri to catch your flight, but not before visiting one last site: the heavenly waterfall Goðafoss.

Eyjafjörður area); these are available at the tourist information centre.

A pleasant but demanding day hike leads up the Glerádalur valley to the summit of Mt Súlur (1213m). The trail begins on Súluvegur, a left turn off Þingvallastræti just before the Glerá bridge. Give yourself at least seven hours to complete the return journey.

Golf

Jaðarsvöllur   GOLF

(☑462 2974; www.gagolf.is) For golf-lovers, there's something strangely appealing about teeing off at midnight. At only a few degrees south of the Arctic Circle, Akureyri's Jaðarsvöllur basks in perpetual daylight from June to early August. In summer you can play golf here around the clock; book ahead for the midnight tee-off. The par-71 course is home to the annual 36-hole Arctic Open (www.arcticopen.is), a golf tournament played overnight in late June. Contact the club for information on green fees and club rentals.

Skiing

Hlíðarfjall Ski Centre   SKIING

(☑462 2280; www.hlidarfjall.is; day pass adult/child Ikr3300/1050) Iceland's premier downhill ski slope is west of town, 5km up Glerárdalur, with 24 pistes covering all categories, from beginner to upper-intermediate. The longest run is 2.5km, with a vertical drop of about 500m. There's also 20km of cross-country ski routes and a terrain park for snowboarders.

The ski season usually runs between December and late April, with the best conditions in February and March (Easter is particularly busy). In the long hours of winter darkness, many of the downhill runs are floodlit. There's ski and snowboard rental, two restaurants and a ski school. In season, buses usually connect the site with Akureyri; check the website for details.

☞ Tours

Most tours can be booked online; you can also visit the information centre for assistance. See p202 for details on the summer fly-in excursion to Grímsey. If you need to return to Reykjavík, consider taking a bus route through the interior highlands, rather than along Rte 1.

TOP
CHOICE **Saga Travel**   TOURS

(☑558 888; www.sagatravel.is; Kaupvangsstæti 4) Offers a rich and diverse year-round pro-

gram of excursions through the north – obvious destinations like Mývatn, Húsavík (for whale watching) and Askja in the highlands, but also interesting tours along themes such as food, art and design, churches or waterfalls. Check out its full program online, or drop by its office (open long hours in summer).

Ferðafélag Akurey   HIKING, SKIING

(FFA; ☑462 2720; www.ffa.is; Strandgata 23) The Touring Club of Akureyri organises a wonderful year-round program of hiking and skiing tours in the area's mountains.

SBA-Norðurleið   TOURS

(☑550 0700/70; www.sba.is; Hafnarstræti 82) The bus company runs a range of sightseeing tours in north Iceland, with popular destinations including Mývatn, Húsavík and Askja.

Nonni Travel   TOURS

(☑461 1841; www.nonnitravel.is; Brekkugata 5) Travel agency able to hook you up with just about any tour in the area.

☆ Festivals & Events

Akureyri's Summer Arts Festival (Listasumar á Akureyri) runs for 10 weeks from Midsummer (around 21 June) to late August, and attracts artists and musicians from around Iceland. There are exhibitions, concerts, theatre performances etc. It culminates in the Akureyri Town Festival, celebrated on the last weekend of August with a street party and parade. For details, check www.visitakureyri.is.

🛏 Sleeping

Akureyri's accommodation scene has undergone a transformation in recent years, with a slew of new, high-quality options at every price level. That said, the town still fills up in summer – book ahead. Bear in mind, too, that there are plenty of options outside the town centre – Akureyri is surrounded by excellent rural farmstay properties (you'll need your own car for these). Consult the handy Icelandic Farm Holidays booklet, *The Ideal Holiday* (www.farmholidays.is).

The tourist information centre can usually help if you arrive without a booking (Ikr500 reservation fee), but your options will be limited, especially in summer. Most accommodation is open year-round. The website of the tourist office (www.visitakurey ri.is) lists practically all options in the area.

Another great source is **AirBnB** (www.air bnb.com), detailing private rooms, cottages, apartments and houses for rent, with strong coverage in Akureyri.

As ever, check websites for up-to-date prices and low-season rates (prices listed here are for the summer peak; some of the rates are from 2012, so expect increases).

Budget

Akureyri Backpackers HOSTEL €
(☑578 3700; www.akureyribackpackers.com; Hafnarstræti 98; dm without bathroom Ikr3990-4990, d without bathroom Ikr11,990; @🛜) Supremely placed in the heart of town, this new backpackers has a chilled travellers vibe and includes a tour-booking service and popular cafe-bar. Rooms are spread over four floors: four- to eight-bed dorms, plus private rooms with made-up beds on the 4th floor. One minor gripe is that all showers are in the basement, as is a sauna (toilets and sinks are on all levels, however). Linen hire costs Ikr990; breakfast is Ikr990.

Akureyri HI Hostel HOSTEL €
(Stórholt; ☑462 3657; www.hostel.is; Stórholt 1; dm Ikr3800, d with/without bathroom Ikr14,000/10,000; @🛜) Well within the city limits though slightly removed from the action, this friendly, well-run hostel is a 15-minute walk north of the city centre. There's a TV lounge and two kitchens in the main house (rooms all have TV), a barbecue deck and two self-contained cottages sleeping up to eight. The owner happily imparts local knowledge; check-in time (from 3pm) is strictly enforced. HI members get a discount of Ikr600 per person; linen hire is Ikr1250.

Gula Villan GUESTHOUSE €
(☑896 8464; www.gulavillan.is; Brekkugata 8; s/d without bathroom Ikr10,000/13,000; 🛜) New owner Sigriður has a background in travel and this cheerful yellow-and-white villa shines under her care. Bright, well-maintained rooms are in a good central location. In a second building, **Gula Villan II** (Þingvallastræti 14; ⊙Jun-Aug) is run by the same folks and offers extra space in summer. Both guesthouses have guest kitchens and breakfast served on request (Ikr1600); BYO sleeping bags to reduce the price.

Centrum Hostel GUESTHOUSE €
(☑892 9838; www.centrumhostel.is; Hafnarstræti 102; s/d without bathroom Ikr9900/12,500; 🛜) Another new and central option, more a guesthouse than a hostel but offering dorm

beds too. Rooms are fresh, with TV and fridge, and there's a communal kitchen-lounge area. You'll save considerably if you use your own sleeping bags (single/double Ikr7900/9500).

City Campsite CAMPGROUND €
(☑462 3379; Þórunnarstræti; sites per person Ikr1000; ⊙mid-Jun–mid-Sep) This central site has a washing machine, dining area and toilets (showers are over the road and cost Ikr100). There's no kitchen. It's handily placed for the swimming pool and a supermarket.

Hamrar Campsite CAMPGROUND €
(☑461 2264; sites per person Ikr1000; ⊙mid-May–mid-Sep; @🛜) This huge site, 1.5km south of town in a leafy setting in Kjarnaskógur woods, has newer facilities than the city campsite, and mountain views.

Midrange

TOP CHOICE **Skjaldarvík** GUESTHOUSE €€
(☑552 5200; www.skjaldarvik.is; s/d without bathroom incl breakfast Ikr12,900/16,900; @🛜) A slice of guesthouse nirvana, this superb option lies in a bucolic farm setting 6km north of town. It's owned by a young family and features quirky design details everywhere you look (plants sprouting from shoes, vintage typewriters as artwork on the walls). Want more? How about a bumper breakfast buffet, horse riding, hot-pot, book swap, and honesty bar in the comfy lounge. The pretty-as-a-picture restaurant (two-course dinner Ikr4500; open dinner mid-May to mid-September) prepares a small but well-executed menu utilising home-grown herbs and vegies; it's open to nonguests, but bookings are essential. Consider its 'Ride & Bite' option to combine dining and a horse ride (see p208).

TOP CHOICE **Sæluhús** APARTMENT €€
(☑618 2800; www.saeluhus.is; Sunnutröð; studio/house €136/219; 🛜) This awesome mini village of modern studios and houses is perfect for a couple of days' R&R. Each house may be better equipped than your own back home: three bedrooms (sleeping seven), full kitchen, washing machine and verandah with hot tub and barbecue. Studios are smaller, with kitchen and access to a laundry (some have hot tub), and are ideal for a couple.

TOP CHOICE **Icelandair Hótel Akureyri** HOTEL €€
(☑518 1000; www.icelandairhotels.is; Þingvallastræti 23; r from Ikr23,870; @🛜) Opened in 2011,

this brilliant hotel showcases Icelandic designers and artists amongst its fresh, white-and-caramel-toned room decor. We love the outdoor terrace, the lounge serving high tea of an afternoon and happy-hour cocktails in the early evening, and the elegant restaurant. The bountiful breakfast buffet is optional (Ikr1700).

Hrafninn HOTEL €€

(📞661 9050; www.hrafninn.is; Brekkugata 4; s/d lkr11,500/16,900; 🛜) Priced below the competition yet delivering well above, beautiful Hrafninn ('The Raven') feels like an elegant manor house without being pretentious or stuffy. The 3rd-floor rooms have recently been renovated, and there's now a spacious 2nd-floor guest kitchen.

Hotel Natur HOTEL €€

(📞467 1070; www.hotelnatur.com; Þórisstaðir; s/d incl breakfast Ikr16,800/24,000; @🛜) About 15km east of Akureyri along Rte 1, this family-run property offers Nordic simplicity in its minimalist rooms, and breathtaking fjord views. The hotel's main accommodation is housed in the farm's old cow barn (but you'd never guess!). The huge dining space and seductive hot-pot add appeal.

Hótel Íbúðir APARTMENT €€

(📞892 9838; www.hotelibudir.is; Geislagata 10; d apt lkr19,700; 🛜) Íbúðir has a choice of seven quite luxurious apartments ranging in size (the largest sleeping eight). With a central location and balconies with town views, they make a fine choice for families.

Hótel Akureyri HOTEL €€

(📞462 5600; www.hotelakureyri.is; Hafnarstræti 67; s/d incl breakfast €125/148; @🛜) Compact, well-equipped rooms are found at this hotel close to the bus station. Front rooms have watery views, back rooms have an outlook on lush greenery. The hotel also has an assortment of apartments and guesthouse rooms in the town centre (with sleeping-bag beds for €25); see the website for a full rundown.

Hótel Edda HOTEL €€

(📞444 4900; www.hoteledda.is; entry on Þórunnarstræti 14; d with/without bathroom lkr23,900/12,900; ⏱mid-Jun–late Aug; @🛜) With its 200-plus rooms, this vast summer hotel in the local school is not a place you'll feel the personal touch. The new wing is surprisingly modern with bright, well-equipped rooms (bathroom, TV, fridge); the considerably cheaper old wing has shared bathrooms and

a dated feel. It's a short walk to the pool and botanical gardens.

Top End

Hótel Kea HOTEL €€€

(📞460 2000; www.keahotels.is; Hafnarstræti 87-89; s/d incl breakfast €169/210; @🛜) Akureyri's largest hotel and popular with groups, the Kea has smart business-style rooms with updated decor and good facilities (including minibar and tea-/coffee-making facilities). There's little local character about it, but some rooms have balconies and views over the fjord. There's a bar, cafe and restaurant here too, but for our money the Icelandair hotel is a fresher (and cheaper) option.

🍴 Eating

TOP CHOICE **Café Björk** CAFE €

(lunchtime buffet lkr1550; ⏱11am-6pm) What could be better than a designer cafe in a botanical garden? This brand-new cafe has gorgeous picture windows, a Scandi-chic feel, good coffee, a big sun terrace and a popular lunchtime soup-and-salad buffet.

Strikið INTERNATIONAL €€

(www.strikid.is; Skipagata 14; light meals lkr1800-2900, mains lkr3500-4900; ⏱11.30am-11pm) Huge windows with fjord views lend a magical glitz to this 5th-floor restaurant. The menu covers all options: go for pizzas and burgers if you must, or order superb-tasting mains showcasing prime Icelandic produce (superfresh sushi, salmon with hollandaise, lobster soup, reindeer burger, beef tenderloin). The three-course chef's menus (Ikr6600 to Ikr6900) are good value.

RUB23 INTERNATIONAL €€€

(www.rub23.is; Kaupvangsstræti 6; dinner mains lkr3790-5990; ⏱lunch Mon-Fri, dinner nightly) This supersleek restaurant revolves around a novel idea: you choose your fish (or meat) main, then pick one of the 11 'rubs', or marinades, that the chef then uses to cook your dish. Go with the chef's suggestions for catfish with smoked barbecue rub, or lamb fillet with citrus-rosemary rub. There's also a separate sushi menu.

Bláa Kannan CAFE €

(Hafnarstræti 96; lunchtime buffet lkr1250; ⏱8.30am-11.30pm) Prime people-watching is on offer at this much-loved cafe (the 'Blue Teapot', in the dark blue Cafe Paris building) on the main drag. The interior is timber-lined and blinged up with chandeliers; the menu offers paninis, bagels, cakes and a good-value daily lunchtime special (Ikr1590). It's a popular drinking hole of an evening.

Kaffi Költ   CAFE €
(Geislagata 10; ⊘10am-11pm Jun-Aug, shorter hours Sep-May; @🛜) A jumble of cool cafe creativity: vinyl records, old sofas, musical instruments, Icelandic craft, tasty cakes and a wonderful yarn-bombed exterior.

Indian Curry Hut   INDIAN €
(Hafnarstræti 100b; dishes Ikr1795-2295; ⊘lunch & dinner) Add a little heat to a chilly evening with a flavourful curry from this popular takeaway hut.

Greifinn   INTERNATIONAL €€
(www.greifinn.is; Glerárgata 20; mains Ikr1640-4830; ⊘11.30am-11pm) Family-friendly and *always* full to bursting, Greifinn is one of the most popular spots in town. The menu favours comfort food above all: juicy burgers, sizzling Tex-Mex, pizzas, salads and devilish ice-cream desserts.

Krua Siam   THAI €€
(Strandgata 13; dishes Ikr1400-2200; ⊘lunch Mon-Fri, dinner nightly) The rotating ceiling fans here call to mind warmer climes, but Krua Siam does a good job of transporting taste buds to the Land of Smiles, despite being a mere 40km from the Arctic Circle.

Bautinn   INTERNATIONAL €€
(Hafnarstræti 92; mains Ikr1460-5250; ⊘lunch & dinner) A local favourite, this unpretentious, family-friendly option has an excellent all-you-can-eat soup and salad bar (Ikr1880), and a big menu featuring everything from pizza, burgers, fish and lamb to such Icelandic favourites as whale.

Örkin hans Nóa   SEAFOOD €€
(Hafnarstræti 22; mains around Ikr4000; ⊘from 2pm Mon-Sat, 6pm Sun) Part gallery, part furniture store, part restaurant – 'Noah's Ark' is certainly unique, and offers a simple food concept done well. The menu features a selection of fresh fish options, which are pan-fried and served with vegetables. Classic, effective, tasty. Cake and coffee are available in the afternoon.

La Vita é Bella   ITALIAN €€
(Hafnarstræti 92; mains Ikr1560-5640; ⊘from 6pm) Come here for delectable Italy-meets-Iceland dishes (eg tagliatelle with lobster tails) plus an unsurprising but well-executed menu of pasta, risotto and pizza.

Brynja   ICE CREAM €
(Aðalstræti 3; ice cream from Ikr310; ⊘9am-11.30pm May-Aug, 11am-11pm Sep-Apr) This legendary sweet shop is known across Iceland for the best ice cream in the country (it's made with milk, not cream). It's not far from the botanical gardens.

Self-Catering

Akureyri has a choice of supermarkets, but none that are very central:

Nettó   SUPERMARKET €
(Glerárgata; ⊘10am-7pm Mon-Fri, to 6pm Sat, noon-6pm Sun) In the Glerártorg shopping mall.

Samkaup-Strax   SUPERMARKET €
(Byggðavegur 98; ⊘9am-11pm Mon-Fri, 10am-11pm Sat & Sun) Near the campsite west of the centre.

Bónus   SUPERMARKET €
(Langholt; ⊘11am-6.30pm Mon-Thu, 10am-7.30pm Fri, 10am-6pm Sat, noon-6pm Sun) Cut-price supermarket, behind the HI hostel. There's an early-opening bakery (from 7.30am) on the premises.

Vín Búð   ALCOHOL €
(Hólabraut 16; ⊘11am-6pm Mon-Thu & Sat, to 7pm Fri) The government-run alcohol shop is near the Borgabíó cinema.

🍷 Drinking

The bar at Akureyri Backpackers is a popular spot for meeting fellow travellers.

Brugghúsbarinn   BAR
(Kaupvangsstræti 23; ⊘from 6pm; 🛜) It's not just any old beer on tap at this candlelit space – it's delicious Kaldi, brewed up the road at the microbrewery in Árskógsströnd. Friendly staff will walk you through the options – five draught Kaldi variants, including a house brew. Food isn't offered, but you can order dishes from the tapas bar upstairs.

Græni Hatturinn   LIVE MUSIC
(Green Hat; Hafnarstræti 96) More traditional and usually less boisterous than Sjallinn, this popular pub is down a lane behind Blaá Kannan. It's the best place in town to see live music.

Café Amour   CAFE, BAR
(Ráðhústorg 9; ⊘11am-1am Sun-Thu, to 4am Fri & Sat) Sophisticated Café Amour tries hard to lure in Akureyri's bright young things with its lengthy cocktail list and New World

wines. The small club upstairs is pretty garish but draws the crowds at weekends.

Kaffi Akureyri   BAR
(Strandgata 7; ☉3pm-1am Sun-Thu, to 4am Fri & Sat) This cafe-bar is one of Akureyri's better live-music venues and gets packed on Friday and Saturday nights when bands play.

Sjallinn   CLUB
(Geislagata 14; ☉to 4am Fri & Sat) Perennially popular and always jammed, this bar, club and live-music venue has DJs playing everything from chart tunes to indie rock and live bands at weekends.

☆ Entertainment

There are two cinemas in the town centre, Borgarbíó (Hólabraut 12) and Nyja-Bíó (Strandgata 2). Both show original-version mainstream films with subtitles.

Keilan   BOWLING
(Hafnarstræti 26; ☉11am-11.30pm) If the weather is against you, Keilan can entertain with ten-pin bowling, pool tables and bar.

Leikfélag Akureyrar   THEATRE
(www.leikfelag.is; Hafnarstræti 57) Akureyri's premier theatre venue hosts drama, musicals, dance and opera, with its main season running from September to June. Check the website for upcoming performances.

🛍 Shopping

Several shops on Hafnarstræti sell traditional Icelandic woollen sweaters (lopapeysur), books, knick-knacks and souvenirs under the tax-free scheme (see p339).

TOP CHOICE **Geysir**   CLOTHING, SOUVENIRS
(www.geysirshop.is; Hafnarstræti 98) We covet everything in this unique store, from the lopapeysa-style capes to the reindeer hides, and the old Iceland maps to the puffin-embroidered slippers.

Eymundsson   BOOKS, SOUVENIRS
(Hafnarstræti 91-93; ☉to 10pm) First-rate bookshop selling maps, souvenir books and a wide selection of international magazines. There's a tasty cafe on-site.

Christmas Garden   SOUVENIRS
(Jólagarðurinn; ☉10am-10pm Jun-Aug, 2-10pm Sep-Dec, 2-6pm Jan-May) If you can handle the Christmas cheer out of season, this gingerbread house sells a super-festive selection of locally made decorations and traditional

Icelandic Christmas foods. It's 10km south of Akureyri on Rte 821.

Viking   SOUVENIRS
(www.theviking.is; Hafnarstræti 104) This hard-to-miss shop lures the masses with its over-sized polar bear plunked out front (not to mention the trolls). There's a good selection of lopapeysas and souvenir knick-knacks.

Fold-Anna   CLOTHING
(Hafnarstræti 100) Staff can be seen knitting behind the counter as you browse this outlet loaded with lopapeysa.

ℹ Information

Emergency
Emergency (☎112)
Police (☎nonemergency 464 7700; Þórunnarstræti 138)

Internet Access
Most lodgings have connections, as do several cafes and museums. There are internet terminals at the tourist information centre and the **library** (Amtsbókasafnið á Akureyri; www.amtsbok.is; Brekkugata 17; ☉10am-7pm Mon-Fri mid-May–mid-Sep, 10am-7pm Mon-Fri, 11am-4pm Sat mid-Sep–mid-May; @📶), for a small fee.

Laundry
Most accommodation offers laundry service for guests.
Þvottahúsið Höfði (Hafnarstræti 34; loads up to 7kg Ikr2000; ☉8am-6pm Mon-Fri) Service laundry.

Medical Services
Akureyri Hospital (☎463 0100; www.fsa.is; Eyrarlandsvegur)
Apótekarinn (Hafnarstræti 95; ☉9am-5.30pm Mon-Fri) Pharmacy.
Heilsugæslustöðin Health Care Centre (☎460 4600; 3rd fl, Hafnarstræti 99; ☉8am-4pm Mon-Fri)

Money
All central banks (open 9.15am to 4pm) offer commission-free foreign exchange and have 24-hour ATMs.
Arion banki (Geislagata 5)
Íslandsbanki (Skipagata 14)
Landsbanki (Strandgata 1)

Post
Main post office (Strandgata 3; ☉9am-6pm Mon-Fri)

Tourist Information
Tourist information centre (☎450 1050; www.visitakureyri.is; Hof, Strandgata 12;

NORTH ICELAND AKUREYRI

⊘8am-7pm mid-Jun–Aug, 8am-5pm Mon-Fri, 10am-2pm Sat & Sun Sep, 8am-4pm Mon-Fri Oct-Apr, 8am-5pm Mon-Fri, 8am-4pm Sat & Sun May–mid-Jun; @⊛) This friendly, efficient office is inside Hof, the town's new cultural centre. There are loads of brochures, maps, internet access and a design store. Knowledge-able staff can book tours and transport for free, and accommodation in the area (Ikr500).

⊕ Getting There & Away

Air

Akureyri airport (www.akureyriairport.is) is 3km south of the city centre. In recent summers it has welcomed a weekly direct flight to/from Copenhagen with Iceland Express, but this service looks doubtful for 2013.

Air Iceland (www.airiceland.is) Runs frequent daily flights between Akureyri and Reykjavík's domestic airport, and from Akureyri to Grímsey, Vopnafjörður and Þórshöfn. Online deals have one-way tickets from around €60.

Icelandair (www.icelandair.com) Has flights from June to September from Keflavík, meaning international travellers arriving into Iceland don't need to travel to Reykjavík's domestic airport to connect to Akureyri.

Bus

Akureyri's **bus station** (Hafnarstræti 82) is the hub for bus travel in the north. To get up-to-date information on schedules and fares, stop by the bus offices (SBA-Norðurleið is inside the bus terminal, Sterna is across the road from it) or the tourist information centre, or check online.

Average fares and journey times (from summer 2012, subject to change): Akureyri–Reykjavík via Rte 1 (Ikr11,800, six hours), Akureyri–Húsavík (Ikr3300, 1¼ hours), Akureyri–Mývatn (Ikr3600, 1½ hours), Akureyri–Egilsstaðir (Ikr8700, four hours).

SBA-Norðurleið (☑550 0700/70; www.sba. is) services:

BUS 62/62A Akureyri–Goðafoss–Mývatn–Egilsstaðir; daily June to mid-September, four times weekly rest of year

BUS 610/610A Akureyri–Reykjavík via the inland Kjölur route; daily mid-June to early September

BUS 640/640A Akureyri–Húsavík; two to four times daily year-round

BUS 641/641A Akureyri–Húsavík–Ásbyrgi–Dettifoss; daily mid-June to August

BUS 680/680A Akureyri–Húsavík–Þórshöfn; three times weekly year-round

Sterna (☑551 1166; www.sterna.is) services include the following:

BUS 60/60A Akureyri–Reykjavík via Rte 1; at least once daily year-round

BUS 35/35A Akureyri–Reykjavík via the Kjölur route; daily mid-June to early September

Hópferðabílar Akureyri (☑898 5156; www.hba. is) services (under the Sterna umbrella):

BUS 620/620A Akureyri–Dalvík–Ólafsfjörður (some extend to Siglufjörður); three times daily weekdays only year-round

Car

After Reykjavik, Akureyri is Iceland's second transport hub. There are several car-hire agencies in town – all the major firms have representation at the airport. See p348 for a list of rental agencies in Iceland. For a fee, most companies will let you pick up a car in Akureyri and drop it off in Reykjavík or vice versa.

Check out www.semferda.is for information about sharing rides with other travellers.

⊕ Getting Around

Central Akureyri is quite compact and easy to get around on foot. Take note of the quirky parking policies if you plan to leave your car in the city centre.

Bicycle

At the time of research, there were no bike-rental agencies in town. Ask at the tourist office to see if this has changed.

Bus

There's a free town bus service on four routes (running regularly from 7am to 10pm weekdays and noon to 6pm weekends) – look for the yellow buses. Unfortunately, no route goes to the airport.

Car

Akureyri has a unique parking system for Iceland (but one that many northern Europeans will be familiar with). When parking in the city centre, you must set a plastic parking clock marking the time you parked, and display it on the dashboard of your car (so as to be seen through the windshield). Parking is free, but spaces are signposted with maximum parking times (between 15 minutes to two hours, enforced from around 10am to 4pm). You'll be fined if your car overstays the advertised time limit. If this sounds too complicated, there is untimed parking by the Hof.

Taxi

The BSO **taxi stand** (☑461 1010; www.bso.is; Strandgata) is opposite the Hof. Taxis may be booked 24 hours a day. BSO's website outlines the cost to hire a car and driver to visit nearby sightseeing destinations.

Around Akureyri

If you have time, it's worth getting off the Ring Road and exploring the region around Akureyri's fjord, Eyjafjörður. The road north along western Eyjafjörður (to Dalvík, Ólafsfjörður and Siglufjörður) is covered in the Tröllaskagi Peninsula section, p196. Eyjafjörður's eastern shore is much quieter than its western counterpart, offering a few interesting places to pause among the sweeping vistas.

The eclectic **Icelandic Folk & Outsider Art Museum** (Safnasafnið; www.safnasafnid.is; adult/child Ikr1000/free; ⊙10am-5pm mid-May–Aug), 12km east of town on Rte 1 (look for the sculpture of a blue man), is a beautiful light-filled (and plant-filled) space. In Icelandic, its name literally means 'the museum museum', a name coined because the curators display just about anything, as long as it was made with an earnest heart.

Further north, Rte 83 branches off the Ring Road to lead you 20km north to the fjordside village of **Grenivík**, with a sweet fishing museum, campsite and grill-bar at the town store. En route are majestic views, plus the photogenic turf roofs at **Laufás** (adult/child Ikr800/free; ⊙9am-5pm Jun-Aug), a preserved manor farm; and the acclaimed stables of **Pólar Hestar** (📞463 3179; www.polarhestar.is), where you can arrange short rides or saddle up for serious week-long journeys into dreamy landscapes (from €950).

Akureyri to Mývatn (Goðafoss)

Travellers heading from Akureyri to Mývatn (or Akureyri to Húsavík if you take a small detour) will happen across heavenly **Goðafoss** (Waterfall of the Gods), which rips straight through the Bárðardalur lava field along Rte 1. Although smaller and less powerful than some of Iceland's other chutes, it's definitely one of the most beautiful.

The falls play an important part in Icelandic history. At the Alþing (National Assembly) in the year 1000, the *lögsögumaður* (law speaker), Þorgeir, was forced to make a decision on Iceland's religion. After 24 hours' meditation, he declared the country a Christian nation. On his way home he passed the waterfall near his farm, Djúpá, and tossed in his pagan carvings of the Norse gods, thus bestowing the falls' present name.

If the sound of pounding water puts you to sleep, a night in the sunny yellow rooms at **Fosshóll** (📞464 3108; www.godafoss.is; sites per person Ikr1000, d with/without bathroom incl breakfast Ikr23,800/18,600; ⊙mid-May–mid-Sep; 📶), next to the falls, might be for you. There's a restaurant here, and orbiting the complex is a petrol station housing an information point, cafeteria and excellent souvenir shop.

MÝVATN REGION

Undisputed gem of the northeast, Lake Mývatn (*mee*-vawt) and the surrounding area are starkly beautiful, an otherworldly landscape of spluttering mudpots, weird lava formations, steaming fumaroles and volcanic craters. The Mývatn basin sits squarely on the Mid-Atlantic Ridge and the violent geological character of the area has produced an astonishing landscape unlike anywhere else in the country; this is the Iceland you've always imagined.

The lake is encircled by a 36km sealed road (Rtes 1 and 848), with the main settlement of Reykjahlíð on the northeast corner. A handy information centre is located here, as are several sleeping options for every budget.

Most of the points of interest are linked by the lake's looping road, including the diverse lava formation in eastern Mývatn, the cluster of pseudocraters near southern Mývatn, and the bird-friendly marsh plains around western Mývatn.

In northern Mývatn, the Ring Road (Rte 1) veers east, away from Reykjahlíð, and takes you over the Námaskarð pass to the Hverir geothermal area. Then, a turn-off to the north (Rte 863) leads to Krafla, 14km from Reykjahlíð.

With your own vehicle this whole area can be explored in one day, but if you're using the bus or a bicycle allow two days. If you want to hike and explore more distant mountains and lava fields, allow at least three.

History & Geology

Ten thousand years ago the Mývatn basin was covered by an ice cap, which was destroyed by fierce volcanic eruptions that also obliterated the lake at its base. The explosions formed the symmetrical *móberg* peaks (flat-topped mountains formed by subglacial volcanic eruptions) south of today's lake, while volcanic activity to the east formed the

Lúdent tephra (solid matter ejected into the air by an erupting volcano) complex.

Another cycle of violent activity over 6000 years later created the Ketildyngja volcano, 25km southeast of Mývatn. The lava from that crater flowed northwest along the Laxárdalur valley, and created a lava dam and a new, improved lake. After another millennium or so a volcanic explosion along the same fissure spewed out Hverfell, the classic tephra crater that dominates the modern lake landscape. Over the next 200 years, activity escalated along the eastern shore and craters were thrown up across a wide region, providing a steady stream of molten material flowing towards Öxarfjörður. The lava dam formed during the end of this cycle created the present Mývatn shoreline.

Between 1724 and 1729 the Mývatnseldar ('Mývatn Fires') eruptions began at Leirhnjúkur, close to Krafla, northeast of the lake. This dramatic and sporadically active fissure erupted spectacularly in 1984, and by the early '90s the magma chamber had refilled, prompting experts to predict another big eruption. As yet this hasn't happened, but it's only a matter of time.

In 1974 the area around Mývatn was set aside as the Mývatn-Laxá special conservation area, and the pseudocrater field at Skútustaðir, at the southern end of the lake, is preserved as a national natural monument.

🏃 Activities

Geothermal Pools

TOP CHOICE Mývatn Nature Baths GEOTHERMAL POOL (Jarðböðin; www.jardbodin.is; adult/child Ikr2800/ free; ⊙9am-midnight Jun-Aug, noon-10pm Sep-May) Northern Iceland's answer to the Blue Lagoon is 3km east of Reykjahlíð. Although it's smaller than its southern counterpart, it's also less hyped (probably a good thing), and it's a gorgeous place to soak in the powder-blue, mineral-rich waters. After a relaxing soak, try one of the two natural steam baths and/or a rich dessert at the on-site cafeteria.

Tours

Tourism reigns supreme at Reykjahlíð and for travellers without transport there are numerous tours around the area (some tours originate in Akureyri). Tours fill up fast during summer, so try to book at least a day before. The information centre handles bookings, or contact operators direct.

MÝVATN

For an abridged (3½-hour, Ikr6100) bus tour of Mývatn's top sights, consider linking up with the sightseeing tour operated by SBA-Norðurleið (✆550 0700/70; www.sba.is). It starts in Akureyri, but you can often hop aboard in Reykjahlíð. There are both summer and winter trips.

Another year-round operator is Akureyri-based Saga Travel (✆558 888; www.sagatravel. is), which has an array of fabulous tours in the region and offers pick-up in Reykjahlíð.

Hiking & Biking

Hike & Bike   HIKING, CYCLING (✆899 4845; www.hikeandbike.is; ⊙8.30am-6pm Jun-Aug) Hike & Bike has a booth by the Gamli Bærinn tavern in Reykjahlíð and a summer program of cycling and hiking tours. At 9am daily, take off on a four-hour guided walk to Hverfell and Dimmuborgir (Ikr7500). At 2pm, there's a three-hour pedal through the backcountry (Ikr8500), or you can opt for an evening cycle that ends with a soak at the Nature Baths (Ikr9500, including admission). Check the website for excellent multiday options (including five days hiking on the Askja Trail), and for winter pursuits (snowshoeing and cross-country skiing tours). Hike & Bike

---

INTO THE MADDING SWARMS

Plague-like swarms of Mývatn's eponymous midges are a lasting memory for many visitors to the area in midsummer. As infuriating as they can be, these pesky intruders are a vital food source for wildlife.

Unfortunately for humans, the midges are attracted to carbon dioxide, so every time you exhale, the little buggers gather around your face and invade your eyes, ears, nose and mouth.

The good news is that only one species bites, so wear a head net (which you can buy at the supermarket in Reykjahlíð), splash on the repellent and pray for a good wind to send the nasty little blighters diving for shelter amid the vegetation.

also rents out bikes for independent exploration (Ikr4000 per day).

Horse Riding

Two companies can get you in the saddle for a short tour – a lovely way to see the landscapes.

Saltvík   HORSE RIDING
(☑847 6515; www.saltvik.is) Just south of Reykjahlíð. Two-hour tours (Ikr8000) are scheduled daily at 10am, 1pm and 4pm June to August. There are also one-hour evening rides at 8pm from late June to late July (Ikr5500).

Safaríhestar   HORSE RIDING
(☑464 4203; safarihestar@gmail.com) One-/two-hour tours (Ikr5000/8000) from Álftagerði III farm on the south side of the lake (400m west of Sel-Hótel).

Sightseeing Flights

Mýflug Air   SCENIC FLIGHTS
(☑464 4400; www.myflug.is; Reykjahlíð airport) Mýflug Air operates daily flight-seeing excursions (weather permitting, of course). A 20-minute trip over Mývatn and Krafla costs €80. A two-hour 'super tour' (€265) also includes Dettifoss, Jökulsárgljúfur, Ásbyrgi, Kverkfjöll, Herðubreið and Askja. You can also take a two-hour Arctic Circle tour that stops in Grímsey for one hour (€220).

LOFTHELLIR CAVE

The dramatic lava cave at Lofthellir is a stunning destination with magnificent natural ice sculptures dominating the interior. Although one of Mývatn's true highlights, the cave can only be accessed on a tour because the cave entrance (suitable only for the svelte) is hard to find along the barren landscape, and special equipment (headlamps, studded boots etc) is required. Saga Travel (☑558 888; www.sagatravel.is) offers tours costing Ikr24,500/18,500 from Akureyri/Reykjahlíð.

ASKJA & THE HIGHLANDS

A fast-growing number of operators run super-Jeep tours to Askja, from mid-June (when the route opens) until as late into September as weather permits. From Akureyri it makes for a long day tour (up to 15 hours); 12-hour tours leave from Reykjahlíð. See the list of operators on p292.

EASTERN LAKESIDE HIKE

Although easily accessible by car, the sights along Mývatn's eastern lakeshore can also be tackled on a pleasant half-day hike. A well-marked track runs from Reykjahlíð village to Hverfell (5km), passing intriguing Stóragjá and Grjótagjá along the way. Then it's on to Dimmuborgir (another 2.5km) with its collection of ruin-like lava. If you start in the late afternoon and time your hike correctly, you'll finish the day with a meal at Dimmuborgir while sunset shadows dance along the alien landscape.

❶ Getting There & Away

All buses pick up/drop off passengers at the tourist information centre in Reykjahlíð. **SBA-Norðurleið** (☑550 0700/70; www.sba.is) services:

BUS 62/62A Akureyri–Mývatn–Egilsstaðir; daily June to mid-September, four times weekly rest of year. Stops at Reykjahlíð and at Sel-Hótel in southern Mývatn.

BUS 650/650A Reykjahlíð–Húsavík; Ikr2700, 40 minutes, twice daily mid-June to August

BUS 661/661A Reykjahlíð to Krafla and Dettifoss; daily mid-June to August. From Dettifoss you have the option of linking with bus 641a to return to Húsavík.

In July and August, **Reykjavík Excursions** (Kynnisferðir; ☑580 5400; www.re.is) operates two scheduled services along the highland Sprengisandur route between Reykjavík or Landmannalaugar and Mývatn; see p291.

❶ Getting Around

There are wonderful hiking trails around Mývatn, but unfortunately they're not all connecting. Without a car or bicycle you may find getting around a bit frustrating, unless you don't mind long walks along the lakeshore road. You can roll the dice and stick out your thumb, although Mývatn isn't always the easiest place to hitch a ride.

You might consider renting a car in Akureyri. During calmer weather, a good option for travellers without a car is to hire a mountain bike from Hike & Bike (p216). The 36km ride around the lake can be done in a day, allowing time for sightseeing at all the major stops.

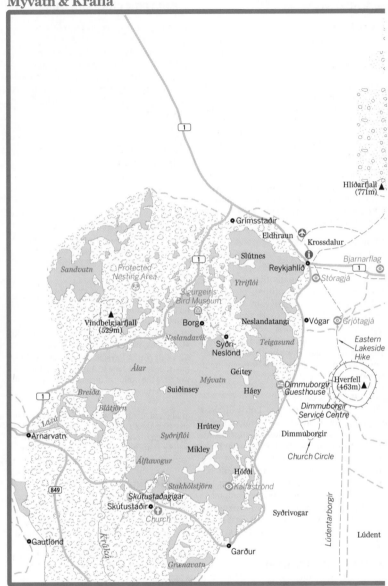

NORTH ICELAND REYKJAHLÍÐ

Reykjahlíð

POP 200

Reykjahlíð, on the northeastern shore of the lake, is the main village and Mývatn's obvious base. There's little to it beyond a collection of guesthouses and hotels, a supermarket, petrol station and information centre.

◉ Sights & Activities

During the huge Krafla eruption of 1727, the Leirhnjúkur crater, 11km northeast of

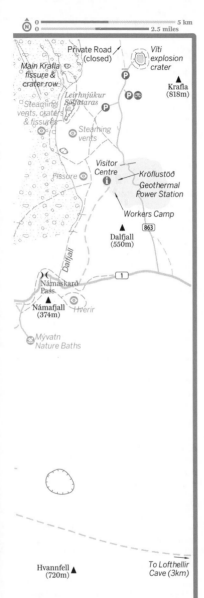

church was spared – some would say miraculously – when the flow parted, missing the church by only a few metres. It was rebuilt on its original foundation in 1876, then again in 1962.

A stormy day is well spent relaxing at the 25m outdoor **swimming pool** (adult/child Ikr400/150; ☺10am-9pm mid-Jun–Aug, shorter hours rest of year).

🛏 Sleeping

Mývatn's popularity means that room rates have soared, and demand is far greater than supply, so don't think twice about booking ahead. Most prices are overinflated, with €200 being the norm for a hotel double room around the lake in summer (that's considerably more than anywhere else in north or east Iceland, and we don't think you get great value for that price).

The following options are located either in central Reykjahlíð or at Vógar, a small cluster of buildings along the lake's eastern shore (about 2.5km south of Reykjahlíð). Additional options can be found at Dimmuborgir and along the southern shore at Skútustaðir. The website www.myvatn -hotels.com gives a rundown of most options.

Prices listed here are generally from summer 2012. See websites for up-to-date rates (and low-season rates). To save money, ask about sleeping-bag options.

Helluhraun 13   GUESTHOUSE €€
(☑464 4132; www.helluhraun13.blogspot.com; Helluhraun 13, Reykjahlíð; s/d without bathroom incl breakfast Ikr11,000/15,500; ☺Jun-Sep) There are just three rooms and one bathroom at this small, homely guesthouse, but they're bright and tastefully decorated. Breakfast is included, as are the views of the lava field out the kitchen window.

Eldá   GUESTHOUSE €€
(☑464 4220; www.elda.is; Helluhraun 15, Reykjahlíð; s/d without bathroom incl breakfast Ikr12,700/17,900; @🛜) This friendly family-run operation owns four properties along Helluhraun and offers cosy accommodation in each (plus one studio apartment sleeping five). There are guest kitchens and TV lounges, and an impressive buffet breakfast is included. All guests check in at this location.

Hlíð   CAMPGROUND, GUESTHOUSE €
(☑464 4103; www.hlidmyv.is; Hraunbrún, Reykjahlíð; sites per person Ikr1300, dm Ikr4100, d incl

Reykjahlíð, kicked off a two-year period of volcanic activity, sending streams of lava along old glacial moraines towards the lakeshore. On 27 August 1729 the flow ploughed through the village, destroying farms and buildings, but amazingly the wooden

breakfast Ikr21,000, cottages Ikr30,000; @🛜) Sprawling, well-run Hlíð is 300m uphill from the church in Reykjahlíð and offers a full spectrum: camping, sleeping-bag dorms and rooms with kitchen access, no-frills huts, self-contained cottages sleeping six and new en-suite guesthouse rooms. There's also laundry, playground and bike hire.

Vogafjós Guesthouse   GUESTHOUSE €€
(📞464 4303; www.vogafjos.net; Vógar; s/d incl breakfast €186/194; 🛜) Fresh scents of pine and cedar fill the air in these log-cabin rooms (cosy with underfloor heating), set in a lava field 2.5km south of Reykjahlíð and a few minutes' walk from the Cowshed restaurant, where breakfast is served. Most rooms sleep two, with family rooms also available.

Bjarg   CAMPGROUND €
(📞464 4240; ferdabjarg@simnet.is; sites per person Ikr1500, d without bathroom Ikr14,000; ☉mid-May–Sep; @🛜) This smaller campsite has a lovely location on the Reykjahlíð lakeshore (just south of the supermarket) and features a kitchen tent, laundry service, summer boat rental and bike hire. Accommodation is also available in a couple of bright rooms in the main building.

Vógar   GUESTHOUSE, CAMPGROUND €€
(📞464 4399; www.vogahraun.is; Vógar; sites per person Ikr1500, d with/without bathroom from €136/81; ☉mid-May–mid-Sep) A range of decent options here, 2.5km south of Reykjahlíð: camping, sleeping-bag accommodation in utilitarian prefab huts, and a new block of compact, en-suite guesthouse rooms.

Lúdent   GUESTHOUSE €€
(📞898 3328; www.ludent.is; Birkihraun 5, Reykjahlíð; d without bathroom incl breakfast Ikr18,500; ☉mid-Jun–mid-Aug) In high summer only, Lúdent offers six simple guesthouse rooms behind Reykjahlíð village. Facilities are homey: three rooms share a kitchen, lounge and bathroom.

Hótel Reynihlíð   HOTEL €€
(📞464 4170; www.myvatnhotel.is; s/d incl breakfast €155/195; @🛜) Scores of tour groups shack up at Mývatn's most upmarket option. In Reykjahlíð, it's a smartly dressed 40-room hotel (plus nine rooms at its new acquisition, the pretty, lakeside Hótel Reykjahlíð). The superior rooms aren't a noticeable upgrade; they only have slightly better views, plus a

little more space. Also here is an upmarket restaurant, plus lounge-bar and sauna.

🍴 Eating & Drinking

The local food speciality is a moist, cake-like rye bread known as *hverabrauð* (often translated as 'geysir bread'). It's slow-baked underground using geothermal heat and is served in every restaurant in town.

In addition to the following, Mývatn Nature Baths has a restaurant.

🏆TOP CHOICE Vogafjós   ICELANDIC €€
(www.vogafjos.net; mains Ikr2200-4700; ☉7.30am-11pm Jun-Aug, shorter hours Sep-May) The 'Cowshed', 2.5km south of Reykjahlíð, is a memorable restaurant where you can enjoy views of the lush surrounds, or of the dairy shed of this working farm (cows are milked at 7.30am and 6pm). Breakfast is open to all. The menu is an ode to local produce: raw smoked lamb, housemade mozzarella, dill-cured Arctic char, geysir bread, homebaked cakes. It's all delicious.

Gamli Bærinn   ICELANDIC €€
(mains Ikr1900-4900; ☉10am-11pm) The cheerfully busy 'Old Farm' tavern beside Hótel Reynihlíð serves up pub-style meals, including fish and steak options. In the evening it becomes the local hang-out – the opening hours are often extended during weekend revelry, but the kitchen closes at 10pm.

Myllan   ICELANDIC €€€
(📞464 4170; www.myvatnhotel.is; mains Ikr4500-6950; ☉6.30-9pm) Hótel Reynihlíð's in-house restaurant is the town's swankiest and features a long list of faves like smoked trout, reindeer and fresh lamb.

Daddi's Pizza   PIZZA €€
(small pizza Ikr1200-1400; ☉11.30am-11pm Jun-Aug) At Vógár campground, this small space cranks out tasty pizzas to eat in or takeaway. Try the house speciality: smoked trout, nuts and cream cheese.

Samkaup-Strax   SUPERMARKET €
(☉9am-10pm mid-Jun–Aug, 10am-6pm Sep–mid-Jun) Well-stocked supermarket (with petrol pumps) next to the tourist info centre. Has a burger grill.

ℹ️ Information

Post office (Helluhraun; ☉9am-4pm) On the street behind the supermarket. Inside is a bank and 24-hour ATM.

Tourist information centre (☑464 4390, www.visitmyvatn.is; Hraunvegur 8; ☺8am-8pm Jun-Aug, 9am-4pm Sep & May, 9am-noon Fri-Mon Oct-Apr) The well-informed centre has good displays on the local geology, and can book accommodation, tours and transport. Pick up a copy of the hugely useful *Visit Mývatn* brochure and *Mývatn Lake* map.

Getting Around

Got a flat tyre from driving over one too many lava flows? You're in luck – Reykjahlíð has a **garage** (☑848 2678; Múlavegur 1) on the corner of Rte 1 and Múlavegur.

Eastern Mývatn

If you're short on time, make this area your first stop. The sights along Mývatn's eastern lakeshore can be linked together on an enjoyable half-day hike (see the boxed text on p217).

STÓRAGJÁ & GRJÓTAGJÁ

About 100m beyond Reykjahlíð is Stóragjá, a rather eerie, watery fissure that was once a popular bathing spot. Cooling water temperatures (currently about 28°C) and the growth of potentially harmful algae mean it's no longer safe to swim in the cave, but it's an alluring spot with clear waters and a rock roof.

Further on at Grjótagjá there's another gaping fissure with a water-filled cave, this time at about 45°C – too hot to soak in, but you can get away with dipping your toes. It's a beautiful spot, particularly when the sun filters through the cracks in the roof and illuminates the interior.

HVERFELL

Dominating the lava fields on the eastern edge of Mývatn is the classic tephra ring Hverfell (also called Hverfjall). This near-symmetrical crater appeared 2700 years ago in a cataclysmic eruption of the existing Lúdentarhíð complex. Rising 463m from the ground and stretching 1040m across, it is a massive and awe-inspiring landmark in Mývatn.

The crater is composed of loose gravel, but an easy track leads from the northwestern end to the summit and offers stunning views of the crater itself and the surrounding landscape. From the rim of the crater the sheer magnitude of the explosion becomes apparent – a giant gaping hole reaching out across the mountain. A path runs along the western rim of the crater to a lookout at the southern end before descending steeply towards Dimmuborgir.

DIMMUBORGIR

The giant jagged lava field at Dimmuborgir (literally 'the Dark Castles') is one of the most fascinating flows in the country. And the story of Dimmuborgir's formation is almost as convoluted as its criss-crossing network of columnar lava. It's commonly believed that these strange pillars and crags were created about 2000 years ago when lava from the Þrengslaborgir and Lúdentarborgir crater rows flowed across older Hverfell lava fields. The new lava was dammed into a fiery lake in the Dimmuborgir basin and, as the surface of this lake cooled, a domed roof formed over the still-molten material below. The roof was supported by pillars of older igneous material, so when the dam finally broke, the molten lava drained and the odd pillars remained.

A series of nontaxing, colour-coded walking trails runs through Dimmuborgir's easily anthropomorphised landscape. The most popular path is the easy Church Circle (2.3km).

Kaffi Borgir (www.kaffiborgir.is; mains Ikr1950-5500; ☺9am-10pm Jun-Aug, reduced hours Sep-May) is a cafe-souvenir shop at the top of the ridge, and a great place to enjoy a late dinner in summer. Grab a table on the outside terrace, sample the house speciality (grilled trout), and watch the sun dance its shadows across the jagged lava bursts.

Dimmuborgir Guesthouse (☑464 4210; www.dimmuborgir.is; s/d Ikr20,000/21,500, d cottages with/without bathroom Ikr33,500/20,000, all incl breakfast; ☎) has a new block of en-suite rooms (with shared kitchen-dining area), plus a smattering of lovely wooden cottages. Breakfast is served in the main house behind big picture windows overlooking the lake. Don't miss the smokehouse hidden in the back – check out the rows of shiny orange salmon, and stock up on the finished product for tomorrow's picnic.

HÖFÐI

One of the area's gentlest landscapes is on the forested lava headland at Höfði. Wildflowers, birch and spruce trees cover the bluffs, while the tiny islands and crystal-clear waters attract great northern divers and other migratory birds. Along the shore you'll see many small caves and stunning *klasar* (lava pillars), the most famous of which are at **Kálfaströnd** on the southern shore of the Höfði Peninsula. Here, the *klasar* rise from the water in dramatic clusters. Rambling footpaths lead across the headland and can easily fill an hour.

Southern Mývatn

Eastern Mývatn may be the ultimate treasure trove of geological anomalies, but the south side of the lake lures with its epic cache of pseudocraters, called **Skútustaðagígar**. The most accessible swarm is located along a short path just across from Skútustaðir, which also takes in the nearby pond, **Stakhólstjörn**, a haven for nesting waterfowl.

SKÚTUSTAÐIR

The small village of Skútustaðir is the only 'major' settlement (and we use that term lightly) around the lake apart from Reykjahlíð. There's a tiny cluster of tourist activity here, including two overpriced hotels often full in summer with tour groups.

🛏 Sleeping & Eating

Skútustaðir Farmhouse
(📞464 4212; www.skutustadir.com; d with/without bathroom incl breakfast Ikr20,000/15,000; @📶) Sensible prices, friendly owners and spotless facilities can be found at this recommended year-round option. Rooms in the homey farmhouse share bathroom, lounge and kitchen, but there's also an annexe of five en-suite rooms, and the new addition of a cottage sleeping four. Ask about

---

PSEUDOCRATERS

Like blasts on the landscape from some sinister alien spacecraft, the dramatic dimples along Mývatn's otherworldly terrain were formed when molten lava flowed into the lake, triggering a series of gas explosions. Known as 'pseudocraters', these hills came into being when trapped subsurface water boiled and popped, forming small scoria cones and craters. The largest clusters, which measure more than 300m across, are east of Vindbelgjarfjall on the western shore of Mývatn. The smallest ones – the islets in the lake – are just a couple of metres wide and are best appreciated from the air.

---

sleeping-bag accommodation outside of summer.

Hótel Gígur   HOTEL €€€
(📞464 4455; www.keahotels.is; s/d incl breakfast €166/208; @📶) The lakeside location compensates for the extra-compact rooms that leave little room for cat-swinging. The pretty green **restaurant** (lunch Ikr990-1890, dinner mains Ikr3190-4490) is the hotel's best feature, offering one of the area's best lake views plus some well-prepared local dishes (such as pan-fried trout, rhubarb pannacotta).

Sel-Hótel Mývatn   HOTEL €€€
(📞464 4164; www.myvatn.is; s/d incl breakfast €169/204; ⊙closed mid-Dec–Jan; @📶) The Sel is looking a bit faded, but its spacious rooms are still comfy. There's a hot-pot, sauna and lounge, plus a souvenir shop-cafeteria (open 8am to 10pm June to August) in the car park. The no-frills restaurant (lunch/dinner buffet Ikr2500/6200) here is home to a few *marimos* (see the boxed text, p223).

Western Mývatn

The clear and turbulent **Laxá** (Salmon River), one of the many Icelandic rivers so named, cuts the western division of Mývatn, rolling straight across the tundra towards Skjálfandi (Húsavík's whale-filled bay). The Laxá is one of the best – and most expensive – salmon-fishing spots in the country. More affordable brown-trout fishing is also available.

The easy climb up 529m-high **Vindbelgjarfjall**, further north along the western shore, offers one of the best views across the lake and its alien pseudocraters. The trail to the summit starts south of the peak, near the farm Vagnbrekka. Reckon on about a half-hour to reach the mount, and another half-hour to climb to the summit.

Birders unite! Western Mývatn offers some of the best birdwatching in the region, with over 115 species present – 42 nesting. Most species of Icelandic waterfowl are found here in great numbers – including 8000 breeding pairs of ducks. Three duck species – the scoter, the gadwall and the Barrow's goldeneye – breed nowhere else in Iceland. Other species frequenting the area include eider ducks, mallards, whooper swans, great northern divers, black-headed gulls, Arctic terns, golden plovers, snipe and whimbrels. The area's bogs, marshes, ponds and wet tundra are a high-density waterfowl

MARIMO BALLS

Marimo balls *(Cladophora aegagropila)* are bizarre little spheres of green algae that are thought to grow naturally in only a handful of places in the world – Mývatn and Lake Akan in Japan (they have also been found in Scotland and Estonia). The spongy balls grow slowly, to about the size of a baseball, rising to the surface of the water in the morning to photosynthesise (when there's enough sunlight) and sinking to the bottom at night.

The name *marimo* is the Japanese word for 'algae ball' – around Mývatn, the locals call 'em *kúluskítur*, which literally means 'ball of shit'. Swing by Sigurgeir's Bird Museum to check out these curious critters – they live in the small pool at the centre of the exhibition space. There are also a few *marimo* balls living in a cloudy aquarium at the Sel-Hótel's restaurant in Skútustaðir.

nesting zone. Off-road entry is restricted between 15 May and 15 July (when the chicks hatch), but hides near the museum allow for birding.

For a bit of background, swing by **Sigurgeir's Bird Museum** (www.fuglasafn.is; adult/child Ikr950/500; ☺10am-7pm Jun-Aug, reduced hours Sep-May), housed in a beautiful lakeside building that fuses modern design with traditional turf house. Inside you'll find an impressive collection of taxidermic avians (more than 180 types from around the world), including every species of bird that calls Iceland home (except one – the grey phalarope). Designer lighting and detailed captions further enhance the experience. The menagerie of stuffed squawkers started as the private collection of a local named Sigurgeir Stefansson. Tragically, Sigurgeir drowned in the lake at the age of 37 – the museum was erected in his honour. The museum also houses a serene cafe and lends out high-tech telescopes to ornithological enthusiasts. Take a look in the small water feature at the centre of the exhibition hall to see the green surprise that lurks inside.

Northern Mývatn

As the lakeshore road circles back around towards Reykjahlíð, the marshes dry up and the terrain returns to its signature stretches of crispy lava. Travellers who continue along the Ring Road towards Krafla will discover a wicked world of orange sky and the gurgling remnants of ancient earthen cataclysms.

The lava field along Mývatn's northern lakeshore, **Eldhraun**, includes the flow that nearly engulfed the Reykjahlíð church. It was belched out of Leirhnjúkur during the Mývatnseldar in 1729, and flowed down the channel Eldá. With some slow scrambling, it can be explored on foot from Reykjahlíð.

If you are hiking directly to Krafla from Mývatn's northern crest, then you'll pass the prominent 771m-high rhyolite mountain **Hlíðarfjall** (also called Reykjahlíðarfjall), just before the halfway mark. Around 5km from Reykjahlíð, the mount can also be enjoyed as a pleasant day hike from the village, affording spectacular views over the lake on one side and over the Krafla lava fields on the other.

EAST OF REYKJAHLÍÐ

Northern Mývatn's collection of geological gems conveniently lie along the Ring Road (Rte 1) as it weaves through the harsh terrain between the north end of the lake and the turn-off to steaming Krafla. Car-less travellers will find plenty of paths for exploring the area on foot.

Bjarnarflag, 3km east of Reykjahlíð, is an active geothermal area where the earth hisses and bubbles, and steaming vents line the valley. Historically, the area has been home to a number of economic ventures attempting to harness the earth's powers. Early on, farmers tried growing potatoes here, but, unfortunately, these often emerged from the ground already boiled. In the late 1960s, 25 test holes were bored at Bjarnarflag to ascertain the feasibility of a proposed geothermal power station. One is 2300m deep and the steam still roars out of the pipe at a whopping 200°C.

Later a diatomite (microfossil) plant was set up and the skeletal remains of a type of single-cell algae were filtered and purified into filler for fertilisers, paints, toothpastes and plastics. All that remains of the processing plant today is the shimmering turquoise pond that the locals have dubbed the 'Blue Lagoon'. This inviting puddle is actually quite toxic and should not be confused with the luxurious Mývatn Nature Baths around the corner, which is sometimes called the 'Blue Lagoon of the North'.

The pastel-coloured Námafjall lies 3km further away (on the south side of the Ring Road). Produced by a fissure eruption, the ridge sits squarely on the spreading zone of the Mid-Atlantic Ridge and is dotted with steaming vents.

HVERIR

As you tumble down the far side of Námafjall, you'll suddenly find yourself in the magical, ochre-toned world of Hverir – a lunar-like landscape of mud cauldrons, steaming vents, radiant mineral deposits and piping fumaroles. Belching mudflaps and the powerful stench of sulphur may not sound enticing, but Hverir's ethereal allure grips every passer-by. Safe pathways through the features have been roped off; to avoid risk of serious injury and damage to the natural features, avoid any lighter-coloured soil and respect the ropes.

A walking trail loops from Hverir up Námafjall ridge. This 30-minute climb provides a grand vista over the steamy surroundings.

Krafla

More steaming vents, craters and aquamarine lakes await at Krafla, an active volcanic region 7km north of the Ring Road. Technically, Krafla is just an 818m-high mountain, but the name is now used for the entire area as well as a geothermal power station and the series of eruptions that created Iceland's most awesome lava field.

The heart of volcanic activity is known as the Krafla central volcano but, rather than a cone-shaped peak, Krafla is a largely level system of north–south-trending fissures underlaid by a great magma chamber. Activity is normally characterised by fissuring and gradual surface swells followed by abrupt subsidence, which triggers eruptions. At present, the ground surface is rising, indicating possible activity in the future. The Institute of Earth Sciences (www.earthice.hi.is) tracks the most recent developments.

From Reykjahlíð, a wonderful hike of around 13km leads to Hlíðarfjall and Leirhnjúkur along a marked path from near the airstrip. Another walking route (about 9km) leads from Namaskarð along the Dalfjall ridge to Leirhnjúkur.

KRAFLA POWER STATION

The idea of constructing a geothermal power station at Krafla was conceived in 1973, and preliminary work commenced with the drilling of holes to determine project feasibility. In 1975, however, after a rest of several hundred years, the Krafla fissure burst into activity with the first in a series of nine eruptions. This considerably lowered the site's projected geothermal potential, but the project successfully went ahead and has been expanded since. The power plant's visitor centre (admission free; ☉10am-4pm Jun-Aug) explains how it all works.

LEIRHNJÚKUR & KRAFLA CALDERA

Krafla's most impressive, and potentially most dangerous, attraction is the Leirhnjúkur crater and its solfataras, which originally appeared in 1727. It started out as a lava fountain and spouted molten material for two years before subsiding. After a minor burp in 1746, it became the menacing sulphur-encrusted mudhole that tourists love today.

From the rim above Leirhnjúkur you can look out across the Krafla caldera and the layers of lava that bisect it. The first of these lava flows was from the original Mývatnseldar, which was overlaid in places by lava from the 1975 eruptions, and again by 1984 lava.

The earth's crust here is extremely thin and in places the ground is ferociously hot. Steaming vents on the rhyolite mountain to the west are the last vestiges of a series of explosions in 1975, when the small grass-filled crater on the western slope of the mountain south of Leirhnjúkur erupted as Kröflueldar, a continuation of Mývatnseldar.

A well-defined track leads northwest to Leirhnjúkur from the Krafla parking area; with all the volcanic activity, high temperatures, bubbling mudpots and steaming vents, you'd be well advised not to stray from the marked paths.

VÍTI

The dirt-brown crater of Víti reveals a secret when you reach its rim – a dark blue pool of floodwater at its heart. The 320m-wide explosion crater was created in 1724 during the destructive Mývatnseldar, and it's just one of many vents along the Krafla central volcano. Behind the crater are the 'twin lakes', boiling mud springs that spurted mud 10m into the air during the Mývatnseldar. They're now down to a mere simmer and Víti is considered inactive.

GJÁSTYKKI

This remote rift zone at the northernmost end of the Krafla fissure swarm was the source of the first eruptions in 1724, and was activated when Leirhnjúkur went off in the 1975 eruptions. Between 1981 and 1984 the area was the main hot spot of activity in the Krafla central volcano, and the current Gjástykki lava fields date from this time. Gjástykki is a very sensitive area and no private vehicles are allowed access. To visit you'll need to join a tour; Saga Travel (☑558 888; www.sagatravel.is) tours the area (Ikr31,000/25,000 from Akureyri/Mývatn), and you can also combine Gjástykki with its tour of the Lofthellir cave.

ⓘ Getting There & Away

From mid-June to early September, **SBA-Norðurleið** (☑550 0700/70; www.sba.is) operates bus 661/661a, running from Reykjahlíð to Krafla at 8am and 11.30am (Ikr1500, 15 minutes), returning at 2.15pm. The latter morning service continues on to Dettifoss.

HÚSAVÍK & AROUND

Húsavík

POP 2240

Húsavík, Iceland's whale-watching capital, is a picturesque harbour town that has become a firm favourite on travellers' itineraries. With its colourful houses, unique museums and stunning snowcapped peaks across the bay, little Húsavík is undoubtedly the prettiest fishing town on the northeast coast.

History

Although the honours normally go to Reykjavík and Ingólfur Arnarson, Húsavík was the real site of the first Nordic settlement in Iceland. Garðar Svavarsson, a Swedish Viking who set off around 850 for the mysterious Thule or Snæland (Snowland), was actually responsible for the island's first permanent human settlement.

After a brief stop-off at Hornafjörður in the south, Garðar arrived at Skjálfandi on the north coast and built a settlement that he called Húsavík. Modestly renaming the country Garðarshólmur (Garðar's Island), he dug in for the winter. At the advent of spring he prepared to depart, but some of his slaves were left behind. Whether by accident or design, these castaways became Iceland's first real settlers, pioneering life in a new country and yet uncredited by the history books.

◉ Sights & Activities

Don't rush off after your whale-watching trip; Húsavík has a few surprises up its sleeve. Sadly, its quirkiest offering, the renowned Phallological Museum, has relocated to Reykjavík.

Museums & Churches

Húsavík Whale Museum   MUSEUM
(Hvalasafnið; www.whalemuseum.is; Hafnarstétt; adult/child Ikr1250/500; ◷9am-7pm Jun-Aug, 10am-5pm May & Sep) Best visited before you head out on a whale-watching trip, this excellent museum tells you all you ever needed to know about these gracious creatures. Housed in an old slaughterhouse at the harbour, the museum interprets the ecology and habits of whales, conservation and history of whaling in Iceland through beautifully curated displays, including several huge skeletons soaring high above (they're real!).

Culture House   MUSEUM
(Safnahúsið á Húsavík; www.husmus.is; Stórigarður 17; adult/child Ikr600/free; ◷10am-6pm Jun-Aug, to 4pm Mon-Fri Sep-May) A folk, maritime and natural-history museum rolled into one complex (together with the town library and a top-floor art gallery), the Culture House is one of the best local museums you'll find in Iceland. 'Man and Nature' nicely outlines a century of life in the region, while the stuffed animals include a frightening-looking hooded seal and a polar bear, which was welcomed to Grímsey in 1969 with both barrels of a gun.

Húsavíkurkirkja   CHURCH
Húsavík's lovely church is quite different from anything else seen in Iceland. Constructed in 1907 from Norwegian timber, the delicately proportioned red-and-white church would look more at home in the Alps. Inside, its cruciform shape becomes apparent and is dominated by a depiction of the resurrection of Lazarus (from lava!) on the altarpiece.

Whale Watching

This is why you came to Húsavík. Although there are other Iceland locales where you can do whale-watching tours (Reykjavík and north of Akureyri), over the last decade or so, this area has become Iceland's premier whale-watching destination, with up to 11

NORTH ICELAND HÚSAVÍK

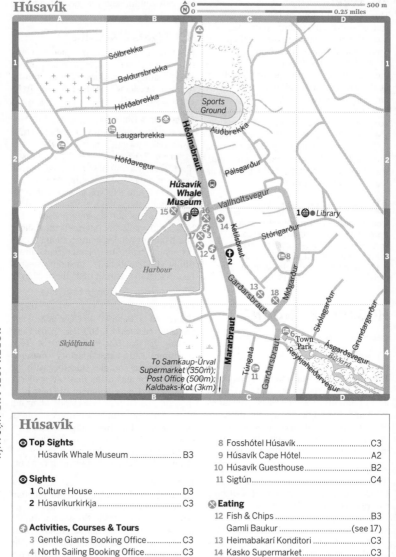

Húsavík

species coming here to feed in summer. The best time to see whales is between June and August. This is, of course, the height of tourist season, but you'll have almost a 100% chance of seeing one.

Two whale-watching companies operate from Húsavík harbour. The original operator is **North Sailing** (☎464 7272; www.northsailing. is; Hafnarstétt), which has a fleet of lovingly restored old-school boats, including the oak schooners *Haukur* and *Hildur*. Its popular four-hour 'Whales, Puffins & Sails' tour stops at the dramatic, puffin-festooned island of Lundey, and overnight trips to Grímsey are possible during the summer.

The second company is **Gentle Giants** (☎464 1500; www.gentlegiants.is; Hafnarstétt), with their flotilla of old wooden fishing vessels and recent glitzy additions of high-speed Zodiac-style boats, offering a way to cover more ground in the fjord. Gentle Giants also runs special trips to Flatey (Flat Island) – you'll most likely see whales along the way.

Don't stress too much over picking an operator; prices are more-or-less standardised and services are comparable for the standard three-hour tour (North Sailing adult/child €58/29 in summer 2013, with Gentle Giants being a fraction cheaper at €56/24). North Sailing offers cinnamon buns while Gentle Giants serves *kleinur* (traditional twisty doughnuts).

Where the differences are clear, however, is in the excursions that go beyond the standard – North Sailing on board its atmospheric old schooners, Gentle Giants on its Zodiacs.

Trips depart throughout the day (June to August) from around 9am to 8pm, and large signs at the ticket booths advertise the next departure time. Boats also run in April, May, September and October with less frequency. You can't miss these offices on the waterfront: North Sailing with its yellow flags, Gentle Giants dressed in blue.

Other Activities

After whale watching, there are plenty of activities around town to keep the blood flowing. Both whale-watching operators offer combo tours that involve whale-watching cruises plus a horse ride. North Sailing has the chance to add on a Mývatn excursion, while Gentle Giants offers fishing or a two-day hiking trip.

Independent hikers should ask at the information centre for details on local trails and hikes around the fossil-ridden Tjörnes Peninsula – pick up the *Útivist & afþreying* #3 map for details.

Short horse rides (two hours, Ikr8000) are available at **Saltvík horse farm** (☎847 9515; www.saltvik.is), 5km south of Húsavík.

The local swimming pool, **Sundlaugin** (Laugarbrekka 2; adult/child Ikr650/300; ⊙7am-9pm Mon-Fri, 10am-6pm Sat & Sun Jun-Aug, shorter hours Sep-May), has hot-pots, and waterslides for children.

And as scenic as the waterfront area is, we recommend a walk through the gorgeously peaceful **town park**, to admire the duck-filled stream. Access is via a footbridge on Ásgarðsvegur, or beside Árból guesthouse.

⛵ Tours

Fjallasýn TOURS
(☎464 3941; www.fjallasyn.is) This Húsavík-based company is well established and does a variety of tours in the area: local to Húsavík or further afield to various parts of northern Iceland and the highlands, day or multiday tours, 4WD, hiking, birdwatching etc.

🛏 Sleeping

TOP
CHOICE **Kaldbaks-Kot** COTTAGES €€
(☎464 1504; www.cottages.is; 2-4 person cabins €135-195; ⊙May-Sep; @🖤) Located 3km south of Húsavík is this cluster of charming timber cottages that all feel like grandpa's cabin in the woods. Choose your level of service (BYO linen or hire it), bring supplies or buy breakfast here (€10) in the magnificent converted cowshed. Then just relax and enjoy the grounds, the hot-pots, the views, the serenity and the prolific bird life.

Sigtún GUESTHOUSE €€
(☎864 0250; www.guesthousesigtun.is; Túngata 13; s/d without bathroom incl breakfast Ikr10,500/17,500; @🖤) Free coffee machine, free laundry and a fancy kitchen are draws at this first-rate guesthouse, under friendly new ownership. Only the downstairs section is open in winter (alas, without the fancy kitchen, but still with cooking facilities).

Húsavík Cape Hotel HOTEL €€
(☎463 3399; www.husavikhotel.com; Höfði 24; d incl breakfast €175; 🖤) A brand-new boutique-y option in a former fish factory above the harbour, with plans for further expansion. Rooms are a good size (some with bunks, for families).

Árból GUESTHOUSE €€
(☎464 2220; www.arbol.is; Ásgarðsvegur 2; s/d without bathroom incl breakfast Ikr10,300/17,500; 🖤) Auður is a sunny hostess at this 1903 heritage house, with a pretty stream and town park as neighbours. Spacious, spotless rooms are over three levels – those on the

ground and top floor are loveliest (the pine-lined attic rooms are particularly sweet). The kitchen can be used by guests of an evening.

Árbót
HOSTEL €

(☑464 3677; www.hostel.is; dm/d without bathroom Ikr3800/10,000; ⊙Jun–mid-Sep; @) One of two HI hostels on rural properties in the area, both about 20km south of Húsavík but the area's only true budget options (you'll need your own transport). Remote Árbót is on a cattle farm off Rte 85 and offers high-quality facilities and comfy common areas. Members get a discount of Ikr600 per person; linen costs Ikr1250.

Húsavík Guesthouse
GUESTHOUSE €€

(☑463 3399; www.husavikguesthouse.is; Laugarbrekka 16; s/d without bathroom incl breakfast €75/110; @☜) From the same owners (a group of brothers) as the nearby Cape Hotel, this comfy guesthouse has seven rooms and shared bathrooms, but no kitchen access. Check-in and breakfast are at the Cape Hotel.

Fosshótel Húsavík
HOTEL €€

(☑464 1220; www.fosshotel.is; Ketilsbraut 22; s/d incl breakfast from Ikr21,100/26,100; ⊙Jan-Nov; @☜) Standard rooms have predictable international-style decor, while superior options feature a few stylish and quirky touches – whale-themed knick-knacks abound. There's an on-site restaurant, which feels like you're eating on a cruise ship from the '70s; check out the movie memorabilia and cool stools at the in-house bar, Moby Dick.

Campsite
CAMPGROUND €

(sites per person Ikr1000; ⊙mid-May–mid-Sep) Next to the sports ground at the north end of town, this popular campsite has such luxuries as heated toilets, washing machine and cooking facilities.

✖ Eating

⌜TOP⌝ CHOICE Pallurinn
ICELANDIC €€

(www.pallurinn.is; Hafnarstétt; mains Ikr1400-2000; ⊙from 6pm Jun-late Aug) The runaway star of 2012 was this summertime 'gourmet tent' behind the Gentle Giants ticket office, run by Iceland's answer to Jamie Oliver, award-winning Völundur Völundarson, aka Chef Völli from the TV show *Delicious Iceland*. The concept was 'Icelandic street food', the cooking apparatus of choice was a giant barbecue (burning birchwood, not charcoals),

prices were reasonable, lamb and seafood were at the forefront, and it was a huge hit, especially with locals. Expect it to return in 2013.

Naustið
ICELANDIC €€

(Hafnarstétt; mains Ikr1500-3000; ⊙noon-10pm) Quietly going about its business at the end of the harbour, no-frills Naustið has been winning praise for its super-fresh fish and a fun, simple concept: skewers of fish and vegetables, grilled to order. There's also fish soup (natch), and weekly specials of sushi or lobster.

Gamli Baukur
ICELANDIC €€

(Hafnarstétt 9; mains Ikr3150-4710; ⊙11.30am-1am or later Jun-Aug, shorter hours Sep-May; ☜) Owned by North Sailing, this timber-framed restaurant-bar serves excellent food (juicy burgers, fish stew, organic lamb) among shiny nautical relics. Live music and a sweeping terrace make it one of the most happenin' places in northeast Iceland. Kitchen closes at 10pm.

Salka
ICELANDIC €€

(Garðarsbraut 6; mains Ikr1750-4800; ⊙11.30am-9pm) Once home to Iceland's first cooperative, this historic building houses a popular restaurant serving everything from smoked puffin to pizza, by way of langoustine and Arctic char.

Fish & Chips
TAKEAWAY €

(Hafnarstétt 19; fish & chips Ikr1300; ⊙11.30am-8pm Jun-Aug) Doing exactly what it says on the label, this small windowfront on the harbour doles out good-value fish (usually cod) and chips, with a few picnic tables out front.

Skuld Café
CAFE €

(Hafnarstétt 9; light meals Ikr650-1200; ⊙from 8am Jun-Aug) Set on the harbourside hill with a tiered outdoor deck overlooking the waterfront, this summer cafe serves up fish soup, sandwiches and baked goods.

Heimabakarí Konditori
BAKERY €

(Garðarsbraut 15; ⊙7.30am-5pm Mon-Fri, 8am-2pm Sat) Sells fresh bread, sandwiches and sugary cakes, and offers a breakfast buffet in summer (Ikr1500, until 10am).

Kasko
SUPERMARKET €

(Garðarsbraut 5; ⊙10am-6.30pm Mon-Thu, to 7pm Fri, to 6pm Sat) Central supermarket.

LOCAL KNOWLEDGE

THE WHALES OF HÚSAVÍK   *BRANDON PRESSER*

Edda Elísabet Magnúsdóttir is a local marine biologist at the Húsavík Research Center (a branch of the University of Iceland), established with a focus on marine mammal studies.

What's so special about Húsavík's geology that brings whales to the area?

Húsavík sits on a scenic bay known as Skjálfandi, which means 'the tremulous one' in Icelandic. The name is appropriate, since little earthquakes occur very frequently in the bay, usually without being noticed. These trembles are caused by the wrench fault in the earth's crust right beneath the bay. Skjálfandi's bowl-shaped topography and the infusion of freshwater from two river estuaries means that there is a great deal of nutrients collecting in the bay. The nutrient deposits accumulate during the winter months, and when early summer arrives – with its long sunlit days – the cool waters of Skjálfandi bay come alive with myriad plankton blooms. These rich deposits act like a beacon, attracting special types of mammals that are highly adapted to life in the cold subarctic waters.

What species of whale visit Húsavík?

Every summer roughly nine to 11 species of whale are sighted in the bay, ranging from the tiny harbour porpoise *(Phocoena phocoena)* to the giant blue whale *(Balaenoptera musculus)*, the biggest animal known to roam the earth.

Plankton blooming kick-starts each year's feeding season; that's when the whales start appearing in greater numbers in the bay. The first creatures to arrive are the humpback whales *(Megaptera novaeangliae)* and the minke whales *(Balaenoptera acutorostrata)*. The humpback whale is known for its curious nature, equanimity and spectacular surface displays, whereas the minke whale is famous for its elegant features: a streamlined and slender black body and white-striped pectoral fin.

Although the average minke whale weighs the same amount as two or three grown elephants, they are known as the 'petite cousin' of the greater rorquals. The minke whale has the tendency to leap entirely out of the water and is likely the only rorqual capable of doing so.

Several minke and humpback whales stay in the bay throughout the year, but most migrate south during the winter. The blue whale, undoubtedly the most exciting sight in Skjálfandi, is a recent summer visitor – they only started arriving around seven years ago. They usually start coming in mid-June and stay until the middle of July. Watching these highly developed hydrodynamic giants in their natural environment is just spectacular.

Other summer sightings in Skjálfandi include the orca, also known as the killer whale *(Orcinus orca;* some come to the bay to feed on fish, others come to hunt mammals), bottlenose whales *(Hyperoodon ampullatus;* a mysterious, deep-diving beaked whale), fin whales *(Balaenoptera physalus)*, sei whales *(Balaenoptera borealis)*, pilot whales *(Globicephala melas)* and sperm whales *(Physeter macrocephalus)*.

Samkaup-Úrval   SUPERMARKET €
(Garðarsbraut 64; ⊙10am-7pm Mon-Sat, noon-7pm Sun) South of town, by the Olís service station.

Vín Búð   ALCOHOL €
(Garðarsbraut 21; ⊙11am-6pm Mon-Thu, to 7pm Fri, to 2pm Sat Jun-Aug, shorter hours Sep-May) Government-run liquor store.

ℹ Information

Íslandsbanki (Stórigarður 1) Opposite the church; bank with ATM.

Library (Stórigarður 17; internet Ikr300; ⊙11am-5pm Mon & Fri, 10am-6pm Tue-Thu) At the Culture House; free wi-fi plus internet access (untimed).

Post office (Garðarsbraut 70; ⊙9am-4.30pm)

Tourist information centre (☑464 4300; www.visithusavik.is; Hafnarstétt; ⊙9am-7pm Jun-Aug, 10am-5pm May & Sep) The ticket desk for the Whale Museum acts as the town's info centre, with plentiful maps and brochures.

ℹ Getting There & Away
Air

Húsavík's airport is 12km south of town. **Eagle Air** (☑562 2640; www.eagleair.is) flies year-round between Reykjavík and Húsavík (one way €134).

Bus

The bus terminal is at the N1 petrol station.
SBA-Norðurleið (☎550 0700/70; www.sba.is) bus services:

BUS 640/640A Akureyri–Húsavík; Ikr3300, 1¼ hours, two to four times daily year-round.

BUS 641/641A Akureyri–Húsavík–Ásbyrgi, then south on Rte 862 to Hljóðaklettar and Dettifoss; daily mid-June to August. From Dettifoss you can return with bus 641a from whence you came, or switch to bus 661a to Mývatn.

BUS 650/650A Reykjahlíð (Mývatn)–Húsavík; Ikr2700, 40 minutes, twice daily mid-June to August.

BUS 680/680A Akureyri–Þórshöfn; three times a week year-round (Monday, Wednesday and Friday). Stops at towns along Rte 85 (including Húsavík and Ásbyrgi) en route.

Húsavík to Ásbyrgi

Heading north from Húsavík along Rte 85 you'll sweep along the coast of the stubby **Tjörnes Peninsula**. The area is known for its fossil-rich coastal cliffs (the oldest layers dating back about two million years).

At the tip of the peninsula is the **Mánárbakki Museum** (adult/child Ikr500/ free; ☺10am-6pm mid-Jun–Aug), home to the eclectic personal collection of friendly farmer Aðalgeir, who will give you a tour of his turf-roofed house and show you various assemblages of photos, furniture and crockery.

Giant cracks, fissures and grabens (depressions between geological faults) scar the earth at low-lying Kelduhverfi, where the Mid-Atlantic Ridge enters the Arctic Ocean. Like Þingvellir, the area reveals some of the most visible evidence that Iceland is being ripped apart from its core.

🛏 Sleeping

There is a handful of comfy farmhouse lodgings in the area; dinner is available at each.

Skúlagarður   HOTEL €€
(☎465 2280; www.dettifoss.is; s/d incl breakfast Ikr16,700/22,500; 🛜) A country hotel behind an unpromising exterior (in a former boarding school). Has compact, modern rooms, a restaurant serving good home cooking, and scruffy sleeping-bag accommodation (Ikr4000). It's 12km west of Ásbyrgi.

Keldunes   GUESTHOUSE €
(☎465 2275; www.keldunes.is; s/d without bathroom incl breakfast Ikr11,900/17,900, cottages Ikr14,900; 🛜) Modern guesthouse with great kitchen-dining area, a hot-pot, and large balconies for birdwatching. There are sleeping-bag options (Ikr5000), and cottages with bathroom. It's 11km west of Ásbyrgi.

Hóll   GUESTHOUSE €
(☎465 2270; d without bathroom incl breakfast Ikr13,000) Four simple rooms in a farmstead, 8km west of Ásbyrgi. Horse riding available.

Lundur   GUESTHOUSE, CAMPGROUND €
(☎465 2280; www.dettifoss.is; sites per person Ikr1100, s/d without bathroom Ikr9200/15,000; ☺Jun-Aug) Basic summer schoolhouse accommodation 7km northeast of Ásbyrgi on Rte 85. Sleeping-bag beds cost from Ikr4300.

JÖKULSÁRGLJÚFUR (VATNAJÖKULL NATIONAL PARK – NORTH)

In 2008 the Vatnajökull National Park – Europe's largest protected reserve – was formed when Jökulsárgljúfur National Park merged with Skaftafell National Park to the south. The idea was to protect the Vatnajökull ice cap and all of its glacial run-off under one super-sized preserve. See p272 for more about the park.

The Jökulsárgljúfur portion of the park protects a unique subglacial eruptive ridge and a 30km gorge carved out by the formidable Jökulsá á Fjöllum (Iceland's second-longest river), which starts in the Vatnajökull ice cap and flows almost 200km to the Arctic Ocean at Öxarfjörður. *Jökulhlaups* (flooding from volcanic eruptions beneath the ice cap) formed the canyon and have carved out a chasm that averages 100m deep and 500m wide.

Vatnajökull National Park's northern section can be roughly divided into three parts. The visitor centre is near the northern entry at Ásbyrgi, a verdant, forested plain enclosed by vertical canyon walls. Vesturdalur's caves and fascinating geological anomalies make up Jökulsárgljúfur's middle section. The mighty falls of Dettifoss anchor the park's southern entrance. Road access is improving but is somewhat convoluted – see p232 for more.

A wonderful two-day hike (see the boxed text, p232) weaves along the canyon, taking in all of the major sights en route. If you're not so keen on hiking, the big attractions, such as the waterfalls at the southern end of the park and horseshoe-shaped Ásbyrgi canyon at the northern end, are accessible by road.

There are considerable changes going on in and around the park, especially regarding road access. Better roads and increased visitor numbers will inevitably result in more facilities and changing transport schedules, so it's worth checking the park website (or with the visitor centre) to see what's new.

Note that from mid-June to mid-August, rangers guide free daily interpretive walks that depart from the visitor centre – a great way to learn about the area. Check the website, or ask staff.

☞ Tours

Summer buses to Ásbyrgi and Dettifoss make it easy to tackle the canyon on your own. If you're after a tour, several companies can oblige, from Mývatn, Akureyri and Húsavík.

Active North ADVENTURE TOUR
(☎858 7080; www.activenorth.is; ☉mid-Jun–mid-Aug) Headquartered opposite the visitor centre, this outfit offers two-hour horse-riding trips around the Ásbyrgi rock canyon (Ikr7900), departing at 10am, 2pm and 5pm. A five-hour tour that includes a cave visit is also available (Ikr15,900).

🛏 Sleeping & Eating

A handful of accommodation providers are within 15km of the park. The petrol station (☉9am-10pm Jun-Aug, 10am-6pm Sep-May) on Rte 85 near the visitor centre at Ásbyrgi has a decent selection of groceries; however, the food at the on-site grill isn't stellar. If you're hiking, it's best to purchase supplies in Akureyri or Húsavík.

Visitor Centre Campsite CAMPGROUND
(☎470 7100; www.vjp.is; sites per person Ikr1300 plus per tent Ikr100; ☉mid-May–Sep; ☎) Camping inside the park boundaries is strictly limited to the official campsites at Ásbyrgi, Vesturdalur and Dettifoss. The large campsite at Ásbyrgi has well-maintained showers (Ikr400) and laundry facilities. Vesturdalur's campsite, near the helpful ranger station, has no power or hot water – toilets are the only luxury here. The free campsite at Dettifoss has limited freshwater supplies, and

Jökulsárgljúfur

the grounds are strictly reserved for hikers doing the popular two-day hike.

❶ Information

Vesturdalur ranger station (☎842 4364; ☉9-11am & 6-8pm early Jun–mid-Sep) The park wardens have created several excellent maps of the region. The park map (Ikr300) is a useful 1:50,000 plan that ranks the local hikes by difficulty. The *Útivist & afþreying* maps are also handy – #3 (Ikr650) zooms in on the Ásbyrgi–Dettifoss route.

Visitor centre (Gljúfrastofa; ☎470 7100; www.vjp.is; ☉9am-9pm mid-Jun–mid-Aug, to 7pm

rest of Jun & Aug, 10am-4pm May & Sep; @🖥️)
The super-helpful office at Ásbyrgi has an
information desk with free brochures and maps
for sale, informative displays on the area, and
knowledgeable staff that can book accommodation, transport and tours in the area.

❶ Getting There & Around

Bus

SBA-Norðurleið (📞550 0700/70; www.sba.is)
services:

BUS 680/680A Akureyri–Þórshöfn; three
times a week year-round (Monday, Wednesday
and Friday in both directions). Stops along Rte
85 (including Húsavík and Ásbyrgi) en route.

BUS 641/641A Akureyri–Húsavík–Ásbyrgi,
then south on Rte 862 to Hljóðaklettar and Dettifoss; daily from mid-June to August. From Dettifoss you can return with bus 641a from whence
you came, or switch to bus 661a to Mývatn.

BUS 661/661A Reykjahlíð (Mývatn)–Krafla–
Dettifoss; daily from mid-June to August. From
Dettifoss you have the option of linking with
bus 641a.

Car

Rte 85 takes you smoothly to the northern section of the park and the visitor centre at Ásbyrgi
(from Húsavík it's 65km).

There are two north–south roads running
parallel on each side of the canyon:

RTE 862 (WEST) From the Ring Road to
Dettifoss (24km), the road is sealed. North of
Dettifoss, the road is gravel for the remaining
37km past Hólmatungur and Vesturdalur to Rte
85 and Ásbyrgi. This section of Rte 862 is no
longer an F road, but it is still tough going in a
2WD. There are plans to seal this route by 2015.

RTE 864 (EAST) This is a poorly maintained
gravel track for its 60km length; it's passable by
2WD vehicles, but its rutted and potholed surface
will tire even the most patient drivers. There are
no plans to improve the road's conditions.

Although the park is open all year, the gravel
roads only open from late May/early June until
sometime between early October and early
November (weather dependent).

Make sure you stick to roads and marked
trails. Off-road driving is hugely destructive to
the country's fragile environment, and illegal.

Ásbyrgi

Driving off Rte 85 on to the flat, grassy plain
at the northern end of the park, there's little
to tell you you're standing on the edge of a
massive horseshoe-shaped canyon. The lush
Ásbyrgi canyon extends 3.5km from north
to south and averages 1km in width, making it difficult to discern at its widest point.
Near the centre of the canyon is the prominent outcrop Eyjan, and towards the south
the sheer, dark walls rise up to 100m. The
cliffs protect a birch forest from harsh winds
and hungry sheep, and the trees here grow
up to 8m in height.

There are two stories about the creation
of Ásbyrgi. The early Norse settlers believed
that Óðinn's normally airborne eight-legged
horse, Slættur (known in literature as Sleip-
nir), accidentally touched down on earth and
left one hell of a hoof-print to prove it. The
other theory, though more scientific, is also
incredible. Geologists believe that the canyon was created by an enormous eruption
of the Grímsvötn caldera beneath distant
Vatnajökull. It released an immense *jökulh-*

ÁSBYRGI TO DETTIFOSS HIKE

The most popular hike in Jökulsárgljúfur canyon is the two-day trip (around 30km) from
Ásbyrgi to Dettifoss, which moves through birch forests, striking rock formations, lush
valleys and commanding perpendicular cliffs while taking in all of the region's major
sights. From Ásbyrgi you can follow the canyon's western rim or river's edge to Vesturdalur (12km, or three to four hours), where you'll spend the night (camping is forbidden
elsewhere). On the second day you'll continue on through to gushing Dettifoss, with two
options: the more difficult involves a spectacular walk via the Hafragil lowlands (18km),
the easier takes a route north of Hafragil (19.5km, six to eight hours). All up, the route is
classified as challenging.

The hike can be done in both directions; however, the park rangers recommend starting in Ásbyrgi, where you can pick up the required maps and brochures. Also, the vistas
reveal themselves more dramatically when travelling in a southerly direction (travelling
north, you'll be walking uphill). Ever-changing bus schedules and plans for sealing more
roads in the area mean that park staff are best placed to answer questions such as how
to leave your car at Ásbyrgi and return to it by bus from Dettifoss at the end of the hike.

laup, which ploughed northward down the Jökulsá á Fjöllum and gouged out the canyon in a matter of days. The river then flowed through Ásbyrgi for about 100 years before shifting eastward to its present course.

From the car park near the end of the road (3.5km south of the visitor centre), several short tracks lead through the forest to viewpoints of the canyon. Heading east the track leads to a spring near the canyon wall, while the western track climbs to a good view across the valley floor. The trail leading straight ahead ends at a small duck-filled pond (Botnstjörn) at the head of Ásbyrgi.

You can also climb to the summit of Eyjan from the campsite (4.5km return) or ascend the cliffs at Tófugjá. From there, a looping track leads around Áshöfði past the gorges. Alternatively, follow the rim right around to Klappir, above the canyon head, from where you can head south to Kvíar (or east to Kúahvammur) and return via the river (the route via Kvíar is about 17km, or four hours return).

Vesturdalur

Off the beaten track and home to diverse scenery, Vesturdalur is a favourite destination for hikers. A series of weaving trails leads from the scrub around the campsite to the cave-riddled pinnacles and rock formations of Hljóðaklettar, the Rauðhólar crater row, the ponds of Eyjan (not to be confused with the Eyjan at Ásbyrgi) and the canyon itself. Reckon on a full day or two to explore the area properly.

HLJÓÐAKLETTAR

The bizarre swirls, spirals, rosettes, honeycombs and columns of basalt at Hljóðaklettar (Echoing Rocks) are a highlight of any hike around Vesturdalur and a puzzling place for amateur geologists. It's difficult to imagine what sort of volcanic activity produced the twisted rock forms here. Weird concertina formations and repeat patterns occur throughout, and the normally vertical basalt columns (formed by rapidly cooling lava) show up on the horizontal here. These strange forms and patterns create an acoustic effect that makes it impossible to determine the direction of the roaring river, a curiosity that gave the area its name.

A circular walking trail (3km) from the parking area takes less than an hour to explore. The best formations, which are also riddled with lava caves, are found along the river, northeast of the parking area. Look out for Trollið, with its honeycomb pattern, Kirkjan, a natural cave in a grassy pit, and Kastali, a huge basalt outcrop. Blueberries abound in late August.

RAUÐHÓLAR

The Rauðhólar crater row, immediately north of Vesturdalur, displays a vivid array of colours in the cinder-like gravel on the remaining cones. The craters can be explored on foot during an interesting 5km loop walk from the parking area.

KARL OG KERLING

Two rock pillars, Karl og Kerling ('Old Man' and 'Old Woman'), believed to be petrified trolls, stand on a gravel bank west of the river, a 2km return walk from the Vesturdalur car park. Across the river is Tröllahellir, the largest cave in the gorge, but it's reached only on a 5km cross-country hike from Rte 864 on the eastern side.

EYJAN

From Karl og Kerling you can return to Vesturdalur by walking a 7km trail around Eyjan, a mesa-like 'island' covered with low, scrubby forests and small ponds. Follow the river south to Kallbjarg, then turn west along the track to the abandoned site of Svínadalur, where the canyon widens into a broad valley, and follow the western base of the Eyjan cliffs back to the Vesturdalur parking area.

HÓLMATUNGUR

Lush vegetation, tumbling waterfalls and an air of utter tranquillity make the Hólmatungur area one of the most beautiful in the park. Underground springs bubble up to form a series of short rivers that twist, turn and cascade their way to the canyon. The most popular walk here is the 4.5km loop from the parking area north along the Hólmá river to Hólmáfossar, where the harsh lines of the canyon soften and produce several pretty waterfalls. From here you head south again on the Jökulsá to its confluence with the Melbugsá river, where the river tumbles over a ledge, forming the Urriðafossar waterfalls. To see the falls, you need to walk along the trail spur to Katlar.

For the best overall view of Hólmatungur, walk to the hill Ytra-Þórunnarfjall, just south of the car park.

Hólmatungur is only accessible by 4WD. If you are travelling by 2WD, you can park your vehicle at Vesturdalur and do a long round-trip day hike. Camping is prohibited at Hólmatungur, but it's a great spot for a picnic lunch.

Dettifoss

The power of nature can be seen in all its glory at the mighty Dettifoss, one of Iceland's most impressive waterfalls. Although Dettifoss is only 44m high and 100m wide, a massive 193 cu metres of water thunders over its edge every second, creating a plume of spray that can be seen 1km away. With the greatest volume of any waterfall in Europe, this truly is nature at its most spectacular. On sunny days, brilliant double rainbows form above the churning milky-grey glacial waters, and you'll have to jostle with the other visitors for the best views.

The falls can be seen from either side of the canyon. A new sealed road, Rte 862, now links the Ring Road with the western bank of Dettifoss, ending in a large car park and toilet facilities. In time, a visitor centre may be built here. From the car park, a 2.5km loop walk takes in the dramatic, canyon-edge viewpoint of Dettifoss plus views of a smaller cataract, Selfoss.

The turn-off to Dettifoss is 27km east of Reykjahlíð; it's then an easy 24km on Rte 862 to reach the falls. North of the falls, Rte 862 is gravel (with plans to seal it by 2015). In the meantime, it's no longer an F road, but it is still tough going in a 2WD (and impassable in winter). Drive accordingly. The same is true of the road on the eastern side of the river, Rte 864.

NORTHEAST CIRCUIT

Bypassed by the tourist hordes who whiz around the Ring Road, this wild, sparsely populated coastal route around Iceland's remote northeast peninsula is an interesting alternative to the direct road from Mývatn to Egilsstaðir. It's an area of desolate moors and wildly beautiful scenery, stretching to within a few kilometres of the Arctic Circle.

❶ Getting There & Around

AIR

Air Iceland (www.airiceland.is) sells flights connecting Akureyri with Þórshöfn and Vopnafjörður. The cheapest online tickets cost around €65 one way.

BUS

SBA-Norðurleið (☑550 0700/70; www.sba.is) runs bus 680/680a year-round three times a week (Monday, Wednesday and Friday) in both directions. It runs between Akureyri and Þórshöfn (Ikr9800, five hours), stopping at towns along Rte 85 (Húsavík, Ásbyrgi, Kópasker and Raufarhöfn) en route. There's no bus to/from Vopnafjörður.

Kópasker

POP 140

Tiny Kópasker, on the eastern shore of Öxarfjörður, is the first place you'll pass through before disappearing into the expansive wilds of Iceland's far northeast.

In 1976 Kópasker suffered a severe earthquake; the small **earthquake centre** (Skjálfta Setrið; Akurgerði; admission free; ⊙1-5pm Jun-Aug) at the school investigates the quake and other tectonics in Iceland. South of the village, the **Byggðasafn** (admission free; ⊙1-5pm Jun-Aug) at Snartarstaðir farm highlights local textile and handicraft traditions. Look for cute, fully dressed scarecrows in the nearby fields.

There's a free campsite on your way into town, but your best bet for a bed is the homely and relaxing **Kópasker HI Hostel** (☑465 2314; www.hostel.is; Akurgerði 7; dm/d without bathroom Ikr3800/10,000; ⊙May-Oct). Rooms are spread across a couple of houses – everything is well maintained, and there's good birdwatching (and sometimes sealwatching) in the neighbourhood. HI members receive a discount of Ikr600 per person; linen costs Ikr1250. Note: no cards accepted, cash only. The town has a small store.

Raufarhöfn

POP 195

Like the setting of a Stephen King novel, distant Raufarhöfn (roy-ver-hup), Iceland's northernmost township, is an eerily quiet place with a prominently positioned graveyard. The port has functioned since the Saga Age, but the town's economic peak came early in the 20th century during the herring boom, when it was second to Siglufjörður in volume. Today, Raufarhöfn's rows of dull prefab housing give few clues to its illustrious past.

There are ambitious plans under way to build a massive stone circle on the hill just north of town. When completed, the **Arctic Henge** (www.arctichenge.is) will be 50m in diameter with four gates (to represent the seasons) up to 7m in height. The plan is to use the stone henge as a finely tuned sundial to celebrate the solstices, view the midnight sun, and explain the strong local beliefs in the mythology of the Edda poem *Völuspá* (Wise Woman's Prophecy). Drop into Hótel Norðurljós to view a model of the henge, and ask about summer guided tours of the site.

If you didn't make it up to Grímsey, **Arctic Travel** (☑893 8386; www.arctictravel. is; ☉mid-Jun–Sep) will take you across the Arctic Circle by boat – it will even give you a little certificate. Sea-angling, sightseeing and midnight cruises are also on offer.

To stay, there's a free **campsite** in the southern part of town, but **Hótel Norðurljós** (Northern Lights; ☑465 1233; www.hotelnordurljos. is; Aðalbraut 2; s/d Ikr11,500/17,900; ☎) is the only formal option. The exterior seems to have been battered by one too many storms, but the inside is quite cosy. Erlingur, the owner, offers up great home cooking at the **restaurant** (2-course lunch/3-course dinner Ikr3100/4500), incorporating local ingredients (often centred on freshly caught fish).

Rauðanes

Heading south from Raufarhöfn, there's excellent hiking at Rauðanes, where marked trails lead to bizarre rock formations, natural arches, caves and secluded beaches. The small and scenic peninsula is edged by steep cliffs full of nesting birds, caves, offshore sea stacks and an exposed rock face, **Stakkatorfa**, where a great chunk of land collapsed into the sea.

The turn-off to Rauðanes is about halfway between Raufarhöfn and Þórshöfn, but the track is only suitable for 4WD vehicles. All cars can park 1.5km from Rte 85, from where it's a 7km loop through the strange terrain.

Þórshöfn & Around

POP 380

The town of Þórshöfn has served as a busy port since Saga times and saw its heyday when a herring-salting station was established here in the early 20th century. Today it's a modest place but makes a good base for heading to the eerily remote Langanes Peninsula or to Rauðanes. The rusty church at **Sauðaneshús** (adult/child Ikr500/free; ☉1-5pm Jun-Aug), 7km north of town en route to Langanes, provides insights into how locals lived 100 years ago. For tourist information in town, stop by the large swimming-pool

> ### ⓘ ROADS IN THE NORTHEAST
>
> A sealed inland Rte 85 has recently been built to link Kópasker with the east, reaching the coast not far from Rauðanes (at the time of research, it was so new it wasn't shown on many maps). From the new Rte 85, Rte 874 branches north to Raufarhöfn.
>
> The new road still carries little traffic, but it means that the unsealed but scenic old coastal route 85 (now labelled Rte 870) around the bleak and little-visited **Melrakkaslétta** ('Arctic Fox Plain') is no longer maintained, so it's rough going but possible in a 2WD.
>
> For 55km between Kópasker and Raufarhöfn, Rte 870 passes through the low-lying flatlands, ponds and marshes of this bird-rich area. There are trails and turn-offs to lonely lighthouses on remote headlands. For a long time Hraunhafnartangi was thought to be the northernmost point of the Icelandic mainland, but recent measurements have pinned that prize on its neighbour, Rifstangi, which falls just 2.5km shy of the Artic Circle.

NORTH ICELAND RAUÐANES

complex **Íþróttahús** (Langanesvegur 18; adult/child Ikr400/150; ☉11am-5pm Mon-Fri, 8am-8pm Sat & Sun Jun-Aug, shorter hours Sep-May).

Þórshöfn has a **campsite** (sites per person Ikr1000) and the appealing **Lyngholt Guesthouse** (☑468 1238; www.lyngholt.is; Langanesvegur 12) near the pool, but there's also the farm property **Ytra-Aland** (☑468 1290; www. ytra-aland.is; d with/without bathroom incl breakfast Ikr18,800/15,200), 18km west of town. Pancakes and big smiles from hostess Bjarnveig greet guests in the morning. Sleeping-bag accommodation is possible (Ikr4500), as is dinner (and kitchen facilities), plus info on fishing and hiking in the area.

Dining options in Þórshöfn are slim. Try the unglamorous **grill** at the N1, pizzas at **Fontur** (Eyrarvegur 3) or self-cater via the **Samkaup-Strax** (☉9.30am-6pm Mon-Fri, 10am-2pm Sat) supermarket.

Langanes

Shaped like a goose with a very large head, foggy Langanes is one of the loneliest corners of Iceland. The peninsula's remarkably flat terrain, cushioned by mossy meadows and studded with crumbling remains, is an excellent place to break-in your hiking shoes.

Rte 869 ends only 17km along the 50km peninsula and, although it's possible to continue along the track to the tip at **Fontur** lighthouse in a 4WD vehicle, parts of the road can be difficult to navigate.

Before exploring the region, base yourself at the excellent **Ytra Lón HI Hostel** (📞846 6448; www.visitlanganes.com; hostel dm/d without bathroom Ikr3800/10,000, apt d from Ikr16,100; 🛜), 14km northeast of Þórshöfn and just off Rte 869. It's part of a working sheep farm run by a young and welcoming Dutch-Icelandic family. The hostel rooms are clean and bright, and there's a comfy common area and hot-pot. Fabulous studio apartments, each with bathroom and kitchenette, are housed in cargo containers and lined up under a greenhouse-style roof. Breakfast is available for Ikr1600; HI members get Ikr600 discount per person on hostel accommodation. Prices listed here don't include linen, which can be hired (Ikr1250).

If you don't have your own vehicle, you can phone ahead to Ytra Lón and the owners will pick you up in Þórshöfn (Ikr1700 per person). Or you can hike from the bus station to Langanes using the 'Back Road', which ends at Hóll. From there, follow the marked trail in a northeasterly direction until you reach Ytra Lón. The hike takes just over three hours if you're travelling light.

Vopnafjörður & Around

POP 700

'Weapon fjord' was once the notorious home of a fearsome dragon that protected northeast Iceland from harm. Today, no dragons,

and it's an agreeably sleepy place. (Note that online information for Vopnafjörður is found under east Iceland, www.east.is, as opposed to north.)

The town's most significant building is the **Kaupvangur** (Hafnarbyggd 6), a restored customhouse. You'll find a small, friendly cafe and **information centre** (📞473 1331, 862 1443; www.vopnafjordur.com; ⊙10am-5pm Jun-Aug; @🛜) on the ground floor. Upstairs there's a well-curated exhibit (in Icelandic only) about two locals, Iceland's version of the Gershwin brothers. Also on the 2nd floor is a small display about east Iceland émigrés; down-on-their-luck locals purchased boat tickets to America from this very building.

The region's biggest attraction is the folk museum at **Bustarfell** (www.bustarfell. is; adult/child Ikr700/100; ⊙10am-6pm mid-Jun–mid-Sep), set in a photogenic 18th-century turf-roofed manor house southwest of Vopnafjörður. Whereas once Bustarfell was on Rte 85, a new route for this road has seen the museum a little stuck in the middle of nowhere. The best option is to take the rough gravel Rte 920 from south of Vopnafjörður; the museum lies about 20km along this road. Rte 920 joins up with the new Rte 85 about 16km past the museum. Ask locally about the condition of Rte 920, as there are plans to improve it.

Another attraction in the middle of nowhere is the riverside swimming pool, **Selárdalslaug** (adult/child Ikr300/150; ⊙7am-11pm), signed 12km north of Vopnafjörður off Rte 85, just south of the river Selá. Stop for a quick soak in the geothermal waters of the hot-pot (and to admire the candlelit change rooms – there's no electricity out here).

HIKE OR DRIVE TO THE END OF THE EARTH

Abandoned farms, lonely lighthouses, seal colonies and craggy windswept cliffs home to prolific bird life – there are few places in the world that feel as remote as Langanes. It's perfect for hiking, and to help plot your route it's worth picking up the handy *Útivist & afþreying #7* map (available at Ytra Lón and local information centres).

If you're short on time, consider doing a 4WD tour – Ytra Lón operates them in conjunction with Húsavík-based tour operator **Fjallasýn** (📞464 3941; www.fjallasyn.is), so you can start the tour from Húsavík or from the hostel. From Ytra Lón, a two-hour tour to the bird cliffs costs €72 (minimum two people), or you can spend five hours touring, including a visit to Fontur (€120). Prebooking is required. Fjallasýn also offers a four-day guided hike through Langanes, beginning and ending at Ytra Lón; see its website for more.

For DIY four-wheel exploration, there is also the option to book a small 4WD jeep locally, by the half- or full day (or longer) from June to September. You'll need to email (hillak@simnet.is) the local car-hire branch in Þórshöfn in advance.

🛏 Sleeping & Eating

Under the
Mountain/Refsstaður II GUESTHOUSE €

(☎473 1562; www.underthemountain.is; s/d without bathroom Ikr5000/8000; 🛜) Cathy, an American of Icelandic descent, has a special knack for hospitality; her farmhouse feels incredibly homey and warm. It's about 9km south of town – first take Rte 917 past the small airstrip, then travel along Rte 919 for 4km. Sleeping-bag beds cost Ikr2500; there is kitchen access, and discounts for longer stays (call ahead in winter). Cathy maintains the local emigration exhibit and provides an interesting perspective on life in rural Iceland.

Campsite CAMPGROUND €

(sites per tent Ikr700, plus per person Ikr350) There's a good campsite with toilets and shower, and views of the fjord and town below. Follow Miðbraut north and turn left at the school. A ranger comes by to collect camping fees.

Hótel Tangi HOTEL €

(☎473 1840; hoteltangi@simnet.is; Hafnarbyggð 17; d with/without bathroom Ikr21,000/14,000) A pleasant surprise hides behind the rundown exterior: modern, sun-filled rooms! Really, these rooms are pretty good – and the popular restaurant (open 6pm to 9pm) isn't half bad either (a good thing, given dining options are limited).

Kauptún SUPERMARKET

(☺9.30am-6pm Mon-Fri, noon-4pm Sat) The supermarket shares a car park with the information centre; there's a **Vin Búð** (☺5-6pm Mon-Thu, 2-6pm Fri) next door.

❶ Getting There & Away

There is no bus service to Vopnafjörður. From Vopnafjörður it's 137km to Reykjahlíð and 95km (via Rte 917) or 136km (via Rte 85 and the Ring Road) to Egilsstaðir, so check fuel levels before you leave town.

NORTHEAST INTERIOR

Travelling between Mývatn and Egilsstaðir, the Ring Road takes a drastic shortcut inland across the stark highlands of the northeast interior. There's little to lure travellers

WORTH A TRIP

ROUTE 917

East of Vopnafjörður, the truly spectacular mountain drive along mostly unpaved Rte 917 takes you over 655m **Hellisheiði** and down to the east coast. The road, which may be impassable in bad weather but in summer is generally doable in a small car, climbs up a series of switchbacks and hairpin bends before dropping down to the striking glacial river deltas on the **Héraðs-sandur**. The views on both sides will be ingrained in your memory forever.

off the road, but the loneliness can be an attraction in itself in this eerie and otherworldly place of endless vistas.

If you won't be travelling into the highlands proper, you'll catch a glimpse of them here. Ostensibly barren, and to some unimaginably dull, the landscape here is dotted with low hills, small lakes caused by melting snowfields, and streams and rivers wandering aimlessly before disappearing into gravel beds. For most of the year it's a grey landscape, but if you're visiting in spring you'll be treated to a carpet of wildflowers that somehow gain root in the gravelly volcanic surface.

It has always been a difficult place to eke out a living, and farms here are few and far between. Isolated **Möðrudalur**, an oasis in the desert, is the highest farm in Iceland at 469m. Here you'll find the charming highland cafe and guesthouse **Fjalladýrð** (☎471 1858; www.fjalladyrd.is; sites per person Ikr1100, d/ cottages Ikr9300/12,900). It's worth spending the night if you're interested in tackling some of Iceland's icy interior; sleeping-bag accommodation is also available (single/double Ikr6200/8900), as are cottages sleeping up to seven (excluding linen Ikr19,500). The busy owners are former highland wardens and run informative 4WD trips to Askja, Herðubreið and Kverkfjöll (p292).

Folks simply passing through should try the succulent lamb dishes at **Fjallakaffi** (mains Ikr1690-5500; ☺May–mid-Oct). Petrol is available here; it's about 7km off the Ring Road on Rte 901 (63km east of Mývatn).

NORTH ICELAND NORTHEAST INTERIOR

East Iceland

Why Go?

Iceland's underrated easterly region doesn't announce itself as loudly as other parts of the country, preferring subtle charms instead of big-ticket attractions. The Eastfjords is the area's most wondrous destination – the scenery is particularly spectacular around the northern fjord villages, backed by sheer-sided mountains etched with waterfalls. If the weather's fine, several days spent hiking or kayaking here may be some of your most memorable in Iceland.

Away from the convoluted coast, the country's longest lake stretches southwest from Egilsstaðir, its shores lined with perfect diversions. Head further inland and you'll come to the forgotten farms, fells and reindeer-roamed heathlands of the empty east, and to Snæfell, one of Iceland's prime peaks.

Most travellers hit the accelerator and follow the over-eager Ring Road as it ploughs through Egilsstaðir and out of this region. Lunacy! They don't know what they're missing.

Best Places to Eat

» Skaftfell (p254)
» Randulffs-sjóhus (p258)
» Hótel Aldan (p254)
» Klausturkaffi (p245)
» Bókakaffi Hlöðum (p244)

Best Places to Stay

» Ferðaþjónustan Mjóeyri (p257)
» Skálanes (p255)
» Hótel Aldan (p254)
» Berunes HI Hostel (p261)
» Kirkjubær (p260)

Road Distances (km)

	Djúpivogur	Reykjavík	Egilsstaðir	Borgarfjörður Eystri	Seyðisfjörður	Neskaupstaður
Reykjavík	552					
Egilsstaðir	85	698				
Borgarfjörður Eystri	155	702	70			
Seyðisfjörður	111	660	27	92		
Neskaupstaður	164	703	72	140	96	
Breiðdalsvík	64	612	84	153	109	100

❶ **Getting There & Around**

The 'Travel Guide' pages of the East Iceland tourism website (www.east.is) outlines transport to/from and within the region, including the boggling schedule of buses in and out of the fjords.

AIR

Egilsstaðir's airport is 1km north of town. **Air Iceland** (Flugfélag Íslands; ☑580 3000; www.airiceland.is) flies daily year-round from Egilsstaðir to Reykjavík (one way from €60).

BUS

TO/FROM THE REGION Egilsstaðir is a major crossroads on the Ring Road. Buses generally arrive at and depart from the N1 petrol station or the nearby tourist information centre. Note that there is no winter bus connection between Egilsstaðir and Höfn.

SBA-Norðurleið (☑550 0700/70; www.sba. is) runs a Akureyri–Mývatn–Egilsstaðir service (bus 62/62a) daily from June to mid-September, four times weekly rest of year; Akureyri–Egilsstaðir takes four hours (Ikr8700).

Sterna (☑551 1166; www.sterna.is) offers a Höfn–Egilsstaðir service (bus 9/9a) once daily from mid-May to mid-September; four hours.

Hópferðabílar Akureyrar (☑898 5156; www. hba.is) runs a Höfn–Egilsstaðir service (bus 1/1a) once daily from June to mid-September (Ikr7500, four hours); stops include Reyðarfjörður, Berunes and Djúpivogur. The company offers a Ikr15,000 pass that allows travel along the route over three days.

WITHIN THE REGION Austfjarðaleið (East Iceland Bus Company; ☑477 1713; www.aust fjardaleid.is) runs buses from Egilsstaðir to villages around the fjords. See the relevant town for details of links.

CAR

The Ring Road steams through Egilsstaðir, but if you want to explore the Eastfjords you need to leave it here. Options:

» **Rte 92** south to Reyðarfjörður and nearby fjord towns

» **Rte 93** east to Seyðisfjörður

» **Rte 94** north to Borgarfjörður Eystri

The Ring Road takes you south then east to Breiðdalsvík and weaves along the coast around to Djúpivogur. A shortcut is provided by the rough (gravel) but scenic Rte 939 via the Öxi mountain pass.

CAR HIRE If you fly into the east, or arrive by ferry from Europe without wheels, **Avis** (www. avis.is), **Budget** (www.budget.is), **Hertz** (www. hertz.is) and **Europcar** (Bílaleiga Akureyrar/ Höldur; www.europcar.is) all have agents in Egilsstaðir.

INLAND

Egilsstaðir

POP 2270

However much you strain to discover some underlying charm, you'll find sprawling Egilsstaðir isn't a ravishing beauty. It's the main regional transport hub, and a centre for local commerce. Sorry, it's about as enchanting as it sounds. Services include an excellent regional tourist office and quality accommodation.

Egilsstaðir's saving grace is its proximity to lovely Lagarfljót, Iceland's third-largest lake. Since Saga times, tales have been told of a monster living in its depths. If you want to do some beastie-hunting, or explore the forest on the lake's eastern bank, Egilsstaðir makes a good base.

⊙ **Sights & Activities**

Thanks to recent high-profile industrial projects (the Kárahnjúkar hydroelectricity dam and Alcoa aluminium smelter – both opposed by environmentalist groups, but welcomed by many locals for bringing jobs to the area), the east has seen an influx of workers, and there has been feverish house-building in Egilsstaðir and other eastern communities. In time, the hub town's entertainment facilities may catch up, but at present there's not a great deal to lure visitors.

Minjasafn Austurlands   MUSEUM
(East Iceland Heritage Museum; www.minjasafn. is; Laufskógar 1; adult/child Ikr1000/free; ⊙1-7pm Mon-Fri, 10am-4pm Sat Jun-Aug, 1-4pm Mon-Fri Sep-May) Egilsstaðir's cultural museum is a sweet little place. Its displays focus on the history of the region.

Sundlaugin Egilsstöðum   SWIMMING POOL
(Tjarnarbraut 26; adult/child Ikr500/250; ⊙6.30am-9.30pm Mon-Fri, 10am-6pm Sat & Sun Jun-Aug, reduced hours Sep-May) The town's impressive swimming pool, with saunas, hot-pots and gym, is north of town.

East Iceland Highlights

1 Arrive in the country in style: sail up a lovely, long fjord to the bohemian village of **Seyðisfjörður** (p251)

2 Chat with the hidden people and snap photos of puffin posses in beautiful **Borgarfjörður Eystri** (p247)

3 Tour the forested shores of **Lagarfljót** (p245) looking for sea monsters

4 Learn the definition of tranquil isolation in ruin-strewn **Mjóifjörður** (p255), verdant **Skálanes** (p255) or horse-happy **Húsey** (p244)

5 Marvel over the magnificent mineral collection in **Stöðvarfjörður** (p260)

6 Inspect the fascinating, trapped-in-time boathouse at **Eskifjörður** (p258)

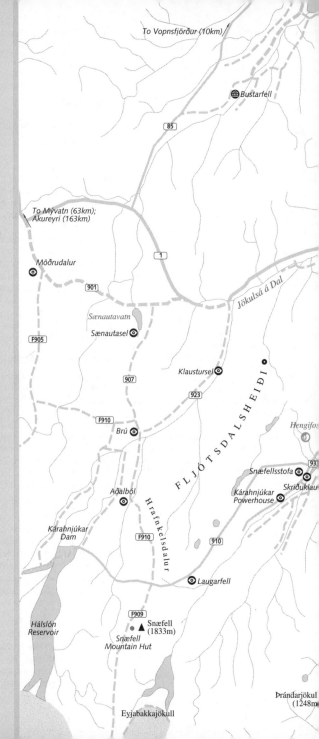

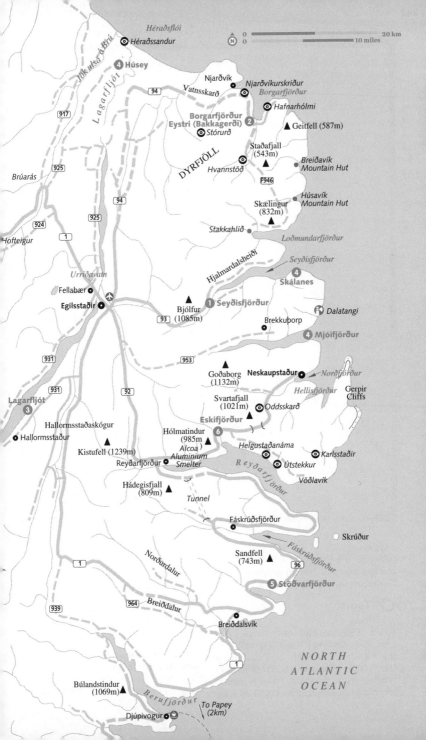

Egilsstaðir

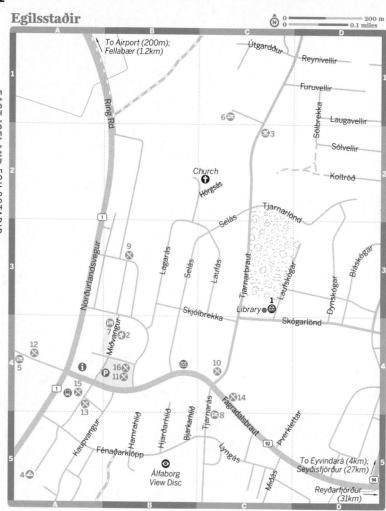

Skógar BICYCLE RENTAL
(Miðvangur 6; 6/24hr rental Ikr1990/3990) You can hire mountain bikes from outdoor store Skógar, opposite the Icelandair hotel.

☞ Tours

Jeep Tours TOUR
(☎898 2798; www.jeeptours.is) Jeep Tours runs 4WD day tours from Egilsstaðir into the highlands, to Askja and Herðubreið (Ikr36,000), to Snæfell (Ikr32,500), or on reindeer-spotting safaris. It's also one of few companies visiting Kverkfjöll as a day tour (Ikr36,000), travelling via the (sealed) Rte 910 to Kárahnjúkar dam before tackling 4WD tracks. Winter tours are a possibility – check the website.

✱ Festivals & Events

See 'What's On' at www.east.is for a run-down of events.

JEA Jazz Festival MUSIC
(www.jea.is) In late June, an annual jazz fest takes place in Egilsstaðir, spreading its wings to include gigs in Seyðisfjörður and Neskaupstaður.

Egilsstaðir

◎ **Sights**

◯ **Activities, Courses & Tours**

◎ **Sleeping**

◎ **Eating**

Ormsteiti   CULTURAL
(www.ormsteiti.is) The possible existence of the lake monster is a good excuse for this weeklong cultural festival during late August.

Dagar Myrkurs   CULTURAL
Over 10 days in early November, in Egilsstaðir and the fjords, the 'Days of Darkness' perversely celebrates the failing light and the onset of winter with ghost stories, Northern Lights spotting and torch-lit processions.

🛏 Sleeping

Book ahead for Wednesday nights in summer, as the ferry to Europe sails from Seyðisfjörður (27km away) on Thursday mornings and beds in the area are in hot demand.

TOP CHOICE **Eyvindará**   GUESTHOUSE €€
(✆471 1200; www.eyvindara.is; d with/without bathroom incl breakfast Ikr21,900/16,400; ☉Mar-Oct; ☏) Set 4km away (on Rte 94), with good views back into town, serene Eyvindará is a delightful place to call home. A handsome, family-run collection of rooms, cottages and motel units sits hidden among fir trees, while delicious reindeer meatballs are served in the button-cute summertime breakfast/dining room.

Lyngás Guesthouse   GUESTHOUSE €
(✆471 1310; www.lyngas.is; Lyngási 5-7; d without bathroom Ikr14,900; ☏) Behind an uninspiring exterior is this new six-room guesthouse, dressed in white and offering fine views, kitchen and a couple of larger, family-friendly rooms. You can save a few krónur with your own sleeping bag. Note the nature photos on the walls, taken by the owner's father.

Egilsstaðir Guesthouse   COUNTRY HOTEL €€
(✆471 1114; www.egilsstadir.com; s/d incl breakfast Ikr21,890/28,490; @☏) The town was named after this splendid heritage guesthouse and farm, on the banks of Lagarfljót, 300m west of the crossroads. Its sensitively renovated en-suite rooms retain a sense of character, and are decorated with antique furniture.

Icelandair Hótel Hérað   HOTEL €€
(✆471 1500; www.icelandairhotels.is; Miðvangur 5-7; r from Ikr27,600; @☏) This bright, friendly business hotel is the plushest in town, and is kitted out with the expected bells and whistles. The stylish restaurant (mains Ikr3000 to Ikr6000) is a good place to indulge. The house speciality is local game, including reindeer and goose.

Campsite   CAMPGROUND €
(Kaupvangur 17; sites per person Ikr1000; ☉Jun-Sep; @) Camping pitches are in utilitarian rows, but it's central and facilities are good – there's a kitchen and laundry, and on-site cafe.

Vinland Guesthouse   GUESTHOUSE €€
(✆615 1900; www.vinlandhotel.com; Fellabær; d Ikr18,000; ☏) Vinland offers six simple but well-equipped motel-style rooms (with TV, fridge, kettle and microwave) just north of Fellabær, a few kilometres from Egilsstaðir. Cute decoration dresses up what is, in effect, a garage-like aluminium exterior.

Hótel Edda   HOTEL €€
(✆444 4880; Tjarnarbraut 25; www.hoteledda.is; s/d Ikr17,100/20,700; ☉Jun–mid-Aug; @☏) Based in the school opposite the swimming pool, this is a typical Edda hotel. Rooms have private bathrooms, and there's a bar and restaurant with panoramic views.

🍴 Eating

Refuelling motorists don't have to look far – quick eats can be found at the busy **Söluskálinn** (☉11am-10pm) inside the N1 petrol station on the Ring Road. Those heading to the fjords can try **Skálinn** (☉8am-9pm

EAST ICELAND EGILSSTAÐIR

Mon-Fri, 9am-9pm Sat & Sun) at the Shell on Fagradalsbraut.

If you're after a taste of top-quality local produce, stop by 'Cowshed Corner', Fjóshorníð (⊙11am-6pm Mon-Fri, 2-5pm Sat & Sun Jun-Aug), beside Egilsstaðir Guesthouse, where you can buy beef and dairy products direct from the farm, or at the food store at organic farm Vallanes (www.vallanes.net; ⊙1-6pm Jun-Aug), selling barley, vegetables and jams and chutneys. Vallanes is about 15km south of Egilsstaðir, off Rte 931 halfway to Hallormsstaður.

TOP CHOICE Bókakaffi Hlöðum
CAFE €

(www.bokakaffi.is; Helgafelli 2; soup buffet Ikr1490; ⊙9am-6pm Mon-Sat; @⊚) In Fellabær, at the western end of the bridge across the river from Egilsstaðir, is this near-perfect cafe: quality coffee, retro furniture, vinyl records, free internet, secondhand books and baked treats. Lunchtime debate: soup-and-salad buffet versus filled crepes?

Egilsstaðir Guesthouse
ICELANDIC €€€

(☑471 1114; www.egilsstadir.com; lunch Ikr990-2190, dinner mains Ikr2490-5690) You'll need time to peruse the menu here – it richly details the locally sourced produce (lamb, beef, fish, game), which is high on quality, low on food miles. The speciality is the beef, raised right here on the farm. Hunger sated, admire the romantic appeal of the lake-view dining room over evening candlelight.

Café Nielsen
INTERNATIONAL €€

(Tjarnarbraut 1; light meals Ikr1250-2400, dinner mains Ikr2550-6900; ⊙11.30am-11.30pm Mon-Fri, 1-11.30pm Sat & Sun) Based in Egilsstaðir's oldest house, cottagey Café Nielsen offers a wide-ranging menu that roams from lobster soup to reindeer by way of nachos and bar-becue pork sandwich. In summer there's a leafy terrace and garden.

Café Valný
CAFE €

(Miðvangur 2-4; ⊙11am-6pm; ⊚) This snug little cafe is a good place to hole up in, with quality coffee or tea accompanied by home-made goodies. Hours can be variable.

Nettó
SUPERMARKET €

(⊙10am-7pm Mon-Fri, 10am-6pm Sat, noon-6pm Sun) Behind the N1 petrol station.

Bónus
SUPERMARKET €

(⊙11am-6.30pm Mon-Thu, 10am-7.30pm Fri, 10am-6pm Sat, noon-6pm Sun) On the Ring Road north of the N1.

Vín Búð
ALCOHOL €

(Miðvangi 2-4; ⊙11am-6pm Mon-Thu, to 7pm Fri, to 4pm Sat Jun-Aug, shorter hours Sep-May) This is a government-run liquor store.

ℹ Information

North past the airport and over the lake, you'll find Egilsstaðir's twin town, Fellabær. It has some accommodation options, but most services are on a large block just off the Ring Road in Egilsstaðir, a good place to position yourself if you're hitching.

Post office (Fagradalsbraut 9; ⊙9am-4.30pm)

Tourist information centre (☑471 2320; www.east.is; Miðvangur 1-3; ⊙8.30am-6pm Mon-Fri, 9am-5pm Sat & Sun mid-May–mid-Sep, 9am-5pm Mon-Fri, 11am-3pm Sat rest of year; @) The excellent regional information centre has enough free brochures to paper your living room. Maps and guides are plentiful – you'll find everything you need to explore the East-fjords and beyond. It offers internet access as well (Ikr300/500 for 15/30 minutes). There's an ATM here (and a bank branch upstairs); be sure to browse Hús Handanna, the art and design store that shares the premises.

WORTH A TRIP

HÚSEY

Reaching Húsey involves a long but scenic drive, 30km off the Ring Road along the rough, unsealed Rtes 925 and 926 beside the Jökulsá á Dal river (all up, about 60km from Egilsstaðir). The only reason to venture out to this isolated farm is a good one: to stay at the simple, rustic Húsey HI Hostel (☑471 3010; www.husey.de; dm/d without bathroom Ikr3800/10,000). There are horses to ride (two-hour seal-watching tours on horseback start at 10am and 5pm daily; €40), birdwatching trails to follow, and seals cavorting in the riverine backdrop. It's worth staying a few days to enjoy the homey atmosphere; longer horse treks are easily arranged. The hostel has cooking facilities but there's nowhere to buy food, so bring supplies. Breakfast can be ordered. Book well in advance, and ask about pick-up options if you don't have your own vehicle. Members get a discount of Ikr600 per person; linen costs Ikr1250.

❶ Getting There & Away

Egilsstaðir is the transport hub of east Iceland. There's an airport, and all bus services pass through. See p239 for transport information.

Lagarfljót

The grey-brown waters of the river-lake Lagarfljót are reputed to harbour a fearsome monster, **Lagarfljótsormur**, which has allegedly been spotted since Viking times. The most recent 'sighting' of the serpentine beast (also called the Worm/Wyrm) caused quite a stir – in February 2012 a local farmer released footage of a large creature moving in the river. The clip has attracted close to five million hits on YouTube, and garnered international news coverage. Read more at www.ormur.com.

Real or imagined, the poor old beast must be pretty chilly – Lagarfljót starts its journey in the Vatnajökull ice cap and its glacial waters flow north to the Arctic Ocean, widening into a 38km-long, 50m-deep lake, often called Lögurinn, south of Egilsstaðir.

Whether you see a monster or not, it's a lovely stretch of water to circumnavigate by car. Rte 931, a mixture of sealed surfaces and gravel (gravel on the less-trafficked western shore), runs all the way around the edge from Egilsstaðir to Fellabær – a distance of around 67km. In July, a new local bus service runs three times a day from the tourist info centre in Egilsstaðir, south to the Kárahnjúkar visitor centre (stopping at Hallormsstaður, Hengifoss and Skriðuklaustur en route, but not taking in the western shore of the lake). If the bus is well utilised, it may extend its seasonal run into June and/or August – make enquiries in Egilsstaðir.

HALLORMSSTAÐASKÓGUR

Iceland's largest **forest**, Hallormsstaðaskógur is king of the woods and venerated by the arborically challenged nation. Although the country's coppices are comical to many foreigners (Q: What do you do if you get lost in an Icelandic forest? A: Stand up), it's rude to snigger.

Although Hallormsstaðaskógur is small by most countries' standards, it's also quite cute – and a leafy reprieve after the stark, bare mountainsides to the north and south of Egilsstaðir. Common species include native dwarf birch and mountain ash, as well as 50 tree species gathered from around the world.

In a cove on the lakeshore, **Atlavík campsite** (sites per person Ikr1000) is an idyllic and extremely popular campsite, often the scene of raucous parties on summer weekends. Pedal boats, rowing boats and canoes can be hired (Ikr1500 per half-hour) for watery pursuits. The smaller, quieter **Höfðavík campsite** (sites per person Ikr1000) is just north of the petrol station.

A veritable campus of buildings hidden amongst the trees, **Hótel Hallormsstaður** (☑471 2400; www.hotel701.is; hotel s/d Ikr21,250/27,320, guesthouse s/d without bathroom Ikr12,350/16,675, all incl breakfast; @🛰🛜) is a bucolic country retreat offering options for most wallets: modern hotel rooms, cottages and guesthouses, plus two restaurants (a renowned dinner buffet in summer), an inviting outdoor area complete with small pool, and bike hire for guests. Beside the summer schoolhouse accommodation, **horse-riding tours** (☑847 0063; 1/2hr Ikr5500/7500) are available.

HENGIFOSS & LÍTLANESFOSS

Crossing the bridge across the lake on Rte 931, you'll reach the parking area for Hengifoss, Iceland's second-highest waterfall. Once you've made the climb up and into the canyon you'll be blown away by the power of the water – after a rainstorm it sounds like a Boeing 747 taking off! The falls plummet 120m into a colourful brown-and-red-striped boulder-strewn gorge.

Getting to Hengifoss requires a return walk of about one hour. From the car park, a long stairwell leads up the hillside – Hengifoss is soon visible in the distance. It's a steep climb in places but flattens out as you enter the canyon. The walk is 2.5km each way; halfway up is a smaller waterfall, Lítlanesfoss, surrounded by spectacular vertical basalt columns in a honeycomb formation.

SKRIÐUKLAUSTUR

Head south from Hengifoss for 5km to reach Skriðuklaustur (www.skriduklaustur.is; adult/child Ikr700/free; ☉10am-6pm Jun-Aug, noon-5pm May & early Sep), site of a 16th-century monastery and the home of an Icelandic author feted by the Third Reich. The unusual black-and-white turf-roofed building was built in 1939 by Gunnar Gunnarsson (1889–1975), and now holds a cultural centre dedicated to him. This prolific writer achieved phenomenal popularity in Denmark and Germany –

at the height of his fame only Goethe out-sold him.

The house also contains an interesting exhibition about the earlier Augustinian monastery, demolished during the Reformation of 1550. Archaeological finds include bones indicating that Skriðuklaustur was used as a hospice. Its most famous artefact is a carved statue of the Virgin Mary, found hidden in an old barn wall. Guided tours of the excavated site (Ikr300, or joint ticket with Skriðuklaustur Ikr800) depart from the reception at 1.30pm and 3.30pm.

TOP CHOICE Klausturkaffi (lunch buffet adult/child Ikr2500/1250), inside Skriðuklaustur, serves an impeccable lunch buffet showcasing local ingredients (seafood soup, reindeer pie, brambleberry puddings). More tantalising, however, is every sweet-tooth's dream: the brilliant all-you-can-eat cake buffet (adult/child Ikr1750/875) served between 2.30pm and 5.30pm.

SNÆFELLSSTOFA
Next door to Skriðuklaustur, this stylish new visitor centre (☎470 0840; www.vjp.is; ☉9am-6pm Mon-Fri, 10am-6pm Sat & Sun Jun-Aug, 10am-4pm Mon-Fri, 1-5pm Sat & Sun May & Sep) covers the eastern territory of the behemoth that is Vatnajökull National Park (see p266 for more on the park). Excellent displays highlight the nature of the eastern highlands, and staff sell maps and offer invaluable advice to travellers wishing to hike or otherwise experience the park (see p295 for information on the Kverkfjöll route).

PIT STOP!

Exactly halfway between Egilsstaðir and Borgarfjörður sits one of east Iceland's quirkier roadside wonders: a pistachio-coloured hut surrounded by miles and miles of nothingness. Built by a local eccentric, the little structure is simply a hut to house a solar-powered refrigerated vending machine. If the power is off, flick the 'on' switch (we're not kidding) and wait two minutes (you can sign the guestbook while waiting). Then, voila: a refreshingly cold beverage or snack.

We're not too sure who takes care of the little booth, but apparently someone swings by once a month to restock and turn the page on the calendar...

KÁRAHNJÚKAR
Two kilometres past Skriðuklaustur is the Végarður visitor centre (☎470 2570; vegardur@lv.is; ☉10am-5pm Jun-Aug) for the Kárahnjúkar hydroelectric project. There's an overview of the project, and you can arrange guided tours of either the power station or the dam area. Dam tours are scheduled twice a week in summer – email for details.

Snæfell
No one seems to know whether 1833m-high Snæfell is an extinct volcano, or if it's just having a rest. Iceland's highest peak outside the Vatnajökull massif is relatively accessible, making it popular with hikers and mountaineers.

Snæfell looms over the southern end of Fljótsdalsheiði, an expanse of spongy tussocks of wet tundra, boulder fields, perennial snow patches and alpine lakes, stretching westwards from Lagarfljót into the highlands. It's part of the vast Vatnajökull National Park – the park website www.vjp.is has useful information, and the national park visitor centre, Snaefellsstofa, has great info, maps and displays. If you want to tour the area with someone else behind the wheel, check the offerings from Jeep Tours (☎898 2798; www.jeeptours.is) in Egilsstaðir.

Work on the controversial Kárahnjúkar dam has brought improved roads around Snæfell, with the paved Rte 910 from Fljótsdalur (the turn-off is just north of Skriðuklaustur) being the best way up. (Beware: although paved, the road is still pretty vertical and hair-raising!) Along the way, watch for wild reindeer, and bring your swimsuit to stop at the hot springs of Laugarfell (☎857 8842; www.laugarfell.is; dm Ikr4000-5000), where a comfy bed and hot food are available.

A 4WD is needed if you wish to get off Rte 910, including to reach Snæfell mountain hut (☎summer 863 9236, year-round 863 5813; www.fljotsdalsherad.is/ferdafelag; N 64°48.250', W 15°38.600'; sites/dm per person Ikr1200/5300) at the base of the peak. The hut sleeps 45, with a kitchen, camping area and showers. From mid-July to mid-August, park rangers guide a one-hour nature walk from the hut at 9am.

Although climbing the mountain itself is not difficult for experienced, well-prepared hikers, the weather can be a concern and technical equipment is required. Ascending from the west is most common – it's a hike of six to nine hours, depending on ice conditions. Discussing your route with the hut warden is always a good idea.

One of Iceland's most challenging and rewarding hikes takes you from Snæfell to the Lónsöræfi district (p283) in southeast Iceland. The five-day, 45km route begins at the Snæfell hut and heads across the glacier Eyjabakkajökull (an arm of Vatnajökull) to Geldingafell, Egilssel and Múlaskáli huts before dropping down to the coast at Stafafell.

This route should not be approached lightly – it's for experienced trekkers only. You'll need a GPS and, for the glacier crossing, you must be skilled at using a rope, crampons and an ice axe. If you're unsure of your skills, you'd be much wiser doing the trip commercially with the likes of **Icelandic Mountain Guides** (IMG; ☑587 9999, www.mountainguide.is) – although IMG's five-day, 50km backpacking tour through Lónsöræfi (from Ikr113,000), called 'In the Shadow of Vatnajökull', begins at Eyjabakkar east of Snæfell and avoids the glacier traverse.

Jökulsá á Dal

A small stream, formed by rivulets from the hillsides, puddles through what was once a riverbed carved out by a more powerful river (now harnessed in the Hálslón reservoir). The part alongside the Ring Road is said to be haunted by mischievous leprechauns and bloodthirsty Norse deities.

If travelling with kids, consider breaking the journey at **Klaustursel** (☑471 1085; adult/child Ikr300/free; ☺10am-7pm Jun-Aug), 12km off the Ring Road along rough Rte 923 (the little bridge you cross was once part of the American railway!). The farm has swans and geese, and you can pat the soft noses of the oh-so-pretty reindeer. Don't miss Ólavía's unique accessories made from tanned hides.

Continuing along Rte 923 leads you to the valley of **Hrafnkelsdalur** (about 100km from Egilsstaðir), full of sites relating to *Hrafnkell's Saga*. The farm **Aðalból** (☑471 2788; www.simnet.is/samur; sites per person Ikr1500, r without bathroom per person Ikr4500-6500; ☺Jun–mid-Sep) was the home of the saga's hero, Hrafnkell Freysgoði, and his burial mound is here. There's a marked saga trail, threading together places mentioned in the story. Meals are available (notice required), as is petrol. The road becomes the F910 before you reach Aðalból, but it's driveable (if

a bit skiddy) in a normal car. It's definitely 4WD-only once you continue past Aðalból – an alternative route to Snæfell, or to the Kárahnjúkar dam.

The reconstructed turf farmhouse **Sænautasel** (☺10am-10pm Jun–mid-Sep), dating from 1843, really brings the past to life... plus it sells pancakes and coffee. This is one of several old farms on Jökuldalsheiði that were originally abandoned when Askja erupted in 1875. The building is beside the lake Sænautavatn, 32km west of Hofteigur and some 13km south of the Ring Road via Rte 907. This area was a source of inspiration for Halldór Laxness' masterwork, *Independent People;* you may notice that many of the farm names here match those of the fictional farms in the book.

THE EASTFJORDS

Unlike the wildly folding Westfjords, the Eastfjords wiggle more modestly around the coast. The difference is akin to an over-theatrical actor chewing up the scenery and an under-emoting character in some Scandinavian art-house film.

Despite (mostly) good surfaced roads and all the Alcoa-related activity, the Eastfjords still seems remote – a feeling enhanced by immense, dramatic mountainsides and the tiny working fishing villages that nestle under them.

The fjords are the true highlight of east Iceland. There are some superb walks, you can kayak to far-off headlands, and thousands of seabirds nest along the cliffs. In a Finest Fjord competition it would be hard to pick a winner – Borgarfjörður has ethereal rhyolite cliffs, Seyðisfjörður fosters a cheery bohemian vibe, Mjóifjörður is riddled with waterfalls, and Norðfjörður has a dizzying ascent/descent. You'll just have to visit and choose your own favourite.

The following section is organised from north to south.

Borgarfjörður Eystri (Bakkagerði)

POP 130

This village, the most northerly in the Eastfjords, is in a stunning location. It's framed by a backdrop of rugged rhyolite peaks on one side and the spectacular Dyrfjöll mountains on the other. There's very little in the village itself, although weird driftwood sculptures, hidden elves, crying seabirds and pounding waves exude a strange charm.

If you're looking for local information, check out www.borgarfjordureystri.is, or stop by Álfheimar or Borg accommodation for hiking brochures (also available from the Egilsstaðir information centre).

Sights & Activities

TOP CHOICE Hafnarhólmi   ISLAND

(www.puffins.is) Five kilometres past the wee church is the photogenic small-boat harbour and islet of Hafnarhólmi, home to a gigantic **puffin colony**. The free viewing platform allows you to get up close and personal with these cute, clumsy creatures (and other seabirds). The puffins arrive mid-April and are gone by mid-August, but other species linger longer.

Lindarbakki   HISTORIC HOUSE

You can't miss the village's hairiest house... bright-red Lindarbakki (1899) is completely cocooned by whiskery green grass, with only a few windows and a giant pair of antlers sticking out. It's a private home and not open to the public, but an information board outside tells you about its history. We particularly liked the estate agent's comments from 1979...

Álfaborg   NATURE RESERVE

Álfaborg (Elf Rock), the small mound and nature reserve near the campground, is the 'borg' that gave Borgarfjörður Eystri its name. Some locals believe that the queen of Icelandic elves lives here. From the 'view disc' on top there's a fabulous vista of the surrounding fields, which turn white in summer with blooming Arctic cotton.

HRAFNKELL'S SORTA-SAGA

The saga of Hrafnkell is one of the most widely read Icelandic sagas, thanks to its short, succinct plot and memorable characters. The tale is particularly interesting because its premises seem to derail any modern notions of right, wrong and justice served. The only conclusions one can really draw are 'it's better to be alive than dead' and 'it's better to have the support of powerful chieftains than rely on any kind of god'.

The main character, Hrafnkell, is a religious fanatic who builds a temple to Freyr on the farm Aðalból in Hrafnkelsdalur. Hrafnkell's prized stallion, Freyfaxi, is dedicated to the god, and Hrafnkell swears an oath to kill anyone who dares ride him without permission. As might be expected, someone does. The stallion himself tempts a young shepherd to leap onto his back and gallop off to find a herd of lost sheep. Discovering the outrage, Hrafnkell takes his axe to the errant youth.

When the boy's father, Þorbjörn, demands compensation for his son's death, Hrafnkell refuses to pay up, offering instead to look after Þorbjörn in his old age. Proudly, the man refuses, and the characters are launched into a court battle that ultimately leads to Hrafnkell being declared an outlaw. He chooses to ignore the sentence and returns home.

Before long, Þorbjörn's nephew Sámur Bjarnason arrives to uphold the family honour, stringing Hrafnkell up by his Achilles tendons until he agrees to hand over his farm and possessions. Sámur then offers him a choice: to live a life of subordination and dishonour, or to die on the spot; you might think a saga hero would go for death, but Hrafnkell chooses life.

Sámur moves into Aðalból and makes a few home improvements. The pagan temple is destroyed, and the horse Freyfaxi weighted with stones, thrown over a cliff and drowned in the water below. Hrafnkell, by now convinced that his favourite god doesn't give two hoots about him, renounces his religious beliefs and sets up on a new farm, Hrafnkelsstaðir. He vows to change his vengeful nature and becomes a kind and simple farmer, becoming so well liked in his new neighbourhood that he gains even more wealth and power than before.

One day, Sámur and his brother Eyvindur pass by en route to Aðalból. Hrafnkell's maid sees them and goads her employer into taking revenge for his earlier humiliation. Hrafnkell abandons the Mr Nice Guy routine, sets out in pursuit of the troublesome brothers, kills Eyvindur, and offers Sámur the same choice that he was offered before – give up Aðalból and live in shame, or be put to death. Sámur also decides not to die. Hrafnkell thus regains his former estates and lives happily ever after at Aðalból.

BORGARFJÖRÐUR TO SEYÐISFJÖRÐUR HIKE

Wildly wonderful and unexplored, the rugged country between Borgarfjörður and Seyðisfjörður makes for one of the best multiday summer hikes in the region. To plan your journey, pick up the widely available *Gönguleiðir á Austurlandi* #1 map, or contact Álfheimar or Borg accommodation in Borgarfjörður if you're looking for a guide. For hut information along this route, check www.fljotsdalsherad.is/ferdafelag.

Day 1: Start at Kolbeinsfjara, 4km outside the township of Borgarfjörður Eystri, and venture up into the mountains along the Brúnavíkurskarð pass (trail #19 on the map). Turn south (along trail #21) at the emergency hut in Brúnavík, passing beautiful Kerlingfjall further on. After your six-to-seven-hour hike (15km), settle in for the night at the outfitted farmhouse/campsite in Breiðavík.

Day 2: Next day features another stunning six or seven hours of hiking (13.5km along trail #30). You'll first walk through the grassy leas below Hvítafjall, then link up with the 4WD track heading south to the Húsavík hut, where you'll spend the second night. The land between Breiðavík and Húsavík is infested with hidden people – the elf sheriff lives at Sólarfjall and the elf bishop lives at Blábjörg further south along the coast.

Day 3: Another 14km of trails are tackled in six to seven hours of hiking (along trail #37) as the path reunites with the sea at silent Loðmundarfjörður. The 4WD track ends at the Klyppstaður lodge on the Norðdalsá river delta at the uppermost point of the fjord.

Day 4: The last day links Loðmundarfjörður to Seyðisfjörður (trail #41). At the highest point of the mountain pass you'll find a logbook signed by previous hikers. As you venture down into Seyðisfjörður, you'll be treated to a watery fanfare of gushing chutes.

EAST ICELAND BORGARFJÖRÐUREYSTRI (BAKKAGERÐI)

Kjarvalsstofa
MUSEUM

(adult/child Ikr500/free; ⏱1-5pm Jun-Aug) Jóhannes Sveinsson Kjarval (1885–1972), Iceland's best-known artist, was brought up on the nearby farm Geitavík and took much of his inspiration from the rhyolite-studded surroundings at Borgarfjörður Eystri. The Kjarvalsstofa, inside the Fjarðarborg community centre, is the village's tribute to him (note that the labelling is only in Icelandic), but we like his unusual altarpiece in the small church Bakkagerðiskirkja more. It depicts the Sermon on the Mount and is directly aimed at his village of fishermen and farmers – Jesus is preaching from Álfaborg, with the mountain Dyrfjöll in the background.

Ævintýraland
CHILDREN'S CENTRE

(Adventure Land; admission Ikr500; ⏱1-5pm Jun-Aug) If you need a break from the kids (or they from you), bring them to Ævintýraland, where they can snuggle up with a colourful pillow and an iPod and listen to several reinterpretations of the local elf stories. There's also dress-ups, painting and magical rock collections. Its future is in doubt for 2013, so ask around.

🎉 Festivals & Events

Bræðslan
MUSIC

(www.braedslan.is) Held in an abandoned herring plant on the third weekend of July, Bræðslan is one of Iceland's best summer concert festivals, earning itself a reputation for great music as well as its intimate atmosphere. Some big local names (and a few international ones) come to play, with past guests including Emiliana Torrini (who used to spend her summer in Borgarfjörður), Damien Rice, Of Monsters and Men and Mugison.

🛏 Sleeping

Blábjörg Guesthouse
GUESTHOUSE €

(📞861 1792; www.blabjorg.is; s/d without bathroom incl breakfast Ikr8900/13,900; 📶) In an old fish factory, this guesthouse boasts pristine white rooms, guest kitchen and lounge, and help-yourself breakfast. Its standout feature is the downstairs sauna and hot-pot with view – open to all from 5pm to 9pm (Ikr2000), or by arrangement.

Guesthouse Álfheimar
GUESTHOUSE €€

(📞861 3677; www.elftours.is; Merkisvegur; d Ikr22,900; ⏱May-Sep; @📶) Easily the most upmarket option (it's the only one with private bathrooms!), Álfheimar has 31 motel-style units in long annexes. The timber-lined rooms have more atmosphere than the newer building but all are spotless and well equipped. The affable owners are a fount of knowledge about the area; guiding and tours can be arranged (the website images will have you entranced). There's a restaurant (two courses Ikr4200) here open to all and offering the dish of the day from the fjord's fishermen or farmers.

Gistiheimilið Borg GUESTHOUSE €
(☑472 9870, 894 4470; gistingborg@simnet.is; r without bathroom per person from Ikr5000) Borg is a good bet for a bed (cheaper sleeping-bag options available), since the owner has a few houses in the village. Rooms are OK if old-fashioned, with cooking and lounge facilities. Hiking, guiding and 4WD tours can be arranged.

Campsite CAMPGROUND €
(sites per person Ikr750; ⊘mid-May–Sep) Beside the church, this quiet green site has a kitchen and showers (Ikr200). The third night is free.

Borgarfjörður HI Hostel HOSTEL €
(Ásbyrgi; ☑472 9962; www.hostel.is; dm/d without bathroom Ikr3800/10,000; ⊘Jun-Aug) Small and homey but looking a little worn out, this small hostel offers beds for up to 20 people. There's a guest kitchen and washing machine. There's Ikr600 discount per person for members. Linen costs Ikr1250.

🍴 Eating

Álfacafé ICELANDIC €
(fish soup Ikr1700; ⊘10am-10pm May-Sep; 🛜) The main place to eat, with large stone-slab tables and fish soup the headlining act (with decent support from the likes of flatbread with trout or herring). Stone knick-knacks are also for sale. Check out the huge piece of raw jasper sitting on the front lawn (it's the biggest piece ever found in Iceland).

Fjarðarborg ICELANDIC €
(meals Ikr1400-1800; ⊘11am-midnight Jun-Aug) Housed inside the community centre, the menu is simple and the decor uninspiring, but it's worth a try for its burgers or lamb stew, and a chat with the locals.

Samkaup-Strax SUPERMARKET €
(⊘12.30-5.30pm Mon-Thu, to 6pm Fri) The tiny Samkaup by the pier sells groceries.

❶ Getting There & Away

Bus

The only public transport is the weekday **postal van** (☑472 9805, 894 8305) between Borgarfjörður Eystri campground (departs 8am) and Egilsstaðir information centre (departs noon). One way Ikr2000.

Car

The village is 70km from Egilsstaðir along Rte 94, about half of which is sealed. It winds steeply up over the Vatnsskarð mountains before dropping down to the coast. There's a card-operated petrol pump by the Samkaup grocery store.

Around Borgarfjörður Eystri

There are loads of trails criss-crossing the northeast – everything from easy two-hour strolls to serious mountain hiking for people with a head for heights! Watch your footing in nonvegetated areas – loose material makes for an experience akin to walking on thousands of tiny ball bearings. Get your hands on the widely available *Gönguleiðir á Austurlandi* #1 map, and check out the boxed text, p249, for a scenic multiday hike that connects Borgarfjörður to Seyðisfjörður.

DYRFJÖLL

One of Iceland's most dramatic ranges, the Dyrfjöll mountains rise precipitously to an altitude of 1136m between the marshy Héraðssandur plains and Borgarfjörður Eystri. The name Dyrfjöll means Door Mountain and is due to the large and conspicuous notch in the highest peak – an Icelandic counterpart to Sweden's famous Lapporten. There are two walking tracks crossing the range, which allow for day hikes or longer routes from Borgarfjörður Eystri.

Stórurð, on the western flank of Dyrfjöll, is a hiker's paradise, an extraordinary place scattered with huge rocks and small glacial ponds. To reach the site on a pleasant half-day hike, start at the red emergency hut along the main road (Rte 94) and follow trail #9, then loop back along trail #8 (clearly marked on the *Gönguleiðir á Austurlandi* map). The 15km trip takes just over five hours.

NJARÐVÍKURSKRIÐUR

A habitual site of accidents in ancient times, Njarðvíkurskriður is a dangerous scree slope on Rte 94 near Njarðvík. All the tragedies were blamed on a nuisance creature (half-man, half-beast), Naddi, who dwelt in a sea-level cave beneath the slope.

In the early 1300s, Naddi was exorcised by the proper religious authorities, and in 1306 a cross was erected on the site bearing the inscription '*Effigiem Christi qui transis pronus honora, Anno MCCCVI*' – 'You who are hurrying past, honour the image of Christ – AD 1306'. The idea was that travellers would repeat a prayer when passing the danger zone and therefore be protected from malevolent powers. The cross has been replaced several times since, but the current one still bears the original inscription.

Seyðisfjörður

POP 675

If you visit only one town in the Eastfjords, this should be it. Made up of multicoloured wooden houses and surrounded by snow-capped mountains and cascading waterfalls, obscenely picturesque Seyðisfjörður is the most historically and architecturally interesting town in east Iceland. It's also a friendly place with a community of artists, musicians and craftspeople.

Summer is the liveliest time to visit, particularly when the Smyril Line's ferry *Norröna* sails majestically up the 17km-long fjord to the town – a perfect way to arrive in Iceland.

If the weather's good, the scenic Rte 93 drive from Egilsstaðir is a delight, climbing to a high pass then descending along the waterfall-filled river Fjarðará.

History

Seyðisfjörður started as a trading centre in 1848, but its later wealth came from the 'silver of the sea' – herring. Its long, sheltering fjord gave it an advantage over other fishing villages, and it grew into the largest and most prosperous town in east Iceland. Most of the unique wooden buildings here were built by Norwegian merchants, attracted by the herring industry.

During WWII Seyðisfjörður was a base for British and American forces. The only attack was on an oil tanker that was bombed by three German warplanes. The bombs missed their target, but one exploded so near that the ship sank to the bottom, where it remains today.

Seyðisfjörður's steep-sided valley has made it prone to avalanches. In 1885 an avalanche from Bjólfur killed 24 people and pushed several houses straight into the fjord. A more recent avalanche in 1996 flattened a local factory, but no lives were lost. The avalanche monument near the church is made from twisted girders from the factory, painted white and erected as they were found.

◉ Sights

Seyðisfjörður is stuffed with 19th-century timber buildings, brought in kit form from Norway: read about them in the brochure *Historic Seyðisfjörður,* available at the tourist office. Several of the historical buildings have been transformed into cosy ateliers where local artisans work on various projects. A quick loop around town will reveal half-a-dozen places to drop some serious krónur, on art, handicrafts and knitwear. Also worth a look is the **gallery space** (Austurvegur 42) above the Skaftfell cultural centre.

Bláa Kirkjan　　　　　　　　HISTORIC BUILDING
(www.blaakirkjan.is; Ránargata) The most prominent of Seyðisfjörður's timber buildings is the pretty Bláa Kirkjan, also known as the Blue Church. On Wednesday evenings from July to mid-August, it's the setting for a popular series of jazz, classical- and folk-music concerts (starting at 8.30pm; tickets Ikr2000); see the website for the program. If you're leaving on the Thursday ferry, this is a great way to spend your final night in Iceland.

Tækniminjasafn Austurlands　　　MUSEUM
(www.tekmus.is; Hafnargata 44; adult/child Ikr1000/free; ◷11am-5pm Mon-Fri Jun–mid-Sep, 1-4pm Mon-Fri mid-Sep–May) For insight into the town's fishing and telecommunications history, stop by this worthwhile technical museum. It's housed in two buildings on Hafnargata: the impressive 1894 home of Norwegian shipowner Otto Wathne, and a workshop from 1907. Seyðisfjörður was at the cutting edge of Icelandic technology in the 19th century – the first submarine telephone cable linking Iceland with Europe was brought ashore here in 1906.

🏃 Activities

Hiking

The hills above Seyðisfjörður are the perfect spot for hiking neophytes. Start by walking up the road past the HI hostel to where a rough 4WD track takes off up the glacial valley to your left. The track peters out after a few hundred metres, but keep walking

Seyðisfjörður

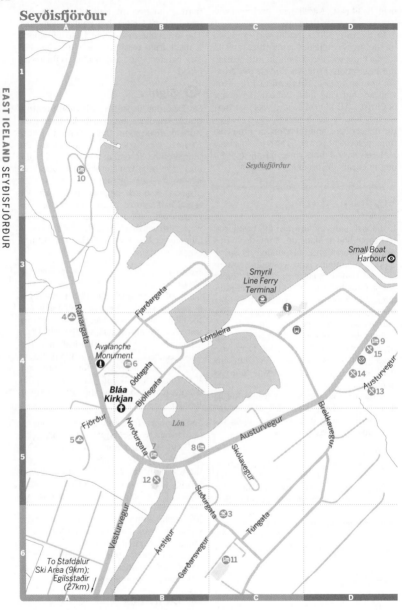

uphill, along the side of the Vestdalsá river. After a couple of hours and several tiers of glorious waterfalls, you'll arrive at a small lake, Vestdalsvatn, which remains frozen most of the year. From the lake you can continue left over the tundra or return down the tiered rows of gushing waterfalls from where you came.

Kayaking & Mountain Biking

For a sublime outdoor experience, contact **Hlynur Oddsson** (📱865 3741; hlynur@hotmail

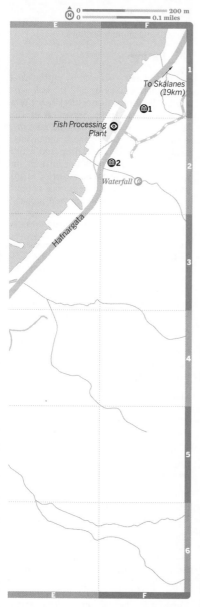

the fjord range from one to six hours, visiting a shipwreck or waterfalls (one/three hours Ikr3500/8000). Experienced kayakers can choose longer trips, perhaps to the uninhabited neighbouring fjord or to Skálanes (full day Ikr22,000, two-day trip with camping Ikr35,000).

Hlynur also takes **mountain-bike tours**, including a four-hour trip out to the Brimnes lighthouse (Ikr5500) or a five-hour tour to Skálanes (Ikr10,000). Alternatively, hire a bike and take off on your own (Ikr2500/3000 for a half/full day).

Other Activities

Sundhöll Seyðisfjarðar SWIMMING POOL
(Suðurgata 5; adult/child Ikr450/free; ⊙6.30-9am & 5-8pm Mon-Fri, 1-5pm Sat Jun-Aug, shorter hours Sep-May) Seyðisfjörður's indoor swimming pool has a sauna and hot-pots.

Stafdalur ski area SKIING
In winter there's downhill and cross-country skiing at the Stafdalur ski area, 9km from

.de; www.iceland-tour.com; ⊙Jun-Aug), a charming Robert Redford-esque character who spends his summers around town and offers tailor-made tours on or around the fjord. With kids, you can opt for an easy half-hour paddling in the lagoon (Ikr1500); options on

Seyðisfjörður on the road to Egilsstaðir – contact the tourist office for details.

🛏 Sleeping

Book ahead for Wednesday nights in summer, as the ferry to Europe leaves on Thursday mornings and beds are in hot demand.

TOP CHOICE Hótel Aldan   HOTEL €€

(☎472 1277; www.hotelaldan.com; reception at Norðurgata 2; s/d incl breakfast from Ikr15,900/21,900; ☏) This wonderful hotel is shared across three old wooden buildings: reception and the bar-restaurant (where breakfast is served) are at the Norðurgata location. The Snæfell location (in the old post office at Austurvegur 3) is a creaky, characterful three-storey place with the cheapest rooms, fresh white paintwork, draped muslin curtains and Indian bedspreads. The Old Bank location (at Oddagata 6) houses a boutique guesthouse with all mod cons. Its luxurious rooms are bright, spacious and furnished with antiques, and beds snuggle under hand-embroidered bedspreads.

Seyðisfjörður HI Hostel   HOSTEL €

(Hafaldan; ☎472 1410; www.simnet.is/hafaldan; dm/d without bathroom Ikr3800/10,000; ⊙Apr–mid-Oct; @☏) Seyðisfjörður's budget digs are housed in two locations: Ranárgata 9, a little out of town past the Blue Church; and at Suðurgata 8, the more-central summertime annexe. The annexe houses the main reception for both buildings from June to August. The thin-walled, unremarkable private rooms at Ranárgata are compensated for by lovely, view-enriched dining and lounge areas. We like the vibe of the annexe more: plants, incense, Indian hangings and funky furniture conceal the fact this used to be the old hospital. There's Ikr600 discount per person for members. Linen costs Ikr1250.

Post Hostel   GUESTHOUSE €

(☎898 6242; www.posthostel.com; s/d without bathroom Ikr9900/13,900; ☏) The name is a little misleading – this fresh-faced guesthouse (in yet another old post office!) has smallish rooms, including some family-friendly ones, plus full kitchen and laundry facilities. There's also a large, luxurious three-bedroom apartment for rent.

Campsite   CAMPGROUND €

(Ránargata; sites per person Ikr1000; ⊙May-Sep) There are two areas for camping – one sheltered, grassy site opposite the church for tents, and another nearby area for vans. The service building houses kitchen, showers (Ikr350) and laundry facilities.

🍴 Eating

TOP CHOICE Skaftfell   INTERNATIONAL €

(www.skaftfell.is; Austurvegur 42; snacks & mains Ikr890-2690; ⊙noon-11pm or later May-Aug, 5pm-2am ferry days & Fri-Sun Sep-Apr; @☏) This fabulous, artsy bistro-bar-cultural-centre is where you can chill, snack and/or meet locals against a cool backdrop, and with a great soundtrack. There's free internet and wi-fi, and a tempting menu (curries, salads, pizzas) that includes decent vegie options. If we lived in Seyðisfjörður, we'd probably come here everyday. Be sure to check out the exhibitions in the gallery space upstairs.

Hótel Aldan   ICELANDIC €€€

(☎472 1277; Norðurgata 2; lunch Ikr2250-3250, dinner mains Ikr3500-7200; ⊙7am-9pm mid-May–mid-Sep) Coffee and delicious cakes are served all day in this country-chic spot, and lunches feature the likes of mussels or lamb chops. In the evening, damask tablecloths and flickering candles prettify the tables, and the menu features traditional Icelandic ingredients (lamb, langoustines, reindeer, fish) with a contemporary touch. Reservations advised.

Skálinn   GRILL €

(Hafnargata 2; ⊙noon-9pm) The grill bar at the petrol station does hot dogs and burgers, as well as cheap cooked lunch/dinner mains.

Samkaup-Strax   SUPERMARKET €

(Vesturvegur 1; ⊙9am-7pm Mon-Fri, 10am-4pm Sat, noon-4pm Sun) For self-caterers.

Vín Búð   ALCOHOL €

(Hafnargata 4a; ⊙5-6pm Mon-Thu, 2-6pm Fri) Government-run liquor store.

ℹ Information

There's free internet access (and wi-fi) at Skaftfell. The website www.visitseydisfjordur.com is invaluable.

Landsbanki Íslands (Hafnargata 2) Bank with 24-hour ATM, which can get crowded when the ferry arrives.

Tourist information centre (☎472 1551; ⊙8am-noon & 1-5pm Mon-Fri; ☏) In the ferry terminal building, helpful staff sell bus passes and maps, and provide information for onward travel. The centre also opens in conjunction with ferry or cruise-boat arrivals.

ⓘ Getting There & Away

Boat

From April to late October, **Smyril Line** (www. smyrilline.com) operates a weekly car ferry, the *Norröna*, on a convoluted schedule from Hirsthals (Denmark) through Tórshavn (Faeroe Islands) to Seyðisfjörður.

From mid-June to August, the *Norröna* sails into town at 9.30am on Thursday, departing for Scandinavia two hours later. From April to mid-June, and again in September and October, the boat pulls in at 9am on Tuesday, leaving Wednesday at 8pm. See p345, and check the website for more info.

Bus

Ferðaþjónusta Austurlands (☑472 1515) runs a bus service between Egilsstaðir and Seyðisfjörður (Ikr1000, around 45 minutes). Services operate year-round, one to three times daily Monday to Saturday (Sunday services operate from mid-June to mid-August). Extra services run to coincide with the ferry arrival and departure. An up-to-date schedule can be found on the Travel page of www.visitseydisfjordur.com.

Around Seyðisfjörður

You might think Seyðisfjörður is the end of the line, but further retreat is possible. The remote farm **Skálanes** (☑690 6966, 861 7008; www.skalanes.com; ⊙May-Sep, by arrangement Oct-Apr), 19km east of Seyðisfjörður along the fjord edge, is a wonderful nature reserve and heritage field centre. The owner has an insatiable passion for the outdoors and has lovingly restored the once-abandoned farmstead into a veritable Eden for amateur scientists, archaeologists (remains from the Settlement Era have been found) and tourists wishing to see pristine bird cliffs (more than 40 avian species). Its isolation inspires nothing but relaxation and will undoubtedly appeal to your inner hermit/naturalist.

A variety of stay-over packages are available, incorporating guided walks, 4WD excursions and meals (there is also a guest kitchen). Straight-up B&B accommodation in cosily refurbished rooms goes for Ikr7500 per night, full board is Ikr12,750.

Getting to Skálanes is an adventure in itself. You could walk all the way from Seyðisfjörður (there are footbridges across the river); you could get there on a mountain bike or in a kayak hired from Hlynur Oddsson (see p252); in a normal car you can drive 13km along the track until you get

to the river, then walk the last bit (which works out to be around 4km); in a 4WD you can drive the whole way there (just be careful as you ford the river!); or you can have the centre pick you up from Seyðisfjörður/the river (Ikr8000/4000 per vehicle).

Mjóifjörður

POP 35

The next fjord south of Seyðisfjörður is Mjóifjörður, flanked by spectacular cliffs and rows of cascading waterfalls. The unsealed road leading into the fjord (Rte 953) pushes the limits of a 2WD, but once you make it in you'll be surrounded by lush hills peppered with fascinating ruins and schools of farmed fish leaping out of the frigid fjord water. A rusted herring vessel sits beached – like a giant ochre carcass – as you tumble down into the fjord basin. Also of interest are the rusting leftovers of the early-20th-century Norwegian whaling station at Asknes (accessible by 4WD only) and the ruined Dalatangi light, Iceland's first lighthouse.

On the north side of the fjord at Brekkuþorp (often labelled Iceland's smallest village), **Sólbrekka** (☑476 0020; mjoi@simnet.is; cottages excl linen Ikr14,000; ⊙Jun-Sep) is the one and only place to stay around here, and it's a welcome sight for hikers. There's an old schoolhouse near the sea (open mid-June to mid-August, camping/sleeping-bag accommodation per person Ikr1000/3500), but the real treat lies up the hill – two gorgeous, self-contained pine cottages each sleeping up to six (BYO food supplies). There's a little afternoon cafe (⊙1-6pm mid-Jun–mid-Aug) at the schoolhouse, and an indoor hot-pot at the cottages (open to all for a small fee). Breakfast, fishing and sightseeing boat trips can be arranged.

There's some brilliant hiking around Mjóifjörður. For a fee, the folks at Sólbrekka can ferry you across the fjord, from where it's a beautiful four-hour hike to Neskaupstaður, or you can climb over northern mountains to reach Seyðisfjörður on a six-hour trek.

It's 30km from Egilsstaðir to the head of Mjóifjörður, then a further 12km to Brekkuþorp. No transport runs here. The road into and out of Mjóifjörður is impassable in winter – access is by boat twice a week from Neskaupstaður.

Reyðarfjörður

POP 1100

In the Prettiest Fjord pageant, Reyðarfjörður could never quite manage to take home the sash and crown. It's a relatively new settlement, which only came into existence – as a trading port – in the 20th century. More recently, however, Reyðarfjörður garnered attention when Alcoa installed a giant 2km-long aluminium smelter just beyond the town along the fjord. Conservationists were up in arms, but the infusion of foreign workers has added a small splash of international flavour in Reyðarfjörður and the surrounding towns. Alcoa jobs have also brought a prosperity best evidenced by the homes being built by new residents (predominantly Icelanders drawn to the area for employment opportunities).

◎ Sights

Íslenska Stríðsárasafnið   MUSEUM

(Spítalakampur; adult/child Ikr1000/free; ◎1-5pm Jun-Aug) During WWII around 3000 Allied soldiers (about 10 times the local population) were based in Reyðarfjörður. At the top end of Heiðarvegur you'll find the excellent Icelandic Wartime Museum, which details these strange few years. The building is surrounded by mines, Jeeps and aeroplane propellers, and holds other war relics. Photographs and tableaux provide a good background to Iceland's wartime involvement. The museum is tucked behind a rusting set of army barracks, built as part of a hospital camp in 1943 but never used for that purpose. No Icelanders actually fought in WWII; however, many locals were killed at sea.

⌂ Sleeping & Eating

There are grill bars at the Shell or Olís petrol stations, and Krónan supermarket (Hafnargata 2; ◎11am-6pm Mon-Thu, to 7pm Fri, to 5pm Sat, noon-4pm Sun) for self-caterers.

TOP CHOICE Reyðarfjörður HI Hostel   HOSTEL €
(Hjá Marlín; ☏474 1220, 892 0336; www.hostel. is; Vallagerði 9 & 14; dm Ikr3800, d with/without bathroom Ikr14,000/10,000; @⑨) Multilingual Marlín (Belgian, but resident in Iceland for over 20 years) is a superb host at this welcoming spot. The primary house has a great bedroom-to-bathroom ratio, plus a cosy restaurant (open 5pm to 8pm) on the 2nd floor; in a large second house down the street there are simple rooms, a barbecue and a sauna. New in 2013 are six rooms with private bathroom, and a brand-new kitchen/dining area. Members get a discount of Ikr600 per person; linen costs Ikr1250.

Tærgesen   GUESTHOUSE €€

(☏470 5555; www.taergesen.com; Búðargata 4; s/d without bathroom incl breakfast €50/85; ⑨) There's loads of cottagey character in these sweet rooms, lined with pine and dressed with white window shutters. They're inside a black corrugated-iron building from 1870, above a good traditional restaurant (snacks and meals Ikr650 to Ikr4450; open 10am to 10pm).

Fjarðahótel   HOTEL €€

(☏474 1600; www.fjardarhotel.is; Búðareyri 6; s/d incl breakfast €100/125; @⑨) The only hotel in town has run-of-the-mill, business-style rooms. An on-site restaurant (mains Ikr2900 to Ikr4700) gets good reviews for its steaks and pizzas.

Sesam Brauðhús   BAKERY, CAFE €

(Hafnargata 1; ◎7.30am-5.30pm Mon-Fri, 9am-4pm Sat) Stop by this cheerful bakery-cafe (near Krónan supermarket) and choose from a cabinet full of sandwiches, salads and pastries, plus a changing lunch special.

❶ Getting There & Away

Austfjarðaleið (East Iceland Bus Company; ☏477 1713; www.austfjardaleid.is) runs the following year-round bus services, which place Reyðarfjörður at their heart. Buses run every day (fewer services on weekends) and are geared to service the needs of Alcoa commuters, but travellers without their own transport will also find them useful (one-way ticket Ikr1500).

» Line 1 Reyðarfjörður–Eskifjörður–Neskaupstaður (Nordfjörður)

» Line 2 Egilsstaðir–Reyðarfjörður

» Line 3 Reyðarfjörður–Fáskrúðsfjörður–Stöðvarfjörður–Breiðdalsvík

Check online for the latest schedule details (www.east.is will have links) or ask at tourist information centres in the area.

Eskifjörður

POP 1000

This friendly, prospering little town is stretched out along a dimple in the main fjord of Reyðarfjörður. Its setting is magnificent: it looks directly onto the mighty mountain Hólmatindur (985m), rising sheer from the shining blue water.

◎ Sights

Sjóminjasafn Austurlands   MUSEUM
(Strandgata 39b; adult/child Ikr1000/free; ⊗1-5pm Jun-Aug) Inside the 1816 black timber warehouse 'Gamlabuð', the East Iceland Maritime Museum illustrates two centuries of the east coast's historic herring, shark and whaling industry. For more salty-dog stories, be sure to check out Randulffs-sjóhus (p258).

Helgustaðanáma   QUARRY
The remains of the world's largest spar quarry, Helgustaðanáma, can be found east of Eskifjörður, past Mjóeyri. Iceland spar (*silfurberg* in Icelandic) is a type of calcite crystal that is completely transparent and can split light into two parallel beams. It was a vital component in early microscopes, and large quantities were exported to some of Europe's top scientists starting from the 17th century until 1924, when the quarry closed. The largest specimen taken from Helgustaðanáma weighs 230kg and is displayed in the British Museum. Science aside, you can still see calcite sparkling in rocks around the quarry. The area is a national preserve, though, so you can't poke out pieces of crystal or take them away. Follow the rough dirt road 8km along the coastline until you get to an information panel; the quarry is then a 400m walk uphill.

Útstekkur   HISTORIC SITE
Abut 1.5km beyond the mine are the ruins at Útstekkur, which was once a bustling trade centre during Danish rule. In its heyday, more than 2400 people lived here, transporting goods from the rural Icelandic countryside onto Europe-bound freighters. Trade centres were also set up at Vopnafjörður and Djúpivogur. After the settlement ruins, the road turns into a rough dirt track for 4WDs, and leads to Vöðlavík – a huge black-sand beach.

⚑ Activities

Hólmanes Peninsula   HIKING
The southern shore of the Hólmanes Peninsula, below the peak Hólmatindur, is a nature reserve. Hiking in the area offers superb maritime views (look out for pods of dolphins) and the chance to observe the protected vegetation and bird life. The Hólmaborgir hike, south of the main road, is a popular loop that takes but an hour or two.

There are also plenty of longer hiking routes up the nearby mountains: Kistufell (1239m), Goðaborg (1132m), Svartafjall (1021m) and Hádegisfjall (809m). Multi-day hikes around the peninsulas east of Eskifjörður abound (consider taking in the dramatic Gerpir cliffs, Iceland's easternmost point), with routes marked on the map *Gönguleiðir á Austurlandi II*, available from Egilsstaðir tourist office. Gönguvikan (Hiking Week) is a big event on the district's annual calendar, falling the week after the summer solstice.

Oddsskarð   SKIING
From Christmas to mid-April, skiing is possible on slopes near Oddsskarð, the pass leading over to Neskaupstaður. The longest run is 327m and is floodlit. See www.oddsskard.is (parts of the site are kept up to date).

🍴 Sleeping & Eating

There's good accommodation in town, and a simple **campsite** (sites per person Ikr1000) in a pretty setting, but it's often busy accommodating Alcoa workers, so it pays to book ahead.

Quick-eat options include a petrol station with a **grill** (⊗9am-10pm), and a **Samkaup-Strax supermarket** (⊗10am-6pm Mon-Fri, to 2pm Sat).

TOP CHOICE Ferðaþjónustan
Mjóeyri   GUESTHOUSE, COTTAGES €€
(☑477 1247, 696 0809; www.mjoeyri.is; Strandgata 120; s/d without bathroom Ikr10,000/13,500, cottages Ikr23,000; 🐾) Right on the eastern edge of town, this charming wooden house has unparalleled views – it literally sits in the middle of the waterway at the tip of a teeny peninsula. Tidy guesthouse rooms off the common space and five family-sized cottages out the back make Mjóeyri a great choice all around. New additions include an amenities block for campers, sauna and one of the finest hot-pots we've seen (in a converted boat). Knowledgeable owners offer an abundance of guiding and tours: hiking, skiing, caving, hunting, fishing and bird-watching. The cottage price doesn't include linen; sleeping-bag accommodation in the guesthouse costs Ikr6000. Breakfast is available (Ikr1500).

Hotel Askja   GUESTHOUSE €
(☑477 1247, 696 0809; www.hotelaskja.is; s/d without bathroom Ikr9700/13,300; @🐾) In a waterfront, corrugated-iron building with king-size

EAST ICELAND NESKAUPSTAÐUR (NORÐFJÖRÐUR)

views to Hólmatindur, Askja has fresh, simple rooms with access to a full kitchen and appealing lounge area. Use your own sleeping bag for Ikr5100.

Hótelíbúðir APARTMENT €€
(☑892 8657; www.hotelibudir.net; Strandgata 26; apt Ikr19,900; ☜) Four spacious, modern, central and fully equipped one-bedroom apartments are offered, sleeping up to four. The price is reduced to Ikr15,000 on your second night.

Kaffihúsið GUESTHOUSE €€
(☑477 1150; www.kaffihusid.is; Strandgata 10; s/d without bathroom Ikr8900/11,900; ☜) You can't miss the oversized coffee cup on the way into town announcing this place, primarily a bar-restaurant (mains Ikr1600 to Ikr4100; open noon to 10pm or later) and hang-out for Alcoa workers, with regular live music. There's also a cluster of rooms in the back; they're simple affairs, all with washbasin and flatscreen TV.

TOP CHOICE Randulffs-sjóhus ICELANDIC €€
(Strandgata 96; mains Ikr1900-3200; ☺5-9pm Jun-Aug or by appointment) This extraordinary old boathouse dates from 1890, and when new owners entered it in 2008, they found that not a soul had been inside for the last 80-odd years. The upstairs sleeping quarters of the fishermen has remained as it was found, while downstairs is an atmospheric restaurant amongst the maritime memorabilia. Unsurprisingly, the menu is heavy on fish. Contact Mjóeyri to see inside the boathouse outside opening hours (Ikr1000); it also arranges boat rental from here.

Neskaupstaður (Norðfjörður)

POP 1500

Just getting to Neskaupstaður feels like a real odyssey. You travel via the highest highway pass (632m) in Iceland, through a single-lane, 630m-long tunnel, then drop from the skies like a falcon into town; attempt to drive further east and you simply run out of road. Although it's one of the largest of the fjord towns, this dramatic end-of-the-line location makes it feel small and far away from the rest of the world.

As with most towns in the Eastfjords, Neskaupstaður began life as a 19th-century trading centre and prospered during the herring boom in the early 20th century. Its future was assured by the building of the biggest fish-processing and freezing plant in Iceland, Síldarvinnslan (SNV), at the head of the fjord.

See p256 for bus information from Reyðarfjörður.

◎ Sights & Activities

Safnahúsið MUSEUM
(Egilsbraut 2; adult/child Ikr1000/free; ☺1-5pm Jun-Aug) Neskaupstaður's three small museums are clustered together in one bright-red warehouse, known as 'Museum House', by the harbour. Art gallery **Tryggvasafn** showcases a collection of striking paintings by prominent modern artist Tryggvi Ólafsson, who was born in Neskaupstaður in 1940. His colourful abstracts, some of which hang in national galleries in Reykjavík, Sweden and Denmark, depict Icelandic scenes and are visually quite striking.

Upstairs, the **Maritime Museum** is one man's collection of artefacts relating to the sea, while on the top floor, the **Museum of Natural History** has a big collection of local stones (including spar from the Helgustaðanáma mine), plus an array of stuffed animals, birds, fish and pinned insects.

Walking & Hiking

At the eastern end of town, where the road runs out, is the nature reserve **Fólksvangur Neskaupstaðar**, perfect for short strolls. Various paths run through long grass, over tiny wooden bridges, and past boulders, peat pits, cliffs and the sea. There are plenty of puffins to watch, as well as gulls and ravens.

For serious hikers, a rewarding route will take you up **Goðaborg** (1132m) from the farm Kirkjuból, 8km west of town. From the summit you can also descend into Mjóifjörður, the next fjord to the north; allow six hours and, due to late snows at higher altitudes, attempt it only at the height of summer.

Horse Riding

Skorrahestar (☑477 1736; http://skorrahestar .123.is; Skorrastaður), west of town, offers horse tours, from one-day rides to six-day farm stays that explore the incredible surrounds. Due to the challenging terrain, these aren't suited to beginners.

★ Festivals & Events

Eistnaflug MUSIC
(www.eistnaflug.is) A metal and punk mayhem festival, Eistnaflug, which could be translated

as 'Flight of Testicles', is held every summer in town on the second weekend in July. Every self-respecting rockin' band shows up, if not to play then to listen and drink!

🛏 Sleeping & Eating

Neskaupstaður's options are pretty lacklustre – we think Eskifjörður makes a better base.

Standard fast-food fare can be found at the grill at **Olís petrol station** (Hafnarbraut 19). Picnic supplies can be picked up at the supermarkets **Samkaup-Úrval** (Hafnarbraut 13; ⊗10am-7pm Mon-Fri, noon-6pm Sat & Sun), near the petrol station, and **Nesbakki** (Bakkavegur 3; ⊗10am-7pm), closer to the campsite.

Hótel Edda HOTEL €€
(☑444 4860; www.hoteledda.is; Nesgata 40; s/d Ikr17,100/20,700; ⊗early Jun–mid-Aug; @🖥) On the waterfront at the eastern end of town, this summer hotel has brilliant views, neat yet predictably plain rooms (all with bathroom), and a reasonable restaurant that stares straight out over the fjord.

Tónspil GUESTHOUSE €
(☑477 1580; www.tonspil.is; Hafnarbraut 22; s/d without bathroom Ikr5900/9900; 🖥) Like an extra in the film *High Fidelity*, you need to ask the dude in the music shop about the rooms above! Which are very, very simple, but there's a handy TV room/kitchen area with washing machine. BYO sleeping bag for reduced prices (Ikr3900 per person). The music shop (worth a look) is open 10am to 6pm Monday to Friday, to 3pm Saturday.

Campsite CAMPGROUND €
(sites per person Ikr1000) High above the town at the avalanche barriers (worth a visit for the great views). It's signposted from the hospital; showers are free.

Hótel Capitanó HOTEL €€
(☑477 1800; www.hotelcapitano.is; Hafnarbraut 50; s/d €108/134) In this bright-blue corrugated-iron building are tired hotel rooms. A last resort.

Nesbær Kaffihus CAFE €
(Egilsbraut 5; lunch Ikr800-1500; ⊗9am-6pm Mon-Wed & Fri, to 10.30pm Thu, 10am-6pm Sat; 🖥) This cafe-bakery-knick-knack shop has a quintessential small-town vibe and offers cakes, sandwiches and soup. It doubles as the town's information point, dispensing a few brochures.

Fáskrúðsfjörður
POP 660

The village of Fáskrúðsfjörður, sometimes known as Búðir, was originally settled by French seamen who came to fish the Icelandic coast between the late 19th century and 1914. In a gesture to the local Gallic heritage, street signs are in both Icelandic and French. The French factor will be further highlighted in a new development for the town, in which the former French hospital and other buildings from that era will be renovated to include a hotel and restaurant. The anticipated opening date of **Franski spítalinn** (the French hospital) is in time for summer 2014.

The full story about the French seamen in Fáskrúðsfjörður can be found at **Fransmenn á Íslandi** (Les Français en Islande; Búðavegur 8; adult/child Ikr700/free; ⊗10am-6pm Jun-Aug), up the hill. The museum uses photographs and paperwork to paint a detailed picture of the interactions between the French and the locals – Icelanders would trade salted fish and the French offered red wine in return (go figure). The museum also has a quaint cafe, which serves a wonderful pie made from fresh rhubarb; the other speciality here is quiche Lorraine. Expect the museum to relocate to the new development when it opens.

At the mouth of the fjord, the island **Skrúður** contains lots of bird life, as well as a large multi-apartment 'puffin cave' – legend has it that it was once a giant's home.

Geologists may get a buzz from the laccolithic mountain **Sandfell** (743m), above the southern shore of Fáskrúðsfjörður, which was formed by molten rhyolite bursting through older lava layers. It's one of the world's finest examples of this sort of igneous intrusion (although Rio's Sugar Loaf Mountain is perhaps a mite more impressive). It's a two- to three-hour walk to the top.

Café Sumarlina (Búðavegur 59; mains Ikr1000-2500; ⊗10am-11pm Sun-Thu, to 3am Fri & Sat; 🖥), at the entrance to town, is a friendly little pub-bar in a creaking wooden house. Self-caterers can visit **Samkaup-Strax** (Skólavegur 59; ⊗10am-6pm Mon-Fri, to 2pm Sat).

Besides the **campsite** (sites per person Ikr1000) at the west end of the village, there's also the quirky **Hótel Bjarg** (☑475 1466; www.hotelbjarg.is; Skólavegur 49; d with/without bathroom incl breakfast €130/110; ⊗Jun-Aug), which feels like an orphanage for unwanted objets d'art. We like BandB Guesthouse (☏868 2687; elinhelgak99@gmail.com; Stekkholt 20; r without bathroom per person Ikr4900), high above town (take Skólavegur then Holtavegur), for its pine-fresh cosiness, sweet host Elín Helga and great views.

See p256 for bus information from Reyðarfjörður.

Stöðvarfjörður

POP 190

Even if geology makes you pass out from boredom, it's well worth stopping in at Steinasafn Petru (www.steinapetra.is; Fjarðarbraut 21; adult/child Ikr900/free; ☹9am-6pm). This exceptional stone collection was Petra Sveinsdóttir's lifelong labour of love. Inside her house, stones and minerals are piled from floor to ceiling – 70% of them are from the local area. They include unbelievably beautiful cubes of jasper, polished agate, purple amethyst, glowing creamy 'ghost stone', glittering quartz crystals…it's like opening a treasure chest. The garden is a wonderfully peaceful place, awash with more rocks, garden gnomes, and beachcombed flotsam and jetsam. Additional collections (including pens, matchboxes and taxidermy birds) show what an incredible hoarder Petra was!

Most people rush from town after seeing the stone show, but there are a few other distractions, including a handicrafts market (Fjarðarbraut 40; ☹11am-5pm Jun-Aug) at the 'Blue House'. Gallerí Snærós (Fjarðarbraut 42; ☹11am-5pm Jun–mid-Aug), one of the oldest galleries in rural Iceland, is the studio of two local artists who dabble in a variety of media.

There's a neat, unmanned campsite (sites per person Ikr1000) just east of the village, but we recommend Kirkjubær (☏892 3319; www.simnet.is/birgiral; Fjarðarbraut 37a; dm Ikr4000-5000), one of Iceland's more memorable lodging options. This tiny old church dates from 1925 but is now in private hands and has been renovated into a cute one-room hostel. The pulpit and altar are still there, and some of the pews are now part of the furniture. There's a full kitchen and bathroom, and the beds (mostly just mattresses) are on the upper mezzanine level. It supposedly sleeps 10, but that would be pretty cosy! We think the best option would be for a family or small group to hire the whole place out (Ikr16,000, excluding linen).

Birgir, the owner, lives in the yellow house below the church at Skolúbraut 1. It's worth asking about boat/fishing trips out onto the fjord.

There are modern rooms (comfy, if a little soulless) at the new guesthouse Saxa (☏511 3055; www.saxa.is; Fjarðarbraut 41; r Ikr16,000-29,600), a former supermarket (!) that also houses a weekend cafe. Across the street is Brekkan (Fjarðarbraut 44; meals Ikr650-1550; ☹9.30am-10pm Mon-Fri, 10am-10pm Sat, 11am-9pm Sun), the local chow house, serving up burgers and toasted sandwiches. There's a stack of groceries in the back.

See p256 for bus information from Reyðarfjörður.

Breiðdalsvík

POP 190

Fishing village Breiðdalsvík is beautifully sited at the end of Iceland's broadest valley, Breiðdalur. It's a quiet place – more a base for walking in the nearby hills and fishing the rivers and lakes than an attraction in itself.

Located in the centre of 'town' (and we're using that term lightly), Hótel Bláfell (☏475 6770; www.hotelblafell.is; Sólvellir 14; d incl breakfast Ikr21,900-26,900; ☏) has freshly furnished, monochrome rooms, free sauna for guests and a superb guest lounge with open fire. Don't be put off by the featureless decor of the restaurant – the summertime evening buffet is justifiably popular. Campers can pitch a tent at the free campsite out the back. Nearby, Kaupfjelagið (Sólvellir 23; ☹10.30am-5pm Jun-Aug) is a cafe and handicrafts store serving up pizzas to passing travellers with a side order of souvenirs. Breiðdalssetur (www.breiddalur.is; Ásvegí; ☹10.30am-6pm Jun-Aug) is a small museum/info centre.

Outside Breiðdalsvík, on Rte 96 heading back towards Stöðvarfjörður, German-owned Café Margret (☏475 6625; cafemargret@simnet.is; s/d incl breakfast €75/120; ☏) is an elegant boutique guesthouse built from Finnish pine. Its four cosy rooms feature quaint antiques and quilts. The attached restaurant (mains Ikr1900 to Ikr3500) is polished, and German-influenced dishes as well as delicious cakes offer a good excuse to stop by, despite the less-than-effusive welcome.

See p256 for bus information from Reyðarfjörður.

Breiðdalsvík to Djúpivogur

BREIÐDALUR

As the Ring Road returns to the coast it passes through the lovely Breiðdalur valley, nestled beneath colourful rhyolite peaks. **Odin Tours Iceland** (☑849 2009; www.odin toursiceland.com) offers horse-riding and hiking tours in the area, and farmhouse accommodation. **Strengir** (☑660 6890; www.strengir. com) brings anglers to the region's salmon-rich waters and runs a luxurious, year-round fishing lodge – see the website for details.

Once a school, **Hótel Staðarborg** (☑475 6760; www.stadarborg.is; s/d incl breakfast from Ikr13,900/18,600; @🛜) has neat, modern rooms, plus sauna and lake-fishing opportunities. Sleeping-bag accommodation is available (Ikr6000), as is dinner (Ikr4500), and campers are welcome. Staðarborg is 7km west of Breiðdalsvík on the Ring Road.

BERUFJÖRÐUR

South of Breiðdalur along the Ring Road is Berufjörður, a longish, steep-sided fjord flanked by rhyolite peaks. The southwestern shore is dominated by the obtrusive, pyramid-shaped mountain **Búlandstindur**, rising 1069m above the water. The westernmost ridge is known as Goðaborg or 'God's rock'. When Iceland officially converted to Christianity in 1000, locals are said to have carried their pagan images to the top of this mountain and thrown them off the cliff.

Around Berufjörður are several historical walking routes through the steeply rugged terrain. The best known of these climbs is from Berufjörður, the farm at the head of the fjord, and crosses the 700m Berufjarðarskarð into Breiðdalur.

TOP CHOICE **Berunes HI Hostel** (☑478 8988, 869 7227; www.berunes.is; dm/d without bathroom Ikr3800/10,000, cabins from Ikr18,000, incl breakfast; ☺Apr-Sep; @🛜) is on a 100-year-old farm with 'a good spirit', according to affable Ólafur, the owner. The wonderfully creaky old farmhouse has little rooms and alcoves, plus a kitchen and lounge; there are also rooms in the newer farmhouse, plus a campsite (sites per person Ikr1200), cottages and two motel-style units with made-up beds and private bathroom (double Ikr20,000). Breakfast (Ikr 1500) includes delicious home-made pancakes; there's also a summertime restaurant (or BYO food supplies for self-catering). Musicians are welcome to play the organ in the neighbouring 19th-century church. HI members get a discount of Ikr600, and linen costs Ikr1250. The hostel is 25km along the Ring Road south of Breiðdalsvík; buses between Egilsstaðir and Höfn stop here.

Djúpivogur

POP 460

This friendly fishing village, at the mouth of Berufjörður, gives summer visitors a flowery welcome. Its neat historic buildings, museum and small harbour are worth a look, but the main reason to visit is to catch the boat to Papey.

Djúpivogur (*dyoo*-pi-vor) is actually the oldest port in the Eastfjords – it's been around since the 16th century, when German merchants brought goods to trade. The last major excitement was in 1627: pirates from North Africa rowed ashore, plundering the village and nearby farms, and carrying away dozens of slaves.

WORTH A TRIP

PAPEY

The name of offshore island Papey (Friars' Island) suggests it was once a hermitage for the Irish monks who may have briefly inhabited Iceland before fleeing upon the arrival of the Norse. This small (2 sq km) and tranquil island was once a farm, but it's now inhabited only by sunbaking seals and nesting seabirds, including a huge puffin posse. Other highlights include the rock Kastali (The Castle), home to the local 'hidden people'; a lighthouse built in 1922; and Iceland's oldest and smallest wooden church (from 1807).

Papeyjarferðir (☑478 8838, 866 1353; www.djupivogur.is/papey; adult/child Ikr6500/3500) runs four-hour tours to the island, spotting wildlife en route and walking the island trails. Weather permitting, tours depart Djúpivogur harbour at 1pm daily from June to August. In fine weather this is a truly magical outing. Bring proper footwear – the island is boggy and wet year-round.

The town has good facilities (supermarket, bank, post office and swimming pool); you can pick up tourist brochures and a map inside Langabúð, or see www.djupivogar.is. Bird life in the area is prolific, and twitchers to the area should check out www.birds.is – it's not completely up to date, but has good general info.

◉ Sights & Activities

Some of the town's handsome wooden buildings date from the late 19th century. The oldest building, the long bright-red Langabúð, is a harbourside log warehouse dating from 1790, which now houses a coffee shop and an unusual local museum (adult/child Ikr500/300; ⊘10am-6pm Jun-Aug). Downstairs is a collection of works by renowned sculptor Rikarður Jónsson (1888–1977), ranging from lifelike busts of worthy Icelanders to mermaid-decorated mirrors and reliefs depicting saga characters. Upstairs, in the tar-smelling attic, is a collection of local-history artefacts.

The town is good for a wander – stop by the Bakkabuð (⊘10am-6pm Mon-Fri, noon-4pm Sat & Sun Jun-Aug) handicraft and design shop near Langabúð. Walk or drive down to the waterfront behind Langabuð and follow the road west to reach the intriguing public artwork Eggin í Gleðivík (The Eggs of Merry Bay), 34 oversized eggs along the jetty, each one representing a local bird. En route you'll pass a quirky little sculpture garden full of mineral rocks, bones and assorted flotsam and jetsam.

🛏 Sleeping & Eating

Hótel Framtíð   HOTEL €€
(📞478 8887; www.simnet.is/framtid; Vogaland 4; d with/without bathroom Ikr24,000/16,950; 🛜) This friendly hotel by the harbour is impressive for a village of this size. Although it's been around for a while (the original building was brought in pieces from Copenhagen in 1906), a newer wing adds modern fixtures to the mix, and there's an abundance of choice (plus bike hire): sleeping-bag accommodation (double Ikr9100), guesthouse rooms, timber-lined hotel rooms, four cute cottages sleeping up to four, or three newer apartments.

Framtíð's elegant restaurant (lunch Ikr1590 to Ikr2420, dinner mains Ikr4650 to Ikr5960) is easily the nicest option in town. Dinner of grilled lobster tails or roast lamb fillet hits the top end of the price-scale and the palate, but there are cheaper pizzas too (from Ikr2000).

Campsite   CAMPGROUND €
(sites per person Ikr1050) Behind the Við Voginn shop, this site is run by Hótel Framtíð, so cough up your pennies at the reception there. It's well equipped, with showers, cooking and laundry facilities.

Langabúð Kaffihús   CAFE €
(lunch Ikr1350-1590; ⊘10am-6pm Sun-Thu, to 11pm Sat & Sun Jun-Aug) The busy cafe inside Langabúð has a suitably old-world atmosphere, and serves cakes, soup and home-made bread.

Við Voginn   GRILL €
(Vogaland 2; mains from Ikr950; ⊘9am-9pm Mon-Fri, 10am-9pm Sat & Sun) A fast-food joint with an attached grocery store, Við Voginn is popular with locals and tourists on the run.

Samkaup-Strax   SUPERMARKET €
(Búland 2; ⊘10am-6pm Mon-Fri, to 4pm Sat, noon-4pm Sun) On the main road into town you'll find a Samkaup-Strax supermarket with a Vín Búð (⊘5-6pm Mon-Thu, 4-6pm Fri) attached.

ℹ Getting There & Away

The summer buses that run between Egilsstaðir and Höfn stop in town (see p239).

Southeast Iceland

Best Places to Eat

» Humarhöfnin (p281)
» Pakkhús (p281)
» Systrakaffi (p267)
» Jöklasel (p282)
» Þórbergssetur (p278)

Best Places to Stay

» Hrífunes (p268)
» Guesthouse Dyngja (p280)
» Viking Cafe (p283)
» Árnanes Country Lodge (p280)

Why Go?

The 200km stretch of Ring Road from Kirkjubæjarklaustur to Höfn is truly mind-blowing, transporting you across vast deltas of grey glacial sand, past lost-looking farms, around the toes of craggy mountains, and by glacier tongues and ice-filled lagoons. The only thing you won't pass is a town.

The mighty Vatnajökull dominates the region, its huge rivers of frozen ice pouring down steep-sided valleys towards the sea. Jökulsárlón is a photographer's paradise, a glacial lagoon where wind and water sculpt icebergs into fantastical shapes.

The bleak coastal deserts of glacial sand are remnants of calamitous collisions between fire and ice. Further inland is the epicentre of Iceland's worst volcanic event, the Lakagígar fissures. With so much desolation on display, it's not surprising that Skaftafell is so popular. This sheltered enclave between the glaciers and the sands throbs with life and colour, and the footfall of hikers.

Road Distances (km)

	Höfn	Reykjavík	Jökulsárlón	Skaftafell
Reykjavík	459			
Jökulsárlón	79	378		
Skaftafell	135	323	57	
Kirkjubæjarklaustur	200	257	122	69

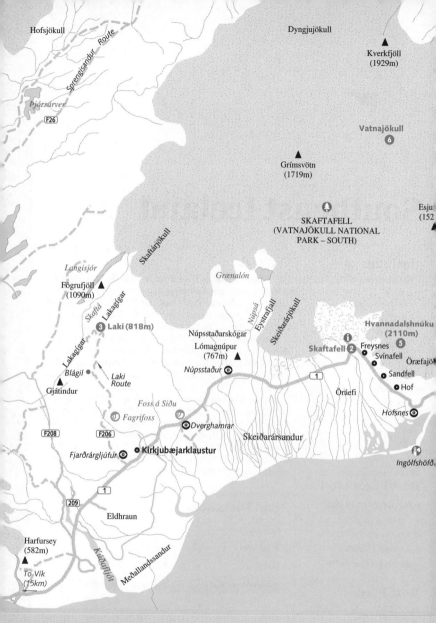

Southeast Iceland Highlights

1 Admire the ever-changing ice sculptures at the bewitching lagoon **Jökulsárlón** (p277)

2 Visit Iceland's favourite national-park pocket, **Skaftafell** (p272), an area of green and lovely life amid the vast sand deltas

3 Stride up **Laki** (p269) for views of three glaciers... and unbelievable volcanic devastation

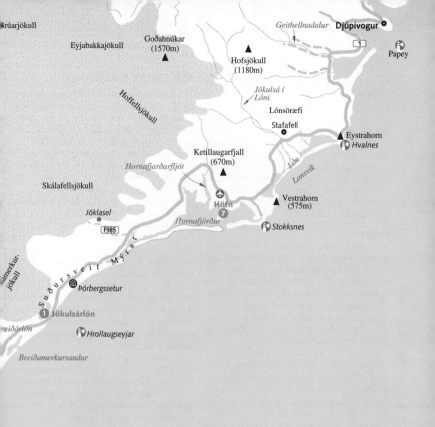

Brúarjökull

Eyjabakkajökull

Goðahnúkar
(1570m)
▲

Geithellnadalur **Djúpivogur** ⊙

Hofsjökull
(1180m)
▲

①

Papey ⊙

Hoffellsjökull

*Jökulsá í
Lóni*

Lónsöræfi

Stafafell ⊙

Eystrahorn ▲
Hvalnes

Ketillaugarfjall
(670m)
▲

Hornafjarðarfljót

Skálafellsjökull

Lón

Lónsvík

Jöklasel

Höfn ✈
⑦

Vestrahorn ▲
(575m)

F985

Hornafjörður

Stokksnes

amerkur-
jökull

S u ð u r s v e i t   M ý r a r

Þórbergssetur 🏛

① Jökulsárlón

eiðárlón

Hrollaugseyjar

Breiðamerkursandur

Ⓝ 0 ———————— 50 km
  0 ———————— 25 miles

N O R T H

A T L A N T I C

O C E A N

④ Don crampons for an easy
but exhilarating **glacier walk**
(p273)

⑤ Rise above all others by
scaling Iceland's highest peak,
Hvannadalshnúkur (p275)

⑥ Try to wipe the smile off
your face as you roar across
the **Vatnajökull ice cap**
(p282) on a snowmobile

⑦ Sample the delicious
seafood treats netted by
the local fishing fleet in the
restaurants of **Höfn** (p281)

Kirkjubæjarklaustur

POP 120

Many a foreign tongue has been tied in knots trying to say Kirkjubæjarklaustur. It helps to break it into bits: *Kirkju* (church), *bæjar* (farm) and *klaustur* (convent). Otherwise, do as the locals do and call it 'Klaustur' (pronounced like 'cloister').

Klaustur is tiny, even by Icelandic standards – a few houses and farms scattered across a brilliant-green backdrop. Still, it's the only real service town between Vík and Höfn, and it's a major crossroads to several dramatic spots in the interior: Landmannalaugar and Laki.

History

According to the *Landnámabók* (a comprehensive account of Norse settlement), this tranquil village situated between the cliffs and the river Skaftá was first settled by Irish monks *(papar)* before the Vikings arrived. Originally, it was known as Kirkjubær; the 'klaustur' bit was added in 1186 when a convent of Benedictine nuns was founded (near the modern-day church).

During the devastating Laki eruptions that occurred in the late 18th century, this area suffered greatly and, west of Kirkjubæjarklaustur, you can see ruins of farms abandoned or destroyed by the lava stream. The lava field, called Eldhraun, averages 12m thick. It contains over 12 cu km of lava and covers an area of 565 sq km, making it the world's largest recorded lava flow from a single eruption.

◎ Sights & Activities

The basalt columns of **Kirkjugólf** (Church Floor), smoothed down and cemented with moss, were once mistaken for an old church floor rather than a work of nature, and it's easy to see why. The honeycombed slab lies in a field about 400m northwest of the N1 petrol station (a path leads to it from beside the information board, or drive down Rte 203, where there's another gate).

Religious connections are particularly strong in this area. The prominent rock pillar **Systrastapi** (Sisters' Pillar), near the line of cliffs west of town, marks the spot where two nuns were reputedly executed and buried for sleeping with the devil and such other no-nos.

At the western end of the village, a lovely double waterfall, **Systrafoss**, tumbles down the cliffs via the Bæjargil ravine. The lake **Systravatn**, a short and pleasant saunter up the cliffs above the falls, was once a bathing place for nuns.

Steingrímsson Memorial Chapel, the triangular, distinctly atypical wood-and-stone chapel on Klausturvegur, was consecrated in 1974. It commemorates Jón Steingrímsson's Eldmessa (Fire Sermon), which 'saved' the town from lava on 20 July 1783.

ⓘ VATNAJÖKULL NATIONAL PARK

Vatnajökull is the world's largest ice cap outside the poles. At 8100 sq km, it's more than three times the size of Luxembourg, and it reaches a thickness of almost 1km (with an average of between 400m and 600m). Under this enormous blanket of ice lie countless peaks and valleys, including a number of live volcanoes and subglacial lakes, plus Iceland's highest point – the 2110m mountain Hvannadalshnúkur.

Huge glaciers, pleated with crevasses, flow down from the centre of Vatnajökull. The best known is probably Skaftafellsjökull, a relatively small glacier that ends within 1.5km of the campsite at Skaftafell. Another famous beauty is Breiðamerkurjökull, which crumbles into icebergs at the breathtaking Jökulsárlón lagoon.

Vatnajökull National Park was founded in 2008, joining the ice cap and the former Skaftafell and Jökulsárgljúfur national parks to form one giant megapark. With recent additions, the park now measures 13,600 sq km – 13% of the entire country. Within its boundaries lies a staggering richness of landscapes, created by the combined forces of rivers, glacial ice, and volcanic and geothermal activity.

There are major park visitor centres at Skaftafell in the south, Jökulsárgljúfur (Ásbyrgi, p231) in the north and Snæfellsstofa (p246) in the east. In the southeast, tourist information centres at Höfn and Kirkjubæjarklaustur work in conjunction with the park.

The best websites for visitors planning a visit to the southern area of the park are **Vatnajökull National Park** (www.vjp.is) and **Visit Vatnajökull** (www.visitvatnajokull.is).

HELLFIRE & BRIMSTONE

The 18th-century eruptions of the volcano Laki brought death and devastation to much of southeastern Iceland, especially Kirkjubæjarklaustur. On 20 July 1783, a particularly fast-moving river of molten lava threatened to engulf the town.

The pastor Jón Steingrímsson, convinced it was due to the wickedness of his flock, gathered the terrified parishioners in the church. There he delivered a passionate hellfire-and-brimstone sermon while the appropriate special effects steamed and smoked outside. By the time the oratory ended, the flow had stopped at a rock promontory – now called Eldmessutangi (Fire Sermon Point) – just short of the town. The grateful residents credited their good reverend with some particularly effective string-pulling on their behalf.

South of the Ring Road is a vast pseudo-crater field known as **Landbrotshólar**. It was formed during the Laki eruptions of 1783, when lava poured over marshland and fast-evaporating steam exploded through to make these barrow-like mounds.

🐾 Tours

Hólasport   JEEP
(📞660 1151; www.holasport.is; ⏱May-Oct) Based at Hótel Laki, just south of Klaustur, Hólasport offers a fun program of super-Jeep tours (full-day tour to Laki for Ikr28,500, or shorter trips into mountains or down to black-sand beaches from Ikr13,500). There are also quad-bike options.

Slóðir   WALKING
(📞852 2012; www.slodir.is; ⏱mid-Jul–mid-Aug) A trio of knowledgeable biologists guides walks with commentary about the geology and history of the area (two-hour evening walk Ikr2000, day trip along sheep-grazing trails Ikr10,000).

Flandur Trips   JEEP, WALKING
(📞899 8767; www.flandur.is) Personalised jeep and/or walking tours of the local wilderness for up to four people (half-/full day from Ikr16,600/28,800) operate year-round.

🛏 Sleeping & Eating

Klausturhof   GUESTHOUSE €
(📞567 7600; www.klausturhof.is; Klausturvegur 1-5; dm Ikr3800-4300, d with/without bathroom Ikr16,200/13,500; 🛜) With pretty Systrafoss waterfall as its neighbour, this bright new complex offers an assortment of compact rooms at reasonable prices, plus guest kitchen and an on-site cafe. Room prices listed are for made-up beds; BYO sleeping bag to save money.

Kirkjubæ II   CAMPGROUND €
(📞894 4495; www.kirkjubaer.com; sites per person Ikr1100; ⏱Jun-Sep) Neat green site with sheltering hedges, right in town. Good facilities include kitchen, hot showers and laundry.

Icelandair Hótel Klaustur   HOTEL €€
(📞487 4900; www.icelandairhotels.is; Klausturvegur 6; d from Ikr27,600; ⏱closed mid-Dec–mid-Jan; 🛜) The Klaustur has sweet management and attractive business-hotel decor, plus a sunny enclosed dining terrace and bar-lounge. The restaurant menu features well-prepared Icelandic mains.

Kleifar   CAMPGROUND €
(sites per person Ikr800; ⏱Jun-Aug) There's a second, very basic campsite (toilets and running water) 1.5km along Rte 203 (signposted towards Geirland), scenically situated by a waterfall.

Systrakaffi   INTERNATIONAL €€
(www.systrakaffi.is; Klausturvegur 12; mains Ikr900-3600; ⏱noon-10pm Jun-Aug, 6-10pm mid-Apr–May & Sep) The liveliest place in town is this beloved cafe-bar. Its varied menu offers pizzas and burgers but plays favourites with local trout and lamb.

Kaffi Munkar   CAFE €€
(Klausturvegur 1-5; mains Ikr1250-3200; ⏱8am-9pm) At the western end of town, Kaffi Munkar is the bright cafe-reception of Klausturhof guesthouse. Pop in for breakfast, or for a plentiful serve of fish stew.

Skaftárskáli   GRILL €
(Rte 1; ⏱8.30am-9pm) For a quick bite, there's the all-day grill-bar at the N1.

Kjarval   SUPERMARKET €
(Klausturvegur 13; ⏱9am-8pm Jun-Aug, 10am-6pm Mon-Fri, 10am-2pm Sat Sep-May) For self-caterers. There's a bank and post office next door.

❶ Information

The **tourist office** (📞487 4620; www.klaustur. is; Klausturvegur 10; ⏰9am-7pm Mon-Fri, 10am-6pm Sat & Sun Jun-Aug, 10am-6pm daily 1-15 Sep) is inside the local visitor centre, Skaftársto-fa, with local info plus coverage of Katla Geopark and Vatnajökull National Park, and a short film on the Laki eruption.

❶ Getting There & Away

Klaustur is a stop on all Reykjavík–Höfn bus routes and it also serves as a crossroads to Landmannalaugar and Laki. Buses stop at the N1.

Sterna (📞551 1166; www.sterna.is) runs a Reykjavík–Höfn service (bus 12/12a) once daily from mid-May to mid-September. Reykjavík–Klaustur costs Ikr8100 (5¼ hours).

Strætó (📞540 2700; www.straeto.is) has a Reykjavík–Höfn service (bus 51) twice daily from June to August, dropping to three times a week in winter (with a need to prebook). Reykjavík–Klaustur costs Ikr5950.

Reykjavík Excursions (Kynnisferðir; 📞580 5400; www.re.is) services:

BUS 10/10A Skaftafell–Klaustur–Eldgjá–Landmannalaugar; once daily mid-June to mid-September. Can be used as a day tour, or as regular transport. Klaustur–Landmannalaugar costs Ikr5200.

BUS 16/16A Skaftafell–Laki; once daily July to mid-September. Used as a tour from Skaftafell or Klaustur, with four hours at Laki. Cost from Klaustur Ikr10,400.

BUS 20/20A Reykjavík–Skaftafell; once daily June to mid-September, with lengthy pauses at south-coast towns. From Skaftafell there are buses further east.

Around Kirkjubæjarklaustur

◉ Sights

Fjaðrárgljúfur   CANYON

This darkly picturesque canyon, carved out by the river Fjaðrá, is a humbling two million years old. A walking track follows its southern edge for a couple of kilometres, and there are plenty of places to gaze down into its rocky, writhing depths.

The canyon is 3.5km north of the Ring Road; you can walk there across lava fields or drive along Rte 206 (take the left fork at the sign for Laki). You'll reach the canyon before it becomes an F road.

Foss á Síðu & Dverghamrar   WATERFALL

Foss á Síðu, 11km east of Kirkjubæjarklaustur, is a head-turning waterfall that normally tumbles down from the cliffs. During especially strong sea winds, however, it actually goes straight up! Opposite the falls is the outcrop Dverghamrar ('Dwarf Cliffs'), which contains classic basalt columns and is thought to be the dwelling place of some of Iceland's 'hidden people'.

🛏 Sleeping & Eating

There's plentiful rural accommodation in the area around Kirkjubæjarklaustur.

Hörgsland   CAMPGROUND, COTTAGES €

(📞487 6655; www.horgsland.is; sites per person Ikr1000, cottages for 2/6 Ikr13,500/25,500, guesthouse d with/without bathroom incl breakfast Ikr19,000/16,000) On the Ring Road about 8km northeast of Klaustur is this mini village of spotless, spacious, self-contained cottages that can sleep at least six. A recent addition is a block of spic-and-span guesthouse rooms. There's also camping, plus outdoor hot-pots, and a simple shop and cafe serving breakfast and dinner.

Hótel Laki   COUNTRY HOTEL €€

(📞487 4694; www.hotellaki.is; d incl breakfast from €195; 🐾) What started as farmhouse accommodation has grown into a sprawling 64-room hotel, on farmland 5km south of Klaustur on Rte 204. As well as comfortable hotel rooms, there are family-sized self-contained cottages, plus a nine-hole golf course, quad-bike and super-Jeep tours (see p267), hot-pot, restaurant and lake fishing.

🏆 TOP CHOICE Hrífunes   GUESTHOUSE €€

(📞863 5540; www.hrifunesguesthouse.is; d with/without bathroom incl breakfast Ikr24,000/19,000; ⏰Jun–mid-Sep; 🐾) On Rte 209, 7km off the Ring Road halfway between Kirkjubæjarklaustur and Vík, is this delightful guesthouse, in an old community house revived with flair (country farmhouse chic plus stunning photos taken by the owner, who runs photography tours). There's a guest kitchen (in a second house), cosy lounge and delicious two-/three-course dinners for Ikr4200/5200. Off-season the guesthouse opens for small groups (minimum four), or you can rent the whole house.

Lakagígar

It's almost impossible to comprehend the immensity of the Laki eruptions, one of the most catastrophic volcanic events in human history.

In the spring of 1783, a vast set of fissures opened, forming around 135 craters that took it in turns to fountain molten rock up to 1km into the air. These Skaftáreldar (River Skaftá Fires) lasted for eight months, spewing out more than 30 billion tonnes of lava, which covered an area of 500 sq km in a layer up to 19km thick. Fifty farms in the region were wiped out.

Far more devastating were the hundreds of millions of tonnes of ash and sulphuric acid that poured from the fissures. The sun was blotted out, the grass died off, and around two-thirds of Iceland's livestock died from starvation and poisoning. Some 9000 people – a fifth of the country – were killed and the remainder faced the Móðuharðindi (Haze Famine) that followed.

The damage wasn't limited to Iceland, either. All across the northern hemisphere, clouds of ash blocked out the sun. Temperatures dropped and acid rain fell from the sky, causing devastating crop failures in Japan, Alaska and Europe (possibly even helping to spark the French Revolution).

Nowadays the lava field belies the apocalypse that spawned it some 230 years ago. Its black, twisted lava formations are overgrown with soft green moss.

The Lakagígar area is contained within the boundaries of Vatnajökull National Park (www.vjp.is). In peak season (mid-July to mid-August), rangers are available at the Laki car park from 11am to 3pm. A new interpretive trail has been established over a gentle 500m walk – pick up the accompanying brochure (or download it) for insight into the fascinating history, geology and biology of the area. You should stick to the paths in this ecologically sensitive region.

Camping is forbidden within the Laki reserve. The nearest campsite, with a toilet and fresh water, is at Blágil, about 11km from Laki. There have been plans mooted to build an information centre and cabins at Galti, but these have been under discussion for quite some time. Check the national park website for the latest.

🚗 Tours

Hólasport JEEP
(☏660 1151; www.holasport.is) Based at Hótel Laki, just south of Kirkjubæjarklaustur, Hólasport offers super-Jeep day tours to Laki (Ikr28,500) from June until the end of September.

Reykjavík Excursions WALKING
(Kynnisferðir; ☏580 5400; www.re.is) The full-day tour breaks for around four hours of walking in the crater area. It departs daily from July to mid-September, at 8am from Skaftafell (Ikr13,800) and at 9am from the N1 at Kirkjubæjarklaustur (Ikr10,400). Bring a packed lunch.

❶ Getting There & Away

Rte F206 (just west of Kirkjubæjarklaustur) is generally passable from mid-June to mid-September (check on www.vegagerdin.is). It's a long, rugged 50km to the Lakagígar crater row. The road is unsuitable for 2WD cars, as there are several rivers to ford. Even low-clearance 4WD vehicles may not be suitable in the spring thaw or after rain, when the rivers tend to run deep. Consider joining a tour if your car is unsuitable.

LAKI

Although the peak called Laki (818m) is extinct, it has loaned its name to the still-volatile, 25km-long Lakagígar crater row, which stretches northeastward and southwestward from its base. Laki can be climbed in about 40 minutes from the parking area, and we highly recommend it. From the top there are boundless 360-degree views of the active fissure, vast lava fields and glinting ice-white glaciers in the distance.

LAKAGÍGAR CRATER ROW

The crater row is fascinating to explore, riddled with black sand dunes and lava tubes, many of which contain tiny stalactites. At the foot of Laki, marked walking paths lead you in and out of the two nearest craters, including an interesting lava tunnel. Another cave, two hours' walk south of the Laki parking area, shelters a mysterious lake.

FAGRIFOSS

Fagrifoss (Beautiful Falls) is not a misnomer: this waterfall must be one of Iceland's most bewitching, with rivulets of water pouring over a massive black rock. You'll come to the turn-off on the way to Laki, about 24km along the F206. Tours to Lakagígar invariably stop here.

The Sandar

The sandar are soul-destroyingly flat and empty regions sprawling along Iceland's southeastern coast. High in the mountains, glaciers scrape up silt, sand and gravel that is then carried by glacial rivers or (more dramatically) by glacial bursts down to the coast and dumped in huge, desert-like plains. The sandar here are so impressively huge and awful that the Icelandic word (singular: sandur) is used internationally to describe this topographic phenomenon.

Skeiðarársandur is the most visible and dramatic, stretching some 40km between ice cap and coast from Núpsstaður to Öræfi. Here you'll encounter a flat expanse of grey-black sands, fierce scouring winds (a cyclist's nightmare) and fast-flowing grey-brown glacial rivers.

Formerly an HI-affiliated hostel, **Hvoll Guesthouse** (487 4785; www.road201.is; d without bathroom from Ikr14,300; mid-Mar–Oct), also known as Road 201, is on the edge of Skeiðarársandur (3.5km south off the Ring Road via a gravel road) and feels very remote despite its large size. There's a busy atmosphere; facilities include several kitchens (bring food – the closest supermarket is 25km away in Klaustur) and a laundry. Downside: no internet or wi-fi. Sleeping-bag doubles cost Ikr11,800; breakfast is available in summer for Ikr1600. It makes an excellent base for exploring Skaftafell and the surrounding sandar. Scheduled passing buses should be able to stop at the Ring Road turn-off.

Just west of Hvoll, **Islandia Hotel Núpar** (517 3060; www.islandiahotel.is; s/d incl breakfast €150/175; mid-May–mid-Sep) offers modern, minimalist rooms, many with good views, and a somewhat soulless restaurant serving buffet dinner.

MEÐALLANDSSANDUR

This region spreads across the Meðalland district south of Eldhraun and east of the river Kúðafljót. The sandy desert is so flat and featureless that a number of ships have run aground on its coast, apparently unaware they were nearing land. Shipwrecked sailors have died in quicksand while trying to get ashore. There are now several small lighthouses along the coast.

SKEIÐARÁRSANDUR

Skeiðarársandur, the largest sandur in the world, covers a 1000-sq-km area and was formed by the mighty Skeiðarárjökull. Since the Settlement Era, Skeiðarársandur has swallowed a considerable amount of farmland and it continues to grow. The area was relatively well populated (for Iceland, anyway), but in 1362 the volcano Öræfi beneath Öræfajökull erupted and the subsequent *jökulhlaup* (flooding caused by volcanic eruption beneath an icecap) laid waste the entire district.

The section of Ring Road that passes across Skeiðarársandur was the last bit of the national highway to be constructed – as recently as 1974 (until then, Höfnites had to drive to Reykjavík via Akureyri). Long gravel dykes have been strategically positioned to channel floodwaters away from this highly susceptible artery. They did little good, however, when in late 1996 three Ring Road bridges were washed away like matchsticks by the massive *jökulhlaup* released by the Grímsvötn (or Gjálp) eruption. There's a memorial of twisted bridge girders and an information board along the Ring Road just west of Skaftafell.

The sands are a major breeding area for great skuas – particularly appropriate birds for such a harsh region.

HOW TO AVOID BEING SKUA-ED

The great sandur regions on Iceland's southern coast are the world's largest breeding ground for great skuas (*Stercorarius skua* in Latin, *skúmur* in Icelandic). These large, meaty, dirty-brown birds with white-patched wings tend to build their nests among grassy tufts in the ashy sand. You'll often see them harassing gulls into disgorging their dinner, killing and eating puffins and other little birds, or swooping down on YOU if you get too close to their nests.

Thankfully (unlike feather-brained Arctic terns), skuas will stop plaguing you if you run away from the area they're trying to defend. You can also avoid aerial strikes by wearing a hat or carrying a stick above your head.

JÖKULHLAUP!

In late 1996 the devastating Grímsvötn eruption – Iceland's fourth largest of the 20th century, after Katla in 1918, Hekla in 1947 and Surtsey in 1963 – shook southeast Iceland and caused an awesome *jökulhlaup* (glacial flood) across Skeiðarársandur. The events leading up to it are a sobering reminder of Iceland's volatile fire-and-ice combination.

On the morning of 29 September 1996, a magnitude 5.0 earthquake shook the Vatnajökull ice cap. Magma from a new volcano, in the Grímsvötn region beneath Vatnajökull, had made its way through the earth's crust and into the ice, causing the eruption of a 4km-long subsurface fissure known as Gjálp. The following day the eruption burst through the surface, ejecting a column of steam that rose 10km into the sky.

Scientists became concerned as the subglacial lake in the Grímsvötn caldera began to fill with water from ice melted by the eruption. Initial predictions on 3 October were that the ice would lift and the lake would spill out across Skeiðarársandur, threatening the Ring Road and its bridges. In the hope of diverting floodwaters away from the bridges, massive dyke-building projects were organised on Skeiðarársandur.

On 5 November, over a month after the eruption started, the ice *did* lift and the Grímsvötn reservoir drained in a massive *jökulhlaup*, releasing up to 3000 billion litres of water within a few hours. The floodwaters – dragging along icebergs the size of three-storey buildings – destroyed the 375m-long Gígjukvísl Bridge and the 900m-long Skeiðará Bridge, both on the Skeiðarársandur. See video footage of the eruption and enormous multi-tonne blocks of ice being hurled across Skeiðarársandur at the Skaftafell visitor centre.

Some other of Grímsvötn's creations include the Ásbyrgi canyon (p232), gouged out by a cataclysmic flood over just a few days. In 1934 an eruption released a *jökulhlaup* of 40,000 cu metres per second, which swelled the river Skeiðará to 9km in width and laid waste to large areas of farmland.

Grímsvötn erupted again in December 1998, November 2004 and most recently in May 2011, when a huge ash plume was released into the atmosphere, disrupting air traffic (but with nowhere near the disruption caused by 2010's Eyjafjallajökull eruption). There was no *jökulhlaup* on any of these three occasions.

NÚPSSTAÐUR & NÚPSSTAÐARSKÓGAR

Bizarrely eroded cliffs and pinnacles tower over the impossibly photogenic old turf-roofed farm at Núpsstaður. The farm buildings date back to the early 19th century, and the idyllic chapel is one of the last turf churches in Iceland. At the time of research the farm was closed to the public (you can't drive onto the property, but you can walk up to it), but is expected to open again perhaps in 2014. Hvoll Guesthouse (☏487 4785) is your best source for information on its status.

Inland is Núpsstaðarskógar, a beautiful woodland area on the slopes of the mountain Eystrafjall. Due to the perils of crossing the Núpsá river, this area is best explored on a tour.

In July and August, Icelandic Mountain Guides (☏587 9999; www.mountainguide.is)

runs a guided four-day (60km) hike through Núpsstaðarskógar, over to Grænalón lagoon, across the glacier Skeiðarárjökull and then into Morsárdalur in Skaftafell. The trip costs from Ikr99,000 with food, camping gear, glacier equipment and transport from Skaftafell included.

GRÆNALÓN

From the southern end of Núpsstaðarskógar, a good two-day hike will take you over the ridges and valleys west of immense Skeiðarárjökull to Grænalón. This ice-dammed marginal lake has the ability to drain like a bathtub. The 'plug' is the western edge of Skeiðarárjökull; when the water pressure builds to breaking point, the glacier is lifted and the lake lets go.

To get there you'll have to join the Icelandic Mountain Guides' Núpsstaðarskógar–Skaftafell tour, as it's impossible to cross the Núpsá and Súlaá rivers on foot.

Skaftafell (Vatnajökull National Park – South)

Skaftafell, the jewel in the crown of Vatnajökull National Park, encompasses a breathtaking collection of peaks and glaciers. It's the country's favourite wilderness: 170,000 visitors per year come to marvel at thundering waterfalls, twisted birch woods, the tangled web of rivers threading across the sandar, and brilliant blue-white Vatnajökull with its lurching tongues of ice.

Skaftafell deserves its reputation, and few Icelanders – even those who usually shun the great outdoors – can resist it. On long summer weekends, all of Reykjavík (including the city's raucous all-night parties) seems to descend on it. However, if you're prepared to get out on the more-remote trails and take advantage of the fabulous hiking on the heath and beyond, you'll leave the crowds far behind.

All flora, fauna and natural features of the park are protected, open fires are prohibited and rubbish must be carried out. In the busy area around Skaftafellsheiði, stick to the tracks to avoiding damaging delicate plant life.

Don't get too close to glaciers or climb on them without the proper equipment and training – the average ice-block calving off Skaftafellsjökull would crush anyone within a few metres of the face.

There's very little accommodation close to the park, so you'll need either a tent or a firm hotel booking if you want to explore the park properly.

History

The historical Skaftafell was a large farm at the foot of the hills west of the present campsite. Shifting glacial sands slowly buried the fields and forced the farm to be moved to a more suitable site, on the heath 100m above the sandur. The district came to be known as Hérað Milli Sandur (Land Between the Sands), but after all the farms were annihilated by the 1362 eruptions, the district became the 'land under the sands' and was renamed Öræfi (Wasteland). Once the vegetation returned, however, the Skaftafell farm was rebuilt in its former location.

Skaftafell National Park was founded in 1967 by the Icelandic Government and the WWF. In June 2008 it was merged with the Jökulsárgljúfur National Park in Iceland's

north to form the massive wilderness area of Vatnajökull National Park.

Activities

There is now a path where mountain biking is permitted. The trail follows a 13km route that crosses the dry riverbed of Skeiðará and travels through Morsárdalur to the woods at Bæjarstaðarskógur.

Glacier Guides (☑571 2100; www.glacier guides.is), with a booking centre at Skaftafell (by the visitor centre), offers independent mountain-bike rental (two/seven/24 hours Ikr1000/6000/7500), and leads a cycling tour ('Skaftafell on Wheels') taking in the trail and a forest walk. The six-hour tour runs four times a week from mid-May to mid-September (Ikr15,990).

Skaftafell is ideal for day hikes and also offers longer hikes through its wilderness regions. Most of Skaftafell's visitors keep to the popular routes on Skaftafellsheiði. Hiking in other accessible areas, such as upper Morsárdalur and Kjós, requires more time, motivation and planning.

Wild-camping is not allowed in the park. Compulsory camping permits (free) for Kjós are available from the information centre. Also enquire about river crossings along your intended route.

Other possibilities for hikes include the long day trip beyond Bæjarstaðarskógur into the rugged Skaftafellsfjöll. A recommended destination is the 862m-high summit of the Jökulfell ridge, which affords a commanding view of the vast expanses of Skeiðarárjökull. Even better is an excursion into the Kjós region.

We recommend asking at the visitor centre for the best map – many options are a little out of date and haven't kept up with the changes this area has undergone since the creation of the new national park. The park itself produces good maps outlining shorter hiking trails (Ikr250 to Ikr350), and stocks larger topo maps from various publishers.

Note that from mid-June to mid-August, rangers guide free daily interpretive walks that depart from the visitor centre – a great way to learn about the area. Check the website, or ask staff.

SVARTIFOSS

Star of a hundred postcards, Svartifoss (Black Falls) is a gloomy waterfall flanked by black basalt columns. It's reached by an easy 1.8km trail leading up from the visitor centre via the campsite (about 1½ hours return).

From Svartifoss, it's worth continuing west up the track to Sjónarsker, where there's a view disc and an unforgettable view across Skeiðarársandur. From here you can visit the traditional turf-roofed farmhouse Sel; this 2½-hour return walk is classified easy. Alternatively, from Svartifoss head east to the viewpoint at Sjónarnípa, looking across Skaftafellsjökull. This walk is classified as challenging; allow three hours return.

SKAFTAFELLSJÖKULL
Another popular trail is the easy one-hour return walk to Skaftafellsjökull. The sealed, marked trail (3.7km) begins at the visitor centre and leads to the glacier face, where you can witness the bumps and groans of the ice (although the glacier is pretty grey and gritty here). The glacier has receded greatly in recent decades, meaning land along this trail has been gradually reappearing. Pick up a brochure that describes the geology of the trail.

SKAFTAFELLSHEIÐI LOOP
On a fine day, the five- to six-hour (15.5km) walk around Skaftafellsheiði is a hiker's dream. It begins by climbing from the campsite past Svartifoss and Sjónarsker, continuing across the moor to 610m-high Fremrihnaukur. From there it follows the edge of the plateau to the next rise, Nyrðrihnaukur (706m), which affords a superb view of Morsárdalur, Morsárjökull and the iceberg-choked lagoon at its base. At this point the track turns southeast to an outlook point on the cliff above Skaftafellsjökull (Gláma).

For the best view of Skaftafellsjökull, Morsárdalur and the Skeiðarársandur, it's worth scaling the summit of Kristínartindar (1126m). The best way follows a well-marked 2km route (classified difficult) up the prominent valley southeast of the Nyrðrihnaukur lookout, and back down near Gláma.

MORSÁRDALUR & BÆJARSTAÐARSKÓGUR
The seven-hour hike (20.6km return) from the campsite to the glacial lake in Morsárdalur is fairly ordinary but enjoyable. Alternatively, cross the Morsá at the foot of Skaftafellsheiði and make your way across the gravel riverbed to the birch woods at Bæjarstaðarskógur. The trees here reach a whopping (for Iceland) 12m, and 80°C springs flow into the tiny but heavenly Heitulækir to the west in Vestragil. The return walk to Bæjarstaðarskógur takes about six

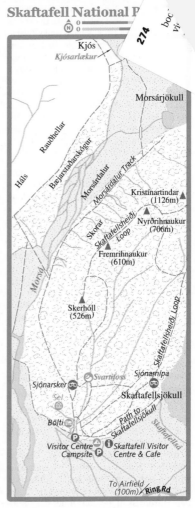

hours (13km return); add on an extra hour to visit Heitulækir.

Tours
The highlight of a visit to Skaftafell is a glacier hike. It's utterly liberating to strap on crampons and stride up a glacier, and there's much to see on the ice: waterfalls, ice caves, glacial mice (moss balls, not actual mice!) and different-coloured ash from ancient explosions.

A number of guides operate in the area. The largest companies, Icelandic Mountain Guides and Glacier Guides, have info and

.ing huts in the car park at Skaftafell ..tor centre, where you can talk to experts ..id get kitted out for glacier walks (warm clothes and hiking boots essential, waterproof gear available for hire). Both companies go further than just easy glacier hikes, offering more-challenging options and ice climbs, right up to summiting Iceland's highest peak. Both offer combos, such as a glacier hike plus Jökulsárlón boat trip or Ingólfshöfði visit. They also pick up from Svínafell campsite and Fosshótel Skaftafell. See the websites for loads of suggestions.

Icelandic Mountain Guides ADVENTURE TOUR
(☑Reykjavík 587 9999, Skaftafell 894 2959, 478 2559; www.mountainguide.is) This long-running operator has highly trained guides leading a range of glacier hikes. Its bestselling walk is the family-friendly 'Blue Ice Experience', with 1½ to two hours spent on the ice at Svínafellsjökull (adult/child Ikr7200/4600, minimum age eight years). These tours run from Skaftafell up to four times daily from March to October, and there are also scheduled Christmas trips. There are longer, tougher walks up the same glacier (from three to 6½ hours).

See the website for IMG's impressive program of multiday cycling, hiking and super-Jeep tours, including a five-day 'Rivers and Glaciers of Vatnajökull' backpacking trip.

Glacier Guides ADVENTURE TOUR
(☑571 2100; www.glacierguides.is) As well as glacier walks of varying duration and difficulty, Glacier Guides also offers rock climbing and mountain biking from Skaftafell.

Its beginner-level walk is family-friendly 'Glacier Wonders', a 2½-hour tour with a stroll up Falljökull (adult/child Ikr7500/5500, minimum age 10 years); trips depart from Skaftafell four times daily mid-May to mid-September. There's also a tougher five-hour walk up the same glacier (per person Ikr11,500, minimum age 15 years).

Local Guide ADVENTURE TOUR
(Öræfaferðir; ☑894 0894; www.localguide.is) There's no physical presence at Skaftafell visitor centre, but this family-run company, based at the farm Hofsnes, offers year-round glacier hikes, ice climbs and cross-country ski tours, plus its well-known summertime tours to Ingólfshöfði.

Atlantsflug SCENIC FLIGHTS
(☑478 2406, 899 2532; www.atf.is) Sightseeing flights offer a brilliant perspective over all this natural splendour, and leave from the tiny airfield on the Ring Road, just by the turn-off to the park visitor centre. Choose between seven tour options, with views over Vatnajökull, Grímsvötn, Lakagígar, Jökulsárlón or the glaciers. Prices start at €145 for 30 minutes.

🍴 Sleeping & Eating

Food in the park is limited to the busy summertime cafe inside the visitor centre, which sells coffee, soup, sandwiches and a tiny selection of groceries.

The nearest hotel is at Freysnes, 5km east of the national park entrance, and there's another at Hof, a further 15km east.

Visitor Centre Campsite CAMPGROUND
(☑470 8300; www.vjp.is; sites per person Ikr1300, plus per tent Ikr100; ☺May-Sep; 🛜) Most visitors bring a tent to this large, gravelly campsite (with laundry facilities, and hot showers for Ikr400). It gets very busy (and loud) in summer. The only other place you're allowed to camp is at the Kjós campsite (free, but you must obtain a permit from the visitor centre before you set off).

Bölti GUESTHOUSE
(☑478 1626; bolti123@gmail.com; Skaftafellsheiði; dm Ikr3700, tw without bathroom excl linen Ikr9800; ☺Mar-Oct) This friendly farm sits high on the hill above the western end of the Skaftafell campsite (2km up a narrow, winding road). There's sleeping-bag accommodation in six-person huts, basic kitchen, outdoor seating with dizzying sandur views, and teensy rooms in the farmhouse. Book ahead, and note that the guesthouse's future was in doubt at the time of research.

ℹ Information

The helpful year-round **visitor centre** (Skaftafellsstofa; ☑470 8300; www.vjp.is; ☺8am-9pm Jun-Aug, 9am-7pm May & Sep, 10am-5pm Mar-Apr & Oct, 11am-3pm Nov-Feb; @) has an information desk with free brochures and maps for sale, informative displays on the Öræfi area, a fascinating 10-minute film about the 1996 Grímsvötn *jökulhlaup*, exhibitions, a summertime cafe and internet access (per 20/40/60 minutes Ikr500/700/1000). The staff here really know their stuff.

ℹ Getting There & Away

Skaftafell is a stop on Reykjavík–Höfn bus routes and also a departure point for wilderness areas such as Landmannalaugar and Laki. Buses stop in front of the visitor centre.

Sterna (☑551 1166; www.sterna.is) runs a Reykjavík–Höfn service (bus 12/12a) once daily from mid-May to mid-September. Reykjavík–Skaftafell costs Ikr10,100 (6½ hours).

Strætó's (☑540 2700; www.straeto.is) Reykjavík–Höfn service (bus 51) runs twice daily from June to August, dropping to three times a week in winter (with a need to prebook). Reykjavík–Skaftafell costs Ikr7700.

Reykjavík Excursions (Kynnisferðir; ☑580 5400; www.re.is) services:

BUS 10/10A Skaftafell–Kirkjubæjarklaustur–Eldgjá–Landmannalaugar; once daily mid-June to mid-September. Can be used as a day tour, or as regular transport. Skaftafell–Landmannalaugar costs Ikr6600.

BUS 15/15A Skaftafell–Jökulsárlón; runs a daily loop between these towns June to mid-September.

BUS 16/16A Skaftafell–Laki; once daily July to mid-September. Used as a tour from Skaftafell, with four hours at Laki (Ikr13,800).

BUS 19/19A Skaftafell–Höfn; Ikr4500, 1¾ hours, once daily June to mid-September.

BUS 20/20A Reykjavík–Skaftafell; once daily June to mid-September, with lengthy pauses at south-coast towns.

Skaftafell to Jökulsárlón

Glittering glaciers and brooding mountains line the 60km stretch between Skaftafell and the iceberg-filled lagoon Jökulsárlón, and the unfolding landscape makes it difficult to keep your eyes on the road.

FREYSNES, SVÍNAFELL & SVÍNAFELLSJÖKULL

The farm **Svínafell**, 8km southeast of Skaftafell, was the home of Flosi Þórðarson, the character who burned Njál and his family to death in *Njál's Saga*. It was also the site where Flosi and Njál's family were finally reconciled, thus ending one of the bloodiest feuds in Icelandic history (see p112). There's not much to this tiny settlement now, but there is a campsite and accommodation here.

In the 17th century, the glacier **Svínafellsjökull** nearly engulfed the farm, but it has since retreated. On the northern side of the glacier (towards Skaftafell), a dirt road leads 2km to a car park, from where it's a short walk to the snout. Tours venture onto the glacier from companies based at Skaftafell.

🍴 Sleeping & Eating

The **petrol station** (◔9am– 8pm Sat & Sun) opposite F﹍ sells burgers, pizzas and ﹍ groceries.

Svínafell CAM﹍

(☑478 1765; www.svinafell.com; sites per p﹍ Ikr1150, cabins per person Ikr3700-4300; 🛜) Thi﹍ well-organised place has a campsite and six basic cabins (sleeping four), and a spotless amenities block with large dining room. If you have your own vehicle, it's an alternative to the campsite at Skaftafell. The owner also offers apartments and rooms of varying size scattered about the village.

Fosshótel Skaftafell HOTEL €€

(☑478 1945; www.fosshotel.is; Freysnes; s/d from €155/172; @🛜) This is the closest hotel to the Skaftafell visitor centre, 5km east at Freysnes. Its 63 rooms are functional rather than luxurious, but staff are helpful. There's a restaurant (mains Ikr2690 to Ikr4690) plating up local produce – be sure to sample the Vatnajökull beer, brewed from 1000-year-old glacier water and flavoured with wild thyme.

ÖRÆFAJÖKULL & HVANNADALSHNÚKUR

Iceland's highest mountain, Hvannadalshnúkur (2110m), pokes out from the ice cap Öræfajökull, an offshoot of Vatnajökull. This lofty peak is actually the northwestern edge of an immense 5km-wide crater – the biggest active volcano in Europe after Mt Etna. It erupted in 1362, firing out the largest amount of tephra in Iceland's recorded history: nearby glaciers are liberally spattered with bits of compressed yellow ash from the explosion. The region was utterly devastated – hence its name, Öræfi (Wasteland).

The best access for climbing Hvannadalshnúkur is from Sandfellsheiði, about 12km southeast of Skaftafell. Climbers should be well versed in glacier travel, and, although most guided expeditions manage the trip in a very long and taxing day (starting around 5am), independent climbers should carry enough supplies and gear for several days. Although there are no technical skills required, the trip is both physically and mentally challenging. Total elevation gain is more than 2000m.

The best time for climbing the mountain is April or May, before the ice bridges melt. Note that each year the ice bridges that make the hike possible are melting earlier and faster, so the climbing season coming shorter. Although trips are ⏉retically possible until September, af-June conditions may force companies ⏉ hire extra guides per group, raising the prices considerably. Check websites for more details.

☞ Tours

The following three tour operators (based in and around Skaftafell, p273) offer ascents of Hvannadalshnúkur; briefings are held the night before.

Icelandic Mountain Guides ADVENTURE TOUR (☑Reykjavík 587 9999, Skaftafell 894 2959, 478 2559; www.mountainguide.is) A guided 12- to 15-hour ascent costs from Ikr26,900 per person (minimum two people), including transport and equipment. Trips run three times a week April to September (conditions permitting). Book in advance, and allow yourself extra days in case the weather causes a cancellation.

Glacier Guides ADVENTURE TOUR (☑571 2100; www.glacierguides.is) Ascents cost Ikr29,990, with a minimum two people, and run daily on demand from mid-May to mid-September.

Local Guide ADVENTURE TOUR (Öræfaferðir; ☑894 0894; www.localguide.is) Ski-mountaineering ascent offered from March to May; price depends on the number of participants (two people costs Ikr45,000). The company owner holds the world record for ascents of Hvannadalshnúkur (more than 270!).

HOF

At Hof there's a picturesque wood-and-peat church, built on the foundations of a previous 14th-century building. It was reconstructed in 1884 and now sits pretty in a thicket of birch and ash with flowers growing on the grassy roof.

Formerly known as Frost & Fire Guesthouse, and beautifully situated beneath the Öræfajökull glacier, the very civilised Hof 1 Hotel (☑478 2260; www.hof1.is; d with/without bathroom incl breakfast Ikr25,500/20,100; ⊙May-Sep) harbours an impressive collection of modern Icelandic art, and an alluring sauna and hot-pot area. There's a variety of rooms scattered in various buildings, and a dining area serving dinner (two courses from Ikr4500).

Nearby, **Lækjarhús** (☑616 1247; www.laek jarhus.is; cabins Ikr16,000; ⊙Feb-Oct) has a trio of super-cosy self-contained cabins sleeping four people in bunk beds (linen costs an additional Ikr1500 per person).

INGÓLFSHÖFÐI

The 76m-high Ingólfshöfði promontory rises from the flatlands like a strange dream. In spring and summer, this beautiful, isolated nature reserve is overrun with nesting puffins, skuas and other seabirds, and you may see seals and whales offshore. It's also of great historical importance – it was here that Ingólfur Arnarson, Iceland's first settler, stayed the winter on his original foray to the country in AD 874. The reserve is open to visitors, but the 6km drive across the shallow tidal lagoon isn't something you should attempt, even in a 4WD.

Luckily, you can get here by hay wagon. The local farm gets out its trusty tractor between May and mid-August and runs tours to the reserve. The half-hour ride across the sands is followed by a 1½-hour guided walk round the headland, with an emphasis on birdwatching. Book through Local Guide (Öræfaferðir; ☑894 0894; www. localguide.is; adult/child Ikr5000/1000; ⊙noon Mon-Sat May–mid-Aug), or simply turn up outside the farm at Hofsnes (signposted, just off the Ring Road) 15 minutes before the tour is due to start. There are additional tours at 9am and 3pm from mid-June to early August.

BREIÐAMERKURSANDUR

The easternmost part of the large sandar, Breiðamerkursandur is one of the main breeding grounds for Iceland's great skuas (see the boxed text, p270). Thanks to rising numbers of these ground-nesting birds, there's also a growing population of Arctic foxes. Historically, Breiðamerkursandur also figures in Njál's Saga, which ends with Kári Sölmundarson arriving in this idyllic spot to 'live happily ever after' – which has to be some kind of miracle in a saga.

The sandur is backed by a sweeping panorama of glacier-capped mountains, some of which are fronted by deep lagoons. Kvíárjökull glacier snakes down to the Kvíár river and is easily accessible from the Ring Road. Leave your car in the small car park just off Rte 1 (you can't drive any further) and follow the walking path into the valley. It's quite an uncanny place: boulders line the huge western moraine like sentinels, the mossy grass is full of fairy rings, and a powerful glacial wind frequently surges down from the ice above.

The 742m-high **Breiðamerkurfjall** was once a nunatak enclosed by Breiðamerkurjökull and Fjallsjökull, but the glaciers have since retreated and freed it.

A small sign off the Ring Road indicates Fjallsárlón, and gives access to two glacial lagoons with a diminutive river flowing between them. Take the left fork for **Fjallsárlón**, where icebergs calve from Fjallsjökull, or right for a lengthier track to **Breiðárlón**, another outlet of Breiðamerkurjökull (also the source of Jökulsárlón). Although neither of these lagoons are as dramatic as Jökulsárlón, they are lovely, thanks to the lack of people. The (very rough) dirt road is extremely off-putting, however. It's possible to get here in a car (but don't blame us if you get stuck), or you can walk. It's 1km from the Ring Road to the first parking area for Fjallsárlón.

Jökulsárlón

A host of spectacular, luminous-blue icebergs drift through Jökulsárlón **glacier lagoon**, right beside the Ring Road between Höfn and Skaftafell. Even when you're driving along, expecting this surreal scene, it's still a surprise. It's worth spending a couple of hours here, admiring the wondrous ice sculptures (some of them striped with ash layers from volcanic eruptions), scouting for seals or taking a boat trip.

The icebergs calve from Breiðamerkurjökull, an offshoot of Vatnajökull, crashing down into the water and drifting inexorably towards the Atlantic Ocean. They can spend up to five years floating in the 18-sq-km-plus, 250m-deep lagoon, melting, refreezing and occasionally toppling over with a mighty splash, startling the birds. They then move on via Jökulsá, Iceland's shortest river, out to sea.

Although it looks as though it's been here since the last ice age, the lagoon is only about 80 years old. Until the mid-1930s Breiðamerkurjökull reached the Ring Road; it's now retreating rapidly (a staggering 200m to 300m per year), and the lagoon is consequently growing.

Jökulsárlón is a natural film set, and a popular backdrop for commercials. It starred briefly in *Lara Croft: Tomb Raider* (2001), pretending to be Siberia – the amphibious tourist-carrying boats were even painted grey and used as Russian ships. You might also have seen it in *Batman Begins* (2005), or the James Bond film *Die Another Day* (2002), for which the lagoon was specially frozen and six Aston Martins were destroyed on the ice!

🏃 Activities

The boat trips are fun, but you can get almost as close to those cool-blue masterpieces by walking along the shore, and you can taste ancient ice by hauling it out of the water. On the Ring Road west of the car park, there are designated parking areas where you can walk over the mounds to visit the lake at less-touristed stretches of shoreline. It's also worthwhile wandering down to the river-mouth, where you'll see ice boulders resting on the black-sand beach as part of their final journey out to sea.

Amphibious Boats   BOAT TOUR
(☑478 2222; www.icelagoon.is; adult/child Ikr3700/1000; ⊙9am-7pm Jun-Aug, 10am-5pm May & Sep) Take a memorable 40-minute trip on the lagoon in amphibious boats, which trundle along the shore like buses before driving into the water. Onboard guides regale you with factoids about the lagoon, and you get to taste 1000-year-old ice. There is no set schedule; trips run from the eastern car park (by the cafe) regularly (at least half-hourly in July and August). Tours are also usually available in April, October and November, depending on demand and weather conditions – contact the operators.

The same company also offers hour-long lagoon tours on Zodiacs (adult/child Ikr5900/2900; not recommended for kids under 10), but demand for the amphibious boats often sees the Zodiacs here being under-utilised.

Ice Lagoon   BOAT TOUR
(☑860 9996; www.icelagoon.com; adult/child Ikr6200/3900; ⊙9am-6pm Jun-Aug, 10am-5pm May-Sep) A second, smaller tour operator sets up in the car park on the west side of the bridge, operating one-hour Zodiac tours on the lagoon. It's a small-group experience, with a maximum 10 passengers per boat, and it travels up to the glacier edge (not done by the amphibious boats). There's also an 8pm tour, in the quiet of evening (Ikr8900; minimum four people; bookings required).

Sleeping & Eating

If you have a campervan with toilet, it's OK to stay in the car park. Otherwise camping by the lagoon isn't condoned (particularly not on the eastern side, where there are lots of nesting birds). The closest hotel is Hali (p278), 12km east.

The year-round **cafe** (⌚9am-7pm Jun-Aug, 10am-5pm Sep-May) beside the lagoon is a good pit stop for information and a snack. Its small space can get overwhelmed in summer.

Getting There & Away

Countless tours take in Jökulsárlón.

Sterna (☎551 1166; www.sterna.is) bus 12/12a between Reykjavík and Höfn runs daily from mid-May to mid-September and stops at the lagoon for an hour (enough time for a boat ride).

From June to mid-September, **Reykjavík Excursions** (Kynnisferðir; ☎580 5400; www.re.is) has two services of note: bus 15/15a runs a daily loop between Skaftafell visitor centre and Jökulsárlón; bus 19/19a runs from Skaftafell to Höfn, stopping briefly at the lagoon.

Jökulsárlón to Höfn

The scenic stretch of Ring Road from Jökulsárlón and Höfn is lined with at least a dozen rural properties (many with glaciers in their backyards) offering high-quality accommodation. Gentle, family-friendly lures include a petting zoo, ice-cream producer, quality museum, bird-filled wetlands and outdoor hot-pots. Those looking for a little more exertion will find walks to (or on) glacier tongues, quad-bike rides and snowmobile safaris.

Sights & Activities

Þórbergssetur MUSEUM
(www.thorbergur.is; adult/child Ikr700/free; ⌚9am-9pm May-Sep, noon-5pm Tue-Sun Oct-Apr) This cleverly crafted museum (its inspired exterior looks like a shelf of books) pays tribute to the most famous son of this sparsely populated region – writer Þórbergur Þórðarson (1888–1974), who was born at Hali in Suðursveit. Þórbergur was a real maverick (with interests spanning yoga, Esperanto and astronomy), and his first book *Bréf til Láru (Letter to Laura)* caused huge controversy because of its radical socialist content. Þórbergssetur also functions as a kind of cultural centre, with changing art exhibitions, and a quality **cafe-restaurant** (lunch Ikr1500-2900, dinner buffet Ikr4900) where the speciality is Arctic char.

Glacier Jeeps ADVENTURE TOUR
(☎478 1000, 894 3133; www.glacierjeeps.is) If you want to get up onto Vatnajökull, the daddy of all local glaciers, for a snowmobile or super-Jeep tour, then this area is where you branch vertically off into the mountains. Rte F985, which leads up to Jöklasel, is about 35km east of Jökulsárlón. See the boxed text, p282, for all the details.

Sleeping & Eating

Accommodation is listed here from west to east. Self-caterers should stock up on groceries in Kirkjubæjarklaustur or Höfn.

Hali COUNTRY HOTEL €€
(☎478 1073; www.hali.is; d with/without bathroom incl breakfast Ikr28,200/19,800; @ Wi-Fi) The Þórbergssetur museum acts as reception and restaurant for this smart option, on a black-sand shoreline. There are hotel and guesthouse-standard rooms, all with access to kitchen and lounge. From October to mid-May, sleeping-bag accommodation is available for Ikr4000 per person.

Vagnsstaðir HI Hostel HOSTEL €
(☎478 1048; www.hostel.is; dm/d without bathroom Ikr3800/10,000; ⌚Apr–mid-Oct; Wi-Fi) Snowmobiles litter this Ring Road property, HQ of Glacier Jeeps. It's a small, bunk-heavy hostel with sunny enclosed dining area. There's Ikr600 discount per person for members. Linen costs Ikr1100.

Smyrlabjörg COUNTRY HOTEL €€
(☎478 1074; www.smyrlabjorg.is; s/d incl breakfast Ikr18,200/26,800; Wi-Fi) A great place if you're after mod cons but still want sheep roaming the car park, mountain views, and peace and quiet. This large, welcoming hotel has a restaurant renowned for country hospitality and a bountiful evening buffet (Ikr6000).

Skálafell GUESTHOUSE €€
(☎478 1041; www.skalafell.net; d with/without bathroom incl breakfast Ikr20,000/17,000; Wi-Fi) At the foot of Skálafellsjökull, this friendly working farm has a couple of rooms in the family farmhouse, and also in motel-style units. There are no cooking facilities, but dinner is available. The knowledgeable owners have set up a marked walking trail from the farm to the glacier. Additionally, **Ice Guide** (☎661 0900; www.iceguide.is; hike Ikr9900) is a local

operator guiding a moderate four-hour glacier walk from the farm.

Hólmur
GUESTHOUSE €

(☑478 2063; www.eldhorn.is/mg/gisting; s/d without bathroom Ikr9000/12,000; @🖥) A perfect pit stop for families, Hólmur offers farmhouse accommodation, a small cafe, spectacular views, and a sweet, smile-inducing farm zoo (adult/child Ikr700/500) with an abundance of feathered and furry friends.

Lambhús
CAMPGROUND, COTTAGES €€

(☑662 1029; www.lambhus.is; sites per person Ikr800, cottages excl linen Ikr14,000-18,500; ⊙Jun-Aug) Ducks, sheep and horses, plus a campsite and eight compact cottages (sleeping four to six and ideal for families), are scattered about this vista-blessed property, owned by an affable, multilingual German-Icelandic family with years of guiding experience.

Brunnhóll
COUNTRY HOTEL €€

(☑478 1029; www.brunnholl.is; d with/without bathroom incl breakfast from Ikr22,900/20,500; ⊙Apr-Oct; @🖥) About 30km from Höfn, the hotel at this dairy farm has decent-sized rooms low on frills but big on views. Outside the June-to-August peak, sleeping-bag accommodation is available from Ikr4000. The good folk at Brunnhóll are also the makers of Jöklaís (Glacier Icecream), which you can sample at the summertime dinner buffet (Ikr5500) open to all. Or stop in anytime to buy a scoop/tub.

Hoffell
GUESTHOUSE €€

(Glacier World; ☑478 1514; www.glacierworld. is; d without bathroom incl breakfast Ikr15,100) The guesthouse at Hoffell has bright, fresh rooms, guest kitchen and a help-yourself breakfast, but what really acts as a drawcard are the activities (also accessible to non-guests): quad-bike tours (from Ikr12,500) to the glacier, and outdoor hot-pots (Ikr500; ⊙7am-11pm).

A rough gravel track heads from the guesthouse 4km to Hoffellsjökull glacier – a 4WD is recommended, as a small ford needs to be crossed. Alternatively, park and walk. There are pedal-boat tours run by the guesthouse at the glacier lake.

Höfn
POP 1640

Although it's no bigger than many European villages, the southeast's main town feels like a sprawling metropolis after driving through the wastelands on either side. Its setting is stunning; on a clear day, wander down to the waterside, find a quiet bench and just gaze at Vatnajökull and its brotherhood of glaciers.

'Höfn' simply means 'harbour', and is pronounced like an unexpected hiccup (just say 'hup' while inhaling). It's an apt name – this modern town still relies heavily on fishing and fish processing, and is famous for its *humar* (often translated as lobster, but technically it's langoustine).

Bus travellers use Höfn as a transit point, and most other travellers stop to use the town's services, so it pays to book accommodation in summer.

👁 Sights & Activities

The 1864 warehouse that once served as the regional folk museum has been moved from the outskirts of town to a prime position on the Höfn harbourfront, and in winter 2012 it was expected to be fitted out as the town's shiny new visitor information centre, possibly incorporating some of the folk exhibits and the glacier expo that resided in the town's old visitor centre (what doesn't fit may find a new home elsewhere in town). Undoubtedly, it will also cover the marvels of the region's flagship national park. Check www.visitvatnajokull.is for the latest details, including opening hours and contact information.

Waterside Paths

There are a couple of short waterside paths where you can amble and gape at the views – one by Hótel Höfn, and another round the marshes and lagoons at the end of the promontory Ósland (about 1km beyond the harbour – head for the seamen's monument on the rise). The latter path is great for watching seabirds, though if you walk to it during nesting season you will be attacked, Hitchcock-style, by Arctic terns on the causeway road.

Other Activities

A visit to this region wouldn't be complete without a pilgrimage to Vatnajökull.

Hornafjödur Bay Cruise (☑894 2391; www.baycruise.is; adult/child Ikr3500/2000) operates one-hour evening tours (departing at 6pm and 8pm according to demand) out on scenic Hornafjördur. Enquire at Hafnarbuðin grill.

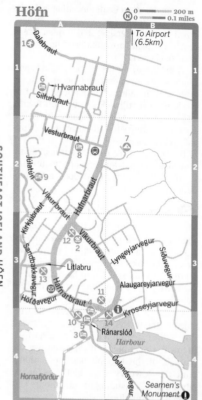

Höfn

The town's outdoor swimming pool **Sundlaug Hafnar** (Víkurbraut 9; adult/child Ikr500/180; ⊙6.45am-9pm Mon-Fri, 10am-7pm Sat & Sun) has water slides, hot-pots and a steam bath. There's also a nine-hole **golf course**, at the end of Dalabraut at the northern end of town.

✦✦✦ Festivals & Events

Humarhátíð   FOOD

Every year in late June or early July, Höfn's annual Humarhátíð (Langoustine Festival) honours this tasty crustacean, hauled to shore in abundance by the local fishing fleet. There's usually a fun fair, flea markets, dancing, music, ice-sculpture competitions, lots of alcohol and even a few langoustines.

🛏 Sleeping

Note that some of the prices listed here are from summer 2012; expect increases.

TOP CHOICE **Guesthouse Dyngja**   GUESTHOUSE €€
(☏690 0203; www.dyngja.com; Hafnarbraut 1; d without bathroom incl breakfast Ikr15,500-19,700; @ 🛜) A lovely young couple have opened this petite five-room guesthouse in a prime harbourfront locale, and filled it with charm and good cheer: rich colours, record player and vinyl selection, delicious breakfasts, outdoor deck and good local knowledge to impart.

Höfn Camping & Cottages   CAMPGROUND €
(☏478 1606; www.campsite.is; Hafnarbraut 52; sites/dm per person Ikr1100/3500, cabins Ikr12,000; ⊙May–mid-Oct; @ 🛜) Lots of travellers stay at the campsite on the main road into town, where super-helpful owners and extensive local info are among the draws. There are 11 good-value cabins, sleeping up to six, plus playground, laundry and bike rental, and a store selling camping gear.

Árnanes Country Lodge   COUNTRY HOTEL €€
(☏478 1550; www.arnanes.is; d with/without bathroom incl breakfast Ikr24,900/19,900; @ 🛜) On the Ring Road 6km west of Höfn, this polished rural locale has motel units and guesthouse rooms; sleeping-bag accommodation (Ikr5300) is available September to May. Árnanes also has a large family home available in a nearby residential area (with five

en-suite bedrooms). There's an agreeable summertime restaurant (mains Ikr3100 to Ikr5500) showcasing the outstanding local produce, and horse-riding tours for all skill levels (open to nonguests).

HI Hostel
HOSTEL €

(☎478 1736; www.hostel.is; Hvannabraut; dm/d without bathroom Ikr3800/10,000; �) Follow the signs from the N1 to find Höfn's best budget option, hidden away in a residential area and with some primo views. It's a sprawling space (a former aged-care home) that's usually bustling with travellers in summer, with the requisite facilities including large rooms, laundry and kitchen (but limited lounge areas). There's Ikr600 discount per person for members. Linen costs Ikr1200.

Hótel Höfn
HOTEL €€€

(☎478 1240; www.hotelhofn.is; Víkurbraut; s/d incl breakfast from Ikr23,300/31,850; @ເ) Höfn's business-class hotel is often busy with tour groups in summer. Nicely renovated rooms feature safe neutral tones and flatscreen TVs, and views are a knockout – you'll want one with a glacier view (but bear in mind that so does everyone else!). There's also a fresh-faced on-site restaurant, Ósinn (lunch Ikr1690-2250, dinner mains Ikr3800-6450).

Höfn Inn
HOTEL €€

(☎478 1544; www.hofninn.is; Vesterbraut 3; s/d incl breakfast from Ikr15,500/21,800; ເ) This newbie offers a dozen spacious rooms next door to the N1 on the road into town. There are some quirky touches (pebble floors, quasikitsch artworks, bizarre 'hand' chairs) but overall facilities are decent, with bathroom, flatscreen TV and kettle in each room.

Guesthouse Hvammur
GUESTHOUSE €€

(☎478 1544; www.hvamminn.is; Ránarslóð 2; s/d without bathroom incl breakfast Ikr10,800/16,500; ເ) Run by the same couple that runs the hostel and Höfn Inn, Hvammur is a large rabbit warren containing 30 simple rooms (most with washbasin and TV) down by the harbour.

Ásgarður Guesthouse
GUESTHOUSE €€

(☎478 1365; www.asgardurhofn.is; Ránarslóð 3; s/d incl breakfast Ikr15,000/21,000; @ເ) Harbourside Ásgarður is more hotel than guesthouse. All rooms have bathroom and TV, and some have glacier views. Decor is a bit bland, but it's in a good location.

Hótel Jökull
(☎478 1400; www.hoteljokull.is; without bathroom Ikr20,700/13 @ເ) As the southeast's o Höfn fills up quickly in Jökull, 8km down the road a good option when all else is full and you have your own wheels. It's a former Edda hotel (in an old school), with friendly owners and an on-site restaurant.

✕ Eating & Drinking

Humar (langoustine, or 'Icelandic lobster') is the speciality on Höfn menus – tails or served whole, grilled with garlic butter is the norm, and prices for main dishes are around Ikr5000 to Ikr6500. If that stretches your budget, you'll find cheaper crustacean-centric options too: bisque, langoustine-decorated pizza or pasta. Mmmm.

TOP CHOICE Humarhöfnin
ICELANDIC €€€

(☎478 1200; www.humarhofnin.is; Hafnarbraut 4; mains Ikr3900-6700; ☒noon-10pm Jun-Aug, 6-10pm Apr-May & Sep) Humarhöfnin offers 'Gastronomy Langoustine' in a cute, cheerfully Frenchified space with superb attention to detail: herb pots on the windowsills, roses on every table. Mains centred on pincer-waving little critters cost upwards of Ikr6000, but there's also a 'small courses' menu boasting a fine langoustine baguette.

TOP CHOICE Pakkhús
ICELANDIC €€€

(☎478 2280; www.pakkhus.is; harbourfront; mains Ikr2790-5990; ☒noon-10pm May–mid-Sep) Newly opened in a harbourside warehouse in 2012, and proudly showcasing local produce, busy Pakkhús has a level of kitchen creativity you don't often find in rural Iceland. First-class langoustine, lamb or Arctic char tempt taste buds, while clever desserts end the meal in style.

Kaffi Hornið
ICELANDIC €€

(☎478 2600; www.kaffihorn.is; Hafnarbraut 42; mains Ikr2120-5250; ☒11.30am-11pm) This log-cabin affair is an unpretentious bar and restaurant where the food comes in stomach-stretching portions. Although the atmosphere is more polished at Humarhöfnin and Pakkhús, the langoustine dishes here are cheaper. There's a lunchtime soup-and-salad buffet (Ikr1980), and a menu stretching from burgers to local trout.

RIDING ON THE VATNAJÖKULL ICE CAP

Although Vatnajökull ice cap and its attendant glaciers look spectacular from the Ring Road, most travellers will be seized by a wild desire to get closer. However, access to Vatnajökull is limited to commercial tours...unless you happen to be set up for a serious polar-style expedition. The ice cap is riven with deep crevasses, which are made invisible by coverings of fresh snow, and there are often sudden, violent blizzards. But don't be disheartened! It's a mind-blowing experience just to get near the glacier, and you can travel way up into the whiteness on organised snowmobile and 4WD tours.

The easiest route up to Vatnajökull is the F985 4WD track (about 35km east of Jökulsárlón, 45km west of Höfn) to the broad glacial spur Skálafellsjökull. The 16km-long road is practically vertical in places, with iced-over sections in winter. Please don't even think of attempting it in a 2WD car – you'll end up with a huge rescue bill.

At the top, 840m above sea level, is Jöklasel, the base for **Glacier Jeeps** (☎478 1000, 894 3133; www.glacierjeeps.is). The **restaurant** (lunch buffet Ikr2800; ⊙lunch 11.15am-2pm Jun–mid-Sep) at Jöklasel must have the most epic views in Iceland – it's like being on top of the world. (Note: there is no accommodation at Jöklasel.)

From here, the most popular tour option is the awesome one-hour **snowmobile ride** (per person Ikr19,500). You get kitted out with overalls, helmets, boots and gloves, then play follow-the-leader along a fixed trail. It's great fun, and although it only gives you the briefest introduction to glacier travel, an hour of noisy bouncing about with the stink of petrol in your nostrils is probably enough for most people! Prices are per person, with two people to a skidoo – there's Ikr8000 extra to pay if you want a skidoo to yourself. If the skidoo isn't your thing, you can also take a more-sedate **super-Jeep ride** (per person Ikr19,500) up onto the ice. The company also offers longer skidoo excursions, or glacier hiking.

If you have your own 4WD transport, the snowmobile or super-Jeep options cost Ikr18,000. For Ikr19,500, you get transport to Jöklasel from the Ring Road. At 9.30am and 2pm daily from May to October, Glacier Jeeps collects people in a super-Jeep from the parking area at the start of the F985. It's essential to call ahead to reserve a space.

Glacier Jeeps runs its snowmobile and super-Jeep tours in the winter months too – times vary, and tours depart from the company's base at Vagnsstaðir hostel (p278).

There are no scheduled buses that work in with the Glacier Jeeps schedule to drop you at a suitable time at the F985 car park. If you're without your own wheels, consider using the services of Höfn-based **Vatnajökull Travel** (☎894 1616; www.vatnajokull.is), which can take you up to Jöklasel and then drive you to Jökulsárlón for a lagoon boat trip. Prices vary according to what you select; contact the company for a quote.

Hafnarbuðin   GRILL €

(mains Ikr290-1350; ⊙noon-9pm) The kind of place where local fishermen go to talk shop, this old-school diner is a fabulous relic with a cheap-and-cheerful vibe, a menu of grill-bar favourites, and even a drive-up window!

Self-Catering

In the Miðbær shopping centre near the library, there's an ATM, a bakery, a **Nettó supermarket** (⊙11am-7pm Mon-Fri, 10am-6pm Sat, noon-6pm Sun Jun-Aug, shorter hours rest of year) and a **Vín Búð** (⊙2-6pm Mon-Thu, 11am-7pm Fri, 11am-4pm Sat Jun-Aug, shorter hours rest of year).

❶ Information

There are two banks on Hafnarbraut, Landsbanki Íslands and Sparisjóðurinn, and an ATM just inside the shopping centre.

Library (internet per 30min Ikr200; ⊙10am-4pm Mon-Fri Jun-Aug, 9am-5pm Mon-Fri Sep-May) Internet access at the library, in the community centre opposite the supermarket.

Post office (Hafnarbraut; ⊙9am-4.30pm Mon-Fri)

Tourist office (☎478 1500; www.visitvatna jokull.is) The tourist office was scheduled to move into new premises down by the harbourfront, next to Pakkhús restaurant, in the winter of 2012. It is expected to be open year-round; check the website for opening hours.

❶ Getting There & Away

Air

Höfn's airport is 6.5km northwest of town.
Eagle Air (☑562 2640; www.eagleair.is) flies year-round between Reykjavík and Höfn (one way €179).

Bus

Buses arrive at and depart from the N1 petrol station, a 10-minute walk from the town centre.

Hópferðabílar Akureyri (☑898 5156; www.hba.is) runs a Höfn–Egilsstaðir service (bus 1/1a) once daily from June to mid-September (Ikr7500, four hours). Stops include Reyðarfjörður, Breiðdalsvík, Berunes and Djúpivogar. The company offers a Ikr15,000 pass that allows travel along the route over three days.

Strætó (☑540 2700; www.straeto.is) has a Reykjavík–Höfn service (bus 51) twice daily from June to August (Ikr10,150, seven hours), dropping to three times a week in winter (with a need to prebook).

Reykjavík Excursions (Kynnisferðir; ☑580 5400; www.re.is) has a Höfn–Skaftafell service (bus 19/19a) once daily from June to mid-September (Ikr4500, two hours). From Skaftafell there are buses further west.

Sterna (☑551 1166; www.sterna.is) services:
BUS 12/12A Reykjavík–Höfn; Ikr13,700, nine hours, once daily mid-May to mid-September.
BUS 9/9A Höfn–Egilsstaðir; four hours, once daily mid-May to mid-September.

Lónsöræfi

If you're in Iceland to get in touch with your inner hermit, the nature reserve Lónsöræfi should be on your list. This protected area, east of Höfn, contains some spectacularly colourful rhyolite mountains, as well as the Stafafellsfjöll peaks, and at 320 sq km is one of Iceland's largest conservation areas.

You can camp at sites in the reserve, and there are mountain huts along the Lónsöræfi–Snæfell hike, which begins at the Illikambur parking area. The only road in the reserve is the F980, a rough track off the Ring Road that ends after 25km at Illikambur (only suitable for *large* 4WDs and experienced drivers – there is a deep, fast-flowing river to cross).

There are many easy day hikes in the hills and valleys north of Stafafell, and longer hikes towards the southeast of Vatnajökull, and northwest to Snæfell. Some of these walks require substantial river crossings (see p350 for advice), so use extreme caution, especially in warm or wet weather.

Although Lónsöræfi isn't part of Vatnajökull National Park, the park's website (www.vjp.is) has information on hiking trails in the area, and the visitor centres at Skaftafell, Höfn and Skríðuklaustur can advise on options. Also excellent for planning is www.stafafell.is and www.stafafell.com.

Ask around for the new hiking map of the reserve, due for publication in early 2013. The area is growing in popularity, and there has been an increase in mountain-hut accommodation and footbridges.

There's nowhere to eat or buy food; bring supplies from Höfn or Djúpivogur.

STAFAFELL

In the middle of nowhere, Stafafell is a lonely farm, lost under the mountains. It's a good hiking base for exploring Lónsöræfi; you can arrange summer tours and hikers' transport, and the farmers here (a trio of brothers) know everything about the area. The farm's website (www.stafafell.is) is rich in local info, and there is a choice of accommodation.

Perhaps the best of the area's day hikes is a well-marked, 14.3km (four- or five-hour) return walk from Stafafell to Hvannagil, a colourful rhyolite canyon on the eastern bank of the river Jökulsá í Lóni. (Pick up a route description from the farmers.)

WORTH A TRIP

VIKING CAFE

About 7km east of the Höfn turn-off, just before the Ring Road enters a tunnel through the Almannaskarð pass, take the signposted road heading south to Stokksnes radar station. After 4.5km, in a wild setting under moodily gothic Litla Horn mountain, you'll find a cool little outpost where 'Berlin goes Icelandic': the Viking Cafe (☑849 4627; www.vikingcafe-iceland.com; ◷9am-9pm Jun-Aug). Indulge in great coffee, waffles and cake, then walk to the neighbouring filmset (a Viking village built by director Baltasar Kormákur, which will hopefully remain in place after its film duties are done) or scour for seals on the surrounding black-sand beaches. You can camp here (with permission), and cabins will be added for summer 2013 – no doubt they will be quite unique.

LÓN

The name Lón (Lagoon; pronounced 'lone') sums up the nature of this shallow bay enclosed by two long spits between the mountains Eystrahorn and Vestrahorn (marked on some maps as Austurhorn and Vesturhorn). To the northwest is the delta of Jökulsá í Lóni, where an enormous colony of swans nests in spring and autumn.

As with other peaks in the region, the batholithic Eystrahorn at the eastern end of Lón was formed as a subsurface igneous intrusion, gradually revealed through erosion. This is the best access for strolls on the Fjörur sand spit enclosing the eastern portion of Lón.

At the western end of Lón, the commanding Vestrahorn and its companion Brunnhorn form a cape between Skarðsfjörður and Papafjörður. Ruins of the fishing settlement Syðri-Fjórður, abandoned in 1899, are still visible. Travel down the signposted road to Stokksnes to explore this area.

Tours

Stafafell HIKING
(☎699 6684; www.stafafell.com) From July to mid-August, one of the farm's owners runs good-value day trips in Lónsöræfi that combine 4WD exploration with a three-hour hike (Ikr8000). Hiker transport to/from trailheads or huts can be arranged, or four-hour horse-riding tours of an evening (Ikr8000).

Icelandic Mountain Guides BACKPACKING
(☎587 9999, www.mountainguide.is) IMG offers regular summer departures for its five-day, 50km backpacking tour through Lónsöræfi (from Ikr109,000), staying in mountain huts. It's in their program under the name 'In the Shadow of Vatnajökull'.

Sleeping

Stafafell CAMPGROUND, GUESTHOUSE €
(☎478 1717; www.stafafell.is; r per person Ikr3000-4500, cottages Ikr12,000) In a rustic farmhouse by the tiny church, there's a simple guesthouse with kitchen facilities (made-up beds available). There are also a couple of self-contained cottages, sleeping four. Next to the farm is a campground, signposted 'Stafafell Nature Park', with campsites for Ikr1000 per person.

Brekka í Lóni GUESTHOUSE €€
(☎849 3589; olgaf@simnet.is; d incl breakfast Ikr17,600) For a little more luxury, Brekka offers four smart, motel-style units on its property just west of Stafafell, by the glacial river. Dinner is offered (Ikr4000).

Getting There & Away

Buses between Höfn and Egilsstaðir pass Stafafell and will stop on request.

The Highlands

Best Natural Wonders

- » Askja (p294)
- » Herðubreið (p294)
- » Hveravellir (p289)
- » Kverkfjöll (p295)
- » Drekagil (p294)
- » Kerlingarfjöll (p289)

Best Places to Take a Dip

- » Víti (p295)
- » Hveravellir (p289)
- » Laugafell (p291)
- » Kerlingarfjöll (p289)

Why Go?

You may have travelled the Ring Road thinking that Iceland is light on towns; that sheep seem to outnumber people; that you haven't encountered an N1 service station for many a mile. Well, you ain't seen nothing yet. In the interior highlands, there are practically no services, accommodation, bridges or guarantees if something goes wrong.

Gazing across the desolate expanses, you could imagine yourself in the Australian outback, or, as many have noted, on the moon. And those aren't overactive imaginations at work – *Apollo* astronauts trained here before their lunar landing!

This isolation, in essence, is the reason that people visit. Although some travellers are disappointed by the interior's ultra bleakness, others are humbled by the sight of nature in its rawest form. The solitude is exhilarating, the views are vast, the access is limited, and it's immensely tough but equally rewarding to hike or bike these cross-country routes.

Good to Know

Kjölur route (Rte F35) North-south route across the country. Served by summer buses. No rivers to ford.

Sprengisandur route (Rte F26) North-south route across the country. Served by summer buses.

Öskjuleið route (Rte F88 or F905/910) Access from Iceland's north to Askja caldera and Herðubreið mountain. Served by numerous tour operators (especially from Lake Mývatn).

Kverkfjöll route (Rte F905, F910, then F902) Access from Iceland's north (or east) to Kverkfjöll ice caves. A few tour operators venture here.

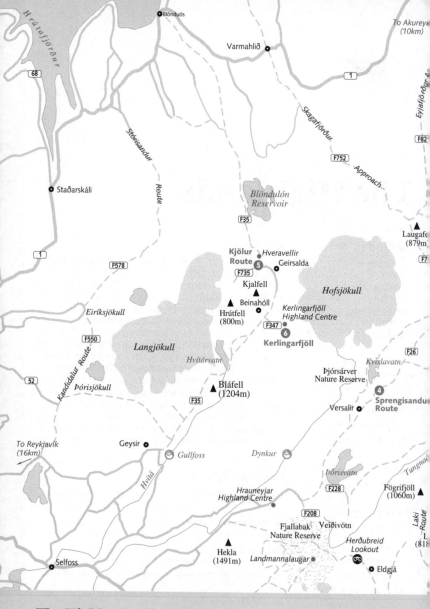

The Highlands Highlights

1 Hike across the lava field at blustery **Askja** (p294), then take a dip in the tepid waters of Víti crater

2 Marvel at icy sculptures hidden in the geothermal caves at **Kverkfjöll** (p295)

3 Pay homage to the Queen of the Mountains, **Herðubreið** (p294)

4 Pity the melancholy ghosts and outlaws on Iceland's longest, loneliest north–south track, the **Sprengisandur route** (p290)

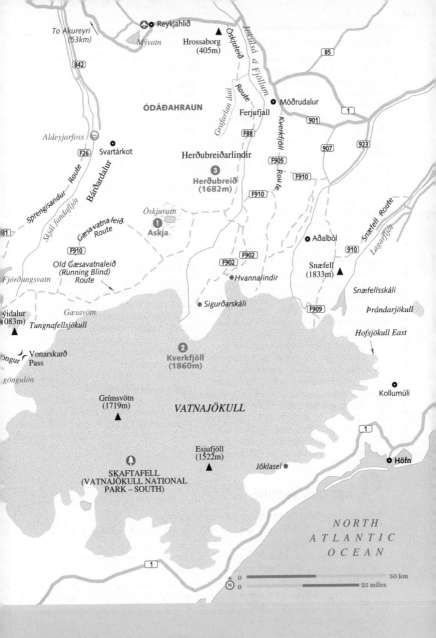

To Akureyri
(53km)

Reykjahlíð

Mývatn

Hrossaborg
(405m)

842

85

ÓDÁÐAHRAUN

Graðarlan dað
Route

Jökulsá á Fjöllum

Öskjuleið

Móðrudalur

1

Ferjufjall

901

F88

Aldeyjarfoss

F26

Svartárkot

Herðubreiðarlindir

Kverkfjöll
Route

F905

F910

907

923

Sprengisandur
Route

Bárðardalur

Skjalfandafljót

3
Herðubreið
(1682m)

F910

Snæfell
Route

Lagarfljót

Gæsavatnaleið
Route

Öskjuvatn

1
Askja

F902

F902

Aðalból

910

81

F910

Old Gæsavatnaleið
(Running Blind)
Route

Snæfell
(1833m)

Fjórðungsvatn

Hvannalindir

Snæfellsskáli

ýidalur
(1083m)

Gæsavötn

Sigurðarskáli

Þrándarjökull

Tungnafellsjökull

F909

Hofsjökull East

öngur
Vonarskarð
Pass

2
Kverkfjöll
(1860m)

göngulón

Grímsvötn
(1719m)

VATNAJÖKULL

Kollumúli

Esjufjöll
(1522m)

1

SKAFTAFELL
(VATNAJÖKULL NATIONAL
PARK – SOUTH)

Jöklasel

Höfn

NORTH
ATLANTIC
OCEAN

1

N
0   50 km
0   25 miles

5 Spice up the endless
vistas of desolation with stops
at hot springs and climbable
crags along the notorious
Kjölur route (p288)

6 Don hiking boots to
investigate the new, improved
trails around the majestic
massif **Kerlingarfjöll** (p289)

Kjölur Route (Kjalvegur)

If you want to sample Iceland's central deserts but don't like the idea of ford crossings, the 200km Kjölur route has had all its rivers bridged. In summer there are even scheduled daily all-terrain buses that use it as a 'shortcut' between Reykjavík and Akureyri. The bus may be an appealing option at first; however, we've received comments from several readers that while the first hour of outback desolation is riveting, the other nine hours can be snooze-inducing if you aren't planning to disembark anywhere along the way.

From the south, Rte F35 starts just past Gullfoss, passing between two large glaciers before emerging near Blönduós on the northwest coast. It reaches its highest point (around 700m) between the Langjökull and Hofsjökull ice caps, near the mountain Kjalfell. Its northern section cruises scenically past Blöndulón, a large reservoir used by the Blanda hydroelectric power station. Road conditions in the north are better than those in the south.

The Kjölur route usually opens in mid-June, and closes sometime in September, depending on weather conditions. Note that on some Iceland maps, the inland route is marked as Rte 35 (not F35); it is still a mountain road, and while it is technically possible to drive a 2WD along the route, it is absolutely not recommended (there are potholes/puddles that could near-swallow a small car, you'll do damage to the car's underside, and your journey will be slow and very bumpy). Car-hire companies expressly forbid the use of 2WD rentals on the route.

Tours

The scheduled buses can be used as a tour along the route. Daily from mid-June to early September, Sterna (☑551 1166; www.sternatravel.com) has a 13-hour day tour from Reykjavík that takes in the Golden Circle and two hours of hiking at Kerlingarfjöll (Ikr24,000).

A bit of online digging will reveal hiking, biking and horse-riding tours along the Kjölur route (also search 'Kjalvegur'). Icelandic Mountain Guides (☑587 9999; www.mountainguides.is) has excellent highland hiking trips.

HVÍTÁRVATN

The pale-blue lake Hvítárvatn, located 35km northeast of Gullfoss, is the source of the glacial river Hvítá – a popular destination for Reykjavík-based white-water rafting operators. A glacier tongue of Iceland's second-largest ice cap, Langjökull, carves into the lake and creates icebergs, adding to the beauty of this spot.

Glacier Lake Hvítárvatn (☑822 1005; www.glacierlake.is) operates boat tours (Ikr15,900) on Hvítárvatn, with the option of a short glacier hike on Langjökull. Cruises are at 2pm daily from mid-June to mid-September; see the website for options

---

 GETTING AROUND

Before you embark on your highlands journey, take note:

» Conditions can be fickle and snow isn't uncommon, even in midsummer. Check www.vedur.is for forecasts.

» Road-opening dates depend on weather conditions, and usually occur any time from early June to early July. Check www.vegagerdin.is.

» The routes described in this chapter are strictly for robust, high-clearance 4WD vehicles, as jagged terrain and treacherous river crossings are not uncommon.

» It's recommended that vehicles travel in pairs, so if one gets bogged or breaks down, the other can drag it out, fetch help or transport all passengers to shelter.

» There are no petrol stations in the highlands, except for at Hveravellir on the Kjölur route, and Hrauneyjar, south of the Sprengisandur route.

» Buses and/or tours make a good alternative to driving yourself. Tour operators offer comfortable vehicles and experienced drivers/guides.

» In the highlands, as with everywhere in Iceland, stick to roads and marked trails. Off-road driving is hugely destructive to the country's fragile environment, and illegal.

THE BADLANDS

Historically in Iceland, once a person had been convicted of outlawry they were beyond society's protection and aggrieved enemies could kill them at will. Many outlaws, or *útilegumenn,* such as the renowned Eiríkur Rauðe (Erik the Red), voluntarily took exile abroad. Others escaped revenge-killing by fleeing into the mountains, valleys and broad expanses of the harsh Icelandic interior, where few dared pursue them.

Undoubtedly, anyone who could live year-round in these bitter, barren deserts must have been extraordinary. Icelandic outlaws were naturally credited with all sorts of fearsome feats, and the general populace came to fear the vast badlands, which they considered to be the haunt of superhuman evil. The *útilegumenn* thereby joined the ranks of giants and trolls, and provided the themes for popular tales such as the fantastic *Grettir's Saga.*

One particular outlaw has become the subject of countless Icelandic folk tales. Fjalla-Eyvindur ('Eyvindur of the Mountains'), a charming but incurable 18th-century kleptomaniac, fled into the highlands with his wife, and continued to make enemies by rustling sheep to stay alive. Throughout the highlands you'll see shelters and hideouts attributed to him and hear tales of his ability to survive in impossible conditions while always staying one jump ahead of his pursuers.

of pick-up in Reykjavík or Gullfoss for those without 4WDs.

In the marshy grasslands northeast of Hvítárvatn is Ferðafélag Íslands' oldest hut, Hvítárnes, built in 1930. From the Kjölur road, where the bus will drop you, it's an 8km walk along the 4WD track to the hut.

KERLINGARFJÖLL

Until the 1850s Icelanders believed that this mountain range (10km off Rte F35 on Rte F347) harboured the vilest outlaws. It was thought they lived deep in the heart of the 150-sq-km range in an isolated Shangri-la-type valley. So strong was this belief that it was only in the mid-19th century that anyone ventured into Kerlingarfjöll, and it was only in 1941 that the range was properly explored by Ferðafélag Íslands.

It's certainly dramatic. The colourful landscape is broken up into jagged peaks and ridges, the highest of which is Snækollur (1477m), and it's scattered with hot springs.

At **Kerlingarfjöll Highland Centre** (summer 664 7878, year-round 664 7000; www.kerlingarfjoll.is; sites per person Ikr1500, d with bathroom incl breakfast Ikr28,800; mid-Jun–mid-Sep;) there is a handful of huts and houses, with various bathroom configurations and linen options (sleeping-bag accommodation Ikr4800 to Ikr6400). There's also a large campsite, guest kitchen, a simple restaurant and hot-pots. Check the website for a detailed list (and maps) of local trails, ranging from 1km to 50km. Petrol is no longer available here (despite its symbol still appearing on some maps and signs).

HVERAVELLIR

Hveravellir is a popular geothermal area of fumaroles and hot springs, signposted 30km north of the Kerlingarfjöll turn-off (approximately 60km north of Gullfoss). Among its warm pools are the brilliant-blue Bláhver; Öskurhólshver, which emits a constant stream of hissing steam; and a luscious human-made bathing pool. Another hot spring, Eyvindurhver, is named after the outlaw Fjalla-Eyvindur. Hveravellir is reputedly one of the many hideouts of this renegade.

At Hveravellir there are two **hikers huts** (summer 452 4200, year-round 894 1293; www.hveravellir.is; sites/dm per person Ikr1200/4000; mid-Jun–mid-Sep) with about 50 beds (linen available for Ikr1200). There's also a campsite, kitchens and a basic cafe. Staff can help with information on local hiking trails, plus arrange glacier exploration of Hofsjökull or horse-riding tours.

In summer, a petrol pump is available at Hveravellir – the only one along the Kjölur route.

🛏 Sleeping

As well as the popular options at Kerlingarfjöll and Hveravellir listed above, two organisations operate huts along the route (BYO sleeping bag). It's wise to prebook.

KJÖLUR HIKING

If you're looking for an independent multiday hiking option in the area:

» **Old Kjalvegur route** (www.fi.is/en/hiking-trails) An easy and scenic three-day hike (39km) from Hvítárvatn to Hveravellir. The trail follows the original horseback Kjölur route (west of the present road), via the Hvítárnes, Þverbrekknamúli and Þjófadalir mountain huts.

» **Hringbrautin** (www.kerlingarfjoll.is/routes) A challenging three-day circuit (47km) around Kerlingarfjöll, starting and ending at Kerlingarfjöll Highland Centre, with recently opened huts at Klakkur and Kisubotnar.

Ferðafélag Íslands   MOUNTAIN HUTS €
(☎568 2533; www.fi.is; dm Ikr3500-4000) The following huts have toilets and a kitchen (no utensils though), and most have running water. Huts are listed from south to north: **Hvítárnes** (N 64°37.007', W 19°45.394'; sleeps 30), northeast of Hvítárvatn lake, with a volunteer warden for most of July and August; **Þverbrekknamúli** (N 64°43.100', W 19°36.860'; sleeps 20), about 4km southeast of the mini ice cap Hrútfell; and **Þjófadalir** (N 64°48.900', W 19°42.510'; sleeps 12), at the foot of the mountain Raudkollur.

Gljásteinn   MOUNTAIN HUTS €
(☎486 5757; www.gljasteinn.is; sites/dm per person Ikr800/4000; ☺mid-Jun–Aug) Has three well-appointed huts on or just off the route. Campers welcome. From south to north: **Fremstaver** (N 64°45.207', W 19°93.699'; sleeps 25), on the south slopes of the mountain Bláfell; **Árbúðir** (N 64°609.036', W 19°702.947'; sleeps 30), on the banks of the Svartá river, right on Rte F35 about 42km north of Gullfoss, which offers a hot shower, has a small cafe and the Sterna bus service (bus 35/35a) stops here; and **Gíslaskáli** (N 64°744.187', W 19°432.508'; sleeps up to 50), 4km north of the turn-off to Kerlingarfjöll, and 1km off Rte F35, which has dining and lounge areas, plus hot showers.

❶ Getting There & Away

Bicycle
Of all the interior routes, Kjölur is probably the best for cycling. For a humorous account, read Tim Moore's *Frost on My Moustache*.

Bus
Daily from mid-June to early September, scheduled buses travel along the Kjölur route between Reykjavík and Akureyri (in both directions). These services are included in a number of bus passports (see p346).

SBA-Norðurleið (☎550 0700/70; www.sba.is) Bus 610/610a takes 10½ hours for the complete journey, with half-hour stops at Geysir and Gullfoss. There's a 15-minute stop at Kerlingarfjöll accommodation, and an hour at Hveravellir (time for a dip). The entire Reykjavík–Akureyri journey costs Ikr13,000. Transporting bikes costs Ikr3000.

Sterna (☎551 1166; www.sterna.is) Bus 35/35a from Reykjavík is a longer day (15 hours), which more resembles a tour if you travel the whole way to Akureyri – there are lengthy stops at Þingvellir, Geysir, Gullfoss and Kerlingarfjöll. The journey in the reverse direction (Akureyri–Reykjavík) is shorter by three hours, with fewer stops. Tickets for the entire route are Ikr12,900; transporting bikes costs Ikr3000.

Car
Drivers with 4WD vehicles will have no problems on the Kjölur route. You won't find a car-rental agency that provides insurance to those with plans of taking a 2WD.

Note that if you're in a 2WD and curious for a taste of the highlands, the first 14km of the route (north of Gullfoss) are sealed.

Sprengisandur Route

To Icelanders, the name Sprengisandur conjures up images of outlaws, ghosts and long sheep drives across the barren wastes. The Sprengisandur route (F26) is the longest north–south trail, and crosses bleak desert moors that can induce a shudder even today in a 4WD!

Sprengisandur offers some wonderful views of Vatnajökull, Tungnafellsjökull and Hofsjökull, as well as Askja and Herðubreið from the western perspective. An older route, now abandoned, lies a few kilometres west of the current one.

The Sprengisandur route proper begins at Rte 842 near Goðafoss in northwest Iceland. Some 41km later, you'll pass through a red metal gate as the road turns into

F26. There's a poster explaining the sights and finer points of the route, and 3km later you'll happen upon one of Iceland's most photogenic waterfalls, Aldeyjarfoss. Churning water bursts over the cliff's edge as it splashes through a narrow canyon lined with the signature honeycomb columns of basalt.

After the falls, the Sprengisandur route continues southwest through 240km of inhospitable territory all the way to Þjórsárdalur. There are two other ways to approach Sprengisandur, both of which link up to the main road about halfway through.

The route generally opens around the start of July.

LAUGAFELL

The main site of interest on the Skagafjörður approach is Laugafell, an 879m-high mountain with some hot springs bubbling on its northwestern slopes. You can stay nearby at the Ferðafélag Akureyrar hut (☑Jul-Aug 854 9302; www.ffa.is; N 65°01.614', W 18°19.923'; dm Ikr4500), with 35 beds, a kitchen and a beautiful geothermally heated pool. There's a warden on-site in July and August.

NÝIDALUR

Nýidalur (known as Jökuldalur), the range just south of the Tungnafellsjökull ice cap, was discovered by a lost traveller in 1845. With a campsite, two Ferðafélag Íslands huts (☑Jul-Aug 860 3334; www.fi.is; N 64°44.130', W 18°04.350'; dm Ikr5000) and lots of hiking possibilities, it makes a great break in a Sprengisandur journey. The huts have kitchen facilities, showers and a summer warden. From mid-July to mid-August, the park ranger guides an evening walk from the hut at 8.30pm.

There are two rivers – the one 500m from the hut may be difficult to cross (even for a 4WD). You can ask locally for advice on conditions.

ÞÓRISVATN

Before water was diverted from Kaldakvísl into Þórisvatn from the Tungnaá hydroelectric scheme in southwest Iceland, it had a surface area of only 70 sq km. Now it's Iceland's second-largest lake at 85 sq km. It's 11km northeast of the junction between Rte F26 and the Fjallabak route.

HRAUNEYJAR

Somewhat unexpectedly, in the bleakest position imaginable (west of Þórisvatn in the Hrauneyjar region), you'll find a year-round guesthouse and hotel! They lie at the crossroads of the Sprengisandur route (F26) and the F208 to Landmannalaugar, so are handy for lots of highland attractions and have marked walking trails in the area.

Hrauneyjar Highland Centre (☑487 7782; www.hrauneyjar.is, d with/without bathroom incl breakfast €155/119; ⑧) offers small, basic guesthouse rooms, and an overpriced sleeping-bag option (single/double €64/79). From mid-June to mid-September there is access to a guest kitchen; there's also a basic restaurant.

If you want luxuries – comfier rooms, bar and smart restaurant (mains Ikr3900 to Ikr5100), hot-pot and sauna – head for Hotel Highland (☑487 7782; www.hotelhighland.is; s/d incl breakfast €209/238; @⑧), 1.4km from the guesthouse.

Petrol and diesel are available. There is sealed road to Hrauneyjar from the west.

VEIÐIVÖTN

This beautiful area just northeast of Landmannalaugar is an entanglement of small desert lakes in a volcanic basin, a continuation of the same fissure that produced Laugahraun in the Fjallabak Nature Reserve. This is a wonderful place for wandering, following 4WD tracks that wind across the tephra sands between the numerous lakes (popular for trout fishing).

🟦 Getting There & Away

Bus

In July and August, **Reykjavík Excursions** (Kynnisferðir; ☑580 5400; www.re.is) operates two scheduled services along the Sprengisandur route between Reykjavík or Landmannalaugar and Lake Mývatn. These services are included in a number of bus passports.

» **Bus 14/14a** Landmannalaugar–Mývatn; 10 hours, 9.30am on Sunday, Tuesday and Thursday. In the other direction, buses depart Mývatn at 8am on Monday, Wednesday and Friday. Although it's a scheduled bus, it's used as a 'tour' of sorts, with extended pauses at Hrauneyjar, Nýidalur, Aldeyjarfoss and Goðafoss. Fare for the entire route is Ikr13,300.

» **Bus 17/17a** Reykjavík–Mývatn; 11½ hours, 8am on Sunday, Tuesday and Thursday. In the other direction, buses depart Mývatn at 8am on Monday, Wednesday and Friday. Again, although it's a scheduled bus, it's used as a 'tour' of sorts, with extended pauses at Nýidalur, Aldeyjarfoss and Goðafoss. Fare for the entire route is Ikr17,600.

THE HIGHLANDS SPRENGISANDUR ROUTE

Car

There's no fuel along the way. The nearest petrol stations are at Akureyri if you come in on the Eyjafjörður approach; at Varmahlíð if you're driving the Skagafjörður approach; at Fosshóll, near Goðafoss, if you're coming from the north along the main route through Bárðardalur; and at Hrauneyjar if you're driving from the south.

» **Eyjafjörður Approach** From the north, the F821 from southern Eyjafjörður (south of Akureyri) connects to the Skagafjörður approach at Laugafell. This route is very pleasant, with few tourists, but it's a more difficult drive.

» **Skagafjörður Approach** From the northwest the 81km-long F752 connects southern Skagafjörður (the nearest town is Varmahlíð on the Ring Road) to the Sprengisandur route. The roads join near the lake Fjórðungsvatn, 20km east of Hofsjökull.

Öskjuleið Route (Askja Way)

The Öskjuleið route runs across the highlands to Herðubreið, the Icelanders' beloved 'Queen of Mountains', and to the desert's most popular marvel, the immense Askja caldera. The usual access road is Rte F88, which leaves the Ring Road 32km east of Mývatn at Hrossaborg, but Askja is also accessible further east via Rte F910. **Hrossaborg** is a 10,000-year-old crater shaped like an amphitheatre and used as a filmset for the Tom Cruise sci-fi film *Oblivion* (2013).

For much of the way it's a flat journey, following the western bank of the Jökulsá á Fjöllum, meandering across tephra wasteland and winding circuitously through rough, tyre-abusing sections of the 4400-sq-km lava flow **Ódáðahraun** (Evil Deeds Lava).

After a long journey through the lava- and flood-battered plains, things perk up at the lovely oasis of Herðubreiðarlindir, at the foot of Herðubreið. The route then wanders westwards through dunes and lava flows past the Dreki huts and up the hill towards Askja, where you leave your car to walk the remaining 2.5km to the caldera.

Askja is part of the vast Vatnajökull National Park, so the park website (www.vjp.is) has excellent information.

🏃 Activities

Hiking

A couple of times a year (usually in July), **Ferðafélag Akureyrar** (FFA; ☎462 2720; www.ffa.is), the Touring Club of Akureyri, organises four-day hut-to-hut hiking tours (Ikr55,500 per person) in the area; see 'Touring Program' on its website for details.

For independent hikers, the FFA's website also outlines details of the **Askja Trail**, the FFA's walking trail with huts across the Ódáðahraun, starting from Herðubreiðarlindir and ending at Svartárkot farm in upper Bárðardalur valley (Rte 843).

Icelandic Mountain Guides (☎587 9999; www.mountainguides.is) runs guided multiday hikes in the area, including a five-day traverse from Mývatn to Askja (from Ikr99,900).

👉 Tours

A growing number of operators run super-Jeep tours to Askja, from mid-June (when the route opens) until as late into September as weather permits. From Akureyri it makes for a long day tour (up to 15 hours); a better base is Reykjahlíð at Mývatn (even then, tour time is around 11 to 12 hours). For all tours, you are expected to bring/order a packed lunch; some operators (Geo, Saga) stop for a late-afternoon coffee at Möðrudalur (p237). Bring your swimsuit and towel, too, should you fancy a dip in Víti.

If you're short on time, scenic flights from Mývatn over Askja are possible (see p217).

Operators (note that some prices are from 2012; see websites for current prices):

Fjalladýrð TOUR
(☎471 1858; www.fjalladyrd.is) Based at Möðrudalur farm, on Rte 901, handily placed for Askja access via F905 and F910. Tours to Askja cost Ikr28,900. Also offers day trips climbing Herðubreið (Ikr31,000) or visiting Kverkfjöll ice caves (Ikr31,000), and two-day trips taking in Askja, Kverkfjöll and Vatnajökull (Ikr65,800).

LUNAR LANDSCAPES

If the endless grey-sand desert and jagged lava formations of Ódáðahraun appear otherworldly, you'll understand why NASA astronauts of the *Apollo* mission twice visited the area around Askja (more specifically, the area south of the F90 east of Askja) for astrogeological field trips in the 1960s.

Herðubreið & Askja Region

Fjallasýn   TOUR

(☑464 3941; www.fjallasyn.is) Tours from Reykjahlíð (Ikr27,500) a few times a week, but can also depart from the company's base in Húsavík. Also offers plenty of guided hiking options in the area, including Kverkfjöll.

Geo Travel   TOUR

(☑864 7080; www.geotravel.is) Recommended small-group tours from Reykjahlíð (€172). Also has day trips climbing Herðubreið (€218).

Jeep Tours   TOUR

(☑898 2798; www.jeeptours.is) Runs tours out of Egilsstaðir in the east (Ikr36,000). It's one of few companies visiting Kverkfjöll as a day tour (Ikr36,000), travelling via the (sealed) Rte 910 to Kárahnjúkar dam before tackling 4WD tracks. Lunch packs available.

Mývatn Tours   TOUR

(☑464 1920; www.askjatours.is) Tours in a large 4WD bus daily mid-July to mid-August, and three times a week the rest of the summer (€130). This is the best option if you want hikers' transport to the area, and to be picked up another day.

Saga Travel   TOUR

(☑558 888; www.sagatravel.is) Reliable option from Akureyri; also picks up in Mývatn (Ikr39,000/33,000 from Akureyri/Mývatn). Hotel pick-ups offered; lunch packs can be ordered.

SBA-Norðurleið   TOUR

(☑550 0700/70; www.sba.is) Runs a popular three-day Askja–Kverkfjöll–Vatnajökull tour, weekly from July to mid-August from Akureyri and Mývatn (see p296).

HERÐUBREIÐARLINDIR

The oasis Herðubreiðarlindir, a nature reserve thick with green moss, angelica and the pinky-purple flower of the Arctic river beauty *(Epilobium latifolium)*, was created by springs flowing from beneath the Ódáðahraun lava. You get a superb close-up view of Herðubreið from here (unless, of course, you're greeted by dense fog and/or a wall of blowing sand, as is often the case).

The mini tourist complex has an information office, a **campsite** (sites per person Ikr1100) and the 30-bed **Þorsteinsskáli hut** (☑mid-Jun–Aug 854 9301; www.ffa.is; N 65°11.544', W 16°13.360'; dm Ikr4500), a comfy lodge with showers, kitchen and summer warden. Free, ranger-led, one-hour walks leave from the hut at 11am daily mid-July to mid-August.

Behind the hut is another Fjalla-Eyvindur 'convict hole'; this one is scarcely large enough to breathe inside. It was renovated in 1922 on the remains of the original, which had long since collapsed. Eyvindur is believed to have occupied it during the winter of 1774–75, when he subsisted on angelica root and raw horsemeat stored on top of the hideout to retain heat inside.

HERÐUBREIÐ

Iceland's most distinctive mountain (1682m) has been described as a birthday cake and a lampshade, but Icelanders call it (more respectfully) the 'Queen of the Mountains'. It crops up time and again in the work of local poets and painters, entranced by its beauty.

If Herðubreið (meaning 'broad shoulders') appears to have been made in a jelly mould, that's not far off base. It's a *móberg* mountain, formed by subglacial volcanic eruptions. In fact, if Vatnajökull was to suddenly be stripped of ice, Grímsvötn and Kverkfjöll would probably emerge looking more or less like Herðubreið.

If you wish to climb Herðubreið, beware that a topographic sheet won't do you any good here. As serenely beautiful as the queen may be, the hike can be unrelenting and frustrating if you are not properly prepared. In the spring, as the weather warms slightly, there are a lot of falling rocks, which can alter paths and topography. Clouds often shroud the mountain, which makes it difficult to find your way. A GPS is a must, as is a helmet, plus crampons and an ice axe (and experience in using them).

From the Þorsteinsskáli hut, a marked trail runs to Herðubreið and you can then hike all the way around it in a day. Herðubreið was once thought to be unclimbable, but it was eventually scaled in 1908. Under optimum conditions you can climb the mountain in summer over one long day. The route to the top ascends the western slope. We don't want you to get the wrong idea, however; this climb is demanding, and the threat of snow, rockfall, landslide or bad weather makes it impossible to tackle without the proper mountaineering gear. Don't go alone, prepare for foul weather, and discuss your intentions with the wardens at Herðubreiðarlindir or Askja. Consider joining a tour.

DREKAGIL

The name of the gorge Drekagil, 35km southwest of Herðubreið, means 'Dragon Canyon', after the form of a dragon in the craggy rock formations that tower over it. The canyon behind the Ferðafélag Akureyrar **Dreki huts** (Askja Camp; ☑mid-Jun–Aug 853 2541; www.ffa. is; N 65°02.503′, W 16°35.690′; sites/dm per person Ikr1100/5000) resembles something out of Arizona or the Sinai; bitter winds and freezing temperatures just don't suit this desert landscape!

The Dreki huts are an ideal base for a day or two of exploring the area. Not only does the dramatic Drekagil ravine offer an easy stroll up to an impressive waterfall, but you can also walk 9km up the road and marked trail to Askja. There is also a marked trail to the Bræðrafell hut. The huts sleep a total of 60, and there are showers, a kitchen, an information centre and a summertime warden. Camping is also permitted (you'll probably see rows of white tents set up for a local touring group), but the wind and cold can become oppressive.

Free, ranger-led, 1½-hour hikes leave from the Askja car park at 1pm daily mid-July to mid-August.

At Dreki the Gæsavatnaleið route (F910) turns off the Öskjuleið to cross some intimidating expanses and connect with the Sprengisandur route at Nýidalur, some 125km away.

ASKJA

Perversely, the cold, windy and utterly desolate Askja caldera is the main destination for all tours in this part of the highlands. As bleak and terrible as it may be, this immense 50-sq-km caldera shouldn't be missed. It's difficult to imagine the sorts of forces that created it.

The cataclysm that formed the lake in the Askja caldera (and the Víti crater) happened relatively recently (in 1875) when 2 cu km of tephra was ejected from the Askja volcano. The force was so strong that bits of debris actually landed in Continental Europe. Ash from the eruption poisoned large numbers of cattle in northern Iceland, sparking a wave of emigration to America. It's quite daunting to realise that such cataclysmic events could be replayed at any time.

After the initial eruption, a magma chamber collapsed and created a craterous 11-sq-km hole, 300m below the rim of the original explosion crater. This new depression subsequently filled with water and became the sapphire-blue lake Öskjuvatn, the second-deepest in Iceland at 220m.

In 1907 German researchers Max Rudloff and Walther von Knebel were rowing on the lake when they completely vanished; their bodies were never found. It was suggested that the lake may have hazardous quirks, possibly odd currents or whirlpools; but a rickety canvas boat and icy water could easily explain their deaths. There's a stone cairn and memorial to the men on the rim of the caldera.

In the 1875 eruption a vent near the northeastern corner of the lake exploded and formed the tephra crater Víti, which contains geothermal water. Although a bit on the chilly side if you're expecting a soothing swim (temperatures range between 22°C and 30°C), a dip in this milky blue pool is one of the highlights of any Askja adventure. The route down is slippery but not as steep as it looks.

ℹ️ Getting There & Away

There's no public transport along the Öskjuleið route, but there are plentiful tours. Alternatively, hire a large 4WD and prepare for a rocky ride (and see p350 for advice on fording rivers). The route usually opens in mid- to late June.

If you take F88 into Askja, it's a good idea to leave along F910 so you don't have to retrace all of your steps. Other options from Askja include heading east towards Egilsstaðir, or west on the Gæsavatnaleið route (F910) to Sprengisandur (ask locally for advice on conditions). To reach Kverkfjöll ice caves, head east on F910, then south on F902.

There are no petrol stations anywhere on the route. The nearest ones are at Möðrudalur (87km from Askja) and Mývatn (100km north of Askja).

Kverkfjöll Route

As its name suggests, this 108km-long route creeps southwards to the amazing Kverkfjöll ice caves. It connects Möðrudalur (65km east of Mývatn, off the Ring Road) with the Sigurðarskáli hut, 3km from the lower ice caves, via the F905, F910 and F902. After visiting Askja, you can follow up with a trip to Kverkfjöll by driving south along the F902.

Along the way are several sites of interest, including the twin pyramid-shaped Upptyppingar hills near the Jökulsá á Fjöllum bridge, and the Hvannalindir oasis where there is another of good ol' Fjalla-Eyvindur's winter hide-outs! Hvannalindir lies about 20km north of the Sigurðarskáli hut.

Kverkfjöll is actually a mountain spur capped by the ice of Kverkjökull, a northern tongue of Vatnajökull. Over time, it's also come to refer to the hot-spring-filled ice caves that often form beneath the eastern margin of the Dyngjujökull ice.

Besides being the source of the roiling Jökulsá á Fjöllum, central Iceland's greatest river, Kverkfjöll is also one of the world's largest geothermal areas. The lower Kverkfjöll ice caves lie between 2km and 3km from the Sigurðarskáli hut, a 15-minute walk in each direction from the 4WD track's end.

Here the hot river flows beneath the cold glacier ice, clouds of steam swirl over the river and melt shimmering patterns on the ice walls, and there you have it – a spectacular tourist attraction. Perhaps this was the source of the overworked fire-and-ice cliché that pervades almost everything ever written about Iceland. Huge blocks of ice frequently crash down from the roof – don't enter the ice caves or you risk being caught in their heated combat. Also, the giant blocks of ice can alter the entrance to the cave – it's best to ask where the safest access point is currently located (there's only one point of entry, and it's not an issue if you are on a tour). There can be a danger of sulphur inhalation further inside the cave. From the lower ice caves, ranger-led tours continue up onto the glacier itself.

The large Sigurðarskáli hut (Kverkfjöll hut; ☎ summer 863 9236, year-round 863 5813; www.fljotsdalsherad.is/ferdafelag; N 64°44.850', W 16°37.890'; site/dm per person Ikr1300/5500; ⊙ mid-Jun–early Sep) has comfortable accommodation and a well-maintained campsite. A 2km-return marked hike from behind the hut takes you up Virkisfell (1109m) for a spectacular view over Kverkfjöll and the headwaters of the Jökulsá á Fjöllum.

The road to Kverkfjöll usually opens around mid- to late June. It's good to get to Kverkfjöll early in the season because there's a higher chance of accessing the caves (warmer weather = tumbling ice blocks and bouts of glacial melting). Ask the ranger first about cave conditions and for recommendations for a successful exploration

THE HIGHLANDS KVERKFJÖLL ROUTE

of the area; consider joining a tour to take advantage of ranger expertise.

Kverkfjöll is part of the vast Vatnajökull National Park, so the park website (www.vjp.is) has information.

☞ Tours

Without a robust 4WD vehicle, the only way to visit Kverkfjöll is on a tour. If you do have your own vehicle you can park and walk up to the ice caves – anywhere further is strictly ill-advised. As well as short walks in the area, the park rangers offer guided hikes from the base hut to the geothermal area and the glacier on all days with good weather (a four-/nine-hour hike costs Ikr7500/13,500, including equipment). Call ✆863 9236 (in summer) for tour details.

Besides the ranger-led tours, there are tour packages involving transport and guiding – see Tours, p292, for operators. Note that Fjallasýn has hiking tours in the area, Jeep Tours offers a day trip here from Egilsstaðir, and Fjalladyrð has two-day tours from Möðrudalur.

Another option to consider is the popular three-day Askja–Kverkfjöll–Vatnajökull tour run by bus company **SBA-Norðurleið** (✆550 0700/70; www.sba.is). It leaves on Mondays from early July to mid-August from Akureyri (8.15am) and Mývatn (10am). The cost is Ikr39,500, which includes transport and guide. You must bring your own food and organise your own accommodation (either book Sigurðarskáli hut or bring a tent).

❶ Getting There & Away

Drivers note: the petrol station at Möðrudalur is the last place to fill up.

Understand Iceland

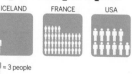

population per sq km

ICELAND   FRANCE   USA

= 3 people

Iceland Today

Crash

Ah, the infamous currency crash – audacious demonstrations of frivolous wealth are 'so 2007', according to locals, but it's still everyone's favourite topic of conversation. These days, however, there's enough distance from the 'crisis' that the nation has had an opportunity to lick its wounds and analyse just how its house of cards was built. Theories have been posited by leading economists – many pointing the finger at the dubious system of privatised fishing quotas and troller loans.

Internationally there was much disdain from foreign investors who watched their funds perform a spectacular vanishing act overnight. A similar sentiment prevailed locally as well, as unscrupulous lending by the conservative banks was brought to light.

By allowing the banks to plummet to their ultimate demise in favour of saving its carefully structured welfare plan, the Icelandic government seems to have found its way back towards the direction of economic prosperity. Job numbers continue to grow, laid-off employees are being reinstated, and everyone is keenly aware that the previous financial decisions are not to be emulated. For more about Iceland's infamous currency crash, see p307.

» Population: 319,800

» Unemployment: 5.8%

» GDP per capita: US$38,500

» Tonnes of fish caught per month: 100,400

» Number of McDonald's: 0

Ash

Earth-rending eruptions are par for the course in Iceland, but Eyjafjallajökull's volcanic blast earned international attention when its thick plumes of smoke caused a record amount of flight cancellations throughout Europe in early 2010. The airline industry, which is estimated to have lost over US$200 million per day, breathed a sigh of relief when the ash cloud stopped on 23 May – as did media broadcasters and commentators, who struggled woefully to pronounce the glacier's name correctly.

Playlist

» Little Talks – Of Monsters and Men
» Big Jumps – Emiliana Torrini
» Boy Lilikoi – Jónsi
» Inside Your Head – Eberg
» Crystalline – Björk
» I'm 9 Today – múm

Top Books

The Draining Lake (Arnaldur Indriðason; 2004) A local favourite
Under the Glacier (Halldór Laxness; 1968) One of the finer works by the Nobel Laureate
The Sagas of Islanders (Jane Smiley et al; 2001) Essential historical reading

Top Films

101 Reykjavík (2000) Comedy with a generous twist of romance
Jar City (2006) Carefully crafted detective thriller set in a windswept small town
Heima (2007) Documentary film following Sigur Rós as they perform throughout Iceland

belief systems
(% of population)

77	3	5
Evangelical Lutheran	Catholic	Free Lutheran
1	9	5
Independent Congregation	Other	No religion

if Iceland were 100 people

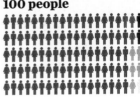

89 would be Icelandic   2 would be Asian
3 would be Polish   **3** would be other
1 would be German   **2** would be other Nordic

Locals sprung into action to relieve the area directly impacted by the storm, as fiery outbursts are quite common, but the international attention that the eruption received was something truly unusual to the local population. The Icelandic tourism board quickly capitalised on the global attention by launching its 'Inspired By Iceland' campaign. The push for more tourists was a smash hit – frustrations from the continent quickly transformed into curiosity, and discounted flights brought over legions of Europeans keen to see what all the fuss was about.

Cash

Although the Icelandic króna is a mere fraction of what it was before the currency crisis of 2008, the country is by no means cheap. The oddly fortuitous crash-and-ash one-two punch gave the nation's tourism industry an unforeseen jolt. Since the summer of 2009, Iceland has been registering record-breaking tourist numbers; the island is expected to hit one million annual visitors by 2015, and there are no signs of slowing down in sight.

Seeing the potential for more serious cash infusion, the government has set about enacting a series of laws in order to trap more of the almighty tourist dollar. At research time, an increase in hospitality tax to 14% was the headlining topic of most news outlets. Local businesses have also followed suit, abiding by the take-from-the-tourists mantra that starkly contrasts the traditional Icelandic style of generous hospitality. The discourse reeks of a certain gold-rush greed as accommodation providers inflate their rates each season with alarming speed. Iceland will undoubtedly reach its glass ceiling – when prices once again outweigh the charms of this naturally gifted island – and it may come sooner than expected if the cost of an Icelandic foray continues to bubble up by 15% to 20% each year.

Most Icelanders don't have surnames, they are given first names and take the name of their father as their last name. As such, the Icelandic phone book is arranged by first names.

Dos & Don'ts

» Do strip and shower thoroughly before entering a hot-pot or pool

» Don't smoke in public places, bars or restaurants

» Do remove your shoes when entering someone's home

» Don't tip in restaurants – it's not customary

» Do leave your pram and baby outside when visiting boutiques and cafes (yes, you read that correctly)

» Don't stand near the edges of bird cliffs – lie on your stomach so as to not spook the wildlife

Top Web Clips

Inspired by Iceland (http://vimeo.com/12236680) Fun-filled, round-the-island romp

London to Iceland (http://vimeo.com/45120368) Inspiring stop-animation short documenting a trip to the island in 52,000 photos

History

Geologically young, staunchly independent and frequently rocked by natural (and more recently financial) disaster, Iceland has a turbulent and absorbing history of Norse settlement, literary genius, bitter feuding and foreign oppression. Life in this harsh and unforgiving landscape was never going to be easy, but the everyday challenges and hardships have cultivated a modern Icelandic spirit that's highly aware of its stormy past yet remarkably resilient, fiercely individualistic, quietly innovative and justifiably proud.

Early Travellers & Irish Monks

History of Iceland, by Jon R Hjalmarsson, is a lively and absorbing account of the nation from settlement to the present day, looking at Iceland's people, places, history and issues.

A veritable baby in geological terms, Iceland was created around 17 million years ago. It was only around 330 BC, when the Greek explorer Pytheas wrote about the island of Ultima Thule, six days' sailing north of Britain, that Europe became aware of a landmass beyond the confines of their maps, lurking in a sea 'congealed into a viscous jelly'.

For many years rumour, myth and fantastic tales of fierce storms, howling winds and barbaric dog-headed people kept explorers away from the great northern ocean, *oceanus innavigabilis*. Irish monks were probably the first to stumble upon Iceland: they regularly sailed to the Faeroes looking for solitude and seclusion. The Irish monk Dicuil wrote in AD 825 of a land where there was no daylight in winter, but on summer nights 'whatever task a man wishes to perform, even picking lice from his shirt, he can manage as well as in clear daylight'. This almost certainly describes Iceland and its White Nights.

It's thought that Irish *papar* (fathers) settled in Iceland around the year 700 but fled when the Norsemen began to arrive in the early 9th century.

TIMELINE

AD 600–700	850–930	871
Irish monks voyage to uninhabited Iceland, becoming the first (temporary) settlers. There is no archaeological evidence, although the element *'papar'* (fathers) crops up in certain place names.	Norse settlers from Norway and Sweden arrive, call the island Snæland (Snow Land), then Garðarshólmi (Garðar's Island), and finally Ísland (Iceland). Scattered farmsteads rapidly cover the country.	Norwegian Viking Ingólfur Arnarson, credited as the country's first permanent inhabitant, sails to the southwest coast and makes his home in a promising-looking bay that he names Reykjavík.

The Vikings Are Coming!

After the Irish monks, Iceland's first permanent settlers came from Norway. The Age of Settlement is traditionally defined as the period between 870 and 930, when political strife on the Scandinavian mainland caused many to flee. Most North Atlantic Norse settlers were ordinary Scandinavian citizens: farmers, herders and merchants who settled right across Western Europe, marrying Britons, Westmen (Irish) and Scots.

It's likely that the Norse accidentally discovered Iceland after being blown off course en route to the Faeroes. The first arrival, the Swede Naddoddur, landed on the east coast around 850 and named the place Snæland (Snow Land) before backtracking to his original destination.

Iceland's second visitor, Garðar Svavarsson, circumnavigated the island and then settled in for the winter at Húsavík on the north coast. When he left in the spring some of his crew remained, or were left behind, thereby becoming the island's first residents.

Around 860 the Norwegian Flóki Vilgerðarson uprooted his farm and family and headed for Snæland. He navigated with ravens, which, after some trial and error, led him to his destination and provided his nickname, Hrafna-Flóki (Raven-Flóki). Hrafna-Flóki sailed to Vatnsfjörður on the west coast but became disenchanted on seeing icebergs floating in the fjord. He renamed the country Ísland (Iceland), and returned to Norway; although he did eventually come back to Iceland, settling in the Skagafjörður district on the north coast.

Credit for the first intentional settlement, according to the 12th-century *Íslendingabók,* goes to Ingólfur Arnarson, who fled Norway with his blood brother Hjörleifur. He landed at Ingólfshöfði (southeast Iceland) in 871, then continued around the coast and set up house at a place he called Reykjavík (Smoky Bay), after the steam from thermal springs there. Hjörleifur settled near the present town of Vík, but was murdered by his slaves shortly thereafter.

As for Ingólfur, he was led to Reykjavík by a fascinating pagan ritual. It was traditional for Viking settlers to toss their high-seat pillars (a symbol of authority and part of a chieftain's paraphernalia) into the sea as they approached land. Wherever the gods brought the pillars ashore was the settler's new home – a practice imitated by waves of settlers who followed from the Norwegian mainland.

Assembling the Alþing

By the time Ingólfur's son Þorsteinn reached adulthood, the whole island was scattered with farms, and people began to feel the need for some sort of government. Iceland's landowners gathered first at regional

Where to Find Viking Vibes

» National Museum, Reykjavík

» Reykjavík 871 +/-2 museum, Reykjavík

» Þingvellir National Park, near Selfoss

» Grettir's Hideout, Drangey

» Eiríksstaðir (reconstruction), Haukadalur

» Stöng farmstead, Þjórsárdalur

» Hrafnkell's burial mound, Aðalból

» Njál's Saga sites, Hvolsvöllur

930	986	1000	1100–1200
The world's oldest existing parliament, the Alþing, is founded at Þingvellir. The Icelanders' law code is memorised by an elected law speaker, who helps to settle legal matters at annual parliamentary gatherings.	Erik the Red founds the first permanent European colony in Greenland, building the settlements of Eystribyggð and Vestribyggð in the southwest of the country.	Iceland officially converts to Christianity under pressure from the Norwegian king, though pagan beliefs and rituals remain. Leif the Lucky lands in Newfoundland, the first European to reach America.	Iceland's literary Golden Age, during which the Old Norse sagas are written. Several are attributed to Snorri Sturluson – historian, poet and the sharpest political operator of this era.

THE VIKINGS

Scandinavia's greatest impact on world history probably occurred during the Viking Age. In the 8th century, an increase in the numbers of restless, landless young men in western Norway coincided with advances in technology, as Nordic shipbuilders developed fast, manoeuvrable boats sturdy enough for ocean crossings.

Norwegian farmers had settled peacefully in Orkney and the Shetlands as early as the 780s, but the Viking Age officially began in bloodshed in 793, when Norsemen plundered St Cuthbert's monastery on Lindisfarne, an island off Britain's Northumberland coast.

The Vikings took to monasteries with delight, realising that speedy raids could bring handsome rewards. They destroyed Christian communities and slaughtered the monks of Britain and Ireland, who could only wonder what sin they had committed to invite the heathen hordes. However, the Vikings' barbarism was probably no greater than the standard of the day – the suddenness and extent of the raids led to their fearsome reputation.

In the following years Viking raiders returned with great fleets, terrorising, murdering, enslaving and displacing local populations, and capturing whole regions across Britain, Ireland, France and Russia. The Vikings travelled to Moorish Spain and the Middle East, attacking Constantinople six times, and even served as mercenaries for the Holy Roman Empire.

Icelandic tradition credits the Norse settlement of Iceland to tyrannical Harald Hårfagre (Harald Fairhair), king of Vestfold in southeastern Norway. Filled with expansionist aspirations, Harald won a significant naval victory at Hafrsfjord (Stavanger) in 890. The deposed chieftains chose to flee rather than surrender, and many wound up in Iceland.

While Viking raids continued in Europe, Eiríkur Rauðe (Erik the Red) headed west with around 500 others to found the first permanent European colony in Greenland in 986. Eiríkur's son, Leif the Lucky, went on to explore the coastline of northeast America in the year 1000, naming the new country Vínland (Wineland). Permanent settlement was thwarted by the *skrælings* (Native Americans), who were anything but welcoming.

Viking raids gradually petered out, and the Viking Age ended with the death of King Harald Harðráði, last of the great Viking kings, who died in battle at Stamford Bridge, England, in 1066.

assemblies to trade and settle disputes, but it became apparent that a national assembly was needed. A national government was a completely novel idea at the time, but Icelanders reasoned that it must be an improvement on the oppressive system they had experienced under the Nordic monarchy.

1104

Hekla's first eruption in historical times. The volcano covers Þjórsárdalur valley and its prosperous medieval farms with a thick layer of ash, rock and cinders.

1200

Iceland descends into anarchy during the Sturlung Age. The government dissolves and, in 1281, Iceland is absorbed by Norway.

KLAUS VEDFELT / GETTY IMAGES ©

» Hekla (p109)

In the early 10th century Þorsteinn Ingólfsson held Iceland's first large-scale district assembly near Reykjavík, and in the 920s the self-styled lawyer Úlfljótur was sent to study Norway's law codes and prepare something similar that would be suitable for Iceland.

At the same time Grímur Geitskör was commissioned to find a location for the Alþing (National Assembly). Bláskógar, near the eastern boundary of Ingólfur's estate, with its beautiful lake and wooded plain, seemed ideal. Along one side of the plain was a long cliff with an elevated base (the Mid-Atlantic Ridge), from where speakers and representatives could preside over people gathered below.

In 930 Bláskógar was renamed Þingvellir (Assembly Plains). Þorsteinn Ingólfsson was given the honorary title *allsherjargoði* (supreme chieftain) and Úlfljótur was designated the first *lögsögumaður* (law speaker), who was required to memorise and annually recite the entire law of the land. It was he, along with the 48 *goðar* (chieftains), who held the actual legislative power.

Although squabbles arose over the choice of leaders and allegiances were continually questioned, the new parliamentary system was a success. At the annual convention of the year 1000, the assembled crowd was bitterly divided between pagans and Christians, and civil war looked likely. Luckily, Þorgeir, the incumbent law speaker, was a master of tact. The *Íslendingabók* relates that he retired to his booth, refusing to speak to anyone for a day and a night while he pondered the matter. When he emerged, he decreed that Iceland should accept the new religion and convert to Christianity, although pagans (such as himself) were to be allowed to practise their religion in private. This decision gave the formerly divided groups a semblance of national unity, and soon the first bishoprics were set up at Skálholt in the southwest and Hólar in the north.

Over the following years, the two-week national assembly at Þingvellir became the social event of the year. All free men could attend. Single people came looking for partners, marriages were contracted and solemnised, business deals were finalised, duels and executions were held, and the Appeals Court handed down judgements on matters that couldn't be resolved in lower courts.

Iceland's 1100 Years: The History of a Marginal Society, by Gunnar Karlsson, provides an insightful, contemporary history of Iceland from settlement to the present.

The word Viking is derived from *vik*, which means bay or cove in Old Norse and probably referred to Viking anchorages during raids.

Anarchy & the Sturlung Age

The late 12th century kicked off the Saga Age, when epic tales of early settlement, family struggles, romance and tragic characters were recorded by historians and writers. Much of our knowledge of this time comes from two weighty tomes, the *Íslendingabók,* a historical narrative from the Settlement Era written by 12th-century scholar Ari Þorgilsson (Ari the Learned), and the detailed *Landnámabók,* a comprehensive account of the settlement.

HISTORY ANARCHY & THE STURLUNG AGE

1241	1397	1402–04	1550
Seventy armed men arrive at Snorri Sturluson's home in Reykholt, ordered to bring him to Norway to face treason charges. Snorri never leaves – he is stabbed to death in his cellar.	On 17 June the Kalmar Union is signed in Sweden, uniting the countries of Norway, Sweden and Denmark under one king. As part of this treaty, Iceland comes under Danish control.	The Black Death sweeps across Iceland, 50 years after its devastating journey across mainland Europe, and kills around half of the population.	King Christian III's attempts to impose Lutheranism finally succeed after the Catholic bishop Jón Arason is captured in battle and beheaded at Skálholt along with two of his sons.

Despite the advances in such cultural pursuits, Icelandic society was beginning to deteriorate. By the early 13th century the enlightened period of peace that had lasted 200 years was waning. Constant power struggles between rival chieftains led to violent feuds and a flourishing of Viking-like private armies who raided farms across the country. This dark hour in Iceland's history was known as the Sturlung Age, its tragic events and brutal history graphically recounted in the three-volume *Sturlunga Saga*.

As Iceland descended into chaos, the Norwegian king Hákon Hákonarson pressured chieftains, priests and the new breed of wealthy aristocrats to accept his authority. The Icelanders, who saw no alternative, dissolved all but a superficial shell of their government and swore their allegiance to the king. An agreement of confederacy was made in 1262. In 1281 a new code of law, the Jónsbók, was introduced by the king, and Iceland was absorbed into Norwegian rule.

Norway immediately set about appointing Norwegian bishops to Hólar and Skálholt and imposed excessive taxes. Contention flared as former chieftains quibbled over high offices, particularly that of *járl* (earl), an honour that fell to the ruthless Gissur Þorvaldsson, who in 1241 murdered Snorri Sturluson, Iceland's best-known historian and writer (see the boxed text, p141).

Meanwhile, the volcano Hekla erupted three times, covering a third of the country in ash; a mini–ice age followed, and severe winters wiped out livestock and crops. The Black Death arrived, killing half the population, and the once indomitable spirit of the people seemed broken.

Enter the Danes

Iceland's fate was now in the hands of the highest Norwegian bidder, who could lease the governorship of the country on a three-year basis. In 1397 the Kalmar Union of Norway, Sweden and Denmark brought Iceland under Danish rule. After disputes between church and state, the Danish government seized church property and imposed Lutheranism in the Reformation of 1550. When the stubborn Catholic bishop of Hólar, Jón Arason, resisted and gained a following, he and his two sons were taken to Skálholt and beheaded.

In 1602 the Danish king imposed a crippling trade monopoly whereby Swedish and Danish firms were given exclusive trading rights in Iceland for 12-year periods. This resulted in large-scale extortion, importation of spoilt or inferior goods and yet more suffering that would last another 250 years. However, one positive thing eventually came from the monopoly. In an attempt to bypass the embargo and boost local industry, local sheriff Skúli Magnússon built weaving, tanning and wool-dyeing factories – the foundations of the modern city of Reykjavík.

The Althing at Thingvellir, by Helmut Lugmayr, explains the role and history of the oldest parliament in the world and includes a section on Þingvellir's unique geology.

The Complete Sagas of Icelanders, edited by Viður Hreinsson, is a must for saga fiends. It's a summary translation of 50 saga tales, featuring all the main yarns, along with a few shorter fantasy tales.

1590	1602	1625–85	1627
Bishop Guðbrandur Þorláksson's lovely – and quite accurate – map of Iceland is published. The sea is sprinkled with whale-like monsters, and it notes that Hekla 'vomits stones with a terrible noise'.	Denmark imposes a trade monopoly, giving Danish and Swedish firms exclusive trading rights in Iceland. This leads to unrestrained profiteering by Danish merchants and Iceland's slow impoverishment.	Period of the notorious Westfjords witch-hunts: 21 Icelanders are executed, beginning with Jón Rögnvaldsson, burned at the stake for 'raising a ghost' and possessing sinister-looking runic writing.	The 'Turkish Abductions' take place: Barbary pirates raid the east of Iceland and the Vestmannaeyjar, taking hundreds of people prisoner and killing anyone who resists them.

Even More Misery

Talk about getting kicked while you're down! As if impoverishment at the hands of Danish overlords was not enough, Barbary pirates got in on the action, raiding the Eastfjords and the Reykjanes Peninsula before descending on the Vestmannaeyjar in 1627. The defenceless population attempted to hide in Heimaey's cliffs and caves, but the pirates ransacked the island, killing indiscriminately and loading 242 people into their ships. The unfortunate Icelanders were taken to Algiers, where most were sold into slavery. Back home, money was scrimped and saved as ransom, and eventually 13 of the captives were freed. The most famous was Guðríður Símonardóttir, who returned to Iceland and married Hallgrímur Pétursson, one of Iceland's most famous poets – the three bells in Hallgrímskirkja are named after the couple and their daughter.

During the same period, Europe's witch-hunting craze reached Icelandic shores. Rather than crazy old ladies, Icelandic witches turned out mostly to be men – of the 130 cases that appear in the court annals, only 10% involve women. The luckiest defendants were brutally flogged; 21 of the unluckiest were burned at the stake, mostly for making their neighbours sick or for possessing magical writing or suspicious-looking amulets.

In 1783 the Laki crater row erupted, spewing out billions of tonnes of lava and poisonous gas clouds for a full eight months. Fifty farms in the immediate area were wiped out, and the noxious dust and vapours and consequent Haze Famine went on to kill around 9000 Icelanders – first the plants died, then the livestock, then the people. The ash clouds affected the whole of Europe, causing freak weather conditions, including acid rain and floods.

Iceland Saga, by Magnús Magnússon, offers an entertaining introduction to Icelandic history and literature, and explains numerous saga events and settings.

HISTORY EVEN MORE MISERY

Return to Independence

Fed up with five centuries of oppressive foreign rule and conscious of a growing sense of liberalisation across Europe, Icelandic nationalism began to flourish in the 19th century. By 1855 Jón Sigurðsson, an Icelandic scholar, had successfully lobbied for restoration of free trade, and by 1874 Iceland had drafted a constitution and regained control of its domestic affairs.

Iceland's first political parties were formed during this period, and urban development began in this most rural of countries. By 1918 Iceland had signed the Act of Union, which effectively released the country from Danish rule, making it an independent state within the Kingdom of Denmark.

Iceland prospered during WWI as wool, meat and fish exports gained high prices. When WWII loomed, however, Iceland declared neutrality

Until 1903 Iceland's coat of arms was a silver stockfish (split, dried cod) topped by a golden crown.

1703	1783–84	1786	1855–90
Iceland's first census reveals that the country's population is a tiny 50,358; 55% are female, 45% male. Men – physical labourers – are more affected by malnutrition and famine.	The Laki crater row erupts, pouring out poisonous gas clouds that kill 25% of the population and over 50% of livestock. The haze covers Europe, causing freak weather conditions, flooding and famine.	The official founding of Reykjavík (currently inhabited by fewer than 200 souls). The settlement is granted a trade charter, and merchants are enticed to settle here with tax breaks.	Iceland moves towards independence, with the restoration of free trade and a draft constitution. Not everyone sticks around to see it: many Icelanders emigrate to start life afresh in North America.

in the hope of maintaining its important trade links with both Britain and Germany.

On 9 April 1940 Denmark was occupied by Germany, prompting the Alþing to take control of Iceland's foreign affairs once more. A year later, on 17 May 1941, the Icelanders requested complete independence. The formal establishment of the Republic of Iceland finally took place at Þingvellir on 17 June 1944 – now celebrated as Independence Day.

WWII & the USA Moves In

Iceland's total lack of military force worried the Allied powers and so in May 1940 Britain, most vulnerable to a German-controlled Iceland, sent in forces to occupy the island. Iceland had little choice but to accept the situation, but ultimately the country's economy profited from British construction projects and spending.

Daughter of Fire – a Portrait of Iceland, by Katherin Scherman, is a beautifully written and evocative historical overview of Iceland, covering the land, the people and the sagas.

When the British troops withdrew in 1941 the government allowed American troops to move in, on the understanding that they would move out at the end of the war. Although the US military left in 1946, it retained the right to re-establish a base at Keflavík should war threaten. After the war, and back under their own control, Icelanders were reluctant to submit to any foreign power. When the government was pressured into becoming a founding member of NATO in 1949, riots broke out in Reykjavík. The government agreed to the proposition on the conditions that Iceland would never take part in offensive action and that no foreign military troops would be based in the country during peacetime.

These conditions were soon broken. War with Korea broke out in 1950, and in 1951 at NATO's request the US, jumpy about the Soviet threat, once again took responsibility for the island's defence. US military personnel and technology at the Keflavík base continued to increase over the next four decades, as Iceland served as an important Cold War monitoring station. The controversial US military presence in Iceland only ended in September 2006, when the base at Keflavík finally closed.

Modern Iceland

Following the Cold War, Iceland went through a period of growth, rebuilding and modernisation. The Ring Road was completed in 1974 – opening up transport links to the remote southeast – and projects such as the Krafla power station in the northeast and the Svartsengi power plant near Reykjavík were developed. A boom in the fishing industry saw Iceland extend its fishing limit in the 1970s to 200 miles (322km). This, however, precipitated the worst of the 'cod wars', as the UK refused to recognise the new zone. During the seven-month conflict, Icelandic ships cut the nets of British trawlers, shots were fired, and ships on both sides were rammed.

1917–18	1918	1940–41	1944
Iceland is struck by the 'Winter of the Great Frosts'. Temperatures plummet to a record low of -38°C (-36.4°F), and icebergs block all ports.	Denmark's grip on Iceland gradually loosens. Following Home Rule in 1904, the Act of Union is signed on 1 December 1918, making Iceland an independent state within the Kingdom of Denmark.	After the Nazis occupy Denmark, the UK sends British troops to invade and occupy neutral Iceland, concerned Germany might acquire a military presence there. A US base is later established at Keflavík.	A majority of Icelanders vote for independence from Denmark, and the Republic of Iceland is formally established on 17 June. King Christian X telegrams his congratulations.

ICELAND'S ECONOMIC MELTDOWN

Everything was looking so rosy. Between 2003 and early 2008, Iceland was full of confidence and riding high. But much of the country's wealth was built over a black hole of debt – its banks' liabilities were more than 10 times the country's annual GDP. The ripples of the worldwide financial crisis became a tidal wave by the time they reached Icelandic shores, washing away the country's entire economy.

By October 2008 the Icelandic stock market had crashed; the króna plummeted, losing almost half its value overnight; all three national banks went into receivership; and the country teetered on the brink of bankruptcy.

Relations between Iceland and the UK were strained following the collapse of Icesave (a subsidiary of Iceland's national bank Landsbanki), in which 300,000 British customers had invested their savings. UK prime minister Gordon Brown invoked antiterrorist laws to freeze Icelandic assets, which was seen by many Icelanders as excessively heavy-handed.

Extra scandal was added with the involvement of two powerful billionaires. Jón Ásgeir Jóhannesson (former boss of Baugur, which bought up British businesses such as Woolworths, Karen Millen Iceland, Marks & Spencer and Hamleys) and Thor Björgólfsson both had major shares in Glitnir, and in Landsbanki and Straumur banks, respectively. Both men have been accused of treating the banks in a cavalier fashion, exposing them to disproportionate risks – accusations that both men strongly denied.

Help came for Iceland in November 2008 with a US$2.1 billion International Monetary Fund (IMF) loan and a US$3 billion bailout from Scandinavian neighbours. Nevertheless, spiralling inflation, wage cuts and redundancies meant that Icelanders' incomes fell by a quarter in real terms. Protestors rioted in Reykjavík, furious with a government they felt had betrayed them by not downsizing the bloated banking system. Prime Minister Geir Haarde resigned in January 2009.

One of the new government's first acts was to apply for EU membership, with a view to changing their currency from the króna to the euro (although this looks a less-than-attractive prospect from the vantage point of 2012).

The crash was a terrible blow to Icelanders, but incredibly the economic situation has already begun to right itself. Where other countries in financial straits chose to bail out their financial institutions, the Icelandic government refused to use taxpayers' money to prop up the failing banks. Instead, it made the Icelandic social welfare system its priority, choosing to help those citizens who were worst affected by the crash and let the private banks' creditors take the hit. This unique decision appears to be paying off – other nations are still floundering in the financial mire, but Iceland appears to be on the rise again.

The fishing industry has always been vital to Iceland, although it's had its ups and downs – quotas were reduced in the 1990s so stocks could regenerate after overfishing. The industry went into recession, leading to an unemployment rate of 3% (a previously unheard of level in Iceland)

1974

The Ring Road around the island is completed when the Skeiðarárbrú bridge opens on 14 July. Until now, Höfn has been one of the most isolated towns in Iceland.

» Ring Road

1986

The beginning of the end of the Cold War? General Secretary Mikhail Gorbachev and President Ronald Reagan agree to meet at a summit in Höfði House, Reykjavík.

HISTORY MODERN ICELAND

and a sharp drop in the króna. The country slowly began a period of economic regeneration as the fishing industry stabilised. Today the industry still accounts for about half of the country's GDP, with the total catch valued at around 150 billion krónur in 2011.

In 2003 Iceland resumed whaling as part of a scientific research program, despite a global moratorium on hunts. In 2006 Iceland resumed commercial whaling, in spite of condemnation from around the globe. The US threatened diplomatic action over the hunting of fin whales, and the company responsible for the majority of fin catches agreed to stop the hunt in 2012. Hunting of minke whales continues, and is likely to be a major issue when the country's EU membership application is formally considered.

The executives of the bankrupt Icelandic banks were awarded the 2009 Ig Nobel Prize for Economics, 'for demonstrating that tiny banks can be rapidly transformed into huge banks, and vice versa'.

Iceland's huge dependence on its fishing industry and on imported goods means that the country has always had relatively high prices and a currency prone to fluctuation. Its exact vulnerability was brought into focus in September 2008, when the global economic crisis hit the country with a sledgehammer blow. Reykjavík was rocked by months of fierce protest, as the then-government's popularity evaporated along with the country's wealth.

Prime Minister Geir Haarde resigned in January 2009. His replacement, Jóhanna Sigurðardóttir, hit international headlines as the world's first openly gay prime minister. Her first major act was to apply for EU membership, with the eventual aim of adopting the euro as the country's new currency. It's a contentious issue: a Gallup poll taken in February 2012 showed 44% of people favoured withdrawing the application, while 43% wanted to continue.

Icelandic volcanism became international news in April 2010, when the ash cloud from the eruption under Eyjafjallajökull glacier shut down European air traffic for six days, causing travel chaos across much of the continent. In comparison to the Eyjafjallajökull eruptions, the Grímsvötn volcano, which erupted the following year, was a mere trifle – its ash cloud only managed to cause three days of air-traffic disruption.

2006	2008	2010	2012
The controversial US military base at Keflavík closes down after 45 years in service; the government also approves the resumption of commercial whaling.	The worldwide financial downturn hits Iceland particularly hard, precipitating the worst national banking crisis ever when all three of the country's major banks collapse.	The volcano under Eyjafjallajökull glacier begins erupting in March. In April its 9km-high ash plume brings European flights to a standstill for six days. The eruption is declared over in October.	Former prime minister Geir Haarde is found guilty of failing to hold emergency cabinet meetings in the run-up to the financial crash, but is cleared of three more serious charges, including gross negligence.

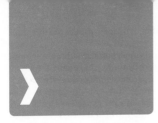

Natural Wonders

It's difficult to remain unmoved by the amazing diversity of the Icelandic landscape. Contrary to popular opinion, it's not an island completely covered in ice, nor is it a barren lunar landscape of congealed lava flows and windswept tundra. Both of these habitats exist, but so too do steep-sided fjords sweeping down to the sea, lush farmland, rolling hills, glacier-carved valleys, steaming fields, bubbling mudpots and vast, desert-like wasteland. It is this rich mix of scenery and the possibility of experiencing such extremes, so close together, that attract, surprise and enthral anyone who has been lucky enough to visit the country.

Iceland is roughly equal in size to England, but with 22 active volcanoes, 250 geothermal areas, 780 hot springs and the world's third-largest ice cap (after Antarctica and Greenland), it's a vast reserve of information for scientists and a stunning playground for the rest of us.

Volatile Iceland

Plonked firmly on the Mid-Atlantic Ridge, a massive 18,000km-long rift between two of the earth's major tectonic plates, Iceland is a shifting, steaming lesson in schoolroom geology. Suddenly you'll be racking your brains to remember long-forgotten homework on how volcanoes work, what a solfatara is, and why lava and magma aren't quite the same thing.

A mere baby in geological terms, Iceland is the youngest country in Europe, formed by underwater volcanic eruptions along the joint of the North American and Eurasian plates 17 to 20 million years ago. The earth's crust in Iceland is only a third of its normal thickness, and magma (molten rock) continues to rise from deep within, forcing the two plates apart. The result is clearly visible at Þingvellir, where the great rift Almannagjá broadens by between 1mm and 18mm per year, and at Námafjall, where a series of steaming vents mark the ridge.

Plants and Animals of Iceland, by Benny Génsböl and Jon Feilberg, is an illustrated guide to all of Iceland's flora and fauna, including birds, marine mammals and 220 species of plants.

Volcanoes

The thin crust and grating plates are responsible for a whole host of exciting volcanic activities. Iceland's volcanoes are many and varied – some are active, some extinct, and some are dormant and dreaming, no doubt, of future destruction. Fissure eruptions and their associated craters are probably the most common type of eruption in Iceland. The still-volatile Lakagígar crater row around Mt Laki is the country's most unearthly example. It produced the largest lava flow in human history in the 18th century, covering an area of 565 sq km to a depth of 12m.

Several of Iceland's liveliest volcanoes are found beneath glaciers, which makes for dramatic eruptions as molten lava and ice interact. The main 2010 Eyjafjallajökull eruption was of this type: it caused a *jökulhlaup* (flooding caused by volcanic eruption beneath an ice cap) that washed away part of the Ring Road, before throwing up the famous ash plume that grounded Europe's aeroplanes. Iceland's most active volcano,

Grímsvötn, which lies beneath the Vatnajökull ice cap, behaved in a similar fashion in 2011.

Iceland not only has subglacial eruptions, but also submarine ones. In 1963 the island of Surtsey exploded from the sea, giving scientists the opportunity to study how smouldering chunks of newly created land are colonised by plants and animals. Surtsey is off-limits to visitors, but you can climb many classical-looking cones such as Hekla, once thought to be the gateway to Hell; Eldfell, which did its best to bury the town of Heimaey in 1974; and Snæfellsjökull on the Snæfellsnes Peninsula.

Recent eruptions in Iceland have tended to be fairly harmless – they're often called 'tourist eruptions' because their fountains of magma, electric storms and dramatic ash clouds make perfect photos but cause relatively little damage. This is partly due to the sparsely populated land, and partly because devastating features such as fast-flowing lava, lahars (mudslides) and pyroclastic surges (like the ones that obliterated Pompeii and Herculaneum) are usually absent in this part of the world. The main danger lies in the gases that are released: suffocating carbon dioxide, highly acidic sulphur-based gases, and the deadly fluorine that poisoned people and livestock during the Laki eruptions. The **Icelandic Met Office** (Veðurstofa Íslands; www.vedur.is) keeps track of eruptions and the earthquakes that tend to proceed them.

For a bit of background information about the country's diverse landscape, check out *Iceland – Classical Geology*, by Þor Þordarson and Armann Hoskuldsson.

Geysers, Springs & Fumaroles

In 2002 scientists discovered the world's second-smallest creature, *Nanoarchaeum equitans,* living in near-boiling water in a hydrothermal vent off the north coast of Iceland.

Iceland's Great Geysir gave its name to the world's spouting hot springs. It was once very active, frequently blowing water to a height of over 100m, but earthquakes have altered the pressures inside its plumbing system and today it is far quieter. Deep under the geyser field, a magma chamber heats rain- and meltwater. Pressurised by overlying water and rock, the water is unable to boil into steam and so it becomes superheated. When a little of the water finally escapes, pressure is temporarily released from the system, which causes the superheated water to flash into steam. The steam takes up to 1600 times as much space as the original volume of water, and this sudden expansion of gas shoots the overlying water skywards. Strokkur demonstrates the effect admirably, blasting a steaming column into the air every six minutes.

Geysers are rare phenomena, with only around 1000 existing on earth. However, in Iceland water that has percolated down through the rock and been superheated by magma can emerge on the surface in various other exciting ways.

GEOLOGICALLY SPEAKING

Everywhere you go in Iceland you'll be bombarded with geological jargon to describe the landscape. The terms following will let you one-up the other geological neophytes.

Basalt The most common type of solidified lava. This hard, dark, dense volcanic rock often solidifies into columns.

Igneous A rock formed by solidifying magma or lava.

Moraine A ridge of boulders, clay and sand carried and deposited by a glacier.

Obsidian Black, glassy rock formed by the rapid solidification of lava without crystallisation.

Rhyolite Light-coloured, fine-grained volcanic rock similar to granite in composition.

Scoria Porous volcanic gravel that has cooled rapidly while moving, creating a glassy surface with iron-rich crystals that give it a glittery appearance.

Tephra Solid matter ejected into the air by an erupting volcano.

Some of it boils its way into hot springs, pools and rivers – you'll find naturally hot water sources all around Iceland, including the springs at Landmannalaugar, the river at Hveragerði and the warm blue-white pool in the bottom of the Víti Crater. Icelanders have long harnessed these soothing gifts of nature, turning them into geothermal swimming pools and spas, the smartest of which are Mývatn Nature Baths and the Blue Lagoon.

Fumaroles are places where superheated water reaches the surface as steam – the weirdest Icelandic examples are at Hverir, where gases literally scream their way from sulphurous vents in the earth. Lazier, messier bloops and bubblings take place at mudpots, for example at Krýsuvík on the Reykjanes Peninsula, where heated water mixes with mud and clay. The colourful splatterings around some of the mudpots are caused by various minerals (sulphurous yellow, iron-red), and also by the extremophile bacteria and algae that somehow thrive in this boiling-acid environment.

Ice & Snow

Glaciers and ice caps cover about 15% of Iceland, many of which are remnants of a cool period that began 2500 years ago. Ice caps are formed as snow piles up over millennia in an area where it's never warm enough to melt. The weight of the snow causes it to slowly compress into ice, eventually crushing the land beneath the ice cap.

Iceland's largest ice cap, Vatnajökull in the southeast, covers almost 13% of the country and is the third-largest in the world. This immense glittering weight of ice may seem immovable, but around its edges, slow-moving rivers of ice – glaciers – flow imperceptibly down the mountainsides. Like rivers, they carry pieces of stony sediment with them, which they dump in cindery-looking moraines at the foot of the mountain, or on vast gravelly outwash plains such as the Skeiðarársandur in southeast Iceland. This can occur very quickly, if volcanoes under the ice erupt and cause a *jökulhlaup*: the *jökulhlaup* from the 1996 Grímsvötn eruption destroyed Iceland's longest bridge and swept Jeep-sized boulders down onto the plain.

Several of Iceland's glaciers have lakes at their tips. Jökulsárlón is a great place to watch icebergs calve from the Breiðamerkurjökull. Luminous-blue pieces tend to indicate a greater age of ice, as centuries of compression squeeze out the air bubbles that give ice its usual silvery-white appearance.

Glaciers have carved out much of the Icelandic landscape since its creation, forming the glacial valleys and fjords that make those picture-postcard photos today. The ice advances and retreats with the millennia, and also with the seasons, but there are worrying signs that Iceland's major ice caps – Vatnajökull, Mýrdalsjökull in the southwest, and Langjökull and Hofsjökull in the highlands – have been melting at an unprecedented rate since 2000. Icelandic Met Office glaciologists believe that some of their attendant glaciers, such as Snæfellsjökull in the west, could disappear completely within a few decades.

Wildlife

Mammals & Marine Life

Apart from sheep, cows and horses, you'll be very lucky to have any casual sightings of animals in Iceland. The only indigenous land mammal is the elusive Arctic fox, best spotted in remote Hornstrandir, in the Westfjords – wildlife enthusiasts can push pause on their holiday and monitor these precious creatures while volunteering at the Arctic Fox Centre. In east Iceland, herds of reindeer can sometimes be spotted from

Iceland isn't truly an Arctic country – the mainland falls short of the Arctic Circle by a few kilometres. To cross that imaginary boundary, you'll need to travel to the island of Grímsey, Iceland's only real piece of Arctic territory.

Imported by the Vikings, the pure-bred Icelandic horse *(Equus scandinavicus)* is a small, tough breed perfectly suited to the country's rough conditions. Icelandic horses have five gaits, including the unusual *tölt* – a running walk so smooth that riders can drink a glass of beer without spilling a drop.

the road. The deer were introduced from Norway in the 18th century and now roam the mountains. Polar bears occasionally drift across from Greenland on ice floes, but armed farmers make sure they don't last long.

In contrast, Iceland has a rich marine life, particularly whales. On whale-watching tours from Húsavík in northern Iceland (among other places), you'll have an excellent chance of seeing cetaceans, particularly dolphins, porpoises, minke whales and humpback whales. Sperm, fin, sei, pilot, killer and blue whales also swim in Icelandic waters and have been seen by visitors. For more information on Iceland's whales, see the boxed text, p229. Seals can be seen in the Eastfjords, on the Vatnsnes Peninsula in northwest Iceland, in the Mýrar region on the southeast coast (including at Jökulsárlón), in Breiðafjörður in the west, and in the Westfjords.

> Arctic terns possess kamikaze instincts and will attack if you venture anywhere near their nests. When hiking in tern territory, wear a hat, raise your hand above your head or carry a long stick – terns go for the highest point when they swoop for a peck.

Birds

Bird life is prolific, at least from May to August. On coastal cliffs and islands around the country you can see a mind-boggling array of seabirds, often in massive colonies. Most impressive for their sheer numbers are gannets, guillemots, razorbills, kittiwakes, fulmars and puffins. Less numerous birds include wood sandpipers, Arctic terns, skuas, Manx shearwaters, golden plovers, storm petrels and Leach's petrels. In addition, there are many species of ducks, ptarmigans, whooping swans, redwings, divers and gyrfalcons, and two species of owl. For information on where to see the birds, see p37.

> Marimo balls (golf-ball-sized spheres of algae) are found naturally in only two places in the world: Lake Akan in Japan and Iceland's Mývatn.

Flowers & Fungi

Although ostensibly barren in places, the vegetation in Iceland is surprisingly varied – you just need to get close to see it. Most vegetation is low growing, staying close to the ground and spreading as much as possible to get a better grip on the easily eroded soil. Even the trees, where there are any, are stunted. As the old joke goes, if you're lost in an Icelandic forest, just stand up.

If you're visiting in summer, you'll be treated to incredible displays of wildflowers blooming right across the country. Most of Iceland's 440 flowering plants are introduced species – especially the ubiquitous purple lupin, once an environmental help, now a hindrance. Throughout Iceland you'll see the bright-pink flowers of the tall Arctic fireweed around riverbeds; the distinctive, graceful bell shape of the purple Arctic

LITTLE NORTHERN BROTHERS

Cute, clumsy and endearingly comic, the puffin (*Fratercula arctica*, or *lundi* as they're called in Icelandic) is one of Iceland's best-loved birds. Although known for its frantic fluttering and crash landings, the bird is surprisingly graceful underwater and was once thought to be a bird-fish hybrid.

The puffin is a member of the auk family and spends most of its year at sea. For four or five months it comes to land to breed, generally keeping the same mate and burrow (a multiroom apartment!) from year to year.

Until very recently, 60% of the world's puffins bred in Iceland, and you would see them in huge numbers around the island from late May to August. However, over the last seven years, the puffin stock has gone into a sudden, sharp decline in the south of Iceland. The reason is uncertain, but it's thought that changing ocean temperatures have caused their main food, sand eels, to drift out of reach. It's also possible that hunting and egg collection have had an unanticipated effect – in 2012 a total ban was proposed.

However, the good news is that puffins in the north seem unaffected. The birds continue to flitter around the cliffs of Grímsey, as well as in Borgarfjörður Eystri and the Westfjords.

WHALING IN ICELAND

In the late 19th century whale hunting became a lucrative commercial prospect with the arrival of steam-powered ships and explosive harpoons. Norwegian hunters built 13 large-scale whaling stations in Iceland, and hunted until stocks practically disappeared in 1913. Icelanders established their own whaling industry between 1935 and 1986, when whale numbers again became dangerously low and commercial hunting was banned by the International Whaling Commission (IWC). Iceland resumed commercial whaling in 2006, to the consternation of environmentalists worldwide. When asked 'why is Iceland whaling today?', the answer is not a simple one.

According to a 2010 Gallup poll, only 5% of Icelanders eat whale meat regularly. Exports are limited: Japan was the main market for fin-whale meat, but lack of demand led to a halt in trade in 2012. Members of Iceland's tourism board are strong objectors, stating that Iceland's whaling industry has a detrimental effect on whale watching (although this is disputed by the Ministry of Fisheries and Agriculture). The industry has also brought international condemnation – in October 2009, 26 nations, including the US, UK, Australia, France, Sweden, Spain and Germany, organised a formal diplomatic démarche against whaling in Iceland.

The arguments against whaling hold little sway in Iceland. A recent poll found that 67% of Icelanders support whale hunting, while 20% are opposed. The fishing industry is of paramount importance to the country, and many believe that culling whales preserves fish stocks (although this is refuted by Whale & Dolphin Conservation Society studies). Older Icelanders view the country's whaling past with nostalgia, remembering when jobs at the whaling station put food on the table. Most of all, whaling has become intrinsically linked to national pride. Icelanders have a long tradition of not letting others dictate their actions, and in the face of worldwide criticism, asking Icelanders whether they support whaling is tantamount to asking whether they support Iceland.

Ironically, most whale meat caught by Icelandic whalers now goes to feeding curious tourists. In 2012 the International Fund for Animal Welfare (IFAW) and Ice Whale (Icelandic Whale Watching Association) launched a high-profile 'Meet Us Don't Eat Us' campaign to encourage visitors to go whale watching rather than whale tasting.

harebell; and several varieties of colourful saxifrage and daisies lining every trail. In grassy lowlands look out for the pale and dainty northern green orchid, and in upland areas the white heads of Arctic cotton, the soft yellow petals of the upright primrose and the small, pretty flowers of the mountain heath. Coastal areas are generally characterised by low grasses, bogs and marshlands, while at higher elevations hard or soft tundra covers the ground.

Another common sight when walking just about anywhere in Iceland is the profusion of fungi. There are about 1500 types of fungi growing in Iceland, and you'll see everything from pale white mushrooms to bright orange flat caps as you walk along trails, by roadsides or through fields.

In southern and eastern Iceland new lava flows are first colonised by mosses, which create a velvety green cloak across the rough rocks. Older lava flows in the east and those at higher elevations are generally first colonised by lichens. Confusingly, Icelandic moss *(Cetraria islandica)*, the grey-green or pale brown frilly growth that you'll see absolutely everywhere, is actually lichen. Over the centuries, Icelanders have eaten it in times of famine – it's very nutritious, but you really would have to be starving to stomach its slimy texture and acid-bitter taste.

Rather sweetly, a nationwide poll was held in 2004 to choose a national flower. The mountain avens *(Dryas octopetala)*, known as *holtasóley* (heath buttercup) in Icelandic, was the worthy winner. Look out for it on gravel stretches and rocky outcrops – its flowers are about 3cm in diameter, with eight delicate white petals and an exploding yellow-sun centre.

A Guide to the Flowering Plants and Ferns of Iceland, by Hörður Kristinsson, is the best all-round field guide to Icelandic flowers.

National Parks & Reserves

Sheep overgrazing has caused dreadful soil erosion. During the 1950s and '60s, it was considered patriotic to sprinkle free Nootka lupin seeds on barren land to combat the problem. Large areas were successfully revegetated, but today the tall flowers are threatening Iceland's biodiversity, blocking light to indigenous mosses, lichens and shrubs.

Iceland has three national parks and more than 80 nature reserves, natural monuments, country parks and wildlife reserves. Umhverfisstofnun (Environment & Food Agency; www.ust.is) is responsible for protecting many of these sites. Its website contains a comprehensive section on each national park. Conservation projects in the parks tend to focus on path-building/maintenance and lupin removal; see the website for details on how to volunteer.

Þingvellir (www.thingvellir.is), Iceland's oldest national park, protects a scenic 84-sq-km lake, the geologically significant Almannagjá rift, and is the site of the original Alþing (National Assembly). The park is administered directly by the prime minister's office and is a Unesco World Heritage Site. See p96 for more details.

Snæfellsjökull (www.ust.is) in west Iceland was established in June 2001. The park protects the Snæfellsjökull glacier (made famous by Jules Verne), the surrounding lava fields and coast; see p151.

Vatnajökull (www.vatnajokulsthjodgardur.is) is the largest national park in all of Europe and covers roughly 13% of Iceland. It was founded in 2008 by uniting two previously established national parks: Skaftafell (p272) in southeast Iceland, and Jökulsárgljúfur (p230) further north. A third visitor centre, Snæfellsstofa, opened recently next door to Skriðuklaustur (see p246) in the east. The park protects the entirety of the Vatnajökull glacier, Dettifoss (the strongest waterfall in Europe) and sundry geological anomalies.

Energy Dilemmas

Iceland's small population, pristine wilderness, lack of heavy industry and high use of geothermal and hydroelectric power give it an enviable environmental reputation. Its use of geothermal power is one of the most creative in the world, and the country's energy experts are now advising Chinese and Indian industries on possible ways to harness geothermal sources. Iceland is also at the forefront of hydrogen-fuel research, and aims to phase out petrol- and diesel-powered cars by 2050.

If hiring a 4WD vehicle, stick to marked trails; off-roading is illegal and causes irreparable damage to the delicate landscape.

However, power supplies provided free by bountiful Nature are not just of interest to Icelanders. Foreign industrialists in search of cheap energy also have their eye on the country's glacial rivers and geothermal hot spots. Alcoa, an American aluminium-smelting company, was responsible for one of Iceland's most controversial schemes. The Kárahnjúkar hydroelectric station in the Eastfjords, completed in 2009, was the biggest construction project in Iceland's history, creating a network of dams and tunnels, a vast reservoir, a power station and miles of high-tension lines to supply electricity to a fjord-side smelter 80km away in Reyðarfjörður. Alcoa was named one of the top sustainable corporations at the World Economic Forum in Davos, Switzerland. The dam, however, has devastated the starkly beautiful landscape and some marvellous natural phenomena that are found nowhere else on earth.

The dam and smelter are a dramatic illustration of the dilemma Iceland faces. Many areas of the country are subject to similar proposals. So how will Icelanders earn their living in the future – through tourism and cultural industries, or by opening up vast tracts of their wilderness to industrial megaprojects? Watch this space...

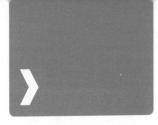

Icelandic Culture: Sagas to Sigur Rós

It might be stuck out on the edge of the Arctic, but Iceland makes up for its isolation and never-ending winter nights with a glowing passion for all things cultural. The country's unique literary heritage begins with the succinct medieval sagas, and stretches right up to today's Nordic Noir bestsellers. Every Icelander seems to play in a band, and the country has produced a disproportionate amount of world-class musicians. Reykjavík's controversial new Harpa concert hall is a glittering, defiant symbol of faith in the arts, constructed during the worst period of the financial crisis.

You might think *Icelandic Folktales*, translated by Alan Boucher, is just a collection of children's tales, but these light-hearted little gems encompass Icelandic history, humour and belief; they're the stories Icelanders have been telling for hundreds of years.

Literature

Bloody, black and powerful, the late 12th- and 13th-century sagas are without doubt Iceland's greatest cultural achievement. But Icelanders aren't resting on their literary laurels: today the country produces the most writers and literary translations per capita of any country in the world.

The Sagas

Iceland's medieval family sagas have often been called the world's first novels. They're certainly some of the most imaginative and enduring works of early literature – epic, brutal tales that suddenly flower with words of wisdom, elegy or love.

Written down during the late 12th to late 13th centuries, sagas look back to the disputes, doomed romances and larger-than-life characters who lived during the Settlement Era. Most were written anonymously, though *Egil's Saga* has been attributed to Snorri Sturluson (see the boxed text, p141).

The sagas, written over the long, desperate centuries of Norwegian and Danish subjugation, provided a strong sense of cultural heritage at a time when Icelanders had very little else. On winter nights, people would gather for the *kvöldvaka* (evening vigil). While the men twisted horsehair ropes and women spun wool or knitted, a family member would read the sagas and recite *rímur* (verse reworkings of the sagas).

Iceland publishes the greatest number of books per capita in the world, and the literacy rate is a perfect 100%.

The sagas are very much alive today. Icelanders of all ages can (and do) read the sagas in Old Norse, the language in which they were written 800 years ago. Most people can quote chunks from them, know the farms where the characters lived and died, and flock to cinemas to see the latest film versions of these eternal tales.

Some of the original saga manuscripts are on display in Reykjavík's Þjóðmenningarhúsið (Culture House; p49).

Eddic & Skaldic Poetry

The first settlers brought their oral poetic tradition with them from mainland Scandinavia, with the poems committed to parchment in the 12th century.

Eddic poems were composed in free, variable meters with a structure very similar to that of early Germanic poetry. Probably the most well known is the gnomic *Hávamál,* which extols the virtues of the common life – its wise old proverbs on how to be a good guest are still quoted today.

Skaldic poems were composed by *skalds* (Norwegian court poets) and are mainly praise-poems of Scandinavian kings, with lots of description packed into tightly structured lines. As well as having fiercely rigid alliteration, syllable counts and stresses, skaldic poetry is made more complex by *kennings,* a kind of compact word-riddle. Blood, for instance, is 'wound dew', while an arm might be described as a 'hawk's perch'.

The most renowned *skald* was saga anti-hero Egill Skallagrímsson. In 948, after being captured and sentenced to death, Egill composed the ode *Höfuðlausn* (Head Ransom) for his captor Eirík Blood-Axe. Flattered, the monarch released Egill unharmed.

Iceland's Viking longhouses have succumbed to the ravages of time. However, traditional turf-and-wood techniques were used right up until the 19th century – there are good examples at Skógar (southwest Iceland) and Glaumbær (north Iceland). *A Guide to Icelandic Architecture* (Association of Icelandic Architects) looks at 250 Icelandic buildings and designs.

Twentieth-Century Literature

Nobel Prize–winner Halldór Laxness is Iceland's undoubted literary genius. Other authors you may come across are the early-20th-century children's writer Reverend Jón Sveinsson (nicknamed Nonni), whose old-fashioned tales of derring-do have a rich Icelandic flavour and were once translated into 40 languages. *At Skipalón* is the only one readily available in English. Two masters of Icelandic literature are Gunnar Gunnarsson (1889–1975) and Þórbergur Þórðarson (1888–1974), who was beaten to the Nobel Prize by Laxness. You'll have to look out for their work in secondhand bookshops.

For more up-to-date and easily available fare, try Einar Kárason's outstanding *Devil's Island,* about Reykjavík life in the 1950s; it's the first of a trilogy, but unfortunately the other two parts haven't been translated into English. Hallgrímur Helgason's *101 Reykjavík* is the book on which the cult film was based. It's a dark comedy following the torpid life and fertile imagination of out-of-work Hlynur, who lives in downtown Reykjavík with his mother. Even blacker is *Angels of the Universe,* by Einar

VIKING EPICS

Egil's Saga Revolves around the complex, devious Egill Skallagrímsson. A renowned poet and skilled lawyer, Egill is also the grandson of a werewolf and a murderous drunk.

Grettir's Saga Brave, rash, unlucky and ultimately doomed, Grettir the Strong is cursed and exiled in this enthralling outlaw saga.

Njál's Saga Two of Iceland's greatest heroes, Njál and Gunnar, are drawn into a fatal 50-year family feud.

Laxdæla Saga A tragic generational saga set in northwest Iceland: bitter marriages, thwarted love and murder abound.

Völsungasaga Parts of this saga may seem familiar – Richard Wagner *(Der Ring des Nibelungen)* and JRR Tolkien *(Lord of the Rings)* both swiped episodes.

Eyrbyggja Saga A minor saga worth reading for its offbeat, supernatural tone; definitely the only medieval Icelandic work where ghosts are taken to court over their hauntings...

HALLDÓR LAXNESS – ICELAND'S FINEST AUTHOR

Over his long lifetime, Nobel Prize–winner Halldór Laxness (1902–98) succeeded in reshaping the world of Icelandic literature. Today he is Iceland's most celebrated 20th-century author.

Laxness was born as Halldór Guðjónsson, but he took the name of his family's farm Laxnes (with an extra 's') as his nom de plume. Ambitious and inquisitive, Laxness had his first work published at the age of 14, and began his restless wanderings at 17. He wrote his first novel, *Undir Helgahnúk* (Under the Holy Mountain), from a monastery during a period of fervent Catholicism. Laxness then left for Italy, where his disaffection with the church and increasingly leftist leanings led to the writing of *Vefarinn Mikli frá Kasmír* (The Great Weaver from Kashmir). In the 1930s he moved to America to try his luck in the fledgling Hollywood film industry, before becoming enthralled with communism and travelling widely in the Soviet Bloc. In 1962 the author settled at Laxnes (now a museum – see the boxed text, p80) for good. It was here that he wrote *A Poet's Time*, a poignant recantation of everything he'd ever written in praise of the Communist Party.

Laxness' works are masterpieces of irony, and his characters, however misguided, are drawn with sympathy. Unfortunately only a portion of his 51 novels and countless short stories, articles, plays and poems are currently available in translation, the most famous of which is probably *Independent People*. This bleak comedy deals with the harsh conditions of early-20th-century Icelandic life, focusing on the bloody-minded farmer Bjartur of Summerhouses. Also fascinating is *Iceland's Bell*, a saga-like portrait of extreme poverty and skewed justice, set in an Iceland subjugated by Danish rule. Other translated works are *World Light, The Fish Can Sing, Paradise Reclaimed, The Atom Station* and *Under the Glacier*.

At the time of writing, Laxness' books were controversial, and his depictions of Iceland as a poor and backwards country hurt the nation's pride. In 1955, however, Laxness won the Nobel Prize for Literature and became – in true Icelandic style – a hero of the people.

ICELANDIC CULTURE: SAGAS TO SIGUR RÓS MUSIC

Már Gudmundsson, which is about a schizophrenic man's spells in a psychiatric hospital.

Currently surfing the Nordic Noir tidal wave is Arnaldur Indriðason, whose Reykjavík-based crime fiction permanently tops the bestsellers list. Nine of his novels are available in English, including *Voices,* the award-winning *Silence of the Grave,* and our favourite, *Tainted Blood* (also published as *Jar City*). Yrsa Sigurðardóttir's thrillers have also been widely translated – her latest is *I Remember You.*

Music

Pop

Internationally famous Icelandic musicians include (of course) Björk. In Reykjavík, look out for the bestselling *Gling Gló*, a collection of Björk-sung jazz standards and traditional Icelandic songs that's quite difficult to find outside the country.

Sigur Rós have followed Björk to stardom; their biggest-selling album *Takk* (2005) garnered rave reviews around the world. It was followed by the poppier *Með suð í eyrum við spilum endalaust* (2007), and after a long hiatus the band released their sixth studio album, *Valtari,* in 2012. Lead singer Jónsi has also had success with his joyful solo album *Go* (2010).

Indie-folk newcomers Of Monsters and Men stormed the US charts in 2011 with their debut album, *My Head is an Animal*. You may also be familiar with Emiliana Torrini, the Icelandic-Italian singer who

An old Icelandic saying is *Betra er berfættum en bókarlausum að vera* ('It's better to be barefoot than bookless'). Icelanders are still passionate about the written word, so it's fitting that Reykjavík became a Unesco City of Literature in 2011.

sang the spooky 'Gollum's Song' in the Lord of the Rings film *The Two Towers*.

Back home, Reykjavík has a flourishing music scene with a constantly changing line-up of new bands and sounds – see www.icelandmusic.is for an idea of the variety. Those who have stayed the course include FM Belfast (who set up their own recording label to release their first album, *How to Make Friends*); múm (electronica mixed with real instruments); Mínus (whose thrashy guitars have supported Foo Fighters and Metallica); Hafdís Huld (spiky female popstress); and ebullient garage-rockers Benny Crespo's Gang.

Reykjavík's live-music venues are ever-changing – the best thing to do is to check the free paper *Grapevine* for current news and listings. As computer-mad internet fiends, a lot of Icelanders spread their music via sites such as MySpace.

The fabulous Iceland Airwaves music festival (held in Reykjavík in October) showcases Iceland's talent along with international acts.

Traditional Music

Until rock and roll arrived in the 20th century, Iceland was a land practically devoid of musical instruments. The Vikings brought the *fiðla* and the *langspil* with them from Scandinavia – both a kind of two-stringed box that rested on the player's knee and was played with a bow. They were never solo instruments but merely served to accompany singers.

In a country permanently on the verge of starvation, instruments were an unheard of luxury. Singing was the sole music. The most famous song styles are the *rímur,* poetry or stories from the sagas performed in a low, eerie chant (Sigur Rós have dabbled with the form), and *fimmundasöngur,* sung by two people in harmony. Cut off from other influences, the Icelandic singing style barely changed from the 14th century to the 20th century; it also managed to retain harmonies that were banned by the church across the rest of Europe for being the work of the devil!

For a list of the latest Icelandic feature films, documentaries and animations to be released, visit the website www. icelandic filmcenter.is.

Cinema

Iceland's film industry is young – regular production started around the early 1980s – but it's thrown out some distinctive work to date. Icelandic short films in particular have received all kinds of international awards. Full-length features are rarer, but they often contain the same quirky, dark subject matter and superb cinematography, using Iceland's powerful landscape as a backdrop.

In 1992 the film world first took notice of Iceland when *Children of Nature* was nominated for an Academy Award for Best Foreign Film. In the film, an elderly couple forced into a retirement home in Reykjavík make a break for the countryside. The film's director, Friðrik Þór Friðriksson, is something of a legend in Icelandic cinema circles, although some of his films are definitely better than others. *Cold Fever* (1994), *Angels of the Universe* (2000) and *The Sunshine Boy* (2009) are three that are well worth watching.

If one Icelandic film *has* put Reykjavík on the cinematic stage, it's *101 Reykjavík* (2000), directed by Baltasar Kormákur and based on the novel by Hallgrímur Helgason. This dark comedy explores sex, drugs and the life of a loafer in downtown Reykjavík. Kormákur's *Jar City* (2006) stars the ever-watchable Ingvar E Sigurðsson as Iceland's favourite detective, Inspector Erlendur. His latest film, *The Deep* (2012), has been a hit with both critics and the public.

ACCESSING ICELAND'S DESIGN SCENE

Iceland's coterie of designers and artists is loosely organised and promoted through the Iceland Design Centre (Hönnunarmiðstöð; www.icelanddesign.is; Vonarstræti 4b, Reykjavík), a mission funded by the Ministry of Education that is also responsible for DesignMarch (www.designmarch.is), an annual event held in Reykjavík during which hundreds of exhibitions and workshops open to the public.

The design centre keeps a regularly updated blog (http://blog.icelanddesign.is) that is well worth checking out during your holiday, as it features the latest and greatest goings-on in the country's design realm. As expected, most of the features focus on the capital; there's an annual online Reykjavík Design Guide, and several handy drop-down lists of designers (from architects to jewellery crafters) that make a great supplement to the Shopping section in the Reykjavík chapter (see p74). Tourists can stop by the design centre (easily spotted with its beautiful mural of cartoon stamps by Siggi Eggertsson at the front) for additional information about design-oriented attractions in Reykjavík and beyond.

In recent years the Designers and Farmers Project (www.designersandfarmers.com/en) was created to unite Iceland's locally sourced harvests with the country's penchant for all things streamlined and thoughtfully designed. The project's biggest success story thus far – a delicious *skyr* candy – was created at Erpsstaðir (p156).

Brandon Presser

Another Icelandic director who has achieved international success is Dagur Kári, whose films include *Nói Albínói* (2003), about a restless adolescent in a snowed-in northern fjord town; and the English-language *The Good Heart* (2009), which received a standing ovation at its premiere at the 2009 Toronto International Film Festival. Also look out for Hilmar Oddsson's *Kaldaljós* (Cold Light; 2004), a slow-moving, poignant film about life in an isolated fjord town, with a stunning performance from the little boy on whom it centres.

Iceland's immense alien beauty and the government's 20% production rebate for film-makers have encouraged Hollywood directors to make movies here. Try to spot the Icelandic scenery in blockbusters such as *Tomb Raider* (2001), *Die Another Day* (2002), *Batman Begins* (2005), *Flags of Our Fathers* (2006), *Stardust* (2007), *Journey to the Centre of the Earth* (2008), *Prometheus* (2012), *Oblivion* (2013), *Star Trek: Into Darkness* (2013) and the HBO series *Game of Thrones*.

Painting & Sculpture

Iceland's most successful artists have traditionally studied abroad (in Copenhagen, London, Oslo or elsewhere in Europe), before returning home to wrestle with Iceland's enigmatic soul. The result is a European-influenced style but with Icelandic landscapes and saga-related scenes as key subjects.

The first great Icelandic landscape painter was the prolific Ásgrímur Jónsson (1876–1958), who produced a startling number of Impressionistic oils and watercolours depicting Icelandic landscapes and folk tales. You can see his work at Reykjavík's National Gallery.

One of Ásgrímur's students was Johannes Kjarval (1885–1972), Iceland's most enduringly popular artist, who lived in the remote east Iceland village of Borgarfjörður Eystri as a child. His first commissioned works were, rather poignantly, drawings of farms for people who were

The cutting-edge Harpa concert hall opened in 2011. Its facade of shining hexagons captures the ever-changing northern light, while its interior has four state-of-the art stages. It was a deeply controversial project and still has its detractors, but absolutely no one has a bad word to say about its amazing acoustics.

emigrating, but he's most famous for his early charcoal sketches of people from the village and for his surreal landscapes.

Iceland's most famous contemporary artist is probably pop-art icon Erró (Guðmundur Guðmundsson), who has donated his entire collection to Reykjavík Art Museum's Hafnarhúsið.

Sculpture is very well represented in Iceland, with works dotting parks, gardens and galleries across the country, and its most famous sculptors all have museums dedicated to them in Reykjavík. Notable exponents include Einar Jónsson (1874–1954), whose mystical works dwell on death and resurrection; Ásmundur Sveinsson (1893–1982), whose tactile work is very wide-ranging but tends to celebrate Iceland, its stories and its people; and Sigurjón Ólafsson (1908–92), who specialised in busts but also dabbled in abstract forms.

Danish-Icelandic artist Olafur Eliasson (1967–) creates powerful installations, such as *The weather project* (2003) for London's Tate Modern, and *New York City Waterfalls* (2008) in New York's harbour. He also designed the facade of Reykjavík's stunning new concert hall, Harpa (2011).

Icelandic Attitudes

Icelanders are unusual people. Centuries of isolation and hardship have instilled particular character traits in the small, homogenous population. The nation's 320,000 souls tend to respond to life's challenges with a compelling mix of courage, candour and creativity, edged with a dark and wintry humour. The failure of politicians to prevent the financial crisis in 2008 sparked righteous fury around the country; it seems typically Icelandic to top that off by electing a comedian as the new mayor of Reykjavík.

The National Psyche

Icelanders have a reputation as tough, hardy, elemental types, and it's true that rural communities are still deeply involved in the fishing or farming industries. Naturally enough for people living on a remote island in a harsh environment, Icelanders are self-reliant individualists who don't like being told what to do. The current whaling debate is a prime example. Although most Icelanders wouldn't dream of eating whale meat, a majority are in support of hunting – a silent sticking-up of two fingers at the disapproving outside world.

But these steadfast exteriors often hide a more dreamy interior world. Iceland has always had a rich cultural heritage and an incredibly high literacy rate, and its people have a passion for all things artistic. This enthusiasm is true of the whole country, but it's particularly noticeable in downtown Reykjavík. Although young Icelanders might adopt an attitude of cool fatalism, get them talking about something they enjoy and you'll see their true can-do ingenuity emerge. Most play in a band, dabble in art, or write poetry or prose – they're positively bursting with creative impulses.

This buoyant, have-a-go attitude was hit hard during the financial meltdown. Soup kitchens sprang up in the city and thousands of younger people left Iceland to try their luck in Norway. But Icelanders have resilience built into their DNA. In just a few short years, emigration rates have fallen, and you can feel tendrils of confidence curling up around the capital once again. The country is regaining its belief in the old saying *'Þetta reddast'* (roughly translated, 'Things will sort themselves out in the end').

Although their pride may have taken a temporary kicking, Icelanders are calmly, rightfully patriotic. Icelandair wishes a heartfelt 'Welcome home!' to its Icelandic passengers when the plane touches down at Keflavík. Citizens who achieve international success are quietly feted: celebrities like Björk and Sigur Rós reflect prestige onto their entire homeland.

Town layouts, the former US military base, the popularity of TV programs such as *Desperate Housewives* and *American Idol,* and the

The Iceland Review website (www.iceland review.com) has a free daily digest of news and cultural events, and its glossy quarterly magazine has some entertaining, light articles about Icelandic people, culture, history and nature.

It's official! Iceland is the most peaceful country on earth, according to the 2012 Global Peace Index. The GPI bases its findings on factors such as levels of violent crime, political instability and what percentage of a country's population is in prison.

ICELANDIC ATTITUDES WORK HARD, PLAY HARD

prevalence of hot dogs and Coca-Cola point to a heavy US influence, but Icelanders consider their relationship with the rest of Scandinavia to be more important.

Although they seem to conform to the cool-and-quiet Nordic stereotype, Icelanders are curious about visitors and eager to know what outsiders think of them: 'How do you like Iceland?' is invariably an early question. And an incredible transformation takes place on Friday and Saturday nights, when inhibitions fall away and conversations flow as fast as the alcohol.

Iceland only had one TV channel until 1988 – which went off air on Thursdays so that citizens could do something more productive instead. It's said that most children born before 1988 were conceived on a Thursday...

Work Hard, Play Hard

In the last century the Icelandic lifestyle has shifted from isolated family communities living on scattered farms in coastal villages to a more urban-based society, with the majority of people living in the southwestern corner around Reykjavík. Despite this more outward-looking change, family connections are still very strong in Iceland, although young people growing up in rural Iceland are more likely to move to Reykjavík to study and work.

Icelanders work hard – the retirement age is 70 – and have enjoyed a very high standard of living in the late 20th and early 21st centuries. But keeping up with the Jónssons and Jónsdóttirs came at a price. For decades, Icelanders straight out of university borrowed money to buy houses or 4WDs and spent the rest of their days living on credit and paying off loans. Then, in 2008, the worldwide financial crisis struck, and that huge national debt suddenly had to be paid back. People wondered how Iceland would ever work itself out of its economic black hole; and yet, with characteristic grit, resilience, adaptability and imagination, Icelanders are hauling their country back from disaster.

The Icelandic addiction to grafting is counterbalanced by recreational indulgences. The bingeing in Reykjavík on Friday and Saturday nights is an example of relaxation gone mad. So too are the hundreds of summer houses you'll see when you're driving around the Golden Circle, and the exceptional number of swimming pools, which form the social hub of Icelandic life.

WHAT'S IN A NAME?

Icelanders' names are constructed from a combination of their first name and their father's (or, more rarely, mother's) first name. Girls add the suffix *dóttir* (daughter) to the patronymic and boys add *son*. Therefore, Jón, the son of Einar, would be Jón Einarsson. Guðrun, the daughter of Einar, would be Guðrun Einarsdóttir.

Because Icelandic surnames only tell people what your dad's called, Icelanders don't bother with 'Mr Einarsson' or 'Mrs Einarsdóttir'. Instead they use first names, even when addressing strangers. It makes for a wonderfully democratic society when you're expected to address your president or top police commissioner as Oliver or Harold!

About 10% of Icelanders have family names (most dating back to early settlement times), but they're rarely used. In an attempt to homogenise the system, government legislation forbids anyone to take on a new family name or adopt the family name of their spouse.

There's also an official list of names that Icelanders are permitted to call their children. Any additions to this list have to be approved by the Icelandic Naming Committee before you can apply the name to your child – so there are no Moon Units, Lourdeses or Apples running around here! Interestingly, there's a lingering superstition around naming newborns: the baby's name isn't usually revealed until the christening, which can take place several months after the child is born.

ICELANDIC ANCESTRY & GENETIC RESEARCH

Biotech research is big in Iceland – thanks, in part, to the 12th-century historian Ari the Learned. Ari's *Landnámabók* and *Íslendingabók* mean that Icelanders can trace their family trees right back to the 9th century. In 1996 neuroscience expert Dr Kári Stefáns-son recognised that this genealogical material could be combined with Iceland's unusu-ally homogenous population to produce something unique – a country-sized genetic laboratory.

In 1998 the Icelandic government controversially voted to allow the creation of a single database containing all Icelanders' genealogical, genetic and medical records. Even more controversially, in 2000 the government then allowed Kári's biotech company deCODE access to it all.

The decision sparked public outrage in Iceland and arguments across the globe about its implications for human rights and medical ethics. Should a government be able to sell off its citizens' medical records? And is it acceptable for a private corporation to use such records for profit?

While the arguments raged, the company set to work, using the database to trace inheritable diseases and pinpoint the genes that cause them. The database was declared unconstitutional in 2004, and deCODE was declared bankrupt in 2010, but not before it succeeded in isolating 15 genes linked to heart attacks, strokes and asthma. Now under new management, deCODE continues to unravel the mysteries of the human genome. In 2012 it discovered a gene that protects individuals from brain impairments, offering new insight into conditions such as Alzheimer's disease.

Women in Iceland

In 2011 *Newsweek* listed Iceland as the best place in the world to be a woman, based on how women fared in the spheres of justice, health, education, economics and politics.

The Viking settlement of Iceland clearly demanded toughness of char-acter, and the sagas are full of feisty women (for example, Hallgerður Höskuldsdóttir, who declines to save her husband's life due to a slap that he gave her years earlier). Women and men struggled equally through Iceland's long, dark history; modern gender equality is a pretty recent phenomenon.

Women gained full voting rights in 1919, but it wasn't until the 1970s protest movements reached Iceland that attitudes really began to change. Particularly powerful was the 'women's holiday' on 24 October 1975: the country ceased to function when 90% of Icelandic women stayed away from work and stay-at-home mums left children with their menfolk for the day.

In 1980 Iceland became the first democracy to elect a female presi-dent, the much-loved Vigdís Finnbogadóttir. In 2009, the world's first openly gay prime minister, Jóhanna Sigurðardóttir, came into power; 50% of her cabinet is female (compare that to Britain's pitiful 18%).

Iceland has one of the world's highest life ex-pectancies – 79.5 years for men and 83.5 years for women.

The social care system is so good that women have few worries about the financial implications of raising a child alone: child care is cheap, and there's no stigma attached to unmarried mothers. The country isn't perfect – sexual violence and unequal pay are still issues – but Icelandic women are well educated and independent. They have the same oppor-tunities as Icelandic men, and they have a government that supports their interests.

Sporting Spirit

Football (soccer) is a national passion for both spectators and players. Al-though Iceland doesn't win a lot of international games, several Iceland-ic players have made it onto top European and English premier-league

SUPERNATURAL ICELAND: GHOSTS, TROLLS & HIDDEN PEOPLE

Once you've seen some of the lava fields, eerie natural formations and isolated farms that characterise much of the Icelandic landscape, it will come as no surprise that many Icelanders believe their country is populated by *huldufólk* (hidden people) and ghosts.

In the lava are *jarðvergar* (gnomes), *álfar* (elves), *ljósálfar* (fairies), *dvergar* (dwarves), *ljúflingar* (lovelings), *tívar* (mountain spirits) and *englar* (angels). Stories about them have been handed down through generations, and many modern Icelanders claim to have seen them...or at least to know someone who has.

As in Ireland, there are stories about projects going wrong when workers try to build roads through *huldufólk* homes: the weather turns bad, machinery breaks down, labourers fall ill. In 2011 tunnelling work in Bolungarvík was thus afflicted: two contractors joined local seers to apologise to the fey folk living inside the mountain. Even politicians show respect: MP Árni Johnsen moved a 30-tonne boulder into his garden in 2012, to thank its supernatural inhabitants for saving his life when he was involved in a car crash.

As for Icelandic ghosts, they're substantial beings – not the wafting shadows found elsewhere in Europe. Írafell-Móri (*móri* and *skotta* are used for male and female ghosts, respectively) needed to eat supper every night, and one of the country's most famous spooks, Sel-Móri, got seasick when he stowed away in a boat. Stranger still, two ghosts haunting the same area often join forces to double their trouble. And Icelandic ghosts can even age – one rather sad *skotta* claimed she was becoming so decrepit that she had to haul herself about on her knees.

Rock stacks and weird lava formations around the country are often said to be trolls, caught out at sunrise and turned forever to stone. But living trolls are seldom seen today – they're more the stuff of children's stories.

A quick word of warning: many Icelanders get sick of visitors asking them whether they believe in supernatural beings. Their pride bristles at the 'Those cute Icelanders! They all believe in pixies!' attitude...and even if they don't entirely disbelieve, they're unlikely to admit it to a stranger.

teams. The biggest national venue is the 14,000-seat Laugardalsvöllur stadium in Reykjavík.

Another fantastically popular team sport is handball, played by two teams of seven. Iceland won silver at the Beijing Olympics – 85% of Icelanders watched the televised match. Team captain Ólafur Stefánsson is a hero to many a young Icelander, and has been voted Sports Personality of the Year four times. You can see handball matches at sports halls around the country – Reykjavík, Hafnarfjörður and Akureyri are good places.

Iceland's most traditional sport is *glíma* (Icelandic wrestling), a unique national sport with a history dating back to Viking settlement in the 9th century. Icelanders still practise *glíma,* but it's not common on a competitive level and you're most likely to see it as a demonstration at a traditional festival.

> Even though Icelanders speak the nearest thing to Viking in existence, Iceland is the least purely Scandinavian of all the Nordic countries. DNA studies have shown that much of Icelanders' genetic make-up is Celtic, suggesting that many Viking settlers had children by their British and Irish slaves.

Religious Beliefs

Norse

At the time of the Settlement Era, Iceland's religion was Ásatrú, which means 'faith in the Aesir' (the old Norse gods). Óðinn, Þór (Thor) and Freyr were the major trinity worshipped across Scandinavia. Óðinn, their chief, is the god of war and poetry, a brooding and intimidating presence. In Iceland most people were devoted to Þór (Icelandic names such as Þórir, Þórdís and Þóra are still very popular). This burly, red-haired god of the common people controlled thunder, wind, storm and natural disaster, so was a vital deity for farmers and fishermen to have on their side. Freyr and his twin sister Freyja represent fertility and sexuality. Freyr brought springtime, with its romantic implications, to both the human and the animal world, and was in charge of the perpetuation of all species.

Icelanders peacefully converted to Christianity more than 1000 years ago, but the old gods linger on. The Ásatrú religion evolved in the 1970s, almost simultaneously in Iceland, the US and the UK. Farmer-poet and high priest Sveinbjörn Beinteinsson managed to get the Íslenska Ása-trúarfélagið (www.asatru.is) recognised by the Icelandic government as early as 1973.

The two main rituals of Ásatrú are *blót* (sacrifice) and *sumbel* (toast). Nowadays sacrifices, which take place on the winter and summer solstices, on the first day of winter and summer, and at Þorrablót (see the boxed text, p327), are usually libations made with mead, beer or cider. The *sumbel* is a ritualised three-part toast: the first is made to the god Óðinn (it's also wise to pour a few drops for Loki, the trickster, to ward off nasty surprises); the second round is to the ancestors and honourable dead; and the third round is to whomever one wishes to honour.

Whereas membership of other religions in Iceland has remained fairly constant, Ásatrúarfélagið is growing. It is now Iceland's largest non-Christian religious organisation, with 1951 registered members and eight priests (five of whom can perform marriage ceremonies).

Christianity

Traditionally, the date of the decree that officially converted Iceland to Christianity has been given as 1000, but research has determined that it probably occurred in 999. What is known is that the changeover of religions was a political decision. In the Icelandic Alþing (National Assembly), Christians and pagans had been polarising into two radically opposite factions, threatening to divide the country. Þorgeir, the *lögsögu-maður* (law speaker), appealed for moderation on both sides, and eventually it was agreed that Christianity would officially become the new religion, although pagans were still allowed to practise in private.

Today, as in mainland Scandinavia, most Icelanders (around 77%) belong to the Protestant Lutheran Church.

Icelanders have a live-and-let-live attitude, but there is a sure-fire way to cause deep offence – by abusing the rules in swimming pools. Icelandic etiquette demands that swimmers wash thoroughly without a swimsuit before hopping into the water (it makes sense hygiene-wise: Icelandic pools don't contain chemical cleaners).

ICELANDIC ATTITUDES RELIGIOUS BELIEFS

Icelandic Cuisine

For much of its history, Iceland was a poverty-stricken hinterland. Sparse soil and cursed weather produced limited crops, and Icelandic farmer-fishermen relied heavily on sheep, fish and seabirds to keep from starving. Every part of every creature was eaten – fresh, or dried, salted, smoked, pickled in whey or even buried underground in the case of shark meat.

Fish, seafood, lamb, bread and simple vegetables still form the typical Icelandic diet. The way in which these ingredients are prepared, however, has changed drastically over the last 25 years. It's now a source of national pride to serve up traditional food as tastily and imaginatively as possible, using methods borrowed from fashionable culinary traditions around the world. The strong Slow Food movement prioritises locally grown food over imports, with restaurants proudly flagging up regional treats.

Dining out in Iceland is expensive, but it's worth spending a little extra to try some of the nation's top restaurants. If you're being determinedly frugal, you'll almost certainly be eating French fries, hot dogs, hamburgers and pizzas.

Food lovers may be tempted by the tasting tour run by Saga Travel (www.sagatravel.is), which allows travellers to sample blue mussels, beef, lamb, beer and ice cream from local food producers on Hrísey island, near Akureyri.

Staples & Specialities

Fish & Seafood

'Half of our country is the sea', runs an old Icelandic saying. Fish is still the mainstay of the Icelandic diet: you'll find it fresh-caught at market stalls and in restaurant kitchens, from where it emerges boiled, pan-fried, baked or grilled.

In the past, Icelanders merely kept the cheeks and tongues of *þorskur* (cod) – something of a delicacy – and exported the rest; but today you'll commonly find cod fillets on the menu, along with *ýsa* (haddock), *bleikja* (Arctic char) and meaty-textured *skötuselur* (monkfish). Other fish include *lúða* (halibut), *steinbítur* (catfish), *sandhverfa* (turbot; not an indigenous fish), *síld* (herring), *skarkoli* (plaice) and *skata* (skate). During the summer you can try *silungur* (freshwater trout) and *lax* (salmon). Wild salmon is called *villtur* and farmed salmon is *eldislax*.

Harðfiskur, a popular snack eaten with butter, is found in supermarkets and at market stalls. To make it, haddock is cleaned and dried in the open air until it has become dehydrated and brittle, then it's torn into strips.

Saltfish (wind-dried, salted fillets of cod) was so important to the Icelanders that it once appeared in the centre of the country's flag.

Shrimp, oysters and mussels are caught in Icelandic waters – mussels are at their prime during both the very beginning and the end of summer. *Leturhumar* are a real treat. These are what Icelanders call 'lobster', although the rest of us know them as langoustine. Höfn, in southeast Iceland, is particularly well known for them and even has an annual lobster festival.

Meat

Icelandic lamb is hard to beat. During summer, sheep roam free to munch on chemical-free grasses and herbs in the highlands and valleys, before being rounded up in the September *réttir* and corralled for the winter. The result of this life of relative luxury is very tender lamb with a slightly gamey flavour. You'll find lamb fillets, pan-fried lamb or smoked lamb on most restaurant menus.

Beef steaks are also excellent but not as widely available, and are consequently more expensive. Horse is still eaten in Iceland, although it's regarded as something of a delicacy – so if you see 'foal fillets' on the menu, you're not imagining things.

In eastern Iceland wild reindeer roam the highlands, and reindeer steaks are a feature of local menus. Reindeer season starts in late July and runs well into September.

Birds have always been part of the Icelandic diet. *Lundi* (puffin) used to appear smoked or broiled in liver-like lumps on dinner plates, although it's a rarer sight these days following a worrying crash in puffin numbers. Another seabird is *svartfugl;* it's commonly translated as 'blackbird' on English-language menus, but what you'll actually get is guillemot *(langvía).* High-class restaurants favouring seasonal ingredients often have succulent roasted *heiðagæs* (pink-footed goose) in autumn.

Sweets & Desserts

Don't miss out on *skyr,* a delicious yoghurt-like concoction made from pasteurised skimmed milk. Despite its rich and decadent flavour, it's actually low in fat and is often mixed with sugar, fruit flavours (such as blueberry) and cream to give it an extra-special taste and texture. *Skyr* can be found in any supermarket (it's a great snack for kids) and as a dessert in restaurants.

Icelandic *pönnukökur* (pancakes) are thin, sweet and cinnamon flavoured. Icelandic *kleinur* (doughnuts) are a chewy treat, along with their offspring *ástar pungur* (love balls), deep-fried, spiced balls of dough. You'll find these desserts in bakeries, along with an amazing array of

Where to Find Fresh...

» **Langoustines** Höfn

» **Tomatoes** Flúðir

» **Reindeer** Eastfjords

» **Lavabread** Mývatn

» **Mussels** Stykkishólmur and Hrísey

» **Foal** Skagafjörður

ICELANDIC CUISINE STAPLES & SPECIALITIES

A BANQUET OF BODY PARTS

Eyeball a plate of old-fashioned Icelandic food, and chances are it will eyeball you back. In the past nothing was wasted, and some traditional specialities look more like horror-film props than food. You won't be faced with these dishes on many menus, though – they're generally only eaten at the Þorrablót winter feast, held (appropriately) in the 13th week of winter.

» **Svið** Singed sheep's head (complete with eyes) sawn in two, boiled and eaten fresh or pickled.

» **Sviðasulta** (head cheese) Made from bits of *svið* pressed into gelatinous loaves and pickled in whey.

» **Slátur** A mishmash of sheep intestines, liver and lard tied up in a sheep's stomach and cooked (kind of like haggis).

» **Blóðmör** Similar to *slátur,* with added blood and bound by rye.

» **Súrsaðir hrútspungar** Rams' testicles pickled in whey and pressed into a cake.

» **Hákarl** Iceland's most famous stomach churner, *hákarl* is Greenland shark, an animal so inedible that it has to rot away underground for six months before humans can even digest it. Most foreigners find the stench (a cross between ammonia and week-old roadkill) too much to bear, but it tastes better than it smells... It's the aftertaste that really hurts. A shot of *brennivín* (schnapps) is traditionally administered as an antidote.

> **EATING PRICES**
>
> The Eating reviews in this book are divided into three categories based on the cost of an average main course.
>
> € Less than Ikr1500 (€10)
>
> €€ Ikr1500–4000 (€10–25)
>
> €€€ More than Ikr4000 (€25)

fantastic pastries and cakes – one of the few sweet legacies of the Danish occupation.

Local dairy farms churn out scrumptious scoops of homemade ice cream by the gallon – they're often featured on the menus of nearby restaurants. Alongside boring old vanilla sit novel flavours such as beer, liquorice and even *slátur* (sheep leftovers cooked in a sheep's stomach).

Drinks

Nonalcoholic

Life without *kaffi* (coffee) is unthinkable. Cafes and petrol stations will usually have an urn of filter coffee by the counter, and some shops offer complimentary cups to customers. A coffee costs around Ikr300, but normally you'll get at least one free refill. Snug European-style cafes selling espresso, latte, cappuccino and mocha are ever more popular, popping up even in the most isolated one-horse hamlets. Tea is available, but aficionados should consider bringing teabags from home – the brand sitting on most supermarket shelves makes a truly feeble brew.

Besides all that coffee, Icelanders drink more Coca-Cola per capita than any other country. Another very popular soft drink is Egils Appelsín (orange soda) and the home-grown Egils Malt Extrakt, which tastes like sugar-saturated beer.

It isn't a crime to buy bottled water in Iceland, but it should be. Icelandic tap water generally comes from the nearest glacier, and is some of the purest you'll ever drink.

Alcoholic

For some Icelanders, drinking alcohol is not about the taste – getting trollied is the aim of the game. Particularly in Reykjavík, it's the done thing to go out at the weekend and drink till you drop. However, drinking during the week has been frowned upon in the past. It's becoming more common, but if you order a midweek pint in the countryside, people may assume you have an alcohol problem!

You must be at least 20 years old to buy beer, wine or spirits, and alcohol is only available from licensed bars, restaurants and the government-run Vín Búð liquor stores (www.vinbud.is). There are roughly 50 shops around the country; most towns have one, and the greater Reykjavík area has about a dozen. In larger places, they usually open from 11am to 6pm Monday to Thursday and on Saturdays, and 11am to 7pm on Fridays (closed Sundays). In small communities, liquor stores are only open for an hour or two in the late afternoon/evening. Expect queues around 5pm on a Friday. The cheapest bottles of imported wine cost from Ikr1200. Beer costs about a third of what you'll pay in a bar.

Petrol stations and supermarkets sell the weak and watery 2.2% brew known as pilsner, but most Icelanders would sooner not drink it at all.

The three main brands of Icelandic beer – Egil's, Thule and Viking – are all fairly standard lager or pils brews; you can also get imported beers such as Carlsberg and (in Irish bars) Guinness. A pint of beer in a pub

Most Icelandic beer is produced by one of two big breweries. If you fancy something a little more niche, head for Reykjavík's tiny Micro Bar, new in 2012. It sells beers from Iceland's best microbreweries, including Gæðingur, Ölvisholt and Kaldi.

costs about Ikr700 to Ikr800; a bottle of house wine in a restaurant will cost at least Ikr3000.

The traditional Icelandic alcoholic brew is *brennivín* (literally 'burnt wine'), a potent schnapps made from potatoes and caraway seeds, with the foreboding nickname *svarti dauði* (black death).

Where to Eat & Drink

Restaurants

Most of Iceland's best restaurants are in Reykjavík, but some magnificent finds do mushroom up beyond the capital. Bear in mind that the price difference between an exceptional restaurant and an average one is often small, so it can be well worth going upmarket. Often, though, in rural Iceland you may not have a choice – the town's only eating place will probably be the restaurant in the local hotel (or the grill in the petrol station).

À la carte menus usually offer at least one fish dish, one vegie choice (invariably pasta) and several meat mains. Many restaurants also have a menu of lighter, cheaper meals such as hamburgers and pizzas. In Reykjavík, and to a lesser extent Akureyri, there are some ethnic restaurants, including Thai, Japanese, Italian, Mexican, Indian and Chinese.

Opening hours for restaurants are usually 11.30am to 2.30pm and 6pm to 10pm daily.

Cafes & Pubs

Downtown Reykjavík has a great range of bohemian cafe-bars where you can happily while away the hours sipping coffee, gossiping, people-watching, scribbling postcards or tinkering with your laptop. Menus range from simple soups and sandwiches to fish dishes and designer burgers. Recent years have seen cafe menus morph into more restaurant-like menus (with an attendant hike in prices).

Beer was illegal in Iceland for most of the 20th century. Several Reykjavík pubs began serving nonalcoholic beer mixed with vodka. When this too was banned in 1985, the nation protested by holding mock funerals and singing dirges. On 1 March 1989 real beer was legalised once more.

ICELANDIC CUISINE WHERE TO EAT & DRINK

FESTIVE FEASTING

February is the month for pagan-like rituals. In Iceland's steepest fjords, the sun vanishes in November and is not seen again until the following year. On the day it finally reappears, villagers gather to celebrate *Sólarkaffi* (Sun Coffee) with pancakes and caraway-flavoured coffee. The infamous Þorrablót winter feast is also held in February (see the boxed text, p327).

Easter was once celebrated by eating porridge, the richest your purse could bear. This custom has fallen out of favour, but two unusual Lenten foodie traditions remain. On Bolludagur (Bun Day; Monday before Shrove Tuesday), Icelanders gorge themselves sick on puff-pastry cream buns. Kids get up early to 'beat' the buns out of their parents with a *bolluvöndur* (literally 'bun wand'). The following day is Sprengidagur (Bursting Day; Shrove Tuesday), when the aim is to stuff yourself with *saltkjöt og baunir* (salted meat and split peas) until you literally can't eat any more.

Continuing the excess, Beer Day (1 March) is a more recent tradition. It dates back to the glorious day in 1989 when beer was legalised in Iceland. As you'd expect, Reykjavík's clubs and bars get particularly wild.

December 23 is Þorláksmessa (St Þorlákur's Day), when the patron saint of Iceland has the dubious honour of being commemorated with a meal of putrefied skate.

On Christmas Day, *hangikjöt* (smoked lamb) is served, with pickled red cabbage and *flatkökur* (unleavened bread, or pancakes, charred on a grill or griddle). In November, traditionalists can hunt the protected *rjúpa* (ptarmigan) to provide the centrepiece for their Christmas table; birds killed in this way are for personal consumption only, so they don't appear on restaurant menus. Jolly old *Jólaglögg* – mulled wine beefed up with vodka – is a popular Yuletide tipple.

ICELANDIC CUISINE VEGETARIANS & VEGANS

ICELANDIC SNACKS

» **Skyr** Rich and creamy yoghurt-like staple, sometimes sweetened with sugar and berries.

» **Hangikjöt** Hung meat, usually smoked lamb, served in thin slices.

» **Harðfiskur** Brittle pieces of wind-dried haddock, usually eaten with butter.

» **Pýlsur** Icelandic hot dogs, made from lamb and topped with raw and deep-fried onion, ketchup, mustard and tangy remoulade (ask for 'ein með öllu' – one with everything).

» **Liquorice** Salt liquorice and chocolate-covered varieties fill the supermarket sweets aisles.

» **Hverabrauð** Rich, dark rye bread baked underground using geothermal heat; try it in Mývatn.

Most of Reykjavík's cafes metamorphose into wild drinking dens in the evenings (Fridays and Saturdays mostly). Suddenly DJs appear, beer is swilled, and merry people dance, screech and stagger around until somewhere between 3am and 6am.

Sweet, peppery caraway is used to flavour Icelandic cheese, coffee, brown bread and *brennivín*. In mid-August, after the plant has flowered, some Reykjavíkurs make a trip to Viðey island to gather caraway seeds.

Hot Dog Stands & Petrol Stations

Icelanders do enjoy fast food! If you see a queue in Reykjavík, it probably ends at a *pýlsur* (hot dog) stand. Large petrol stations often have good, cheap, well-patronised grills and cafeterias attached. They generally serve sandwiches and fast food from around 11am to 9pm or 10pm. Some also offer hearty set meals at lunchtime, such as meat soup, fish of the day or plates of lamb.

Supermarkets & Bakeries

Every town and village has at least one small supermarket. The most expensive are 10-11 and 11-11. Bónus (easily recognised by its garish yellow-and-pink piggy sign) is the country's budget supermarket chain. Others include Hagkaup, Krónan, Nóatún, Samkaup-Strax and Samkaup-Úrval. Opening times vary greatly; in Reykjavík most are open from 9am to 11pm daily, but outside the capital hours are always shorter.

We can't praise the wonderful Icelandic *bakarí* (bakeries) enough. Every town has one, generally open from 7am or 8am until 5pm on weekdays (sometimes also Saturdays). They sell all sorts of inexpensive fresh bread, buns, cakes, sandwiches and coffee, and usually provide chairs and tables.

Check out *50 Crazy Things to Eat in Iceland*, by Snæfroður Ingadóttir and Þorvaldur Örn Kristinundsson, for a few fun pictorials of Iceland's traditional eats.

Iceland has to import most of its groceries, so prices are exorbitant – roughly two or three times what you'd pay in North America, Australia or Europe. Fish (tinned or smoked) and dairy products represent the best value and are surprisingly cheap. Some fruit and vegetables are grown locally, and these tend to be fresh and tasty, but imported vegetables usually look tragic by the time they hit the supermarket shelves.

Vegetarians & Vegans

You'll have no problem in Reykjavík – there are several excellent meat-free, organic cafe-restaurants in the city, and many more eateries offer vegetarian choices. Outside the capital most restaurants have at least one vegie item on the menu – although as this is routinely cheese-and-tomato pasta or pizza, you could get very bored. Vegans will have to self-cater.

It's unlikely that you'll ever have to explain yourself in Icelandic but, just in case, *'Ég er grænmetisæta'* means 'I'm a vegetarian' and *'Ég borða ekki kjöt'* means 'I don't eat meat'.

Survival
Guide

Directory A-Z

Accommodation

Iceland has a full spectrum of accommodation options, from spartan mountain huts through to hostels, working farms, guesthouses and school-based summer rooms to luxury hotels. It must be said, however, that accommodation is often of a lower standard than you might expect from a developed European destination. Although rooms are generally spotless, they are usually small, with thin walls and limited facilities.

PRICE RANGES

The Sleeping reviews in this book are divided into three categories based on the high-season price of a double room:
€ less than Ikr15,000 (approx €100)
€€ Ikr15,000–30,000 (€100–200)
€€€ more than Ikr30,000 (€200)

In the Sleeping reviews of this book, please note the following:

» We recommend that between June and August travellers book all accommodation in advance (note there is rarely any need to prebook campsites).

» Our book is not a directory covering all the accommodation options in Iceland. This is due to space constraints, as well as our desire to cover the best selection for travellers. Note, too, that new places are opening all the time, to cope with the rapid rise in tourist numbers.

» Tourist information centres will generally have details of all the accommodation in their town/region. Larger centres have a booking service for travellers, where they will book accommodation for a small fee (usually around Ikr500). Note that this service is for visitors to the centre, not for prebooking via email.

» Prices for the peak season of 2012 (June to August) are listed in our reviews – or prices for summer 2013, where these were available. Travellers must expect that prices will rise from year to year. Websites will invariably list up-to-date prices.

» From September to May, most guesthouses and hotels offer discounts of 20% to 50% on their summer prices. Again, check websites for up-to-date prices.

» Many hotels and guesthouses close during winter; where this is the case, opening times are shown in the review. Many hotels and guesthouses close over the Christmas–New Year period. If no opening times are shown, accommodation is open all year.

» Some Icelandic hotels list prices in euros only. Where this is the case, we have followed suit.

» Many guesthouses and farmstays offer numerous options: camping; rooms with/without bathrooms, with made-up beds or sleeping-bag options; cottages with/without kitchen and/or bathroom. Where possible, we have tried to explain all that is available, but listing prices for all permutations is close to impossible. Check websites for full coverage.

» Our reviews indicate whether a private bathroom is offered; whether linen is included or there is a sleeping-bag option; and if breakfast is included in the price.

Camping

» *Tjaldsvæði* (organised campsites) are found in almost every town, at farmhouses in rural areas and along major hiking trails. The best sites have washing machines, cooking facilities and hot showers, but others just have a cold-water tap and a toilet block. Some are attached to the local *sundlaug* (swimming pool), with shower facilities provided by the pool for a small fee.

» It is rarely necessary to book a camping place in advance. Many small-town campsites are unstaffed – there is a contact number for a caretaker posted on the amenities block, or an instruction to head to the tourist information centre/swimming pool to pay; alternatively, a caretaker may visit the campsite of an evening to collect fees.

» Wild camping is possible in some areas but in practice it is often discouraged. In national parks and nature reserves you must camp in marked campsites, and you need to get permission before camping on fenced land in all other places.

» When camping in parks and reserves the usual rules apply: leave sites as you find them, use biodegradable soaps, carry out your rubbish and bury your toilet waste away from water sources.

» Campfires are not allowed, so bring a stove. Butane cartridges and petroleum fuels are available in petrol stations and hardware shops. You can often pick up partly used canisters left behind by departing campers at the campsites in Reykjavík and Keflavík.

» Camping with a tent or campervan/caravan usually costs Ikr800 to Ikr1200 per person. Electricity is often an additional Ikr800. Some campsites charge for showers.

» A new 'lodging tax' of Ikr100 per site per night was introduced in 2012; some places absorb this cost in the per-person rate, others make you pay it in addition to the per-person rate.

» Consider purchasing the **Camping Card** (www.campingcard.is), which costs €99 (in 2013) and covers unlimited camping for the season at 44 campsites throughout the country for two adults and up to four

WARNING – POTENTIAL PRICE HIKE

In mid-2012, the Icelandic government floated the idea of increasing the VAT paid on restaurant meals, tourist attractions and hotel rooms (always incorporated into prices, rather than a separate charge paid by visitors) from 7% to a hefty 25.5%. It was a deeply unpopular move within the tourist industry, as it was feared that visitor numbers would fall in response to dramatically higher prices.

Common sense has prevailed, and in late 2012 the government announced that the hospitality VAT would rise from 7% to 14%, effective from September 2013. Needless to say, prices post-September 2013 may look quite different to those listed in this book. Our best advice is to always check websites for up-to-date information.

children (but doesn't include the new Ikr100-per-site tax). Full details are on the website. Icelandic weather is notoriously fickle, and if you intend to camp it's wise to invest in a good-quality tent.

» Most campsites open from June to August or early September only. If it's a large campsite that also offers huts or cottages, these may be open year-round.

» The free directory *Tjalds-væði Íslands* (available from tourist information centres) lists many of Iceland's campsites.

Emergency Huts

» There are bright-orange survival huts on high mountain passes and along remote coastlines (usually marked on country maps in some way). The huts are stocked with emergency rations, fuel and blankets (and a radio to contact help). Note that it is illegal to use them in a non-emergency.

Farmhouse Accommodation

» Throughout Iceland, many rural farmhouses offer campsites, sleeping-bag spaces, made-up guestrooms and cabins and cottages. Over time, some 'farmhouses' have evolved into large country hotels.

» Facilities vary: some farms provide meals or have a guest kitchen, some have outdoor hot-pots (hot tubs) or a geothermal swimming pool, and many provide horse riding or can organise activities such as fishing. Roadside signs signal which farmhouses provide accommodation and what facilities they offer.

» Rates are similar to guesthouses in towns, with sleeping-bag accommodation costing around Ikr6000 and made-up beds from Ikr9000 to Ikr14,000 per person. Breakfast (if not included in the room price) costs around Ikr2000, while an evening meal (usually served at a set time) costs around Ikr8000.

» Some 180 farm properties are members of **Icelandic Farm Holidays** (www.farmholidays.is), which publishes an annual listings guide called *The Ideal Holiday*, available free from most tourist information centres.

BOOK YOUR STAY ONLINE

For more accommodation reviews by Lonely Planet authors, check out http://hotels.lonelyplanet.com. You'll find independent reviews, as well as recommendations on the best places to stay. Best of all, you can book online.

Guesthouses

» The Icelandic term *gisti-heimilið* (guesthouse) covers a wide variety of properties, from family homes renting out a few rooms to custom-built motels.

» Guesthouses vary enormously in character from stylish, contemporary options to those overwhelmed by chintzy decor. A surprisingly high number of them offer rooms only with shared bathroom.

» Most are comfortable and homey, with guest kitchens, TV lounges and buffet-style breakfast (either included in the price or for around Ikr1500 to Ikr2000 extra).

» Some guesthouses offer sleeping-bag accommodation at a price significantly reduced from that of a made-up bed. Some places don't advertise a sleeping-bag option, so it pays to ask (especially outside the peak June-to-August season, when guesthouse owners are more inclined to let you use your sleeping bag).

» As a general guide, sleeping-bag accommodation costs Ikr4500 to Ikr6000, double rooms from Ikr12,000 to Ikr20,000, and self-contained units from Ikr14,000 per night.

» Some guesthouses open only from June to August; others take in students in the winter months – especially in Reykjavík.

Hostels

» Iceland has 36 well-maintained youth hostels administered by **Hostelling International Iceland** (www.hostel.is). In Reykjavík and Akureyri, there are also independent backpacker hostels. Bookings are recommended at all of them, especially from June to August.

» A number of hostels close for the winter, so check reviews in this book or online for info on opening times.

» All hostels offer hot showers, cooking facilities, luggage storage and sleeping-bag accommodation, and most offer private rooms. If you don't have a sleeping bag, you can hire linen (Ikr1250 per stay at HI hostels).

» Breakfast (where available) costs Ikr1500 to Ikr2000.

» Join **Hostelling International** (HI; www.hihostels.com) in your home country to benefit from HI member discounts of Ikr600 per person on hostel rates. Nonmembers will pay around Ikr3800 for a dorm bed; single/double rooms cost Ikr6200/10,000 (more for private bathrooms). Children aged five to 12 years pay half-price.

Hotels

» Every major town has at least one business-style hotel, usually featuring comfortable but innocuous rooms with private bathroom, phone, TV and sometimes minibar. Invariably the hotels also have decent restaurants.

» Summer prices for singles/doubles start at around Ikr17,000/22,000 and include a buffet breakfast. Prices drop substantially outside high season (June to August), and cheaper rates can often be found if you book online.

» Two of the largest local chains are **Fosshótel** (www.fosshotel.is) and **Icelandair Hotels** (www.icelandairhotels.is).

SUMMER HOTELS

» Once the school holidays begin, many schools, colleges and conference centres become summer hotels offering simple accommodation. Most are open from early June to late August, and 12 are part of a chain called **Hótel Edda** (www.hoteledda.is), overseen by the Icelandair Hotels chain.

» Accommodation tends to be simple: rooms are plain but functional, usually with twin beds, a washbasin and shared bathrooms, although a number of the hotels have rooms with bathroom, and a handful offer 'Edda Plus' rooms, with private bathroom, TV and phone.

» Some Edda hotels have dormitory sleeping-bag spaces; most Edda hotels have a restaurant.

» Expect to pay from Ikr3000 to Ikr4500 for sleeping-bag accommodation, Ikr10,600/12,900 for a single/double with washbasin and Ikr19,500/23,900 for an 'Edda Plus' single/double.

Mountain Huts

» Private walking clubs and touring organisations maintain *sæluhús* (mountain huts) on many of the popular hiking tracks around the country. The huts are open to anyone and offer sleeping-bag space in basic dormitories. Some also have cooking facilities, campsites and a warden.

» The huts at Landmannalaugar, Þórsmörk and around Askja are accessible by 4WD, and you can get to the huts in Hornstrandir by boat, but most are only

---

SLEEPING WITH THE LOCALS

Two recommended websites can help you find a bed with a local host:

AirBnB (www.airbnb.com) Has private rooms, cottages, apartments and houses for rent throughout Iceland, with a large concentration in the capital.

CouchSurfing (www.couchsurfing.com) Access a great network of travellers hosting travellers.

SLEEPING-BAG ACCOMMODATION

Iceland's best-kept secret is the sleeping-bag option offered by hostels, numerous guesthouses and some hotels. For a fraction of the normal cost you'll get a bed without a duvet or blanket; just bring your own sleeping bag and you can keep costs down substantially. Taking the sleeping-bag option doesn't mean sleeping in a dorm – generally you can still book a single or double room, just minus the linen. The sleeping-bag option usually means BYO towel, too (a pillowcase is also worth packing). Sleeping-bag prices will never include breakfast, but you'll often have the option of purchasing it.

accessible on foot. Even so, it's essential to book with the relevant organisation as places fill up quickly.

» The main organisation providing mountain huts is **Ferðafélag Íslands** (Icelandic Touring Association; ☑568 2533; www.fi.is; Mörkin 6, IS-108 Reykjavík), which maintains 38 huts around Iceland (some in conjunction with local walking clubs). The best huts have showers, kitchens, wardens and potable water; they cost Ikr4000 to Ikr5000 for nonmembers. Simpler huts cost Ikr3500 and usually just have bed space, toilet and a basic cooking area. Camping is available at some huts for around Ikr1100 per person. GPS coordinates for huts are included in the destination chapters.

» The following also provide huts:

• **Ferðafélag Akureyrar** (Touring Club of Akureyri; ☑462 2720; www.ffa.is; Strandgata 23) Runs huts in the northeast, including along the Askja Trail.

• **Útivist** (☑562 1000; www.utivist.is; Laugavegur 178, IS-105 Reykjavík) Runs huts at Básar and Fimmvörðuháls Pass in Þórsmörk.

Activities

Iceland's dramatic scenery, vast tracts of wilderness and otherworldly atmosphere make it a superb playground for outdoor enthusiasts. See Outdoor Adventures (p32) for more information.

Business Hours

Many attractions and tourist-oriented businesses in Iceland are only open for a short summer season, typically June to August. As tourism figures increase at a rapid pace, some businesses are vague about their opening and closing dates (increasingly, seasonal restaurants or guesthouses may open sometime in May, or even April 'if there's enough tourists around'; conversely, they may stay open until the end of September if demand warrants it).

Note that most museums (especially outside the capital) only have regular, listed opening hours during summer (June to August). From September to May they may advertise very restricted opening hours (eg, a couple of hours once a week), but many places are happy to open on request, with a little forewarning – you don't need to be a large group, just get in touch via the museum website or the local tourist office.

Note that most Icelandic hotels and guesthouses generally shut down from Christmas Eve to New Year's Day.

Opening hours in general tend to be far longer from June to August, and shorter from September to May.

Standard opening hours are as follows:

» **Banks** 9.15am to 4pm Monday to Friday

» **Cafe-bars** 10am to 1am Sunday to Thursday, 10am to between 3am and 6am Friday and Saturday

» **Cafes** 10am to 6pm

» **Offices** 9am to 5pm Monday to Friday

» **Petrol stations** 8am to 10pm or 11pm

» **Post offices** 9am to 4pm or 4.30pm Monday to Friday (to 6pm in larger towns)

» **Restaurants** 11.30am to 2.30pm and 6pm to 10pm

» **Shops** 10am to 6pm Monday to Friday, 10am to 4pm Saturday; some Sunday opening in Reykjavík malls and major shopping strips

» **Supermarkets** 9am to 8pm (later in Reykjavík)

» **Vín Búð (government-run alcohol stores)** Variable; many outside Reykjavík only open for a couple of hours per day

Children

Iceland is a fairly easy place to travel with children, and although there aren't many activities especially aimed at youngsters, the dramatic scenery, abundance of swimming pools and the friendliness of the locals help to keep things running smoothly. If your kids like science projects, they will probably love the bird colonies, waterfalls, volcanic areas and glaciers. A number of activities can keep them busy, such as short hikes, super-Jeep tours, horse riding, whale watching, boat rides and easy glacier walks (for the latter, the minimum age is around eight to 10 years).

Once you've decided on a family holiday in Iceland, one of the biggest considerations will be what to see and where to go, as distances can be long between attractions. It may be a good idea to limit yourselves to one part of the island to avoid boredom-induced tantrums and frequent bouts of carsickness. Reykjavík is the most child-friendly place simply because it has the greatest variety of attractions and facilities.

Practicalities

» For kids, admission to museums and swimming pools varies from 50% off to free. The age at which children must pay adult fees varies from place to place (anywhere from 12 to 18 years).

» On internal flights and tours with Air Iceland, children aged two to 11 years pay half-fare and infants under two fly free.

» Most bus and tour companies offer a 50% reduction for children aged four to 11 years; Reykjavík Excursion tours are free for under 11s, and half-price for those aged 12 to 15.

» All international car-hire companies offer child seats for an extra cost (these should be booked in advance).

» The changeable weather and frequent cold and rain may put you off camping as a family, but children aged two to 12 are usually charged half-price for camping, hostel, farmhouse and other accommodation. Under-twos can usually stay for free.

» Many places offer rooms accommodating families, including hostels, guesthouses and farmstays. Larger hotels often have cots (cribs), but you may not find these elsewhere.

» Many restaurants in Reykjavík and larger towns offer discounted children's meals, and most have high chairs.

» Toilets at museums and other public institutions usually have dedicated baby-changing facilities; elsewhere, you'll have to improvise.

» Attitudes to breastfeeding in public are generally relaxed.

» Formula, nappies (diapers) and other essentials are available everywhere.

Climate Chart

Akureyri

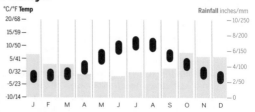

Reykjavík

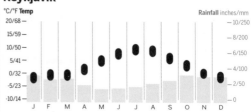

Vík

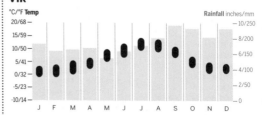

Customs Regulations

» Iceland has quite strict import restrictions. For a full list of regulations, see www.customs.is.

» Alcohol duty-free allowances for travellers over 20 years of age:

* 1L spirits and 1L wine and 6L beer OR
* 3L wine and 6L beer OR
* 1L spirits and 9L beer OR
* 1.5L wine and 9L beer OR
* 12L beer

» Visitors over 18 years can bring in 200 cigarettes or 250g of other tobacco products.

» You can import up to 3kg of food (except raw eggs, meat or dairy products), provided it's not worth more than Ikr18,500. This may help self-caterers to reduce costs.

» To prevent contamination, recreational fishing and horse-riding clothes require a veterinarian's certificate stating that they have been disinfected. Otherwise officials will charge you for disinfecting clothing when you arrive. It is illegal to bring used horse-riding equipment (saddles, bridles etc) into Iceland.

» Many people bring their cars on the ferry from Europe. Special duty-waiver conditions apply for stays of up to one year (see p347).

Electricity

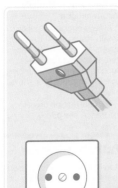

230V/50Hz

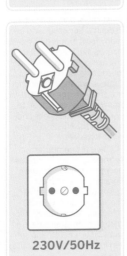

230V/50Hz

Embassies & Consulates

Up-to-date details of embassies and consulates within Iceland and overseas can be found (in English) on the **Icelandic Ministry of Foreign Affairs** (www.mfa.is) website.

Note that Australian and Irish residents need to contact their respective embassies in Copenhagen; New Zealanders need to contact their representatives in Stockholm; and the Dutch must contact their embassy in Oslo – contact details are on www.mfa.is.

A handful of countries have formal embassies in Reykjavík:

Canada (575 6500; www.canada.is; Túngata 14)

Denmark (575 0300; http://island.um.dk/; Hverfis gata 29)

Finland (510 0100; www.finland.is; Túngata 30)

France (575 9600; www.ambafrance.is; Túngata 22)

Germany (530 1100; www.reykjavik.diplo.de; Laufásvegur 31)

Japan (510 8600; japan@itn.is; 6th fl, Laugavegur 182)

Norway (520 0700; www.noregur.is; Fjólugata 17)

Sweden (520 1230; www.swedenabroad.com/reykjavik; Lágmúli 7)

UK (550 5100; www.britishembassy.is; Laufásvegur 31)

USA (595 2200; www.usa.is; Laufásvegur 21)

Food

» You'll find information on food and special dishes in the Icelandic Cuisine chapter (p326).

» For cafe and restaurant standard opening hours, see p335.

Gay & Lesbian Travellers

» Icelanders have an open attitude towards homosexuality, though the gay scene is quite low-key, even in Reykjavík. Aggression against gays and lesbians is rare.

» The main GLBT organisation is **Samtökin '78** (552 7878; www.samtokin78.is; 4th fl, Laugavegur 3, Reykjavík;

office 1-5pm Mon-Fri), which doubles as an informal gay community centre with a drop-in cafe (open from 8pm to 11pm Thursdays year-round).

» Reykjavík's **Gay Pride** (www.gaypride.is) is held annually on the second weekend in August.

» **Pink Iceland** (www.pinkiceland.is) is a Reykjavík-based LGBT tour specialist with some good tips on its website.

» Useful source of information on news, events and venues: www.gayice.is.

Health

Travel in Iceland presents very few health problems. Tap water is absolutely safe to drink, the level of hygiene is high and there are no endemic nasties. Specific travel vaccinations are not required for visitors to Iceland.

Health Care

The standard of heath care is extremely high and English is widely spoken by doctors and medical clinic staff. Note, however, that there are limited services outside of large urban areas. For minor ailments, pharmacists can dispense valuable advice and over-the-counter medication (look for signs for *apótek*, or pharmacy). They can advise when more specialised help is required.

Citizens of other Nordic countries need only present their passport to access health care. Citizens of the European Economic Area (EEA) are covered for emergency medical treatment on presentation of a European Health Insurance Card (EHIC). Enquire about EHICs at your health centre, travel agency or (in some countries) post office well in advance of travel.

Citizens from other countries can obtain medical assistance but must pay in full (and later be reimbursed

PRACTICALITIES

» **Discount Cards** Students and seniors qualify for discounts on internal flights, some ferry and bus fares, tours and museum entry fees, but you'll need to show proof of student status or age.

» **DVDs & Videos** Iceland uses the PAL video system, and falls within DVD zone 2.

» **Newspapers & Magazines** The daily paper *Morgunblaðið* (www.mbl.is) is in Icelandic; its website has local news in English. For tourist-oriented and daily-life articles about Iceland in English, check out the freebie newspapers *Iceland Review* (www.icelandreview.is) and *Reykjavik Grapevine* (www.grapevine.is).

» **Radio** RÚV (Icelandic National Broadcasting Service; www.ruv.is) has two radio stations: Rás 1 (news, classical music) and Rás 2 (pop music, current affairs). Rás 1 (in Reykjavik, FM 92.4 and 93.5) has a short broadcast of news in English at 7.30am Monday to Friday from June to August. BBC World Service is available at FM 94.3.

» **Smoking** Illegal in enclosed public spaces, including in cafes, bars, clubs, restaurants and on public transport. Most accommodation is nonsmoking.

» **Weights & Measures** Metric

by their insurance provider, if they have one). Travel insurance is advised. For more detailed information on health care for visitors, see www.sjukra.is/english/tourists/.

Hypothermia & Frostbite

The main health risks are caused by exposure to extreme climates; proper preparation will reduce the risks. Even on a hot day in the mountains, the weather can change rapidly – carry waterproof garments and warm layers, and inform others of your route.

» Acute hypothermia follows a sudden drop of temperature over a short time. Chronic hypothermia is caused by a gradual loss of temperature over hours. Hypothermia starts with shivering, loss of judgement and clumsiness. Unless rewarming occurs, the sufferer deteriorates into apathy, confusion and coma. Prevent further heat loss by seeking shelter, wearing warm dry clothing, drinking hot sweet drinks and sharing body warmth.

» Frostbite is caused by freezing and the subsequent damage to bodily extremities. It is dependent on wind chill, temperature and the length of exposure. Frostbite starts as frostnip (white, numb areas of skin), from which complete recovery is expected with rewarming. As frostbite develops, however, the skin blisters and becomes black. Loss of damaged tissue eventually occurs. Your should wear adequate clothing, stay dry, keep well hydrated and ensure you have adequate kilojoule intake to prevent frostbite. Treatment involves rapid rewarming.

Insurance

» Although Iceland is a very safe place to travel, theft does occasionally happen, and illness and accidents are always a possibility. A travel-insurance policy to cover theft, loss and medical problems is strongly recommended.

» Always check the policy's small print to see if the policy covers any potentially dangerous sporting activities, such as hiking, rock climbing, horse riding, skiing or snowmobiling.

» For information on car insurance, see p349.

Internet Access

» In this book, we have used the 🛜 symbol to indicate where wi-fi is available to guests/customers. The @ symbol is used where there is a computer for guest use.

» Wi-fi is common in Iceland: with a laptop or smartphone, you can pick up a signal in most cafes, bars and hotels in central Reykjavík, and in many farm properties, guesthouses and hotels across the rest of the country. Often wi-fi is free for guests/customers, but sometimes there is a small charge involved. In many places you'll need to ask staff for an access code. Many of the N1 service stations have free wi-fi.

» There are computer terminals for public internet access in most Icelandic libraries, even in small towns (often with a small fee, around Ikr200 for 30 minutes). Many tourist information centres also have a public internet terminal, often free for brief (15-minute) usage.

Legal Matters

Icelandic police are generally low-key and there's very little reason for you to end up in their hands. Worth knowing:

» Drink-driving laws are very strict – one drink can put you over the legal limit of 0.05% blood-alcohol content. The penalty is loss of your driving licence plus a large fine.

» If you are involved in any other traffic offences – speeding, driving without due care and attention etc – you may be asked to go to the station to pay the fine immediately.

» Drunk and disorderly behaviour may land you in a police cell for a night, but you will usually be released the following morning.

» Penalties for possession, use or trafficking of illegal drugs are strict (long prison sentences and heavy fines).

Maps

» In general, maps of Iceland are not fantastic. Few seem able to keep up with the recent spate of road-building and the sealing of gravel stretches.

» Tourist information centres have useful free maps of their town and region. They also stock the free tourist booklet *Around Iceland*, which has bags of information and town plans. Tourist info centres, petrol stations and bookshops all sell road atlases and maps.

» The map publisher **Ferðakort** (www.ferdakort. is) sells its selection of maps online and has a dedicated map department at **Iðnú bookshop** (Brautarholt 8, Reykjavík; ☉9am-5pm Mon-Thu, 9am-4pm Fri).

» A good map for general driving around Iceland, Ferðakort's 1:500,000 *Touring Map Ísland* (Ikr1790) includes all the larger villages and roads, and many small farms and B&Bs. The more in-depth 1:200,000 *Road Atlas* (Ikr3970) has full mapping plus details of accommodation, museums and swimming pools.

» More-detailed Ferðakort maps include the four 1:250,000 maps of northwest, northeast, southwest and southeast Iceland (Ikr2190 each); and 1:100,000 hikers' maps for areas including Hornstrandir,

Skaftafell, Húsavík and Lake Mývatn, and Þórsmörk and Landmannalaugar (Ikr1440 to Ikr1965 each).

» Serious walkers are best asking at the local tourist information centre, which often sell excellent regional walking maps, or at national park visitor centres. The visitor centres for Vatnajökull National Park, for example, stock excellent maps detailing hiking trails in particular areas of the park (Ikr250 to Ikr350).

Money

Iceland is an almost cashless society where the credit card is king. Locals use plastic for even small purchases. As long as you're carrying a valid card, you'll have little need for travellers cheques and will need to withdraw only a limited amount of cash from ATMs.

If you prefer more traditional methods of carrying money, travellers cheques

and banknotes can be exchanged for Icelandic currency at all major banks.

ATMs

» Almost every town in Iceland has a bank with an ATM, where you can withdraw cash using MasterCard, Visa, Maestro or Cirrus cards.

» Diners Club and JCB cards connected to the Cirrus network have access to all ATMs.

» You'll also find ATMs at larger petrol stations and in shopping centres.

Credit & Debit Cards

» Visa and MasterCard (and to a lesser extent Amex, Diners Club and JCB) are accepted in most shops, restaurants and hotels.

» You can pay for the Flybus from Keflavík International Airport to Reykjavík using plastic – handy if you've just arrived in the country.

» If you intend to stay in rural farmhouse accommodation or visit isolated villages, it's

TAX-FREE SHOPPING

» Anyone who has a permanent address outside Iceland can claim up to a 15% refund on purchases when they spend over Ikr4000 (at a single point of sale). Look for stores with a 'tax-free shopping' sign in the window, and ask for a form at the register.

» If the refund amount on a single form exceeds Ikr5000, you have to show the goods to customs when leaving the country and receive a customs stamp (note, this doesn't apply to woollen goods).

» There are three options for getting your refund:

* Credit card refund – write your credit card number on the tax-free form/s and mail it for a refund to your card.

* Cash refund – present the form/s to an agent when you leave Iceland (at airports, or on board cruiseships or the Smyril Line ferry).

* Prepaid refund – get your refund while still in the country, at the Reykjavík tourist information centre or the larger Reykjavík malls. Then put your form/s in the mailbox at Keflavík International Airport or mail it from home.

» Full details are outlined at www.taxfreeworldwide. com/Iceland.

a good idea to carry enough cash to tide you over.

Currency

» The Icelandic unit of currency is the króna (plural krónur), written as Ikr in this book, and often written elsewhere as ISK.

» Coins come in denominations of one, five, 10, 50 and 100 krónur.

» Notes come in 500-, 1000-, 2000- and 5000-krónur denominations.

» Some accommodation providers and tour operators give their prices in euro. Where this is the case, we have listed the euro prices in this book.

» In July 2009 the Icelandic parliament applied for EU membership, and talks started in mid-2010. It is expected that Iceland will vote on accession in early 2013. Whether the country will in time adopt the euro as its currency remains to be seen. It is a contentious issue among Icelanders (see p306).

» For exchange rates, see p17, or www.xe.com.

Tipping

» As service and VAT are always included in prices, tipping isn't required in Iceland.

Post

» The **Icelandic postal service** (Pósturinn; www.post ur.is) is reliable and efficient, and rates are comparable to those in other Western European countries.

» A postcard/letter to Europe costs Ikr175/300; to places outside Europe it costs Ikr230/475. A full list of postal rates is online.

Public Holidays

Icelandic public holidays are usually an excuse for a family gathering or, when they occur on weekends, a reason to rush to the countryside

and go camping. If you're planning to travel during holiday periods, particularly the August bank holiday, you should book camping areas, mountain huts and transport well in advance.

Most Icelandic hotels and guesthouses generally shut down from Christmas Eve to New Year's Day.

National public holidays in Iceland:

New Year's Day 1 January
Easter March or April Maundy Thursday and Good Friday to Easter Monday (changes annually)
First Day of Summer First Thursday after 18 April
Labour Day 1 May
Ascension Day May or June (changes annually)
Whit Sunday and Whit Monday May or June (changes annually)
National Day 17 June
Commerce Day First Monday in August
Christmas 24 to 26 December
New Year's Eve 31 December

School Holidays

» The main school summer holiday runs from June to late August, which is when most of the Edda and summer hotels open.

» There are big student parties when school breaks up and when school restarts, so popular camping areas may be packed out.

» The winter school holiday is a two- to three-week break over the Christmas period (December to January).

Safe Travel

Iceland has a very low crime rate and in general any risks you'll face while travelling here are related to road safety, the unpredictable weather and the unique geological conditions.

A good place to learn about minimising your risks while travelling in Iceland is **Safetravel** (www.safetravel.is).

The website is an initiative of the Icelandic Association for Search and Rescue (ICE-SAR); it also outlines the 112 Iceland app for smartphones, and explains procedures for leaving a travel plan with ICE-SAR or a friend/contact.

Road Safety

» Beware: locals universally ignore the speed limit, cut corners and weave out of their lanes.

» There are also unique hazards for drivers, such as livestock on the roads, single-lane bridges, blind rises and rough gravel roads.

» For road conditions, see www.vegagerdin.is or call ☐1777.

» For more information on driving in Iceland, see p347.

Weather Conditions

» Never underestimate the weather. Proper clothing and equipment is essential.

» Visitors need to be prepared for inclement conditions year-round. The weather can change without warning, and it's essential for hikers to get a reliable forecast before setting off – call ☐902 0600 (press 1 after the introduction) or visit www.vedur.is/english for a forecast in English.

» Emergency huts are provided in places where travellers run the risk of getting caught in severe weather.

» If you're driving in winter, carry food, water and blankets in your car.

» Car-hire companies can provide snow tyres or chains in winter.

Geological Risks

» When hiking, river crossings can be dangerous, with glacial run-off transforming trickling streams into raging torrents on warm summer days. See p350 for more information on how to cross rivers safely.

» High winds can create vicious sandstorms in areas

where there is loose volcanic sand.

» Hiking paths in coastal areas are often only accessible at low tide, so seek local advice and obtain the relevant tide tables.

» In geothermal areas, stick to boardwalks or obviously solid ground, avoiding thin crusts of lighter-coloured soil around steaming fissures and mudpots.

» Be careful of the water in hot springs and mudpots – it often emerges out of the ground at 100°C.

» In glacial areas beware of dangerous quicksand at the end of glaciers, and never venture out onto the ice without crampons and ice axes (even then, watch out for crevasses).

» Snowfields may overlie fissures, sharp lava chunks or slippery slopes of scoria (volcanic slag).

» Always get local advice before hiking around live volcanoes.

» Only attempt isolated hiking and glacier ascents if you know what you're doing. Talk to locals and/or employ a guide.

» It's rare to find much by way of warning signs or fences in areas where accidents can occur (large waterfalls, glacier fronts, cliff edges). Use common sense, and supervise children well.

Telephone

» Public phones are elusive in mobile-crazy Iceland. There may be a payphone outside the post office or bus station, and at the local petrol station. Many payphones

EMERGENCY NUMBERS

For police, ambulance and fire services in Iceland, dial ✆112.

accept credit cards. Local calls are charged at around Ikr20 per minute.

» To make international calls while in Iceland, first dial the international access code ✆00, then the country code (listed in telephone directories), the area or city code, and the telephone number.

» To phone Iceland from abroad, dial your country's international access code, Iceland's country code (✆354) and then the seven-digit phone number (note: Iceland has no area codes).

» Toll-free numbers in Iceland begin with ✆800, and most seven-digit mobile phone numbers start with ✆8.

» There's an online version of the phone book at http://en.ja.is/.

» Useful numbers:

• Directory enquiries (local) ✆118

• Directory enquiries (international) ✆1811

• International collect (reverse-charges) calls ✆800 8050

Mobile Phones

» The cheapest and most practical way to make calls at local rates is to purchase an Icelandic SIM card and pop it into your own mobile phone. Before leaving home, make sure that your phone isn't blocked from doing this by your home network. If you're coming from outside Europe, also check that your phone will work in Europe's GSM 900/1800 network (US phones work on a different frequency).

» You can buy a prepaid SIM card at bookstores, grocery stores, post offices and petrol stations throughout the country. Top-up credit is available from the same outlets. When purchasing a SIM card, there are two main players: Iceland Telecom **Síminn** (www.siminn.is) provides the greatest network coverage; **Vodafone** (www.vodafone.is) is not far behind.

BY THE BOOK

Due to the unique way in which surnames are formed in Iceland (girls add the suffix -dóttir, daughter, to their father's first name; boys add the suffix -son), telephone directories are alphabetised by first name. Hence, Guðrun Halldórsdóttir would be listed before Jón Einarsson.

Both companies have starter packs including local SIM cards for as little as Ikr2000 (including Ikr2000 in call credit).

Phonecards

» The smallest denomination phonecard (for use in public telephones) costs Ikr500, and can be bought from grocery stores, post offices, petrol stations and Síminn telephone offices.

» Low-cost international phonecards are also available in many shops and youth hostels.

Time

» Iceland's time zone is the same as GMT/UTC (London), but there is no daylight-saving time.

» From late October to late March Iceland is on the same time as London, five hours ahead of New York and 11 hours behind Sydney.

» In the northern hemisphere summer, Iceland is one hour behind London, four hours ahead of New York and 10 hours behind Sydney.

Tourist Information

Icelandic tourist information centres are helpful, friendly and well informed, and can be invaluable in helping you find accommodation, book tours or see the best an area has to offer. Employees usually speak several European languages including English.

We have listed tourist information centres for individual destinations throughout this book. Note that if you arrive in a town after the tourist information centre has closed, the local petrol station is often a good bet for maps and information.

Websites

The official tourism site for the country is **Visit Iceland** (www.visiticeland.com), which has comprehensive information and brochures to download.

Each region also has its own useful site/s:

Reykjavik (www.visitreykjavik.is)

Southwest Iceland (www. visitreykjanes.is, www.south.is)

West Iceland (www.west iceland.is)

The Westfjords (www. westfjords.is)

North Iceland (www.north iceland.is, www.visitakureyri.is)

East Iceland (www.east.is)

Southeast Iceland (www. south.is, www.visitvatnajokull.is)

Publications

Look out for the following useful booklets, published annually and available free at most tourist information centres:

Áning – guide to accommodation

Around Iceland – general tourist guide

The Ideal Holiday – guide to farmhouse accommodation

Tjaldsvæðl Íslands – guide to camping in Iceland

Travellers with Disabilities

Iceland can be trickier than many places in northern Europe when it comes to access for travellers with disabilities.

» For details on accessible facilities, get in touch with **Sjálfsbjörg** (☑550 0360; www.sjalfsbjorg.is; Hátún 12, IS-105 Reykjavík). Sjálfsbjörg's website (click on 'English', then 'For travellers') has excellent information on resources and organisations.

» Another good resource is the website **God Adgang** (www.godadgang.dk), a Danish initiative adopted in Iceland in 2011. Follow the instructions to find Icelandic service providers that have been assessed for the accessibility label.

» Most museums and other attractions offer reduced admission prices for travellers with disabilities. For travel, Air Iceland offers reduced rates, as does the Smyril Line ferry.

» Reykjavík's city buses have a 'kneeling' function so that wheelchairs can be lifted onto the bus; elsewhere, however, public buses don't have ramps or lifts.

» **Hertz** (www.hertz.is) has a wheelchair-accessible minivan for hire.

» The company **All Iceland Tours** (www.allicelandtours. is/Disabled_Travel.html) offers tailor-made trips around the country. Its website also has good general info.

» Sjálfsbjörg has guest apartments for rent. Otherwise, the website www.whenwetravel.com lists which hotels in Iceland are wheelchair accessible. (Once you've clicked on the destination, then on hotels, a Wheelchair Accessible option appears in the menu.) All farms in the **Icelandic Farm Holidays** (www.farmholidays. is) network have been evaluated for accessibility; you can search for accessible properties.

Visas

Iceland is one of 26 member countries of the Schengen Convention, under which the EU countries (all but Bulgaria, Romania, Cyprus, Ireland and the UK) plus Iceland, Norway, Liechtenstein and Switzerland have abolished checks at common borders.

The visa situation for Iceland is as follows.

» Citizens of Denmark, Faroe Islands, Finland, Norway and Sweden – no visa or passport required.

» Citizens of other EU and Schengen countries – no visa required for stays of up to three months.

» Citizens or residents of Australia, Canada, Japan, New Zealand and the USA – no visa required for tourist visits of up to three months. Note that the total stay within the Schengen area must not exceed three months in any period of six months.

» Other countries – check online at www.utl.is.

» To work or study in Iceland a permit is usually required – check with an Icelandic embassy or consulate, or online.

Volunteering

A volunteering holiday is a worthwhile (and relatively inexpensive) way to get intimately involved with Iceland's people and landscapes.

Volunteer Abroad (www.vol unteerabroad.com) Offers an overview of possible projects in Iceland. Note that many of the projects listed are under the remit of Iceland's Environment Agency (Umhverfisstofnun), but arranged through various international volunteering organisations.

Umhverfisstofnun (UST; www.ust.is/the-environment -agency-of-iceland/volunteers/) Iceland's Environment Agency recruits more than 200 volunteers each summer for work on practical conservation projects around the country, mainly creating or maintaining trails in Vatnajökull National Park. Places on its short-term programs (under four weeks) are usually arranged through its partner volunteer organisations, including UK-based **The Conservation Volunteers** (www.tcv.org.uk) and **Working Abroad** (www.workingabroad.org), or Iceland-based SEEDS and Worldwide Friends. Longer-term placements are also possible on Trail Teams that work together for 11 weeks over the summer; see the UST website for details.

SEEDS (SEE beyonD borders; www.seeds.is) Iceland-based SEEDS organises work camps and volunteering holidays, primarily focused on nature and the environment (building trails, ecological research), but also construction or renovation of community buildings, or assistance at festivals and events.

Worldwide Friends (Veraldarvinir; www.wf.is) Iceland-based Worldwide Friends runs work camps that largely support nature and the environment, but there are also options for involvement in community projects, and art and cultural events.

Transport

GETTING THERE & AWAY

Iceland has become far more accessible in recent years, with more flight options from a growing list of destinations. Ferry transport is also possible and makes a good alternative for European travellers wishing to take their own car.

Flights, tours and rail tickets can be booked online at www.lonelyplanet.com/travelservices.

Entering the Country

» As long as you are in possession of the right documentation, immigration control should be a quick formality at the air- or ferry port where you arrive.

» Citizens of Schengen nations, the European Economic Area (EEA), the US, Australia, New Zealand, Japan, Canada, Israel and several Latin American nations can travel in Iceland without a visa for up to three months. Other nationalities require a visa; for more information, see p342.

Air

Airports & Airlines
AIRPORTS

» Iceland's main international airport is **Keflavík International Airport** (www. kefairport.is), 48km southwest of Reykjavík.

» Internal flights and those to Greenland and the Faeroes use the small **Reykjavík Domestic Airport** (www. reykjavikairport.is) in central Reykjavík.

» A couple of international flights from Copenhagen land at tiny **Akureyri Airport** (www.akureyriairport.is) in Iceland's 'second city' in the north.

AIRLINES FLYING TO/FROM ICELAND

A growing number of airlines fly to Iceland; many have scheduled services only in the peak summer months (June to August).

Air Berlin (www.airberlin.com)

Air Greenland (www. airgreenland.com)

Air Iceland (Flugfélag Íslands; www.airiceland.is)

Atlantic Airways (www. atlantic.fo)

Austrian (www.austrian.com)

Delta (www.delta.com)

easyJet (www.easyjet.com)

Germanwings (www.germanwings.com)

Iceland Express (www. icelandexpress.com)

Icelandair (www.icelandair.com)

Lufthansa (www.lufthansa.com)

Norwegian (www.norwegian.com)

SAS (www.flysas.com)

Transavia France (www. transavia.com)

WOW air (www.wowair.com)

CLIMATE CHANGE & TRAVEL

Every form of transport that relies on carbon-based fuel generates CO_2, the main cause of human-induced climate change. Modern travel is dependent on aeroplanes, which might use less fuel per kilometre per person than most cars but travel much greater distances. The altitude at which aircraft emit gases (including CO_2) and particles also contributes to their climate change impact. Many websites offer 'carbon calculators' that allow people to estimate the carbon emissions generated by their journey and, for those who wish to do so, to offset the impact of the greenhouse gases emitted with contributions to portfolios of climate-friendly initiatives throughout the world. Lonely Planet offsets the carbon footprint of all staff and author travel.

Sea

» **Smyril Line** (www.smyril line.com) operates a pricy but well-patronised weekly car ferry, the *Norröna*, on a somewhat convoluted schedule from Hirsthals (Denmark) through Tórshavn (Faeroe Islands) to Seyðisfjörður in east Iceland.

» Boats run all year, but Iceland is only part of the itinerary from April until late October. (Between November and March the ferry only travels between Denmark and the Faeroes.)

» Fares vary widely, depending on when you travel, whether you are travelling with a car/campervan/motorbike etc, and what sort of cabin you choose.

» Sample one-way fares from Hirtshals to Seyðisfjörður (journey time approximately 47 hours) for a car and two passengers in high season (mid-June to mid-August) is €738, before cabin choice is factored in. For a solo traveller (without vehicle), the one-way base fare is €203.

» High-season cabin prices start at €58 per person for a dorm-style 'couchette', €92 for a berth in a four-berth cabin (with linen and bathroom).

» It's possible to travel from Denmark to Iceland with a stopover in the Faeroes. Contact Smyril Line or see the website for information about trip packages.

GETTING AROUND

There is no train network in Iceland. The most common way for visitors to get around the island is to rent a car and drive (see the Ring Road Planner, p30, for advice on this). There is also a good bus network operating from approximately mid-May to mid-September to get you between major destinations, but don't discount

internal flights that can help you maximise your time in Iceland.

Air

» Iceland has an extensive network of domestic flights, which locals use almost like buses. In winter a flight can be the only way to get between destinations, but weather at this time of year can play havoc with schedules.

» Note that almost all domestic flights depart from the small Reykjavík International Airport in central Reykjavík (ie, not the major international airport at Keflavík).

» There are a handful of airstrips offering regular sightseeing flights – at Mývatn and Skaftafell, for example.

Airlines in Iceland

Air Iceland (Flugfélag Íslands; www.airiceland.is) Destinations covered in its network: Reykjavík, Akureyri, Grímsey, Ísafjörður, Vopnafjörður, Egilsstaðir and Þórshöfn. Offers some fly-in day tours from Reykjavík (including to destinations in Greenland). Online deals for domestic flights start at around €60 one way.

Eagle Air (www.eagleair. is) Operates scheduled flights to smaller airstrips: Vestmannaeyjar, Húsavík, Höfn, Bíldudalur and Gjögur. Flights cost €130 to €180 one way. There is also a number of day tours.

Air Passes

Air Iceland offers a couple of air passes, available year-round, which must be purchased either outside Iceland or in Icelandic travel agencies catering for foreign visitors.

» The Air Iceland Pass is available with four/five/six sectors for €384/445/512 in high season (mid-June to mid-August).

» The Fly As You Please pass gives 12 consecutive days of unlimited flights in Iceland for €508 in high season, excluding airport taxes (€8 per departure).

Bicycle

» Cycling through Iceland's dramatic landscapes is a fantastic way to see the country, but you should be prepared for some harsh conditions along the way. Gale-force winds, driving rain, sandstorms, sleet and sudden flurries of snow are all possible at any time of year.

» An excellent resource: the English pages of the website of the **Icelandic Mountain Bike Club** (http://fjallahjolak lubburinn.is).

» It's essential to know how to do your own basic repairs and to bring several puncture-repair kits and spares, as supplies are hard to come by outside Reykjavík.

» Reykjavík has several well-stocked bike shops. Two of the best include **Örninn** (☑588 9890; www.orninn.is; Skeifan 11d, IS-108 Reykjavík) and **Markið** (☑517 4600; www.markid.is; Ármúli 40, IS-108 Reykjavík).

» If you want to tackle the interior, the Kjölur route has bridges over all major rivers, making it fairly accessible to cyclists. A less-challenging route is the F249 to Þórsmörk. The Westfjords also offer some wonderful cycling terrain, though the winding roads and steep passes can make for slow progress.

Transporting Bicycles

» Most airlines will carry your bike in the hold if you pack it correctly. You should remove the pedals, lower the saddle, turn the handlebars parallel to the frame and deflate the tyres.

» The Smyril Line ferry from Denmark transports bikes for €15 each way.

» Buses charge Ikr2500 to Ikr3000, but space may be a problem so show up early or book ahead.

» If you've brought your own bicycle, you can store your bike box at the campsite in Keflavík (at Guesthouse Alex) for free for the duration of your visit.

Hire

» Various places around Iceland rent out mountain bikes, but in general these are intended for local use only, and often aren't up to long-haul travel. If you intend to go touring, it's wise to bring your bike from home or purchase one when you arrive.

Boat

Several year-round ferries operate in Iceland. See the relevant regional sections for more detailed information.

Major routes:

» car ferry *Herjólfur* between Landeyjahöfn (about 20km southeast of Hvolsvöllur – take Rte 254 off the Ring Road) and Vestmannaeyjar (see www.herjolfur.is). Note that there are occasions, in inclement weather, when the ferry cannot use the Landeyjahöfn port, and reverts to its old dock at Þorlákshöfn (a much longer sea route to the islands).

» car ferry *Baldur* between Stykkishólmur on the Snæfellsnes Peninsula to Brjánslækur in the Westfjords, stopping at the island of Flatey (see www.seatours.is)

» car ferry *Sæfari* between Dalvík and Hrísey or Grímsey (see www.landflutningar.is)

» passenger ferry *Sævar* between Arskógssandur and Hrísey (see www.hrisey.net)

From June to August, Bolungarvík and Ísafjörður have regular ferry services to several different points in Hornstrandir. There is no ferry service from the Strandir region into Hornstrandir.

Bus

» Iceland has an extensive network of long-distance bus routes with services operated by a number of bus companies. They're overseen by BSÍ (Bifreiðastöð Íslands; www.bsi.is), based in the BSÍ bus terminal in Reykjavík.

» The booking desk at the BSÍ bus terminal sells tickets and distributes the free Iceland on Your Own brochure, which contains timetables for some (but not all) services.

» From roughly mid-May to mid-September there are regular scheduled buses to most places on the Ring Road, and to larger towns in the Westfjords and on the Reykjanes and Snæfellsnes Peninsulas. There are also services along the highland Kjölur and Sprengisandur routes (inaccessible to 2WD cars). During the rest of the year services range from daily to nonexistent.

» In small towns and villages, buses stop at the main petrol station.

Companies

Main bus companies:

Reykjavík Excursions (Kynnisferðir; ☑580 5400; www.re.is) Serves the Reykjanes Peninsula and operates the Flybus to/from Keflavík International Airport, plus some scheduled southern routes, and summer buses across the interior.

SBA-Norðurleið (☑550 0700/70; www.sba.is) North Iceland.

Sterna (☑551 1166; www.sterna.is) Services countrywide.

Stjörnubílar (☑456 5518; www.stjornubilar.is) Westfjords.

Bus Passes

Iceland's bus operators are coming out with new and improved bus passes every year to make public transport around the island as easy as possible. (Nevertheless, it's still significantly more convenient to hire your own vehicle.)

Visit www.re.is/Iceland OnYourOwn/Passports/ and www.sterna.is/en/bus-passport for a longer list of passports. Following are some options (note: prices listed are for summer 2012):

Beautiful South Passport (3/7/11 days Ikr20,700/37,600/51,000) Valid from June to mid-September. Unlimited travel along the south coast and to Þórsmörk, Landmannalaugar and Lakagígar. Offered by Reykjavík Excursions.

Combo Pass-port (7/11/15 days Ikr49,000/65,000/77,000) The Big Kahuna of passports, from Reykjavík Excursions (working with SBA-Norðurleið) and taking in the Ring Road, the northeast circuit (Húsavík to Þórshöfn), Golden Circle and both highland routes (but not Westfjords or Snæfellsnes), valid from early June to mid-September.

Full Circle Passport (Ikr37,000) Sterna's pass is valid from mid-May to mid-September for one circuit of the Ring Road in one direction, stopping wherever you like. Reykjavík Excursions has a similar pass for Ikr35,000 (the Ring Road Passport), with slightly shorter validity.

Golden Circle Passport (Ikr9000) Valid from June to mid-September, and a decent alternative to taking a day excursion. Covers Þingvellir, Geysir and Gullfoss, and Selfoss. Offered by Sterna.

Highland Circle Passport (Ikr35,600) Valid from mid-June to early September (depending on when the highlands roads are open) for one circular route taking in the Sprengisandur and Kjölur routes. Offered by Reykjavík Excursions.

Hiking Passport (Ikr10,500) Reykjavík Excursions offers return bus journey to southwest hikers from their start/

end point, choosing two of three destinations: Skógar, Landmannalaugar and Þórsmörk.

Snæfellsnes & National Park Passport (Ikr17,000) Valid from mid-June to August for one circuit of Snæfellsnes Peninsula, starting and ending in Reykjavík. Offered by Sterna.

West & Westfjords Passport (Ikr27,000) Valid from June to August for one circuit of the Westfjords, to/from Reykjavík and including the ferry across Breiðafjörður. Offered by Sterna (in conjunction with Stjörnubílar). Sterna also offers a Full Circle (Ring Road) plus Westfjords option (Ikr59,000).

Car & Motorcycle

» Driving in Iceland gives you unparalleled freedom to discover the country and, thanks to good roads and light traffic, it's all fairly straightforward. See the Ring Road Planner (p30) for information on planning your driving itinerary.

» The Ring Road (Rte 1) circles the country and is mostly paved. Beyond the Ring Road, fingers of sealed road or gravel stretch out to most communities. Off the Ring Road you are likely to pass no more than a handful of cars each day, even in high season.

» In coastal areas driving can be spectacularly scenic, and incredibly slow as you weave up and down over unpaved mountain passes and in and out of long fjords. Even so, a 2WD vehicle will get you almost everywhere in summer (note: not into the highlands).

» In winter heavy snow can cause many roads to close and mountain roads generally remain closed until June. Some mountain roads start closing as early as September after the warm summer months. For up-to-date information on road conditions, visit www.vegagerdin.is.

Bring Your Own Vehicle

» Car hire in Iceland is shockingly expensive, so taking your own vehicle to the country may not be as crazy as it sounds. The Smyril Line ferry from Denmark is busy in summer bringing vehicles to Iceland from all over Europe.

» For temporary duty-free importation, drivers must carry the vehicle's registration documents, proof of valid insurance (a 'green card' if your car isn't registered in a Nordic or EU-member country) and a driving licence.

» Permission for temporary duty-free importation of a motor vehicle is granted at the point of arrival for up to 12 months, and is contingent upon agreeing to not lend or sell your vehicle. For more information, contact the **Directorate of Customs** (www.customs.is).

Driving Licences

You can drive in Iceland with a driving licence from the US, Canada, Australia, New Zealand and most European countries. If you have a licence that is not in Roman script, you need to get an International Driving Permit, which is normally issued by the automobile association in your home country.

Fuel & Spare Parts

» There are regularly spaced petrol stations around Iceland, but in the highlands you should check fuel levels and the distance to the next station before setting off on a long journey.

» At the time of research, unleaded petrol cost about Ikr260 (€1.70) per litre, diesel about Ikr265 per litre. Leaded petrol isn't available.

» Most smaller petrol stations are unstaffed, and almost all pumps are automated – though there is the time-consuming option of going inside the service station to ask staff to manually switch on the pump, enabling you to fill up and pay for your fuel afterwards.

» To fill up using the automated service, put your credit card into the machine's slot (you'll need a card with a PIN) and follow the instructions. Enter your PIN, then enter the maximum amount you wish to spend, then wait

---

ESSENTIAL WEB RESOURCES

Four websites every traveller should know about:

Safetravel (www.safetravel.is) Learn about minimising your risks while travelling in Iceland.

Car Pooling in Iceland (www.samferda.is) Handy carsharing site that helps drivers and passengers to link up around the country. A savvy alternative to hitching. Passengers often foot the petrol bill.

Icelandic Met Office (www.vedur.is) Never underestimate the weather in Iceland, or its impact on your travels. Get a reliable forecast before you go anywhere from this site (or call ☎902 0600, and press 1 after the introduction).

Vegagerdin (www.vegagerdin.is) Iceland's road administration site details road openings and closings around the country. Vital if you plan to explore Iceland's little-visited corners and remote interior.

while the pump authorises your purchase. (Note that you will only be charged for the amount of the fuel put into your vehicle, not the maximum amount you enter.) If you require a receipt, re-enter your card into the slot. It's a good idea to check that your card will work by visiting a staffed station while it is open, in case you have any problems.

» Some Icelandic roads can be pretty lonely, so carry a jack, a spare tyre and jump leads just in case. In the case of a breakdown or accident, your first port of call should be your car-hire agency.

» Although the Icelandic motoring association **Félag Íslenskra Bifreiðaeigenda** (FÍB; www.fib.is) is only open to residents of Iceland, if you have breakdown cover with an automobile association affiliated with ARC Europe you may be covered by the FÍB – check with your home association.

» FÍB's round-the-clock breakdown number is ☎511 2112. Even if you're not a member, it can provide information and phone numbers for towing and breakdown services all around Iceland.

Car Hire

» Travelling by car is often the only way to get to parts of Iceland. Although car-hire rates are expensive by international standards, they compare favourably against bus or internal air travel within the country, especially if there are a few of you to split the costs.

» To rent a car you must be 20 years old (23 to 25 years for a 4WD) and you will need to show a valid driving licence.

» The cheapest cars on offer, usually a Hyundai i10, Toyota Yaris or similar, cost from around Ikr16,000 per day in high season (June to August). Figure on paying from around Ikr25,000 for the smallest 4WD. Rates include unlimited mileage and VAT, and usually collision damage waiver (CDW). From September to May you should be able to find considerably better daily rates and deals.

» Be sure to check the small print, as additional costs such as extra insurance, airport pick-up charges and one-way rental fees can add up.

» You'd think that with such high prices it would be easy to find a car. Think again. In the height of summer many dealerships completely run out of rentals. Book ahead.

» There are dozens of registered car-hire companies in Iceland. If you arrive in Iceland without any prior car-hire arrangements, it's worth looking around and asking at your accommodation if it offers any discounts.

» Many travel organisations (eg Hostelling International Iceland, Icelandic Farm Holidays, Air Iceland) offer package deals that include car hire.

» Most companies are based in the Reykjavík and Keflavík areas, with city and airport offices (larger companies may have a branch at Reykjavík domestic airport). Larger companies have extra locations around the country (usually in Akureyri and Egilsstaðir).

» Ferry passengers entering Iceland via Seyðisfjörður will find car-hire agencies in nearby Egilsstaðir.

CAR-HIRE COMPANIES

The following list is far from exhaustive.

Átak (www.atak.is)

Avis (www.avis.is)

Budget (www.budget.is)

Europcar (Bílaleiga Akureyrar/Höldur; www.europcar.is) The biggest hire company in Iceland.

Geysir (www.geysir.is) Lists its daily/weekly summer and winter prices for each of its vehicles on its website.

Go Iceland (www.goiceland.com) Also rents out camping equipment (tents, mattresses, stoves).

Hasso (www.hasso.is)

Hertz (www.hertz.is)

SADcars (www.sadcars.com) Older fleet, therefore cheaper prices.

Saga (www.sagacarrental.is)

CAMPERVAN HIRE

Combining accommodation and transport costs into campervan rental is a popular option. The large car-hire companies usually have campervans for rent, but following are some more offbeat choices.

Camper Iceland (www.campericeland.is)

F ROADS

We can think of a few choice F words for these bumpy, almost nonexistent tracts of land, but in reality the 'F' stands for *fjall* – the Icelandic word for mountain. Most F roads only support 4WDs and, while some of them may almost blend into the surrounding nature, off-road driving is strictly prohibited everywhere in Iceland.

Before tackling any F road you should educate yourself as to what lies ahead (river crossings, boulders etc) and whether or not the entire route is open. See www.vegagerdin.is for road closure details. Note, too, that if you travel on F roads in a hired 2WD, you invalidate your insurance. Not only that, you're guaranteed a seriously bumpy, slow, unpleasant journey – F roads are not meant for 2WD travel. Do yourself a favour and steer clear. If you want to explore F roads, hire a 4WD.

Happy Campers (www.happycampers.is)

JS Camper Rental (www.campers.is) Truck campers on 4WD pickups.

Kúkú Campers (www.kukucampers.is) Artwork-adorned campers (celebs like Chuck Norris or the Hoff), plus gear rental (tent, fishing gear, barbecue, acoustic guitar, surfboard etc).

Snail.is (www.snail.is)

MOTORCYCLE HIRE

Biking Viking (www.bikingviking.is) Motorcycle rental, tours and service.

Insurance

» A vehicle registered in Nordic or EU-member countries is considered to have valid automobile insurance in Iceland. If your vehicle is registered in a non-Nordic or non-EU country, you'll need a 'green card', which proves that you are insured to drive while in Iceland. Green cards are issued by insurance companies in your home country; contact your existing insurer.

» When hiring a car, check the small print carefully; most vehicles come with third-party insurance and collision damage waiver (CDW) to cover you for damage to the hire car. Also check the excess (the initial amount you will be liable to pay in the event of an accident) as this can be surprisingly high.

» Hire vehicles are not covered for damage to the tyres, headlights and windscreen, or damage caused to the underside of the vehicle by driving on dirt roads, through water or in ash- or sandstorms. Many companies will try to sell you additional insurance to cover these possibilities.

» Some policies prohibit 'off-road driving'. This usually refers to mountain roads (F roads) and 4WD tracks, but check with the car-hire company to be sure.

DRIVE SAFELY

Road Rules

» Drive on the right
» Front and rear seat belts are compulsory
» Dipped headlights must be on at all times
» Blood alcohol limit is 0.05%
» Mobile phone use is prohibited except with a hands-free kit
» Children under six years must use a car seat
» Do not drive off-road

Speed Limits

» Built-up areas 50km/h
» Unsealed roads 80km/h
» Sealed roads 90km/h

» Car-hire agreements also do not cover damage to the hire car caused by collisions with animals.

Parking

» Other than in central Reykjavík, parking in Iceland is easy to find and free of charge. For information on parking in the capital, see p79.

» Note that Akureyri has a different system for parking (involving the use of plastic clocks). See p214 for details.

Road Conditions & Hazards

Good road surfaces and light traffic make driving in Iceland relatively easy, but there are some specific hazards that drivers will encounter. Watch the 'How to Drive in Iceland' video on www.drive.is.

» **Livestock** Sheep graze in the countryside over the summer, and often wander onto roads. Take care, and slow down when you see livestock on or near roadsides.

» **Malbik Endar** Not all roads are sealed, and the transition from sealed to gravel roads is marked with the warning sign 'Malbik Endar' – slow right down to avoid skidding when you hit the gravel. Most accidents involving foreign drivers in Iceland are caused

by the use of excessive speed on unsurfaced roads. If your car does begin to skid, take your foot off the accelerator and gently turn the car in the direction you want the front wheels to go. Do not brake.

» **Blindhæðir** In most cases roads have two lanes with steeply cambered sides and no hard shoulder; be prepared for oncoming traffic in the centre of the road, and slow down and stay to the right when approaching blind rises, marked as 'Blindhæðir' on road signs.

» **Einbreið Brú** Slow down and be prepared to give way when approaching single-lane bridges (marked as 'Einbreið Brú'). Right of way is with the car closest to the bridge.

» **Sun glare** With the sun often sitting so low to the horizon, sunglasses are essential for driving.

» **Winter conditions** In winter make sure your car is fitted with snow tyres or chains. Be sure to carry a shovel, blankets, food and water. Take extra care when driving on compacted snow.

» **Ash & sandstorms** Volcanic ash and severe sandstorms can strip paint off cars and blister your windows; strong winds can even topple over your vehicle.

CROSSING RIVERS

While trekking or driving in Iceland's highlands you're likely to face unbridged rivers that must be crossed – a frightening prospect for the uninitiated. Don't panic – there are a few simple rules to follow.

» Melting snow and ice cause water levels to rise, so the best time to cross is early in the morning before the day warms up, and preferably no sooner than 24 hours after a rainstorm.

» Avoid narrow stretches, which are likely to be deep – the widest ford is likely to be shallowest. The swiftest, strongest current is found near the centre of straight stretches and at the outside of bends. Choose a spot with as much slack water as possible.

» Never try to cross just above a waterfall and avoid crossing streams in flood (identifiable by dirty, smooth-running water carrying lots of debris and vegetation). A smooth surface suggests that the river is too deep to be crossed on foot. Anything more than thigh deep isn't crossable without experience and extra equipment.

» Before attempting to cross deep or swift-running streams, be sure that you can jettison your pack in midstream if necessary. Unhitch the waist belt and loosen shoulder straps, and remove long trousers and any bulky clothing that will inhibit swimming. Lone hikers should use a hiking staff to probe the river bottom for the best route and to steady themselves in the current.

» Never try to cross a stream barefoot – slicing your feet open on sharp rocks will really spoil your holiday. Consider bringing a pair of wetsuit boots or sandals if you want to keep your hiking boots dry.

» While crossing, face upstream and avoid looking down or you may risk getting dizzy and losing your balance. Two hikers can steady each other by resting their arms on each other's shoulders.

» If you do fall while crossing, don't try to stand up. Remove your pack (but don't let go of it), roll over onto your back and point your feet downstream, then try to work your way to a shallow eddy or to the shore.

» Crossing glacial rivers can be dangerous in a vehicle. It's best to wade across your intended route first, as described above, to check the depth. Work with the water – drive diagonally across in the direction of the current, making sure you're in a low gear. Drive steadily, without stopping or changing gear, just slightly faster than the water is flowing (too slow and you risk getting stuck, or letting water up the exhaust). If you're not travelling in convoy, consider waiting for other traffic. Watch where and how experienced drivers cross.

At-risk areas are marked with orange warning signs.

» **F roads** Roads suitable for 4WD vehicles only are F-numbered. It's a good idea to travel in tandem on these roads and carry emergency supplies and a full tool and repair kit. Always let someone know where you are going and when you expect to be back.

» **River crossings** Few interior roads have bridges over rivers. Fords are marked on maps with a 'V', but you may need to check the depth and speed of the river by wading into it.

Hitching

» Hitching anywhere in the world is never fully without risk. Nevertheless, we met scores of tourists that were hitching their way around Iceland and most of them had very positive reports. Single female travellers and couples tend to get a lift the quickest.

» Of course, when it comes to hitching, patience is a prerequisite, and logic is important too – be savvy about where you position yourself. Don't stand in the middle of a long straight stretch of highway because drivers will zoom right by before they even notice you. Try standing at junctions, near petrol stations or even by Bónus supermarkets.

» When you arrive at your accommodation for the night it doesn't hurt to let everyone else know where you're trying to get to the next day. Chances are there's another traveller going that way who can give you a ride.

» Summer is by far the best time to hitch a ride and you'll find that both locals and tourists are up for helping hitchers out. You'll get picked up in the winter out of pity – but there aren't too many people driving around at that time of year.

» If the idea of hitching makes you uncomfortable, check out www.samferda.is, a handy car-sharing site.

Local Transport

Bicycle

» You can hire bicycles for local riding from some tourist offices, hotels, hostels and guesthouses. The standard daily charge is about Ikr3000

per day, plus a deposit (a credit-card imprint will usually suffice). Helmets are a legal requirement for children aged under 15.

Bus

» Reykjavík has an extensive network of local buses connecting all the suburbs, and running all the way to Akranes, Borgarnes, Hveragerði, Selfoss and Hvalfjarðarsveit. See www.straeto.is for information on timetables, schedules and routes.

» Free local bus networks operate in Akureyri and Ísafjörður, and the Reykjanesbær area (www.sbk.is) has a municipal service as well.

Taxi

» Most taxis in Iceland operate in the Reykjavík area, but many of the country's larger towns also offer a service. Outside of Reykjavík, it's usually wise to prebook.

» Cabbies offer sightseeing tours of the city and nearby attractions. See the destination chapters for more information.

» Taxis are metered and – like all other transport in Iceland – they can be quite pricey. Tipping is not expected.

Tours

See the planning section, p38, for information about organised tours within Iceland.

Language

WANT MORE?

For in-depth language information and handy phrases, check out Lonely Planet's phrasebooks range. You'll find them at **shop .lonelyplanet.com**, or you can buy Lonely Planet's iPhone phrasebooks at the Apple App Store.

Icelandic belongs to the Germanic language family, which includes German, English, Dutch and all the Scandinavian languages except Finnish. It's related to Old Norse, and retains the letters 'eth' (ð) and 'thorn' (þ), which also existed in Old English. Be aware, especially when you're trying to read bus timetables or road signs, that place names can be spelled in several different ways due to Icelandic grammar rules.

Most Icelanders speak English, so you'll have no problems if you don't know any Icelandic. However, any attempts to speak the local language will be much appreciated.

If you read our coloured pronunciation guides as if they were English, you'll be understood. Keep in mind that double consonants are given a long pronunciation. Note also that öy in our pronunciation guides is like the '-er y-' in 'her year' (without the 'r') and that kh is like the 'ch' in the Scottish *loch*. Stress generally falls on the first syllable in a word.

BASICS

Hello.	*Halló.*	ha·loh
Goodbye.	*Bless.*	bles
Please.	*Takk.*	tak
Thank you.	*Takk fyrir.*	tak fi·rir
Excuse me.	*Afsakið.*	af·sa·kidh
Sorry.	*Fyrirgefðu.*	fi·rir·gev·dhu
Yes.	*Já.*	yow
No.	*Nei.*	nay

How are you?
Hvað segir þú gott? kvadh se·yir thoo got

Fine. And you?
Allt fínt. En þú? alt feent en thoo

What's your name?
Hvað heitir þú? kvadh hay·tir thoo

My name is ...
Ég heiti ... yekh hay·ti ...

Do you speak English?
Talar þú ensku? ta·lar thoo ens·ku

I don't understand.
Ég skil ekki. yekh skil e·ki

DIRECTIONS

Where's the (hotel)?
Hvar er (hótelið)? kvar er (hoh·te·lidh)

READING ICELANDIC

Letter	Pronunciation
Á á	ow (as in 'how')
Ð ð	dh (as the 'th' in 'that')
É é	ye (as in 'yet')
Í í	ee (as in 'see')
Ó ó	oh (as the 'o' in 'note')
Ú ú	oo (as in 'too')
Ý ý	ee (as in 'see')
Þ þ	th (as in 'think')
Æ æ	ai (as in 'aisle')
Ö ö	eu (as the 'u' in 'nurse')

Can you show me (on the map)?
Geturðu sýnt mér ge·tur·dhu seent myer
(á kortinu)? (ow kor·ti·nu)

What's your address?
Hvert er heimilisfangið kvert er hay·mi·lis·fan·gidh
þitt? thit

EATING & DRINKING

What would you recommend?
Hverju mælir þú með? kver·yu mai·lir thoo medh

Do you have vegetarian food?
Hafið þið ha·vidh thidh
grænmetisrétti? grain·me·tis·rye·ti

I'll have a ...
Ég ætla að fá ... yekh ait·la adh fow ...

Cheers!
Skál! skowl

I'd like a/the ..., please.	*Get ég fengið ..., takk.*	get yekh fen·gidh ... tak
nonsmoking section	*reyklaust borð*	rayk·löyst bordh
smoking section	*borð þar sem má reykja*	bordh thar sem mow rayk·ya
table for (four)	*borð fyrir (fjóra)*	bordh fi·rir (fyoh·ra)

I'd like (the) ..., please.	*Get ég fengið ... takk.*	get yekh fen·gidh ... tak
bill	*reikninginn*	rayk·nin·gin
drink list	*vínseðilinn*	veen·se·dhit·lin
menu	*matseðilinn*	mat·se·dhit·lin
that dish	*þennan rétt*	the·nan ryet

bottle of (beer)	*(bjór)flösku*	(byohr)·fleus·ku
(cup of) coffee/tea	*kaffi/te (bolla)*	ka·fi/te (bot·la)
glass of (wine)	*(vín)glas*	(veen)·glas
water	*vatn*	vat

breakfast	*morgunmat*	mor·gun·mat
lunch	*hádegismat*	how·de·yis·mat
dinner	*kvöldmat*	kveuld·mat

Signs

Inngangur	Entrance
Útgangur	Exit
Opið	Open
Lokað	Closed
Bannað	Prohibited
Snyrting	Toilets

Numbers

1	einn	aydn
2	tveir	tvayr
3	þrír	threer
4	fjórir	fyoh·rir
5	fimm	fim
6	sex	seks
7	sjö	syeu
8	átta	ow·ta
9	níu	nee·u
10	tíu	tee·u
20	tuttugu	tu·tu·gu
30	þrjátíu	throw·tee·u
40	fjörutíu	fyeur·tee·u
50	fimmtíu	fim·tee·u
60	sextíu	seks·tee·u
70	sjötíu	syeu·tee·u
80	áttatíu	ow·ta·tee·u
90	níutíu	nee·tee·u
100	hundrað	hun·dradh

EMERGENCIES

Help!	*Hjálp!*	hyowlp
Go away!	*Farðu!*	far·dhu

Call ...!	*Hringdu á ...!*	hring·du ow ...
a doctor	*lækni*	laik·ni
the police	*lögregluna*	leu·rekh·lu·na

I'm lost.
Ég er villtur/villt. (m/f) yekh er vil·tur/vilt

Where are the toilets?
Hvar er snyrtingin? kvar er snir·tin·gin

SHOPPING & SERVICES

I'm looking for ...
Ég leita að ... yekh lay·ta adh ...

How much is it?
Hvað kostar þetta? kvadh kos·tar the·ta

That's too expensive.
Þetta er of dýrt. the·ta er of deert

It's faulty.
Það er gallað. thadh er gat·ladh

There's a mistake in the bill.
Það er villa í thadh er vit·la ee
reikningnum. rayk·ning·num

Do you accept credit cards?
Tekur þú kreditkort? te·kur thoo kre·dit·kort

Where's the ...?	Hvar er ...?	kvar er ...
bank	bankinn	bown·kin
market	markaðurinn	mar·ka·dhu·rin
post office	pósthúsið	pohst·hoo·sidh

TRANSPORT

Can we get there by public transport?
Er hægt að taka   er haikht adh ta·ka
rútu þangað?   roo·tu thown·gadh

Where can I buy a ticket?
Hvar kaupi ég miða?   kvar köy·pi yekh mi·dha

Is this the ...	Er þetta ...	er the·ta ...
to (Akureyri)?	til (Akureyrar)?	til (a·ku·ray·rar)
boat	ferjan	fer·yan
bus	rútan	roo·tan
plane	flugvélin	flukh·vye·lin

What time's	Hvenær fer ...	kve·nair fer ...
the ... bus?	strætisvagninn?	strai·tis·vag·nin
first	fyrsti	firs·ti
last	síðasti	see·dhas·ti

One ... ticket	Einn miða	aitn mi·dha
(to Reykjavík), please.	... (til Reykjavíkur), takk.	... (til rayk·ya·vee·kur) tak
one-way	aðra leiðina	adh·ra lay·dhi·na
return	fram og til baka	fram okh til ba·ka

I'd like a taxi ...	Get ég fengið leigubíl ...	get yekh fen·gidh lay·gu·beel ...
at (9am)	klukkan (níu fyrir hádegi)	klu·kan (nee·u fi·rir how·de·yi)
tomorrow	á morgun	ow mor·gun

How much is it to ...?
Hvað kostar til ... ?   kvadh kos·tar til ...

Please stop here.
Stoppaðu hér, takk.   sto·pa·dhu hyer tak

Please take me to (this address).
Viltu aka mér til   vil·tu a·ka myer til
(þessa staðar)?   (the·sa sta·dhar)

GLOSSARY

See the Icelandic Cuisine chapter (p326) for useful words and phrases dealing with food and dining, and the Transport chapter (p349) for road safety terms and signs.

á – river (as in Laxá, or Salmon River)
álfar – elves
austur – east

basalt – hard volcanic rock that often solidifies into hexagonal columns
bíó – cinema
brennivín – local schnapps
bær – farm

caldera – crater created by the collapse of a volcanic cone

dalur – valley

eddas – ancient Norse books

ey – island

fell – see *fjall*
fjall – mountain
fjörður – fjord
foss – waterfall
fumarole – vents in the earth releasing volcanic gas

gata – street
geyser – spouting hot spring
gistiheimilið – guesthouse
gjá – fissure, rift
goðar – political and religious leaders of certain districts in the times before Christianity (singular *goði*)

hákarl – putrid shark meat
hestur – horse
hot-pot – outdoor hot tub or spa pool, found at swimming baths and some accommodation; in Icelandic, hot-pot is *heitur pottur*
hraun – lava field

huldufólk – hidden people
hver – hot spring
höfn – harbour

ice cap – permanently frozen glacier or mountain top
Íslands – Iceland

jökull – glacier, ice cap

kirkja – church
kort – map

Landnámabók – comprehensive historical text recording the Norse settlement of Iceland
laug – pool; one that is suitable for swimming
lava tube – underground tunnel created by liquid lava flowing under a solid crust
lón – lagoon
lopapeysa/lopapeysur (sg/pl) – Icelandic woollen sweater
lundi – puffin

mudpot – bubbling pool of superheated mud

mörk – woods or forest; colloquially *mörk* also refers to the goals in football, and the earmarks of sheep

nes – headland

norður – north

puffling – baby puffin

reykur – smoke, as in Reykjavík (literally 'Smoky Bay')

safn – museum

sagas – Icelandic legends

sandur – sand; can also reference a glacial sand plain

scoria – glassy volcanic lava

shield volcano – gently sloped volcano built up by fluid lava flows

sími – telephone

skáli – hut, snack bar

stræti – street

suður – south

sumar – summer

sundlaug – heated swimming pool

tephra – rock/material blasted out from a volcano

tjörn – pond, lake

torg – town square

vatn – lake, water

vegur – road

vestur – west

vetur – winter

vík – bay

vogur – cove, bay

Behind the Scenes

SEND US YOUR FEEDBACK

We love to hear from travellers – your comments keep us on our toes and help make our books better. Our well-travelled team reads every word on what you loved or loathed about this book. Although we cannot reply individually to postal submissions, we always guarantee that your feedback goes straight to the appropriate authors, in time for the next edition. Each person who sends us information is thanked in the next edition – the most useful submissions are rewarded with a selection of digital PDF chapters.

Visit **lonelyplanet.com/contact** to submit your updates and suggestions or to ask for help. Our award-winning website also features inspirational travel stories, news and discussions.

Note: We may edit, reproduce and incorporate your comments in Lonely Planet products such as guidebooks, websites and digital products, so let us know if you don't want your comments reproduced or your name acknowledged. For a copy of our privacy policy visit lonelyplanet.com/privacy.

OUR READERS

Many thanks to the travellers who used the last edition and wrote to us with helpful hints, useful advice and interesting anecdotes:

Irisa Albion, Greg Barbutti, Paul Bennett, Amy Billings, Greta Maria Bjornsdottir, Maja Branovacki, Douglas Buck, Benoit Cambron, Ling Chan, Natalie Cherchas, Dan Chiasson, Kit Conn, Lianne Damen, Inge De Kort, Clive Deacon, Paul Dest, Silke Diedenhofen, Anke Dijkhuis, D Drake, Elisabet Engdahl, Val Featherby, Irini Gavrielidou, Mario Giaquinto, Steve Glennie-Smith, Koen Goorman, Maria Gough, Elísa Gyrðisdóttir, Julia Haag, Marije Hettinga, Ben Hosford, Jelly Julia, Trip Kennedy, Stephanie Klempfner, Martin Kooiman, Matthias Kranke, Alastair Learmont, Jenny Littlefield, Janine Luck, Siobhan Madden, Meghan Makielski, Coco Manson, Ilse Marien, Ruben Mooijman, Christian R Musil, Serge Nadeau, Ivo Nemec, Karvel Ogmundsson, Mary Paul, Dalia Petersil, Laurel Plewes, Juri Rebkowetz, Charles Scheim, Sam Simonds-Gooding, Katarzyna Skawińska, Pétur Snaebjornsson, Marijana Sostaric, Pnina Spector, Rebecca Stephany, Lucy and Stuart Stirland, Ondrej Valina, Pieter Van Der Woude, Matt Vitug, Kristi Weidlein, Ed Weiss, Simon Wickens, Moritz Ziegler, Hrafnhildur Ævarsdóttir

AUTHOR THANKS

Brandon Presser

A huge thank you to three very special people: Manny, Pálli and Nanna Hlín – I couldn't have done it without you. Takk fyrir to the inspiring Vilborg Árna, the intrepid Siggi Bjarni, the thoughtful Sigursteinn, and to Ester Rut, Bergþór Karlsson, Rósa Björk, Kristján Pálsson, Gústaf Gústafsson, Addý Ólafssdóttir and Jón Trausti. At Lonely Planet, thanks to everyone on the editorial and production team who helped put this book together, especially Katie, Kristin, Fran, Sasha and James. A massive thank you to Joanne for always being there, and finally to Carolyn Bain, my genius coauthor, for the endless laughs and Pinochet candy.

Carolyn Bain

Huge thanks to Katie O'Connell at Lonely Planet for commissioning me for my dream job, and to Yarctic explorer Jenny Blake for coming to play for a few days in Niceland. I could list half the Icelandic phonebook given the number of friendly, generous and wise locals who helped me out on this trip – instead, I'll say a sincere takk fyrir to everyone, but especially to Bergþór Karlsson, Ásbjörn Björgvinsson, Cosima Zewe, Regína Hreinsdóttir, Helga Árnadóttir, Sigrún Lóa Kristjánsdóttir, Arny Bergsdóttir, Egill and Sæmundur Þór Sigurðsson, Kristján at Glacier Jeeps, Mirjam and Halldóra, Emilia and Juan Carlos, Kiwis Karen and Diane, and Cathy Josephson. Finally, my heartfelt gratitude goes to my coauthor and friend, Brandon Presser. BP, from trip planning in Tallinn to the Djúpavík welcome and the Blue Lagoon debrief, it's been a pleasure working with you. A million thanks for your professional generosity, for sharing your local knowledge and contacts, for support during write-up, and for the many laughs along the way.

Fran Parnell

Thanks to fellow authors Brandon Presser and Carolyn Bain for all their input, and to Lonely Planet's in-house team, particularly Katie O'Connell and Kristin Odijk for patience in the face of procrastination. Heartfelt thanks to Erpur S Hansen of Náttúrustofa Suðurlands for such an articulate and comprehensive overview of Icelandic bird life.

ACKNOWLEDGMENTS

Climate map data adapted from Peel MC, Finlayson BL & McMahon TA (2007) 'Updated World Map of the Köppen-Geiger Climate Classification', *Hydrology and Earth System Sciences*, 11, 163344.
Cover photograph: Strokkur geyser, Geysir; Richard l'Anson/LPI

BEHIND THE SCENES

THIS BOOK

This 8th edition of Lonely Planet's *Iceland* guidebook was researched and written by Brandon Presser, Carolyn Bain and Fran Parnell. The 7th edition was written by Fran and Brandon, and the 6th edition was written by Fran and Etain O'Carroll. This guidebook was commissioned in Lonely Planet's London office, and produced by the following:
Commissioning Editor Katie O'Connell

Coordinating Editors Carolyn Boicos, Kristin Odijk
Coordinating Cartographer James Leversha
Coordinating Layout Designer Mazzy Prinsep
Managing Editor Sasha Baskett
Senior Editors Andi Jones, Catherine Naghten
Managing Cartographers Anita Banh, Adrian Persoglia
Managing Layout Designer Jane Hart
Assisting Editors Janet

Austin, Pat Kinsella, Rosie Nicholson, Christopher Pitts
Cover Research Naomi Parker
Internal Image Research Chris Girdler
Language Content Branislava Vladisavljevic
Thanks to Joe Bindloss, Bruce Evans, Ryan Evans, Larissa Frost, Trent Paton, Kirsten Rawlings, Raphael Richards, Jessica Rose, Kerrianne Southway, Gerard Walker, Clifton Wilkinson

index

INDEX K-M

366

INDEX W-Ö

how to use this book

These symbols will help you find the listings you want:

- ◉ Sights
- 🐾 Beaches
- 🏃 Activities
- 🤿 Courses
- 👉 Tours
- 🎉 Festivals & Events
- 🛏 Sleeping
- 🍴 Eating
- 🍷 Drinking
- ⭐ Entertainment
- 🛍 Shopping
- ℹ Information/Transport

Look out for these icons:

- TOP CHOICE — Our author's recommendation
- FREE — No payment required
- 🌿 — A green or sustainable option

Our authors have nominated these places as demonstrating a strong commitment to sustainability – for example by supporting local communities and producers, operating in an environmentally friendly way, or supporting conservation projects.

These symbols give you the vital information for each listing:

- ☏ Telephone Numbers
- ⊙ Opening Hours
- Ⓟ Parking
- ⊝ Nonsmoking
- ❄ Air-Conditioning
- @ Internet Access
- 📶 Wi-Fi Access
- 🏊 Swimming Pool
- 🥗 Vegetarian Selection
- 📖 English-Language Menu
- 👪 Family-Friendly
- 🐾 Pet-Friendly
- 🚌 Bus
- ⛴ Ferry
- Ⓜ Metro
- Ⓢ Subway
- 🚋 Tram
- 🚆 Train

Reviews are organised by author preference.

Map Legend

Sights
- Beach
- Buddhist
- Castle
- Christian
- Hindu
- Islamic
- Jewish
- Monument
- Museum/Gallery
- Ruin
- Winery/Vineyard
- Zoo
- Other Sight

Activities, Courses & Tours
- Diving/Snorkelling
- Canoeing/Kayaking
- Skiing
- Surfing
- Swimming/Pool
- Walking
- Windsurfing
- Other Activity/Course/Tour

Sleeping
- Sleeping
- Camping

Eating
- Eating

Drinking
- Drinking
- Cafe

Entertainment
- Entertainment

Shopping
- Shopping

Information
- Post Office
- Tourist Information

Transport
- Airport
- Border Crossing
- Bus
- Cable Car/Funicular
- Cycling
- Ferry
- Monorail
- Parking
- S-Bahn
- Taxi
- Train/Railway
- Tram
- Tube Station
- U-Bahn
- Underground Train Station
- Other Transport

Routes
- Tollway
- Freeway
- Primary
- Secondary
- Tertiary
- Lane
- Unsealed Road
- Plaza/Mall
- Steps
- Tunnel
- Pedestrian Overpass
- Walking Tour
- Walking Tour Detour
- Path

Boundaries
- International
- State/Province
- Disputed
- Regional/Suburb
- Marine Park
- Cliff
- Wall

Population
- Capital (National)
- Capital (State/Province)
- City/Large Town
- Town/Village

Geographic
- Hut/Shelter
- Lighthouse
- Lookout
- Mountain/Volcano
- Oasis
- Park
- Pass
- Picnic Area
- Waterfall

Hydrography
- River/Creek
- Intermittent River
- Swamp/Mangrove
- Reef
- Canal
- Water
- Dry/Salt/Intermittent Lake
- Glacier

Areas
- Beach/Desert
- Cemetery (Christian)
- Cemetery (Other)
- Park/Forest
- Sportsground
- Sight (Building)
- Top Sight (Building)

OUR STORY

A beat-up old car, a few dollars in the pocket and a sense of adventure. In 1972 that's all Tony and Maureen Wheeler needed for the trip of a lifetime – across Europe and Asia overland to Australia. It took several months, and at the end – broke but inspired – they sat at their kitchen table writing and stapling together their first travel guide, *Across Asia on the Cheap*. Within a week they'd sold 1500 copies. Lonely Planet was born.

Today, Lonely Planet has offices in Melbourne, London and Oakland, with more than 600 staff and writers. We share Tony's belief that 'a great guidebook should do three things: inform, educate and amuse'.

OUR WRITERS

Brandon Presser

Coordinating Author; Reykjavík, Southwest Iceland & the Golden Circle, West Iceland, The Westfjords, Iceland: Nature's Wonderland, Iceland Today Growing up in northern Canada, Brandon was all too familiar with sweeping, desolate terrain and shiver-worthy landscapes. But no snowdrift was big enough to prepare him for the sheer awesomeness of the remote Icelandic countryside. It was a simple transcontinental layover that turned harmless curiosity into full-blown infatuation and now, a decade later, he's checked off almost every fjordhead and mountain pass from his to-do list. He's even received compliments on his Icelandic pronunciation! (His grammar, however, is improving at glacial speeds.) Brandon spends most of the year writing his way across the globe – he's authored around 40 Lonely Planet guidebooks and explored over 75 countries. For more about Brandon, check out www.brandonpresser.com.

Read more about Brandon at:
lonelyplanet.com/members/brandonpresser

Carolyn Bain

Month by Month, North Iceland, East Iceland, Southeast Iceland, The Highlands, Directory A–Z, Transport Melbourne-born Carolyn has had an ongoing love affair with the Nordic region, a love that began when she was a teenager living in Denmark and that has been regularly rekindled over 12 years of writing guidebooks to destinations such as Denmark, Sweden and Nordic-wannabe Estonia. Researching this book fulfilled a long-held ambition and has taken her Nordic adulation to dizzying new heights. New and/or rekindled obsessions include *skyr*, snowmobiles, fjords, hot-pots, Northern Lights, puffins, *lopapeysur* and Of Monsters and Men.

Read more about Carolyn at:
lonelyplanet.com/members/carolynbain

Fran Parnell

History, Natural Wonders, Icelandic Culture, Icelandic Attitudes, Icelandic Cuisine Fran's passion for Scandinavia began while studying for a masters degree in Anglo-Saxon, Norse and Celtic. A strange university slide show featuring sublime Icelandic mountains and a matter-of-fact man who'd literally dug his own grave awakened a fascination that has kept on growing. Deserted valleys and blasted mountain tops are her chosen lurking places, and Hekla is her favourite volcano. Fran has also worked on Lonely Planet's guides to Scandinavian Europe, Sweden, Finland, Denmark and Reykjavík.

Published by Lonely Planet Publications Pty Ltd
ABN 36 005 607 983
8th edition – May 2013
ISBN 978 1 74179 942 2
© Lonely Planet 2013   Photographs © as indicated 2013
10 9 8 7 6 5 4 3 2 1
Printed in China

Although the authors and Lonely Planet have taken all reasonable care in preparing this book, we make no warranty about the accuracy or completeness of its content and, to the maximum extent permitted, disclaim all liability arising from its use.

All rights reserved. No part of this publication may be copied, stored in a retrieval system, or transmitted in any form by any means, electronic, mechanical, recording or otherwise, except brief extracts for the purpose of review, and no part of this publication may be sold or hired, without the written permission of the publisher. Lonely Planet and the Lonely Planet logo are trademarks of Lonely Planet and are registered in the US Patent and Trademark Office and in other countries. Lonely Planet does not allow its name or logo to be appropriated by commercial establishments, such as retailers, restaurants or hotels. Please let us know of any misuses: lonelyplanet.com/ip.